V'Khol Banayikh: Jewish Education For All

A Jewish Special Needs Resource Guide

Edited by Sara Rubinow Simon,
Linda Forrest and Ellen Fishman

ISBN 10 1-934527-20-3

ISBN 13 978-1-934527-20-7

Copyright © 2008 Sara Rubinow Simon, Linda Forrest, Ellen Fishman.

Published by Torah Aura Productions. All rights reserved.

Torah Aura Productions • 4423 Fruitland Avenue, Los Angeles, CA 90058

(800) BE-Torah • (800) 238-6724 • (323) 585-7312 • fax (323) 585-0327

E-MAIL <misrad@torahaura.com> • Visit the Torah Aura website at www.torahaura.com

MANUFACTURED IN CHINA

ACKNOWLEDGEMENTS & DEDICATION

The process of compiling and refining this resource guide has tightly bound the three of us together so that what was originally a professional relationship has been transformed into a deep and abiding friendship. We learned to capitalize on individual strengths and to accommodate individual styles. In essence, we modeled the processes that are described in *V'Khol Banayikh: Jewish Education for All*.

We gratefully acknowledge the encouragement and patience of our husbands Matthew, Richard, and Martin, and that of our children (and grandchildren) through the many years as we diverted a considerable portion of our "leisure time and energy" to the project.

We deeply appreciate the support of the Covenant Foundation and its faith in this project. The Covenant Foundation continues to play a significant role in encouraging innovation in Jewish education and professional development of Jewish educators.

We thank our colleagues in the Consortium of Special Educators in Central Agencies for Jewish Education, under the aegis of the Jewish Education Service of North America (JESNA), who contributed articles to the guide or who provided helpful feedback that shaped its scope. Their experience and expertise were invaluable throughout. Through their input, we were able to identify authors from their communities whose articles have added so much to the breadth and depth of the resource guide.

We especially want to thank Elana Naftalin Kelman for her significant assistance in preparing these materials for publication.

We want to thank Jane Golub for her patience, editorial skills, and commitment *l'hotzi la'or*—to bring *V'Kol Banayikh: Jewish Education for All, A Jewish Special Needs Resource Guide* to see the light of day.

We applaud the many educators who have stretched their original view of the teaching process to successfully include in their instruction students with special learning needs. We salute the Jewish communities who have responded so generously to the compelling mandate of which we speak, that of making it possible for every Jewish individual to learn about his heritage and to participate in all facets of Jewish life to the best of his ability. Dynamic lay leadership, with the encouragement of skilled communal professionals, provide the funding that makes Jewish programming for people with special needs a reality. In addition to Federation allocations, we must recognize the benefactors and foundations who provide necessary support.

We dedicate this resource guide to the families of our students. They courageously entrusted their children to us as we embarked on the uncharted course of Jewish special education. And, finally, we turn to our past, present, and future students. We trust that we will be able to enrich your lives as Jews.

I

Dear Linda, Ellen, and Sara,

I want to congratulate and thank you on behalf of JESNA for putting together this wonderful volume, *V'khol Banayikh: Jewish Education for All, A Jewish Special Needs Resource Guide.* We are proud that through our sister organization, the Covenant Foundation, we have been able to contribute in some small measure to its publication.

Making Jewish education accessible, joyful, and effective for all is more than a worthy goal; it is a *mitzvah,* an obligation that we in the Jewish community have yet to fulfill. Happily, progress is being made, thanks in no small measure to the work of you and your dedicated colleagues who have contributed to this book.

V'khol Banayikh is both a gift and a goad. It is a gift to every child, every parent, every teacher, and every administrator who refuses to accept that Jewish learning is only for *some* Jews. And it is a goad to policy-makers, philanthropists, and institutional leaders who will now have at their fingertips the evidence that Jewish special needs education has come of age, that the knowledge and tools exist to educate every Jewish child *al pi darko,* in an individually appropriate way. What we need, of course, are the will and the resources to translate what is in the pages of this marvelous book into the practice of hundreds of Jewish educational settings.

It is a privilege to help you disseminate this milestone work. *Kol hakavod* to you, who refused to give up on this project, to the contributors, and to the publisher.

With my warmest good wishes.

Sincerely,
Jonathan S. Woocher
Chief Ideas Officer, Director of the Lippman Kanfer Institute, JESNA

וְכָל-בָּנַיִךְ לִמּוּדֵי יי וְרַב שְׁלוֹם בָּנָיִךְ.

**When all of your children are
taught of the Eternal, great will be
the peace of your children.**

(Isaiah 54:13)

CONTENTS

ACKNOWLEDGEMENTS & DEDICATION
INTRODUCTION

JOURNEYS 13

Everyone Is Someone's Jacob: What I've Learned from My Autistic Son—
   Rabbi Bradley Shavit Artson 15

My Special Daughter (and Her Special Brother)—Rabbi Bradley Shavit Artson 19

A Parent's Perspective: My Son Is Formed in the Image of God, Too—Becca Hornstein 21

A Sibling's Perspective: He's a Part of Me—Shana Hornstein 25

Light in the Darkness—Rabbi Shawn Fields-Meyer 29

A Personal Story—Yonatan Y. Koch 33

Jacob Artson's Message—V'khol Banayikh 35

OUR SOURCES TELL US 39

DNA Analysts—Danny Siegel 41

Meshaneh Ha-Briyyot: A New Jewish Approach to Disabilities—Rabbi Elliot Dorff 43

Special Education in Judaic Literature—Rabbi Martin Schloss 53

PART 1: AN HISTORICAL PERSPECTIVE OF SPECIAL EDUCATION PROGRAMS AND SERVICES 59

A Time Line of Special Education Programs and Services in the United States 61

An Overview of the Americans With Disabilities Act 65

Chapter 1: Yesterday, Today and Tomorrow: Special Education—Rabbi Martin Schloss 67

Chapter 2: Jewish Special Education: A Fifty Year Perspective—Rabbi Bennett M. Rackman
   and Sara Rubinow Simon 71

PART 2: BUILDING AN INCLUSIVE JEWISH COMMUNITY 81

Chapter 3: A Rabbi's Guide to the Person With Special Needs—Rabbi Robert Layman 83

Chapter 4—Welcoming People With Disabilities Into Our House Of Worship—That All May
   WorshipNational Organization on Disability 89

Chapter 5: The Journey Of A Congregation—A Self-Assessment and Learning Tool of the
   Accessible Congregations Campaign, National Organization on Disability 91

Chapter 6: Welcoming All Families—Janice P. Alper and Linda Zimmerman 95

Chapter 7: PPAC (Parallel Professional Advisory Committee) For Special Needs, Greater
   Washington—Sara Rubinow Simon 101

The Jewish Federation of Greater Washington Parallel Professional Advisory Committees . . 103

Chapter 8: Coordinated Network of Services for Persons with Disabilities, Atlanta—
   Sheryl Arno and Linda Zimmerman 105

Chapter 9: A Community Responds:Minneapolis Jewish Community Inclusion Program for
   People with Disabilities—Shelly Christensen 109

Chapter 10: Parent-to-Parent: Parent Networking And Support—Shelley Siegel 113

Chapter 11: Finding Your Voice…Advocating for Your Child—Shelly Christensen 119

PART 3: JEWISH FORMAL EDUCATION 125

Chapter 12: Towards an Inclusive *K'lal Yisrael*: What's Reasonable?—Ellen Fishman and
Sara Rubinow Simon 127

Chapter 13: The Role of the Jewish Preschool—Mara Bier 129

Day School Special Needs Continuum Of Services 143

Chapter 14: Day School Special Needs Program Options—Sara Rubinow Simon 145

Chapter 15: Supporting Students With Learning Differences in the Jewish Day School—
Judith Stern. 149

Chapter 16: The Amit Community School Program—A School Within A School—
Linda Zimmerman 159

Chapter 17: Navigating the Special Education System—Identification, Referral, Evaluation and
PlacementFor Students with Special Needs—Shana Erenberg 167

Supplementary School Program Options—Sara Rubinow Simon 175

Chapter 18: Setting Up A Resource Program in a Congregational School—
Sara Rubinow Simon and Phyllis S. Greene. 177

PART 4: "THE INCLUSIVE CLASSROOM"TEACHING TO DIVERSE LEARNING STYLES 189

Chapter 19: Learning Styles—An Overview—Flora Kupferman 191

Chapter 20: Many Types of Smart:Using Multiple Intelligences to Enhance Learning—
Linda L. Forrest 199

Chapter 21: Multiple Intelligences in a Jewish Setting—Logical-Mathematical—
Deborah Gettes 205

Chapter 22: Creating Inclusive Classrooms with Differentiated Instruction—
Sandy Miller-Jacobs 213

Chapter 23: Cooperative Learning and the 21st-Century Classroom—Ellen Fishman. 219

Chapter 24: That Each May Learn: Educational Technology in the Inclusive Classroom—
Caren N. Levine and Sara Seligson. 225

Chapter 25: The Learning Center Model—Ann Litwack. 241

Chapter 26: Instructional Games—Jennifer Malka Rudo 253

Chapter 27: Building Bridges Through Music and Movement Experiences in the Classroom—
Ronna S. Kaplan. 259

Chapter 28: The Magic and the Art of Story:Storytelling and Creative Dramatics in the
Classroom—by Cherie Karo Schwartz 271

PART 5: CLASSROOM AND MATERIAL ACCOMMODATIONS 279

For All Students and Especially Students Who May Have a Variety Of Learning
Disabilities 281

Chapter 29: Suggested Classroom Accommodations for Students with Attention Deficit
Disorder—Gary Smith, Marilyn Eyler Conaway, and Carolyn Croft Lodwig. 283

Chapter 30: Classroom Modifications—Anita Naftaly. 289

PART 6: BEHAVIOR 305
Chapter 31: Behavior—What is the Student Trying to Tell Us?—Miriam Gluck. 307
Chapter 32: Behavior Management Concepts and Techniques—Sara Portman Milner 315
Code Of Conduct: Ohr Kodesh, Chevy Chase, MD 323
Behavioral Intervention Plan 327

PART 7: HEBREW LANGUAGE INSTRUCTION 329
Chapter 33: Natural Hebrew: A Common-Sense Framework for Teaching Hebrew Reading—
Sharon S. Schanzer. 331
Reading Problems in Hebrew. 349
Diagnostic Reading Test Score Sheet. 351
Hebrew Finger Spelling 352

PART 8: CURRICULAR EXCERPTS 353
Chapter 34: *Sh'ma V'ezer* Program 355
Chapter 35: ETGAR Holiday Curriculum. 357
Chapter 36: My Book of Jewish Holidays—Marlene N. Marcus and Mary F. Meyerson. 361
Chapter 37: A Time to Rejoice—Miriam Wolf, Marlynn Dorff, Kenneth Schaefler 365

PART 9: PROFESSIONAL DEVELOPMENT/STAFF TRAINING 377
Chapter 38: *Sh'lom Kitah*: A Model to Train Congregational School Learning Specialists—
Lenore Layman 379
Chapter 39: The Role of Instructional Aides In A Day School Setting—Ellen Fishman 387
Chapter 40: Teenade: Jewish Continuity Through Special Education—Sandy Miller-Jacobs . 389

PART 10: BAR/BAT MITZVAH PREPARATION 397
Chapter 41: Bar/Bat Mitzvah Preparation for Children With Special Learning Needs:
An Overview—Sara Rubinow Simon 399
Chapter 44: Bar Mitzvah Stories—Rabbi Daniel T. Grossman 403
Chapter 43: Michael's Perfect Bar Mitzvah—Beverly Weaver. 407
Bar/Bat Mitzvah Preparation For Children With Special Learning Needs 413
Siddur Tefillah Yehoshua Hazak. 415

PART 11: INFORMAL EDUCATION 417
Chapter 44: Social/Recreational Activities for Children With Disabilities—
Sara Portman Milner 419
Chapter 45: Recruitment and Training of "Non-Professional" Support Staff—
Sara Portman Milner 423
Chapter 46: The Tikvah Story—Howard Blas 427

PART 12: TRANSITION TO ADULTHOOD 435
Chapter 47: Transitioning from School to Adulthood: A Parent's Perspective—
Becca Hornstein 437

Chapter 48: Jewish Living In Group Homes—Marcia Goldberg. 441

Chapter 49: Adult B'nai Mitzvah—Marcia Goldberg 449

Chapter 50: Shabbat in a Box for Jews with Special Needs—Becca Hornstein. 453

Chapter 51: Adult Jewish Education:A Model for Individuals with Developmental Disabilities—
Elliot Fix 455

PART 13: DISABILITY AWARENESS/SENSITIVITY. 459

Chapter 52: Let My House Be Open—Pearl Schainker 461

Chapter 53: Justice, Justice for All—Marlynn Dorff, et al. 467

Attending a Bar Mitzvah Ceremony 468

APPENDICES 471

APPENDIX A: DISABILITY/ACCESSIBILITY STATEMENTS 473

Jewish Reconstructionist Federation 475

Orthodox Union. 477

Union For Reform Judaism—Department Of Lifelong Jewish Learning. 479

United Synagogue of Conservative Judaism—Special Education Committee Of The
Commission On Jewish Education 481

Measures For Persons With Disabilities. 483

APPENDIX B: GLOSSARY OF SPECIAL NEEDS TERMINOLOGY 485

Glossary of Special Needs Terminology 487

APPENDIX C: OVERVIEW OF EXCEPTIONALITIES 505

Learning Disabiblities 507

Attention Deficit Hyperactivity Disorder—Shana R. Erenberg 511

Autism Spectrum Disorder/Pervasive Developmental Disorder

Sensory Integration Disorder—Mimi Goss. 527

Teaching The "Twice Exceptional" Student: Gifted And Learning Disabled—
Limor Dankner. 531

The Non-Elitist Gifted Student. 543

The Child With a Hearing Impairment in the Jewish Classroom—Batya Jacob 545

APPENDIX D: SYNAGOGUE ACCESSIBILITY SURVEY 547

Synagogue Accessibility Survey 549

Welcoming a Person Into Our House Of Worship: That All May Worship 553

By Using Words with Dignity, We Encourage Equality for Everyone 561

APPENDIX E: RESOURCES FOR JEWISH EDUCATORS 563

Special Needs Related Resources 564

INTRODUCTION

As we have trained teachers, it has become increasingly apparent that we could not find a compendium of best practices in the field of Jewish Special Education.

Despite the growth of Jewish Special Education programs in recent years, there was a dearth of readily-available resources that provided Jewish educators with a familiarity with the language and perspective of special education so that they could adapt it to their particular Jewish religious and cultural settings.

Through our many years of work in our respective Jewish communities, we were able to identify a number of the issues facing an individual with special needs and his family. We collected materials from a variety of sources and shared them with our colleagues, "field-testing" them in our programs—but there was still no single guide book that we could use.

We are fortunate to have colleagues from Jewish communities across North America with whom to consult. Through the Consortium of Special Educators in Central Agencies for Jewish Education, we have come in contact with an extraordinarily capable and dedicated cadre of professionals whom we could ask for input regarding topics, formats and contributors. This resource guide contains many of their contributions.

We should not forget the important role the family members play when we work with a student with special needs. Included in this guide are "Family Journeys", providing insight into caring for a family member with special needs.

The creation of this guide was a labor of love. The enormity of the task we undertook was not apparent to us when we accepted the challenge to compile a comprehensive guide for individuals with special needs of all ages and for their families to help them make their way in their Jewish community. We believe that it is a work in progress, to be completed by you.

Dear Reader, we hope that *V'khol Banayikh: Jewish Education for All* will spark your imaginations and spur you to look with enthusiasm and optimism at the rewarding opportunity of reaching and teaching each of your students so that they, too, are able to benefit from the beauty and wisdom of our Jewish heritage.

B'Hatzlahah—much success in your holy work!

Sara Rubinow Simon
Linda Forrest
Ellen Fishman

INTRODUCTION

JOURNEYS

EVERYONE IS SOMEONE'S JACOB: WHAT I'VE LEARNED FROM MY AUTISTIC SON

Rabbi Bradley Shavit Artson

My wife and I endured a difficult pregnancy with our twins. She was bedridden from 26 weeks and ultimately required an emergency C-section that delivered our children six weeks premature. They say that it takes a village to raise a child. We know that from firsthand experience, since we would never have survived had it not been for our caring community—congregants who helped us with meals, inquired about Elana and the children's wellbeing, held our hands, and comforted us during a frightening time. When the children were born and the doctors finally let us bring them home, it seemed like a miracle for us and for the entire community. I remember the day we celebrated Jacob's *Brit Milah* and Shira's *Simhat Bat*, how the sanctuary was overflowing with people and food and joy. It was a celebration in which everyone participated and everyone made possible.

I don't need to detail the hopes that parents have with their children. I don't need to explain how the entire promise of life itself gets concentrated into one little tiny baby lying in a crib (in our case, two very tiny babies). Yet all of the effort and all of the struggle seem insignificant when looking into the pure eyes of those babies and the hope that they embody for the future.

They were beautiful babies, and they developed beautifully. We watched in wonder as they emerged into the world: sitting up at the same time, learning to stand at more or less the same time, even beginning to walk and climb stairs together. Then, somehow, in the second year something changed and our Jacob stopped growing. Our little boy, who had been developing just like his sister, stopped. Shira continued to surge: mastering new challenges, surpassing herself, and delighting in her new abilities. Jacob was still Jacob, but somehow he was pulling away, somehow sliding into some other world, behind some wall that we couldn't penetrate. Our Jacob, who had been so vivacious and so energetic and so enthusiastic, would play by himself for hours, compulsively repeating meaningless motions, endlessly plucking leaves or throwing pebbles, one after another.

His behavior wasn't the only source of distance between us. Jacob's words never came out. He wouldn't talk. It doesn't take a lot of imagination to feel the pain that a parent would endure seeing that. You can understand the delusion that we constructed to fool ourselves into thinking that nothing was wrong, that our boy was just developing differently from his sister, that's all. The horror was so vast that we willingly agreed with the popular pabulum that people offered us: we shouldn't be pressuring him to be like her. We need to let him grow to be who he is. We shouldn't label that boy. And so we repeated to ourselves, our desperate, misguided mantra until we couldn't honestly say it any longer. Until the reality was so pressing that it shredded our denial. Finally, we took Jacob to a specialist for a diagnosis. After a frustrating and futile effort to get Jacob to engage in the diagnostic test, the doctor told us that Jacob suffered from something we had never hear of, PDD, Pervasive Developmental Disorder.

As if this new PDD weren't bad enough, while he was telling us about PDD the doctor kept referring to autism. I felt as though the entire universe had caved in, that we were the living dead. I had been betrayed by God, and the cosmos, and by everything. For months the pain was so great that I couldn't speak about it to anybody. I couldn't share it. I couldn't face it. I couldn't confront it on my own. Jacob, my son, my son!

Since that time, our life has become a battleground. Our home is ground zero in the private war against autism. We are fighting for a beautiful boy who's locked somehow inside himself, who needs to learn how to emerge. Every day is a struggle. The things that other parents don't have to worry about, we worry about. Well intended opportunities confront us with insurmountable challenges. How can we accept an invitation to someone's house when Jacob is going to sit by himself the whole time? How are we going to be able to play with other children when Jacob doesn't really know how to play, when he has to be guided, and when the other children have to be taught how to play with him? How can we bring Jacob to any new place when all new places are frightening? How can we bring him into a crowd (we live such public lives) when being with masses of people is the very thing of which he's most terrified?

This message is not meant to be just another anguished parent venting in public. I'm sharing this, my pain, because of all of us carry pain, and all of us carry wounds, and all of us bear disappointments. I want to share with you what my Jacob has taught me about life because what he has taught me is precious and applies to us all.

Jacob has taught me to let go of the future. Jacob taught me all the thousands of expectations and impositions that I didn't even know I had and that I had to give up. And I discovered that I counted on them only when I realized I couldn't have them anymore. We tell ourselves, "Oh, our children can grow up to be anything, they can grow up to do anything, they can have whatever life they want to have," and it's nonsense. We don't even know the extent of what we demand of them until they won't do it. And then suddenly we realize how very much we want for them and from them. I now admit that I don't know Jacob's future. Nobody knows Jacob's future. I pray that he will have one that is full and rich. I pray that he will have a good life, but what it is will be his to create. Jacob reminded me of something I knew intellectually, but he has taught it to me in a deeper way: all we have is today, now. Tomorrow may never be, and it will certainly not be what we expect it to be. So don't postpone joy, or reconciliation, or love until tomorrow. Life is to be lived now, on this day, because this day is what we have and it is all we have. In the words of Israel Zangwill, "for Judaism the center of gravity is here and now. The whole problem of life faces us today." The Sages of the Mishnah counsel, "Don't say you will study tomorrow for tomorrow you may not have time." Don't put off righting a wrong until tomorrow, tomorrow may never come." Now, today. "If not now," says Hillel, "then what?" Jacob made me a gift of the present.

The second gift Jacob gave me is that he forced me to reassess what is really important in the world, what it is that really matters in our loved ones. When I first found out that Jacob was autistic, I confess that I experienced fantasies of his dying. I imagined being rid of him, of starting over. I couldn't face the fear and the pain of now knowing whether he would ever come out of his shell. I didn't know if I would hear him speak to me. I didn't know what his future would be. I feared that he would have to endure a lonely old age in which nothing would make sense, his Abba and his Ema would no longer be there for him, no one would appreciate or love him. That nightmare terrifies me still. And so in those first horrible months, I would toy with the idea of his death.

Those daydreams made me realize that the only possibility more terrifying than living with Jacob and his illness is the thought of living without him. His sweetness lights up my soul. When he looks at the Torah and smiles and says "bye-bye Torah" at the end of the Torah Service, something inside me glows. With all of my fear of the future, with all of the suffering and uncertainty his autism entails, Jacob is a blessing as he is. Every child is a blessing as they are. I thank God for Jacob because he is a gift every morning when he crawls into bed with me. Jacob has taught me that what really matters isn't the IQ, although it's nice. It isn't accomplishments, although those are also beautiful. But what's really the core, what we can't give up, what is the essence is soul. What is the essence is sweetness and goodness and loving and caring.

Our worth is not what we do; it is that we are. What is precious is simply that being ourselves, we bring something precious into the world. We don't have to earn God's love, and we don't have to earn each other's. Each of us is infinitely precious being ourselves and we need to acknowledge that (a gift from my son). The Talmud teaches us *"rachmana leiba'i,"* God wants only the heart. And if we have heart, we have everything and if we don't have heart, no degree, no income, no wealth and fame can compensate for its lack. Finally, I can see in my son, a beautiful soul, and a *"zisen neshomeh"* trying to express itself, and I see his sickness trying to shut him in. I see Jacob beating against the limits of his autism, struggling to emerge. I know my Jacob from the inside out, and I know that my Jacob is not his illness. But I also see people shying away from Jacob, confusing his illness for him and not seeing the beautiful boy but seeing instead a label, autism. Jacob isn't autism and Jacob isn't autistic. Jacob is Jacob. And he is like every other child, precious, and sweet, and beautiful if you can learn to address him in a way to which he can respond to. It takes effort. It takes starting with Jacob's illness and working toward Jacob's soul, so that his label is a tool, not an obstruction. We live in a world of labels; we live in a world of division. We live in a world that sees only the label and dismisses the person beyond the label. We don't take time to see the person who that label is hiding, who that label is distorting and covering. I have learned that everybody is somebody's Jacob. And every Jacob has parents who, like me, pray that someone out there will be able to see their "Jacob" with love and with compassion. That some kind soul will look beyond the label and will care for their child with kindness and warmth.

We all need to see other people as worthy of our love, not just the ones who are easy to love or to respect, but most particularly those who are not: the nudnik who won't leave you alone, that's somebody's Jacob. The person at work who keeps saying those annoying things, that's somebody's Jacob. The fellow congregant everyone avoids after services, she is somebody's Jacob. If all we have is the present (and we do) and if everybody is someone's Jacob (and they are) then they deserve your empathy now! Enough with the bickering, enough with discounting each other, enough with ignoring each other's humanity and needs, that time is gone.

My Jacob has taught me more than all of my professors at Harvard or in rabbinical school could ever have hoped to, because my Jacob taught me to live now. He taught me that all that really matters is in the heart. He reminds me to love the unlovable, because the great miracle of life is that, if we love the unlovable, they become really loveable indeed.

MY SPECIAL DAUGHTER (AND HER SPECIAL BROTHER)

Rabbi Bradley Shavit Artson

Let us bless the Source of life in its infinite variety,
Who creates all of us whole, none of us perfect.

Judith Glass, "Afterbirth"

My son, Jacob, believes that Disneyland is the happiest place on earth. For my daughter, Shira, it may or may not be a happy place, but Disneyland is certainly the place where she is happiest to be Jacob's sister. Because Jacob is autistic, we don't have to wait on line to enjoy any of the rides. Instead, we flash his IEP (Independent Education Plan, given by the public school system and attesting to his condition), Disney bestows a VIP pass on Jacob, we skip the line and get stared at by all the other guests. As we breeze onto the ride, Shira beaming, I routinely overhear people mumbling, "What's so special about them?"

What is so special indeed?

In the language of our age, our son is "special" and our daughter is "typical." Ten years earlier, he would have been "disabled" and she, "normal." A decade passes, the compass shifts, the language moves. But having a special child often doesn't feel special. It feels hard, burdensome, relentless, a joke. When our twins were born, we had dreams of them as inseparable, a playmate always at the ready. We dreamed of their always having an intense connection with someone who would understand them on an intuitive level. Those dreams have withered, scorched in an inferno of special therapies, medications, procedures, and behaviors. Dare I cling to the hope that Shira will feel a connection to Jacob when they are grown? Will she make for him a loving presence in her heart and her life?

Jacob is "special," and that will be Shira's burden throughout her life. Should any child have to mature in the shadow of that additional responsibility? Jacob may be special, but Shira isn't typical, which is fortunate; she can't afford to be.

- At three years old, Shira wanted to join me in greeting congregants arriving at Rosh Ha-Shanah services. I told her she could pick her own clothes, so she picked two items that expressed the fullness of her own unique personality: her Cinderella ballroom gown, and her arba knafot underneath (complete with *tzitzit* hanging out below). Thus attired, she reached up and shook hundreds of hands, wishing them a smiling "Shanah Tovah!" That is no typical child.

- As a child of four, Shira found out that people die. During one of several conversations about mortality, Shira informed me that, when the time came, she would hold my hand and die with me. When I told her that I hoped she would live for many, many years after I

17

did, she burst into tears. "Abba, I don't want to live if you aren't living!" That's not typical either.

- At age seven, still a white belt in karate, Shira's instructor gave her a wooden board by mistake (only the higher belts get their own boards). When her teacher tried to retrieve it, Shira was so adamant that he relented. Shira smashed it in two with her first kick.

Shira knows who she is, feels passionately, and lives without restraint. I can't help but suspect that, in part, she is so special because she has a "special" brother.

Once, Elana (my wife/her mother) was reading Shira *Mori's Story*, a wonderful book about an autistic boy written by his wise eleven-year-old brother. Shira began to cry when we got to the parent's loving decision to place their autistic child with a foster family who could provide him with the care he needed. "We won't ever do that to Jacob, will we?" She cried, horrified at the possibility. We explained that each family was different, and had different needs. Jacob would stay with us.

Shira, in the middle of nothing in particular, announces that it is unfair that she has an autistic brother when none of her friends do. She plugs both ears when Jacob makes his nonsense sounds, his "silly talk." She rolls her eyes in disgust when he emerges from the bathroom with his pants still around his ankles. She deliberately picks the video that she knows will make him scream, cry, and fling himself to the ground.

But Shira is also the one attracted to friends who are distinctive and unusual children. She is the sister who hands Jacob half her french fries, without his asking, because she knows he likes them. Or her leftover brownies. Shira is the first to try to assure him that the hotel room is safe and secure, when it feels unknown and threatening to him. And if we discuss some future plan without mentioning Jacob, Shira is the one to insist, "Jacob too!"

Raising a child with special needs is challenge enough. But raising that child's sibling is a task requiring no less consciousness, planning, and consideration. In the press of an autistic melt-down, Shira's more subtle needs can easily appear less pressing. Because she is more verbal, her acting like a seven-year-old feels petulance when Jacob's problems rise to the surface. And, finally, because Jacob requires constant attention and assistance, it's easy to let Shira fade into the background. Her very sweetness, understanding, and sympathy make it easier to give her short shrift.

For all that, it is also true that having to make room for an autistic brother, mentally, emotionally, and in the prosaic details of her family, Shira has developed a depth and a caring that takes my breath away.

Shira is a miracle in our lives. And like all miracles, she defies simple understanding, eludes neat categorization. There is no one quite like her. It turns out that she is, in her own way, special too.

And isn't that typical?

A PARENT'S PERSPECTIVE: MY SON IS FORMED IN THE IMAGE OF GOD, TOO

Becca Hornstein

When faced with devastating news, it is natural to turn to your family for love and support. Upon receiving the diagnosis that your child has a disability, it is understandable that parents would turn not just to their immediate family, but also to their family-at-large, the Jewish community. Sadly, and too often in the past, parents found themselves denied any comfort or support from their synagogue or religious school. Rabbis, cantors, and teachers may have been trained on how to respond to a death in the family, but they were unprepared to handle the news of a child's physical or developmental disability. Brushed aside by the religious community that they expected to embrace and comfort them, many of these parents turned their backs on Judaism.

As the parent of Joel, an adult son who has autism, I faced that kind of rebuff in the 1970s and early 1980s. I realize now that the rabbis, cantors and religious school teachers were uninformed, unprepared, and more than a little frightened by the parent who brought them an atypical child. How does a religion that requires the performance of daily prayer teach a child who cannot hear or speak? How does a religion that mandates study of Torah and Talmud teach a child who learns in a distinctly different way from his/her peers? How do "the people of the book" educate the child who cannot see the book, hold the book, or understand the book? Faced with these dilemmas, many religious schools in past decades retreated from the challenge.

Despite Joel's disability, I would not accept that my precious son could not be a part of the Jewish community. After years of rejection, in 1984 I was blessed to find Temple Chai, a small congregation in Phoenix that opened its doors to every Jew. Starting with the premise that every person is formed in the image of God, the rabbi, cantor, school director and I created an educational program that recognized the unique strengths and challenges Joel possessed. We individualized his religious school goals, and we adapted the curriculum to meet his special needs. A special education teacher was employed and a teenager who knew sign language became the *madrickah* (aide). From the commitment to "educate each child according to his ability," a special needs classroom was born. Nearly 20 years later, my congregation now provides an educational spectrum that offers classes, resource rooms and full inclusion to more than 100 students.

Looking back at Joel's Bar Mitzvah, his unexpected triumphs in learning to speak Hebrew, read Torah, and lead the congregation in prayers, my heart swells and my eyes fill with tears. The entire congregation became involved in Joel's special Jewish education and each one of them felt proud of his achievement. On the Friday evening before a child's bar mitzvah, it is our congregation's tradition to call the child up to the bima to chant the kiddush and thus prepare him to face a sanctuary full of people the next day. When Joel strode to the bima, lifted the kiddush cup and began to chant in perfect Hebrew, the entire congregation held their collective breathes. Upon his conclusion, the room exploded with the mass release of air and hearty cheers of "mazel tov!"

At his bar mitzvah, Joel performed flawlessly in Hebrew and English, leading the congregation in prayer and chanting his *parsha* confidently. This shy, quiet teenager who normally hovered around the periphery of any gathering stood before 200 people and beamed with pride in his accomplishment that day. But the modification of a bar or bat mitzvah should not be the conclusion of any person's participation in Jewish life. It is the portal to a lifetime of joyous participation.

As the result of what I had started at Temple Chai, I was asked by community leaders to create an agency to assist children and adults who have disabling conditions to facilitate their participation in our Jewish community. For Joel and many other young adults in our community who are active members of Yad B'Yad, a social and educational group for adults with special needs, there are twice monthly meetings to continue their Jewish studies and celebrate all of the holidays and unique elements of Judaism. Among other things, they have learned some Yiddish, donned costumes to put on the Purim spiel they created, conducted their own mock wedding under a chuppah and performed a wide variety of mitzvah projects for others in the community. Each of these several dozen men and women speak with pride and confidence about the importance of Judaism in their lives and how much they value their inclusion in our Jewish community.

In 2001, we opened our first Jewish group home for men who have developmental disabilities. As the three residents and their parents gathered around the table for their first Shabbat dinner, I looked at each young man. Jason is the gregarious one, and he tells the most amazing stories, some of which may actually be true! Kevin is more intense, eager to please others and very focused on the matters at hand. Joel is the quiet one, his limited communication skills reflecting the symptoms of autism. The house manager joined us for dinner, and I suddenly realized that we were taking the first steps toward forming a new family in Shalom House. The men were bubbling over with questions and comments: "I like these kiddush cups. Do we get to keep them? Joel knows the kiddush by heart. Did you hear how good he said it? Next week, can I light the candles? I know the blessing real good!"

After dinner, the men cleared the table and rinsed their dishes. Without any prompting, they suddenly broke into song, singing two of their favorite melodies "Shabbat Shalom" and "Sim Shalom." Jason and Kevin raised their arms and began to dance like "Tevya." Jason reached out and drew Joel into their dance. I saw them forming a small circle as they sang lustily (and off-key) and moved about the room, laughing with pure delight.

Nothing could prevent the tears from filling my eyes as I witnessed my son's first Shabbat in Shalom House. To live Jewishly with the support of family, friends and community is a reasonable goal for any person. Because Yad B'Yad meets in Shalom House and the parents see it every time they drop off their adult children, our group home has inspired others to replicate it. Another group of families opened their own supervised Jewish residence this past month and more group homes are in the planning stages.

Today, congregants still warmly greet my 34-year old son at services, chat with Joel about his job and hobbies, and frequently reminisce about his remarkable bar mitzvah. They all sound like proud aunts and uncles, just like a family that lovingly embraces and applauds the achievements of all of their children. This, then, is what I sought so long ago from my family-at-large, my Jewish community.

Parents of children who have mental or physical disabilities, sensory impairments or learning disabilities, emotional problems or attention deficits do not expect their child to "perform" in the same manner as a typical child. They realize that this child's education will require modifications to the standard curriculum and possibly a special bar or bat mitzvah that will accommodate his/her special qualities. What the parents seek, even when they cannot articulate it, is the opportunity for their child to attend religious school alongside his/her siblings and peers, to be surrounded by the sights and sounds of their parents' and grandparents' religion, and to be accepted as a person of dignity and value who brings a unique element to the overall composition of a school and congregation.

To include a special child requires disability awareness, sensitivity, compassion and a little extra effort. The rewards to all who make these efforts are immeasurable. Thankfully, with the growing number of special education resources in the Jewish community, assistance to schools and teachers is available for many communities. Jewish education and a lifetime of inclusion in the Jewish community must be available to every child.

A SIBLING'S PERSPECTIVE: HE'S A PART OF ME

Shana Hornstein

To others, having an older brother with a disability probably seems like a "unique experience." I've never thought there was anything unique about it because I've never known anything else. Perhaps my perspective on disabilities is atypical because my mother has worked in the field of disabilities for my entire life, and I was always around children and adults who have special needs. It seemed like a very "normal" thing for me to spend time with people using wheelchairs or sign language or Braille books.

In my experience talking with other siblings, one of the most difficult things was feeling embarrassed at school when your peers saw your brother or sister behaving differently. At those times, siblings might feel embarrassed or even ashamed. They also feel protective and angry if peers tease or make jokes about their sibling. I never experienced this because my neighborhood school did not include many students with disabilities. My brother Joel attended a different school that provided the special education classes he needed. Because of this, I had two identities: my school identity which did not reveal that I had a brother with autism, and my identity within the Jewish community in which I was known to be the sister of the boy with autism who attended Temple Chai's special needs class.

If there were any questions when my classmates saw Joel, they were usually expressions of curiosity: "What's wrong with him? Why does he carry that Magic Slate all the time? Can I play with it, too?" I had a short and simple answer for each question: He has autism; he likes to draw letters and numbers on it; and no, he doesn't like anyone else to touch it. If they pursued the topic, my friends might ask: "Are you close to him?" (Absolutely) "Can you talk to him?" (Yes, but he doesn't always answer me); and, now that Joel is an adult, "What does he do? Does he live at home?" (He works full time in a library and lives in a Jewish group home my parents created for him and two other men).

How I answered all depended on my mood when the question was asked. Sometimes I would answer patiently, slowly giving a detailed explanation so the person received a clear understanding of my brother and his disability. Other times, I just didn't want to talk about it, explain about autism, hear about how the other person knew someone once or saw a movie about a person with disabilities, blah blah blah. At those times, I might be a bit curt or abrupt. From the very beginning, my parents told me that I could choose whether or not I wanted to talk about my brother or autism. I knew that as his sister I had a responsibility (along with my parents) to shield and protect Joel from the world as well as educating the public so that others could accept Joel.

I was, and continue to be, very protective of my brother Joel and his feelings. I was highly selective of who I invited to my home. In effect, my friends had to earn the privilege of meeting my brother by first earning my trust and confidence in them. After graduating from high school and moving away from my parents' home, I once again established two separate identities. I have my present "local identity" with people who know many aspects of my life and personality, one of which is my profession working with children who have autism. Then there is my "hometown identity" with people who knew me in Phoenix where a large part of my identity still includes being "Joel's sister" and where I am inextricably entwined with the world of autism and special needs. I have often felt odd about making friends in these new cities. Even though these valued friends are kindred spirits and we care about each other deeply, I feel that they don't really know all of me because they've never met Joel. Joel is such an essential part of me that no one can really know and understand me without knowing and understanding him.

Because my brother has autism and didn't speak until he was nearly eight years old, he needed a lot of attention from my parents. When Joel was upset about something, it occasionally required both parents to physically control him and calm him. He needed a great deal of assistance in personal hygiene, medical care and dental appointments. It was hard for me to hear Joel screaming in fear at the dentist's office, knowing that there was nothing I could do to help, and I desperately did want to help. While I may have resented the hours that Joel's needs took my parents' attention away from me, I also sincerely wanted to be his "caretaker," too. In my talks with other siblings, I've discovered that they are fairly evenly divided between wanting to help care for their sibling and resenting the demands of their sibling. Siblings often feel both of these emotions at the same time.

My parents made every effort to give me "special time," quite often without my brother. There were the "Daddy and Me" classes we took, the surprise outings to a movie or the season's tickets for Mom and me to see touring Broadway musicals together. I understood and appreciated my parents' efforts to give me singularly focused attention.

Although we observed Jewish holidays at home, it took many years for my family to find a synagogue or religious school that would welcome Joel and accept his autistic qualities. After a long search, we joined Temple Chai, in Phoenix, AZ, then a small congregation that warmly welcomed Joel as well as the rest of our family. From the very first day, Rabbi William Berk, Cantor Sharona Feller, the teachers and the congregational families made a concerted effort to get to know Joel.

While I don't remember being teased about Joel on the religious school playground, I do remember awkward moments when we all assembled for "tefillah." Some of the typical students would notice the small group of students with special needs speaking or singing louder than the others, and occasionally I would overhear their whispered comments. Looking back, I realize my closest friends today are my kind, caring classmates from religious school, and not the public school friends who didn't know Joel. Back then, I was glad to have a separate school identity that did not include Joel or autism. Now I realize that people who don't know that side of me don't really see the "complete" Shana.

There weren't any sibling support groups available until I was 13 years old. By the time I attended that group, I had worked through most of my sibling issues. There were no other Jewish kids in the group that I attended, and none who had a brother or sister with autism. I didn't meet others who had a sibling with autism until I was in high school and worked at the school district's Extended School Year summer programs. The one Jewish person I met had a sister with Down Syndrome and she held the opposite attitude toward her sibling; she wanted to get as far away from her as possible. While she didn't want to have *anything* to do with her sister, I wanted to have *everything* to do with my brother!

I was only 10 years old at the time of my brother's bar mitzvah, but I clearly remember helping him learn his prayers and Torah portion in Hebrew, listening to him perform perfectly from the bima, admiring the "special occasion clothes" Joel and I got to wear, and being surrounded by my entire extended family and nearly everyone who had a part in Joel's life. I had only attended a few other b'nai mitzvah, so I didn't really know what they were supposed to be like. Nonetheless, I sensed that there was something very, very special happening to everyone in the sanctuary as Joel performed beyond anyone's expectations. To others, this was a unique experience. To me, it was just Joel doing his very best, just as I had taught him!

I am so grateful to our rabbi, cantor and everyone in our congregation. Without their warmth and affection for Joel, our family probably would not have been the active participants in the synagogue and Jewish community that we are today. I fear that we would have become secular Jews, left with a bitter taste in our mouths by the rejections of other congregations that wouldn't even attempt to accommodate Joel's special needs.

As a youngster, I attended Jewish Community Center day camps. I was involved in the first efforts to include campers who had special needs. Just as I witnessed the creation and growth of special education classes at our religious school, I saw the numbers of special needs campers increase in all of the local Jewish camps. After my bat mitzvah, I spent the summers as a "special needs counselor" at Jewish camps and the rest of the year as a "special needs madrikha" in religious school. In my middle school and high school, I always spent at least one hour a day in special education classes as a peer tutor. I was drawn to help these children who struggled each day and whose achievements were so very remarkable.

After high school, I continued to spend summers working with children with a variety of disabilities in summer camps and home therapy programs. I completed my bachelor's degree in Psychology and Special Education at the University of Arizona in 1999. I moved to Seattle, Washington where I received my master's degree in Early Childhood Special Education and teaching certificate in 2001. I taught a classroom for children with autism in the Seattle School District for three years. While in Seattle, I tutored three children with a variety of significant disabilities to prepare them for their bar mitzvoth. Each one was unique and each family has a very special place in my heart.

I also ran sibling support groups called "Sibshops" in Seattle for four years. My last year in Seattle, I found a little start-up congregation and taught Hebrew to non-disabled students; being part of a Jewish community without the disability connection was wonderful. It warmed my heart to know that this congregation would warmly welcome a child with a disability.

I spent a year in London, England where I was a Program Supervisor at a private school for children with autism. I supervise the teachers, teaching assistants and children in three classes. It was fascinating to view my past experiences in autism, teaching, Jewish community, family and friends from the perspective of living in another country. I told my English friends and colleagues stories about Joel so they could learn about a real person who has autism and therefore learn more about me, but it is difficult to describe and communicate. I am presently in an early childhood special education program.

It is the accumulation of all of these "unique experiences" that convinces me that I will always be involved with helping people who have disabilities find their place in the Jewish community.

LIGHT IN THE DARKNESS

Rabbi Shawn Fields-Meyer

Adam Ha-Rishon, the first man, was created on the eve of the first Shabbat, before nighttime, and then fell asleep. The next morning he awoke and again saw daylight. But as the hours went on, and night began to fall, Adam Ha-Rishon grew terrified. He did not know what darkness was, and felt himself becoming enveloped in a sea of blackness. So he screamed. He cried out to God: "What is happening? I can't see anything! I can't move! Help me!" He groped in the darkness, hoping for divine intervention.

When my second of three sons was two and a half years old, we began to notice some unusual behavior. Day by day, as he played, and ate, and spoke; at school, in stores, at synagogue, in the back yard: nothing seemed quite right. Ezra was hard to grasp. He would not connect.

At home, his favorite thing to do was to drag a blanket outside, turn on the garden spigot so there was the sound of a trickle, and roll himself in the blanket until he was fully cocooned inside. He would lie there for long stretches of time, just listening to the sound of the water. Other times he would burrow himself in his brother Noam's crib, under huge piles of stuffed animals. One afternoon, I became panicked because I could not find him anywhere. After a long search, I finally discovered by son on a shelf in the back of a deep linen closet, in the dark, hugging pillows.

When I told him how upset I'd been, he just walked away silently.

At school, he interacted with no one. He had no interest in friends. He seemed to look right through everyone: teachers, peers, even his own brothers. He was most animated with his menagerie of plastic dinosaurs and jungle creatures.

Ezra had an odd rigidity, unmatched by other children we knew: he would only eat white food. He insisted on wearing corduroy pants exclusively. He had an insistent, almost urgent desire for certain sensory experiences, but an extreme dislike of others. He could not stand to hold a hand, or have his head stroked, or keep his clothes on. Haircuts were torment. This made ordinary family life very difficult.

His speech was odd. He mimicked words and phrases from books, tapes and videos (Winnie the Pooh, Sesame Street). He repeated them tens of times in a row, like a broken record. You never knew if you were talking to Ezra, or to a character in a story.

But most disturbing was Ezra's almost haunting retreat from the world. And every time we tried to bring him into our orbit, we were met by either tortured screams or an empty, far-away stare. Nothing we did seemed to bring him back.

All this came to the surface one morning a month before his third birthday, at a parent-teacher conference at his nursery school. The teacher gave us example after example of Ezra's distance and withdrawal. I asked her what she was doing to help him. She shrugged, and said, "I don't know what to do. I'm telling you."

That night, I could not sleep. In the darkness and silence, I asked myself: what is wrong with this child? Finally, I sat up in bed and, in tears, wrote out a list. Under the heading "Who and what is my son Ezra?" I wrote down every detail I could think of what he liked, what he felt, how he did things. And I finally concluded the answer to my own question: I don't know.

Every parent has dreams. Fantasies of what might be. You hold a little baby in your arms, you feed him and sing to him you rock him and comfort him. And as the hours and days go by, you just dream and dream. And plan. And expect. And all of us know, that life never turns out the way you planned it.

But months of living with this beautiful, sweet, little boy; months of watching our formerly normal child slip away to some alternate reality; months of looking him in the eye and having him look the other way; this was more than unplanned. This was out of control. This was chaos! Like Adam on that first day, we stumbled in the darkness.

Stumbling through the darkness means not knowing where you're going. It means being filled with fear, insecurity, aloneness, limitations, uncertainty, powerlessness, and even some shame and embarrassment. My husband and I stumbled there for a long while. Really, we just stood there, groping around in the darkness.

In the still moments, out of the silent darkness, we began to discern something. We began to hear a word: Autism. It was a word. Just a name. A concept. But it was hearing that word, speaking it, that brought the very first spark of light into that darkness.

The word was in fact spoken by many people, but the first time I heard it with real comprehension was from the mouth of a psychiatrist who is also a rabbi. He said to us: Not only is there a name for this collection of symptoms, thereis something you can do to help him. A spark.

We began to follow some of the many leads given to us by him and others—many others. Slowly, tentatively at first, and then with growing speed and agility we learned to navigate the waters of what my husband Tom has described as a neurological disorder whose cause is not known, whose diagnosis is vague, whose prognosis is uncertain and whose treatment is constantly under dispute. But there were sparks – sometimes even rays – of light.

For many years, Ezra visited an occupational therapist who helped him discover physical activity to regulate himself. The minutes of swinging before dinner could make the difference between chaos and calm. Rolling in blankets regulated his system and helped him sleep at night. The therapist called it a sensory diet. We built these activities into our daily lives. Sparks.

We found that what appears to be withdrawal is in fact masking an almost desperate desire for human connection. I used to refer to his retreat as "Planet Ezra". But we learned to travel to that planet, to follow his lead, his interests. To wait patiently for him on his planet, communicate with him there, and then ask him to come with us. And he does. Sparks of light.

And we have learned that we are not the only ones. Stumbling in the darkness in those earliest days, we felt isolated. These days, we swap concerns and success stories with other parents. And we study Torah and offer support with a Jewish group we created of special needs moms and dads. We have drawn a circle of love and light around us: teachers, specialists, family, and friends who love Ezra. Sparks.

I recall the time that I was in the car with Ezra – he was five at the time – and, as usual, I told him what I tell him and his brothers countless times every day: "I love you," I said. "I love you, Ezra." He paused, and looked me in the eye. "I love you too, Ima." And I realized, that was the first time, in his nearly 5 years of life, that he had ever spoken those words.

He's older now. My son, who once would pass through our house seeming not to notice anyone around him, now asks friends and family members to play a game with him, to talk to him, to connect. My son, who once constructed lonely, impenetrable worlds of plastic zebras and giraffes now invites us over to join him as he pets a poodle at the park. My son, whose love of books once meant sitting alone and flipping rapidly through pages, ignoring words, now emails everyone he knows to tell them about his interests, and to ask them about theirs. Little by little, light is dispelling the darkness.

In our family, we don't really talk about a cure. Rather, the task is to nurture our child, to respect his unique personality; not to change him, but to give him tools.

In the Garden of Eden, what did God do, when God heard Adam's cry? How did God respond to the human's terror, to his utter paralysis in the enveloping darkness of the Garden of Eden? Because we have read the rest of the Bible, we know this is the God who can make miracles happen – He can send the plagues and part the waters and cause the sun to stand still. So what did God do for the man stumbling, frightened of the black night? Did God perform a miracle? Turn day into night? Lighten up the horizon? No.

Instead, God said to the man: Feel around you. See, there are two flints by your feet. Take those flints, and run them together until you see a spark. Eventually you will create a flame, and with that flame you will light up the darkness and stop stumbling.

God long ago created all the miracles-to-be. They are out there. Now, God points us to the tools, the ones often in our own gardens, that help us light the sparks that dispel our darkness.

A PERSONAL STORY

Yonatan Y. Koch

Lately I have been doing workshops for many different groups and organizations. Why me? Who am I that I am able to bring my knowledge and share it with all of you?

That's simple. I'm Yonatan Koch, a Special Education teacher in the New York City Public Schools. I am working on a doctorate in Administration of Special Education Programs and doing lectures while writing a book.

But wait, I wasn't always able to do all of this. In fact, had you met me about 22 years ago you would never know I was the same person. Why is this you ask? That is a good question and I am glad you asked.

When I was five I was unable to read, write, walk, or talk intelligibly. I was my mom's "ga" boy. I would point to an object and say 'ga'. She knew what I meant. I remember looking down from the top of a hill and although my grandfather was only maybe five steps away, I feared that I could not walk down the hill. He and my father stood at the bottom of the hill and encouraged me to try. I remember how scared I was to try riding a bike. My therapists assured me that I could do it.

I had these misconceptions because of the fact that I have a Learning Disability or Learning Differences. This means that I have some trouble remembering things that you would find very easy to remember. It also means that I have a harder time at learning things that you would learn easily. A learning disabled person has to work harder to keep up with their classmates..

It was because of the positive, encouraging attitudes and actions of my parents, grandparents, teachers, and therapists that I was able to overcome the obstacles as I have. The other encouraging factor to overcome these obstacles, to this day, is self determination.

Kol Ha-Olam Kulo, Gesher Tsar Me'od—the entire world is a narrow bridge and the main thing is not to be afraid

This is the attitude I have had for the last number of years. This thinking helped me in overcoming obstacles—I know it sounds hard to believe but, due to visual perceptual deficits while attending college on Long Island, New York, I was unable to leave the island because I was scared to drive on the Long Island Expressway. To this day, reading is a challenge because my reading comprehension skills are not as strong as my peers due to my academic challenges,

As I prepare for the upcoming year, a year that promises to be nothing short of challenging—as I embark on a doctorate program at Columbia University while teaching full time—I know that I have the support networks set up in my favor. I have the contacts that I can use as valuable resources. My life experience has taught me this. I didn't get where I am today without a struggle. My path in life was not presented to me on a silver platter, but I was given many obstacles—some doctors even told my parents that due to my learning disabilities I would not succeed in life. Just goes to show what they know.

The obstacles have not subsided, nor do I ever expect them to—what I will do is continue to implement strategies that will help me locate the proper accommodations in order to succeed.

Yesterday was *Shabbat Nahamu*. Following Tisha B'Av and the destructions it commemorates the Haftarah from Isaiah shows the Prophet being told to comfort God's People in the face of their despair. Following a national catastrophe despair is obvious; but what of the quiet despair that often besets individuals who find themselves unjustly shunned and shut out of the world simply because they are different in physical, emotional, or mental capabilities? Do we not bear a burden to bring them comfort by assisting them to integrate into society as respected people?

Recently I have been pondering the question, "Why must we educate students with Learning Differences or Disabilities?" It would be much easier to say; "Yankel has Learning Differences, let's leave him alone," and that would be the end of that.

However, our texts tell us that this mode of thought is unacceptable. Torah teaches that, "You shall not insult the deaf nor place a stumbling block before the blind; you shall revere your God—I am Adonai," (Lev. 19:14).

Right here it is written; God commands our reverence, our respect. To respect God is to respect all created in the Divine image, including those with differences and special needs, be they strangers, friends, or our students. In respecting God we need do what God commands. If that means removing all obstacles found in the path of the blind then so we must. As Amy Weiss points out in a D'var Torah she did on Emor for the Union for Reform Judaism in *Torat Hayim*, "...by ignoring their needs [those of the disabled], we do inadvertently place a stumbling block before them." My colleagues, removing stumbling blocks is not merely an option; it is a requirement. We must work diligently to help each and every one of our students.

In Leviticus we are charged,*"K'doshim tih'yu, ki kadosh ani Adonai Eloheikhem; you will be kadosh because I, Adonai your God, am kadosh."* Kuf-Daled-Shin can carry a meaning of maximizing potential, i.e. to be the very best we can be. In a D'var Torah he wrote on Va-Yikra, Rabbi Norman Koch said, *"K'dushah,* 'holiness,' might be seen as a maximizing of potential: making the best of self, moment, or situation...this verse beckons us, beings created in the image of the Divine, to maximize our potential, as God, our template, is the maximum of all potential." If we are not helping our students to work to their full potential then we are not working to ours. Yes, all students have potential, despite the obstacles they may encounter. Most of you are unaware that at the age of five I was unable to read, write, walk properly, or talk in an intelligible fashion. Had my parents not acted with the fullness of their strengths and talents I would not be standing before you working in fulfillment of my potential. They, and so many others, helped me understand and access the potential I have to complete the doctoral degree I am currently pursuing.

In Judaism numbering is very important. We number ten for a Minyan; we number thirteen years to Bar or Bat Mitzvah; we number six days in a week leading up to Shabbos. When we fail to think about working with a student just because they have learning differences we send that child a message that they aren't among our number. How as Jews can we tell any child that she doesn't count? Who are we to tell a child that he doesn't belong and therefore cannot be numbered among us?

Judaism also underscores the idea of saving a life. "Save a life and you have saved the whole world; destroy a life and you have destroyed the whole world. Well, if you ignore the student with learning differences in your classroom you are, in a way, destroying that child's life, hence destroying the world. Each of our students can succeed if given the right help. How can we ignore the student who cannot achieve the desired outcome without modifications? It is our duty to provide the accommodations necessary.

Sadly, there are places in Torah where those with disabilities are excluded. One example of this is in the Priesthood, where those with disabilities weren't allowed to serve. Unfortunately, we often exclude those who are different. We exclude some from Shul when we fail to provide adequate access to the building; or, if they are able to enter, we fail when, absent a ramp, they are unable to ascend the bima for an aliyah. In my experience, the majority of people who are excluded by our lack of awareness or our lack of attention to the details of their need won't say anything. Not wanting to burden others, or being shy, or frustrated by prior experience, or fear of rejection will often deter self-advocacy. What we should all realize is that they shouldn't have to speak up; it is up to us to be proactively inclusive. We need remember and internalize the teachings of Torah as an impetus to action and thus can we honor our God. It is up to us, thus should we endeavor to not insult the deaf nor should we inadvertently place a stumbling block before the blind. I pray that we enable ever-greater access and inclusion and thus fully revere our God.

JACOB ARTSON'S MESSAGE

Hi. My name is Jacob Artson and I am a person just like you. I am part of a wonderful Jewish family, I go to our local public high school where I am in mostly regular classes, I play sports, I love to travel, and I enjoy hanging out with my friends and girlfriend. The only difference between you and me is that I have lots of labels attached to me like nonverbal, severely autistic and developmentally disabled.

You have probably never met anyone like me who cannot speak but who can communicate by typing. I am a perfect example of how someone can be very impaired in one area but have great strength in other areas. Actually, I think that is true of all people, but it is especially true about people with autism. When I was diagnosed at age 3, I could not speak or move my body properly, and 13 years later that remains true. However, if success and worth are measured by being a mentsch and giving back to others, then I would classify my life as a success. You can be the judge.

There are lots of myths and misconceptions about autism out there. Many purported experts claim that individuals with autism are not interested in socializing. This is totally ridiculous. I love people, but my movement disorder constantly interferes with my efforts to interact. I cannot start and stop and switch my thinking or emotions or actions at the right time. This can make being in a big group very lonely and that is the worst thing about autism. So next time you see someone like me at your synagogue or at your event, remember that they probably feel really lonely and you could be the person to make their day by smiling at them and letting them know that they exist.

Another myth is that the majority of kids with autism are mentally retarded. In fact, our bodies are totally disorganized but our cognitive skills are intact and our minds are hungry for knowledge. For the first seven years of my life, I was considered profoundly retarded. Then a speech therapist introduced me to facilitated communication, which involves typing with support. Facilitated communication literally saved my life. As a toddler and young child, my life was ruled by anxiety about my disability and fear that it would isolate me forever. As I developed the ability to type, I gradually was able to break out of my autistic prison and create social connections with family and, for the first time, friends. Later I was able to share my writings with my classmates and synagogue community, and I have also become something of a spokesperson for the silent autistic masses, which feels like a tremendous privilege. For me, communication is the key to being engaged in the world, and I think every facilitated communication user would agree with that statement. In the autism world we say that not being able to speak doesn't mean that you don't have anything to say. In my experience, the converse is also true – just because you can speak doesn't mean that you have anything worth saying.

Every person alive is encumbered by challenges and blessed with gifts. I used to think that my ratio of challenges to gifts was higher than most, but now I realize that my challenges are just more obvious. I have learned that there are actually many positive aspects of autism. For example, I get a VIP pass at Disneyland and I get to kiss all the beautiful counselors at camp and pretend I don't know any better. On a serious note, not being able to speak means that you spend lots of time listening. In fact, much of what I know I've learned from listening to conversations that other people didn't think I could hear, or listening through the wall to what the teacher in the next classroom was saying. People often ask me how I became such a good writer. The answer is that my inability to speak gives me lots of time to contemplate and imagine and also forces me to hear everyone's perspective and think about it because I cannot interrupt or monopolize the conversation like people who have oral speech.

There are many factors that have influenced who I have become. First and foremost, my family has never wavered in their belief that I am a child of God with an equal claim to dignity and respect as any typically developing child. I know that it has taken a heavy toll on them, but it has been a lifesaver for me. My amazing twin sister, Shira, is my best friend, hero, social secretary, advocate, fashion consultant, role model and cheerleader. My Ema has been my tireless advocate and my rock. My Abba, whom I adore more than anyone on earth, has given me a model to strive to emulate.

Second, I benefited tremendously from floortime therapy, which involves many hours of structured, interactive play. Floortime taught me to smile spontaneously, and that is the most important skill I have ever learned because it has ensured that I am not lonely and invisible like I was as a toddler. Wherever I go, even when I have been the most motorically challenged person present, I have always made friends and even been popular because floortime taught me to love life and to live it with joy and laughter. Now, as a teenager, I may still passionately hate autism, but I love life more than I hate autism.

Third, I have been blessed with a wonderful therapeutic team. When I moved to Los Angeles at the age of 6, I was a classic case of severe autism. My behavior was so awful I hated myself. Almost everyone I met gave up on me almost immediately and believed I would never amount to anything. But there was one doctor who saw the gem locked inside my prison of autism. She smiled at me in a way that reflected her belief that I was a worthy person with the ability and desire to engage, and she waited the very long time it took for me to smile back. That was the beginning of my long and wonderful relationship with Dr. Ricki Robinson, who has been my mentor and guide as I struggle to reach my goals of becoming a productive member of society and a person worthy of respect. At school, at least since 5th grade, my teachers have consistently given me opportunities to develop my academic abilities and have focused on my accomplishments rather than my anxieties. I also have had two amazing aides who have stuck with me and have shown me that I can achieve anything I focus on 100% because I know I have someone supporting me who believes I am capable of flying.

Beyond those central supports, I am surrounded by a community of friends who treat me like a regular kid and think of our family as just another typical Jewish family. Even though at this point in time I cannot calm down enough to participate in many shul or community activities, it is very important to me to be invited – it symbolizes for me a belief that I will eventually reach the stage of participating more fully. At our shul, I know that the invitations are genuine, not mere window dressing, so they provide a tremendous motivation to control my awful behavior.

I have found great support in God, Torah, and the Jewish community. The greatest single day of my life was my bar mitzvah because everyone there accepted and celebrated me for exactly who I am. At the end of the service, everyone came up on the bima for Adon Olam. I will carry in my mind and heart forever the picture of everyone there smiling at me. I had wonderful experiences when I was in a Jewish preschool and later kindergarten, even though my teachers had never had a child with autism in their class. What made those experiences successful was the way the teachers modeled inclusion for the other kids. They treated me as a person made in God's image and not as different in any way. Through the years, I've also had wonderful buddies from The Friendship Circle, attended several Jewish camps, participated in a Jewish musical theater program called The Miracle Project, and prayed at Koleinu, a service at our synagogue for kids with special needs.

But there have been obstacles as well. I have never attended religious school because I was bored in the special ed Hebrew school and the typical classes did not allow a place for me to engage either. When I was younger, I went to synagogue every Shabbat but the other kids ignored me. As a teenager, I have attended Jewish camps and youth groups, but the first reaction is that I am too disabled to attend, or that I don't participate once I'm there. So whether I'm invited seems to depend on the particular director that year.

So here is my advice for those of you who run Jewish schools or organizations: The best peers and aides I have had didn't have any special background. It doesn't actually take any training to be a leader who models inclusion. It just takes an attitude that all people are made in God's image and it is our job to find the part of God hidden in each person.

Because I have had to struggle every day of my life to do things that other kids take for granted, I think that I have experienced God's love in a way that most kids have not. Also, it takes struggle to gain wisdom, so I have had many opportunities to acquire wisdom. I used to get very offended at the notion of being someone's community service project. But then I realized that while my buddies were teaching me how to be like other kids, I was teaching them how to appreciate the beauty of God's world in a new way. All in all, who gets the greater benefit?

Kids with special needs don't need to be reinforced like dogs with good job and good listening and similar phrases used for animal training. All we need is stimulation, patience, and someone to notice our little triumphs and comment on them. When all those little triumphs combine over days and weeks and months and years, the results can be truly miraculous!

OUR SOURCES TELL US

DNA ANALYSTS

Danny Siegel

Moses had a speech impediment. He wasn't born with it, but, as the story goes, he put a hot coal in his mouth, causing burns that left him damaged. The story seems to be one of the three most well-known in most kids' Jewish education, along with Abraham breaking his father's idols and the angel that slaps you on the mouth when you are born and make you forget all the Torah you knew in the womb.

And yet, something is wrong. No one—at least in my day—has taught this midrash as a point of departure for sensitizing us to people with certain limitations and disabilities. It is a sorely missed opportunity. It seems strange now, in my 50's, that as I review biblical and Talmudic tests, people with disabilities keep popping up all over the place. I had thought (or I think I thought) that all Jews were whole, fully functioning. But, in the Bible:

Issaac was blind.

Jacob limped.

Moses, of course, had his speech impediment. (Exodus 4:10).

Miriam had to contend with leprosy (or whatever the disease was).

One *midrash* (Numbers Rabbah, Naso 7:1) indicates that most of the Jews who left Egypt had disabilities (industrial accidents through all the building projects).

Job was disfigured and ugly from the boils with which he was stricken early on in the book (Chapter 3), and not cured until the end (Chapter 42).

In Talmudic literature:

Rabbi Preda had a student with whom he had to review all the material 400 times in order for him to understand it.

Rav Sheshet was blind.

Rav Yosef was blind.

The selfsame Rav Yosef also had some kind of disability that made him forget whatever Torah he had been learning, and his student, Abayye had to remind him (Nedarim 41a).

On that same page, we are told that Rabbi Yehuda HaNasi, certainly one of the preeminent Talmudic personalities, suffered from a similar malady—and Rabbi Chiyya and others helped him to remember.

Rav Yosef taught (Mena<u>h</u>ot 99a). "Take care of, and with, an elder who has forgotten his Torah because of circumstances beyond his control...Not only the second (whole) tablets were in the Ark, but the shattered pieces of the first tablets." When Moses broke the first tablets, the pieces were still holy, so he gathered the fragments and put them in the Ark with the new ones.

People who are not as complete as other people are also holy, and entitled to be treated with the same sense of *kavod*—dignity—as anyone else, entitled to the same priviledges and same entre to everything the Jewish community has to offer. Who better to teach it than Rav Yosef? And, one last point, taught to me by one of my students -The Levites had a double burden in the desert: the Ark was that much heavier because it held the two sets of tablets.

That is the "price" we pay to make sure that everyone remains part of *Klal Yisrael*, the Jewish people. *Klal Yisrael* means all Jews—all of them.

Including me, with my learning disability.

MESHANEH HA-BRIYYOT: A NEW JEWISH APPROACH TO DISABILITIES

Rabbi Elliot Dorff

I want to suggest a virtual Copernican revolution in how the Jewish tradition, and Jews along with it, should understand and treat disabilities. In order to describe this new view, I need first to summarize what the Jewish tradition has said in the past.

A SUMMARY OF THE TRADITION'S TREATMENT OF DISABILITIES

I think it is fair to say from the very start that traditional Judaism's approach to disability is remarkably enlightened and compassionate, especially when compared to the treatment disabled people got in other cultures. Before we get to the specific legal aspects of this, note that almost all of the biblical heroes were disabled in some way. Sarah, Rebekah, Rachel, and Hannah are all barren for some time in their lives,[1] Isaac and Jacob suffer from blindness in their old age,[2] Jacob was lame for much of his life,[3] and even the greatest biblical hero, Moses, suffered from a speech impediment.[4] Similarly, a number of talmudic rabbis were disabled; for example, Nahum of Gimzo, Dosa ben Harkinas, Rav Joseph, and Rav Sheshet were all blind.[5] The more "manly" biblical models—Esau, Gideon, Samson, and even David—are all portrayed as flawed in character. In contrast, the heroes of Greek and Roman culture were all physically perfect—even extraordinary. American secular culture applauds those who overcome disabilities, along with those who triumph over any obstacles, and some popular movies, like Philadelphia, and some country songs, like Mark Wills' "Don't Laugh at Me," warn us not to ignore or denigrate the homeless or ill, but very few, if any, commercials depict disabled people or even old people because Americans honor youth and ability. That is why Franklin Delano Roosevelt insisted on hiding his wheelchair in the last years of his presidency. Thus the fact that so many of the biblical and rabbinic heroes were disabled in various ways speaks volumes about how our tradition from its very beginnings thought of this group of people: in contrast to the Greek, Roman, and American cultures, in Jewish sources the disabled were to be construed like everyone else, and they were often leaders.

This stems from some deep Jewish convictions. For the Jewish tradition, we are all created in the image of God,[6] and, as such, we have divine worth independent of whatever we do. That does not mean that we may do whatever we want; quite the contrary, God gives us 613 commandments, and the Rabbis add many more. Moreover, the fact that each person is created in the image of God does not mean that we have to like everyone or what everyone does. It does mean, though, that even when we judge a person harshly for his or her actions, we must still recognize the divine worth inherent in that person. The extreme illustration of that is that the

43

Torah demands that "If a man is guilty of a capital offense and is put to death, and you impale him on a stake, you must not let his corpse remain on the stake overnight, but must bury him the same day. For an impaled body is an affront to God"[7]—literally, "a curse of God." That is, the image of God inherent in even such a person must be honored. How much the more so must we honor the image of God in those who have not committed heinous crimes but happen to be disabled in some way.

The Jewish tradition is remarkable not only in how it thought about the disabled, but in the actions it demanded with and for them. In Greek and Roman cultures, "imperfect" infants were put out to die, and disabled adults were left to fend for themselves and often mocked to boot. In Jewish culture, in contrast, killing an infant for any reason constitutes murder,[8] and the Torah specifically prohibits cursing the deaf or putting a stumbling block before the blind.[9]

As Jews, we dare not forget these fundamental features of our tradition's thought and practice. On the contrary, given how other cultures treated the disabled, we should take pride in the fundamental humanity embedded in our own tradition.

With this as a background, though, it is also important that we acknowledge that Jewish sources did put the disabled at some disadvantage. This especially affected the Temple and the biblical concept of the holy. Specifically, while disabled men born into the priestly class were not denied their part of the priestly portions, they were not allowed to serve in the Temple and were instead put to menial work such as cleaning the kindling wood from worms, for which a special area was set aside: "No one at all who has a defect shall be qualified [to offer a sacrifice], no man who is blind, or lame, or has a limb too short or too long; no man who has a broken leg or a broken arm; or he who is hunchback, or a dwarf, or who has a growth in his eye, or who has a boil-scar, or scurvy, or crushed testes."[10] Maimonides explains the exclusion on the grounds that "most people do not estimate a person by his true form, but by his limbs and his clothing, and the Temple was to be held in great reverence by all."[11] Somehow, for the Torah and Maimonides, one could be disabled and still function as the people's political leader, but one could not serve in the sacred precincts of the Temple. One verse in Deuteronomy even says that a man who has crushed testes or a severed penis "may not enter the congregation of the Lord"; it is not clear whether that only refers to a man who voluntarily maimed himself that way in service of some Canaanite god, or whether it refers to any man in that condition, and we also do not know the meaning or implications of "not entering the congregation of the Lord,"[12] but it clearly constitutes an exclusion of such men from normal status.

Now, as we turn from ancient rites to Jewish law now in practice, I shall summarize the various categories of disability and how the Rabbis treated them. In all fairness, by and large the Rabbis limited any legal restrictions on the disabled to the specific tasks the disability prevented them from doing, seeing such people otherwise as full-fledged Jews. That is, the Rabbis did not dismiss the disabled categorically from Jewish responsibilities and roles; they instead sought to empower them as much as possible. Still, Rabbinic law does impose some limitations on them in both ritual and civil law.

The disabilities the Rabbis discuss are the following: one who is insane or sufficiently mentally retarded to lack the mental ability to be held legally responsible (*shoteh*); blind (*suma*); epileptic (*nikhpeh*); sexually neuter (*tumtum*) or hermaphrodite (*androgenus*); or sterile (*saris* for a male; *aylonit* for a female). In addition, they speak about a heresh, a term the Mishnah defines as someone who is both deaf and mute, but the Talmud defines *heresh* as someone who is deaf but not mute, *ileim* being used to describe a mute.[13] That ambiguity will affect later rulings about that category.

Here, then, are some of the rulings regarding the disabled in Jewish ritual law:

1. Blind people should say the blessing before the Shema that praises God for creating light because even though they cannot see the light of day, they benefit from it because others see them and keep them from accidents.[14]

2. Similarly, even though the third paragraph of the Shema (Numbers 15:39) commands us to wear fringes so that we may see them and thereby remember God's commandments, blind people are obligated to wear fringes because others can see them.[15]

3. Along the same lines, even though the Shema begins with "Hear O Israel," a deaf person, who by definition cannot hear either the command or his or her own voice saying the prayer, can nevertheless fulfill the commandment of reciting the Shema because others can hear him or her saying the prayer.[16]

4. Since the Torah must be read and not recited by heart, blind people may not serve as the Torah reader, but they may be called up to recite the blessings over the Torah and they may read the Haftarah from a Braille text or even recite it by heart.[17] A deaf person may read from the Torah as well as recite the blessings over it.[18]

5. A blind person may lead the congregation in prayer because blindness does not free a Jew from the duty to pray and, contrary to reading the Torah, one may pray by heart.[19]

6. A *heresh* (probably here a deaf-mute) cannot fulfill the obligation of the community to hear the Purim megillah read because such a person cannot speak audibly.[20]

7. Despite some arguments to the contrary, a blind person is obligated to recite the Haggadah of Passover, as two great, blind talmudic scholars, Rav Sheshet and Rav Joseph, did.[21]

8. A blind person may not serve as a kosher slaughterer, for one must see clearly to cut firmly and quickly to minimize the animal's pain. A deaf-mute or even a shoteh, however, may serve in this capacity if they are supervised by a person who knows how to do this and who attests that the slaughter fulfilled the requirements of Jewish law.[22]

9. Finally, a *heresh*, *shoteh*, and a minor are not obligated to hear the *shofar* blown on Rosh Hashanah and therefore are not eligible to fulfill the commandment for others if they blow the *shofar*. The later codes specify that this applies only to a deaf person, but a hearing person, even if mute, is obliged to hear the *shofar* blown and therefore can fulfill the commandment for others.[23] This is a good example of a general tendency embedded in all of these Jewish ritual laws and in Jewish civil law as well—namely, that the Rabbis restricted a disabled person's duties and eligibility only to those areas affected by the disability.

Now let us look at a few of Jewish civil laws related to the disabled. In general, deaf-mutes were categorized together with insane people and minors because the Rabbis had no way of knowing whether deaf-mutes understood what was happening or not; as a result, deaf-mutes, like minors and the insane, were not given much legal status. The blind and the crippled, on the other hand, were presumed to have full legal competence, except in areas that required someone to see or to walk. In other words, Jewish law worried most about legal competence (what American lawyers call *"mens rea"*), and that was much more likely to be compromised by mental, rather than physical, disabilities.

Here, then, are some examples, of Jewish civil laws relating to the disabled:

1. An insane person and a minor who does not realize the value of an object cannot acquire title for themselves or for others; only an agent of sound mind (such as a parent) can acquire title for them. A deaf-mute and a minor who *can* understand an object's value, however, can acquire title for themselves, although not for others.[24]

2. Because inheritance to and from blood relatives requires no legal transfer of property but rather occurs automatically at death, both an insane person and a deaf-mute can make bequests and receive them. In both cases, though, a trustee or guardian must be appointed to look after their affairs.[25]

3. An insane person cannot buy or sell property, but a deaf-mute and even a minor can buy or sell movable property (but not real estate) in order to sustain themselves.[26] Special care had to be taken, though, to assure that the witnesses to the sale correctly understood the gestures made by the deaf-mute to indicate an intention to buy or sell.[27] Someone who was mute but not deaf, however, could effect an acquisition or sale even of real estate.[28] Someone who sometimes was of sound mind and sometimes not, such as an epileptic, has full ability to buy or sell both movable property and real estate while of sound mind, but the witnesses must take steps to ensure that that is indeed the case during the transaction.[29]

4. Even though there were restrictions on the ability of deaf-mutes, insane people, and minors to acquire property, someone who took away anything such people found had committed theft.[30]

5. Insane people were not held liable at law, and if the situation required it, a guardian was appointed to protect the interests of both the insane person and those who might suffer as a result of his or her legal immunity.

6. An insane person may never serve as a witness, and even a sane person who is confused about a given matter may not serve as a witness about that matter. Those who are sometimes sane and sometimes insane must be tested to ascertain their eligibility as a witness.[31] The deaf and mute were also excluded from most testimony because the Rabbis, interpreting Leviticus 5:1, determined that one must be able not only to hear, but to speak in order to testify.[32] The deaf and mute could, however, testify to free a woman from becoming chained to her first husband and thus unable to remarry (an *agunah*).[33] The Torah's verse requiring that witnesses see what happened also excluded the blind from testifying, even if they recognize the voices of the parties.[34] Moreover, since these disabilities barred a person from serving as a witness, they also excluded them from being eligible to serve as a judge.[35]

7. An insane person could not marry because such a person could not legally consent, but a deaf-mute could.[36] Sterile people could marry as long as both parties were aware of that fact at the time of marriage, but otherwise the marriage was void. Someone who exhibits no sexual characteristics (a *tumtum*) could marry either a woman or a man, although the marriage had doubtful status. A hermaphrodite (*adrogenus*) may marry a woman but not a man because the Rabbis considered such a person male.[37]

8. Finally, and perhaps most indicatively, just as a person who disgraces an able-bodied person must compensate the victim with money as well as seek forgiveness, so too anyone who demeans a disabled person must pay such damages. Only an insane person is not paid for this, according to the Talmud, because being insane, in the Rabbis' judgment, already constituted a disgrace second to none.[38] That last provision may disturb us, but what is remarkable is that Jews were forbidden to embarrass all other categories of disabled people and had to pay damages if they did.

MY COPERNICAN REVOLUTION

Dayyenu, that is enough to give you a good sense of the tradition's treatment of disabilities. It is not a perfect picture; there are parts of the story and the law that we might wish were different. Those who would like to see changes in Jewish attitudes toward the disabled or the laws governing them base their arguments on the immense changes that have taken place in recent times in technology and medicine, enabling even paraplegics to get around, the deaf to communicate through sign language, and the blind to read texts translated into Braille. Psychotherapy and drug therapies have made good progress in relieving a variety of psychological disorders. Obviously, such disabilities often still compromise a person's competence to do some things, but, many maintain, the advances in what the disabled can do should move us to change Jewish law in a number of particulars. I completely agree with such moves, and I think that they are completely in line with the Rabbis' careful analysis of identifying exactly what people suffering from a particular disability can and cannot do.

In this paper, though, I want to try a completely different approach. I call it "a Copernican revolution" because like Copernicus, who got us to think of the Earth as going around the sun rather than the other way around, I similarly want to prod us to think of the world from the vantage point of the disabled. That is, I want to suggest that we think of a world in which *the norm* is what we now call "disabled," and we able-bodied and sane people are the abnormal ones. What would—or should—Jewish perspectives and law look like then?

This project of mine may seem a little crazy to you, and so before I go any further with it, I would like to point out two things that might make it seem considerably more reasonable. First, the idea struck me because of what a disabled person told me long ago—namely, that from the point of view of the disabled, all the rest of us are *"temporarily abled"*! How do you like *that* description of yourself? But we all know, of course, that they are right: Even Olympic athletes will, in the course of life, most likely lose at least some of their vision and hearing, and even the most nimble and those who exercise regularly will not escape the slowing down and the aches and pains that age inevitably brings. We nervously joke about it, but even our mental processes may dull; you do not have to have full-blown Alzheimer's to become increasingly forgetful—and yes, often more crotchety—as time goes on. As my wife, Marlynn, told me, the first time she heard about disabilities was at a conference of the Bureau of Jewish Education in Los Angeles in 1971, when a young woman who was wheelchair-bound told the assembled teachers: "Don't care about the disabled out of sympathy. Care for them for your own selfish reasons, for you too will be like me some day." My intention is not to depress you; it is only to point out that it is not so far-fetched to think of everyone as disabled, especially as the American and Jewish populations age.

Second, one is not just abled or disabled; there are *degrees* of disability. I, for example, have worn glasses since I was 17, and it was also during that year that I had my first asthma attack.

Ever since then I have lived with these disabilities. The asthma, in particular, prevents me from engaging in fast sports. In my younger days, when the test of a male's masculinity was all-too-often connected with his athletic abilities, and when asthma medications were much less helpful than they are now, that particular malady took quite a toll on my psychological well-being and my social standing. I mention these things not to seek your sympathy, but just to indicate that each one of us is disabled in some ways—physical, mental, interpersonal, or all of the above—and even if we learn to cope with these problems, they do change our image of ourselves and what we can do. So all of us who think of ourselves as able-bodied should not have too much difficulty picturing ourselves as at least partially disabled.

In such a world, then, in which the norm is being disabled and the unusual thing is to have full control of one's physical and mental faculties and full ability to interact socially with people without any psychological problems whatsoever, how would we want Judaism to treat disabilities? I guarantee you that our whole attitude would change. Instead of thinking about humane treatment for the disabled as being motivated by our own compassion or God's commandment, we would see it as simply caring for ourselves—much as we see any of the services that we Americans expect the government or others to provide for us.

With that as the norm, wheelchair access, for example, would not be a new and sensitive thing; it would be what we just normally assume. "Walk" and "Don't Walk" lights at intersections would naturally have ticking sounds so that the blind would not have to depend on the sighted or what traffic they hear to know when to cross. As many college classrooms are now equipped with internet access, so too they would have facilities for Braille transcriptions of materials being discussed in class, and they would be routinely staffed by people who sign for the deaf. The same would be true for business meetings, court proceedings, and the like. Even private homes would be easily accessible for people in wheelchairs and would be arranged to ensure that the blind would have an easy time finding their way without tripping.

As the objects of society—the nouns—would change, so too would daily activities—the verbs, so to speak. That is, daily activities and special events, including trips, would be planned assuming that most people are disabled in some way. So, for example, there might still be sports for the able-bodied, together with teams and league competition, and there might even be professional sports teams for the able-bodied, but such activities would be seen simply as a subset of the larger social efforts to provide athletic expressions for all of society's members. Thus, just as there are now professional men's and women's basketball teams for the able-bodied, so too there would be professional teams for the blind, deaf, and wheelchair-bound, perhaps differentiated by sex as well. Courses in schools and colleges would be taught in a multi-media way so that people of all kinds of abilities and disabilities could participate. It would be obvious that school districts needed to schedule and pay for classes for autistic children and those with other developmental disabilities, with teachers specially trained for helping such children. Business meetings, court proceedings, and visits to the doctor, the accountant, the barber, and everyone else who provides a service or sells a product would all be easily handled by all people, regardless of their forms and levels of ability or disability. Even those inviting others to their homes would automatically think about not only the activities that they plan, but even how to give directions to get to their home for people of varying abilities and disabilities.

What kind of society would this be? Clearly, our whole way of looking at the world and what we expect of people would change. That would bring with it a number of objective, subjective, and interpersonal innovations.

First, objectively, massive economic and social changes would be entailed in the kind of Copernican revolution I am proposing. As I indicated through only a few examples, both the objects and activities of our lives would have a very different character. Much of that would cost considerable sums of money, and that is a real concern, but, truth to tell, the economic outlays to make this happen would be nothing like the 14% of Gross National Product that we currently spend on cosmetics.

The real difference would be one of attitude. Instead of thinking of ourselves with all kinds of abilities and coping with whatever disabilities we have, and instead of modeling ourselves after people with no apparent disabilities, we would instead think of human beings as coming in all kinds of shapes and sizes, abilities and disabilities.

THE COSTS AND BENEFITS OF SUCH A COPERNICAN REVOLUTION

While I very much encourage us to entertain my proposal, I must warn you that it entails significant costs. First, in the most literal sense of the word "cost," my plan, as I indicated above, would require major financial expenditures. There is no getting around that, and it is a major concern. To do anything like what I am proposing would require major outlays of money. We have already tasted that in the costs of complying with the Americans with Disabilities Act, but my proposal would require much more. If anything, American society today seems to be moving in the opposite direction, as we have seen the United States Supreme Court chip away at the ADA's protections and its costs over the last several years. The current Administration, and American society generally, may not be ready to spend more money on these issues, and that raises real questions about the viability of what I am suggesting.

Even apart from current spending priorities, it must be acknowledged that one important reason why society is structured as it is does not stem from fear of the disabled or prejudice against them, but from the fact that the vast majority of us, for the vast majority of our lives, are, in fact, remarkably abled. We may require glasses, asthma medications, and the like; but God has given most of us bodies that enable us to do many things for many years, and God's agents in the form of doctors and other mental and physical health care personnel are extending our abilities and their longevity yet further. Thus there is a certain plausibility in treating the abled as the norm and the disabled as the exception, not only in conception, but in creating social policy.

Furthermore—and this really gives me pause—I fear that my proposal may understate the pain involved in being disabled. After it is all said and done, it is harder to cope with life if you are blind and most people are sighted, deaf when most people are hearing, unable to walk when most people can, or unable to learn or interact with people as most people do. This increased difficulty encompasses not only the physical trials of getting around in the world of the abled, but the emotional challenges of feeling a sense of self-worth and the social obstacles of creating friendships. I certainly do not want to minimize those problems in the least; on the contrary, my proposal aims at mitigating them by resetting the default option in society, as it were—that is, by making us think of everyone as disabled in some way. Even less do I want to stand in the way of efforts to develop cures for disabilities or better tools to cope with them; on the contrary, I want to encourage such efforts as much as possible. So my proposal of making the disabled the norm should not be construed as minimizing the pain involved in disabilities or as discouraging efforts to alleviate that pain.

Moreover, to do what I am proposing would require us to do some considerable emotional work in readjusting our American way of thinking and feeling about ourselves. Currently, with the exception of doctors and other mental and physical health care personnel, most of us live in a state of denial for most of our lives about the disabilities that we ourselves will most probably incur at some later date. We do that, in part, by choosing to engage with only able-bodied people in at least the vast majority of our daily activities. We avoid visiting the sick at hospitals, not only because it is a bother and poses a real risk for infection, but also because hospitals remind us of our own vulnerability and even our own mortality, and we do not like to think about that or feel insecure.

In the society that I am proposing, though, very much like the society of our great-grandparents, people will encounter others of all ages of ability and disability on a daily basis; the disabled will not be sequestered into specific institutions for them, but will rather live at home and will regularly study and work with the more able-bodied. That may make some of us today, who are used to being protected from daily reminders of our vulnerability, terribly uncomfortable. Such feelings may pass, however, as we again get used to such a society. In many ways, this is similar to the process by which Jews of my generation gradually accepted women—and, for that matter, men—participating in many areas of life where they had never been before. But like the opening of roles in society to people of both genders, so too the opening of society's spaces and activities to people of all levels and forms of ability and disability will, at least, take some getting used to.

So much for the costs of my proposal. What are its benefits? First of all, making the disabled the norm would make all of us feel better about ourselves, for such a society would be much more accepting of high degrees of disability in the various areas of life. That would not stop a bad baseball player from striving to be a better one, or a person ignorant of science from becoming more adept at it, for we would still try to develop our physical and mental abilities, as we do today.

On the other hand, this social arrangement would help to control our egos, for it would remind us that our human claim to worth is not a function of our abilities. In the Torah, God warns us against claiming that "My own power and the might of my own hand have won this wealth for me. Remember that it is the Lord your God who gives you the power to get wealth"[39]—and, for that matter, to do anything else. We certainly can and should feel proud of our achievements, but seeing the world from the vantage point of the disabled should restore and reconfirm in us a needed sense of humility.

My proposal would also make society as a whole a kinder, gentler, more inclusive place to be. People would not be judged primarily by how much they can do or how beautiful they look; since the norm would be a lack of many abilities, people would be judged primarily by what they do to help others in coping with life. That is, character world have a much greater chance to be the criterion of worth in such a society—and that, I dare say, is a very nice result.

And what about the trappings of Jewish law? The intriguing part of this proposal is that it might prompt us to look with a completely new lens at a number of the details of Jewish law regarding the disabled. As I indicated above, in most cases Jewish law makes every effort to include the disabled as much as their disabilities will permit, and we should be proud of the extent to which ancient Jewish law did just that. Some provisions of Jewish law, though, would become hard to justify if we look at the world from the vantage point where most of us are disabled. For example, if most of us were blind, we certainly would not require the Torah to be read from a scroll that is only accessible to the sighted; we might allow reading from such a scroll, but we would presume that most people would read from a Braille text. Similarly, if most of us were deaf or blind, we certainly would not exclude deaf or blind people from giving testimony to what they did perceive through their functioning senses. Now that we know that mute people are not necessarily or even usually insane, we would treat them at law like everyone else. And we probably would maintain, contrary to the Talmud but very much in line with its reasoning regarding those asleep, that those who insult the insane would be liable for damages because others hearing the disparaging remark would understand it as an insult.[40] Thankfully, there are only a few such cases in which Jewish law would need to be changed, but looking at the world through the lens I am suggesting makes those areas that need to be changed crystal clear.

EPILOGUE

And now, with apologies to you all, I am going to pull what football players know as a "double reverse." We owe God daily thanks that most of us, for most of our lives, do not suffer from debilitating conditions that make living life hard. Because that is the case, and because we do need to work to ameliorate the difficulties faced by people who suffer from such maladies, the norm will inevitably—and properly—continue to be people with what we have come to expect as normal human abilities.

At the same time, I hope that this thought experiment will motivate us to think much more deeply about disabilities in our society generally, and in Judaism in particular. Only when we walk in the disabled community's moccasins, at least in our imaginations, aided by what we can learn from what the disabled themselves tell us about what they face, can we begin appropriately to judge how we think about the disabled and how we treat them in society generally and in Jewish life in particular. In the meantime, may our journey into the world of the disabled—and into the upside-down world in which they are the vast majority—make us better, more sensitive people and Jews.

NOTES

In the following, M. = Mishnah (edited c. 200 C.E.); T. = Tosefta (also edited c. 200 C.E.); J. = Jerusalem (Palestinian) Talmud (edited c. 400 C.E.); B. = Babylonian Talmud (edited c. 500 C.E.); M.T. = Maimonides' *Mishneh Torah* (1177 C.E.); and S.A. = Joseph Karo's *Shulhan Arukh* (1567 C.C.), with glosses by Moses Isserles.

1. Genesis 15:2–4; 18:1–15; 25:21; 30:1–8, 22–24; 35:16–20; I Samuel 1:1–20.

2. Isaac: Genesis 27:1; Jacob: Genesis 48:10.

3. Genesis 32:25, 31–32.

4. Exodus 4:10.

5. Nahum of Gimzo: B. *Ta'anit* 21a. Dosa ben Harkinas: B. *Yevamot* 16a. Rav Joseph and Rav Sheshet: B. *Bava Kamma* 87a. There were also a number of anonymous, blind scholars: B. *Haggigah* 5b; J. *Pe'ah*, end.

6. Genesis 1:27; 5:1; 9:6.

7. Deuteronomy 21:22–23.

8. M. *Oholot* 7:6.

9. Leviticus 19:14.

10. Leviticus 21:17–21.

11. Maimonides, *Guide to the Perplexed* 3:45.

12. Deuteronomy 23:2; see commentary on that verse in *Etz Hayim* (Philadelphia: Jewish Publication Society, 2002), p. 1122.

13. *Heresh* as deaf-mute: M. *Terumot* 1:2. *Heresh* as deaf but not mute, with ileim describing a mute: B. *Haggigah* 2b.

14. B. *Megillah* 24a–24b; S.A. *Orah Hayyim* 69:2.

15. M.T. *Laws of Fringes* 3:7.

16. I am drawing this list from the work of Carl Astor, *"Who Made People Different: Jewish Perspectives on the Disabled"* (New York: United Synagogue of America, 1985), Chapter Four, a book that I heartily recommend in its entirety. In the Talmud, whether the deaf are obligated to recite the Shema is disputed (B. Berakhot 15a), but the codes rule that a deaf person can fulfill the commandment: M.T. *Laws of Reading the Shema* 2:8; S.A. *Orah Hayyim* 62:3.

17. That the Torah must be read: B. *Gittin* 60b. That blind people are therefore excluded from reciting it for the congregation: S.A. *Orah Hayyim* 53:14; 139:4. That the blind may be called to recite the blessings over the Torah: Moses Isserles, gloss and the commentary of the TaZ (Turei Zahav) by Rabbi David ben Samuel Ha-Levi there.

18. Astor, *"Who Makes People Different,"* pp. 75, 107-109.

19. S.A. *Orah Hayyim* 53:14.

20. B. *Megillah* 19b; S.A. *Orah Hayyim* 689:2. M.T. *Laws of the Megillah* 1:2, however, leaves out the heresh as an excluded category.

21. B. *Peshaim* 116b.

22. M.T. *Laws of Slaughter* 4:5; see, however, B. *Hullin* 2a, where this special circumstance permitting the animals that they slaughter for consumption is not mentioned.

23. S.A. *Orah Hayyim* 589:1-2 with the glosses of R. Moses Isserles and the *Magen Avraham* there.

24. M.T. *Laws of Acquisition (Zekhiyah)* 4:6-7.

25. M.T. *Laws of Inheritance (Nahalot)* 6:1; 10:5. As for inheritance from one's spouse, marriage to a deaf-mute or insane person is valid only by rabbinic, and not by biblical authority, because such people could not be presumed to be of sound mind and could not pronounce the blessings with the proper intent. Therefore the usual, biblical laws of inheritance, where property is passed on automatically to relatives in a prescribed order, do not apply, and the property is treated as gifts. A deaf-mute cannot give gifts but can receive them. Thus a woman who is deaf cannot transfer property to her husband, but a man who is deaf can receive property from his hearing wife (M.T. *Laws of Marriage* 22:4).

26. M.T. *Laws of Sale* 29:1.

27. B. *Gittin* 59a, 67b.

28. M.T. *Laws of Sale* 29:3-4.

29. M.T. *Laws of Sale* 29:5.

30. B. *Gittin* 59b.

31. M.T. *Laws of Testimony* 9:9.

32. B. *Gittin* 71a.

33. M.T. *Laws of Testimony* 9:11.

34. M.T. *Laws of Testimony* 9:12.

35. B. *Niddah* 50a.

36. B. *Yevamot* 112b.

37. B. *Yevamot* 81a.

38. B. *Bava Kamma* 86b.

39. Deuteronomy 8:17-18; see verses 11-18 to understand the context.

40. B. *Bava Kamma* 86b.

SPECIAL EDUCATION IN JUDAIC LITERATURE

Rabbi Martin Schloss

INTRODUCTION

In 1975, the United States Congress passed landmark education legislation that dramatically altered the educational landscape for future generations. The legislation known as Public Law 94-142, mandated the education of all children in the United States, with a specific focus on youngsters with learning and other disabilities. The legislation bundled a variety of federal, state and local mandates that included the development of an educational contract called the "Individualized Education Plan" (IEP) to ensure an appropriate education for each and every child (Hallahan & Kaufman, 2000). Indeed, PL 94-142 firmly established the birthright of each and every citizen of the United States to a meaningful and appropriate education—an education that maximizes his/her opportunities for an active and productive life in the mainstream of American society. Since 1975, other countries around the world (Israel, Canada, England, etc.) have followed the US lead and adopted similar legislation. Thus, one could say that the global growth of services for persons with special needs can be attributed, in large measure, to the passage of PL 94-142.

With the above in mind, the question of the Judaic perspective demands exploration. Does Judaic literature deal with education for students with special needs? The response is that Halakhic Judaic Literature does indeed grapple with this issue. A review of Biblical, Talmudic and Halakhic literature demonstrates that concern for the education of each individual child, including those with special needs, is intrinsic to the basic mandate of Jewish education dating back more than two millennia. Unfortunately, an extensive treatment of this topic is beyond the purview of this paper. (In fact, a segment of this topic serves as the focus of my own dissertation.) Nonetheless, a sampling of Judaic thought and practice regarding education and disability will be presented.

SELECTIONS FROM BIBLICAL, TALMUDIC AND HALAKHIC LITERATURE

In Deuteronomy (chapter 33, verse 4), Moses, in his final address to the Jewish people, explains, "The Torah that Moses commanded us is the heritage of the Congregation of Jacob" (The Stone Edition Chumash, 1993, p.1112). In a monograph dedicated to Jewish philosophy and Jewish education, noted Jewish educator and psychologist, Rabbi Dr. Aharon Herschel Fried, cites the Biblical exegete, *Bnei Yisosschor*, who comments on the words *"Congregation of Jacob."* He states, "Let no man say, this son of mine is not fit for Torah and will not succeed in learning Torah—No man should ever say this for our Creator has already promised us, 'and all your children shall be learned of the Lord ...' " (Fried, 1983). The intent of this citation is to establish the Biblical position that Jewish education is intended, to the extent possible, for every child—even those whose learning is difficult. This Biblical declaration was made well over three thousand years ago.

The next Biblical citation explores recommendations to help individuals best meet the above declaration. King Solomon writes in Proverbs (chapter 22, verse, 6), "Train [educate] the youth [child] according to his way; even when he grows old, he will not sway from it " (Mesorah Publications Tanach, 1996). The eighteenth Century exegete, *Metzudas Dovid* explains this citation to mean, "Accustom [educate] the child to perform God's service according to his intelligence, whether excessive or limited, so that even when he grows old, he will never veer away from it..." (Judaica Press Inc., 1993, p.134). According to the *Metzudas Dovid*, King Solomon reminds us that successful Jewish education is individualized and based on each child's particular intellectual abilities regardless if those abilities are excessive or extremely limited. Thus, according to King Solomon, intellectual prowess is never criteria for educational entitlement—that entitlement is unconditional. Rather, he informs us, that intellectual ability is significant in helping determine appropriate educational methodologies and strategies designed to maximize each individual's capacity to serve God.

The exploration of Judaic literature on this topic continues with the Talmud. The Talmud is comprised of two distinct components: the *Mishnah* and *Gemarah*. The *Mishnah* represents rabbinical teachings of the *Tanaim*, Rabbis from a little before the Common Era to the beginning of the third Century. The *Mishnah* was compiled by Rabbi Yehudah Hanasi who collected the information and arranged it into six areas dealing with Jewish life. The second component is called, *Gemarah*, which represents rabbinical teachings of the *Amoraim*, Rabbis from the beginning of the third century until the end of the 5th century who commented on the *Mishnah*. The *Gemarah* is subdivided into the Babylonian Talmud and the Jerusalem Talmud. This division represents the teachings of the Gemarah in two distinct geographical locations: Jerusalem and Babylon (Dimont, 1994; Wein, 1996). The Jerusalem *Gemarah* was compiled by Rabbi *Yochanan* while the Babylonian *Gemarah* was compiled by *Ravenah* and *Rev Ashi* (Introduction to the *Mishnah Torah* of Maimonides, 1180).

The first Talmudic source is from a *Mishnah* in the Tractate of *Avot* (chapter 2, Mishnah 5). "Hillel said, 'Don't say that something is impossible to understand because in the end it will be understood' "(Bunim, 1964). In his popular commentary on *Pirkai Avot*, Bunim suggests that the intent of this *Mishnah* is to indicate that significant learning challenges can be overcome through diligence and persistence (Ibid.).

The notion of overcoming learning difficulties is continued in the teachings of the *Gemarah*. The Jerusalem Talmud's Tractate of *Horiot* discusses how Moses internalized the Torah given on Mount Sinai. The Talmud states, "Rebbe *Yochanan* says that each of the forty days that Moses was on Mount Sinai he learned the entire Torah and then forgot it. In the end, the Almighty infused Moses with the Torah as a present. Why was Moses subjected to this experience? [Answer] To bring the *'Tipshim* [challenged learners] closer to the Torah." (Jerusalem Talmud *Horiot*, p.18b.).

The *Pnei Moshe*, an 18th century Commentary on the Jerusalem Talmud, clarifies the *Gemarah's* question of why "Moses was subjected to this experience" by explaining that since God saw his difficulty in learning the Torah, why didn't He simply give Moses the Torah as a present on the first day [rather than have Moses endure this challenge for 39 days]?" He then proceeds to interpret the *Gemarah*'s answer of, "to bring the *Tipshim* [whom he defines as individuals with short/long term memory problems] closer to the Torah", that no one in the Jewish community should ever ask the question why must we teach individuals who demonstrate extensive difficulty in mastering information. The response to such a potential query comes directly from the experience of Moses our Teacher. Moses reviewed the material numerous times and was still unable to successfully internalize the lessons. Nevertheless, he continued to dedicate himself to the task of learning and was ultimately successful in acquiring the information." (Ibid.)

The message from the above selection is that no Jewish educator should ever entertain excusing children with learning problems from studying the Torah. It is the responsibility of each teacher to be determined and diligent in exploring various methods and strategies to better assist the student with his/her learning. Furthermore, this message comes from Moses himself. If we were to have excused individuals with learning problems from Jewish education, we would have forfeited our greatest teacher

The following Talmudic citation demonstrates the Talmudic concept of a special educator practicing special education. The Tractate of *Eruvin* in the Babylonian Talmud states:

"R. Pereda had a pupil whom he taught his lesson four hundred times before the latter could master it. On a certain day having been requested to attend to a religious matter he taught him as usual but the pupil could not master the subject. 'What', the Master asked, 'is the matter today?'—'From the moment', the other replied, 'the Master was told that there was a religious matter to be attended to I could not concentrate my thoughts, for at every moment I imagined, Now the Master will get up or now the Master will get up. 'Give me your attention ', the Master said, 'and I will teach you again', and so he taught him another four hundred times (Babylonian Talmud *Eruvin*, 54b)

Rav Pereda could clearly be considered one of the first special educators in world history. He discovered a successful individualized strategy and utilized it. At no time did Rav Pereda entertain the thought of ceasing to educate his student because of his apparent learning challenge. And, when Rav Pereda encountered student failure, he pursued and persevered until his student was successful—indeed, a true special educator.

One could question the above citation; however, as to whether this was simply a practice of one dedicated teacher or a mandate for all teachers. The following Talmudic source responds to that question. The *Gemarah* in the Babylonian Talmud of Tractate *Sanhedrin* states:

Rav Yehudah said in the name of Rav: Whoever withholds the teaching of the law from the mouth of a student, i.e. whoever neglects to teach Torah to a student, is as if he robs [the student] of his ancestral heritage. For it is stated: The Torah that Moses commanded us is the heritage of the congregation of Jacob. This means: It is a heritage to all of Israel since the six days of creation (The Art Scroll Babylonian Talmud, Tractate *Sanhedrin*, 91b).

The *Maharshah*, a 17th century commentary on the Talmud, explains that the Talmud is instructing all educators to maximize their efforts so that no child will be lacking information that he/she could have mastered. Furthermore, he informs us that this mandate also includes students who possess learning difficulties similar to those encountered by the student of Rav Pereda (as per citation above). He continues this theme by indicating that any teacher who withholds information from this type of student by virtue of inadequate instruction is no less than a common thief who has robbed a child of his birthright and entitlement [guaranteed to the student] from the time of creation (Babylonian Talmud Tractate *Sanhedrin*, p.71b).

Thus, the *Maharshah* responds to query as to whether every teacher ought to educate his students as did Rav Perada. The answer is clear. Yes!

The next citation is taken from Maimonides's Code of Jewish Law, The *Yad Hahazakah*, written in the late 12th century. In the section on Education, Maimonides instructs teachers and students on how to deal with students who experience learning difficulties. The importance of this particular quotation is that Maimonides incorporated the above listed Talmudic sources into Judaic law. Maimonides states:

If a teacher has taught a subject and the pupils failed to understand it, he must not be angry with them nor get excited, but should review the lesson with them many times until they finally grasp it. Neither should a pupil say, 'I understand' when he does not, but should keep on asking questions repeatedly. If his teacher gets angry and excited on account of him, he should say to him, 'Teacher, this is the Torah! I must study it, even though [my] capacity is limited.

A student must not feel ashamed on account of his colleagues who have apprehended a subject at once, or soon after it was taught a second time, while it has taken him many times to grasp it. If he were to feel embarrassment because of this, he would be attending school without learning anything. For this reason, the early sages declared, 'the bashful cannot learn, nor can the quick-tempered teach' (Ethics of the Fathers 2:5). (Birnbaum, 1967, p.27—translation of Maimonides' *Yad Hahazakah*, 1180)

As an aside, it is interesting to note that there exists a dispute among Jewish historians as to Maimonides' own learning ability. A number of Jewish publications, including the *Seder HaDorot* (a respected Jewish history text by Rabbi Yechiel Heilpern written in 1711), suggest that Maimonides grew up with severe learning disabilities—so severe, that according to some, until the time of his Bar Mitzvah he was incapable of proficient reading. It was only after his encounter with Rabbi Yosef Ibin Migash that Maimonides developed into the brilliant Torah luminary as he is known today (Heilpern, 1993; Yaffe, 1992). If accurate, this would suggest that two of Judaism's greatest leaders and teachers experienced significant learning disabilities: Moses and Moses Maimonides.

Finally, Rabbi Dr. David Bleich, a current Orthodox Rabbinical Halakhist, addresses the issue of educating youngsters with mental retardation in one of his Responsa. He cites a Talmudic selection which discusses the Biblical Commandment of mandating fathers to educate their children without regard to the level of the child's intellectual ability (Babylonian Talmud, Tractate *Kiddushin*, p.29a). Rabbi Bleich writes:

The Commandment, "And you shall teach them to your sons is not at all predicated upon the capacity of the child to perform the *mitzvot* upon reaching the age of halachic capacity. A father is obligated to instruct his son in the biblical passages concerning Shabbat and Tefillin, not in order that he become a Sabbath observer and don tefillin, but by virtue of the intrinsic *mitzvah* of *Talmud Torah*. The father is Biblically obligated to teach Torah to his son just as he is obligated to study Torah himself. The paternal duty of *Talmud Torah* is not predicated upon the mental competence of the child and is limited in extent solely by the child's ability to absorb instruction" (Bleich, 1983).

The above citation represents a focus of my own dissertation, *Halakhah* and Mental Retardation. At a later date, I hope to write extensively on this topic representing a wealth of Judaic thought in this area.

CONCLUSION

The purpose of this paper was to indicate that special education as it is interpreted today by variations of Public Law 94-142 has for thousands of years been an integral component of Judaic thinking, literature, tradition and law. I believe that this rather small sampling of the wealth of Judaic literature demonstrated this notion. However, the most important component of this paper is its message to the organized Jewish community. Aside from federal, state and local legislation mandating education for all children, Judaic law mandated such education thousands of years ago. How close are we now to meeting our religious mandate? And, what do we still need to do to make education a true birthright of all children regardless of ability? It is, after all, the essence of our survival and the guarantee of our future.

BIBLIOGRAPHY

Birnbaum, Philip. *Maimonides' Mishneh Torah*. New York, New York: Hebrew Publishing Company, 1967.

Bleich, J. David. *Contemporary Halakhic Problems Vol. II*. New York, New York: KTAV Publishing House Inc., 1983.

Bunim, Irving M. *Ethics From Sinai* (Pirkei Avot). New York, New York: Philipp Feldheim, Inc., 1964.

Edels, Shmuel. *Maharsha* (in Talmud Bavli/Tractate Sanhedran). New York, New York: Israeli Trading Corp., 1972.

Dimont, M.I. *Jews, God and History*. New York: Penguin Books USA, Inc., 1994.

Fried, Aaron, Hershel. *The Jewish Center for Special Education Reader*. Brooklyn, New York., 1983.

Goldin, Hyman E. *Ethics of the Fathers* (Pirkei Avot). New York, New York: Hebrew Publishing Company, 1962.

Hallahan, D. P. & Kauffman, J. M. *Exceptional Learners: Introduction to Special Education* (8th edition). Boston, Massachusetts: Allyn and Bacon, 2000.

Heilprin, Yechiel. *Seder Hadorot*. Jerusalem, Israel: Even Yisroel Publishing.

Kantor, Mattis (1989). *The Jewish Timeline Encyclopedia*. Northvale, New Jersey: Jason Aaronson Inc., 1993.

Maimonides, Moses. *Mishnah Torah* (1180). New York, N.Y., Hebrew Publishing Company, 1967.

Margolis, Moshe. *Pnei Moshe*. (in Talmud Yerushali/Tractate Horiot) Jerusalem, Israel: Esther Offset., 1970.

Proverbs. Brooklyn, New York: Judaica Press, 1993.

Talmud Bavli/Tractate Eruvin. London, England: The Soncino Press, 1984.

Talmud Bavli/Tractate Kiddushin. Brooklyn, New York: Mesorah Publications Ltd., 1992.

Talmud Bavli/Tractate Sanhedrin. Brooklyn, New York: Mesorah Publications Ltd., 1995.

Talmud Yerushalmi/Tractate Horiot. Jerusalem, Israel: Esther Offset, 1970.

The Stone Edition Tanach. Brooklyn, New York: Mesorah Publications, Ltd., 1996.

The Stone Edition Chumash. Brooklyn, New York: Mesorah Publcations, Ltd., 1993.

Wein, B. *Echoes of Glory: The Story of the Jews in the Classical Era 350 BCE-750 CE*. Broolyn,NY: Shaar Press, 1996.

Yaffe, Rochel. *Rambam: The Story of Rabbi Moshe Ben Maimon*. Brooklyn, N.Y.: Hachai Publishing, 1992.

PART 1:
AN HISTORICAL PERSPECTIVE OF SPECIAL EDUCATION PROGRAMS AND SERVICES

A TIME LINE OF SPECIAL EDUCATION PROGRAMS AND SERVICES IN THE UNITED STATES

1700's: Dr. Benjamin Rush first introduces the idea of educating persons with disabilities

1800's: Learners with disabilities begin to be deemed worthy of education
Residential institutions are established for teaching children who were deaf or blind.

1829: Samuel Gridley Howe opens the New England Asylum for the Blind (now the Perkins School for the Blind) in Boston, the first center school for the blind in the United States, which continues to operate today.

Louis Braille, a frenchman who was blind, develops a tactile system for reading and writing that used an embossed six-dot code, which is the Braille system today.

1854: Congress authorizes establishment of a school for the deaf, dumb and blind, which became Gallaudet College for the education of the deaf.

1842-1918: States, one by one, adopt publicly supported education—all pass compulsory attendance laws

1880's: Remedial programs are opened for people with specific disabling conditions

1900: The first public school class for the blind is established in Chicago.

1900's: Institutionalized, segregated education is the norm

1904: Alfred Binet, along with a group of colleagues, develops the first intelligence test to identify students "at risk" of failure so they can receive remedial help.

1911: New Jersey becomes the first state to mandate the establishment of special classes for the deaf, blind and educationally retarded students.

1950's/1960's: Special classes in public schools become the preferred education delivery system. The most significantly disabled remain in residential settings

1954: Brown vs. Board of Education of Topeka (Kansas)
Chief Justice Earl Warren rules "Separate Is Not Equal."

1966: The U.S. Bureau of Education for the Handicapped (Office of Special Education) is established within Health, Education and Welfare

1968: Handicapped Children's Early Education Programs begin

1973: Rehabilitation Act of 1973: Section 504 (P.L. 93-112)
Guarantees the rights of persons with disabilities in employment and in educational institutions that receive federal monies

LANDMARK LEGISLATION

1975: Education of All Handicapped Children Act (Public Law 94-142)
"to the maximum extent appropriate, handicapped children, including those children in public and private institutions or other care facilities, are educated with children who are not handicapped, and that special classes, separate schooling, or other removal of handicapped children from the regular educational environment occurs only when the nature or severity of the handicap is such that education in regular classes with the use of **supplementary aids and services** cannot be achieved satisfactorily" (Section 1412 [5] [B]

Guarantees free appropriate education for all children regardless of type and severity of the disability

Parents have a right to due process if services are not provided

Services must be provided in the least restrictive environment

Necessary related services must be provided

Meaningful individualized educational plan (IEP) must be developed._

Public Law 99-457 (Amendments to Public Law 94-142)—extending services to children birth to age five

Lowers the mandated age for special education birth to age 3

Child Find system set up to:

Provide a free multidisciplinary evaluation

Locate and identify children eligible for services

Part H (now Part C) provides financial assistance to states to implement programs of early intervention services for infants and toddlers with developmental delays or at risk (birth to age 3) and their families

Services offered in natural environments

Services and supports offered through interagency collaboration

Families make their choices known through an Individualized Family Service Plan (IFSP)

Families have a right to service coordination

1990: **Americans with Disabilities Act (ADA)** Public Law No. 101-336 mandates equal access for individuals with disabilities to employment, state and local government services, transportation, public accommodations and services provided by private entities, and telecommunications.

1990 **Individuals with Disabilities Education Act (IDEA) Public Law 101–470**

(Changed the name of 1975 Education of All Handicapped Children Act)

substituted the term disability for handicap

broadened scope of eligible disabilities (autism and traumatic brain injury)

placed emphasis on preparing students for life after special education

added assistive technology, transition services and rehabilitation counseling enhanced services to younger children and minorities

changed overall focus from handicapping condition to individual

2004 Reauthorization of Individuals with Disabilities Education Improvement Act (IDEIA)

The core components of the legislation remains the same. Certain changes have been instituted regarding some of the disability categories, such as speech and learning disabilities.

EDUCATIONAL IMPLICATIONS BASED ON LEGISLATION

Use of individualized approaches to curriculum and assessment for all students

All students are given the opportunity to learn to think and be creative

Heterogeneous and cooperative group arrangement of students is encouraged

Staff, students, parents and community collaborate

The social and emotional development of each student needs to be considered and school staff facilitates in promoting appropriate skills in these areas

AN OVERVIEW OF THE AMERICANS WITH DISABILITIES ACT

EXCERPTED FROM LOVING JUSTICE, NATIONAL ORGANIZATION ON DISABILITY

The Americans with Disabilities Act (ADA), Public Law No. 101-336, signed into law on July 26, 1990, mandates equal access for people with disabilities to employment, state and local government services, transportation, public accommodations and services provided by private entities, and telecommunications.

Seventeen percent of the general population have one or more disabilities. For purposes of the ADA, the definition of disability is very broad-based and includes, among others, mobility and sensory impairments, mental illness, mental retardation, and learning disabilities. This definition of disability includes diabetes, cancer, HIV/AIDS, arthritis, respiratory and cardiac conditions, and chronic back pain.

Title V of the ADA addresses a variety of issues, some of which apply to religious organizations and the entities they control.

The legal requirements of the ADA as applied to the religious community and spelled out in *Loving Justice* are complex. It may also be advisable to consult with an attorney on these matters.

It is encouraging to note that congregations and religious institutions throughout the country are voluntarily removing barriers of architecture, communication, and attitude, thus promoting the full participation of people with disabilities in all aspects of worship and programming.

Much of the material printed here was originally published by the Religion and Disability Program of the National Organization on Disability (N.O.D.) and is reprinted here with permission.

Further information can be found on the N.O.D. website at www@NOD.org. The N.O.D. phone number in Washington, DC, is (202) 293-5960. The guide *Loving Justice* can be ordered online.

CHAPTER 1

YESTERDAY, TODAY AND TOMORROW: SPECIAL EDUCATION

Rabbi Martin Schloss

It is sobering to note that organized special education classes in Jewish schools are, at least, a century old. This information was documented at a 1994 international conference on Jewish special education held at University of Tel Aviv, Israel. In a stimulating presentation, Dr. Carlebach of Hebrew University delivered a paper on Jewish special education in pre-World War I Hamburg, Germany. The principal of the Hamburg Jewish day school, Rabbi Dr. Joseph Carlebach (the presenter's father), created a class for students who encountered learning difficulties and for whom the school's curriculum was clearly inappropriate. Of particular interest to me was the fact that my own grandfather (after whom I am named) was one of the instructors of that special education class. Aside from historical interest in this knowledge, there are compelling educational comparisons between that program and our current programs. The important question is, "What, if anything, has changed after nearly a century of special education classes in Jewish schools?"

To date, the author of this article has not had the opportunity to examine the curricula, materials and structure of that class—and probably never will. Nonetheless, one can assume some obvious differences between then and now. Clearly, some differences directly relate to the research and developments culled from the scientific world of special education during the interim. It is noteworthy that the Hamburg Jewish special education class existed as Simon and Binet were in the process of cultivating the field of intelligence assessment—a significant component in understanding special education. Additionally, the contributions of Piaget, Skinner, Strauss, Frostig, Valet, Vellutino, Wiig and Semel, Kohlberg, Schumaker and Deshler, Shepherd and Fried, just to name a few, were unknown. Most of the research that platforms current special education thinking wasn't even contemplated at that time.

On the other hand, one can only assume that concepts of inclusion, adaptation, modification and alternative instruction were prominent in Rabbi Dr. Carlebach's thinking, as were responding to parental concerns, anxiety and frustrations. Mastery of the traditional Judaic texts of Bible, *Mishnah, Talmud* and *Halakhah* posed similar educational challenges as it does today. And, most likely, Rabbi Dr. Carlebach confronted the special education dilemmas of educational standards and school reputation. In Germany, all students were subjected to important 4th grade exams, not unlike today's students. Those exams, however, dictated a student's academic future. Test results determined whether a child would be permitted to pursue an academic track leading to a potential university education or a vocation track. One can only imagine the pressure on day school leaders at that time to demonstrate academic excellence in Jewish day schools. No doubt, as today, parents compared the academic effectiveness of the Jewish day schools with that of non-Jewish day schools. Thus, a plausible perspective in a centennial comparison of Jewish special education would yield a result of some similarities and some differences.

In reality, however, the above analysis is somewhat frivolous. Not at all tangential to these educational comparisons are the societal and environmental variables. Success in an increasingly technological society demands skills not conceived of at the turn of the 20th century—skills that directly challenge those with learning and developmental disabilities.

This last statement brings us to the far more pertinent challenge of today, namely, "What have we learned about special education during the last century that will better assist us as we begin a new millennium?" Whereas, there are probably countless responses to this query, I would like to focus on two: *Prevention* and *Technology*.

The most critical stage for effective educational intervention is the earliest moment that a potential problem is detected. Research by social psychologist Dr. Carol Dweck, often cited by Dr. Margaret Jo Shepherd of Columbia University, demonstrates the devastating impact of persistent and consistent academic failure on self-efficacy and ultimately upon self-motivation. In a creative experiment, Dr. Dweck examined various children's reactions to academic failure. The results indicated that the child's age contributes to the perception of that failure. Youngsters between the ages of about 4-7 equated intelligence with effort: "If I try harder, I'll get smarter." The youngsters in this age group attributed their failure to their level of effort. Thus, failure was less devastating to them. They simply maintained that if they would try harder they would do better—a dynamic view of intelligence. This perception changes when the same children become ten years old and older. The child then personalizes success and/or failure. Intelligence is now viewed as an aspect of the individual and is not subject to change: "I am either smart or dumb. And, if I am dumb, then nothing I do can change that notion." More disturbing is that even if the child were to succeed at a given task, he/she would attribute this success to the task being so easy that anyone could do it, to having been "lucky" or to the teacher having simply given him/her this mark out of kindness, when it was not really earned. This self-perception, if not corrected, can become a true lifelong disability that permeates and negatively affects all facets of the child's life. Special education literature refers to this condition as "learned helplessness." Thus, delays in recognizing potential problems often result in far-reaching devastation well beyond the learning problem itself.

Unfortunately, the challenge to early intervention has been the relative inability of teachers to detect potential problems at the most critical stage—before the child experiences academic failure. Many of the difficulties encountered by children with learning disabilities manifest themselves in the capacity to read. This is a skill that is often difficult to determine until the individual actually begins to learn to read—late in the optimum intervention process. This condition is exacerbated by the inability of various screenings and assessments in the pre-reading youngster to accurately identify potential precursors to reading difficulties.

The good news is that the 21st century begins with a strong indication that the above challenge may well be on the road to being positively addressed. For close to a decade, Drs. Frank Vellutino and Donna Scanlon, among others, have been conducting significant research correlating pre-reading language behaviors with later reading capacity. Their published findings suggest that not only are many reading difficulties identifiable in the pre-reading stage of development but also, with guided prescriptive classroom instruction, correctable. Their studies demonstrate that many students who are identified as learning disabled in the area of reading, in fact have no disability and that if these students receive appropriate instruction in their early childhood classes, they will never experience school failure. This is not to say that all children may be spared learning disabilities in reading. Indeed, there are children who possess true reading disabilities who will not respond as successfully as others. It does suggest, however, that at-risk children who are not truly disabled may be successfully prevented from experiencing school failure, while children who are truly disabled may receive special education intervention at the most propitious time.

Based on the above, and accompanied by the support of two foundations, the Board of Jewish Education of Greater New York (BJE) initiated a longitudinal pre-reading intervention pilot project in Jewish schools, directed by Dr. Jed Luchow and in collaboration with Drs. Vellutino, Scanlon, Shepherd, Robbins and Tannenbaum. The four pilot schools receive ongoing staff development in the assessment tools used by Scanlon and Vellutino, as well as in the instructional components of the Scanlon and Vellutino program. Student progress is monitored and evaluated on an ongoing basis. The purpose of this activity is to ascertain whether the initial findings of Scanlon and Vellutino is replicable in Jewish schools and whether the findings in English language are applicable to those in Hebrew language. The potential benefits of this effort include the enormous impact on early childhood and special education in Jewish schools—not to mention the thousands of children whose lives will be profoundly enriched.

Technology represents the second Jewish special education frontier for this millennium. The changes in technology are fast and furious. Every day is accompanied by new innovations that impact the way we go about every aspect of our daily lives. And, because we have become so accustomed to technological development, it is taken for granted. Didn't we always have cell phones, the Internet, ATM's, MetroCards and E-Z pass? Did doctoral candidates actually use typewriters for their dissertations? What did they do when they realized they had omitted a few paragraphs in the middle of their tests?

There is, unfortunately, one discipline that has been sluggish in maximizing the potentials of technological advancement—education. A prominent topic for the New York State Education Department Commissioner's Advisory Panel on Special Education was how to assist educators in incorporating technology into their classroom instruction. This topic is not only germane for general and special education, but for Jewish education as well. Millions of dollars worth of the latest technology remain in original packaging because too few Jewish educators have the knowledge, skill and capacity to best utilize the increasingly growing universe of educational technology. Not a week goes by that we do not see new software, both general and Judaic, that could have a profound impact on successful student learning. There are new and exciting software developments in Hebrew reading, Bible, *Mishnah*, and *Talmud*. My father, who has suffered retinal damage resulting in significant reading difficulty, has successfully maintained his learning of the "daily Talmud page" through a CD that has both auditory and visual components of each Talmudic tractate. Within a week, the Board of Jewish Education's Instructional technology department viewed two Judaic text software packages that were designed to make text learning more exciting and successful. What is meaningful for educators is that the new software packages take complicated abstract Judaic concepts and concretize them into understandable sequential segments. The packages also contain student evaluation units that not only assess student outcomes, but also provide targeted programmatic review for mastery—clearly a valuable educational tool.

Once again, NYC's Board of Jewish Education (BJE) has responded to this challenge by partnering with a major university specializing in instructional technology. BJE's newly constructed technology lab houses federally funded staff development courses for nonpublic schoolteachers. In addition, the BJE Department of Instructional Technology with a grant from the Covenant Foundation has negotiated a joint Master's Degree program in Instructional Technology with the New York Institute of Technology. Unique to this joint program is the additional course-work focus on Judaic content areas.

As we emerge into the 21st Century, serious attention ought to be paid to the development of the above two areas. Both will undoubtedly factor heavily in the progress of Jewish special education during this millennium. Just imagine what a difference the above would have meant to Rabbi Dr. Joseph Carlebach one hundred years ago.

CHAPTER 2

JEWISH SPECAL EDUCATION: A FIFTY YEAR PERSPECTIVE

Rabbi Bennett M. Rackman
and Sara Rubinow Simon

The earliest reported program to provide religious education for Jewish children with disabilities was reported in *The American Journal of Mental Deficiency* in 1955. Louis Birner described a Sunday School program for "retarded children" that was conducted at The Jewish Temple in order to prepare the participants for their Bar Mitzvah. The children were described as either withdrawn, aggressive, or friendly. The program was instituted to "provide them with a type of learning experience that would facilitate their social and emotional growth." In teaching the religious subject matter, there was "a need for both repetition and simplicity." The goal of the lessons was "to make the subject matter an active part of the life and play experience of the group." This model of a Sunday School or supplementary school program is essentially the prototype followed by others. (Aron, 1956; Kaiman, 1963; Kohn, 1957; Lerner, 1964; Rosenkranz, 1976; E. Schwartz, 1973 and 1975; Shapiro, 1964;Silver, 1957; Syden, 1960; Weisberg, 1964.)

Rebecca Lister (1959), with assistance from Saul Hofstein, attempted to publicize the existing programs that were providing Jewish education for special education. Her publication was mainly targeted toward professionals. She hoped to encourage them to establish additional programs. Her extensive "Guide" of about eighty pages contained reports of several successful supplementary school programs, suggestions for replicating these special classes in new locations, and sample lesson plans to be used by Jewish special educators. She also felt that laymen needed to recognize the benefits that such programs provided for special children. This early attempt to enlighten educators to the needs of the atypical child served notice to the Jewish community that such programs can be successful. It encouraged more parents of children with developmental disabilities to request of their congregations and Jewish schools that similar classes be established. Another early Sunday School program, still functioning, was started by Sylvan Kohn in the Metrowest area of New Jersey.

In that same year, Maimonides Institute for Exceptional Children was established in Middle Village, New York. The school's objective was to provide a Jewish environment in which both Judaic studies, as well as a general curriculum, could be taught to children with mental retardation. Later, the school's population also contained children with other diagnoses such as learning disabilities, brain injuries, speech and language impairments, and emotional disturbances.

The three founders of this unique school were a special educator and two rabbis, one of whom was a social worker. No money was yet available from public sources. Costs were kept to a minimum: rent was almost free and food was prepared by volunteers. Transportation was subsequently provided by the New York Board of Education. But teachers had to be paid and supplies for the students had to be purchased. Eventually, through a Women's Auxiliary, funds were raised for the fledgling school. In addition, proposals were submitted to obtain grants from State and Federal sources.

A network of community classes was also affiliated with the Institute, which provided supplementary religious education to children with disabilities in synagogues throughout the New York metropolitan area. Innovations such as monthly field trips to sights of Jewish interest like the Jewish Museum and participation in an annual Shabbaton in a largely Jewish neighborhood introduced the students to the greater Jewish community.

The unique feature of the Institute was that the curriculum was not divided into two components: religious studies and general studies. Rather, the curriculum, as designed by Hershel M. Stiskin, was meant to integrate the two areas. If educators were teaching about Shabbat, they would not just teach the rituals and prayers connected to that day. They would focus on cleaning the house for the special day, shopping for food, preparing the food, hygiene and cleanliness, etc. Social interactions with people in the community were all connected to the goal of properly observing the Sabbath day. The children needed to develop a sense of religious identity and purpose. Stiskin maintained that, by first involving special children in the social and cultural life of their Jewish homes, and then in the neighborhood and synagogue, it would be easier to integrate them into the larger community. Stiskin felt that this integration of religious and general education was truly reflected in the meaning of Jewish Special Education. Shulman (1969) similarly wrote of the need for Jewish educational planning for children with brain injuries.

Out of this small beginning, Maimonides Institute grew to become the non-sectarian Maimonides School with residential and day treatment programs and was eligible for public funding. The religious components became an auxiliary to the school. By 1979, Maimonides School had to close its doors due to financial difficulties.

Other all-day schools emerged in the New York area to service the needs of Jewish special children. Among them were the Brooklyn (Hebrew) Day School for Special Children (HASC), and the Hebrew Institute for the Deaf (and Exceptional Children.) Some of these schools also eventually had to become non-sectarian as the cost for providing a special education rose. State funding was needed. (The Lexington School for the Deaf and Pleasantville Cottage School for children with emotional disturbances had originally been founded many years earlier by the Federation of Jewish Philanthropies but they had long since become non-sectarian.)

Recognition must be given to the Jewish Center for Special Education, established in 1976, to educate Hassidic and Orthodox children with learning disabilities [by Rabbi Aharon Hersh Fried]. It was to serve as a model school for educating students with mild disabilities. After a few years, these students who might have become "useless," were integrated back into their local yeshiva or day school, later to become productive members of their Jewish community. Dr. Fried was assisted by Mrs. Helene Ribowsky in developing the curriculum for the school. In a sense, "Chush," as the school was called in Hebrew, was the experimental model school that one generally finds within a university setting. Curricula and teaching materials were developed, refined, and disseminated to Jewish special educators throughout the country.

Chush was one of the first day schools to consistently employ audio-visual materials every day in the classroom. (Fried and Ribowsky, 1977; Fried,1979; Ribowsky, 1979.)

In the late 1960's, Hershel M. Stiskin served as a part-time consultant to the Jewish Education Committee (later renamed the Board of Jewish Education of New York, the BJE), dealing with parents seeking advice and placements for their children with special needs. In addition, he was a part-time consultant to the American Association for Jewish Education (AAJE), later renamed JESNA, the Jewish Education Service of North America, the national umbrella organization for Jewish education. He also became the first chairman of the United Synagogue Special Education Committee. At the time, he was the only national "lobbyist" in Jewish education trying to improve the inadequate state of services for students with special needs. Stiskin left Maimonides to found the Summit School in 1970, and later in 1972, moved to Israel.

Rabbi Joseph Kelman, who succeeded Stiskin as chairman of the United Synagogue Special Education Committee, was a leading advocate in Canada. In 1964, he had outlined a curriculum of study for two programs conducted for students with special needs in Toronto. Both the Kadima School and the Ezra School were established to provide supplementary Jewish education to youngsters with disabilities. The former program serviced children with IQs "from about fifty up." The classes met once a week. The curriculum encompassed "Shabbat and Jewish holidays, customs and ceremonies, prayers, Bible stories, Hebrew, dramatics, arts and crafts, music, and special programs." The latter program serviced students with learning disabilities those who were "slow learners." Classes met twice weekly. The curriculum paralleled the curriculum of the regular congregational school, with accommodations made for the learning differences of the participants. (See also Schwartz, 1973, 1975.)

In addition, Kelman was responsible for establishing the Reena Foundation and Camp Reena in 1975, for children and adults with special needs. This residential camp did not integrate the campers with disabilities with the other campers. Rather, the goal was to prepare the campers with disabilities for independent living within the community. It was hoped that they would "establish patterns of behavior that will be sustained throughout the year." (Reena Foundation, 1976)

A 1972 survey conducted in the Greater New York area by the BJE indicated that ten out of the two hundred Sunday and supplementary religious schools had already established classes for children with disabilities. In 1974, funds were allocated through the BJE to provide the needed subvention, guidance, and supervision. A part-time consultant, Dr. Bennett M. Rackman, was hired to deal with Jewish Special Education. His primary role was to allocate funds to existing programs, generally self-contained classes for students attending special self-contained classes in their secular schools. The BJE supervised and directly funded a small number of Sunday School programs in neighborhoods that required additional support. Only after the tremendous needs of full-day programs were demonstrated, was the Jewish Federation later persuaded to provide financial assistance to these schools as well. The resource room model was the usual choice of Jewish day schools to support their students with learning disabilities. The BJE consultant visited all the schools that applied for funding and certified that their programs were indeed serving children with special needs. Teachers were provided supervision and advice from the BJE consultant when it was requested.

During this same period, the central agency for Jewish Education in Atlanta created and administered the Havanah program and the Board of Jewish Education of Greater Washington hired a part-time special needs consultant, Sara Rubinow Simon, and created and administered the

Sh'ma V'Ezer School for Special Education. In Chicago, the United Synagogue and Associated Talmud Torahs, the two central agencies for Jewish education, hired Dr. Richard Malter as special needs consultant to work with congregational and day schools. The central agency in Cleveland benefited from the pioneering work of Isadore Reisman and the Bureau of Jewish Education in Rhode Island coordinated a Jewish Special Education Program. Simon saw the role of the Sh'ma V'Ezer School as providing "...a transideological community school to children with special learning needs. Each group would no longer be operating in isolation. The key to Sh'ma V'Ezer's considerable development is its continuity and the support of the Jewish community." In several communities across North America, parents were the catalyst for individual classes for their children with special needs. These isolated classes, often sponsored by, or housed in, synagogues, were usually short-lived and ended with the Bar Mitzvah of its few students.

A major task facing the central agencies for Jewish education was development in the area of public relations. The Jewish communities had little familiarity with the needs of Jewish children with "learning disabilities," a term that was becoming increasingly popular. Through press releases and radio spots, the availability of Jewish educational services for students with special learning needs was advertised. Working together with both public and private schools and parents' groups, children were identified and invited to participate in Jewish educational programs. Workshops for mainstream teachers were also conducted. Listings of available classes were compiled and disseminated to all those requesting this information.

There were few resources available to assist the fledgling Jewish special education programs. The only materials prepared especially for students with mental retardation and learning disabilities were a series of workbooks authored by Hershel M. Stiskin. Between the years 1962 and 1965, he had put together special reader-activity books based on the Jewish calendar. These workbooks, published by the Jewish Education Committee Press, contained simple reading and uncomplicated professional illustrations. The series covered Shabbos, Rosh Hashanah, Succos, Chanukah, Passover, and Purim. Apart from these, early childhood materials were adapted and used.

In 1971, Barbara and Herbert Greenberg developed "The Sabbath," a popular curriculum kit that was published jointly by the United Synagogue of America and the Union of American Hebrew Congregations. *Sins of Omission: The Neglected Children*, written originally in 1977 by Edward Kaminetsky as his doctoral dissertation and later published, reviewed the field of special education. He then cited the opinion of Jewish religious sources for the necessity of providing this education and the reality of what was available for these children in the early 1970's. He exhorted the Orthodox Jewish community to recognize its responsibility to offer all children a chance to have a religious education.

But there was a paucity of information on how to apply special education strategies to a Jewish setting. In 1976, Torah Umesorah disseminated *Implementation of a Diagnostic and Remedial Program at a Hebrew Day School*, a 30 page "cookbook" describing the establishment and operation of a resource room program at the Hillel Day School in Denver. Dr. Reuven Hammer wrote *The Other Child in Jewish Education: A Handbook on Learning Disabilities*, published by United Synagogue in 1979. In the same year, *A Question in Search of An Answer: Understanding Learning Disability in Jewish Education* was written by Roberta Greene and Elaine Heavenrich and published by the Union of American Hebrew Congregations.

Another problem that soon became evident was the lack of communication between the teachers and administrators of the schools that serviced Jewish students with disabilities, both within the same city and between cities. Much effort was being wasted as each educator set about "re-inventing the wheel."

The National Commission on Torah Education (NACOTE), an affiliate of Yeshiva University, held a conference in December 1974 entitled "The Special Child in the Jewish School." This meeting of hundreds of educators and parents was the start of many new developments that would follow.

Torah Umesorah, the National Society for Hebrew Day Schools, through TOUCH (Torah Umesorah Clearinghouse for the Handicapped) disseminated educational materials to be used in instructing students with disabilities and sponsored a conference on "Special Education in the Jewish Community" in 1979, publishing its proceedings.

The BJE of New York sponsored three annual conferences on Special Education in Jewish Schools: "Programs and Techniques for the Learning Handicapped Child" in June, 1977; "Adaptations in Curriculum and Methodology" in April, 1978; and "Integrating Individualized Instruction and Mainstreaming," in May, 1979. All three conferences featured a keynote address by a pioneer in the field of Jewish Special Education. Workshops were conducted that addressed the needs of administrators and supplementary school and day school Judaic and general studies teachers. Participants, including parents and interested people from other communities, had the opportunity to share names, addresses, and experiences with colleagues trying to deal with the same challenges that they had previously thought were uniquely their own. Vendors and suppliers of Jewish educational materials were invited to display their wares at the conferences as well. These events also generated publicity in the Jewish press and periodicals.

Shalaym, a parent advocacy group that functioned under the umbrella of the United Synagogue of America, lobbied for the establishment of supplementary school programs in Conservative congregations, as well as year-round programming including camping. *Shalaym* parents helped to make the Tikvah Program for teens with special needs at the Ramah Camps a reality. This group also encouraged the United Synagogue of America Commission on Jewish Education's Special Education Committee to convene its first national conference for Jewish Special Education professionals, again attended by individuals from across the country. The February 1979 conference was titled "How Appropriate Jewish Observances can Address the Special Child 's Needs." Its emphasis was inclusion in every day Jewish living outside the classroom. The keynote address, delivered by Dr. Morton Siegel, spoke of the special needs of our Jewish patriarchs, matriarchs, and "heroes." The sessions by Edya Artz and Rabbi Robert Layman described in detail the ways to include the youngster with special needs in Jewish practices in the home and the synagogue. During the five years from 1979 to 1985, five conferences were held. Conference proceedings were made available through the United Synagogue's Department of Jewish Education. A conference on the topic of Shabbat was co-sponsored by United Synagogue and the Union of American Hebrew Congregations, under the guidance of Howard Bogot, a strong advocate for inclusion of people with disabilities in all aspects of Jewish life.

In the Orthodox community, a parent advocacy group was established in 1976 by the name of P'TACH (Parents for Torah for All Children), headed by Dr. Joel S. Rosenshein. These parents were dedicated to ensuring that students with special needs would be accommodated in a yeshiva or Jewish day school setting. The group became a powerful force in the establishment and maintenance of resource room and self-contained programs on both elementary and high school levels within existing day schools. Starting in 1976, P'TACH convened annual professional conferences. With the rapid growth of P 'TACH in the New York area and across North America, Torah Umesorah suspended its operations in this area, as did NACOTE.

Rabbi Rackman established the Special Education Program at BJE in 1974. He served as the part-time consultant to existing programs. But, the need for new services was ever present. After consultations with several agencies serving the retarded, a proposal was presented to Federation of Jewish Philanthropies (New York) to establish programs for retarded youngsters in communities in which this population was not being served. In 1978, Rabbi Martin Schloss was hired to head the Jewish Heritage Program for Retarded Adolescents and Adults. Rabbi Schloss then assumed leadership of the fledgling department and Chana Zweiter guided the Heritage Program. Eventually Ms. Zweiter moved this innovative project to the National Council of Synagogue Youth (NCSY), an affiliate of the Union of Jewish Congregations of America and Canada. Renamed *Yachad,* meaning "together," the program provided young people with educational, recreational, and social activities through weekend and holiday classes, programs, and retreats. *Yachad* members were mainstreamed into the NCSY youth groups whenever feasible, as were members of "Our Way," a similar program for young people with hearing impairments (also under NCSY sponsorship). Both programs are still functioning and thriving.

Between 1974 and 1979, informal contact was maintained with colleagues at other central agencies for Jewish education and other educators in metropolitan areas such as Miami, Baltimore, Washington, DC, Atlanta, Denver, Chicago, Los Angeles, Montreal, and New York City, as communities began Jewish special education programs. At the international convention of the Council for Exceptional Children held in Atlanta in April 1979, an organizational meeting was held to establish a national trans-ideological professional association called Jewish Education for Exceptional Persons (JEEP). The Council for Exceptional Children was asked for assistance and recognition through their sub-group, Religious Education for Exceptional Persons (REEP.) The American Association for Jewish Education (AAJE), the umbrella organization for Jewish education, was also requested to sponsor the Ad Hoc National Commission for Religious Education for the Special Child, with Dr. Bennett M. Rackman and Sara Rubinow Simon as co-chairs.

The birth of the Coalition for Alternatives in Jewish Education (CAJE) in 1976 provided impetus for a national grassroots network of educators, learning together at the annual conferences in different locations across the country and linked by newsletters. Meeting at CAJE conferences, people interested in Jewish special education developed strong personal as well as professional bonds that sustained them when they returned to their own communities to try to establish Jewish special education programs. The CAJE Special Needs Task Force, later re-named the Special Needs Network, was co-founded by Howard Adelman and Sara Rubinow Simon in 1980. Their goal was to disseminate program information and materials appropriate for students with special learning needs as well as to publish newsletters and convene mini-conferences, prior to the regular huge CAJE conference, in which there were intensive seminars and peer consultations. The CAJE Special Needs Task Force held its first mini-conference in Spring, 1980 in Washington, D.C., co-hosted by the Sh'ma V'Ezer Special Education Program of the Board of Jewish Education of Greater Washington.

In Fall 1979, the AAJE devoted an entire edition of *The Pedagogic Reporter,* its journal on Jewish education, to Jewish Special Education. Academicians and practitioners contributed articles on a range of topics dealing with programs for students with special needs, including the gifted and talented.

The Union of American Hebrew Congregations established the *Liheyot* Program in the early 1980's, providing comprehensive curricular and sensitization materials for Reform congregations and religious schools, under the guidance of Dr. Howard Bogot and Dr. Zena Sulkes. Reform educators were trained to include students with special needs and there were summer camp sessions for young people who were deaf. The first national conference on the congregational response to persons with disabilities was held in October, 1988 at Temple Chai in Phoenix, Arizona in collaboration with the Union of American Hebrew Congregations, the Central Conference of American Rabbis, and the National Association of Temple Administrators. The two days of workshops included presentations on developing awareness of the special needs of persons with disabilities, modifying curriculum, providing inclusion in youth groups, becoming a welcoming congregation, and funding the special programs. There was a certification process established in becoming a *Liheyot* congregation.

In the meantime, there was increasing pressure in the secular educational world to identify and accommodate students with special needs in the least restrictive environment. Across North America, Jewish communities were impacted by changing parental expectations and demands that their children be integrated into the regular early childhood programs as well as the regular Jewish day school and congregational supplementary school programs. Boards of Jewish Education were looked to for support. In response, central agencies in both large and small Jewish communities created staff positions for special educators.

The BJE in New York City, as the largest central agency for Jewish education, established the Association of Jewish Special Educators (AJSE) in 1981 to further reduce the sense of isolation among Jewish special educators and to facilitate communication among them. The AJSE has several hundred members and sponsors workshops and seminars during the course of the year focusing on topics of both Jewish and general special education interest. The Special Education Department became the expanded Special Education Center in 1986, with Rabbi Martin Schloss as director. It serves as a model for other communities with its comprehensive goals that include early identification and intervention for children who are at risk, referral and placements services, professional growth opportunities, curriculum development and dissemination, resource library, etc.

Many of the new central agency special education professionals came to CAJE conferences and participated in the lehrhauses and modules taught by their colleagues. It became apparent that they had additional concerns and perspectives that were not being addressed through the CAJE framework, despite the advantages of interacting with professionals and interested educators from a range of different settings and backgrounds. In 1985, Rabbi Martin Schloss and Sara Rubinow Simon approached Jewish Education Services of North America (JESNA) the national umbrella organization for Jewish education that replaced AAJE, requesting that the network of special educators in central agencies for Jewish education be permitted to operate under its aegis. The resulting Consortium of Special Educators in Central Agencies for Jewish Education holds an annual Colloquium in cities around North America, maintains a listserve of members, and publishes an annual newsletter that is distributed nationally to leadership and educators. Its Call to Action states:

In recognition of the obligation to provide a religious education for all Jewish persons with special needs, the Consortium of Special educators in Central Agencies for Jewish Education, in conjunction with the Jewish Education Service of North America (JESNA) urges all Jewish communities throughout North America to develop and support systems to :

identify Jewish persons with special needs including individuals with developmental, learning, behavioral, neurological, physical, medical, and sensory disabilities;

deliver Jewish educational services to special persons that will enhance and enrich their Jewish lives and those of their families. Such services include special educational programming in early childhood; day and supplementary schools; continuing adult education programs; and programs in residential, social/recreational, and camping settings;

explore various funding sources for the provision of these services through federal, state, and local government entitlements and foundations as well as local community and private sources.

The Consortium, in conjunction with JESNA, endorses this proactive approach to provide services to Jewish individuals with special needs. "It is enough that an individual has a disability. Let us not disable him or her as a Jew as well."

Jewish special education programming continued to blossom and flourish. In 1991, Caren N. Levine and Dr. Leora W. Isaacs of JESNA compiled *A Preliminary Survey and Listing of Jewish Special Needs Programs and Classes in North America*. This data base, for use by practitioners, planners, researchers and parents, provided helpful information that facilitated networking among people with common interests and goals. In addition, each ideological group within Judaism formed its own internal committees to focus on disability/special education issues.

Whereas, in the pioneering stages of Jewish special education it was possible to identify the relatively few individuals and programs, although unfortunately we clearly have missed some, the tremendous, and much-needed, proliferation of programs in recent years makes it difficult to find and list them all. Now, the lists of articles, books, web sites, personalities and programs are impressively long and they are difficult to keep up to date, no matter how intensive our research.

Today, several of the Jewish teacher training institutions and schools of education offer courses in special education and inclusion. Jewish special education opportunities now begin in early childhood and continue through adult education, in both formal and informal settings. Many, if not most, Jewish day schools provide support to students with special learning needs. In addition, a growing number of communities have programs that enable children with more complex and severe disabilities to attend day school programs. Similarly, many, if not most, congregational religious schools accommodate students with a range of learning differences. Every Jewish youngster has the chance to celebrate becoming Bar/Bat Mitzvah, as do many adults who never had the opportunity when they were young because of their special needs.

We recognize that we stand on the shoulders of our courageous predecessors, those early visionaries who struggled to enable <u>all</u> Jews to learn about their heritage. The past fifty years have seen great advances and strides in Jewish Special Education. The Jewish community at large can be proud of the fact that we are trying to fulfill the mandate of "Educate the child according to his needs..." (Proverbs, XXII, 6). There is still more work that must be done in the years ahead.

REFERENCES

Aron, Ruth S. "A Special Project for Slow Learners." *The Jewish Teacher*. Union of American Hebrew Congregations, Vol. 24, No. 2, pp. 10-14. January 1956.

Birner, Lous. "An Experimental Program for Retarded Children in a Part-Time Congregational Religious School," *American Journal of Mental Deficiency*. Vol. 60, No.1, pp.95-97. July 1955.

Fleischmann, Rienne. *Curriculum Guide to the Ezra-Kadima School.* Beth Emeth Bais Yehuda Synagogue. Downsview, Ontario, Canada. 1976

Fried, Aharon H. "Mekoros for Special Education." *Special Education in the Jewish Community-Porceedings of the Greater New York Conference on Special Education.* Torah Umesorah (National Society for Hebrew Day Schools), pp.54-64. March 1979.

——Aharon H. and Helene Ribowsky. *Learning to Learn*. Brooklyn, New York: Jewish Center for Special Education, June 1977 (unpublished program for First Annual Tea.)

Friedman, Erwin. "Mental Retardation and Jewish Law". *Information Service-Sharing in Religion with Persons Who are Retarded* (an official publication of the Religion Division, American Association on Mental Deficiency), Vol. 9, No.4, pp.22-27. November 1980.

Greenberg, Barbara and Herbert A. Greenberg. "The North Bellmore Experience." *The Synagogue School*. Summer 1973.

——"The Tikvah Program." *The Pedagogic Reporter*. Vol. 31, No. 1. pp. 31-33. Fall 1979.

Greenberg, Herbert A. "Integration of Children with Learning and Emotional Difficulties: An Evaluation and Descriptive Analysis." *Tikvah Program, Summer 1971, Phase II-Camp Ramah in Glen Spey.* (paper read at the Second Annual Ramah Special Education Conference, 9 pp. August 1971.

Greenberg, Herbert A. and Barbara Greenberg. *The Sabbath Kit.* New York: Union of American Hebrew Congregations and United Synagogue of America. 1971.

Greene, Roberta M. and Elaine Heavenrich. *A Question in Search of an Answer: Understanding Learning Disability in Jewish Education*. New York: Union of American Hebrew Congregations. 174 pp. 1979.

Hammer, Reuven. *The Other Child in Jewish Education*. New York: United Synagogue Commission on Jewish Education. 314 pp. 1979.

Isaacs, Leora W. and Caren N. Levine. *Preliminary Survey and Listing of Jewish Special Needs Programs and Classes*. New York: JESNA. Fall 1991.

Kaminetsky, Edward. *Sins of Omission: The Neglected Children*. New York: Studies in Torah Judaism, Yeshiva University Press. 134 pp. 1977.

Kelman, Joseph. "Special Education for All," *The Synagogue School*, Vol. 23, No. 2, pp.4-21. Winter 1965.

Kohn, Sylvan. "A Torah Workshop for the Handicapped Children," *The Synagogue School*, Vol. 16, No. 22, pp. 21-23. December 1957.

Lerner, Jack. "The Brain Injured Child." *The Synagogue School,* Vol. 12, No. 1, pp. 10-11. Fall 1963.

Levinson, Boris. "The Intellectually Exceptional Child, Part I, The Mentally Defective Child." *Yeshiva Education*, Vol. 3, No. 1. pp. 5-17. Fall 1959.

Lister, Louis. "Religious Education for the Emotionally Disturbed." *The Southwest Teacher,* Vol. 1, No.3. Winter 1967-Spring 1968. (Guest Issue: The Exceptional Child and his Jewish Education)

Lister, Rebecca. *Jewish Religious Education for the Retarded Child*. New York: Union of American Hebrew Congregations. 1959.

Margolis, Isidore. "Yeshiva Special Education." *Yeshiva Education*. Vol. 3, No. 1, pp. 3-4. Fall 1959.

Ribowsky, Helene. "Jewish Education and the Learning Disabled." *The Jewish Press*. Brooklyn, New York. Four part series: January 5, 12, and 19, 1978 and March 2, 1979.

Rogow, Sally. "The Child with Learning Disabilities in the Synagogue School." *The Synagogue School*. Summer 1974.

Rosenkranz, Samuel. "The Steps We Took with Tommy," *The Southwest Teacher,* Vol. 1, No. 3. Winter 1967/ Spring 1968. (Guest Issue: The Exceptional Child and his Jewish Education)

Schwartz, Elliot S. "A Very Special World." *The Synagogue School.* Vol. 31, No. 4 (Summer 1973). pp. 12-25.

——*A Manual for Organizing Classes for Jewish Special Children.* New York: United Synagogue Commission on Jewish Education, 1975. 14 pages.

Schwartz, Larry. "Educable Retarded Children," *The Southwest Teacher,* Vol. 1, No. 3. Winter 1967/Spring 1968. (Guest Issue: The Exceptional Child and his Jewish Education).

Shapiro, Helen. "Jewish Religious Education for Retarded Children." *Mental Retardation,* Vol. 2, No. 4, pp. 213-216. August 1964.

Silver, Daniel. "The Retarded Child and Religious Education," *Religious Education,* Vol. 52, No. 5, pp. 362-364. September/October 1957.

Stiskin, Hershel M. "Jewish Education for the Special Child." *Your Child,* Vol. 1, No. 1. Fall 1968. United Synagogue Commission on Jewish Education.

——"Religious Education for the Retarded." *Digest of the Mentally Retarded,* Vol. 1, No. 2, pp. 104-108, 1965.

——"The Slow Learner and the Yeshiva," *The Jewish Parent Magazine,* Vol. 17, No. 1, October 1965.

——*Survey of Jewish Religious Programs for the Handicapped,* American Association for Jewish Education, 1968.

Syden, Martin. "Religious Education for the Jewish Retarded Child," *American Journal of Mental Deficiency,* Vol. 64, No. 4. pp. 689-694, January 1960.

Teller, Hanoch. "The Stone Rejected by the Builders..." *The Jewish Observer.* Vol. 13, No. 3. pp. 25-29. May 1978.

Volstad, Naomi. "Jewish Education for Very Special Children." *Hadassah Magazine.* pp. 14-15, 24. February 1979.

PART 2: BUILDING AN INCLUSIVE JEWISH COMMUNITY

CHAPTER 3

A RABBI'S GUIDE TO THE PERSON WITH SPECIAL NEEDS

Rabbi Robert Layman

PREFACE

The following is intended as a guide for clergy and was written by a rabbi who has had personal experience as a parent of a child with special needs. Rabbis' specific contributions in this area are spelled out forthrightly by Sara Rubinow Simon. Ms. Simon, in a 1980 letter to the members of the Rabbincal Assembly, wrote:

"You are in a unique position. Through sermons, direct action and personal leadership, you are able to set a positive tone for your congregation and your community.

For many rabbis, the first problem is often identifying individuals with disabilities. Because of previous negative experiences, their families may shy away from the synagogue. It cannot be overemphasized that their involvement begins with your reaching out to them. They must be persuaded to come to the synagogue, and to you for comfort, guidance, and acceptance. If you make clear your interest and concern and if you help your congregation to start thinking in terms of the individual's potentials rather than the deficits which make him different, you will be gratified by the numbers who approach you."

National ideological organizations are recognizing the need to acquaint clergy with a problem which, for some time, remained virtually unrecognized by the organized Jewish community and was a source of embarrassment and deep malaise to parents. Because of the high premium that our people have placed on education and academic achievement, those families who have had children with mental, emotional, or learning disabilities have had to deal with an enormous emotional burden. There has been, in the past, a great reluctance to admit openly that such family members exist and to take measures to provide an appropriate Jewish education for them.

A biography of Golda Meir, for example, contains the startling revelation that among her survivors is an adult granddaughter with Down Syndrome. In all of her own writings, Mrs. Meir never acknowledged the existence of this person, nor did she ever speak about her. The granddaughter herself was aware of her distinguished grandmother's neglect and encountered disbelief whenever she identified herself as a grandchild of Golda Meir.

The late Prime Minister's attitude may not be typical of her generation but neither is it an isolated case. In recent years, the Jewish community and Jewish families have taken a more positive and realistic approach to the person with special needs, his/her educational needs and integration into the family and into Jewish life. National ideological groups, along with a number of local agencies in major metropolitan areas, have undertaken an elaborate program of educational activities on behalf of Jews with special needs.

Congregations and community groups have been sensitized to the need for and desirability of offering Jewish experiences for individuals with learning differences and other special needs. Numerous classes have been established during the past three decades and there has been a significant growth in the number of teachers who are qualified specialists in this field.

Because congregational rabbis must deal with a variety of personal problems and have become increasingly involved in such issues as divorce, family instability, aging, the attraction of cults, etc., it is equally important that they develop an awareness of a problem which affects more families than they may realize. Within each congregation there are probably several families who have children with disabilities or have relatives with similar problems who may never have communicated with their rabbi about these matters, either because of their own embarrassment or what they perceive to be the rabbi's lack of sensitivity or information about these matters.

THE RABBI'S ROLE IN THE CONGREGATIONAL RELIGIOUS SCHOOL

One area where a rabbi may become aware of some of the conditions is in the Religious School classroom. Teachers and administrators who are unfamiliar with special education are apt to present the rabbi with a problem which they cannot handle themselves, a problem which they are likely to see as disciplinary in character. The claims may vary: the student is a slow learner; he refuses to take direction; he cannot sit still; he is constantly disruptive.

What is commonly viewed as a "discipline problem" may be something quite different. The student's behavior combined with his lack of academic achievement may be symptomatic of an underlying problem. There may be a temptation, however, to dismiss the student's shortcomings as typical evidence of lack of motivation and commitment and the other deficiencies that are normally associated with Jewish education and the families who participate in the process ambivalently or reluctantly.

In situations where the education director has experience with special learning needs, the rabbi should be informed of the accommodations being made and should be updated periodically. When a child's behavior appears to be beyond the control of the teacher and the school administrator or he shows consistent evidence of significant special learning needs that are not being fully addressed, the rabbi would be well advised to interview the child and to observe his behavior first hand. It is best to be forearmed with a knowledge of the literature on special education and the person with special needs in order to be able to recognize the characteristics and to analyze them intelligently.

When the rabbi is satisfied that the problem does not stem from boredom, unimaginative teaching, or other classroom conditions which do not make for a healthy environment, he should invite the parents to a conference. This may prove to be a difficult challenge, especially dealing with typical Jewish parents who, as noted above, place a high value on academic achievement. The education director can provide background information prior to the conference, and may choose to participate in the conference.

The following are two of the obstacles that the rabbi is likely to encounter in his conversations with the parents:

Defensiveness. The parents may, at first, be unwilling to acknowledge that a problem exists. They are likely to place the blame on the school: poor teaching, lack of concern and compassion for the individual as a human being, and the built-in deficiency of the supplementary school which demands alertness and achievement after a full day of secular school studies. The parents may reinforce their contention with the claim that the child has no such problems in public school. This claim may be easily checked by contacting the school authorities, who are generally cooperative. By and large, it will come as no surprise to learn that behavior and learning patterns manifested in religious school have a correlation with those manifested in the secular school.

Guilt. Assuming that the parents are convinced that a problem exists, they are likely to focus the blame on themselves or on each other. It is not unusual for a crisis to develop between the parents of children with special needs because of mutual recrimination. The rabbi will have to use all of his skills as a counselor, or recommend outside counseling, to forestall a marital rift at a time when the child with special needs requires all of the moral support he can get. The rabbi must exercise skill in deflecting the guilt feelings of the parents and directing them to take the steps necessary to deal with the child's disability as well as adjusting their own lives to this newly acknowledged reality.

THE RABBI'S ROLE IN THE SYNAGOGUE AND THE COMMUNITY

Before taking concrete steps to deal with the needs of people with disabilities in his congregation, the rabbi should develop an awareness of the nature of their disability. As an interpreter of tradition, the rabbi may consult the classical sources to ascertain the rabbinic approach and attitude to people with mental and functional disorders. In terms of our sophisticated, modern knowledge of this field, the rabbi may find the sources wanting or ambivalent at best. There is much literature on the *shoteh* which has been variously defined as "imbecile" or "madman" and whose status in Jewish law is something less than admirable. There may be a temptation to categorize the mentally or emotionally disabled person as a *shoteh* and thus adopt a somewhat unsympathetic view of him. In the light of modern trends in all ideological movements such as the Conservative Movement's Tikvah Program of Camp Ramah and Kadima's *Yad b'Yad* project, a sympathetic and sensitive approach is a *sine qua non* for the rabbi in dealing effectively with the special person, his problem, and his family.

An understanding rabbi can play a variety of significant roles in the congregation and the community.

DETERMINING THE AVAILABILITY OF SPECIAL EDUCATION PROGRAMS

In a fairly large, well-established Jewish community, there should be opportunities for special children. Congregations, regardless of ideological orientation, should pool their resources and organize such programs. The local Federation should be invited to participate by providing subsidies. Such programs, ideally, should be open to all Jewish families regardless of affiliation. Payment of tuition should be based on a policy which makes special education available to all regardless of income. Keep in mind that these families may face financial burdens which far exceed those of the average family.

In a community which does not offer Jewish special education services, the rabbi can serve as the initiator of such a program. He should consult with experts in the field of secular special education and confer with his own school committee to determine the most effective means of providing these opportunities. Acting in concert with colleagues, irrespective of ideological differences, he can be instrumental in organizing a community-based program.

In a small community where there may be very few special children, a specialist should be engaged to provide consultation and support. The congregation's board should be persuaded to provide a subvention to cover the tutor's fee.

SENSITIZING THE CONGREGATION TO THE PRESENCE OF INDIVIDUALS WITH SPECIAL NEEDS IN ITS MIDST

Because of the benighted attitudes toward developmental and learning disabilities which persist to this day, some congregants may not be receptive to the inclusion of individuals with special needs in the synagogue's activities. The rabbi, together with the education director, the cantor, and the teaching staff, should work to overcome these prejudices and gain acceptance of the special person at religious services and social activities. There is probably no more compelling event that can move hearts and minds than the Bar/Bat Mitzvah of a child with special needs who has studied diligently and painstakingly for this occasion. It is important to learn the techniques for preparing such a child for the ceremony as well as preparing the congregation for it. As Dr. Reuven Hammer notes: "A congregation should learn, if it does not already know, that deviations from the norm of performance are desirable for a purpose such as this."

In a situation where parents have requested a Bar/Bat Mitzvah ceremony and no one else has taken the initiative to organize a class or to provide instruction, the rabbi could demonstrate his interest and concern by initiating the Bar/Bat Mitzvah training program himself.

In brief, people with special needs can be integrated into the mainstream of congregational life with the moral support of the rabbi and caring members of the professional staff and the congregation at large.

DEVELOPING A CURRICULUM

It stands to reason that, while the curriculum of the special education program may parallel that of the religious school, there will be significant differences based on time limitations, attention span and ability to comprehend, among other factors. A determination must be made concerning the extent to which Hebrew will be taught and where major emphasis will be placed. Of necessity, stress will be placed on the concrete, such as Shabbat and holiday observances with their rich symbolism, while abstract concepts can be adapted to the comprehension levels of the students. Historical ideas and personalities can be integrated in the teaching of holidays, e.g. Hanukkah and Purim. In addition, biographies of famous personalities through the ages can be introduced.

Knowledge of basic Jewish beliefs and Jewish living skills constitute the core of the curriculum. Hebrew may be used as deemed appropriate. The rabbi may be called on, depending on his expertise as an educator, for consultation in the development of curriculum for students with special needs.

HELPING THE FAMILY AT HOME

Publications are available that contain a wealth of suggestions relating to the participation of the person with special needs in home rituals and religious observances and for helping him develop an awareness of his Jewish identity. Among the activities in which he can participate, as suggested by Dr. Morton K. Siegel, are daily routines in *Kashrut* observance such as selecting the proper dishes for meat and dairy, joining in the *Berakhot* before and after the meal, lighting the candles of the *Hannukiyah*, and saying the Four Questions, however imperfectly, on *Pesah*. The possibilities and opportunities are innumerable. The rabbi should meet with the family, prepare an outline of possibilities, and encourage the family's perseverance in involving the special member.

RECRUITMENT

For years, Jewish educators, rabbis, and committed lay leaders have faced the challenge of convincing Jewish parents of the need for providing their children a Jewish education. Many studies have revealed the paltry number of children who receive any kind of Jewish education in relation to the potential, particularly in large metropolitan areas. How much more difficult it is to persuade the parents of children with disabilities of this need. Yet, a person with a disability is entitled to the same Jewish self-awareness as his "typical" counterpart.

The problem is compounded by the widespread reluctance of Jewish parents to make public the existence of a person with a disability in the family. As I have noted elsewhere, "it is… difficult to face other Jews in the community, with its clearly defined goals and values regarding individual achievement."

The rabbi can play a significant role by seeking out those parents who are committed to Jewish special education and persuading them to encourage their friends and acquaintances who also have children with special needs to come forward and enroll them. Parents of children with disabilities in the same community generally get to know each other through their contacts in the secular school or because they are brought together by mutual friends. On the theory of *tzarat rabim hatzi nehamah* (the concerns shared by many are partial consolation), recruitment can be rather successful.

ACHIEVING COMMUNITY SUPPORT

In this era of sharp cutbacks in government funding, Jewish Federations may be regretfully reluctant to allocate funds for a new venture in special education. Federation leaders may express sincere interest in the project but will justifiably insist that the funds simply are not available. An influential rabbi, along with equally influential lay leaders, may be instrumental in assuring that a line be included for special education in future Federation budgets. It is unlikely that anyone will, in principle, at least, reject such a request. In the meantime, the rabbi and his committee should actively pursue other sources, e.g. affluent, concerned individuals or foundation grants.

HELPING INDIVIDUALS WITH PHYSICAL DISABILITIES

Society has, of late, taken greater cognizance of the needs of individuals with physical disabilities. Accommodations range from close-captioned television programs for those with hearing impairments, to oversize print for individuals with visual impairments, to "kneeling" buses, to ramps as alternatives to stairs for wheelchairs. In addition, accommodations have been mandated by the Americans with Disabilities Act (ADA).

Again, the synagogue can play an important role in integrating a congregant with a physical disability into the life of the congregation and the rabbi should be the central figure in that role. Just as with members with cognitive disabilities that affect one's learning, the rabbi and other professional personnel can work together to sensitize congregants to the needs of the individuals with physical disabilities so that they are not made to feel like outcasts.

AN AFTERWORD ON THEOLOGY

One may suggest that this should have begun with fundamental questions relating to the acceptance of disabilities. Those questions cover a wide range of emotions and are articulated in a manner that challenges our assumptions about God and His role in the lives of human beings. A rabbi must not only be prepared to resolve these difficulties in his own mind but to respond to the challenges presented by individuals with disabilities and their families. Among the difficult questions the rabbi can expect to hear are: "Why me?" "Why is God punishing me (or my loved one)?" "How can a good God permit such suffering?" Some may go so far as to deny the existence of God because of the calamity which has befallen them.

How the rabbi responds depends, to be sure, upon his own theological conceptions. To suggest, for example, that God is testing the person or his family as He tested Abraham at the *Akedah* may be a hollow and inadequate response. There is no rule of thumb that anyone can presume to set forth. This writer, who is the father of a child with special needs, is not ready to blame God for what some may perceive as a misfortune. Let us rather suggest that anyone who works to aid people with disabilities, to alleviate their suffering and the anguish of his family is doing God's work. Such an approach is offered by Rabbi Harold Kushner in his acclaimed book, *When Bad Things Happen To Good People*, a work which every rabbi should read and which should be lent or presented to every family with a loved one who is disabled.

CHAPTER 4

WELCOMING PEOPLE WITH DISABILITIES INTO OUR HOUSE OF WORSHIP

That All May Worship
National Organization on Disability

There are forty-three million people with disabilities in America. They differ in strengths and weaknesses, abilities and needs, as much as individuals in any group differ. Our synagogues should welcome each one of them!

IMPROVING PERSONAL INTERACTIONS

Talk directly to the person with a disability, not to the nearby family member, companion or interpreter.

Offer assistance but do not impose. Allow a person to retain as much control as possible, doing things for himself or herself, even if it takes longer.

Ask the person with the disability about the best way to be of assistance. Personal experience makes him or her the expert.

Do not pretend to understand if the speech or ideas of the person are unclear. Request that the person clarify. Continue speaking to the person rather than asking a companion to answer for him or her.

Work to control reactions of personal discomfort when someone behaves in an unexpected way or looks somewhat different. Try to see the wholeness of spirit underneath and overcome the tendency to turn away or ignore the person with the disability.

WIDENING CONGREGATIONAL HOSPITALITY

Use multi-sensory approaches to involve all listeners when preaching, teaching or making presentations. Everyone will benefit.

Encourage people with disabilities to participate in the full range of congregational experiences.

Follow announcements of general invitation with personal invitations and arrangements for transportation. Persons with disabilities may not really believe the invitation is "for them" if they have had disappointing or isolating experiences in the past.

Nominate people with needed skills to be contributors and leaders in positions of responsibility. Never decide for someone with a disability that getting to meetings or doing the work is "too hard." Invite first, then leave it up to them.

Be sure that people with disabilities are asked to plan and review progress on both programmatic and architectural changes.

Provide notetakers for meetings.

Develop transportation to religious and social activities for people with a wide variety of conditions.

Develop a job placement program and support group for those in the congregation who are out of work. Two-thirds of people with disabilities, who are of working age and want to work, are unemployed, and many who work are underemployed. When the congregation provides affirming support, it empowers the person's job search.

Be aware that accommodations for one group can cause difficulty for another. For example, discuss the proposed placement of ramps and curb cuts with members who have impaired sight and could trip on edges and grading.

Support the families of those with disabilities for they experience stress and isolation.

Locate and support local chapters of organizations which offer services to people with disabilities and their families. Such services may include recreation, respite care, advocacy, financial assistance and health care.

CHAPTER 5

THE JOURNEY OF A CONGREGATION

A Self-Assessment and Learning Tool of the Accessible Congregations Campaign, National Organization on Disability

The Accessible Congregations Campaign was developed by the National Organization on Disability to gain the commitment of 2,000 congregations by December 31, 2000, to include people with all types of disabilities as full and active participants. To help congregations assess their progress along the journey, the following tool was developed. The Accessible Congregations Campaign did meet their goal and the number of congregations continues to increase each month.

THE VISION

Congregations across America are opening their hearts, minds, and doors to people with disabilities and to older adults, recognizing their unique needs while appreciating their unique gifts and talents.

ACCESS: IT BEGINS IN THE HEART.

How well are you doing?

For each of the 15 levels in the journey of your congregation, select the item that best matches current progress. You will notice that each level of the Journey represents a greater commitment on the part of the congregation toward the goal of full participation of people with disabilities.

THE JOURNEY OF A CONGREGATION

	not started	getting started	well on our way	we're there
AWARENESS. Recognition by some congregation members or the ordained religious leadership that certain barriers were preventing children or adults with physical, sensory, or mental disabilities from accessing a full life of faith (including worship, study, service, and leadership)				
ADVOCACY. (Internal) Growing advocacy within the congregation to welcome people with disabilities as full participants and to remove barriers (architectural, communications, and attitudes) to this participation				
DISCUSSIONS. Concerns raised regarding ability of the congregation to meet the challenges (e.g., Are there enough people with this need to justify the expense? Will people with disabilities feel comfortable in joining us once barriers have been removed?) and then solutions identified—ideally with input from people with disabilities and other experts				
PLANS. Invitation of people with disabilities to join the congregation as full members (including participation in rites of passage and initiation), action plans devised to achieve barrier-removing goals, and formal commitment made to welcome people with disabilities				
ACCOMMODATIONS. Accommodations made to improve the participation of people with disabilities (e.g., large print bulletins, trained ushers, accessible parking spaces, ramps and pew cuts, improved lighting and sound systems, appropriate religious education for children with disabilities)				
WELCOMING ENVIRONMENT. Appreciation expressed for the changes being made and friendships extended to people with disabilities and their family members by increasing numbers within the congregation				
HURDLES. Identification of architectural (e.g., elevator, accessible restroom, ramp to the altar, or bimah), communications (e.g., sign language interpreter or alternative formats for materials), transportation (e.g., wheelchair accessible van) , financial, or other barriers and ways found to move forward in spite of them				

	not started	getting started	well on our way	we're there
INCLUSION. Increased participation of people with disabilities in worship, study, and service to others, as well as increased comfort levels of members with a more diverse congregation				
OUTREACH (Local). Options explored and action plans formulated for partnership opportunities with local agencies and organizations serving people with disabilities				
LEADERSHIP. Recruitment of lay members with disabilities for leadership roles within the congregation and a willingness demonstrated to accept and accommodate an ordained leader with disability				
NEW CONSCIOUSNESS. Resistant barriers of attitude within the congregation toward people with disabilities addressed (e.g, through adult education forums, interactive experiences for children, consciousness raising by the leadership of the congregation, and one-on-one friendships)				
TRANSFORMATION. Ongoing transformation of the congregation (through enriched opportunities, responsibilities, and friendships) into a place where children and adults with disabilities are welcomed, fully included, and treated with respect				
ADVOCACY (External). An expanded advocacy role for congregation members regarding the needs and rights of persons with disabilities in the community-at-large				
OUTREACH. Successful strategies, insights, and effective practices compiled and shared with other congregations and communities				
SHARING THE STORY. The story of the transformation of the congregation publicized through articles, presentations, and/or media events				

How, specifically, is your congregation welcoming children and adults with disabilities, as well as older adults? Can you describe up to three congregational actions or programs that have increased accessibility for people with disabilities and moved the congregation forward on its journey?

CHAPTER 6

WELCOMING ALL FAMILIES

Janice P. Alper and Linda Zimmerman

In the last few years, there has been a virtual explosion of information about building inclusive communities and on providing better support for families who have members with diverse abilities. In schools, businesses and organizations that help people with disabilities, community building is being seen as central to creating better outcomes and addressing problems that face us.

New approaches and methods of supporting the celebration of diversity are being developed throughout the country. A wide range of efforts have been underway over the last twenty years that support "community inclusion" of people with disabilities. This is a way of strengthening the community itself.

The Jewish community has reached out to include all people into its synagogues, supplementary schools, day schools and community centers. Jewish organizations nationwide have begun providing services to individuals with disabilities. However, we often leave out the crucial component of creating an environment in which families can truly feel part of *Klal Yisrael*.

While there is no one uniform definition of community building, we do see key principles and themes beginning to emerge:

Valuing Diversity
Sense of Belonging
Community Support

The following series of suggestions and activities can be used by facilitators to include families in community activities. There is an emphasis on planning to ensure success as well as other suggestions for welcoming families where there are diverse needs of some family members.

I. PREPARING FOR AN EVENT:

A. **Whenever your organization publicizes an event it is important to include language that lets all individuals know they are welcome to attend. For instance:**

In announcing a preschool story hour in our library we include the words:

Please call ahead if you and/or your child need special accommodations.

These few words indicate to families whose children have special needs that they are welcome and that their individual needs will be met.

B. You may facilitate participation in public places such as synagogues and community centers in the following ways:

In synagogues have items available such as:

- Braille and large print *Siddurim* and <u>*Humashim*</u>
- Personal amplification systems
- A TTY for telephone communication with people who have hearing impairments
- A list of sign language interpreters to use as needed
- A collapsible wheelchair and oxygen tank with mask
- A wheelchair lift or ramp to the *bima* or other hard places to reach in the synagogue.

Make it known to all congregants that you can accommodate them in this way by publishing it in your newsletter and weekly announcements on a regular basis and encourage people to call ahead so you can be prepared for them at services and life cycle events.

Community centers should have:

- Signs in Braille and large print
- Either ramps into the pools or equipment to lower individuals into the pool
- Exercise equipment that can be modified for individuals in wheelchairs
- Opportunities for individuals with developmental disabilities and other special needs to participate in social, sporting and camp programs.

C. Sensitivity Awareness Training

One can never assume that all people will be comfortable in new situations. In order for all members of your community to feel comfortable, it is important to offer many opportunities to help people become more sensitive and aware of people's differences.

This can be accomplished through rabbis' sermons, bringing in individuals trained in the field of disabilities to lead workshops, including diversity training in school curricula, and asking individuals in your community who have disabilities to share their life stories with members of your organization.

D. Planning activities that encourage group participation

A wonderful activity to use at a retreat or opening event is "Information Sharing".

Have a sheet of paper with a variety of questions such as:

- *Do you have a family member who was born in another country?*
- *What is your favorite joke/movie/song/book?*
- *Do you speak a different language?*
- *Do you like spicy food?*
- *Do you know how to knit?*
- *You can think up many more on your own...*

(Tip: If you have advance information about participants, you can really have a good time by tailoring the questions for the group.)

Everyone goes around the room and talks to different people to find out who fits into which answer. Each person's name can appear only once. In order to complete the task, talk to people you may never have met before or might not single out in other situations.

When planning an activity, be sure that everyone in attendance will be able to participate. This does not mean that you cannot do a particular activity, rather be creative in how everyone can have a part.

Defining specific role(s) in advance often works well for individuals who have developmental disabilities such as:

- Asking them to be in charge of giving out supplies
- Cleaning up
- Collecting finished products and helping to make displays
- Teaching them something in advance, such as a simple dance step or song, so that they can help you teach it to the group

When preparing for individuals with mobility issues, you may want to ensure that there is space for them to move around. Appropriate chairs and seating arrangements for all enable them to not feel singled out, but included in the group.

Everyone can participate in a treasure hunt or ecology project. Everyone can participate in creating artifacts if you have the right kind of materials, such as fat crayons or markers, pens or pencils with grips, scissors for left handed people, and unfinished models so that people do not think theirs has to look exactly like yours!

II. DURING THE PROGRAM/ACTIVITY

A. Give instructions so that everyone understands what to do.

It is important for the leader to be aware of the audience and to encourage individuals to call ahead if they are going to attend in order for accommodations to be made. This may mean hiring a sign language interpreter or having extra volunteers to work one-on-one with the individual.

Also, all information should be offered in written and oral format. If necessary the information can be printed in Braille by a local association for people who have visual impairments. For instance, if you are discussing the organization's budget at an annual meeting, it would be helpful to have copies of the budget in large print.

B. Establish a buddy system

If you are aware of individuals in your community who have disabilities, it is beneficial to have a core group of staff or volunteers who have been trained to provide support. These individuals do not have to have a background in special needs, they only have to have the desire to help others. Look for individuals in the community who are capable of leading seminars on how to assist individuals without taking over for them.

It is important for volunteers to understand that persons with a disability should be allowed to make their own decisions and participate in the activity of their choosing. The volunteer should never assume to know what the individual wants.

C. Consider alternate activities that accommodate different abilities and assist siblings or other family members in getting equal attention.

When including families in programming, you must remember that not everyone in the family has a disability. Parents and siblings often need to have an opportunity to be heard and have their own personal needs to be met. We tend to identify a family by the one member who has a disability. Although it is important to create opportunities for the entire family to be included, we must remember to give equal attention to siblings who are often relegated to second place.

There are many ways to include people with different abilities into most activities. Examples:

- Select a person in a wheelchair to be the score keeper for the relay race at a family retreat.
- An individual with intellectual disabilities can work as an usher; helping people find their seats, handing out the weekly brochure, monitoring entering and leaving the sanctuary, etc.
- Encourage volunteerism by having an individual come in to prepare mailings, answer phones, be an aide in a classroom, etc.
- Look for individual strengths and encourage participation in those areas; i.e. assisting with audio-visual set ups, leading parts of the service, designing the brochure and other computer-related activities, participating in phone chains, being in charge of correspondence for the Sisterhood or Men's Club, etc.

By planning ahead, activities can be organized to allow for all individuals, regardless of age or ability, to participate. Examples include:

- A cooking activity could include individuals measuring, reading the recipe, locating the ingredients, mixing, putting on the tray, putting in and taking out of the oven, packaging, etc.
- Encourage entire families to come up to the bima to light Shabbat Candles or say the *Kiddush*.
- At a gathering where there will be singing or movement, individuals with mobility issues can play a musical instrument or be in charge of the audio visual equipment.
- Have puppets and a costume box on hand for people to dress up or act out characters and stories.
- Prepare several stations so that people have choices of activities—i.e. if you want to teach a song, you can have a listening center with earphones and one where there is a group with a song leader, both accomplishing the same thing; an alternative to a writing station is to have a place where people can cut out or draw pictures which express their ideas, someone can even be assigned to write down the thoughts/ideas. The same holds true for crafts. Not everyone is artistic, as noted above. You need the right materials, but you can make a *mezuzah* in a simple way or in a more complex fashion. You decide.
- There is always a need for a photographer. Have disposable cameras handy and set up a rotation for taking pictures. Be sure to have a public display place on which to post the pictures subsequent to events and activities and give credit to the picture takers. Leave them out on a table for individuals to collect. Families love these as souvenirs!

Sample: A *Yom HaAtzma'ut* Celebration—A Virtual Walk Through Jerusalem

Computer

Touch the stones

Write a note for the wall

Listen to the music

Smell the fruit and spices

Create an Israeli stamp

Make a photographic display from the images on the screen

III. FAMILY INCLUSION

A. Encourage families to interact and celebrate with each other. Organize them by children with similar ages/diverse families/surrogate grandparents and extended families/similar interests, etc.

Form neighborhood *havurot* for celebration, walks, story time, cooking/singing/camping/bicycling together, etc.

Commit to Mitzvah projects such as:

* cooking a meal at a local shelter;
* visiting a local Jewish home for the aged or a nursing home and talking to the residents; recording family histories, and participating in armchair exercises;
* calling someone on the phone who is unable to leave his/her home on a regular basis (weekly or monthly) just to chat and say hello;
* cleaning up a yard or garden; planting trees; Habitat for Humanity...

Encourage play dates and Mommy and Me programs as well as library visits for story hour for families with pre-school children.

B. Encourage individuals to share their strengths by teaching others how to do something.

* Magic tricks and origami
* Construct things, such as birdhouses, cabinets or models
* Teach a song
* Bake a pie

Find out the strengths of *ALL* individuals in your community and encourage them to share their abilities at meetings, programs and events.

* Make *mezuzot*
* Perform drama programs
* Celebrate—sing songs, act out or lead rituals, such as candle lighting, *motzi* or *kiddush*
* Services—learn a specific part and lead it
* Nature walks—recognize plants, flowers, trees; go on a treasure hunt
* Build *sukkot*
* Use the computer to create a data base of important Jewish dates, such as birthdays, marriage dates and birth and death dates of family ancestors
* Illustrate Bible stories, parts of the service or the *Haggadah*.
* Develop movement activities or lead a dance.
* Play a musical instrument, especially percussion, such as drum or tambourine; recorder, guitar; accordian.

C. Fit siblings into the scene

In planning family activities it is important to remember that siblings who do not have special needs are a part of the family. Too often, they are relegated to the role of caregiver for their brother, sister, aunt, uncle or parent. It is important for all children to be able to interact with age appropriate peers. It is sometimes a good idea to ask the sibling if he/she would like to be in a particular group or interface with particular individuals.

Try to create environments where families interact with other families. This allows siblings to be with a peer group of friends who may share similar interests and abilities. It also assists parents in making contact with other families who have learned to accept diversity and welcome socialization and ongoing relationships.

BIBLIOGRAPHY

Alper, Janice P. *Learning Together: a Sourcebook on Jewish Family Education*. Denver, CO: Alternatives in Religious Education, 1987. *A collection of programs, including one-time, multi-session, and ongoing programs, for topics such as Shabbat, bar/bat mitzvahs, holidays, Jewish identity, and life cycle events. Also includes a section on Jewish family life education.*

Appleman, Harlene Winnick. *J.E.F.F.: Jewish Experiences For Families: a Model For Community Building and Family Programming*. Southfield, MI: Jewish Experiences for Familiies, 1995. *A model of programming, including philosophy, planning, marketing, and resources. Programs for families with children of all ages include crafts, recipes, lessons, and events.*

Cotter, Suzanne Amerling. *Family Education Programs Kindergarten-sixth grade: a Resource Syllabus*. New York: UAHC Department of Education, 1993. *Techniques and a syllabus, with a different topic for every age.*

Grishaver, Joel Lurie. *Jewish Parents: a Teacher's Guide: Strategies For Developing Active Partnerships Between the Classroom and Home*. Los Angeles: Torah Aura, 1997. *Stories, ideas, and supplemental materials covering topics such as family homework, communication techniques, problem solving and activity planning.*

Isaacs, Leora W. *Jewish Family Matters: a Leader's Guide*. New York: Commission on Jewish Education, United Synagogue of Conservative Judaism, 1994. *Programs for Shabbat and holidays, including stories, games, and songs.*

Kelman, Vicky. *Family Rooms: Linking Families Into a Jewish Learning Community*. Los Angeles: The Shirley and Arthur Whizin Institute for Jewish Family Life, 1995. *Games, activities, and supplements, from warm-up to closing, covering such topics as creation, holidays, prayers, and Israel.*

Kelman, Vicky. *Jewish Family Retreats: a Handbook*. New York: Melton Research Institute of JTS & Whizin Institute for Jewish Family Life, 1992. *A resource book for retreats, from philosophy and setup to programming, staffing, and lesson suggestions.*

Miller, Lisa Farber, ed. *Apples & Honey: Helping Parents Create a Jewish Home*. Denver, CO: A.R.E. Publishing, 1997. *Articles on the spiritual development of children, making Shabbat special, and many others, with supplemental activities, midrash, and resource listings.*

Schein, Jeffrey, and Judith S. Schiller. *Growing Together*. Denver, CO: A.R.E. Publishing, Inc., 2001.

Wolfson, Ron, and Bank, Adrianne, eds. *First Fruit: a Whizin Anthology of Jewish Education*. Los Angeles, CA: The Whizin Institute for Jewish Family Life, 1998. *Essays including personal journey experiences, home, synagogue, and school issues, theology, education and development, and case studies of some major community ventures.*

CHAPTER 7

PPAC (PARALLEL PROFESSIONAL ADVISORY COMMITTEE) FOR SPECIAL NEEDS, GREATER WASHINGTON

Sara Rubinow Simon

For more than thirty years, the Greater Washington Jewish Community has been a leader in providing programs and services to individuals with disabilities and their families.

By the mid-1970s, programs were already in place in the Jewish Community Center, the Board of Jewish Education, and the Jewish Social Service Agency. Youngsters who attended the Board of Jewish Education's Shema V'Ezer School for Special Education on Sunday mornings, a program for students who could not function effectively in their own congregation's religious school because of their disabilities, then were able to participate in special recreational programs at the Jewish Community Center. They and their families could also receive counseling and support from the Jewish Social Service Agency.

Professionals from these three agencies found that they were in constant contact regarding "their" families. Each agency created a committee dealing with special needs which they staffed. It became increasingly apparent that, in order to coordinate services, a more formalized way of communicating was necessary.

In 1979-80, the United Jewish Appeal Federation of Greater Washington (UJAF), the umbrella organization of the community, undertook an extensive survey of the programs and services of its beneficiary agencies. The chairman of the Unmet and Unclassified Needs Division's Committee on Handicapped (sic) was the father of a child who participated in these programs. His familiarity with the issues was important as unmet needs were identified and program and budget proposals were developed to meet those needs.

Under the aegis of the UJAF, and facilitated by a member of their Budget and Planning Department, the PPAC on the Handicapped met monthly. They served as a resource to UJAF and also were able to report back to their agencies on emerging needs and new programs.

Now called the PPAC for Special Needs, the group continues to meet regularly and works collaboratively on behalf of the community's members with disabilities and their families. Membership has expanded to included the Jewish Foundation for Group Homes, campus activities at Gallaudet through Hillel of Greater Washington, the Hebrew Home for the Aged, the Jewish Information Service and the Jewish Vocational Service. The PPAC also offers collegial support and professional consultation to its members, who genuinely like, respect, and trust each other—a value often overlooked in such groups.

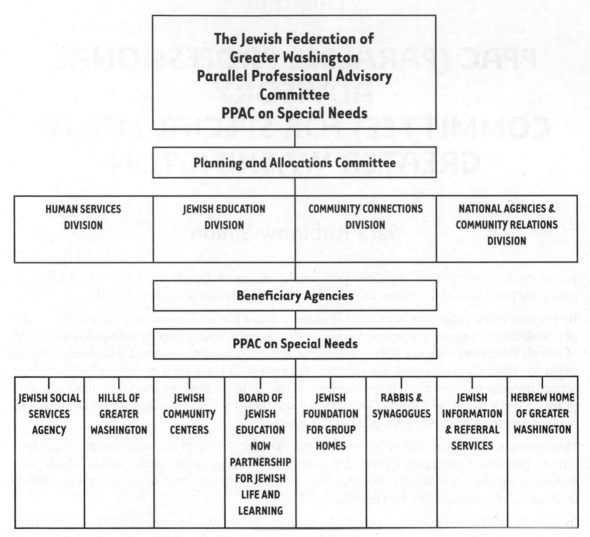

The Jewish Federation of
Greater Washington
Parallel Professioanl Advisory
Committee
PPAC on Special Needs

Planning and Allocations Committee

| HUMAN SERVICES DIVISION | JEWISH EDUCATION DIVISION | COMMUNITY CONNECTIONS DIVISION | NATIONAL AGENCIES & COMMUNITY RELATIONS DIVISION |

Beneficiary Agencies

PPAC on Special Needs

| JEWISH SOCIAL SERVICES AGENCY | HILLEL OF GREATER WASHINGTON | JEWISH COMMUNITY CENTERS | BOARD OF JEWISH EDUCATION NOW PARTNERSHIP FOR JEWISH LIFE AND LEARNING | JEWISH FOUNDATION FOR GROUP HOMES | RABBIS & SYNAGOGUES | JEWISH INFORMATION & REFERRAL SERVICES | HEBREW HOME OF GREATER WASHINGTON |

NOTES:

1. Federation P&A is comprised of community lay leadership.
2. PPAC is comprised of agency professionals who are responsible for delivering/supervising services to special needs populations.
3. PPAC recommendations for new services are considered by the appropriate agency for inclusion in budget. Informal advice is forwarded directly to Divisions.
4. Agency budget requests are reviewed by P&A Divisions and P&A Committee.
5. PPAC chaired and staffed by Federation; meetings are every four to six weeks.

THE JEWISH FEDERATION OF GREATER WASHINGTON
PARALLEL PROFESSIONAL ADVISORY COMMITTEES

PURPOSE OF PPAC

1. Formalizes interagency coordination and collaboration.
2. Provides ongoing forum for communication program development, assessment and planning.
3. Creates a single clearinghouse for all concerns of special needs individuals.
4. Ensures a comprehensive perspective for community evaluation of programs and services.
5. Offers collegial support and professional consultation.

WHY PPAC WORKS:

1. All of the professionals are cooperative, goal-oriented people who genuinely like, respect, and trust each other.
2. There is something in our cooperative arrangement for everyone. We really do need each other.
3. Each participating agency has clearly delineated functions, which do not ordinarily overlap. Whenever there is a possible overlap in function, the agencies work cooperatively to protect the PPAC relationship and to deliver the best service to the clients.
4. There is regular and frequent communication between staff, board members, and executive directors.
5. None are wholly dependent on the others.
6. We have more clout as a group of agencies than we do individually.
7. There is an overriding commitment to a shared set of values and goals, which goes beyond the specific function of each agency. This commitment includes beliefs about people with disabilities as well as religious and ethnic values. The absence of "a pride of ownership" for any portion of the total community program stems from the shared belief that all of us are doing God's work. We do not own any portion of it, personally.

CHAPTER 8

COORDINATED NETWORK OF SERVICES FOR PERSONS WITH DISABILITIES, ATLANTA

Sheryl Arno and Linda Zimmerman

The Atlanta Jewish Federation initiated a long-range planning process in 1987 called the "Year 2000." One area of need identified in the findings was in the area of programming and services for people with developmental disabilities. In response to this need, the Jewish Federation of Greater Atlanta (JFGA) created the Coordinated Network of Services for Persons with Disabilities. Through coordination, cooperation, and collaboration among the Jewish agencies in Atlanta and several nonsectarian disability providers, there has been an incredible growth in services to this population. Overall coordination is provided by Jewish Family Services (JFS) as the lead agency.

In 2004 a new position was funded by JFGA with the title of Disability Information & Referral Coordinator. This individual provides information in response to telephone and internet inquiries about services for persons with disabilities and is actively involved in the general community to advocate for individuals with a variety of needs.

COORDINATED NETWORK FOR PERSONS WITH DISABILITIES (THE NETWORK)

The Network is made up of staff and lay people from three Federation beneficiary agencies in Atlanta; the Center for Jewish Education & Experiences—Amit Community School Program, Jewish Family & Career Services and the Marcus Jewish Community Center of Atlanta. Within The Network, families are able to access information and support in several areas. The core services in the Network are designed to meet the expressed needs of children and adults with disabilities for counseling and/or case management, work, housing, recreation, and education.

CENTER FOR JEWISH EDUCATION & EXPERIENCES—AMIT COMMUNITY SCHOOL PROGRAM

Amit's vision is to ensure that all children regardless of ability have equal access to quality Jewish programming. A variety of services have been put in place to achieve this:

Amit Sunday School—A Sunday morning Judaics class for children with developmental disabilities.

B'Yachad—An opportunity for young people with and without disabilities to interact for religious & socially programming.

Ability Awareness Training—Includes: description of disabilities, ability vs. disability, appropriate terminology, simulation exercises, and more. This program is offered to schools, businesses & community organizations.

Facilitation—Amit provides a trained instructional aide to "shadow" students in a typical day school or congregational school classroom setting. The classroom teacher maintains responsibility for all academic programming. Amit supervises and trains all instructional aides.

Gar'inim—Is a modified self-contained class, housed in a day school. This program is for children with moderate to severe learning disabilities and/or developmental disabilities. The children receive small group and individualized instruction in academics and are included with students of the host school for non-academic subjects and school wide programming. Speech and Occupational therapy sessions are integrated into the program.

Information & Referral—Staff is available to assist families with questions and concerns regarding their child's education. The Amit Educational Consultant is also available to assist schools and parents in parent-school communication.

Learning Disability Networks—Provides the opportunity for teachers in Jewish day schools to discuss issues relating to teaching children who learn differently, learn new teaching techniques and engage in group problem-solving.

Learning Lab—A resource program for day schools, staffed by Amit special education teachers, which offers academic support in reading/language arts and math to children with learning disabilities. Instruction is offered in small groups and individualized to each student's unique learning styles. This program allows children to remain in their Jewish day school and receive the support needed in order to be successful academically.

Parent Seminars—An opportunity for parents to come together to network with each other as well as hear from professionals in the field of special education and parenting.

Resource Center—a place to review or check out books, videos, curriculum ideas and other materials related to learning differently.

Teacher Education—Seminars and classes taught by professionals in the field of Special Education. Teachers are assisted in learning the necessary skills to work with a variety of learning styles in their classrooms.

Technological Support—Amit provides adaptive equipment as needed in order for a child to participate fully in the school.

Yad B'Yad—Support and matching funds to congregational schools to ensure that children who learn differently can receive a quality Jewish education.

JEWISH FAMILY & CAREER SERVICES (JF&CS)

JF&CS was designated as the lead agency in the coordination of The Network. The key service components provided by JF&CS include residential services, vocational services, transportation services and respite services. Through JF&CS, persons with disabilities and their families are also provided overall client coordination as well as information, counseling services, and referrals for social/recreational activities and educational services.

Programs offered:

The Zimmerman-Horowitz Independent Living Program—Our program focuses on helping each participant reach his or her full potential. Independent living skills are taught by professional consultants in the participant's own apartment or home. Participants are assisted in finding an appropriate roommate and living site. This program emphasizes choice and options for service and the need for full community inclusion.

Transition program—This program is part of the Zimmerman-Horowitz ILP. Participants for the program share a home together Sunday through Friday. Individualized plans are developed so each participant works on specific goals for living independently. This program is housed at the Sanford and Barbara Orkin Home on the Zaban campus of the MJCCA. This is a collaborative effort with the two agencies which represents a maximum use of the facility.

Respite Services—JFS provides two types of respite service so parents can have a break from parenting: in-home (a caregiver comes to your home) and host-family (your loved one is cared for at the caregiver's home). The family chooses the option that best meets its needs and then selects a provider from a list of approved JFS providers. This program is a member of the MARC (Metro Atlanta Respite Cooperative) which enables them to offer a sliding scale and give families more options.

Alterman/"JETS" Transportation Service(JF&CS Escorted Transportation Services)—There is a multifaceted service available also to the elderly clients of the agency. JF&CS provides rides to and from work, medical appointments, and social and recreational outings. There is a fee for this service.

Vocational Services—The vocational program assists individuals with disabilities in becoming gainfully employed in competitive or supported employment. The services include: Comprehensive Vocational Evaluation; Vocational Counseling; Supported Employment; The C.R.E.W., a community based project for people with developmental disabilities who enjoy volunteering and purposeful activities to enrich their lives; and a processing center in which mature adults work with people with developmental disabilities to complete work orders.

Bregman Educational Series—This is an annual conference for adults with developmental disabilities, their families and caregivers. It is held on the campus of a local community college and allows the participants to socialize and enjoy a unique learning experience.

THE MARCUS JEWISH COMMUNITY CENTER OF ATLANTA (MJCCA)

The Blonder Family Department For Developmental Disabilities at the MJCCA provides year round high quality and nationally recognized social, recreational and educational programs open to the entire community. The MJCCA provides a wide range of activities for children and adults with developmental disabilities including:

The Sanford and Barbara Orkin Respite Center—The MJCCA makes it possible for parents and caregivers to have some time to themselves, while assured that their loved one is being taken care of in a warm and safe environment. Quality respite care is provided on weekends at the center for children and young adults who are developmentally disabled. The MJCCA is a member of the MARC (Metro Atlanta Respite Cooperative) which enables them to offer a sliding scale and offer many options.

Chaverim Connection—After school care is provided for school age children with developmental disabilities. During school vacations the MJCCA offers "camps".

Camping Programs—There are special units for campers with developmental disabilities at each of the MJCCA Summer camps. They are Camp Barney Medintz, an overnight camp in Cleveland, GA, The Get Set, the work program at Camp Barney Medintz, Camp Isidore Alterman day camp at Zaban Park in Dunwoody and Camp Chai day camp at Shirley Blumenthal Park In Marietta, GA.

Habima Theater—This is Georgia's only theatrical company directed and produced by professionals, with a unified cast featuring actors with developmental disabilities and without disabilities. Each year a full-scale adaptation of a musical theatrical production is presented and every year performances sell out.

Debra "Debbie" Sonenshine SOAR Program—This is a sports program that encompasses soccer, basketball and baseball. Skills are taught and enhanced during weekday practice sessions with games.

Social Groups—The MJCCA provides ongoing social programming for children and adults with developmental disabilities. VSP serves ages 21 and older; Transition Club serves ages 18–21; Teens in Motion serves ages 13-18; Kids in Motion serves ages 8-13 and Children in Motion ages 5-8.

Trips—At least once per year, the MJCCA provides trip for the participants of the Teens in Motion, Transition Club and VSP. Trips have included trips to Cancun, Mexico, California, Disney World, and first trips to Israel, independently and included in a JFGA Mission.

For more information contact www.amitatlanta.org.

CHAPTER 9

A COMMUNITY RESPONDS: MINNEAPOLIS JEWISH COMMUNITY INCLUSION PROGRAM FOR PEOPLE WITH DISABILITIES

Shelly Christensen

"All I've ever wanted to do was to belong."

Anna (name changed) was in her mid forties when she told me her story. Born with cerebral palsy, she grew up in a small Jewish community where access to her synagogue was accomplished only when her father could be there to carry her up the many steps to the building entrance. Once inside, having a disability posed so many barriers that she was essentially denied access to educational, worship and social opportunities.

Anna grew up yearning to be a member of her Jewish community. Although her participation was limited, she wanted to belong in the same way as her non-disabled peers. All Anna wanted was access to her synagogue. As an adult, she moved to Minneapolis where the opportunities for participation seemed to be greater.

Anna began her journey in her new community, trying to attend services at a variety of synagogues. Some told her that they didn't have wheelchair access, others told her she could attend services where she sat alone every time. She felt invisible every time she attempted to initiate her own inclusion. She had no partners on her journey and no one to turn to on this lonely path.

Anna's story is familiar to many Jews with disabilities and their families. Limited or no access to preschools, day and religious schools, bar and bat mitzvah training, youth groups and all of the programs supporting the development of lifelong Jewish learning and involvement were often denied to children and adults with disabilities. In 2001, that all began change with the creation of the Minneapolis Jewish Community Inclusion Program for People with Disabilities.

Parents of children with disabilities, accustomed to inclusion in public schools, actively advocated for inclusion in religious schools, bar and bat mitzvah studies and youth groups. The Individuals with Disabilities Education Act (IDEA) was influential, creating expectations from parents that their children could have opportunities for meaningful participation in their Jewish community. A group of parents of children with disabilities, along with staff from Jewish

Family and Children's Service of Minneapolis (JFCS), began to envision a community-wide approach to facilitate inclusion of their children in mainstream Jewish life.

JFCS, the Minneapolis Jewish Federation, and the Sabes JCC, along with the generous support of the Rose and Jay Phillips Family Foundation, collaborated to create the Minneapolis Jewish Community Inclusion Program for People with Disabilities. An advisory committee, comprised of parents, professionals and concerned individuals, was formed to define the mission and vision for the program.

Mission. The mission of the Inclusion Program is to lead the Jewish community to become inclusive and welcoming, where all people with special needs have an opportunity to fully participate in educational, spiritual, social and recreational activities.

Vision. The vision of the Program is to be a caring and responsible community that respects every individual's right to participate in all aspects of Jewish life.

IN THE BEGINNING

The Minneapolis Jewish community participated in a survey to determine the extent of need among people with disabilities and their family members. Individuals with disabilities and their families were surveyed in order to understand the barriers to inclusion that they had encountered. Professionals were surveyed in order to understand the obstacles they encountered while trying to provide support and service.

The results of the survey indicated that inclusion affected people at all phases of their lives. For children, inclusive Jewish education in formal and informal settings was the greatest need. For teens and young adults, continued involvement in the Jewish community, social and educational opportunities and transportation were needed. And for adults, affordable and well-run Jewish housing, opportunities for worship, social and educational opportunities and transportation represented their greatest needs.

In addition to surveying the community, I met with rabbis, educators, youth and executive directors to understand the unique needs and perspectives on each organization. Every organization had a unique understanding and approach to inclusion and it was exciting to realize the opportunities that lay ahead for us to work together.

Some rabbis shared stories of bar and bat mitzvahs of children in their congregations. These *simchas* were transformational for they helped others see that someone of different abilities could make that leap to Jewish adulthood in the tradition of the congregation. Community professionals understood that inclusion was something that they supported and wanted. Many were looking forward to having a community partner to help guide them in their efforts.

It was obvious from the research and interviews that inclusion needed to be woven into the entire fabric of Jewish life, not just into a few segments. The Inclusion Program addresses the needs of Jews with disabilities of all ages in all aspects of Jewish life. The Inclusion Program also supports the efforts of synagogues, schools, agencies and organizations in the community as a partner, collaborator and resource.

The Inclusion Program represents a significant commitment by the Minneapolis Jewish community to welcome Jews with disabilities and their families and to provide meaningful and appropriate opportunities for participation. We realized that for each person who is able to participate meaningfully in our Jewish community, so many more people are not yet connected. Where once a program for adults with developmental disabilities might have included people with cognitive disorders, it was not appropriate to serve the growing number of people with autism spectrum disorders and other non-cognitive conditions. By meeting the needs of students in religious and day schools through Sha'arim, the community special education agency, we realized that teens and young adults needed other types of connections to the community, such as participation in youth groups and camps. We understood that just opening doors was not enough to someone who had never been welcome in a synagogue before. Inclusion of people with disabilities is not something that happens in a vacuum. Inclusion, if not considered carefully and respectfully, can tax an organization's resources in many ways. Systems had to be changed in order to start the inclusion initiatives in our organizations.

A COMMUNITY RESPONDS

Lay leaders in our schools and synagogues began meeting regularly to share ideas, resources, challenges and successes. Coined the "Liaison Committee," members set about developing their own inclusion or special needs committees, and met with their rabbis, boards and staff to begin to raise awareness.

After several years, Liaison Committee members recommended that we develop a manual or guidebook to help them move inclusion forward. The organizations needed additional guidance to navigate their own journeys of inclusion.

After six months of planning and considering how this manual could be tailored to each organization's needs, we began to create the Community Inclusion Guide. The Community Inclusion Guide reflects the areas that need to be considered when planning a journey of inclusion. Those areas are Raising Awareness, Evaluation and Assessment, Creating Your Own Roadmap, and Evaluating the Journey.

Support from the Inclusion Program is built into the process for using the Inclusion Guide. The organizations will have a visioning session with the Inclusion Program Manager to set goals and priorities for inclusion. They will use the evaluation tools created by lay leaders and professionals in the community to assess their current level of inclusion. With guidance from the Inclusion Program, the organizations will then create a roadmap to reach their goals. Finally, when these goals have been reached, they will evaluate their success and determine where they will take their journey next.

The Community Inclusion Guide can be tailored to each organization. There are evaluation tools, resources and ideas to address these principal areas: worship, education, social, organizational and recreational. The Inclusion Guide is written to accommodate usage by synagogues, schools and agencies. The built-in flexibility and the support of the Inclusion Program will help each organization develop a meaningful roadmap. By raising awareness of the barriers to inclusion, Jewish organizations will be more responsive and welcoming to people with disabilities and their families.

We believe that inclusion is not a solo effort. No one does this alone. With the richness of our Jewish tradition guiding us, we may all enjoy the participation of all members of our community. By raising awareness and working together as a community, we anticipate that many Jews with disabilities will enter through newly opened doors.

A DOOR OPENED FOR ANNA

Anna, through her persistence and with the support of the Inclusion Program, finally found her spiritual home. Her synagogue's *bimah* is only accessed by a ramp, so that all who are called to the Torah ascend the same way. Anna has been studying Hebrew and is now preparing for her Bat Mitzvah. She is the secretary of her synagogue's Inclusion Committee. When Anna was called to the Torah for an *aliyah* for the first time, her congregation celebrated with her, understanding the long and difficult road she had traveled so that she too could take her place among the Jewish people. When I asked Anna what it was like for her to be so active and involved, she looked up at me with a radiant smile and said, "I love my new life!"

We look out over the community and we see so much that is new: ramps to *bimahs*, automatic door openers, better lighting and signage, inclusion facilitators and staff, special educators. People with disabilities are reading Torah, celebrating life cycle events with their congregations, and contributing in ways to the life of this community that would have been impossible five years ago. We see people having a place to call for support, encouragement and connection to the Jewish community. We are beginning to understand that all people, regardless of their abilities, have a strong need to belong to a community, to worship, to study, to make friends, to share and to give back.

If we hold this vision in our hearts and in our minds, we will continue to reach out to those who are not yet in this picture. We stand together, as Moses did with all the people before they entered the Promised Land, as one people, destined to take this journey of inclusion together. We do not know all we need to know, but, like our ancestors, we have learned much along the way that will help us move forward together.

For more information contact www.jfcsmpls.org.

CHAPTER 10

PARENT-TO-PARENT: PARENT NETWORKING AND SUPPORT

Shelley Siegel

Community *(ke·myoo·ni·te)*. 1. a social, religious, occupational or other group sharing common characteristics or interests and perceived or perceiving itself as existing in some respect from the larger society within which it exists. (Random House Webster's Unabridged Dictionary)

Belonging to a community is a way of making connections and feeling comfortable in the larger world around us. We all do it, we may be official members of organizations that make up communities such as professional groups, religious groups, school groups, or sporting clubs. We also belong to communities in less official capacities: neighborhood friendships, joggers crossing the same path every morning, shoppers frequenting the same market every other afternoon, parents talking together in the park while their children play.

Being a part of what is going on around us is important to us as Americans. We are taught from an early age that it's good to belong! Play groups, Boy Scouts, Girls Scouts, dance classes, team sports, and religious affiliation, are some of the avenues in which modern friendships are made. We develop interests and look for like-minded people to share those interests. Identifying with a larger group provides us with feelings of strength, security and confidence.

Independent or different-minded individuals often find it hard to be a part of established communities. The unique beliefs and thoughts of the diverse person can make being a part of a larger group difficult; feelings of belonging are incomplete. Differences become more acute and a type of isolation (sometimes self imposed) can occur. Modern society has a way of shunning differences while simultaneously giving lip service to diversity and individuality.

Peripherally belonging to a community isn't enough for many people, yet the search for those who share similar experiences and ideals can be exhausting and self-defeating. People who think of themselves as existing from the larger society often struggle between the reality of who they are and the pressure of what the community is willing and able to accept.

The Jewish people have struggled with this dilemma for centuries. We want to be part of the larger community, yet we desire distinction. We want to embrace and be embraced by our world at large, yet we strive to be true to our unique values and beliefs. We try not to conform so much that we lose the essence of who we are. We are a proud people who enjoy our connection with each other. We find comfort and security within our sameness. We have built communities within communities to support us in the way we choose to live our lives.

The Jewish family of a child with a disability faces this "belonging" issue every day. Where do we fit in? Who is our community? Parents of children with special needs find themselves on the periphery of many communities, part of the group, but not really. Something is different for these families. As much as we are included, and as much as the community tries, there are times we are left behind. Whether it is a comment that stings, or a physical activity that limits our family from participation, we feel it. The need to share our dreams, struggles and glories with others who understand intensifies. The need for an environment where we do not have to explain what makes up the core of our being deepens. There are times we need to be surrounded by people who just "know".

When a family finds that they have a child with a disability, the communities they are involved in may not feel as comfortable as they once were. The family's interests may be changing. Their emotional state, and needs from those around the, may prove to be difficult for the community to fully appreciate, or address. A search for another community may ensue. How sad it can be to feel one must leave the arena they have lived in with satisfaction and step into new territory, alone.

Judaism is made up of many types of people with varying interests, and diverse characteristics. We are a sampling of the world around us. The belief in one God is the commonality that holds us all together. We don't have to leave our community to find others who are similar to us: they are here with us. We must learn to be confident enough within our communities to share our differences and to reach out to others in comparable situations to create smaller communities that remain a part of the whole.

Offering support to families of children with special needs through the Jewish community is one way to keep our community thriving. Organizing parents together in meaningful ways that address their exceptional lives, within the framework of a community to which they already belong, will keep the family feeling less vulnerable and more connected. The greater community will prosper due to the diversity of its population, as well as the satisfied sense of belonging of all who participate.

STRATEGIES FOR SUCCESSFUL SUPPORT GROUPS

A. FACILITATORS

Experience shows that parents of children with special needs are best at offering emotional support to other families facing similar challenges.

It is necessary to have a facilitator at support meetings; this should be a parent.

The role of facilitator should rotate from meeting to meeting, thus allowing the facilitator to receive support as well as give it.

The facilitator's duties include defining the theme for the meeting, keeping the group on task and on track, allowing people to express themselves without dominating the discussion, and beginning and ending the meeting.

B. ADMINISTRATIVE SUPPORT

Support groups offered through an organization should have clear means of administrative support. Such support is vital for the group to flourish, and can often lead to the breakdown of communication.

Roles should be well defined. Decisions must be made regarding how information is to be disseminated to members and potential new members.

Who is responsible for calendar, announcements, and phone calls?

Is it necessary to follow up with personal phone calls ensuring attendance at get-togethers?

Who is responsible to make sure that staff is made aware of the wishes of the group?

C. CHILD CARE

Providing childcare allows families easier access to participation.

Local babysitting services have competent people willing to work with several children at a time, including children with special needs.

Most families are willing to pay for this service.

Children discover an opportunity to socialize with each other.

Bringing children must be optional.

D. ACCESSIBILITY

When planning events take into consideration the physical requirements of participants. Make involvement easy!

E. RULES

Groups will look different depending on the types of individuals involved. Support groups should establish rules to meet the needs of participants. Some universal rules follow:

Gatherings should not turn into gripe sessions.

Those who wish to speak should receive the opportunity to do so.

Those who wish to remain silent should not feel pressure to offer thoughts.

Confidentiality above all else is essential.

Assumptions are not permitted.

Not all problems can be solved.

All members have contributions to offer group, and should be respected.

Other things to take into consideration when setting rules:

How often will group meet?

Will group hold social activities?

What types of programs are members interested in?

What expertise do members have that they are willing to share?

Where will group meet? (Homes, schools, synagogues, restaurants)

Does group want to utilize speakers? (If so, how often?)

How does group outreach to others?

F. ESTABLISH RAPPORT

Having a child with a disability does not inexorably mean one will forge close relationships with every other parent of a child with special needs!

Plan activities to help participants get to know each other. Use icebreakers, and teambuilding situations. (see below)

Leave time for individual discussions to develop.

Members of support groups may choose not to associate with each other outside group. Group takes burden off family and friends by providing a forum willing to listen and share. Participants may want to keep this separate form their everyday lives.

G. ICEBREAKERS AND TEAMBUILDING IDEAS

Food and drink! People are comfortable when they have something to do! Eating and drinking are familiar comfortable activities.

Ask members to share something other than I.D. from their purse or wallet that tells a little about who they are.

In the event publicity, ask participants to bring a favorite picture of their child. Encourage everyone to share and tell why they chose the picture they did.

Ask members to think about a situation that is bothering them currently regarding their child. Pass out slips of paper so that worries can be written down. If members are comfortable doing so, have them fold up papers and place them in a basket. Next, members are invited to pull out a worry, and share it with the group. Brainstorm ideas on how to handle situation. At the end of the meeting, ask if anyone is willing to shred their worry.

Invest in a Trainers' Guide, available at most bookstores. Tailor the activities suggested to meet the needs of your group.

H. THEMES

At first, dialogue may be slow in coming. Prepare a topic to be discussed and include it in your invitation.

Facilitator must be flexible and attuned to the group's needs and interests.

Focus may shift during meetings. Facilitator must take pulse of the group often.

Suggested Topics or Themes

How Did You Spend Your Summer Vacation?

Remember How to Laugh (how humor can get us through even difficult times)

Reading, Writing, and Arithmetic (school issues)

Clues for Making Life Work For You (coping strategies for busy parents, guest speaker)

Nobody Likes Me, Everybody Hates Me (sibling rivalry)

Read Any Good Books Lately? (have parents bring with them their favorite books regarding their child or disability.)

Dreams and Nightmares, What Do You Hope For? What Are You Afraid Of?

Bring an object or cute story about your child to share with the group.

I. DIRECTION

Support groups will eventually take on a life of their own. Participants may come and go.

Continually invite new faces to join the group.• (outreach ideas to follow.)

Parents of older children have much to offer through their experiences.

Parents of younger children have a fresh perspective that can open the eyes of veteran parents to new ways of thinking.

Within the group individual connections will develop, opening doors to new possibilities of, mentoring, friendship and a feeling of connectedness.

•Outreach

Encourage members to invite friends.

Place announcements in synagogue and association (secular and special education) newsletters.

Send fliers home with religious school, pre-school and day school students.

Send press releases or articles to local Jewish newspapers. (See page 117 for such an article.)

Supporting families within a familiar framework makes a difference, in both the private life of the family, and the larger life of the community. The word community can be welcoming and warm if you are on the inside. The word community from the outside, may be cold and rejecting. It is up to each of us, educators, parents, rabbis, students and professionals to be sure that people of diversity are included in our communities and that we all find comfort from being there.

PARENTS WANTED!

PARENTS OF CHILDREN ALL AGES ACCEPTED!

REQUIREMENTS:

- Willing to listen patiently
- Able to share innermost feelings
- Can laugh hard, and cry just as powerfully
- Should be an active thinker, able to offer suggestions
- Knows when there are no suggestions to offer
- Must be comfortable with a warm hug
- Experience helpful, but not necessary
- On site training provided

EDUCATIONAL BACKGROUND:

- M.A. in rushing out the door with only the most essential tasks complete.
- PhD. in negotiating
- R.N. or M.D. strongly suggested
- Advanced degrees in physical, occupational, and speech therapy
- JD specializing in taking on the system
- Teaching certificates for all levels of schooling
- Weight trainer—in many cases applicant must be able to bench press 150 lbs of uncooperative weight and equipment
- Dieticians license
- Experience in juggling helpful
- Must be willing to take crash course in any and every new situation that arises, which could occur on a daily basis

Do you possess some, or most of these skills? Then come meet other parents in similar situations, as we get together once a month to talk, laugh, and share. We are parents of children with disabilities. We are strong individuals. We have to be. We have learned to be.

To the general public, we keep most of our extraordinary talents hidden from view, and function just like parents of typical children do in a hurry up world. We work, drive car pools, cook, clean, and make minor and monumental decisions for our children in the blink of an eye. We anchor our family by playing the role of the nurturer, and the days pass quickly by.

Just when life seems to be running smoothly, we slam into a situation that requires us to quickly slip into a phone booth and change costumes. In goes "run of the mill parent," and out steps "SUPER PARENT"; advocate, rescuer, purveyor of peace, shield against evil, and all around great person! We may have to play this role for only seconds, or it may last for days and weeks. At some point, the unrest settles enough for us to change back into our original role, and we trudge bravely on, with our fear hidden just beneath our "run of the mill parent" clothes, resting just above our hearts.

To share your accounts of metamorphosis, and to meet other "run of the mill parents", please call.................

CHAPTER II

FINDING YOUR VOICE... ADVOCATING FOR YOUR CHILD

Shelly Christensen

Jacob was diagnosed with Attention Deficit Hyperactivity Disorder (ADHD) when he was eight years old. His mother felt a crushing moment of seeing her hopes and dreams for her child in jeopardy. "When will he outgrow this?" she wanted to ask. But to speak the words would be to acknowledge that Jacob had something wrong. "There must be a medication," she rationalized. Conflicting emotions raged through her mind, but this was surely a job for the professionals. They could fix Jacob.

I remember that day so well. I am Jacob's mother.....and I am his partner, his advocate and his cheerleader. But, when he was diagnosed, I was a passive parent, hoping that if I would just let go, the school professionals could make Jacob "normal."

That phase did not last long for me because I soon realized that Jacob was not going to stop having ADHD. In fact, it became a component of his true diagnosis, Asperger syndrome. The path to a new and accurate diagnosis was discovered only because I became Jacob's advocate. In fact, the suggestion that Asperger syndrome might be a correct diagnosis came from Jacob's religious school teacher.

Deciding to become your child's advocate is not a simple decision. As parents, our goal is to build a successful team, a partnership that includes educational professionals, with our child as the main focus.

It sounds so easy.

FEELING THE FEELINGS

When parents learn their child has a disability, they begin a journey that was not in the master plan for their child or their family. Life becomes filled with powerful emotions, difficult choices, interactions with many different professionals and specialists, and a constant need for information and services.

Uncertainty and fear are prevail until a complete diagnosis is made. Parents want some certainty of what the future may hold for their child when often that information is not yet available. Parents are fearful because they do not know where their child will be in five or 10 years, or whether their child can achieve any of the things they had dreamed. Worry over the severity of the disability, questions about society's rejection, fears about the impact on brothers and sisters, and even doubts about how to love this child make parents emotionally weary. The effect can be immobilizing.

Faced with emotional turmoil, parents approach professionals warily. At conferences, the preschool teacher who reports that a child is having difficulties in social situations with her peers may suddenly become a target of anger. It may not matter that this news affirms what parents themselves are seeing outside of preschool. Parents have lost something very precious—control of their child's life. Not knowing what the future may hold and experiencing myriad emotions, they may feel unsure of their role.

As parents, we must learn to adapt to this redefined role as the parent of a child with special needs. We must meet our own needs for informational, emotional and social support. Once we begin this new journey and understand more about the barriers we encounter, the more effective we become as advocate and partner to our professional counterparts.

PARENT AS ADVOCATE

When Jacob was entering eighth grade I attended a workshop at the Minnesota Parent Training Center, PACER Center. I learned about the Individuals with Disabilities Education Act (IDEA). I knew my child was possibly eligible for a *free appropriate public education* in the *least restrictive environment*, and that in Minnesota, parents could request that an appropriate evaluation be done to determine eligibility.

So, when the assistant principal of Jacob's school called to inform me that my son received in-school suspension for poking a hole in a concrete wall with a pencil, I semi-explosively asked, "Well, before you go ahead and do that, I am going to ask you how you intend to provide my son with a *free appropriate public education in the least restrictive environment* today."

Before he could reply, the assistant principal was hit with a barrage of my questions, delivered in a clipped and angry voice. "What do you know about ADHD anyway? Why hasn't anyone at the school responded to my request over a month ago to do an appropriate evaluation?"

I was so outraged and articulate in my advocacy for Jacob, that my office colleagues gave me a standing ovation when my tirade was done and I hung up the phone.

But I was appalled at my behavior. How could I help my son if I was so angry? How was it possible to take my knowledge and use it to help realize educational goals for our son?

After the anger subsided, I began to realize how emotionally invested parents are in our children. When the dream of the perfect child is unrealized, what are we supposed to do? When we lose our hope, how do we reclaim it?

Fighting the system because our anger is unresolved indicates that we have not come to terms emotionally with our grief and our loss of dreams. That was the wisdom I gained from my outburst at the assistant principal.

I realized that there were going to be many interactions with educational professionals. Until this point, the little contact I had with educational experts revolved around what Jacob was not doing. It became my responsibility to share information about Jacob that could not be observed in a six hour school day. I had to be his biggest champion, talking about his strengths, gifts, and interests as well as working with the professionals to discover ways to provide his free appropriate public education in the least restrictive environment.

Educating our children with disabilities is not the sole responsibility of our educational professionals. Parents have a significant role to play as a partner and member of the team, sometimes even managing or leading the team.

Parents are the one constant in our children's lives. Year after year, we watch the changes in our child. We become their best advocates, expressing our belief in their capacity to learn. When we work in collaboration with school professionals, we create a partnership that then includes people who have different experiences with our child. As a team, when we focus on the child and eliminate unhealthy tension, and when we embrace the spirit of educating all children according to their needs, our hopes and dreams for our children can become reality.

PARENT ADVOCATES ARE PARTNERS

Parents can and do evolve into the kind of partners that educational professionals cherish. Educational professionals are no different than parents when it comes to wanting to be valued and respected. When you believe that everyone has honorable intentions toward the process and your child, the parent-school collaboration will be stronger and more effective.

The following ideas can help you become a parent advocate who believes in your own ability to be a partner with educational professionals.

Information gathering. Learn about your child's disability. Know what fits for your child and what does not. Disabilities occur on a spectrum, and not every child is going to fit the classic model described in educational labels. Learn about the rights of students under the Individuals with Disabilities Improvement Act (IDEIA). Gather resources about accommodations and modifications for your child's disability and know where to access information so you can share it with school professionals.

Communication. At a team meeting, decide how each team member prefers to communicate with each other. Preschool parents may opt to share a daily note with their teachers. For day and congregational schools, weekly e-mails from the special education coordinator or classroom teacher can alert parents and the school alike to homework assignments.

Although some parents have difficulty sharing information for fear of their child being labeled, providing information about your child that will help them educationally and socially should not be withheld.

Every year, I wrote a letter to Jacob's teachers describing his personality, his hopes and dreams, his strengths and his challenges. I wanted them to know that Jacob was not a label, but a real person. In my letters, I also wrote about the importance of partnership and collaboration, sometimes highlighting the successful accommodations and modifications that resulted from a robust team process. I also provided a copy of the letter to his congregational school director so she could share it with her team.

Listen. Use your eyes as well as your ears to listen to others on your child's team. You can set a positive tone by asking for clarification when you do not understand what someone has said. You can also affirm that you are listening to them when you rephrase a comment in your own words. Listening helps everyone feel valued and respected.

Understand the system. Parents want what is best for their child, and often that means we ask that our child receive additional resources. While day and supplemental schools are making strides in budgeting for special education and inclusion services, some of your requests may not be feasible. We know, for example, that pulling a child from their classroom to attend speech and language therapy at a nearby public school can be disruptive to them. Yet, the system is set up so that children are entitled to receive services outside of their private school at no cost to the parents or school. To provide repetitive services in a day school setting may strain the budget, taking valuable resources away from other children who also have needs.

Being an advocate for your own child means that you understand the limitations of the educational system. Some parents opt for private services outside of school. Some utilize the day schools' process for receiving special education and related services.

Parents want what is best for their child. Sometimes parents want *the* best, when the school can afford to provide what is adequate. As a parent advocate, you must communicate your concerns and listen to the response of educational professionals. Somewhere in the differences may be a solution—and as collaborative partners, it is incumbent upon each of you to work toward a reasonable solution.

Build relationships with educational professionals. When my husband and I attended our first Individual Educational Program (IEP) meeting, we sat quietly while the special education teacher told us what Jacob's IEP was going to say. We signed the IEP and left. The teacher told us that she had many students on her caseload, and I marveled at the challenge of her job. She was not just working with many students, she was responsible for meeting with families, drafting IEPs and completing a monumental amount of paperwork.

How was Jacob going to stand out among the rest of her students? I wondered. Maybe I could help him by standing out myself.

Over time I learned that building a respectful and honorable relationship is how parents can stand out. Listening, sharing information, communicating on a regular basis are all ways to build that very important relationship.

Have a conversation. Tell your educational partners that this is a journey and that you are working together to create a roadmap for your child. Everyone brings something of value to the conversation. The conversation is not going to conclude in one day; it will be on-going. For you as the parent, it will go on for many years with many different professionals. Through conversation you will all work together, creating a valuable partnership. When the strengths of each member of this partnership are recognized and valued, the roadmap you will create for your child will be so much more effective.

Say thank you. The smiles of appreciation and recognition are one of the rewards granted to you when you show gratitude. Remember, parents and professionals alike want to feel valued. A simple thank you goes a long way toward building your relationship.

Records. Keep all the paperwork you receive from school in an organized binder. This will help you locate the evaluation report or IEP quickly. Parents should be able to access this information efficiently.

Share the Information. A common thread in formal and informal Jewish education is that parents seem reluctant to share their school IEPs with congregational and supplemental schools, camps and youth groups advisors. Fear of their child being labeled may surpass the importance for parents to share information to achieve a successful educational experience.

When diagnostic and educational information is available, sharing the resources is essential. When religious schools can benefit from the information, the chances of providing appropriate modifications and accommodations are greater.

Share Your Goals. Every parents has goals for their child's education. Communicate your goals clearly. If one of your goals is for your child to participate in a *bar* or *bat mitzvah* ceremony, let the education professionals know that. Then you will all work together to ensure that it will happen.

Share the goals in your child's IEP with teachers and tutors in your supplemental school. That way everyone will be aware of what your expectations are, and can support your child in this setting, too.

Be Realistic. For many parents, this is the most difficult task of all. Being realistic means that you have begun to let go of your old hopes and dreams. It also means that you are beginning to embrace new ones based on the reality of your child's abilities and strengths. By being a realist, you and your team will set a plan in motion that will allow your child to succeed and feel good about his or her accomplishments. Being realistic means that your child may need accommodations or modifications that level the playing field, that teach them basic skills, and that may take additional time. Being realistic and having hope are compatible with each other.

Your child will demonstrate success time after time as long as you have realistic hopes and dreams based on your child's abilities.

Jacob will soon graduate from his transition program. He has received special education services since he was nine. I have been there with him, supporting him and cheering him on. I have cried so many times, frustrated because having a disability just isn't fair. But for all those tears I shed, I think about all the pride in Jacob's accomplishments. As Jacob's mom, I will always celebrate those sweet moments. Perhaps they are the true consequence for loving my child enough to change myself.

PART 3:
JEWISH FORMAL
EDUCATION

CHAPTER 12

TOWARDS AN INCLUSIVE
K'LAL YISRAEL:
WHAT'S REASONABLE?

Ellen Fishman and Sara Rubinow Simon

Mishnah Sanhedrin 4:5 reminds us that "a human being mints many coins from the same mold and they are all identical. But the Holy One, Blessed be He, strikes us all from the mold of the first Adam and each one of us is unique." Each one of us, regardless of our abilities or appearances, must be treated with *kavod,* with respect.

Aviva has been attending a Jewish school since early childhood. Now in the second grade at a day school, her teachers have serious doubts about her ability to perform in the rigorous dual curriculum and it is clear that there are some academic and social issues that require assessment. Test results are reviewed and placement is recommended. Aviva's parents want her to remain in the school since they are very committed to Jewish education and Aviva's two siblings attend the same day school. After many meetings and unhappy feelings, the school administration decides that Aviva will have to attend the local public school in the coming academic year.

Ari was born with Down Syndrome. He, too, comes from a very committed family that is anxious for him to learn Jewish rituals, celebrate becoming a Bar Mitzvah like his brothers, and participate in Jewish communal life. The synagogue to which his family belongs has no special needs support services, nor does his Jewish community. He was able to attend the primary grades in his family's congregational religious school and, fortunately, his Gimmel teacher last year had some special education training and was able to integrate him into the classroom. She has moved away and is not available to help his Dalet teacher, who has no experience with students with disabilities and has become frustrated and unwilling to devote the extra effort to including Ari in class activities.

These may seem like unusual cases, but educators and school administrators are hearing more and more similar stories. For these families, and the growing numbers like them, the challenge is enormous. It is against this backdrop that one looks at our Jewish communities, many of which are responding to these emerging expectations and are listening to the increasingly vocal demands of families with children with special needs.

The current special education environment was shaped by the landmark 1975 Education for All Handicapped Children Act (Public Law 94:142), revised as the Individuals with Disabilities Education Act (IDEA). Federal law requires that children with special needs be educated in their local public schools in the most appropriate and least restrictive environment possible. The direct, though not necessarily deliberate, result of the federal legislation has been to apply pressure on educators to place students with special needs in the regular classroom.

But is this to the benefit of these students, let alone the other children in the classroom? Even with the best of intentions, any given learning environment may be restrictive for an individual student unless a continuum of options is available. Possible placement options can include: support for the regular teacher to help him build in accommodations and modifications through consultation, resource help through specific skill instruction geared to individual needs, team teaching of special education and regular classroom personnel, or special self-contained classes that provide intensive, highly individualized instruction.

The following questions need to be considered: What is reasonable? What about including the student who is on grade level but is very disruptive? What about the other students in the class who may not get the most efficient and effective instruction because the teacher is dealing with the students with special needs? Who is responsible for the extra staffing and the financial aspects of the support being provided? Who makes up the team that decides placement in a Jewish school? Where does parent advocacy fit in the puzzle?

Communities need to be much more proactive and develop written policies for admitting, maintaining, and, sadly, "counseling out" students. This is not a legal obligation but a moral mandate that entitles every Jewish family to find a place in the Jewish community. It is not a question of "them" and "us" but all of us together in *K'lal Yisrael*.

In some communities, youngsters like Aviva may be able to remain in the day school system if support can be obtained from the local public school system to supplement the day school's resource program support services that are already available. Her classmates can be helped to appreciate individual differences as a Jewish value, while she benefits from interacting with her typical peers.

Ari's Jewish educational journey appears to be more complicated. However, there are probably Jewish special educators in the community's public school system who could help to design a suitable program for Ari. His current secular school teacher could provide specific information on how Ari learns best. Moreover, the rabbi can seek out congregational resources or contact the national movement's office for assistance. Ari can, and shall, celebrate becoming a Bar Mitzvah and can be taught Jewish living skills that he can use throughout his life.

CHAPTER 13

THE ROLE OF THE JEWISH PRESCHOOL

Mara Bier

INTRODUCTION

"In the Beginning" there is preschool. It is, for most young children, the first group experience. It is, for most families, the first opportunity to see their child interact in a peer group and respond to adults outside of the home. Most young children thrive in the preschool's nurturing and educationally stimulating environments. For some children, however, the preschool classroom is more challenging. Children with special needs come to our schools. Some children enroll with no documented disability or delay. Their parents are often unaware that there are any developmental concerns. Or, families may suspect a delay or disability but, for many reasons, have not yet sought professional consultations. Other children enroll in our schools already having received a diagnosis of a special need. These families secure therapeutic interventions for their children and look to our classrooms to provide an opportunity for their child to interact with typically developing peers. Each child and each family presents special challenges. Each deserves special support.

Current research validates what early childhood educators have always known. The early years are a time of rapid brain growth and development and provide a "window of opportunity" for intervention. Scientists know that the first five years of life provide "sensitive periods when learning is easier and more natural." We must take advantage of this period in a child's life to "feed the brain". This is important for all children and even more critical for the child with a delay or disability.

Public laws mandate early intervention services. Although The Education for All Handicapped Children Act of 1975 mandated a free appropriate public education in the least restrictive environment for children and youth, it was not until 1986 that our preschool classrooms were directly affected. In 1986, Public Law-99 part B extended the school's responsibility to include the education of children ages three to five, and part H (now Part C) established programs for infants and toddlers with special needs. In 1990, Congress passed the Individuals with Disabilities Education Act (IDEA) and re-authorized it in 1997. This law entitles all students with disabilities to an education in the "least restrictive environment" and "to the maxim extent appropriate." The federal law means that children should be receiving an education in their "natural" environment, while receiving the support necessary to meet their diagnosed special needs. Although not legally bound to do so, Jewish educators should be compelled to provide supportive services to young children with special needs in our Jewish educational settings.

Increased public awareness has led to increased parent requests for services for children with special needs in typical preschool classrooms. Parents want their children to attend the preschool in their neighborhood or their synagogue. They want their child with disabilities to attend the same school that their typically developing siblings attended. They want their child with disabilities to benefit from the enrichment of a Jewish preschool education.

We have an equally strong motivation to help children with undiagnosed disabilities receive a thorough evaluation and intervention. Not only are preschool teachers able to observe the "red flags" of a delay or disability, but we are in a prime position to help each family develop an understanding of their child's development and guide them to secure appropriate services for their child. In order to accommodate children with special needs in the preschool setting, we must be prepared to support staff, parents, and all the children we see.

SUPPORTING CHILDREN

As we observe children in our programs, we have the opportunity to document their growth and development. Classroom teachers and directors should be knowledgeable about typical growth and development as well as "red flags" which might indicate a delay or disability. Since the children in our programs are so young, and for most this is their first group experience, it is common for a delay or disability to first become observable while a child is enrolled in our programs. Once we identify concerns we need to help children receive appropriate comprehensive diagnostic evaluations and therapeutic interventions. **It is not the role of the school to diagnose. We are the observers of behavior. It is our role to accurately report our observations to parents and to encourage and support them in seeking further diagnostic information.** It is our role to provide inclusive settings for children with diagnosed special needs in our preschool classrooms.

SUPPORTING FAMILIES

All parents have a dream for their children. Learning that your child has a special need can shatter that dream. For many families preschool is the arena where that dream is shattered. It is the first time that parents hear words like "I have a concern about Josh's motor skills" or "I've noticed that it is hard for Sarah to interact with friends in the housekeeping corner" or "Aaron's language skills do not seem to be typical for a child his age." It is imperative, if we are to provide appropriate quality services to young children, that we understand and support the needs of their parents. Many parents, upon learning of their child's disability, will go through a grieving process. They mourn the loss of a cherished dream. They mourn the loss of the child that was meant to be. They pass through the stages of grieving and experience denial, anger, acceptance, and chronic sorrow. Parents need support as they begin to adjust to the knowledge of their child's diagnosis. Parents also need information. Our schools should be prepared to serve as resources to families and provide them with information regarding disabilities, diagnostic services, therapeutic intervention services, support groups, and placement options.

Many families are unfamiliar with special education terminology and may be overwhelmed by the information they confront. Parents often over or under estimate the impact of their child's disability on their family. Families frequently need time to adjust to the knowledge of their child's disability. Our schools are in a prime position to be able to provide support and guidance to parents as they seek appropriate services for their children. Directors need become knowledgeable about the local professional diagnostic and support services available in their area in order to provide parents with a referral list.

SUGGESTED REFERRAL LIST

Families should be encouraged to explore the services provided by both the public and private sector.

Allergists

Behavioral Therapists

Clinical Social Workers

Developmental Neurologists

Developmental Pediatricians

Educational Diagnosticians

Hospital Child Diagnostic Clinics

Nutritionists

Occupational Therapists

Physical Therapists

Psychiatrists

Psychologists

Public School Systems Diagnostic Services

Sensory Integration Therapists

Special Education Private Schools Diagnostic Services

Speech and Language Therapists

Support Groups

Vision Therapists

SUPPORTING STAFF

If we are to provide appropriate services to children with special needs in our preschools, we must adequately prepare our staffs. Many preschools staff members have limited or no training in special education. Staff training should be provided to increase skills and knowledge of typical growth and development as well as what constitutes variance from typical growth and development. Teachers need knowledge of "red flags" signaling a possible delay or disability in areas of fine motor, gross motor, speech and language development, sensory integration, cognitive development, social-emotional developm ent, behavioral characteristics, attention and health related issues. Teachers should be trained in observation and documentation.

When children with diagnosed special needs are integrated into our classrooms teachers need training to increase their knowledge of elements that would contribute to the success of such an inclusionary program.

Many teachers feel that interacting with parents is their most difficult job related task. Few teachers have received formal training in communicating with adults. Gaining the respect and trust of parents is the first step in being able to help children. Teachers must be well trained in communication skills so that they will be able to be skillful when working with parents of children with special needs.

Staff training can be provided through workshops, conferences, university courses, seminars, staff meetings and suggestions from visiting consultants.

In addition to increased staff training it is important for preschools to provide adequate on site support for staff. Children with special needs often require increased individual attention in a busy preschool classroom. Often the services of an additional classroom assistant will be necessary. By reducing the student teacher ratio we are better able to meet the needs of all students in our preschool classrooms.

Working with Paraprofessionals

Increasingly, children with significant special needs are attending preschool with an individual facilitator or shadow teacher. The role of the facilitator varies from situation to situation. Some children require an extra set of hands to assist in manual or physical activities or in self-help skills. Some children need one on one support to redirect inappropriate interactions with other children. Other children benefit from having an adult to facilitate language and play. Inviting another adult into the classroom is often the key to providing successful inclusion for many children. It is however, a situation that requires careful planning.

Other considerations include the following:

The director, in consultation with the child's parents and the diagnostic team, should decide what level of training is necessary in each situation. Some children need an extra pair of hands and a kind word. Other children require an aide trained in specialized techniques such as Sensory Integration Therapy, Lovas, or Child Centered Therapy.

Abide by your school and local policies for employment (Tuberculosis tests, background check, fingerprinting etc.)

Clarify what will happen in the event of an absence of the child or the facilitator.

Include parent(s), director, and classroom teachers in the interview process when possible.

Be clear about the role of the facilitator in the classroom. Will s/he be responsible only for one child or will s/he be willing to, or expected to, have other responsibilities.

Plan for continued meetings with the facilitator, teacher and director. Decide with the child's parents if they will be attending all of these meetings or only selected meetings.

Plan for meetings with the child's private therapists. Elicit their suggestions for classroom modifications and adaptations.

Decide with the family how the role of the facilitator will be explained to the other parents. Some families will want to share information about their child's disability and the role of the facilitator with the other class parents. Other families strongly object to identifying their child with a special need. It is often sufficient to say, "Our children are all working on individual goals. _____(name of facilitator) is here to help one of the children work on his goals. "

Establish a "Communication Log" to travel between home and school. The facilitator can write a short daily message to the parents. Parents will respond and use the log to ask questions.

Extra effort should be taken by the classroom teacher to make sure that the child and the family feel a part of the class.

Possible sources of eligible facilitators include: current employees, former employees, university and college Early Education and Special Education programs, referrals from therapists, nannies, university Hillel programs.

Possible sources of funds include: school budget, private pay by family, rabbi's discretionary funds, synagogue special needs funds, Sisterhood and Men's Club, donations, etc. In some jurisdictions, public school on-site support is provided.

PROCESS AND PROCEDURES
WORKING WITH A CHILD WITH A DIAGNOSED DELAY OR DISABILITY

Ever-increasing numbers of children with diagnosed special needs are requesting placement in our preschool programs. Careful preparation will help us provide the best programming for each student. It is suggested that every school develop a special needs policy and procedure. Although this can be altered each year as your program expands, it provides a guideline to follow. The following are suggested steps to follow:

Conduct an intake conference with the child's family gathering information concerning

Diagnosis

Required accommodations

Previous school experiences

Names of professionals providing intervention services

Consult with service providers (after securing written release of information form)

Meet the student or, if possible, observe student at home or in another educational or group setting

Conduct a team meeting with all staff projected to be working with the student. Include "specialists" such as music, art, and movement teachers. If teachers are unable to attend this meeting it is important that all information be shared with them before they have the opportunity to work with the student.

Decide on accommodations your school will be able to provide

Meet with family to confirm schedule and accommodations

Plan for continuous team meetings and parent conferences

Plan for transition meeting (when student is ready to move to another class or to another school)

WORKING WITH A CHILD WITH A SUSPECTED DELAY OR DISABILITY

Often it is the preschool classroom teacher who raises the first concern for a child's growth and development. Careful observation, documentation, and sharing of information with parents will ensure the proper evaluation of all children.

Suggested steps to follow include:

Teacher observes child and documents behaviors and skill performance;

Teacher shares concern with the director;

Set conference with parents to share observations and concerns and to make appropriate referrals and recommendations;

Maintain communication with parents and out of school professionals;

Provide continued support for parents and staff;

Provide resource materials for parents and staff;

Although many parents, when learning of the schools concerns about their child's development, seek immediate evaluation and, if necessary, therapeutic intervention, some do not. These families require extra understanding and support before they are ready to pursue evaluation of their children.

THE CONFERENCE

Slow, careful, and supportive are the words we need to describe the approach to take we when talking to parents about their child's diagnosed or suspected delay or disability. The attitude and presentation displayed at the initial information sharing conference can enhance or confuse the parents' understanding of the school's concerns. The attitude and presentation displayed can encourage or deter the action parents choose to take. The initial conferences will set the tone for the way we will be able to work with each family. Here is where we establish or destroy the trust families place in us.

FACTORS TO CONSIDER FOR SUCCESSFUL PARENT CONFERENCES

Physical Setting: The conference should be held in a comfortable room that affords privacy. The best location is one away form the hustle and bustle of parents and staff, without telephone interruption.

Physical Comfort: Hold the conference in a conference room or in the director's office. If the preschool does not have a conference room, consider using the synagogue conference room, or converting a classroom into a permanent or temporary meeting room. Not only will this increase comfort level, it also adds to the dignity and seriousness of the meeting. If your preschool does not have the luxury of a "conference room" try to create the most comfortable situation possible by bringing adult-size chairs into a classroom. Provide tissues, pens, and writing paper. Pay particular attention to the seating arrangement. It is threatening to have several staff members lined up on one side of a long table and the parent seated across the table. Optimum seating would be at a round table.

Scheduling: Leave enough time. This conference will take one hour. Indicate to staff and parents that you have set aside this amount of time. Be prompt. Do not leave parents alone in the room to make small talk with a teacher.

Be aware of the high level of anxiety that parents are experiencing leading up to the conference. Be direct. Explain to parents as soon as you begin the conference exactly what the agenda of the meeting will be.

Example: "We are here to talk about Sara. We all know that Sara is a great kid with many wonderful attributes but we do have some concern about her_____development. What we are going to do in the next hour is share our observations of Sara with you, listen to your observations and concerns, if any, about Sara and decide together what follow-up should take place at this point. "

Be alert to when the conference is over. When parents or teachers themselves ask for answers that we are unable to generate at this time, it is time to end the conference.

Make sure parents leave the conference with written information. You can summarize the conference's main points and list for parents what it is that they are requesting from the referral source. List names and phone numbers of referrals. Do not come into the conference with this list already prepared. The list should be generated at the conference based on the information shared.

Provide follow-up to each conference. A follow-up conference can be scheduled for a future date allowing enough time for a parent to investigate recommendations or to put a treatment plan in place. The director can invite a parent to call or stop by her office if she has questions or concerns. Remember that this is a confusing period for parents. They may need encouragement and support. If, however, the director or the teacher feels that the parent requires more information another conference should be scheduled as soon as possible.

STEPS TO FOLLOW TO SUPPORT PARENTS

Parents will benefit from additional conferences in order to get more feedback from teachers.

Provide articles or books for parents to read which will add to their knowledge in areas where school has a concern.

Invite parents to observe their child in the classroom setting. This may aid them in gaining insight into your concerns.

Some parents may be willing to have an educational diagnostic consultant observe their child in the classroom. Often the "advice of experts" convinces a parent that it is necessary to obtain more information about their child's growth and development.

INCLUDING CHILDREN WITH SPECIAL NEEDS IN THE PRESCHOOL CLASSROOM

There are many factors to take under consideration when placing a child with a special need in a regular classroom. It is important to select a classroom that will provide the optimum opportunity for success.

FACTORS TO CONSIDER FOR SUCCESSFUL PLACEMENT:

Teacher Attitude: The most successful placements occur in classrooms where the teacher is open to the concept of inclusion. Many teachers express fears over having a child with special needs in their classroom. With guidance and support, a hesitant teacher can become comfortable.

Other Students: Pay attention to the number and ages of students in the class. How many other students with special needs are in the class? How will they interact? Are there several active or aggressive students in the class?

Physical Accommodations: Pay attention to the location of the classroom. Is there a better choice because of distance to the entranceway, playground, and bathrooms? Is the physical layout of the classroom arranged so that the child with special needs can easily access all areas?

PARTIAL INCLUSION

When full-time inclusion in a preschool classroom turns out not to be the best program for a student, partial inclusion should be considered. Some students may not be able to sustain a full morning in an integrated setting. For other students, certain activities prove to be successful for inclusion while others may be more problematic. For example, some children respond to the structured environment of circle time but have difficulty during free play. Or, a child may do well on days when the schedule provides for a lot of classroom time but have difficulty on days when there are many transitions (music, movement, Shabbat sing, etc.) At times, demanding therapy schedules may overlap with school schedules resulting in creating a "partial" day schedule. It is important to be flexible when arranging a child's schedule. The amount of time a student spends in a classroom needs to be constantly reevaluated and changes made when necessary.

TRANSITIONS

Transitions are difficult for all young children and even more so for many children with special needs. We can think of many types of transitions: daily movement to different activities and locations in the building, transitions to different classes and transitions to different schools. There are also planned and unexpected and unplanned transitions (teacher leaving in the middle of the year). All of these are better faced with planning and communication with both the children and the adults.

FACTORS TO CONSIDER FOR SUCCESSFUL TRANSITIONS

For daily transitions: Utilize picture cards and photographs. Actual photographs of children in your room engaged in activities works particularly well. Make a daily schedule chart using pictures and photographs to help child see what activity is about to happen.

Use clear and repetitive transition tools (songs, music, chimes etc.)

Give several notices of an upcoming transition For example: "Friends, in five minutes, we will be cleaning up our toys and getting ready for snack."

Minimize transitions in your daily schedule

After informing the class that a change of activity is coming, give a special personal alert to children having difficulty with transitions. For example: "Josh, in five minutes all of your friends will be cleaning up toys and getting ready for snack. I will help you."

Have someone offer personal assistance to the special needs child during transition times.

DISABILITY AWARENESS

In general, young children are very accepting of differences. They are keen observers of behavior and learn quickly about the strengths and challenges of both the children and the adults in their world. Their innate sense of curiosity and lack of understanding of "socially acceptable rules" gives them the freedom to both look and openly question what they do not understand. It is therefore not usually necessary to teach "Disability Awareness" as a separate theme in the early childhood classroom. Instead, it should become part of every day conversations and activities. The exposure to peers with disabilities in their classrooms will give them the understandings that they need.

The beauty of working with young children is that they are so observant. Walk into a pre-school classroom with a child with special needs and any other child will be willing to accurately describe that special child to you:

"Joshua doesn't like loud noises so he covers his ears"

"Rebecca doesn't talk yet"

Children are so open about their questions: *"Why does he walk funny?"*

They live it… they learn it!

BARRIERS TO INCLUSION IN THE PRESCHOOL PROGRAM

New ideas create real and perceived concerns. We ask a great deal from programs that support children with special needs. Schools that are committed to the success of inclusionary programs will need to address both real and these perceived concerns. Barriers to successful inclusion of young children with special needs in our preschools exist. It is important that each school look at which barriers may be preventing them from beginning or expanding their special needs programs and then work to break down those barriers.

Possible Barriers to Successful Programs may include any number of the following:
- Philosophy and attitude of directors, teachers, parent leadership and synagogue boards
- Communication
- Funding
- Staff training
- Ability and willingness to integrate related services into school programs
- Class size and student teacher ratio
- Scheduling

A FEW WORDS FOR DIRECTORS

Your commitment to families and children with special needs serves as the model for your staff. Families and teachers look to you for guidance regarding the challenging issues of working with children with special needs.

Some tips to follow:

Have clear, published procedures for working with identified special needs as well as procedures to follow when you suspect a special need.

Be aware of your staff's various skill levels and experience dealing with special needs.
- Mentor new teachers to familiarize them with your schools attitude and policy.
- Offer staff training in all aspects of special needs and parent communication
- Insist on careful record keeping
- Attend parent conferences when sensitive issues are being discussed

WHEN IT DOES NOT WORK

Ideally, all children with special needs would be accommodated in our Jewish preschool programs. This, however, is not the case. We must be able to look realistically at a situation which is detrimental to the individual child or to the class, and know when alternative placement would be more appropriate.

Possible situations that would require disenrollment of a student include:

When the child's therapeutic needs are greater than can be provided outside of the regular preschool day.

When the health or safety of any student or teacher is at risk.

When physical space or financial aid can not be arranged to accommodate special needs.

Parents can be guided to look at other preschool programs that may be better suited to accommodate their child's specific needs, or special/ therapeutic preschools in the public or private sector.

CONCLUSION

"In the beginning there is preschool." Research shows that children with disabilities have a greater chance of reaching their full potential when they are included in activities with typically developing children. Acceptance in a developmentally appropriate early childhood program can be great opportunity for a child with special needs to learn appropriate skills, establish friendships and develop a positive self-image. By building a partnership with the parents and outside resources, not only does the child with special needs benefit, the overall quality of the early childhood program is enhanced for all children.

With a desire to make it happen, with increased education, and with the financial support of our community, we can insure that "in the beginning there is Jewish preschool" for all our children!

RESOURCES:

Bailey, Pam and others. *Active Learning for Children with Disabilities: A Manual for Use with the Active Learning Series.* New York: Addison-Wesley Publishing Co., 1996.

Bredekamp, S. and C. Copple (Editors). *Developmentally Appropriate Practice in Early Childhood Programs: Revised Edition.* NAEYC, 1997.

Chandler, Phyllis A. *A Place for Me.* Washington, D.C.: National Association for the Education of Young Children, 1992.

Cook, Ruth E., Annette Tessier, and M. Diane Klein. *Adapting Early Childhood Curricula for Children in Inclusive Settings.* Upper Saddle River, NJ: Merrill, 2000.

Deiner, Penny Lou. *Resources for Teaching Children with Diverse Abilities: Birth through Eight (second edition)* Orlando, Florida: Harcourt Brace and Company, 1993.

Dombro, Amy L., Laura J. Colker; and Diane Trister Dodge. *The Creative Curriculum for Infants and Toddlers.* Washington, DC: Teaching Strategies, 1999.

Essa, Eva. *A Practical Guide to Solving Preschool Behavior Problems.* 3rd Ed. Albany, NY: Delmar Publishers, 1995.

Klein, M. Diane and others. *Strategies for Including Children with Special Needs in Early Childhood Settings.* Albany, NY: Delmar Publishing, division of Thomson Learning, 2001.

Krajiceck, Marilyn and others. *First Start Program: Handbook for the Care of Infants, Toddlers, and Young Children with Disabilities and Chronic Conditions,* Pro-Ed, 1997

McCarney, Stephen B. *The Early Childhood Behavior Intervention Manual.* Columbia, MO: Hawthorne Educational Services, Inc., 1992.

Meisels, Samuel J. and Atkins-Burnett, Sally. *Developmental Screening in Early Childhood: A Guide.* Washington, D.C.: National Association for the Education of Young Children, 1994.

Mulligan, S., Morris, S., Miller Green, K. and S. Harper-Whalen. *Child Care Plus+ Curriculum on Inclusion: Practical Strategies for Early Childhood Program.* Missoula, Montana: Child Care Plus+, 1999.

Wolery, Mark and Wilbers, Jan S. Editors. *Including Children with Special Needs in Early Childhood Programs.* Washington, D.C.: National Association for the Education of Young Children, 1994.

Youcha Rab, V. and K. Ikeda Wood. *Child Care and the ADA: A Handbook for Inclusive Programs.* Baltimore, MD: Paul H. Brooks Publishing, 1995.

For more information, contact www.pjll.org.

PERIODICALS:

Early Childhood Today
Child Care Information Exchange ,
Exchange Press Inc.
PO Box 3249, Redmond, WA 98073
(800) 221-2864 • (425) 702-0678

Scholastic Early Childhood Today
2931 E. McCarty Street
PO Box 3710, Jefferson City, MO 65102
(800) 544-2917 • Fax: (303) 604-7644

Young Exceptional Children
Council for Exceptional Children—
Division of Early Childhood
1920 Association Drive, Reston, VA 20191-1589
(703) 620-3660

Young Children
National Association for the
Education of Young Children (NAEYC)
1509 16th Street, NW, Washington, DC 20036
(202) 232-8777 • (800) 424-2460
Fax: (202) 328-1846

Exceptional Parent
EP Foundation
555 Kinderkamack Road,
Oradell, New Jersey 07649
(800) EPARENT • www.parent.com

Journal of Early Intervention
Council for Exceptional Children
Division of Early Childhood
1920 Association Drive, Reston, VA 20191-1589
1-888-232-7733

Jewish Education News
Coalition for the Advancement of
Jewish Education (CAJE)
261 W. 35th Street Floor 12A,
New York, NY 10001
(212) 268-4210 • Fax: (212) 268-4214

ORGANIZATIONS

Council for Exceptional Children (CEC)
Division of Early Childhood (DEC)
1920 Association Drive, Reston, VA 20191-1589
1-888-232-7733

Coalition for the Advancement of Jewish Education (CAJE)
261 W. 35th Street Floor 12A, New York, NY 10001
(212) 268-4210 • Fax: (212) 268-4214

National Association for the Education of Young Children (NAEYC)
1509 16th Street, NW, Washington, DC 20036
(800) 424-2460 • Fax: (202) 328-1846

National Jewish Early Childhood Network

Child Care Plus
Montana University Affiliated Rural Institute on Disabilities
634 Eddy, The University of Montana, Missoula, MT 59812-6696
1-800-235-4122 • (406)243-5467 Voice/TTY

National Information Center for Children and Youth with Disabilities
P.O. Box 1492, Washington, DC 20013-1402
(800) 695-0285 (Voice/TTY)

National Early Childhood Technical Assistance System (NEC•TAS)
500 NationsBank Plaza
137 East Franklin Street, Chapel Hill, NC 27514-3628
(919) 962-2001

AUTHORIZATION FOR RELEASE OF INFORMATION

I_____Parent's Name(s)

Authorize _____, Early Childhood Special Needs
Consultant, Board of Jewish Education to:

☐ Obtain from: _____

☐ Release to: _____

the following information:

☐ Counseling/psychotherapy reports other (specify) _____

_____

☐ Psychological/educational testing reports

☐ Psychiatric reports

☐ Medication information

☐ Medical information/history

☐ School observations

The purpose of this disclosure is_____

_____

_____

_____

Date of Consent _____

Parent Signature _____

PARENT/PROFESSIONAL CONTACT FORM

Date_____

Child's Name _____

Parent/Professional Name_____ Phone (___) _____

Information _____

_____

_____

_____

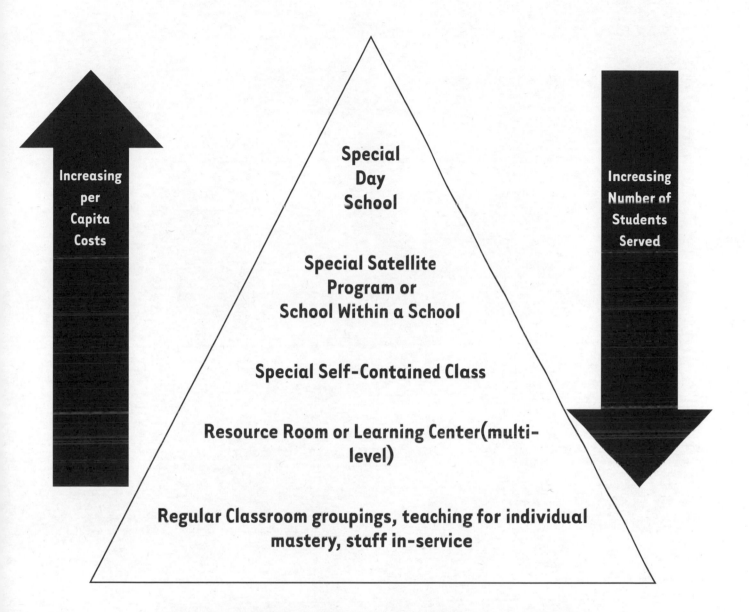

Increasing per Capita Costs

Increasing Number of Students Served

Special
Day
School

Special Satellite
Program or
School Within a School

Special Self-Contained Class

Resource Room or Learning Center(multi-level)

Regular Classroom groupings, teaching for individual mastery, staff in-service

DAY SCHOOL SPECIAL NEEDS CONTINUUM OF SERVICES

CHAPTER 14

DAY SCHOOL SPECIAL NEEDS PROGRAM OPTIONS

Sara Rubinow Simon

I. The regular classroom: the "first line of defense"

The classroom teacher is able to observe the student at length in a variety of activities and interactions and s/he can

- Recognize individual learning styles
- Create small groups and learning stations
- Modify materials and assignments for individual students
- Teach for mastery

II. The combination, cluster or transitional class

- Individualizes to help compensate for maturational lags
- Allows students to progress at own faster or slower rate

III. The Learning Center: A multi-level intervention plan

The non-categorical multi-level "resource room" provides assistance in general education skills, e.g., reading and math and Judaic/Hebraic studies, ESOL, enrichment, special behavior management, and in-service workshops.

The Center is staffed by learning specialists with special education certification, at least one of whom has dual expertise in Hebrew as well as special education, and with aides. All tutoring is coordinated by the Learning Center. Staff works closely with other support personnel, e.g., psychologist, guidance counselor, speech-language specialist, etc.

Supplemental and alternative pedagogic materials are available for teachers' use.

The optional levels of service are:

LEVEL A: Consultative services to classroom teacher and/or provision of special materials and equipment.

LEVEL B: Direct services to students in Learning Center or classroom (short term) to demonstrate techniques to teacher.

LEVEL C: The development of an individualized remedial educational plan to be implemented by the classroom teacher and, one to three times a week, by the learning resource specialist. Projects and activities for the gifted can be short or long term.

LEVEL D: Long term diagnostic/prescriptive assistance in specific subject area(s). Students are taken out of their classroom for all instruction in that area, creating a good scheduling procedure and preventing them from missing "other" work. (This requires the commitment of the classroom teacher to adhere to the same timetable). The Learning center gives homework, tests, and grades in that subject.

IV. Self-contained tracking (ability grouping)

- Curriculum modification
- Pace modification

V. Alternative day school program (for children with more complex disabilities)

- Self-contained community-based satellite to existing day school
- Option of joint participation in appropriate activities

VI. Outside agency

- Contract to deliver diagnostic, remedial, enrichment, staff development services
- School sends bills and collects fees
- Percentage of fees may be rebated to school

VII. Community-based diagnostic team

Benefits of a community-based diagnostic team include increased efficiency and reduced costs in the diagnostic process and the enabling of day school learning specialists to devote additional time to the actual remediation rather than testing. The experience of other communities with centralized Educational Counseling Centers should be considered.

IMPLEMENTING A RESOURCE PROGRAM: ROLE AND SERVICE DELIVERY MODELS

To implement a special education resource program, careful planning and coordination are required.

A. Role of the Resource Program Teacher

The primary function of the resource program specialist is to improve instructional programs for students with special learning needs. This function may be accomplished in a variety of ways: through consultation, assessment/diagnostics, and instructional programming. The following diagram depicts these three major functions:

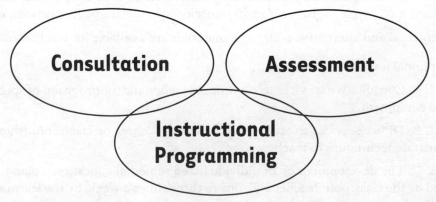

As indicated above, these three roles are clearly interrelated. However, the major emphasis must be on instructional programming to students.

B. Models: Options for Service Delivery

While the three roles identified above are all responsibilities of the learning resource specialist, implementation of each role may vary among schools depending on the needs of students, the needs of staff, and the organization of the general education program. Models for implementing instructional services to students follow. Each model contains all three roles; yet each model offers a different focus in the service delivery of the instructional programming.

1. "Pull Out" Model

   In this model, the primary function of the learning resource specialist is to teach students in the resource room. The specialist is responsible for addressing certain agreed upon objectives from the individualized educational plan. Assessment and consultation with other staff continue to be performed, but the majority of the special time is spent in working directly with students within the resource room.

2. "Plug In" Model

   An adaptation of the above model is the "plug in" model. In this model, the primary function of the learning resource specialist is to teach students; however teaching takes place within the regular classroom while the regular teacher also teaches. The resource specialist has a small group of students (which may also include some other students in the class) and plans and implements the strategies for accomplishing instructional objectives.

3. Consultative Model

   In this model, the primary function of the learning specialist is to provide consultation and suggestions to staff after becoming thoroughly acquainted with a student's needs and learning style. This may involve a variety of strategies. The resource specialist may observe a student in a various settings including the regular classroom. A student may be individually taught, or a small group of students may come to the resource room for diagnostic teaching. The resource teacher may also utilize "demonstration teaching" through large group instruction of the total regular classroom in order to gain additional diagnostic information about a specific student. This approach may also serve to demonstrate effective instructional strategies or behavior management techniques in the classroom. In this model, the regular education staff has the primary responsibility for implementing a student's program but uses the resource specialist to assist in designing instructional strategies, suggesting and preparing materials, as well as specifying techniques for behavior management where appropriate. This model includes preparing a detailed prescription of activities, strategies, and materials that may be appropriate for a given student. It also involves assisting the teacher in successful implementation of that prescription.

4. Team-Teaching Model

   In this model, the learning specialist provides the majority of services in conjunction with another service provider. This may be with a regular classroom teacher, a reading specialist, an alternative teacher, an ESOL teacher, or any other appropriate staff member. It may occur in the regular classroom or in the resource room. The responsibility for meeting students' objectives is shared. Both teachers would be involved in planning instructional strategies and in on-going assessment.

5. Combined Models

It is important to note that combinations of these options may be appropriate. Regardless of the option(s) selected for service delivery, selections should be based on the needs of students and staff in a given school.

CHAPTER 15

SUPPORTING STUDENTS WITH LEARNING DIFFERENCES IN THE JEWISH DAY SCHOOL

Judith Stern

Jewish schools with a commitment to educating a broad spectrum of students from their community face the challenge of meeting the needs of a diverse population of learners with special needs as well as those of the other students. As identification of learning and attention problems becomes more common in the child population as a whole, Jewish educators find themselves refining their own attitudes and techniques in order to effectively teach the "average" student, as well as his gifted and disabled peers found in the same classroom. Newly trained teachers are required to take special education courses to be eligible for regular teaching certificates, while more seasoned educators are discovering that understanding special education has become an essential tool for working with students in private as well as public schools.

With the additional mission of providing children with a strong religious education, as well as a working knowledge of Hebrew, Jewish day schools must inevitably examine how they can match these goals with the varied learning profiles of the students they admit to their programs.

The task is an arduous one, usually involving numerous participants. The combination of good parent-school teamwork working with a motivated student can often prove to be a winning one. However, ongoing commitment and communication, appropriate staffing, and flexibility of educators, all contribute as well to the success of mainstreaming the student with special needs. The stakes may be high when something is left out. A disatisfied parent may air grievances about the school to the outside community. A poorly prepared or overworked teacher will be unable to meet her students' needs. An under-served or ignored student may deprive tomorrow's Jewish community of a valuable citizen.

In fairness to the high expectations of a dual curriculum program, a Jewish day school can best meet the needs of students who have at least average intellectual skills. From there, it is reasonable to expect that a fairly wide variety of children will be able to receive a quality education in their community's day schools. However, it is important for an individual school to clearly define for parents the students they believe they will truly be able to serve. Without this honest understanding, there is greater likelihood of an eventual mismatch. As difficult as it may be to inform parents that the school cannot adequately serve an entering kindergartner, it is far more complex to turn away a child who has been enrolled a the school for several years and can no longer manage the curricular demands. Unfortunately, it is not always possible to know which five year old may eventually be classified as a student with special needs. It is hoped that a well designed screening procedure, combined with a carefully planned model of special needs educational services, will help identify students who are suited for the school and deal eventually with those who later surface with learning and attention issues.

When a Jewish day school has the staff needed to provide services to students with special learning needs, a wide variety of students can be better accommodated. Students with a formal Learning Disability diagnosis are considered eligible for special education services within public school systems. In the dual curriculum parochial school, it is most likely that these students will also require additional services to meet the high educational demands. The day school may also choose to provide extra services to students who do not meet all the necessary criteria for the public school's definition of learning disabilities, although they have sufficient learning difficulties to impact their learning and work production. Given the fast pace of the dual curriculum and the introduction of a second language to all students, it is to be expected that students with mild learning difficulties may also experience some level of distress, even if they are not performing two years below level in an academic subject, a prerequisite for special services in many public school systems.

Another category of students found with regularity in most classrooms is the child with Attention Deficit Hyperactivity Disorder (AD/HD). As diagnosis and treatment of this disorder become more common, schools must address the needs of these students as effectively as possible. With a host of intervention techniques and medication now available, the child with AD/HD can be expected to function well. However, the implication is that extra work on the school's part must be a part of the picture.

Students experiencing extreme difficulties with organization that require them to have additional services constitute another category. They are a tremendous challenge to their teachers, and almost always benefit from some form of additional attention. Whether or not these children have a formal diagnosis of a learning or attention disorder, disorganization prevents them from performing to their potential. The school that is prepared to help this sub-group of students will be better able to meet the needs of a significant set of its population.

A varied service delivery model best meets the needs of a diverse student population. While it is not uncommon for private schools to relegate any necessary supplemental services to private tutors, this is hardly comparable to an in-school system that provides ongoing coordination, communication and quality control as a means of insuring that students with problems have their educational needs met. If a day school has taken on the commitment to educate many different children, it must accept the extra responsibility that this brings. "Contracting out" services will leave many needs unmet: regular meetings, consultation with teachers, ongoing educational monitoring from year to year and appropriate curriculum adaptations. While private tutors can be a useful adjunct to a teaching staff, this will not work as a replacement for a special education team employed by the school.

A Resource Room provides a location for a school to center its special education activities. It can serve as a pull-out classroom for students requiring direct services from a learning specialist. It can be a place where teachers and parents stop by with questions and concerns. Books and materials related to learning disabilities and AD/HD can be housed here. Meetings to discuss students can be held in this room, away from the more public areas of the school.

When a student is eligible for extended time testing, the Resource Room provides a quiet, distraction-free setting.

A school needs to determine which students require additional services outside of the mainstream classroom. Since standards for eligibility for these services are looser in the private school setting, it is possible to accommodate students in need through the availability of a continuum of services. Realistically, the child in a dual curriculum program can only afford to work apart from his class for a maximum of several sessions a week, in order to avoid missing too much of what is happening in his classroom. Making a decision to pull a student out for additional services is a balancing act. Some of the regular classroom routine may be missed. However, individual or small group time instruction by a skilled special educator can be an invaluable asset for the child who is experiencing learning difficulties. This is a good opportunity to provide a student with remedial instruction in a variety of academic areas. For the student with attentional or organizational problems, weekly resource sessions are good times to receive additional support and supervision.

Another model for working with the student with special needs involves having the learning specialist provide services in the child's classroom. The regular classroom teacher and the special education teacher serve as co-teachers in order to meet the needs of specific students. While this model eliminates concerns about the student being isolated from classmates, it needs to be evaluated for its effectiveness with specific students. For the child who is highly distractible or in need of an individualized remedial program, working on specific skills in a classroom where other activities are going on may prove to be an inefficient use of teacher time.

When the learning specialist who is accessible and well-trained becomes an accepted member of the teaching staff, she will be able to play the role of consultant and sounding board throughout the school year. Inevitably, she will be consulted about the students receiving direct resource services. However, in an environment dedicated to meeting the needs of a variety of students, consultation will also occur about other students and may include curriculum based questions as well. Having a special educator on site helps to solve problems earlier, along with the possibility of identifying special needs of students before they become too complex to manage. It also provides a sense of support to the classroom teacher, who may feel overburdened by the presence of students with special needs in the classroom.

By the end of each year, some students will have made sufficient progress to be released from the resource program. Developing a system to monitor these children during the following years provides a way to check in and determine if further intervention will be necessary. In addition, specific students with very mild learning difficulties may be monitored by the special education staff as a way to keep track of any special problems that might surface.

Availability of individualized educational testing within the school is a luxury that is not always available. However, if a teacher trained in administering some of the more common learning disabilities tests is able to fit in this responsibility within a job definition, the school will have access to useful information in designing instructional plans for specific students.

A good resource program requires careful staffing. When a school is large enough, several teachers may be needed to handle the caseload. Since at least ten percent of students may have special needs, even a small department can stay very busy throughout the year. It is preferable to have certified special education teachers as members of the resource staff. Expertise in reading is especially helpful, given the prevalence of reading and language problems in the learning disabled population. If a school has made the important decision to provide resource services for Judaic studies as well, this will necessitate choosing a teacher with Hebrew/Judaic skills as part of the resource team.

Initially, the establishment of a formal referral process may create more work for a school's staff. However, there are clear advantages to the process. Rather than asking a resource teacher to make arbitrary decisions when stopped "in the hall" by a teacher convinced that one of her students needs extra help, a formal referral process encourages a classroom teacher to provide a more specific description of her concerns. This helps supply the resource team with enough information to assist in a subsequent meeting to determine how to best meet a student's learning needs. Since no school has unlimited resources, difficult decisions can more effectively be made when children are screened in some way to judge their appropriateness for receiving extra services.

A referral form in a checklist format is relatively easy for a teacher to complete. It also provides valuable information about where the actual concerns exist. Instead of a child being identified in vague terms, such as "something is just not right," teachers are encouraged to look at a variety of areas when they report their concerns. A school's forms should contain categories for academic problems as well as behavioral, attentional and organizational concerns. Space should also be provided on the form for teachers to write their narrative comments. Whenever possible, the student's general studies and Judaic studies teachers should fill in referral forms.

Since day schools essentially function as self-contained educational units, they do not necessarily follow the child study team formats used in public school settings. However, these types of meetings offer a positive model that should be considered in almost any school. The essential function of bringing together parents, teachers and counselors to discuss and formulate learning plans for special needs students is an extremely effective means of communication and cooperation. Scheduling may prove to be somewhat of a challenge, since ideally meetings should include both the general and Judaic studies teachers who work with the student.

A team meeting may be used in a variety of ways. It can be scheduled on an occasional basis to include teachers, administrators, and counselors, in order to address the many issues that relate to educating students with special needs. Team meetings can also be scheduled on a regular basis to serve as opportunities for the school staff to meet with parents to discuss newly referred students, to determine what type of services will best meet their needs. Students who have been receiving ongoing services should also be discussed at these meetings in order to evaluate progress, changing needs and new concerns. The advantage of incorporating in-house team meetings on a regular basis is that relevant staff members are brought together to focus clearly on a student. Expertise and ideas are shared, while parents feel included in the educational planning for their children with special needs.

When children have learning or attention problems, their needs are often more complex, their progress more erratic, and they are more likely to require the services of varied professionals. These factors contribute to the necessity of establishing and maintaining communication between all the personnel involved with the student. While team meetings provide this opportunity occasionally during the year, more informal efforts at communication should also occur. The teachers who work with the student should maintain an ongoing dialogue with each other to insure educational consistency for the child, as well as a sharing of successful techniques and concerns. When the child is working with a special educator or tutor, assignments and goals should be coordinated on a regular basis. The special education staff and counselor should be included in the network of people who stay in contact regularly with the classroom teachers to check in on specific students. The extra time spent on this type of weekly or monthly discussion invariably pays off in the sense that everyone is alerted to problems before they become unmanageable. On the positive side, student progress and accomplishments can also be discussed, providing teachers with strong reinforcement for their extra efforts and accommodations.

Placing students carefully each year is a significant way to minimize problems. Whenever possible, the child with special learning needs should be placed with the teachers on the grade level who have some specialized training in learning differences, as well as flexibility in their teaching styles. Generally, students with learning and attention issues manage better in a classroom environment that is structured and well-run. It is essential, however, for administrators to support balanced placement decisions. Putting too many students with special needs with one teacher needs to be avoided. In some cases, it may be necessary to provide other teachers with additional training and mentoring, so that they are better able to share the load with their more qualified colleagues.

Since the special education field continually sees new developments, it is important for educators who work with students to keep up their own professional training. Workshops, both in and out of school, should be made available to classroom teachers so they can continue to add to their repertoire of instructional techniques that are suggested for students with special needs. Classroom teachers profit from learning a variety of strategies for managing challenging children within a heterogeneous classroom. Curriculum adaptations, new teaching methods and behavioral interventions are all helpful tools to be considered. The more teachers are able to expand their areas of expertise, the more their students will benefit. In addition, professional training on special needs issues should be ongoing requirements for the school's special education team and administrators.

PROCEDURES FOR RESOURCE SPECIALIST UTILIZATION

1. Classroom teacher completes Special Needs Referral form for a student having difficulty in the learning situation.

2. Parents are informed that resource specialist will be asked to observe because of these difficulties.

3. Classroom observation time is established with teacher for a minimum of fifteen to twenty minutes. Observation notes are written on back of referral form.

4. After observation, resource specialist and classroom teacher meet to share information and, if possible, restructure classroom situation to meet will notify resource specialist.

5. Parents are informed of results of observation and plan for providing support. If possible, arrange meeting with parents and review plan based on input from teacher, resource specialist, and parents. Format and content are written out and filed in school office.

6. Schedule periodic follow up contacts/meetings with parents, teacher, and resource specialist.

DAY SCHOOL STUDENT REFERRAL FORM (Page 1 of 3)

Date_____

Student's Name _____ Date of Birth _____

Teachers: General _____ Judaic _____ f

Last Year's Teacher_____ Referring Person_____

1. Reason for referral (Describe behaviors and issues that have prompted you to make this referral). Attach work samples when useful. _____
   _____
   _____

2. What do you hope to obtain from this referral? _____
   _____
   _____

3. What do you see as the student's strengths?_____
   _____
   _____

4. What classroom modifications have been useful with this child?_____
   _____
   _____

5. Please check any areas of concern. Your comments are especially useful.
   - ☐ Speech and language:
   - ☐ Difficulty with concepts and/or categories
   - ☐ Difficulty articulating speech sounds
   - ☐ Unusual voice quality
   - ☐ Problems with syntax
   - ☐ Difficulty using oral language to express thoughts and ideas
   - ☐ Limited speaking vocabulary
   - ☐ Word retrieval problems
   - ☐ Other (Comments): _____
     _____
     _____
     _____

DAY SCHOOL STUDENT REFERRAL FORM (Page 2 of 3)

Behavior

- ☐ Difficulty with separation
- ☐ Overactive
- ☐ Lacks self-control
- ☐ Frequent sudden changes in mood throughout the school day
- ☐ Excessive inconsistency in performance from day to day, even hour to hour
- ☐ Needs constant approval or reassurance
- ☐ Unusually aggressive toward others
- ☐ Unusually shy or withdrawn

- ☐ Easily frustrated
- ☐ Difficulty with changes in routine
- ☐ Difficulty interpreting verbal and nonverbal social cues
- ☐ Exhibits disruptive behavior
- ☐ Appears nervous or worried
- ☐ Difficulty with peer group
- ☐ Apathetic
- ☐ Sleepy

Mathematics

- ☐ Difficulty with numbers
- ☐ Difficulty with concepts

- ☐ Difficulty with basic operations:
  - ☐ Addition
  - ☐ Subtraction
  - ☐ Division

- ☐ Difficulty understanding place value
- ☐ Difficulty solving word problems
- ☐ Other (Comments): _____
  _____
  _____
  _____
  _____

Motor Skills

- ☐ Difficulty with eye-hand coordination
- ☐ Fine motor problems
- ☐ Gross motor problems
- ☐ Other (Comments): _____
  _____
  _____

- ☐ Difficulty with visual tracking
- ☐ Confusion of left/right

DAY SCHOOL STUDENT REFERRAL FORM (Page 3 of 3)

Memory

- ☐ Difficulty recalling newly learned material
- ☐ Difficulty retaining information over time
- ☐ Visual memory difficulty
- ☐ Other (Comments): _____
_____
_____
_____
_____

Attention

- ☐ Fidgety
- ☐ Impulsive
- ☐ Difficulty beginning tasks
- ☐ Difficulty maintaining attention
- ☐ Easily distracted
- ☐ Difficulty completing tasks
- ☐ Other (Comments): _____
_____
_____
_____

Organization Skills

Difficulty organizing:

- ☐ Materials
- ☐ Time
- ☐ Work
- ☐ Belongings
- ☐ Problems with sequencing
- ☐ Other (Comments): _____
_____
_____

RECORD SHEET OF PHONE CONFERENCE CALLS
COPY IS ALSO SENT TO GUIDANCE COUNSELOR

Name of Student _____

Resource Teacher: _____

General Studies Teacher: _____

Judaic/Hebrew Teacher(s) _____

Date of Phone Call:_____

Summary of Discussion: _____
_____
_____
_____
_____
_____
_____
_____

Concerns:_____
_____
_____
_____
_____
_____
_____
_____
_____
_____

Is there a need for follow up (e.g. meetings, another parent or teacher contact)? If so, please describe. _____
_____
_____
_____
_____

SUMMARY OF MEETING

Used to record notes at all team meetings with parents, teachers, and resource staff. A copy is given to parents and all participants at the meeting.

Student's Name: _____

Grade: _____

Date: _____

Participants: _____

_____

Area of Strengths: _____

_____

_____

Area of Concern:_____

_____

_____

Recommandations: _____

_____

_____

Signatures:

Parent _____

School _____

CONFERENCE SUMMARY

Date_____

Child's Name :_____

Date of Birth _____ Age _____

School: _____

Teacher: _____

Attendance:

_____	_____	_____
name	title	signature
_____	_____	_____
name	title	signature

Summary:_____

_____

CHAPTER 16

THE AMIT COMMUNITY SCHOOL PROGRAM
A SCHOOL WITHIN A SCHOOL

Linda Zimmerman

The Amit Community School Program began as the Special Needs Department of Jewish Educational Services in Atlanta, Georgia. This department was created in 1995 to provide consultative services and professional development opportunities to the Jewish preschools, synagogue supplementary schools and day schools in the community. However, this added service was not enough for the parents whose children were still being asked to leave the Jewish day schools because of their learning difficulties, or for the parents of children who were never accepted in the first place due to the severity of their learning disability.

The Atlanta metropolitan area has four Jewish elementary day schools for students in kindergarten through 8th grade, and four Jewish high schools. Yet, in order to attend these schools children must be able to survive in a highly competitive, advanced learning program.

Year after year, children have been asked to leave the day schools due to their inability to flourish academically with the high standards required by the school. These children often end up in other private "clinical" schools or in public schools that may or may not be able to accommodate their specific learning styles, but do not provide the Jewish component that their parents so desperately want for their children.

The students who leave these day schools generally have only mild to moderate learning disabilities. But there is another population of students who have never had the opportunity to attend a Jewish day school, namely, children who have severe learning disabilities and/or developmental disabilities. For this population the doors to a Jewish day school education in Atlanta have never been opened.

HOW DOES THE AMIT PROGRAM PLAN TO MEET THIS NEED?

Staff and lay people from the Amit Steering Committee visited and contacted many programs around the country that provide support services to children with mild to severe learning disabilities in Jewish day schools. The information which was collected nationally, as well as data from a locally conducted survey, helped lay the foundations for a unique program that addresses the needs of the Atlanta metropolitan community that previously went unmet.

The Amit Community School Program focuses on four areas: *Support Services, Modified Self-Contained Classrooms (Gar'inim), Teacher Education and Disability Awareness.*

Support Services are available to children with moderate learning disabilities whose needs are not currently being met in the Atlanta day schools. These services to be offered on site at participating schools, will include one or more of the following: a learning disabilities specialist on site to provide pull-out services in an Amit Learning Lab, a facilitator to attend class with a student, a modified curriculum to meet the individual needs of the student, available speech and occupational therapy services on site, resource materials, technological assistance, adaptive equipment and general information and referral.

Gar'inim, the Amit *"School Within a School"* is a modified self-contained class housed in a day school in which eventually a wing will be designated to allow for the growth of the program from kindergarten through eighth grade. In kindergarten all academic and Judaic subjects are taught in the classroom, while the children attend all non-academic classes with their peers in the regular school program. Starting in first grade, children who show strengths in specific academic areas are able to mainstream into typical classes in the host school.

The target population for the Gar'inim classroom includes children with severe non-specific learning disabilities and developmental disabilities.

An extensive *Teacher Education* program is being established to teach the faculty of the schools hosting the various Amit programs, how to include children with different learning styles into their classrooms. In addition, classes will be offered on a regular basis to teachers in all Jewish day schools on how to teach material creatively in order for all children to benefit.

Through the *Ability Awareness & Sensitivity* program, teachers, parents and students are learning to remove the social barriers which are regularly faced by people with disabilities. This program teaches that it is not the disability itself which inhibits individuals, but the attitudes and lack of acceptance by others, caused by ignorance, indifference or discomfort. Through the sensitivity program, Amit staff and volunteers hope to work towards removing these barriers, which will help *all* children reach their full potential. The understanding and support of differences can help create a climate that values each individual's worth and abilities.

MENU OF OPTIONS

As a fledgling program Amit was asked by a granting organization to begin work on formulating a strategic plan. Due to the unique nature of the services provided, the Amit planners decided to create a "Menu of Options" which would guide the future growth of the program. We are not just a school which can plan for future growth by knowing that each year we will add a grade with one or more classrooms. Our main goal is to allow as many children as possible to remain in the school of their choice by providing the necessary supports in order for them to be successful. This "menu" includes a variety of services that are either currently available, or ones that the agency hopes to provide as the financing becomes available. The menu items are listed below with the fee for the service in parenthesis:

1. *Consultation Services* ($100.00/hr)—An experienced Learning Specialist is available to provide consulting services to school administrators and teachers in curriculum modification, case management, individual student planning, purchasing of resource materials, adaptive equipment and teacher mentorship.

2. *Staff Development/Parent Education* (fees vary)—Workshops and seminars for schools, parents and the community.

3. *Resource teacher* ($50.00/hr): Amit will provide a teacher to offer remediation/tutor services for identified individual students who would benefit from assistance with a frequency of 30 minutes one time per week to one hour five days per week.

4. *Learning Lab* ($5,000/yr full program—$2,000 to $3,000/yr transition program): Students enrolled in the school of their choice will receive one to two hours per day of individual and small group instruction in the areas of Language Arts and Math. In addition, the Amit teacher works with classroom teachers of all subjects to monitor the children's academic progress and advise on modifications as necessary. The teacher conducts an after-school homework hour twice a week.

5. *Facilitation* ($5,000 to $18,000/yr): Amit provides a trained instructional aide to "shadow" one to three students on site. The classroom teacher maintains responsibility for all academic programming. Amit supervises and trains the instructional aides.

6. *Technology/Adaptive Equipment* (fees vary, if any): Amit will provide adaptive equipment as specified in a child's learning plan or as needed for the child to participate fully in the school.

7. *Therapies* ($75/hr): Amit will facilitate the planning, scheduling and implementation of speech/language and occupational therapy services.

8. *Gar'inim (Amit's "School Within a School")*: A self-contained full-day program housed at a Jewish Day School for children with severe learning disabilities and/or developmental disabilities. Students will receive secular and Judaic academic instruction in the Gar'inim classroom and will integrate into the host schools' program as appropriate.

The rest of this chapter will focus on three areas of direct service, which we are currently offering parents and schools.

WHAT IS FACILITATION?

A facilitator is a trained instructional aide hired to "shadow" one to three students in the child's own classroom. The classroom teacher maintains responsibility for all academic education while the facilitator oversees the child's ability to stay on task and learn.

In addition to reading, writing and arithmetic, there are many learning opportunities throughout every day at school. They include reinforcement of academic skills, social skills (working in groups, intrapersonal relationships, self-motivation, etc.) and the building of self-esteem. A child with disabilities often misses out on the subtle cues given off by other children and adults that allow them to become socially adept. The facilitator insures not only that the child stays on task and is able to learn academics, but also works toward helping the child to "fit in" among his/her peers.

The facilitator also works closely with the parents and with the therapists that the child sees during the week in order to carry over behavior modifications and therapeutic techniques into the child's schedule throughout the school week.

In a private school setting, facilitation is a costly endeavor. However our hope is that this service will be more widely available in the future through establishment of an Endowment Fund and by working with the local public school districts to share resources.

WHAT IS A LEARNING LAB?

The Amit Learning Lab is an innovative approach for teaching children with diagnosed learning disabilities. Amit piloted the Learning Lab concept with children in fourth through seventh grades at The Alfred & Adele Davis Academy, a Reform Jewish day school in Atlanta. The students are enrolled in the host school and pay full tuition. In addition, Amit charges a fee for the services of the Amit Lab.

Students are referred to the Amit Lab after being identified by teachers and/or parents as having difficulties in the classroom. If the school feels that the child's needs are more than can be handled by the school's Resource Program, then the family is referred to the Lab. The admissions process for the Lab requires the parents to submit an application including; background information, school reports, a psycho-educational evaluation, therapy reports, etc. This material is reviewed by the Amit Admissions Criteria Committee, and if it is determined that the child's learning needs can be met in the Learning Lab they are admitted into our program.

All of the students in the Lab require assistance in reading and language arts instruction. Some also receive support in mathematics. The students come to the Lab when their classmates are receiving instruction on the same topic so that they do not miss their other subjects. The Lab teacher uses a variety of teaching methods and materials to instruct the child and to help him/her develop techniques to compensate for their learning weakness. The teacher also follows the child's academic progress in their other subjects by meeting regularly with teachers and offering advice and assistance when necessary. The Lab teacher is also available twice a week for an optional homework hour after school as well.

CREATING THE GAR'INIM PROGRAM—THE "SCHOOL WITHIN A SCHOOL"

Gar'inim (Hebrew word for *seeds)* is the name given to the Amit modified self-contained program, our *School Within a School*. Although the current trend in education is full inclusion, this is not always feasible in the private school setting. First of all, many private schools have designed a college preparatory curriculum that often pushes the average child to perform above typical grade standards. Secondly, the costs involved in hiring sufficient staff to insure that each child reaches their ultimate potential is often prohibitive to the school and the families involved. During our visits to other locations, we noticed that children who were supposedly "included" in typical classrooms were often alone in another room with their own instructor in order to learn the material at their level. If they were in the classroom they were in the back of the room learning alone with their facilitator.

Gar'inim was created to provide as much inclusion as possible in a typical private Jewish day school program while also addressing the individual learning styles and needs of children with severe learning problems and other associated sensory difficulties.

Many of the local day schools were approached to house Gar'inim. Atlanta's Jewish schools are fortunate to have the problem of full capacity, and unfortunately this means a lack of spare rooms. One of our schools was in the process of a capital campaign that would result in a new middle school building within the next two years. This school, The Alfred & Adele Davis Academy was very excited over the prospect of offering Amit space for many reasons, the main one being the impact it would have on its current student body. The Head of School, Rabbi Steven Ballaban, needed no help in seeing the many benefits to his school and his students. He understood that having children with developmental disabilities in his school would not only open the doors to a Jewish day school experience for the children but would help teach his current student body acceptance of all people. In addition, he had the foresight to see that families would want to enroll the siblings of the Gar'inim students into his school.

With a location secured, Gar'inim was born. An agreement was written between The Davis Academy and the Amit Community School Program outlining the financial obligations of both schools, staff concerns and other administrative issues. Due to the lack of space at the current school, while the new building was being built, two modular units were rented and installed on the school campus. The Davis Academy assisted in the costs of setting up the units and Amit pays the rental fees. Each unit has two classrooms. The Gar'inim program is currently using one full unit and The Davis Academy uses the other. The first kindergarten class began in the fall of 2002 with 3 students.

The Gar'inim students are not officially Davis students. The families pay tuition to Amit and Amit hires and supervises the staff, equips the room and oversees all aspects of the program. The Davis Academy has been very accommodating, allowing our students to participate, accompanied by our staff, in all non-academic programming in the school such as physical education, music, art, lunch, recess, Shabbat programming and field trips.

The Gar'inim students are divided and assigned to a Davis Academy classroom of the same grade. They attend all non-academic programming with that class and participate in other activities including "center time". The children are made to feel that they are an integral part of the classroom. If a Gar'inim child shows strength in a particular academic area, the child is permitted to go to the Davis Academy classroom when that subject is being taught. For example a child who will be age appropriate for first grade next year will attend math class in a Davis Academy classroom. An aide from the Gar'inim classroom will be with him until it is determined that he can function on his own.

A TYPICAL GAR'INIM WEEK

The curriculum and scheduling of the Gar'inim class is designed to meet the individual needs of the children as well as to allow for maximum opportunity for mainstreaming into the classes of the host school. The Gar'inim teachers meet weekly with the host school teachers to adjust the class schedule as needed in order for the children to participate in all extra-curricular activities with their peers in the host school.

SAMPLE SCHEDULE (M = MAINSTREAMING WITH HOST SCHOOL)				
MONDAY	**TUESDAY**	**WEDNESDAY**	**THURSDAY**	**FRIDAY**
Prayers/Calendar	Prayers/Calendar	Prayers/Calendar	Prayers/Calendar	Prayers/Calendar
Reading/LA	Speech/Lang. Therapy	Reading/LA	Speech/Lang. Therapy	Kabbalat Shabbat (M)
PE (M)	Reading/LA	Music (M)	Reading/LA	Reading/LA
Lunch/Recess (M)	PE (M)	Lunch/Recess (M)	PE (M)	Lunch/Recess (M)
Math	Lunch/Recess (M)	Math	Lunch/Recess (M)	Host school buddies visit
Occupational Therapy	Math	Occupational Therapy	Math	Library
Themed activities	Themed activities	Themed activities	Themed activities	Themed activities
Center time (M)	Center time (M)	Center time (M)	Center time (M)	Center time

The above schedule is a general overview. The children we serve thrive on structure and repetition. Although there are set times of the day that the teachers put aside for academic instruction, the reality is that this occurs throughout every day. The teachers take advantage of every activity planned or un-planned to reinforce what the children are learning.

Children with developmental disabilities are also unpredictable. On any given day one child may enter the room in a hyper state, the other children react to the behavior, and the best laid plans of the teacher go out the window. The teachers must be flexible and have the ability to take any situation and make it into a fruitful learning experience.

The Gar'inim class uses an integrated curriculum. In addition to the daily prayers, the children learn about their Jewish history and the holidays through their daily academic activities. For example; when the children were learning about the holiday of Tu B'shevat, the Jewish New Year for Trees, they learned the customs associated with the holiday and also learned the letters T (trees) and S (seeds). For a science project they planted grass seeds and for math they collected nuts and used them for counting exercises. The students then went on a field trip to the park with the students of the host school.

CONTINUUM OF SERVICES

There are two main issues involved in providing services to children with learning disabilities and/or developmental disabilities in a private school setting. One is the ability to meet the individual needs of each student in a cost effective manner, and the other is the desire of most private schools to provide a highly competitive college preparatory educational curriculum.

The Amit Community School Program was designed to help the schools meet the unique learning needs of children with diagnosed learning disabilities in a cost effective manner and without compromising the academic standards of the school. This is done through a continuum of services that allows each child to receive the support they need in the least restrictive environment possible for a private school.

Gar'inim is the *school within a school*, for children who need highly structured small group instruction with small teacher-student ratios. A classroom will have no more than 10 students with one lead teacher, one assistant teacher and one para-professional. The children have the opportunity to mainstream throughout each day with students in the host school. This is an ideal program for children with developmental disabilities or severe learning disabilities with associated behavior or sensory problems. Some children will remain in the Gar'inim program throughout their academic career. Others will mainstream out of the program to the day school of their choice.

The Learning Labs provide support to children who are able to remain in a typical classroom with their peers, however, due to their moderate learning disabilities need the assistance from a special educator to be successful. They spend between one to two and a half hours per day in the Lab and may return after school twice a week for "homework hour". And a facilitator allows for the child to remain the entire day in a typical classroom.

Special education is very expensive. The Gar'inim program, when full, will break even financially, but will not bring in the extra funds needed to provide additional services or cover administrative costs. The Learning Labs actually bring in additional funds due to the number of children that can be served by each teacher and the lower overhead costs. Facilitation is the most expensive service offered and is not covered by tuition alone. By offering a wide range of services the overall cost of the program is more manageable.

In addition, through combined services most children, regardless of the severity of their learning or developmental disability can be successful in a Jewish day school environment. As the student's needs change they are able to move from one "menu option" to another, thereby, allowing the child to reach their ultimate potential.

WHERE DID THE ORIGINAL FUNDING COME FROM AND HOW WILL IT BE FUNDED IN THE FUTURE?

The start-up funds for the Amit program and the Gar'inim classroom came from individuals in our community and a grant from the Partnership for Excellence in Jewish Education. The research had shown that the cost of a "school within a school" program would probably never be fully covered by tuition. This is why the Amit Community School Program was developed. By offering a variety of services to many different schools, joint purchasing, sharing staff and administration and increasing the number of children receiving some type of support services, the money raised through fees would increase while expenses would be streamlined.

In addition the Board of Directors has developed a fundraising/income/development strategy that is broad, long-term, multi-faceted and creative. This way the program will always be able to keep pace with increasing needs. The Fundraising Committee has developed a plan that includes five fund raising programs: *Annual Membership Campaign, Special Events, Endowment/ Planned Giving, Foundations/Grants,* and *a Capital campaign.*

CLOSING THOUGHTS

The first few years of any new program are difficult. The community has to be convinced that the program is needed. Parents have to have trust in the school in order to send their children to a new program which has yet to establish a history. And foundations and individuals have to share the dream of providing equal access to all children in parochial and non-sectarian private schools.

The other factors that the Amit Program had to deal with were the attitudes of the parents of the host schools whose children do not have learning problems. They feared that the highly academic program would be "watered down" once children with more severe learning difficulties where allowed to attend the schools. And the teachers of the schools had to be convinced that their workload would not increase with the new students.

Both of these issues were addressed through open forums and community education. Within the first few weeks of the school year all initial concerns seemed to be forgotten. The teachers realized that the Amit Learning Lab and Gar'inim teachers were readily available to answer their questions and to give advice on all of the children in the classroom, not just those receiving support services. By the middle of the year, the host school teachers would routinely come to the Amit classrooms to borrow material or to ask for advice on a particular student. The parents were also more at ease when they came to realize that the classroom teacher now had more time to spend with their child. And their child's teachers began making changes in their teaching styles that benefited the entire classroom.

For more information, contact www.amitatlanta.org.

CHAPTER 17

NAVIGATING THE SPECIAL EDUCATION SYSTEM IDENTIFICATION, REFERRAL, EVALUATION AND PLACEMENT FOR STUDENTS WITH SPECIAL NEEDS

Shana Erenberg

For parents with a child with special needs, navigating the special education system can be challenging and intimidating. Parents are often faced with a barrage of terms and acronyms that are confusing, as well as diagnostic reports that are difficult to understand. Obtaining services for their child can seem like moving through an impossible, frustrating labyrinth.

It is crucial that parents are active and vocal advocates for their child with special needs. Frequently, parents will find that the school team is supportive and committed to providing the best possible services for the child. In some cases, however, parents may find themselves at loggerheads with the district over the child's needs. In either case, parents must be familiar with special education policies and procedures to insure that their child's unique needs will be met. Education is the key to effective advocacy.

The Individuals with Disabilities Education Act (IDEA) is a federal law that provides mandates for the education of students with special needs, from birth through age 21. Each state implements the IDEA in conjunction with State rules and regulations. (Readers are referred to the State Board of Education for their particular state for specific policies and procedures.) Both IDEA and State Administrative Codes delineate the process by which children with special needs are identified, referred for evaluation, assessed, and served.

1. THE CHILD IS IDENTIFIED AS POSSIBLY NEEDING SPECIAL EDUCATION AND RELATED SERVICES, AND REFERRED FOR AN EVALUATION.

By law, a state must identify, locate, and evaluate all children with disabilities in the state who need special education and related services. To do so, states conduct "Child Find" activities. These activities may include advertisements of services, offerings of screenings, and informational meetings for parents.

In addition, parents may request that the school district conduct an initial case study if the child has special needs. This request may be verbal or in writing, but it is advisable that all requests be put in writing and dated. The school district may also refer a child for an evaluation if it is suspected that the child has special needs. Parental consent is required before a case study is conducted. The case study evaluation must be completed within a reasonable time period, usually no more than 60 school days from the time of the request.

When a child is referred for evaluation, the district may first conduct a preliminary screening, such as observation of the child, assessment for instructional purposes, consultation with the teacher or other referring agent, and a conference with the child. The district will then determine whether or not a full case study evaluation is warranted. The district must notify the referring party and the parent of the decision and the basis on which it was reached.

2. A CASE STUDY IS CONDUCTED AND THE CHILD IS EVALUATED.

Each district must have written policies pertaining to the evaluation process. The case study is a multidisciplinary effort, involving specialists from a variety of professional domains. The team usually included the school psychologist, a learning disabilities specialist, the school nurse, and a social worker. Speech and Language therapists, as well as Occupational and Physical Therapists may be part of the team if the student's special needs require it. A variety of assessment tools and strategies must be used by qualified specialists, and no single measure may be used alone to determine the presence of a disability.

Tests and other materials used to evaluate a child cannot be discriminatory on a racial or cultural basis. The assessments must be administered in the child's native language or other mode of communication, unless it is clearly not feasible to do so. The tests must be technically sound and designed to assess the relative contributions of cognitive, behavioral, physical, and developmental factors; and shall be used in a manner consistent with the instructions provided by their publishers.

3. A MULTIDISCIPLINARY CONFERENCE (MDC) IS HELD TO DISCUSS THE TEST RESULTS AND DETERMINE ELIGIBILITY.

Upon completion of the case study evaluation, an MDC is held to review the results with the parents. The MDC must be held no later than 60 days after the initiation of the case study process. Parents must be advised in writing of the date of the MDC, usually no less than ten days before the scheduled meeting. Each evaluator prepares a written report of the diagnostic findings and shares this information with the team. Parental input and concerns must be considered and addressed at the MDC.

The team will then determine whether or not the child is eligible for special education services. Eligibility criteria may differ from state to state. Under the IDEA, students may be eligible for special education and related services under one or more of the following categories:

Autism: A developmental disability significantly affecting verbal and nonverbal communication and social interaction, generally evident before age three, that adversely affects a child's educational performance. Other characteristics often associated with autism are engagement in repetitive activities and stereotyped movements, resistance to environmental change or change in daily routines, and unusual responses to sensory experiences. The term does not apply if a child's educational performance is adversely affected primarily because the child has an emotional disturbance.

Deaf-Blindness: Concomitant hearing and visual impairments, the combination of which causes such severe communication and other developmental and educational needs that they cannot be accommodated in special education programs solely for children with deafness or children with blindness.

Deafness: A hearing impairment that is so severe that the child is impaired in processing linguistic information through hearing, with or without amplification, that adversely affects a child's educational performance.

Emotional Disturbance (includes schizophrenia but does not apply to children who are socially maladjusted, unless it is determined that they have an emotional disturbance): A condition exhibiting one or more of the following characteristics over an extended period of time and to a marked degree that adversely affects a child's educational performance:

- An inability to learn that cannot be explained by intellectual, sensory, or health factors;
- An inability to build or maintain satisfactory interpersonal relationships with peers and teachers;
- Inappropriate types of behavior or feelings under normal circumstances;
- A general pervasive mood of anxiety or unhappiness or depression; or
- A tendency to develop physical symptoms or fears associated with personal or school problems.

Hearing Impairment: An impairment in hearing, whether permanent or fluctuating, that adversely affects a child's educational performance but that is not included under the definition of deafness.

Mental Retardation: Significantly sub-average general intellectual functioning, existing concurrently with deficits in adaptive behavior and manifested during the developmental period, that adversely affects a child's educational performance.

Multiple Disabilities: Concomitant impairments (such as mental retardation-blindness, mental retardation-orthopedic impairment, etc.), the combination of which causes such severe educational needs that they cannot be accommodated in special education programs solely for one of the impairments (does not include deaf-blindness).

Orthopedic Impairment: A severe orthopedic impairment that adversely affects a child's educational performance; includes impairments caused by congenital anomaly (e.g., clubfoot, absence of some member, etc.), impairments caused by disease (e.g., poliomyelitis, bone tuberculosis, etc.), and impairments from other causes (e.g., cerebral palsy, amputations, and fractures or burns that cause contractures).

Other Health Impairment: Limited strength, vitality or alertness, including a heightened sensitivity to environmental stimuli, that results in limited alertness with respect to the educational environment, that is due to chronic or acute health problems such as asthma, attention deficit disorder or attention deficit hyperactivity disorder, diabetes, epilepsy, a heart condition, hemophilia, lead poisoning, leukemia, nephritis, rheumatic fever, and sickle cell anemia; and adversely affects a child's educational performance.

Specific Learning Disability: A disorder in one or more of the basic psychological processes involved in understanding or in using language, spoken or written, that may manifest itself in an imperfect ability to listen, think, speak, read, write, spell, or do mathematical calculations, including such conditions as perceptual disabilities, brain injury, minimal brain dysfunction, dyslexia, and developmental aphasia. (the term does not include learning problems that are primarily the result of visual, hearing or motor disabilities, of mental retardation, of emotional disturbance, or of environmental, cultural, or economic disadvantage.)

Speech or Language Impairment: A communication disorder, such as stuttering, impaired articulation, a language impairment, or a voice impairment, that adversely affects a child's educational performance.

Traumatic Brain Injury: An acquired injury to the brain caused by an external physical force, resulting in total or partial functional disability or psychosocial impairment, or both, that adversely affects a child's educational performance. The term applies to open or closed head injuries resulting in impairments in one or more areas, such as cognition; language; memory; attention; reasoning; abstract thinking; judgment; problem-solving; sensory, perceptual, and motor abilities; psychosocial behavior; physical functions; information processing; and speech. The term does not apply to brain injuries that are congenital or degenerative or to brain injuries induced by birth trauma.

Visual Impairment: An impairment in vision that, even with correction, adversely affects a child's educational performance (includes both partial sight and blindness).

The MDC can sometimes prove to be overwhelming for parents. They are hearing information about their child that may be difficult to process and accept. In addition, there are often numerous district personnel in attendance, and the parents may feel "outnumbered". In such cases, it is advisable for the parents to bring along another individual for support. This person may be a special needs advocate, a private specialist, or even a friend. (Check your community resources for low-cost or free advocacy services). In contentious cases, parents may choose to bring an attorney to the MDC. It is, however, in everyone's best interest to keep the process as amicable as possible, and for all participants to work cooperatively on behalf of the child.

If the parents disagree with the district evaluation, they have the right to take their child for an Independent Educational Evaluation (IEE). They can ask that the school system pay for this IEE.

4. IF THE CHILD IS DETERMINED ELIGIBLE FOR SPECIAL EDUCATION, THE TEAM AND PARENTS MEET TO DEVELOP AN INDIVIDUALIZED EDUCATION PLAN (IEP) OR INDIVIDUAL FAMILY SERVICE PLAN (IFSP) FOR YOUNGER CHILDREN, AND DETERMINE PLACEMENT.

The IEP meeting must be held within thirty days after the determination of eligibility. Usually, the IEP meeting is held immediately subsequent to the MDC. The IEP must be developed before actual placement, and initiation of special education and related services. No special education and related services can be provided prior to the development of the IEP.

Parents must be notified in writing of the date and time of the IEP meeting at least ten days in advance. The meeting must be held at a mutually convenient time and place. If a parent cannot participate in the IEP meeting, the district must take steps to insure that parental input is considered and the results of the meeting conveyed to the parents.

The IEP committee *must* be composed of at least the following:

- A school administrator or designee who is authorized to make and supervise placement decisions
- The child's classroom teacher and the special education teacher

- Parent/legal guardian or surrogate parent
- The student (the student may opt to not participate in the IEP meeting)
- A member of the evaluation team or someone knowledgeable about the evaluation procedures used with the student and the results of the evaluation. This person is usually the school psychologist.

Additional participants in the IEP meeting may include:
- General education teacher(s)
- Physical, occupational, and speech therapists
- Vocational counselors
- Representatives of community agencies (e.g., Community Service Boards, Rehabilitation Counselors)
- Pupil personnel staff
- Others at the discretion of the school and/or parent

The IEP is considered to be a legal document that delineates academic goals, related services, and accommodations that the child requires. It must be calibrated to convey an educational benefit for the child. The development of the IEP precedes placement decisions, and cannot be designed to reflect a specific placement. The IEP is based on assessment data as well as input from parents and professionals, and drives all educational decisions for the child.

The IEP must contain the following components:

Present Levels of Educational Performance is a written statement that describes the student's strengths, weaknesses and learning styles in academic areas; vocational, social, behavioral, perceptual, physical, communication; and/or life skills, as appropriate. This information should be current, and based on relevant assessment data.

Annual Goal(s): An annual goal(s) is a statement(s) of what a student with a disability can reasonably be expected to accomplish in a years time in a specific area(s). It is written to address an area of weakness identified in the Present Level of Educational Performance.

Short-Term Objectives: Short-term objectives include a number of steps in the sequence of steps moving the student toward each annual goal. The objectives must be stated in behavioral, measurable terms and state what the student will accomplish. Short-term objectives include benchmarks that identify the amount of progress a student is expected to make in a given period of time.

Evaluation Criterion: Evaluation criterion is the level of performance necessary for mastery of a given objective. This can be expressed in percentage of accuracy required, number of times a certain performance is required, etc. Evaluation criterion also include the means by which performance is assessed, as well frequency.

Special Education and Related Services: The IEP must list all special education and related services required by the student to benefit from the student's special education program. The determination of the special education and related services is based upon the student's IEP goals and objectives that correlate to the student's present level of educational performance. The IEP must specify the amount of minutes per week or month that the services will be offered, as well as the personnel required to provide the services.

Related services may include:

- Speech and language therapy, occupational therapy, physical therapy, transportation, and other developmental, corrective and supportive services the child may need.

- Social work services, counseling services, including rehabilitation counseling, and certain medical services (for diagnostic and evaluation purposes only) as may be required to assist a child with a disability to benefit from special education.

- Transition Services: The IEP for students beginning no later than the age of sixteen (16) and annually thereafter (and at a younger age, if determined appropriate) must contain a statement of needed transitional services. This includes when appropriate, a statement of the interagency responsibilities or linkages (or both) before the student leaves the school setting.

    Transportation, if needed.

    Assistive technology, as needed.

Accommodations: The IEP will contain a list of accommodations including supplementary aids and services needed by the student to assist the student in both special and general education settings. Accommodations may include instructional and behavioral modifications, assessment modifications, adaptive equipment, and/or assistive technology devices.

Participation in General Education and Nonacademic Activities: Students with disabilities must be given the opportunity to participate with their non-disabled peers to the maximum extent appropriate in general education, nonacademic and extracurricular activities. The extent to which the student participates needs to be documented on the IEP. If a student is unable to participate in the general education curriculum, justification for this decision must be listed in the IEP.

5. ONCE THE GOALS AND SERVICES HAVE BEEN DELINEATED IN THE IEP, A PLACEMENT DECISION IS MADE.

After the IEP is developed and agreed to, the next step is to determine where the student will receive the services outlined in the IEP. Placement is driven by the IEP, and must provide a free and appropriate public education (FAPE) in the Least Restrictive Environment (LRE). The Least Restrictive Environment requires that:

- The child has the opportunity to participate with typical peers in academic, nonacademic, and extracurricular activities unless otherwise indicated.

- The child is educated in a setting similar to that which the student would be served if he/she did not have a disability.

- The amount of time and the distance the student must be transported from his/her home must be considered.

- The student is removed from the regular educational environment only when the nature and severity of the disability is such that education in regular classes with the use of supplementary aids and services cannot be achieved.

- Consideration is given to any potential harmful effects the placement may have on the student.

To assist in determining the placement, the IEP team considers a continuum of services. From least to most restrictive, placements may range from:

- Direct instruction and/or consultative services within the regular classroom.

- Resource room services for less than 50% of the school day.

- Resource room services for more than 50% of the school day.
- A self contained class (within the home school or elsewhere), with integration with typical peers as appropriate.
- A self-contained without integration.
- Separate public day school for students with disabilities.
- Separate private day school for students with disabilities.
- Public and private residential facilities.
- Homebound services
- Hospitalization

The team must consider and discuss more than one placement option. Placement options are then either rejected or accepted. A justification statement for each decision must be included in the IEP.

If the school district is unable to provide FAPE in the LRE for the child, it is required to fund a private placement. It is important to note that the standard that is generally applied is reflected in the analogy that the school must provide a "serviceable Chevy" rather than a "Cadillac" for educational placements. Parents always have the option of unilateral placement of their child in a "Cadillac" school, however, if the district has viable placement options it will not be required to pay for the private placement.

If the parents agree to the IEP and placement recommendations, services must commence within ten days. Parents can waive the ten day requirement so that services can begin sooner.

6. PARENTS MUST BE GIVEN THEIR RIGHTS AT THE MDC/IEP MEETING, INCLUDING THE RIGHT TO DUE PROCESS IF THEY DO NOT AGREE WITH THE TEAM'S DECISION.

At each MDC/IEP meeting, parents must be given a written copy of their rights under IDEA. These rights include Due Process procedures that can be applied should their be a disagreement regarding the evaluation, IEP, or placement. Due Process refers to a legal option that parents of a child with special needs may pursue if the student's needs are not being met. The parents and school district will present the issue along with documentary evidence to an Impartial Hearing Officer, who will rule on the matter. Parents should refer to an attorney or special education advocate before filing for Due Process to ascertain that proper procedures are followed. While advisable, an attorney or advocate are not required for a parent to file Due Process. A school district also has the right to file Due Process.

Parents who seek to file due process have the option to request mediation. The mediation process is an intermediate step in attempt to reconcile the issues prior to a due process hearing. Mediation is not binding on either party.

While Due Process is an important right for children with special needs, it can be emotionally draining and time consuming for parents. In addition, if the parent engages an attorney and experts, the process can be financially burdensome (although there is a provision for the recovery of fees for the prevailing party). As such, Due Process should not be taken lightly, nor filed for frivolous issues. It is always preferable for the parents and school district to come to a mutually acceptable agreement that will provide an educational benefit for the child. That caveat being noted, parents should not hesitate to exercise their right to due process for significant issues pertaining to their child's education. If a parent files a Due Process request, the IEP and current placement remain in place until the matter is resolved. This process is known as "stay put".

7. ANNUAL REVIEW

At a minimum, the IEP must be reviewed annually. The IEP team reconvenes with the parents to review progress made by the students towards the goals. New goals will be written for the following school year. The team, including the parents, will also review the child's strengths, continued needs. Determinations may be made regarding the need to increase, decrease, or maintain special education and related services for the child. These changes cannot be implemented without parental consent. While the district must formally review and update the IEP annually, parents may request that progress meetings be held periodically throughout the year. The child may be included in the review process if appropriate.

8. TRIENNIAL RE-EVALUATION

Every three years following the initial evaluation in which a child was found to have disabilities requiring special education and related services, the school district must re-evaluate the student. All of the same policies, procedures and safeguards from the initial assessment apply to the triennial reevaluation.

GLOSSARY OF ACRONYMS:

CEC: Council for Exceptional Children
CSE: Case Study Evaluation
FAPE: Free and Appropriate Public Education
FERPA: Federal Education Records Privacy Act
IEP: Individual Education Plan
ISFP: Individual Family Service Plan
IDEA: Individuals with Disabilities Education Act (Reauthorized 04-05)
LDA: Learning Disabilities Association
LEA: Local Educational Agency
LRE: Least Restrictive Environment
MDC: Multidisciplinary Conference
NCLB: No Child Left Behind

REFERENCES

Tomey, Harley A. Individualized Education Program
The Process. Virginia Department of Education
Special Education Law in Illinois

LINKS

MY CHILD'S SPECIAL NEEDS: A Guide to the Individualized Education Program
IEP/CSE Information and Forms

GENERAL INFORMATION

A Guide to the Individualized Education Program, U.S. Department of Education

SUPPLEMENTARY SCHOOL PROGRAM OPTIONS

Sara Rubinow Simon

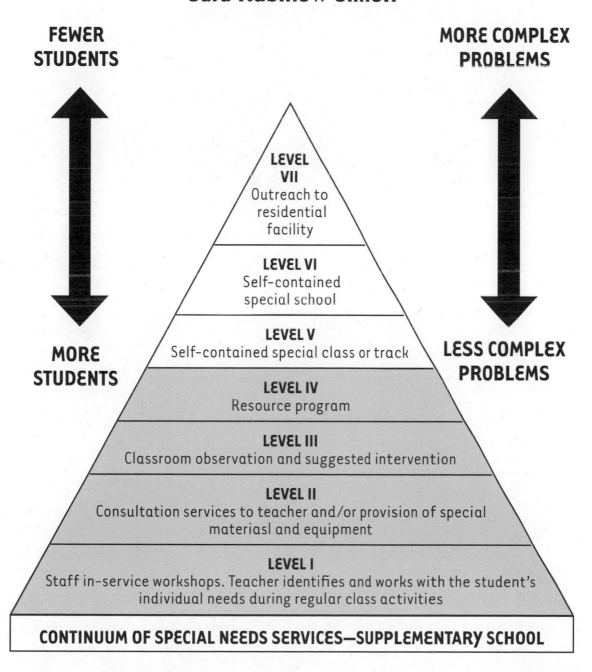

FEWER STUDENTS

MORE COMPLEX PROBLEMS

MORE STUDENTS

LESS COMPLEX PROBLEMS

LEVEL VII
Outreach to residential facility

LEVEL VI
Self-contained special school

LEVEL V
Self-contained special class or track

LEVEL IV
Resource program

LEVEL III
Classroom observation and suggested intervention

LEVEL II
Consultation services to teacher and/or provision of special materiasl and equipment

LEVEL I
Staff in-service workshops. Teacher identifies and works with the student's individual needs during regular class activities

CONTINUUM OF SPECIAL NEEDS SERVICES—SUPPLEMENTARY SCHOOL

CHAPTER 18

SETTING UP A RESOURCE PROGRAM IN A CONGREGATIONAL SCHOOL

Sara Rubinow Simon and Phyllis S. Greene

HOW TO BEGIN

A school should make every effort to meet the needs of all its students whenever possible. There may be students in many supplementary and day schools who can remain regular classes if special modifications are made in the programs.

To implement a special education resource program in either a day or supplemental school program, careful planning and coordination are required. The keys to success are a supportive educational director, school committee and faculty. The educational director must recognize the need in the school for a resource program and be willing to devote time to its development.

It is to the educational director's benefit to assemble a task force comprised of congregants with backgrounds in special education and others who are interested in the creation of such a program. This task force can define the scope of the program and identify possible ways in which it may be implemented. Community resources such as the Board of Jewish Education, the Jewish Community Center, the public school system and local college faculty may also give support and advice concerning the initiation of a special needs program. The program should then be presented to the school committee and the Board of Directors for funding and approval.

An additional element essential to the success of this program is the faculty. The faculty must have the flexibility to participate in a team approach for solutions to educational problems. They must allow the resource teacher to observe students in the classroom and participate in discussion of appropriate solutions for each student who is a candidate for a resource program.

From the beginning, parents of such students must be informed and included in the process and be continually notified of their child's progress.

Each person must see himself or herself as part of a community of professionals willing to listen to one another, share expertise, and contribute to the educational success of all students.

ROLE OF THE RESOURCE PROGRAM TEACHER

The primary function of the resource program specialist is to improve instructional programs for students with special learning needs. This function may be accomplished: through consultation, assessment/diagnostics, and instructional programming.

These three roles are clearly interrelated. However, the major emphasis must be on instructional programming for identified students.

MODELS: OPTIONS FOR SERVICE DELIVERY

While the three roles identified above are all responsibilities of the learning resource specialist, implementation of each role may vary among schools depending on the needs of students, the needs of staff, and the organization of the school's educational program. Models for implementing instructional services to students are described below. Each model contains all three roles; yet each model offers a different focus in the delivery of the instructional support.

"PULL-OUT" MODEL

In this model, the primary function of the learning resource specialist is to teach students in the resource room. The specialist is responsible for addressing certain agreed-upon objectives from the individualized educational plan. Assessment and consultation with other staff continue to be occur, but the majority of the specialist's time is spent working directly with students within the resource room. Hebrew decoding skills are the most frequent focus in this model.

"PLUG-IN" MODEL

An adaptation of the "pull-out" model is the "plug-in" model. In this model, the primary function of the learning resource specialist is to teach students; however teaching takes place *within the regular classroom* while the regular teacher also teaches. The resource specialist has a small group of students (which may also include some other students in the class) and plans and implements the strategies for accomplishing instructional objectives.

CONSULTATIVE MODEL

In this model, the primary function of the learning specialist is to provide consultation and suggestions to staff after becoming thoroughly acquainted with a student's needs and learning style. "Becoming thoroughly acquainted with a student's needs and learning style" may involve a variety of strategies. The resource specialist may observe a student in various settings including the regular classroom. A student may be individually taught, or a small group of students may come into the resource room for diagnostic teaching. The resource teacher may also utilize "demonstration teaching" through large group instruction of the entire regular classroom in order to gain additional diagnostic information about a specific student. This approach may also serve to demonstrate effective instructional strategies or behavior management techniques in the classroom. In this model, the regular education staff has the primary responsibility for implementing a student's program but uses the learning resource specialist to assist in designing instructional strategies, suggesting and preparing materials, as well as specifying techniques for behavior management where appropriate. This model includes preparing a detailed individualized educational plan (IEP) of activities, strategies, and materials that may be appropriate for a given student. It also involves assisting a teacher in successful implementation of that prescription.

TEAM-TEACHING MODEL

In this model, the learning specialist provides the majority of services in conjunction with the regular classroom teacher. The responsibility for meeting students' objectives is shared. Both teachers are involved in planning instructional strategies and in on-going assessment.

COMBINED MODELS

Combinations of these options may be appropriate. Regardless of the option(s) selected for service delivery, selections should be based on the needs of students and staff in a given school.

REFERRAL PROCESS
IDENTIFICATION OF STUDENTS WITH SPECIAL NEEDS

In general, schools have a population of students whose needs are not being met. Currently, statistics indicate that 2-20% of students may have specific learning disabilities, although many cannot be coded according to formal criteria.

PARENTAL IDENTIFICATION

In some cases, the parents voluntarily identify their child's special needs and discuss them with the rabbi and/or educator in advance of the start of school. When this occurs, everyone benefits because everyone knows what to expect. There are no surprises to the teacher, no time wasted in trying to ascertain the child's needs after school has already started, and no frustration for the child who would otherwise be expected to perform at a level not possible for him/her.

Every student's ability to access the social and educational programs offered by the synagogue must begin before the child (or the family) enters the building on the first day of school. Every school has a registration form, and questions about special education needs should be a part of the enrollment process.

TEACHER IDENTIFICATION

Many parents do not identify their children's special needs prior to the start of school. Some hope that the "problems" will not surface in the religious or Hebrew school setting. Some may deny that their children have special needs at all. Some, ashamed of their children's disabilities or special needs, do not want their friends and acquaintances at the synagogue to know. The reasons are as varied as the children's needs, but the bottom line is that in withholding information, these parents are doing both their children and their teachers a disservice.

Students who do not receive appropriate educational interventions soon become frustrated. Their self-esteem drops as their failures increase, and they often develop behavior and discipline problems as well.

The classroom teacher who is able to identify a child's special needs early in the year can help the individual student and the entire class in a significant way. An observant teacher can spot significant trends in a student's performance in class and alert the educator and/or special education teacher on staff. The earlier a referral of this type is made, the better the chances of providing the child with interventions which will make the classroom environment more conducive to everyone's learning.

PROCEDURES FOR RESOURCE TEACHER UTILIZATION

Copies of the resource teacher referral form is given to each classroom teacher at the beginning of the school year. Explanation of the school's procedure in this process should be part of the staff development meeting at the beginning of each school year.

Upon observation and documentation of concerns with a student's ability to perform in the classroom, the teacher completes the referral form. A copy should also be given to the education director.

The classroom teacher or educational director contact the parents to gain input on the situation and to request their permission to have the resource teacher observe the student.

Classroom observation time is established; observation notes can be written on the back of the referral form. Minimum observation time should be 15 or 20 minutes. Appropriate time is set with the classroom teacher.

Resource and classroom teachers meet to share information. Ideas in restructuring classroom situation to meet the student's specific needs are explored. If additional help is warranted, the classroom teacher will notify the resource teacher.

Arrange a meeting between the classroom teacher, resource teacher, education director (their discretion) and parents when the student needs direct resource help. At this conference, a plan is established based on input from all involved. The format and content are written out and filed in the school office.

Inform all teachers who work with this student of the outcomes of the meeting.

Schedule periodic follow up meetings with the parents.

For a resource program to be successful, it is essential that lines of communication are always open between the education director, resource specialists, teachers and parents. An efficient method of record keeping is important in order to keep track of each student involved in the program. In addition, workshops and trainings should be offered to allow all those involved to acquire a working knowledge of the total resource program.

Lastly, the education director must continue to study the ongoing issues in special education. It is essential to be familiar with the definitions and procedures currently in use and to have an awareness of the process in the secular educational system so that there is an appropriate Jewish educational option for each child in the congregation.

RESOURCES:

Greene, Phyllis S. and Simon, Sara R. *The Resource Program Guide for a Congregational School*. Rockville, MD: BJE of Greater Washington, 1990.

Kupferman, Flora. *Handbook for Special Education Programs in the Synagogue Schools*. San Francisco, CA: Bureau of Jewish Education of San Francisco, 1996.

Naftaly, Anita. *Opening The Doors Special Education Partnership Program: Partnership Schools Handbook of Procedures and Forms*. Southfield, MI: Agency for Jewish Education, 1999.

STUDENT HEALTH AND INDIVIDUAL NEEDS FORM (Page 1 of 2)

Student's Name Last_____ First _____ Grade_____

Parent's Name Last_____ First _____ Phone _____

The philosophy of _____ emphasizes the uniqueness of each student. Therefore, it is of great importance that we have specific information about each child—information that only a parent or guardian can provide. Your detailed reply, which will be kept strictly confidential, will help us enrich your child's experience at _____.

Does your child have any issues that may affect his/her learning in school, cause you any concern, and/or may be important for the school staff to know? Please check the appropriate column for each of the following health areas.

	Yes	No	Don't Know	Comments (attach extra sheets if needed)
General health (e.g., fatigue, low energy level, frequent illness)	☐	☐	☐	
Specific physical condition/illness past or present (e.g., cerebral palsy, epilepsy, asthma, diabetes)	☐	☐	☐	
Allergy (e.g., insect stings, food, drugs, pollens)	☐	☐	☐	
Vision/eye (e.g., contact lenses, glasses)	☐	☐	☐	
Hearing/ear (e.g., frequent infections, draining ear, hearing loss, hearing aid)	☐	☐	☐	
Speech (e.g., delay, stuttering, difficulty understanding speech)	☐	☐	☐	
Learning or perceptual problems (in particular, difficulty in learning to read phonetically)	☐	☐	☐	
Gross motor or fine motor impairment	☐	☐	☐	
Hyperactivity and/or attention deficit disorder	☐	☐	☐	
Special dietary needs	☐	☐	☐	
Organizational/memory skills	☐	☐	☐	
Is your child taking any regular medication?	☐	☐	☐	Specify:
Behavior/personal relationships (e.g., very active, easily upset, shy, difficulty making friends)	☐	☐	☐	
Major changes or disruptions in your child's life	☐	☐	☐	When: Specify:

Is there anything else that might contribute to your child's success at school? _____

Are there any other concerns? _____

Please feel free to call the education office at _____to schedule an appointment with the educator, teacher, or special education consultant.

(Please fill out reverse side)

STUDENT HEALTH AND INDIVIDUAL NEEDS FORM (Page 2 of 2)

Please describe any special needs you child has. _____
_____
_____
_____
_____
_____

Does your child receive any special services at school? ☐ Yes ☐ No
Please indicate which:

    Resource Room program _____
    Speech and language assistance _____
    Special education class _____
    Instructional aide _____
    Other (describe) _____
_____
_____

Has your child been considered for special services? ☐ Yes ☐ No

Have you requested special services? ☐ Yes ☐ No

If yes, please describe. _____
_____
_____

Does your child have an IEP. (Individual Education Plan) at his/her secular school? ☐ Yes ☐ No
If yes, please describe how we can best implement the plan in our program. ____
_____
_____
_____

Would you provide us with a copy of the IEP? ☐ Yes ☐ No
Please describe any accommodations your child requires to be successful at out school. _____
_____
_____
_____

Is there someone at the child's secular school with whom we could be in contact?
Name _____ Title/Role _____ Phone (____) _____

Other professionals we should contact?
Name _____ Title/Role _____ Phone (____) _____

SUPPLEMENTARY SCHOOL REFERRAL FORM (Page 1 of 2)

School _____

Student Name _____Date_____

Grade _____ Age _____Home Phone (_____) _____

Classroom Behavior	Most of the time	Sometimes
Easily distracted	☐	☐
Withdrawn	☐	☐
Talks out of turn	☐	☐
Responds to questions inappropriately	☐	☐
Unable to sit still	☐	☐
Impulsive	☐	☐
Unable to pay attention	☐	☐
Does not complete assignments	☐	☐
Has difficulty getting along with peers	☐	☐
Comes to class without books/supplies	☐	☐
Works better alone	☐	☐
Works better in groups	☐	☐
Does not participate in class discussions	☐	☐
Short-term memory (same day)	☐	☐
Long-term memory (retention)	☐	☐

Academic Concerns	Most of the time	Sometimes
Reverses letters/omits letters	☐	☐
Confuses similar letters	☐	☐
Has difficulty learning/remembering letters/words	☐	☐
Has difficulty with crowded page	☐	☐
Unable to copy from blackboard correctly	☐	☐
Holds books close to eyes	☐	☐
Difficulty forming letters	☐	☐
Has difficulty following oral directions	☐	☐
Has difficulty learning sounds or reproducing sounds of letters	☐	☐
Misunderstands what is said	☐	☐
Needs directions repeated frequently	☐	☐

SUPPLEMENTARY SCHOOL REFERRAL FORM (Page2 of 2)

	Most of the time	Sometimes
Works better in groups	☐	☐
Does not participate in class discussions	☐	☐
Short-term memory (same day)	☐	☐
Long-term memory (retention)	☐	☐
	☐	☐
Hebrew Phonetic Reading Ability		
At class level	☐	☐
Below class level	☐	☐
Impulsive	☐	☐
Unable to pay attention	☐	☐
Does not complete assignments	☐	☐

1. Describe any difficulties/concerns you have observed that are not listed _____
_____
_____

2. Describe student's strengths _____
_____
_____

3. List parental contacts regarding your concerns _____
_____
_____

4. Describe classroom interventions you have tried _____
_____
_____

Teacher completing this form _____ Position (grade) _____

Signature _____ Date _____

SECULAR SCHOOL REPORT

Date of Report: _____

Student's Name: _____

Grade: _____

Present Level of Performance: _____

Reading Level: _____

Writing Level: _____

Strengths: _____

_____

_____

Needs: _____

_____

_____

Learning Style: _____

_____

_____

Behavior: _____

_____

_____

Classroom Modification:_____

_____

_____

Comments/Recommendations: _____

_____

_____

_____

_____

In order that we may further contact you if any questions arise, please provide name, position of person completing this form, and telephone number.

Name:_____

Position:_____

Telephone number: _____

Source: *The Resource Program Guide for a Congrgation School* by Phyllis S. Greene and Sara R. Simon. Board of Jewish Education of Greater Washington, © 1990.

RESOURCE PROGRAM PARENTAL NOTIFICATION

Date_____

Dear Parent,

_____will be participating in the RESOURCE PROGRAM at _____ .

The schedule will be:_____ .

_____ .

_____ .

We will be covering the following skills:_____ .

_____ .

If you have any comments and suggestions, please feel free to contact me. You will be receiving reports on your child's progress as part of his report card.

Thank you,

Resource Teacher _____

LETTER TO CLASSROOM TEACHERS FOR THEIR INPUT PRIOR TO MID-YEAR "CHECK-IN" CALLS TO PARENTS OF ALL RESOURCE STUDENTS

To: _____

From: _____

I am in process of preparing my midyear Resource Program reports for parents. I would appreciate your input on _____ . Please let me know if you have any specific concerns or academic areas where you would like to see further remediation. Of course, positive changes should also be shared!

If you prefer to give me this information by meeting with me, I will be glad to arrange a time.

Thank you.

Comments: _____

_____

_____

_____

PROGRESS REPORT

Resource Teacher _____ Date _____

Student _____ Grade _____

I. Skills Covered _____

_____

II. Evaluation _____

_____

III. Additional information (secular school, family sources, etc.) _____

_____

IV. Recommendations _____

_____

V. Parent comments _____

_____

Resource Teacher _____ Parent Signature _____

Classroom Teacher _____ Director of Education _____

Please return a signed copy of this report.

END-OF-YEAR CONFERENCE FORM

Date _____

Dear Parent,

Your child, _____, has been involved in the Resource Program this year. We would like to schedule a conference with you on _____ at _____

to discuss you child's progress and to plan for next year. Please call the school office if this is not convenient for you.

Thank you.

Resource Teacher _____

PART 4: "THE INCLUSIVE CLASSROOM" TEACHING TO DIVERSE LEARNING STYLES

CHAPTER 19

LEARNING STYLES— AN OVERVIEW

Flora Kupferman

INTRODUCTION

Learning styles. What are they? Can they be changed every month or two, like hairstyles? Do we gradually settle into them like lifestyles? Do we choose them, or are we born with them? What can we do about them once we know about them? Are they important to us in our learning, our teaching, or both? This chapter will explore what learning styles are, what learning style theory teaches about students and teachers, and how to make use of this knowledge in practical ways.

Just as everyone has a personality and personal style, each person also has a unique learning style. Learning styles influence the ways people process or take in information from the outside world. Most people use the five senses of sight, hearing, touch, taste, and smell to learn about the world. Some see the big picture, while others focus on the details. Some people learn through personal interactions, while others prefer to think things out alone. When babies begin to learn, their senses of touch and taste provide vast amounts of information. A baby who wants to know more about a block, a rattle, a crayon, or a feather will put it in her mouth. Although people make use of all their senses in different situations throughout their lives, most people have a preferred mode of learning. The educational system traditionally has had a tendency to emphasize only certain types of learning. Children are expected to sit quietly and listen to what the teacher says or look at or read the materials he presents. Learning takes place in even the worst situations, but a little knowledge about learning styles and teaching techniques makes a huge impact on every child's success in the classroom.

ASSUMPTIONS ABOUT LEARNING STYLES[1]

Before exploring the various learning styles and their implications in the classroom, we need to be aware of several underlying assumptions:

- Learning style is neutral, and no learning style is better or worse than any other. Visual learners are no smarter than kinesthetic learners. Global learners do not have the advantage over analytical learners. Teachers who are auditory learners are no more or less effective than other teachers. But people who have an understanding of learning styles

---

[1] *Teaching to Learning Styles Leader's Guide* (Alexandria, VA: Association for Supervision and Curriculum Development, 1992), pp. 3–4.

are better teachers because they consciously address all their students' strongest learning modalities more often than teachers who teach in only one way.

- Teaching to learning styles is a philosophy and an approach to education in which all students' strengths are valued and supported. Teachers who accommodate students' learning styles do not have a step-by-step program manual that tells them how to do it.

- Learning styles should not be used as an excuse for not learning. Students can use different styles to master the same skills. Additionally, students may have strength in one area, they can still take in information through the other modalities. The fact that they usually learn best visually does not rule out their ability to stretch her other styles and learn in another way. A person's learning style tends to remain relatively stable over time, however.

- A teacher who addresses a variety of learning styles will not necessarily solve all the educational problems that may occur in the classroom. A class in which all students' learning styles are accommodated will be an exciting learning environment, but there are often other educational issues that require other interventions.

LEARNING STYLES

VISUAL LEARNERS

One of the most common ways to take in information from the environment is through our sense of sight. People who learn best by looking at or reading things are considered visual learners. In the classroom, the visual learners will notice what people write on the chalkboard, what the bulletin boards look like, what is on the overhead projector, and what movies are shown. The visual learners will remember what they see much better than what they hear. They will prefer to put their own thoughts on paper or in some format where they can look at them. Visual learners may not necessarily be excellent readers, but they learn most effectively from what they see, and they can picture things in their minds.

AUDITORY LEARNERS

Another way to get information is through our ears or sense of hearing. Those who remember what they hear or say are called auditory learners. The auditory learners in the class will enjoy discussions, lectures, and interviews. They will tune in to conversations and sounds in the room, and they will remember oral directions. The give and take of a classroom in which students can talk to each other is an ideal environment for auditory learners. Reading aloud to themselves or verbalizing the processes they are using to solve problems are good ways for auditory learners to master written material.

KINESTHETIC LEARNERS

> "Tell me, and I forget,
> Show me, and I remember,
> Involve me, and I understand."

This Chinese proverb could have been written for kinesthetic learners, for these are the students who remember best what they do and experience firsthand. These students need to be actively involved in order to learn and remember material. They will be the students who want to get their hands on manipulatives and other learning aids. They want to participate actively in discussions and activities. Kinesthetic learners are often restless and inattentive in class. The kinesthetic learners are the students who benefit least from the traditional teaching methods of lecture and individual reading, which are more suited for auditory and visual learners.

GLOBAL LEARNERS

Herman Witkin, a cognitive psychologist, describes a mode of perception called field-dependent or global. He found that the context or field surrounding the object influences global learners; in other words, they see the "whole picture" or the forest. Global learners make connections between related items and look for patterns and relationships. They learn best by relating new material to their own experiences and to what they already know.

ANALYTICAL LEARNERS

Witkin describes analytical or field-independent learners as those who see an object as separate from the surrounding field. These are the people who look at details first, who move from the parts to the whole. They see the trees. Analytical learners prefer accurate, detailed information, and they want the teacher to focus on specific tasks and content. These students often prefer to work independently and to do things their way.

INTROVERTED LEARNERS

Carl Jung, the psychologist, in his attempt to understand human psychology, divided behavior into categories he called psychological types. In his model there are eight psychological type preferences[2], but two of them are the most useful in learning styles theory. Introverted learners tend to look inward. They like to think things through before starting a task or answering a question. They need to process their ideas inside their heads before participating in group discussions. These students tend to be private and are harder to get to know. When introverted students don't understand something, they prefer to watch someone else doing it before trying it out themselves.

EXTROVERTED LEARNERS

The extroverted learners in the classroom are the ones who like to think out loud. They understand concepts best when they talk about them. They prefer to have feedback from others in order to know how they are doing. These students are usually friendly and talkative, and they like to learn with others. They are usually action-oriented and like to move quickly from one activity to another.

TEACHING STYLES AND TECHNIQUES

Students are not the only people who learn in different ways. A teacher's style will reflect her own learning style. Thus a teacher whose learning strength is in the visual modality will decorate the room with attractive bulletin boards, charts, pictures, and other visual aids. The teacher who is an auditory learner will be more likely to lecture to the students or lead class discussions. The analytical teacher will provide detailed lists of facts, and the teacher whose style is introverted will make sure the students have plenty of quiet time to process information on their own. It is important for a teacher to recognize his own learning style and then to constantly stretch to include other methods in the classroom.

---

[2]Carolyn Mamchur, *A Teacher's Guide to Cognitive Type Theory & Learning Style* (Alexandria, VA: Association for Supervision and Curriculum Development, 1996), p. 4.

In order for all students, regardless of their learning style, to learn effectively, a teacher must make a conscious effort to teach to all styles. Teaching lessons in different ways to address the students' different learning strengths and preferences will never harm any of the students, but students whose learning strengths are not addressed regularly will suffer in the classroom. Exposure to the same material in different forms is always beneficial, and teachers must make sure that they provide meaningful learning opportunities to students with every learning style. The following lists provide some ideas for teaching to different styles.

SUGGESTED TEACHING STRATEGIES

VISUAL LEARNERS

- Keep oral directions short and simple.
- Give oral directions one at a time.
- Have students repeat oral directions.
- Write directions as you say them.
- Color-code Hebrew vowels, directionality, papers, etc.
- Use visual aids (charts, pictures, graphs, photos, films, overhead projectors) with auditory presentations.
- Speak slowly and clearly.
- Vary voice tone and pitch.
- Show students examples of finished products.
- Have students make and use flashcards.
- Provide students with written copies of what is presented.
- Label objects in the room in English and/or Hebrew.
- Post word and *alef bet* charts around the room.
- Use colored chalk on chalkboards or markers on dry erase boards.

AUDITORY LEARNERS

- Read directions aloud to the student.
- Use music, songs, and trope often.
- Use tape recorders.
- Read aloud.
- Speak and demonstrate at the same time.
- Do storytelling without visual cues.
- Use clapping, drums, and bells for auditory patterning.
- Memorize poems, rhymes, and songs.
- Play Simon Says/*Shimon Omer*.
- Make written material neat, clear, and simple.
- Have a "buddy" read directions aloud to the student.
- Provide cardboard markers or frames for reading.
- Allow students to complete half a page (or every other item) of written work.

KINESTHETIC LEARNERS

- Assign role-playing or interviewing activities.
- Encourage large writing in the air or on the chalkboard.
- Trace Hebrew letters on another student's back with fingers.
- Use clay or dough to make Hebrew letters.
- Play active games. (One example: Make a large game path on the floor with chalk or masking tape, and let the children be the game pieces.)
- Use trays or box lids and finger paint, shaving cream, whipped cream, pudding, sand, cornmeal, etc. for tracing letters or words.
- Use flashcards made from yarn, buttons, beans, sandpaper, glitter, dried glue, etc.
- Schedule small-group discussions or cooperative learning activities.
- Allow time for students to move around.
- Form Hebrew letters with the students' whole bodies.

GLOBAL LEARNERS

- Make mind maps or flow charts.
- Relate new material to the students' personal experiences.
- Emphasize the major concepts.
- Connect new material to recent learning.
- Use cooperative learning techniques.

ANALYTICAL LEARNERS

- Provide specific and detailed information.
- State learning objectives clearly.
- Allow time for independent work.
- Give students choices.

INTROVERTED LEARNERS

- Make time for silent reading in class.
- Give students think time before asking them to answer questions.
- Use private study areas.
- Allow children to work on individual projects.

EXTROVERTED LEARNERS

- Encourage whole-class or small-group discussions.
- Allow children to do group projects.
- Use skits or plays.
- Let students give speeches or monologues.
- Provide time and space for active projects.

Teaching to learning styles includes more than merely addressing various modalities in the presentation of material. A teacher must also give the students opportunities to process new information in a variety of ways. In other words, the students should be able to decide how to organize material in ways that match their learning styles.

- Visual learners may draw a diagram of the information to be studied.
- Kinesthetic learners prefer making a model.
- Global learners could draw out a mind map.
- Analytical learners write a detailed outline.

Allowing students to process material in different ways creates no extra work for the teacher. It requires flexibility and a greater tolerance for activity within the classroom, but once the teacher provides a menu of options that students use in their classroom study time or homework assignments, the students take charge of their own learning.

Teachers should also allow students to demonstrate their learning in their strongest style. This means that there is no need for every student's assignment or final project to be in the same format. For example, a student could show her understanding of a unit on the events leading up to the declaration of Israeli statehood in a wide variety of ways.

- Visual learners make a series of drawings with captions.
- Introverted learners write a report.
- Extroverted and/or auditory learners present a group project in which they interview important historical figures.

Teachers can provide students with a list of project options and let them choose how they will demonstrate their knowledge or mastery of the material. Here is an example of such a list.

SAMPLE STRATEGIES FOR STUDENTS TO DEMONSTRATE KNOWLEDGE OR MASTERY OF MATERIAL

VISUAL LEARNERS
- Cartoons
- Drawings or paintings
- Collages
- Diagrams

KINESTHETIC LEARNERS
- Models
- Skits, plays
- Puppet shows

ANALYTICAL LEARNERS
- Lists
- Outlines
- Tree with leaves, each containing one fact

INTROVERTED LEARNERS
- Written reports
- Individual projects

AUDITORY LEARNERS
- Monologues or dialogues
- Tapes
- Songs, raps, poems
- Interviews

GLOBAL LEARNERS
- Personal stories
- Large diagrams
- Time lines
- Mind maps

EXTROVERTED LEARNERS
- Speeches
- Oral presentations
- Group projects
- Game-show formats

SUMMARY

When teachers use learning style theory in their classrooms, all students can be successful. They have opportunities to learn and process new material and are able to demonstrate their understanding through their areas of strength. A teacher new to learning style theory need not feel overwhelmed by the prospect of suddenly having to teach in many new ways. If teachers want to explore using learning style theory, they could begin by choosing one new area to address. For example, if teachers are auditory learners, they may decide to incorporate visual techniques in the classroom for a month or two. When they become more comfortable with these approaches, other strategies can be added.

Teachers who already use a variety of techniques need not worry about addressing all learning styles in every lesson. As long as lessons and assignments are varied, students will benefit. Teachers who present lessons in more than one modality might want to begin providing the students with more choices in how they process and/or demonstrate understanding.

Knowing more about learning styles will alert teachers to their own style preferences and to those of their students. Teachers with this knowledge will consciously teach in ways that reach more of their students, thus creating an atmosphere of increased excitement and learning in the classroom. Students will have the opportunity to process the material they are learning as well as to demonstrate what they know in ways that accentuate their areas of strength. If we as Jewish educators follow the words of Proverbs 22:6 and "teach (the) child according to his way," we will have done our best.

BIBLIOGRAPHY

Burke Guild, Pat, and Stephen Garger. *Marching to Different Drummers*. Alexandria, VA: ASCD, 1985.

Overview of learning, teaching, and supervisory styles intended for educators.

Mamchur, Carolyn. *A Teacher's Guide to Cognitive Type Theory and Learning Style*. Alexandria, VA: ASCD, 1996.

Overview of learning style and cognitive type theories with practical suggestions for classroom teachers.

Teaching to Learning Styles. Alexandria, VA: ASCD, 1992.

Thirty-minute video for elementary through high school teachers about learning styles and teaching techniques.

Teaching to Learning Styles Leader's Guide. Alexandria, VA: ASCD, 1992.

Workshop leader's guide includes handouts for introductory or in-depth workshops about learning styles and teaching techniques.

CHAPTER 20

MANY TYPES OF SMART: USING MULTIPLE INTELLIGENCES TO ENHANCE LEARNING

Linda L. Forrest

According to the book of Genesis (*Bereshit*), all humans are created *b'tzelem elohim*—in the image of God. Accepting this as indisputable, our concept of God must include male and female, a fantastic spectrum of hues of skin color, and a complete continuum of ages. If we acknowledge that we are *all* created in God's image, wouldn't individuals who fit any possible combination of these descriptions be included in a definition of "typical"? Wouldn't that definition also include ranges of sight and hearing and speech? In other words, each and every one of us, regardless of our appearance and natural abilities, embodies a divine image. If we are willing to embrace this concept, it would seem unreasonably restrictive to believe that our likeness to God is limited to our physical attributes or talents. Wouldn't the multitude of manners in which we think and behave, learn and grow also constitute part of being created in God's image?

If we apply this thinking process to an educational setting, we realize that some students might learn better in a traditional classroom with a teacher lecturing, while others might learn better by singing, interacting with others, performing experiments, choreographing a dance, or solving real-world problems. Fortunately, this theoretical framework has been extensively researched and documented by individuals in the education community.

The current conception of giftedness indicates that many educators and parents believe that intelligence can be objectively measured using standardized testing that results in an IQ score. Focusing on research done at Harvard University, neuropsychologist Howard Gardner challenges this definition of intelligence, looking at traits and talents such as leadership, creativity, and curiosity as forms of giftedness. Gardner questions the validity of paper-and-pencil tests to determine a person's intelligence; he feels that individuals learn and process information in many different ways.

In his groundbreaking work *Frames of Mind*, Gardner suggests that there are additional ways to consider and measure intelligence beyond a single standardized intelligence quotient test. He defines seven possible intelligences, or multiple intelligences: linguistic, logical-mathematical, spatial, musical, bodily kinesthetic, interpersonal, and intrapersonal. Gardner distinguishes specific qualities that make up an intelligence so as to differentiate it from talents or abilities. Since his initial work, he has also added an eighth intelligence that he has classified as naturalist.

The following is a brief description of each of the eight intelligences.

- **Linguistic intelligence** includes the range of verbal skills, both oral and written.
- **Logical-mathematical** is what we might call scientific thinking, or the ability to construct a problem rather than articulate it.
- **Spatial intelligence** incorporates the ability to visualize and manipulate objects, to navigate.
- Perception and production are integral components of the **musical intelligence**.
- **Bodily kinesthetic intelligence** is not just movement, but responding to problematic situations in an effective manner.
- **Interpersonal** encompasses all of the skills that we use in relating to others, while **intrapersonal** intelligence has to do with metacognition, reflecting on one's inner thoughts.
- **Naturalist** intelligence involves the sensitivity to natural phenomena, looking at the flora and fauna of one's environment.

Gardner suggests that each of us possess all eight intelligences. However, our eight intelligences are not on equal levels—some tend be more developed than others. The combination of our eight intelligences is what allows us to solve problems that we are confronted with every day in all types of situations.

Try to imagine a famous individual, a former or current student who clearly stands out as being particularly or uniquely intelligent in just one of these areas. With Gardner's model, every student has a chance to be "gifted" in something. One student might be weak in spelling, be a whiz at math, be a mediocre athlete, and have a large number of friends. Another student loves to read, plays two musical instruments, struggles with math, and enjoys being by himself. Even students with developmental disabilities can show high levels in the musical, interpersonal, and/or bodily kinesthetic intelligences.

How can we, as educators, use Gardner's intelligence theory to help identify students' gifts and tailor their school learning activities to their particular strengths and needs? Students tend to learn best when they are able to call upon their more developed intelligence(s). They also tend to "act out" in the classroom using these same intelligences. Based on the above premise, it would only be natural that teachers feel the most comfortable in the classroom when they are able to use their stronger intelligences. It can take much more energy to develop an assignment that they themselves might not feel comfortable doing as a student. Consider the consequences that can occur when the teacher's and student's stronger intelligences differ. Can the learning environment of the classroom be affected? How may that affect a student's learning potential?

In order to best serve the educational needs of each student, a teacher must be able to identify a student's stronger intelligences. Informal methods using observation seem to be effective, as there is not a standardized test available to provide this information.

1. Take note of what a student does during free time at school. Observing students when they initiate an activity on their own sheds light on how they learn most effectively.

2. Observe how a student "misbehaves" in class. Take note when a student talks out of turn, doodles, fidgets in the seat, daydreams, or socializes with other students at inappropriate times.

Students should have numerous opportunities to learn and achieve through the modality(or modalities) in which they may have the greatest opportunity for academic success. The possibilities for using multiple intelligences in class are endless. Every lesson can incorporate one or more of the intelligences. Attempting to include three or four in one assignment can make for an outstanding lesson, while trying to integrate all eight may prove overly ambitious. Keep it simple. Begin with one per lesson, and after you've tried all eight, endeavor to apply combinations of the intelligences. Allow students to demonstrate their understanding of the material by designing a mural or developing a simulation.

Consider the following questions when planning lessons based on a particular topic:

1. Linguistic—How can I use the spoken or written word?
2. Logical-mathematical—How can I bring in numbers or critical thinking skills?
3. Spatial—How can I use visual aids?
4. Musical—How can I bring in music or environmental sounds?
5. Bodily kinesthetic—How can I involve the whole body or use hands-on experiences?
6. Interpersonal—How can I engage students in peer sharing, cooperative learning, or large-group simulation?
7. Intrapersonal—How can I evoke students' personal feelings or memories?
8. Naturalist—How can I incorporate living things, natural phenomena, or ecological awareness?

If you are planning a class period about Shabbat, you may want to consider the following:

Linguistic—Talk about the customs of Shabbat.

Logical-mathematical—Present the sequence of the days of Creation.

Spatial—Develop a web about Shabbat.

Bodily-kinesthetic--Act out preparing the home for Shabbat.

Musical—Prepare a tape of melodies for Shabbat prayers and *zemirot*.

Interpersonal—Collaborate to design simulation of preparation for and welcome of Shabbat.

Intrapersonal—Relate own feelings about Shabbat and its practices.

Naturalistic—Describe sunset *(ha-ḥamah mairosh ha-ilanot....)* and approach of Shabbat on *Erev Shabbat*. Talk about looking for three stars and darkness as Shabbat leaves.

Multiple intelligences can also be considered when teaching Hebrew. When learning *Shema*, the following is a sampling of the various activities that can be used.

Topic: *Shema*

	Hebrew	**English**
Linguistic	Read the first paragraph of the *Shema*.	Recite the first paragraph of the *Shema*.
Logical-mathematical	List and count the mitzvot in the first paragraph of the *Shema*.	Count the number of times the word "you" or "your" appears in the first paragraph of the *Shema*.
Spatial	Arrange flash cards in their proper order.	Place the translation under the Hebrew sentences.
Bodily-kinesthetic	Act out the mitzvot.	Draw the mitzvot and make a mezuzah.
Musical	Learn the trope and sing it.	Learn the song "And You Shall Love," (the English version of the *Shema*).
Interpersonal	Read for mastery with a partner.	Discuss with a partner how to "love God with all your heart, with all your soul, and with all your might."
Intrapersonal	Choose the key words that are most meaningful to you and tell why.	Choose a way to tell, in your own words, the meaning of the *Shema*.

ASSESSING STUDENT'S LEARNING BASED ON MULTIPLE INTELLIGENCES

Not only is it important to think about a student's multiple intelligences when teaching subject matter, it should also be considered when assessing the student's learning of the topic presented. The following provides various ways a student can share knowledge of the subject matter.

_____ Write a report

_____ Create a comic strip

_____ Build a board game

_____ Produce a videotape

_____ Design a photo essay

_____ Conduct an interview

_____ Develop a class newspaper

_____ Create a rap, chant, song

_____ Keep a journal

_____ Teach the topic to the class

_____ Create a mind map

_____ Design a mural, collage, mobile, photo album

_____ Build a model

_____ Set up an experiment

_____ Choreograph a dance

_____ Engage in a debate or discussion

_____ Develop a statistical chart

_____ Create a play or musical

_____ Compile a scrapbook

_____ Create a group project

_____ Set up an interactive computer presentation

Adapted from _Multiple Intelligences in the Classroom,_ Thomas Armstrong, 2nd Edition, 2000.

The theory of multiple intelligences allows teachers to accept each student _b'tzelem elohim,_ in the image of God. Providing a variety of learning activities and assessment alternatives, teachers allow all students the opportunity to feel successful using their areas of strength. Multiple intelligences theory has changed the notion of intelligence enabling all individuals, no matter what their IQ score, to be "smart."

BIBLIOGRAPHY

Armstrong, Thomas. _Awakening Your Child's Natural Genius: Enhancing Curiosity, Creativity, and Learning Ability._ New York: Jeremy P. Tarcher, Inc., 1991.

Armstrong, Thomas. _In Their Own Way: Discovering and Encouraging Your Child's Personal Learning Style_ (revised). Los Angeles: Jeremy P. Tarcher/Putnam, 2000.

Armstrong, Thomas. _Multiple Intelligences in the Classroom_ (2nd Edition). Alexandria, VA: Association for Supervision and Curriculum Development, 2000.

Armstrong, Thomas. _Seven Kinds of Smart: Identifying and Developing Your Multiple_ Intelligences (revised). New York: Plume/Penguin, 1999.

Gardner, Howard. _Frames of Mind: The Theory of Multiple Intelligences._ New York: Basic Books, 1983.

Gardner, Howard. _Multiple Intelligences: The Theory in Practice._ New York: Basic Books, 1993.

Gardner, Howard. _The Unschooled Mind: How Children Think and How Schools Should Teach._ New York: Basic Books.

Lazear, David. _Multiple Intelligence Approaches to Assessment: Solving the Assessment Conundrum._ Tucson: Zephyr Press.

Lazear, David. *Eight Ways of Knowing: Teaching for Multiple Intelligences* (3rd Edition). Palantine, IL: IRI/Skylight Publishing, Inc.

Lazear, David. *Eight Ways of Teaching: The Artistry of Teaching with Multiple Intelligences* (3rd Edition). Palantine, IL: IRI/Skylight Publishing, Inc.

CHAPTER 21

MULTIPLE INTELLIGENCES IN A JEWISH SETTING— LOGICAL-MATHEMATICAL

Deborah Gettes

It is our goal to stimulate your thinking and encourage you to integrate multiple intelligence strategies into your lessons. The first intelligence the Auerbach Central Agency is highlighting is

LOGICAL-MATHEMATICAL. There are two components to the information that follows:

1. Examples of how to incorporate the logical-mathematical intelligence into the subject areas Hebrew, Israel, *mitzvot*, holidays, *tefillah*, and Torah.

2. A chart to view all subject areas and the integration of the logical-mathematical intelligence at a glance.

The graphic organizers in this reference are based upon the materials in the website Enchanted Learning—http://www.enchantedlearning.com/graphicorganizers/.

I. HEBREW

A. Action Verbs and Student Behaviors

Begin your activity with a word such as

- Differentiate

- Discriminate

- Translate

Examples: Can you discriminate the difference between Hebrew letters that look alike?

Can you discriminate the differences between Hebrew letters that sound alike?

B. Student Products and Performances

Create a chart with colors, numbers, shapes, food, things found in a desk, home, outside, etc. Include the picture and the word in Hebrew.

C. Assessment Formats

Create a list of words the students should be able to read and ask them to read them aloud. When they are able to read all of the words on the list they can move to the next list.

D. Curriculum Outcomes

Demonstrate understanding of the *shoresh* (*kof, dalet, shin* קד״ש) by making a list of words that use the *shoresh*.

II. ISRAEL

A. Action Verbs and Student Behaviors

Begin your activity with words such as

- Account for
- Contrast
- Determine

Examples: Contrast life in Israel before 1948 to what it is like in 2006.

Contrast the various geographical areas of Israel.

Contrast the people who live in Israel (different types of Jewish people, different ethnic groups).

B. Student Products and Performances

Cause-and-effect relations: Artifacts guessing game—Show students an ancient object found in an archeology dig in Israel (use a replica of an object or a picture). Give them twenty guesses to discover what it is and what it was used for.

Time Lines: Continuum or timeline diagrams are a type of graphic organizer that is used to represent a continuum of data that occur in chronological (time) order or in sequential order.

If the topic has definite beginning and/or ending points, and the data points in between are not discrete, use a continuum/timeline.

For example, a continuum or timeline diagram can be used to explain important periods in Israel's life.

In making a timeline the student must first determine appropriate endpoints for the timeline and important points/dates to label on the continuum.

C. Assessment Formats

"What if" exercises (What if the Temple had not been destroyed?)

D. Curriculum Outcomes

Create a timeline of important periods in Israel's history.

III. MITZVOT

A. Action Verbs and Student Behavior

Begin your activity with words such as

- Conclude
- Demonstrate
- Find examples

Examples:

Tikkun Olam is repair of the world.

- Conclude what the world would be like if no one cared about the environment.

- Conclude what your synagogue would be like if no one cared about keeping up the maintenance in the synagogue.
- Conclude what your yard would be like if everyone threw trash on it, no one cut the grass, no flowers or plants were in the yard.

B. Student Products and Performances

Graphic Organizers: Cause and Effect

Cause and effect diagrams, also called sequence-of-events diagrams, are a type of graphic organizer that describes how events affect one another in a process. Students can create a visual representation of what happens when one does a particular mitzvah. What happens as a result of this mitzvah being done?

The student must be able to identify and analyze the cause(s) and the effect(s) of an event or process. In this process the student realizes how one step affects the other.

C. Assessment Formats

Read/Relate Challenges:

Read about the mitzvah of *hakhnasat orhim,* welcoming strangers. When, how, and where can you welcome a stranger?

D. Curriculum Outcomes

Predict the consequences of following or not doing mitzvot.

IV. SHABBAT

A. Action Verbs and Student Behavior (begin your activities with words such as these)

- Brainstorm
- Demonstrate
- Distinguish

Example: Distinguish the difference between things you do on Shabbat and the things you do not do on Shabbat. What makes the Shabbat things special?

B. Student Products and Performances—Symbols

Time Sequence Charts:

Create a chart of the flow of Shabbat in time order.

C. Assessment Formats

Notebooks: Keep a notebook of what you do on Shabbat from sundown to sundown. Put a star next to every Shabbat practice you do to make Shabbat special.

D. Curriculum Outcomes

Create a flow chart of preparation for Shabbat: Friday night, Saturday, and Havdalah.

The website Enchanted Learning (http://www.enchantedlearning.com/graphicorganizers/) has hundreds of graphic organizers that can be used to help teach using the logical-mathematical intelligence.

V. TEFILLAH

A. Action Verbs and Student Behavior (begin your activities with words such as these)

- Classify

- Interpret
- Show understanding

Example: Classify the prayers that praise God and those that ask God for something in the *Amidah*.

B. Student Products and Performances: Charts

Webs—Web diagrams are a type of graphic organizer that condenses and organizes data about multiple traits, facts, or attributes associated with a single topic.

Web diagrams are useful for basic brainstorming abut a topic or simply listing all of the major traits related to a theme.

For example, a web diagram can be used to create a graphic display describing all you know about a prayer. What are the parts of the prayer? What is the prayer about? Who says the prayer? When is it said?

C. Assessment Formats

Formula: Use the formula for blessings (*Barukh Ata Ado-nai…*) to create your own blessing.

D. Curriculum Outcomes

Compare and contrast two prayers.

VI. TORAH

A. Action Verbs and Student Behavior (Begin your activities with words such as these)

- Extrapolate
- Simplify
- Wonder

Examples: Wonder why Sarah laughed when she was told she would have a child.

Wonder why it took so many plagues to finally allow Pharaoh to let the Jewish people go.

B. Student Products and Performances: Predictions

Story Grids

Story grids are graphic organizers that can be useful in helping a student analyze or write a story.

This type of analysis is especially good for examining Torah stories, fables, and folktales.

Story grid graphic organizers help the student identify the elements of the story and the theme or moral of the story. Some of the many elements of a story include the important characters (their appearance, personality traits, and motivations), the setting of the story (time and place), the problem faced by the characters, how the problem is approached, and the outcomes.

There are many types of story grids that examine different elements of the story (and reveal different structures within a story).

Some summarize the beginning, middle, and end of a story.

Some list the five W's: the "who, what, where, when, and why" of a story.

Some list the title, setting, characters, problem, solution, and moral or theme of the story.

C. Assessment Formats

Critiques: What do you think of Moses telling all of the Jewish people to walk in the Red Sea?

D. Curriculum Outcomes

Analyze several mitzvot and put them into categories.

The website Enchanted Learning (http://www.enchantedlearning.com/graphicorganizers/) has hundreds of graphic organizers that can be used to help teach using the logical-mathematical intelligence.

For a further explanation and description of each intelligence, click on http://www.arches.uga.edu/~hmt/webwrite/printable1.htm.

For additional examples, refer to *Curriculum & Project Planner for Integrating Learning Styles, Thinking Skills, and Authentic Instruction* by Imogene Forte and Sandra Schurr, published by Incentive Publications.

MATHEMATICAL-LOGICAL INTELLIGENCE IN THE JEWISH CLASSROOM

SUBJECT AREA	ACTION VERBS & STUDENT BEHAVIOR	STUDENT PRODUCTS & PERFORMANCES	ASSESSMENT FORMATS	CURRICULUM OUTCOMES
HEBREW	Differentiate Discriminate Can you discriminate the difference between Hebrew letters that look alike? Can you discriminate the differences between Hebrew letters that sound alike? Translate	Charts Create a chart with colors, numbers, shapes, food, things found in a desk, home, outside, etc. Include the picture and the word in Hebrew.	Checklist Create a list of words the students should be able to read and ask them to read them aloud. When they are able to read all of the words on the list, they can move to the next list.	Demonstrate understanding of the *shoresh*
ISRAEL	Account for Contrast Contrast life in Israel before 1948 with what it is like in 2006. Contrast the various geographical areas of Israel. Contrast the people who live in Israel (different types of Jewish people, different ethnic groups) Determine	Artifacts guessing game: Show students an ancient object found in an archeology dig in Israel (use a replica of an object or a picture). Give them twenty guesses to discover what it is and what it was used for. Cause and Effect Relations Time Lines	"What if" exercises What if the Temple had not been destroyed?	Create a timeline of important periods in Israel's history
MITZVOT	Conclude *Tikkun Olam* is repair of the world. Conclude what the world would be like if no one cared about the environment. Conclude what your synagogue would be like if no one cared about keeping up the maintenance in the synagogue. Conclude what your yard would be like if everyone threw trash on it, no one cut the grass, no flowers or plants were in the yard. Demonstrate Find examples	Graphic organizers Cause and Effect diagrams, also called sequence-of-events diagrams, are a type of graphic organizer that describe how events affect one another in a process. Students can create a visual representation of what happens when one does a particular mitzvah. What happens as a result of this mitzvah being done?	Read/Relate challenges Read about the mitzvah of welcoming strangers. When, how, and where can you welcome a stranger?	Predict consequences of doing or not doing mitzvot.

SHABBAT	Brainstorm Distinguish Distinguish the difference between things you do on Shabbat and the things you do not do on Shabbat. What makes the Shabbat things special? Demonstrate	Time Sequence Charts Create a chart of the flow of Shabbat in time order. Symbols	Notebooks After Shabbat, keep a notebook of what you do on Shabbat from sundown to sundown. Put a star next to every Shabbat practice you do to make Shabbat special.	Create a flow chart of Shabbat practices.
TEFILLAH	Classify Classify the prayers that praise God and those that ask God for something in the Amidah. Show understanding Interpret	Charts Webs Web diagrams are a type of graphic organizer that condense and organize data about multiple traits, facts, or attributes associated with a single topic.	Formula Use the formula for blessings (Barukh Ata Ado-nai...) to create your own blessings.	Compare and contrast two prayers.
TORAH	Wonder Wonder why Sarah laughed when she was told she would have a child. Wonder why it took so many plagues for Pharaoh to finally allow the Jewish people go. Simplify Extrapolate	Story grids Story grids are graphic organizers that can be useful in helping a student analyze or write a story. This type of analysis is especially good for examining Torah stories. Predictions	Critiques What do you think of Moses telling all of the Jewish people to walk into the Red Sea?	Analyze several people from Torah stories and categorize them according to their personality traits.

CHAPTER 22

CREATING INCLUSIVE CLASSROOMS WITH DIFFERENTIATED INSTRUCTION

Sandy Miller-Jacobs

Joseph bounds into the classroom eager to share his family's Shabbat dinner experience with his new friend and classmate. Max slides into the room and into his seat without looking at anyone. Maya gallops into the room all sweaty, bouncing a ball, and blasting out the number of baskets she just landed. Deena practically knocks over a classmate, her nose buried in a great classic book that keeps her enthralled. These are a few of the children who make up your classroom.

All these children are in the same class and are approximately the same age but have different concerns, interests, styles, and abilities. They are not the same, so why would anyone think they could be taught the same way? Children are different in size, personality, motivation, and in the way they process information and learn. Not all children are interested in the same subjects; not all children like to read; not all children learn at the same pace. Yet when teaching a classroom of twenty-plus students it is difficult to take all these differences into account. Adding students with special learning needs to the already diverse classroom can bring one to the tipping point that leaves a teacher feeling overwhelmed and even unsuccessful.

WHAT IS DIFFERENTIATED INSTRUCTION?

Differentiated instruction is a philosophy of instruction that helps create classrooms where children and teachers feel successful. Based on this philosophy, a teacher recognizes and appreciates children's varied strengths and weaknesses and provides lessons that take them into account. In this manner the teacher is respectful of the children's abilities and provides learning activities that fully engage the children in the learning process. Used in the area of gifted education for the past several decades, differentiated instruction is now also seen as a way to improve the performance of students with learning problems.

Carol Tomlinson (1995) has written extensively on differentiated instruction and sees it as a key in creating effective inclusive classrooms. She suggests there are four characteristics that mark the differentiated classroom.

1. Instruction is concept-focused and principle-driven. All students have the opportunity to explore and apply the key concepts of the subject being studied.

2. Ongoing assessment of student readiness and growth are built into the curriculum.

3. Flexible grouping is consistently used.

4. Students are active explorers. Teachers guide the exploration.

Prior to differentiated instruction, teachers were expected to individualize instruction for the students in their classroom. Teachers spent hours creating different lesson plans for individuals or small groups of children. Students might all be studying science, but sometimes as many as fourteen different lessons were simultaneously going on in the classroom. With differentiated instruction, students learn the same material but learn it in ways that take into account their strengths and preferred learning styles.

WHAT DOES DIFFERENTIATED INSTRUCTION INVOLVE?

Differentiated instruction recognizes that differences seen in students' interests, learning styles, and readiness levels need to be addressed in the classroom in order for students to participate in the learning process. The basis of differentiating instruction lies in the teacher's ability to offer a variety of approaches to the content, process, and product of the lessons and units.

The *content* of the lesson is the topic being taught. Every lesson offers students the opportunity to learn specific knowledge, skills, and/or attitudes. Content is the "what" of the lesson—what is it the students will be able to do after this lesson? What is the objective of the lesson? What is the powerful or big idea of the lesson? Let's suppose the class is studying Shabbat observance. The objective could be any of the following: The students will be able to recite the Kiddush. The students will be able to describe three laws that pertain to the observance of Shabbat. The students will be able to compare and contrast two different family celebrations of Shabbat. Differentiating the content enables all the students to have access to the same content. Some students might be reading the laws concerning Shabbat in the Torah; some might be reading articles or easier books about the laws; others might be viewing a video. In each case the student has access to the content because it is presented in a manner that takes into account the student's academic level, interest, and learning style.

The *process* of the lesson can be considered what the children do as they "mess about" with the information they are learning. The process of the lesson is the core of the lesson—the activities the children do to help them learn the content. For teachers, this is the creative part of teaching. It's the "how" of the lesson—that is, how will the students learn this material? What activities will the students enjoy doing as they learn the content? It is important to offer a variety of learning opportunities that enable the students to achieve the objectives of this specific lesson. In our Shabbat example, some children might be interviewing others about how they observe Shabbat, some might be organizing Shabbat pictures according to the different laws they represent, and others might be writing specific family observances that reflect the laws. Still other students might be reading the Kiddush together, while others might be listening to a tape.

The *product* of the lesson is the way the student shares what s/he has learned. This is how you know whether the student has mastered the objectives of the lesson. Without clearly stated objectives, students cannot show you what they have learned, so it is important to determine the powerful ideas you want the students to gain before you determine the activities and the products. Products can be differentiated based on students' learning styles, readiness, and interests. Not every lesson has to be evaluated by a written test, an essay, or an oral presentation. Again, teachers can be creative, offering a varied list of products. Allowing students to choose the product they will share empowers their learning. Going back to our Shabbat example, students can complete a graphic organizer such as a web on Shabbat laws. They can create a video of different Shabbat observances, explaining the laws being observed. They can create a folder game with questions about Shabbat. A musical rap could be sung highlighting Shabbat laws. (JibJab.com created a very clever rap for Pesa<u>h</u> that could be used as a model.) A new tune for Kiddush could be created. (Debbie Friedman wrote a melody for the *Meshebairach* prayer that is now used in many synagogues.)

WHAT STRATEGIES HELP A TEACHER CREATE A DIFFERENTIATED CLASSROOM?

Once the teacher has determined the content and drafted the objectives, powerful ideas, and skills, the first step is to determine what the students already know by conducting a *pre-assessment*. In a math lesson on multiplication, for example, the students might complete a matrix so the teacher can determine which facts are known, which can be completed with a bit more time to think, and which are still unknown. Suppose a student did the facts first with a blue pencil and was able to complete the matrix for the ones, twos, and fives. Given more time and a green pencil, the student might be able to complete those facts where the number is multiplied by itself (e.g., 3 x 3, 4 x 4, etc.). With this information the teacher can flexibly group the children for direct instruction based on which facts they still need to learn. There would be nothing more boring than having to sit through a day's lesson on multiplication of the fives if you already know them! Such groups give students access to the material they need to learn while respecting the knowledge they have already mastered.

The process used for learning activities can also be varied. *Flexible grouping* is one way to provide variety as students work together to learn the content. Groups can be formed based on learning style. Students who learn best auditorily can learn 8 x 8 = 64 with the rhyme "My gate, my gate has a sticky door." The threes table can be sung to "I've been working on the railroad." Students who learn kinesthetically can learn the nines tables by using a simple finger play. Put your fingers out in front of you. Your left pinky is number 1, ring finger is 2, etc. Bend under the finger that is being multiplied. Each finger to the left of the turned-down finger counts as ten, and each finger to the right of the turned-down finger is one. Thus for 9 x 3 = 27 you turn down your third finger—tall man on left hand. There are two fingers to the left, which makes twenty, and seven fingers to the right, which are ones, resulting in the correct answer, 27. These are ways to help the children hold on to the facts so they can develop automaticity in their responses.

Cubing is another strategy often used in differentiated classrooms. The teacher can create a small three-dimensional cube with written questions or activities on each side of the cube. For example, when studying the history of state of Israel, the cube might have these tasks: Welcome to Israel. First task, write a letter to your parents, who will soon join you; compare the ideas expressed in an Israeli song of the 1940s with those in a current song; complete a timeline of ten major events that took place in the land of Israel; tell three things a person living on a kibbutz might do today; prepare a day of sightseeing in Jerusalem, describing three sites and the reason for their selection; and select one important Israeli and state why s/he is famous. Cubes of different colors can be used, making the tasks easier. For example, one cube might ask a child to compare and contrast kibbutz life from the 50s with that of today, while a different cube might separate this into two different questions by asking on one side of the cube to list three things they would do if they lived on a kibbutz in 1950 and on another side to list three things they would do on a kibbutz today. Instead of creating a timeline, the students might be asked to put a series of events in chronological order. Using different groupings and assigning the students to different-colored cubes, the teacher provides tasks geared to the students' interests and abilities. The tasks outlined on the cubes could be the products that show what the students have learned. The process would be how they gather the information via books, videos, CDs, and websites.

Another strategy is the use of *graphic organizers*. These are visual representations of content in diagram format. A Venn diagram (two intersecting circles) is frequently used to help students compare and contrast information about two different things, such as how two characters in a book are the same and what's unique about each. A story web would have several circles attached to one middle circle by connecting lines. The main topic is written in the middle circle, and the outer circles contain related information. If the center circle is labeled *kashrut*, the surrounding circles might be labeled laws & fish; laws & animals; laws & poultry; kashering dishes, pots, and utensils. Such graphic organizers help students to organize the content they are learning and to remember the specific information. Once the graphic organizers are completed, they can be used as a basis for expanding the information into a story or essay. However, for some children the graphic organizer might be the product that shows the teacher how much they have learned.

HOW DOES A DIFFERENTIATED CLASSROOM FOSTER INCLUSION?

By offering learning activities that are geared to different learning styles and academic levels, the differentiated classroom offers students with special needs the opportunity to actively engage in learning and to succeed in mastering the content. Giving the students choices of activities and final tasks empowers them and gives them control over their learning. If a student learns the content, it really doesn't matter which activity they have completed. Think about how different people study for a test—some rewrite their notes, some pace and recite facts, some make up mnemonics to help them remember. (Do you remember Roy G. Biv? He visits me every time I see a rainbow colored **r**ed, **o**range, **y**ellow, **g**reen, **b**lue, **i**ndigo, **v**iolet!)

In a differentiated classroom, the teacher must be very clear about the lesson's objectives, giving the student a clear structure within which to function. Tasks are clearly laid out, often defined by the use of rubrics. These spell out exactly what is expected so that students can successfully complete the project. Students are actively involved in their learning, allowing the teacher to provide individual and small-group direct instruction while students work independently.

Remember our classmates Joseph, Max, Maya, and Deena? Joseph and his friend are drawing a Shabbat mural depicting their meal together. Maya is creating a basketball game with Shabbat questions for her classmates to answer. Deena is writing about how her book's main character, who is not Jewish, celebrates a Sabbath day and how it is similar yet different from the way we celebrate Shabbat. With all the students busily at work, the teacher has the opportunity to talk with Max, who shares his concerns about his brother's upcoming surgery and agrees to create a special blessing of his own to say over the Shabbat candles this week. All are engaged in meaningful and respectful tasks that foster a deeper appreciation for how Shabbat helps enrich their lives.

RESOURCES

Bender, W.N. *Differentiating Instruction for Students with Learning Disabilities: Best Teaching Practices for General and Special Educators.* Thousand Oaks, CA: Corwin Press and Council for Exceptional Children, 2002.

Forsten, C., J. Grant, & B. Hollas. *Differentiated Instruction: Different Strategies for Different Learners.* Peterborough, NH: Crystal Springs Books, 2002.

Heacox, D. *Differentiating Instruction in the Regular Classroom: How to Reach and Teach All Learners, Grades 3–12.* Minneapolis, MN: Free Spirit Publishing, 2001.

Tomlinson, C. *Differentiating Instruction for Advanced Learners in theMmixed-ability Middle School Classroom.* ERIC, *EC Digest* #E536, October,1995.

Tomlinson, C. *How to Differentiate Instruction inMmixed-abilityCclassrooms.* Alexandria, VA: Association for Supervision and Curriculum Development, 1995.

Tomlinson, C. *The Differentiated Classroom: Responding to the Needs of All Learners.* Alexandria, VA: Association for Supervision and Curriculum Development, 1999.

Willis, S., & L. Mann. "Differentiating Instruction: Finding Manageable Ways to Meet Individual Needs." *Curriculum Update*, Winter 2000, Web document. **www.ascd.org/readingroom/cupdate/2000/1win.html** (11/20/2000)

Witherell, N., & M. McMackin. *Graphic Organizers and Activities for Differentiated Instruction in Reading.* Scholastic, 2002.

CHAPTER 23

COOPERATIVE LEARNING AND THE 21ST-CENTURY CLASSROOM

Ellen Fishman

BACKGROUND

Cooperative learning is rooted in the old-fashioned _hevruta_ learning system of "studying with, and being responsible to, one another." In current practice, research indicates that this strategy provides a broad range of learning opportunities for the diverse needs of students in the classroom. Cooperative learning offers full participation in academic pursuits and fosters the development of interpersonal relationships.

WHAT IS COOPERATIVE LEARNING?

When we think about the classroom we generally think about three different environments: competitive, individualistic, and cooperative. The competitive classroom is the one we see most often. It is a classroom in which activities are organized so that some will succeed and others will fail. That is, a system of spreading grades equally across the A–F continuum. It seems strange that any teacher would want a percentage of students to fail. Indeed, one would expect teachers to want every student to succeed. In a competitive environment, however, that is virtually impossible.

A second category of classroom, one that is also prevalent in our system of education, is the individualistic environment. In this system students are encouraged to complete seatwork by themselves and share little information with their classmates. It isn't unusual to see students cover their papers and refrain from communicating with their peers. In both of these techniques teachers utilize the "pour-in method," wherein the teacher is the "expert" who possesses all the knowledge and students are the receptacles who receive the information. Discovery and inquiry are not part of the process. Generally students are asked to memorize the facts and spit back the information. The cooperative learning classroom, on the other hand, is a method that employs inquiry, discovery, and active learning. All of the research indicates it is a method that supports a much deeper understanding of the material while at the same time fostering relationships among students who might otherwise not have any interactions with one another. In a classroom where teachers employ cooperative learning, they must be well prepared to launch a cooperative learning unit. The unit must be well conceived, materials must be readily available, and student groupings and roles must be predetermined for successful implementation. Without establishing the necessary foundation, success will be elusive. In short, cooperative learning requires careful preparation and patience, since in the beginning there is a significant amount of trial and error. The payoff, however, is substantial.

As teachers launch their cooperative learning units, experts advise them to choose a content area in which they feel very comfortable and a cohesive class where students naturally work well together. Further, it is recommended that teachers find a core professional group with which to talk, discuss problems and issues, and perhaps even find opportunities for team teaching. Research indicates that it takes three to five years to acquire solid cooperative learning skills and truly incorporate this methodology into the classroom. It is well worth the effort! In a method that fosters higher-level thinking skills, students are constantly pushed to inquire and uncover answers. Cooperative learning lessons, when properly constructed, create a learning community where the responsibilities for learning fall as much on the students as on the teacher, where competition is *not* present and students support each other in the pursuit of learning.

Cooperative learning contains five significant elements that are central to the methodology and that must be present for success. Although we assume that our students know how to employ these skills, in fact, they need to be taught directly. They include:

- Face-to-face interaction: Students sit "eye to eye, knee to knee."
- Positive interdependence: Students are responsible for a specified aspect of the assignment.
- Social skills: Students learn appropriate interpersonal interactions.
- Individual accountability: Students are responsible for knowing all of the information.
- Processing: Students reflect on the group's successes and analyze areas for improvement (Johnson & Johnson).

Many teachers believe that they are incorporating cooperative learning methods in their teaching. A closer look reveals, however, that they are actually using group work strategies. While it is not possible in this lesson to furnish in-depth directions, this chapter will provide suggestions for implementation throughout the lesson. (See cooperative learning sources for a detailed understanding of the methodology.)

TEACHER'S ROLE

In a cooperative learning activity the teacher's role changes. No longer does the teacher hold all of the information; rather, the teacher makes information available to students through various sources. The traditional teacher becomes "a guide on the side." In this role teachers act as resources and facilitators for the students. While they continue to teach, they put the work of learning into the hands of the students.

There are a number of things to consider as the teacher examines the lesson and environment. Some questions to keep in mind include:

- Are the teams cohesive?
- Is the material appropriate to the method?
- Has the teacher provided the students with enough information to get the job done?
- Is accountability built into the lesson?
- Do all of the aspects of the lesson support success?
- Where are teams failing?

- What is the status of individual students in the group?

Throughout the lesson the teacher maintains an active role, listening to and monitoring student activity. Using a clipboard, the teacher can document how often students participate and the way in which they do so. At the conclusion of the lesson, during the processing phase, the teacher can use the data to help students think about their interactions and modify the way in which they accomplish their tasks. The teacher listens in on the groups and guides them in their study. If student's are "stuck," it is customary for the teacher to act as facilitator and turn the questions back to the team to find their own answers. This encourages problem solving and deepens students' ability to find answers on their own. According to Robert Slavin, "teachers should employ the 'three before me' rule, which requires students to ask three classmates before requesting assistance from the teacher." Students should also be encouraged to seek understanding from peers in other teams if their own teammates can't assist. (For more in-depth information on the role of the teacher, refer to the bibliography.)

PHYSICAL PLANT AND CLASSROOM ORGANIZATION

Desks are arranged in squares to allow three to five students at each, with four as the optimal number. If the classroom has tables, place chairs at each. Alternatively, allow students to sit on the floor in different areas of the classroom.

DIVIDING THE GROUPS

Divide students into groups of four, if at all possible. Four is the optimal number for cooperative learning activities. There are various ways in which to create the groups, which include, but are not limited to:

> Student choice
> Random assignment
> Sociogram
> Teacher choice

In order to provide the maximum opportunity for interaction, interdependence, and accountability, it is recommended that the teacher select the student groupings. These groups should be heterogeneous and consist of a strong, a weak, and two average students. Where appropriate, gender should be taken into account as well (Slavin).

ASSIGNING ROLES

Either the teacher or the groups can choose the roles that students will assume in the cooperative groups. The roles will depend on the type of activity in which students are involved. Assigning a role to each student provides opportunities for full participation and interaction in the cooperative work. Suggested roles include:

- Reader—This individual is responsible for reading all of the material.
- Recorder—This individual records all of the information, either specific answers or a summary of the discussion.
- Reporter—This individual reports back to the larger group.
- Chairperson—This individual ensures that every student understands the material, the directions, and every aspect of the work the group must accomplish.

- Encourager—This individual supports team members by using phrases such as: "great job," "nice work."
- Cheerleader—The cheerleader praises students as they accomplish tasks.
- "Go-Fer"—This individual gathers all of the materials so students can complete the assigned work. This may be a student for whom the work is difficult, but without whom the group cannot succeed.

Note: The above roles depend on the nature of the activity. Assignments should be differentiated to meet the needs of individual students. It is not necessary for everyone to be working on the same material.

EVALUATING THE WORK USING RUBRICS

Rubrics are instruments for evaluating instruction and achievement based on predetermined expectations and standards. Provide students with a rubric (see samples). Using the rubric as a guide, groups can decide how they plan to accomplish the tasks.

SAMPLE LESSONS

In the examples below, the teacher might choose the following roles: chairperson, reader(s), reporter, encourager, go-fer.

LESSON 1

The following cooperative learning lesson is based on the story "The Shabbat Snowstorm" by Roberta Goldshlag, Melton Aleph Curriculum, Volume 3.

1. In pre-assigned groups, students read the story. Students can elect to do this in a number of ways, or the teacher can decide on their behalf. Examples include taking turns, assigning a reader, or allowing each student to read silently. Group members should determine the best strategy for their individual groups. Groups do not all need to choose the same procedure.

2. Materials (great job for the "go-fer")
   - one story for every two students
   - a different colored pen for each
   - one index card that contains the following question: What lesson does this story teach us?

   After the group has completed the reading, the "go-fer" should obtain the card from the designated materials area.

3. Each group discusses the question and, with consensus, decides on the group answer. (No put-downs; every contribution is valued.) Taking turns and using assigned colored pens, each student contributes a sentence or two to the answer. If one of the students has difficulty thinking of a sentence, it is absolutely permissible and encouraged to receive assistance from other group members.

   Important points to consider:
   - Everyone must contribute.
   - Each group member should make an equal contribution to the final product.

- The multicolored record sheet indicates full participation by group members.
- When all groups have concluded this portion of the assignment, each reporter shares the results with the entire class.

LESSON 2—SHABBAT SYMBOLS ACTIVITY

Teacher's role:

- Divide students into groups of four (if possible).
- Provide pre-cut poster board sections to each group.
- "Guide on the side" circulates among groups listening to comments, assisting when there is a need for redirection.

Students' role:

- Select group roles.
- Individually choose four symbols that represent Shabbat.
- With consensus, prioritize the symbols and use the top four.
- Agree on the appearance of the finished product.
- Decide on necessary materials, e.g., magazines, glue, markers.
- The "go-fer" picks up the items.
- Complete assigned section of the poster.
- Together, glue the four sections together and present to other groups.

Note: By putting this decision in the hands of the group, each is able to produce a unique product.

CONCLUSION

To suggest that cooperative learning is an easy skill to acquire would be less than truthful. There is no question that it requires a great deal of effort and time in the planning and implementation phase. Moreover, it takes patience to iron out the wrinkles of a new classroom strategy. Nonetheless, for those educators who presevere and practice using the strategy in their classrooms and with their colleagues, they will derive much reward from the hard work. It may take time, but when every student has access to the material and learns to work with diverse peers, we will have accomplished a great deal. Good luck to all who take the leap!

BIBLIOGRAPHY

Cohen, Elizabeth G. *Designing Groupwork: Strategies for the Heterogeneous Classroom.* 2nd ed. N.Y.: Teachers College Press, 1994.

Glasser, William. *Control Theory in the Classroom.* New York: Harper and Row Publishers, Inc.,1986.

Johnson, D.W., et al. *The New Circles of Learning: Cooperation in the Classroom.* Alexandria, VA: ASCD, 1994.

_____, *The Nuts & Bolts of Cooperative Learning.* Edina, MN: Interaction Book Company, 1994.

Putnam, JoAnne W. *Cooperative Learning and Strategies for Inclusion.* Baltimore, MD: Paul H. Brookes Publishing Co., 1993.

Slavin, Robert. E. *Learning to Cooperate, Cooperating to Learn.* New York: Plenum Press, 1985.

_____, *Using Student Team Learning.* 4th ed. Baltimore, MD: The Johns Hopkins University, 1994.

CHAPTER 24

THAT EACH MAY LEARN: EDUCATIONAL TECHNOLOGY IN THE INCLUSIVE CLASSROOM

Caren N. Levine and Sara Seligson

OVERVIEW

The purpose of this chapter is to provide educators and parents with an introductory overview of technology-based resources that are available to assist learners in inclusive day school and congregational education settings.

The chapter includes:

a) a general overview of educational technology to facilitate inclusive learning;

b) frameworks for evaluating websites and software;

c) a case study describing the BJE/Chai Lifeline Telecommunications Network;

d) resources for special needs education and inclusion.

Pugach and Warger (2001) noted that the passing of IDEA '97 (Individuals with Disabilities Education Act) represented a watershed in how technology was perceived for accommodating special needs. Previously assistive technologies had been primarily viewed as rehabilitative or remedial; with IDEA '97 schools considered technology as a means for accommodating learners with special needs to access the general curriculum. They point out that access to the general education curriculum has two components: (a) participation in instruction alongside peers without disabilities, and (b) the opportunity to actually learn the curriculum outcomes (p. 228).

Other initiatives such as the Assistive Technology Act of 1998 and the Individuals with Disabilities Education Improvement Act of 2004 further refined concepts related to the use of technology to accommodate learning for all students. Research on the use of computers by children with special needs is mixed, and more is needed to better understand issues related to the effectiveness of different technologies in learning (Woodward, Gallagher, and Rieth, 2001).

There are a growing number of initiatives in Jewish education that seek to take advantage of assistive technologies to facilitate enriched Jewish experiences for diverse learners. The Tikvah Program of Camp Ramah uses Kurzweil reading and learning software to help campers study Jewish text, learn songs, and create original written materials. Sasone, a program of the Jewish Federation of Greater Kansas City and its educational arm, CAJE, assists in the provision of adaptive technology, among other services. Communities also offer professional development opportunities, such as the Brookline Area Special Education Collaborative, which is supported by the Combined Jewish Philanthropies and Bureau of Jewish Education of Greater Boston. The Collaborative works with staff of synagogue inclusive special education programs and focuses on the use of technology.

Educational technology can help facilitate the participation and engagement of students with diverse learning abilities in Jewish schools, children and adults alike.

This chapter provides a brief survey of ways to integrate technology into the inclusive classroom in order to facilitate learning for every student in ways that can individualize and transform learning in Jewish educational settings.

INTEGRATING TECHNOLOGY FOR INCLUSIVE EDUCATION

There are many ways to use technology to provide an inclusive learning environment and to enhance the learning experience. In addition, there is a growing movement toward using technology tools to design learning that is accessible to all learners. The use of computer-based technologies should therefore be part of every educator's toolkit of strategies and resources to support and facilitate the learning process.

Pugach and Warger (op. cit.) suggest that technology in the inclusive classroom plays at least two other roles. Used appropriately, and with a variety of supports, it can foster class social dynamics; and it can facilitate access to the curriculum for each learner. The use of educational technology does not in itself guarantee success, but it can facilitate access to the curriculum by helping students become more actively engaged with their own learning. Access may mean different things to each student. It may mean developing learning skills specific to his or her own disability, or it may mean accessing content through accommodations such as written notes or audio reinforcement. Technology may also help students participate in an inclusive classroom by providing means for better communication and group interaction with peers.

New technologies not only help extend a person's capacities, they also change the way people learn. Rose and Meyer point out that there is a cycle of technology adoption. New technologies are generally utilized to perform specific tasks more easily and with greater efficiency. There is, however, a point of technological evolution in which concepts of learning and teaching become transformed. For example, the new media can be customized to meet individual needs by providing multiple means of representation, expression, and engagement. New media, and how they are designed, can play important roles in understanding how learning is achieved.

Determining appropriate resources is central to the successful learning experience. There are several factors to consider in selecting appropriate technologies, including, but not limited to, the following:

- Does the resource reinforce the learning goals of the curriculum? How?
- What kinds of activities can the teacher create to integrate the resource seamlessly into the curriculum?
- How can the resource help to individualize learning?
- Can the resource be used in flexible ways—for example, as a group activity?
- Does it take into account multiple ways of learning? Does it address multiple intelligences?
- Does the resource provide complex and helpful feedback?

- Does it teach or reinforce learning strategies?
- Is it engaging and motivating for the user?
- Is the content well organized? Does it facilitate organization of content for the user?
- What skills does the user need to acquire in order to fully benefit from this resource?
- What additional types of content supports does the teacher need to provide?

Specific criteria for evaluating software and websites are cited elsewhere in this chapter.

Traditionally, computers have been used in the classroom to provide remediation through tutorials and drill and practice exercises; to produce learning materials and student-made items; to express student learning and creativity; to reward students; to extend and enrich the curriculum; and as a means of integrating secular and Judaic studies.

Not every school has easy access to technologies. However, the school can work in partnership with parents, who generally have computers at home, to provide resources for home study In addition, administrators, faculty, board members, and parent associations can advocate for experimenting with different in-school options and acquiring appropriate resources. Classrooms with access to one computer can invest in a video display device to connect a computer with a larger-screen video monitor for group activities and presentations, or as a learning station with reference tools and resources for guided individual and small-group work. Classrooms that do not have on-site access to computers can use school labs, resource centers, and synagogue libraries, or laptops and portable keyboards like AlphaSmart that can be signed out for individual use or circulated to different classrooms. Other strategies for one-computer classrooms can be found in articles listed on Kathy Schrock's review of the literature (http://kathyschrock.net/1computer/1computer.htm).[1]

Issues such as sustained technology planning, building community readiness in educational settings, in-service and pre-service teacher training and professional development, classroom design, and other factors that ensure appropriate integration of technology into education are beyond the scope of this chapter. Resources for planning and integrating educational technology may be found on many of the websites cited in this text and in the accompanying bibliography.

What follows is a summary of how technology can be integrated into the inclusive day school or congregational school classroom in ways that can benefit all learners.

RESOURCES FOR LEARNING

There are many different types of technology-based resources that can assist learners. This article will focus on an introduction to assistive technologies (also known as adaptive technologies) as well as resources and strategies for technology-based learning. These resources and strategies primarily include computer-based learning and may be familiar to those who already integrate educational technology into their teaching.

ASSISTIVE TECHNOLOGIES IN THE CLASSROOM

Once a student's IEP (Individualized Education Program) team determines that an inclusive class is appropriate for a child, they will need to evaluate suitable assistive technology devices

---

[1] Please note: Websites and software cited in this chapter portray only a sampling of such resources and are not intended to represent a comprehensive listing. Every attempt has been made to provide accurate information as of publication; however, websites and web addresses often change over the course of time.

and services. Assistive technologies generally address issues of communication, manipulation, positioning and mobility, and access to learning.

The Assistive Technology Act defines assistive technology as "any item, piece of equipment, or product system, whether acquired commercially, modified, or customized, that is used to increase, maintain, or improve the functional capabilities of individuals with disabilities." The Wisconsin Assistive Technology Initiative's (WATI) *Resource Guide for Teachers and Administrators* defines assistive technologies as tools that can help a learner who has a disability do a task "that he or she could not otherwise do without it, or any tool the student uses to do a task more easily, faster, or in a better way." These technologies may be high-tech, like voice synthesizers, portable word processing devices, or "Readingpens," or low-tech, like book holders, sticky notes, and highlighter pens. Some resources may already be included in standard computer setups. For example, text-to-speech capabilities are generally built into popular word processing software, and most programs feature shortcut keys that perform standard functions, which can be helpful to those with limited mobility. In addition, enlarging the size of text or changing the text and/or background colors of a document can assist visual learning.

When considering appropriate assistive tools, it is important to base decisions on both the specific disability/ies and the resources required for implementing specific tasks. For example, assistive technologies for a disability such as vision impairment might include eyeglasses, computer screen magnifiers, and screen readers. Assistive technologies for a skill that uses vision, such as reading, can include a talking word processor that vocalizes text.

Other technological innovations include mobility devices, Braille printers, adaptive keyboards, touch screens, vibrating pagers, switches, remote-controlled appliances, voice recognition software, speech synthesizers, word prediction software, augmentative and alternative communication (AAC) devices, pencil grips, special mice, pointers, joysticks, and more. There are many resources available online to help develop assessments for a student's IEP; WATI (www.wati.org) is a fairly comprehensive site that includes forms for assessments and other resources that can be adapted for learning in multiple contexts. Checklists and charts for matching tools with needs are available online at assistive technology clearinghouses like WATI.

COMPUTER-ENRICHED ACTIVITIES AND CURRICULA

Schools typically use computer-based activities such as tutorials, drill and practice, problem-solving software, instructional games, exploratory activities, puzzles, interactive communications, presentations, simulations, and creativity/productivity tools. Many learners with special needs benefit from drill and practice repetitions. These learners often find computer programs more motivating than traditional worksheets and flashcards. The better programs also provide additional feedback to support the learning process. The use of technology provides accommodations to gifted and talented students. For example, students who are comfortable using Hebrew can download Israeli radio broadcasts over the Internet and develop reading skills through Hebrew language websites and Israeli newspapers. All learners should be provided with a variety of computer-based activities, including access to authoring software and multimedia design packages, so that they have opportunities to express themselves and engage in higher-order thinking and creativity.

Some software and websites are specifically designed to support differentiated learning. For example, MyJewishLearning.com organizes its guided learning according to different levels of interest by offering primers, topical overviews, deeper explorations, and analysis and interpretation. Another example of a website organized around concepts of differentiated learning is The Brain from Top to Bottom (www.thebrain.mcgill.ca). The site is an online tutorial about the brain that offers guided tours and materials geared toward beginner, intermediate, and advanced learners.

Software and Internet-based activities, like any other curricular piece, need to be set in the larger context of learning goals by the teacher. A searchable, annotated database of Judaic websites and software is found on the JESNA website (www.jesna.org) and is useful for identifying such resources. Some software, for example, takes advantage of audio and graphic supports to help learners develop their Hebrew reading skills. Hebrew and English word processors allow students to order and highlight text to assist in reading and understanding grammar relationships. Hebrew language websites and sites with Jewish games like ZigZagWorld (www.zigzagworld.com) and Jewish Funland (www.bus.ualberta.ca/yreshef/funland/funland.html) and software like Gemara Berurua (www.gemaraberura.com) provide new motivations for authentic learning and interactive reinforcement.

There are many ways of developing technology-based curricular material. Judi Harris identified three genres of educational Internet activities (http://virtual-architecture.wm.edu): interpersonal exchange; information collection and analysis; and problem solving. Interpersonal exchange refers to activities in which students connect electronically with other students or experts in a field. This might include cultural exchanges or twinning projects with "keypals" as sponsored by the Pedagogic Center of the Department of Jewish Zionist Education (www.jafi.org.il/education). "Ask An Expert" services like AskMoses.com and "telementoring" involve outside experts working with students in a particular content area. Information collection and analysis activities help students transform information that they uncover. For example, classes can exchange messages and student-written articles comparing Jewish customs in their community with those of Jews around the world or go on "virtual field trips" by participating remotely in on-site expeditions to places beyond the four walls of the classroom. Problem-solving activities include peer feedback events in which students (in the class, beyond the class) offer constructive feedback on a project or writing activity. An example of a sequential creation is an ongoing story to which each group contributes. Students in the inclusive classroom can be assigned different roles for group work that capitalize on strengths and interests and help bolster areas of weakness.

Tom March (www.ozline.com) describes technology-enriched curriculum in terms of learning-centered scaffolds. Different types of activities are suited to specific learning process goals. For example, a collection of predetermined websites to guide students to appropriate sites, or "Topic Hotlist," provides learners with an open exploration of a topic. A "Concept Builder" activity, in which examples are selected to help students derive critical attributes of a particular concept, moves the learner to higher-order thinking. WebQuests—inquiry-based activities that use pre-defined resources (online and off)—are appropriate formats for cooperative learning, problem solving, and investigating complex topics (http://webquest.sdsu.edu). Examples of WebQuests with Jewish content have been collected and organized by the Jewish Education Center of Cleveland (www.jecc.org). TorahQuests (www.jrf.org/torahquest) are another type of activity that supports the creation of Torah commentary.

The use of any media, whether computer, video, television, or print, also requires consumers to be able to critically evaluate materials and make appropriate choices. Media literacy is key to providing structures for supporting successful lifelong learning.

DISTANCE LEARNING

Another way of using technology is through distance learning. Learners access courses remotely through the Internet or from classrooms through devices such as videophones and videoconferencing. The BJE of Greater New York and Chai Lifeline, for example, co-sponsor the BJE/Chai Lifeline Telecommunications Network, which links critically ill children who are at home to their classrooms and to one another through the use of videophones and the Internet (see the case study below). Some schools arrange for gifted and talented students to take distance learning courses for advanced work in a specific subject area. Schools can also take advantage of distance learning opportunities for their students if they are unable to offer a particular course due to inadequate resources or class size. Many Jewish institutions of higher learning offer distance learning courses for credit.

PRESENTATION TOOLS, CAMERAS, AUDIO, AND GRAPHICAL ORGANIZERS

Computers provide a means for learners to represent and manipulate data in different ways to facilitate greater understanding and analysis. Multimedia programs such as PowerPoint are excellent tools for students to use to develop and present their learning—and for teachers to provide multi-modality teaching—through storyboarding, audio, video, and graphic representations. They can also be used as dynamic "chalkboards" for presentations that can be saved, shared and reviewed by students at their own pace.

Jewish clip-art images can be found in clip-art software packages and websites. Jewish museum websites are wonderful resources for visualizing cultural artifacts; online exhibitions provide users with a wealth of information and contexts for better understanding the Jewish material world. Digital cameras and web cameras can also be used to provide visual support and motivation and to allow the student to create original materials.

Graphical organizers, visual learning tools, and brainstorming software such as Inspiration and Kidspiration (www.inspiration.com) help students organize information and develop ideas through concept mapping and flow charts. Timelines assist learners in visualizing sequences of events. Some examples of websites with timelines and/or maps of Jewish history include, among others, online encyclopedias, the Jewish Virtual Library (www.jsource.org), the National Museum of American Jewish History, (www.nmajh.org), the Pedagogic Center of the Department of Jewish Zionist Education (www.jafi.org.il/education/pedc.html), and Bible Atlas Online by the Access Foundation (www.anova.org/sev/atlas/htm). DVDs like PBS's Heritage set and accompanying website (www.pbs.org) include many primary and secondary historical sources and objects. Audio files can reinforce classroom work, help students learn prayer and cantillation skills, and support other text study. These files can be downloaded to home computers, CD-ROMs, or portable devices like iPods.

PERSONAL DIGITAL ASSISTANTS/HANDHELD COMPUTERS

PDAs provide relatively inexpensive and highly portable access to computer resources. Students can use PDAs such as the PalmPilot as personal organizers to keep track of tasks, class schedules, and other important information, including locker combinations, student ID numbers, and library and assignment due dates. Other resources include administration tools such as attendance keepers and software for students and teachers to keep track of grades and assignments. Keyboards and other accessories can be added to facilitate note taking and manipulating the small interface. PDA versions of software applications such as word processors, graphing tools, calculators, and Internet access are available to users. In addition, Hebrew language, Jewish calendars, timelines, databases of Jewish interest, and electronic texts including blessings, the Bible and other religious texts, dictionaries, newspapers, and Jewish learning can be downloaded from the PilotYid site (www.pilotyid.com). PDAs are also useful for data collection and information sharing that can be beamed to others in the class. For example, teachers can download lesson plans and beam worksheets to students. Upon completion, students can beam them back for assessment.

LESSON PLANNING, CLASSROOM MANAGEMENT, AND ADMINISTRATION

Teachers use computer software for creating learning materials and for administration. Word processors and online templates are useful for designing lessons, for creating specialized "tip" sheets to scaffold learning, and for designing worksheets and quizzes. Sites like Kathy Schrock's Teaching Tools (http://school.discovery.com/teachingtools/teachingtools.html) include links to templates for creating worksheets, lesson plans, quizzes, and puzzles. Puzzlemaker (http://puzzlemaker.school.discovery.com), for example, lets teachers and students create materials to demonstrate mastery in a fun way. Email can be used to communicate with students, other faculty, school administrators, and parents. Databases and spreadsheets can be used to help keep track of detailed student records, grades, and assignments.

RESOURCES FOR PROFESSIONAL DEVELOPMENT

TEACHER SITES

Educators use the Internet and the World Wide Web to further their work and their own professional growth. Teachers use email, discussion groups, and bulletin board services to link with other teachers for collegial exchanges and sharing. They investigate teacher-oriented websites for curricular resources, lesson plan ideas, teaching strategies and "best practices," research, online assistance, and publications. Examples of teacher-oriented sites include Kathy Schrock's Guide for Educators (school.discovery.com/schrockguide), CAJE: Coalition for the Advancement of Jewish Education (www.caje.org), Lookstein Virtual Resource Center for Jewish Education (www.lookstein.org), and e-Chinuch.org: Pinchas Hochberger Creative Learning Pavilion (www.echinuch.org). Lesson plans and ways to adapt them are also available online. TeacherVision, for example, provides suggestions for adapting curriculum design to reach all learners in conjunction with the Council for Exceptional Children in its section on classroom management and the art of teaching, and it houses a collection of other useful classroom resources in its special needs area (www.teachervision.fen.com). Other sites that primarily address assistive technologies are cited throughout this chapter and are included in a listing that follows.

ONLINE LEARNING

Teachers may elect to take online courses to strengthen their understanding of particular content areas or to learn more about instructional strategies. Many Jewish institutions of higher learning now offer access to their faculty and academic resources through online courses. Initiatives such as JSkyway (www.jskyway.com), the Lookstein Center (www.lookstein.org), and the Jewish Agency's Contact Center (www.jacontact.org) offer professional development courses on Jewish content and educational techniques.

Online courses are available for educators from organizations that specifically focus on educational technology and special needs. Some of these are free tutorials; others are more formal, tuition-based workshops. Examples can be found at the following sites: Assistive Technology Training Online Project (ATTO: www.atto.buffalo.edu), ASCD (www.ascd.org), Council for Exceptional Children (www.cec.sped.org), and PBS Teacherline (http://teacherline.pbs.org). An example of a WebQuest that was designed to help teachers identify "twice exceptional students" is included in a following section.

TECHNOLOGY STANDARDS IN EDUCATION

Familiarity with assistive technologies is called for by the National Educational Technology Standards (NETS: www.iste.org) developed by ISTE and by associated technology standards determined by the National Council for Accreditation of Teacher Education (NCATE: www.ncate.org). WATI (www.wati.org) posts best practices, including "AT Competencies" developed for school district staff members working in the area of assistive technology. Many school-based IT staff and technology coordinators may be familiar with these standards and how they are applied to curriculum integration, but they are less conversant with assistive technologies, which generally fall under the domain of the special needs professional. Ideally these specialists will work together as a team to enhance their students' learning. Teachers in inclusive settings must be able to recognize the needs of each learner, the technologies available to them, how to adapt them, and how to assess their effectiveness.

In addition to educational standards, there is a movement in the technology community toward instructional and communications design standards that facilitate accessibility for all learners. These include initiatives such as the National Instructional Materials Accessibility Standard (NIMAS: http://nimas.cast.org), Bobby-approved web accessibility (http://webxact.watchfire.com), and universal design (www.washington.edu/doit/Resources/udesign.html). Educators and designers of Jewish resources should be cognizant of these educational and design standards.

FOSTERING THE HOME–SCHOOL CONNECTION
CLASS WEBSITES

There are a number of ways that technology can be used to build stronger communication between the home and the school. Class websites can be used to post assignments and to keep parents updated on classroom activities. Even if the school does not sponsor a website, or if the teacher does not know how to create a webpage, there are online teacher sites that offer templates for creating and storing online resources that can be accessed through the web. Some of these sites also allow teachers to post assignments and grades that students and parents can review on a password-protected site. Educators are experimenting with podcasts, blogs, and other new media to supplement class activities.

ASSESSMENT TOOLS AND ELECTRONIC PORTFOLIOS

Internet sites such as SurveyMonkey.com and 4Teachers (www.4teachers.org) provide tools for designing traditional and alternative assessments. These can be created by teachers or by students who are interested in self-assessment of their learning. Portfolios developed by students in conjunction with teachers highlight individual students' work and progress over time. These electronic portfolios can be stored online and often feature interactive capabilities so that the learner and teacher can share an ongoing dialogue. Many portfolios include multimedia material, which is another way of integrating technology into the classroom. Electronic-Portfolios (http://electronicportfolios.com/) offers more information on the rationale for and development of these tools.

HOMEWORK HELPERS

Well-chosen ancillary materials help learners better understand content and provide a means of deepening their engagement with the material. Different students will require different supports; for example, some might need more instructional scaffolding, while others might benefit from more challenging content. Outreach to families and communication with parents are keys to supporting student learning and to building community beyond the classroom. Teachers and administrators can use the Internet to email regular class updates to parents. Teachers can also send parents suggested resources for learning more about holidays, suggested activities for home rituals and projects, and useful sites that focus on parenting skills. In addition to materials produced by teachers, there are online "homework helper" sites that provide background information on Jewish subject areas to supplement in-class learning. About. com, for instance, has compiled a number of annotated links for assistance in learning Hebrew, including a number of online tutorials that take advantage of audio and visual aids. These online tutorials can serve as practice for students and as refresher courses for parents. Sites such as MyJewishLearning.com, Judaism 101 (www.jewfaq.org), and Rabbi Scheinerman's Judaism site (www.scheinerman.net/judaism) provide content and links for parents to explore Jewish content and concepts. Educators in Jewish settings can also direct students to resources and materials related to the Jewish experience that can be incorporated into their general studies curriculum. For example, a child who is developing a presentation on immigration for social studies can be encouraged to integrate materials that focus on the Jewish experience.

SUPPORT, INFORMATION, AND LEARNING STRATEGIES

Other online resources include information, self-assessments, and strategies related to different learning styles that can be helpful for students, parents, and teachers. The Center for Advancement of Learning (www.muskingum.edu/%7Ecal/database), for example, developed a database to help students assess their learning styles and identify strategies based on content and on types of learning. LDPride.net offers a number of resources, including information on learning styles and multiple intelligences. Resources are also available for supporting tutors engaged in reading and literacy skills, such as Web-Based Tutor Training (www.nwrel.org/learns/web-based/index.php).

The Internet also provides emotional and informational supports through discussion groups, blogs, and chats in which parents and teachers can share ideas and children can develop social relationships with peers. A partial listing of online resources follows.

EVALUATING SOFTWARE AND WEB-BASED RESOURCES

SOFTWARE

Evaluating the appropriateness of software for individual and group activities is a key element in its successful implementation. Because the software experience is an interactive and multidimensional one, it is imperative that the evaluation process include not only the pedagogy the software embodies, but its design features as well. Some questions to consider are:

- What is the intended purpose of the software—e.g., a specific skill or a fun experience? *Alef Bet Schoolhouse I, II,* and *III* (www.davka.com) provides both drill and games to teach Hebrew letter identification, vowels, words, and basic Hebrew grammar skills.

- In what setting is the primary use intended—i.e., the home or the classroom? *JBOP, Interactive Haggadah,* and *Who Stole Hanukkah* (www.ejemm.com) are primarily for individual or family use but were also designed with a teacher's guide for classroom integration.

- What is the developmental level of the intended audience? *Aleph to Tav* (www.davka. org) offers young children an interactive Hebrew letter tutor. Older children may prefer the graphics and sound in *Hebrew World* (www.davka.org), which can even be used by adults.

- Does the program offer accommodations for different abilities?

- Are there authorship tools? For example, can the educator or parent adapt it for individualized programming? Both *Hebrew Word Quest* (www.jewishsoftware.com), and *Jewish IQ Baseball,* included in the Davka Classic Game Pack (www.davka.com) offer opportunities to create one's own content for the games.

- How easily can the user access the program's components, including the help menu? The *Beit Hamikdash* (www.jewishsoftware.com) offers a "remote control" that allows users to easily access a library and a picture gallery of vessels and to explore the rituals of the sacrifices. The user can also switch between Hebrew and English in just one click.

Educators have to learn how to apply the appropriate evaluation criteria to software in order to determine the effectiveness of the product for its intended goal. Educators and parents who rely on software evaluations that have been conducted by others must consider that information may be out of date, incomplete, or biased for purposes of marketing.

Jewish software lists and reviews can be found on several websites, including Associated Talmud Torahs of Chicago (www.att.org), JESNA (www.jesna.org), and the Jewish Education Center of Cleveland (www.jecc.org).

WEB-BASED RESOURCES

Critical to creating and using the Internet in such individualized learning activities is the ability for the educator and/or student, depending on his or her abilities, to evaluate the websites in question. There are many rubrics available for evaluating online content. In general, evaluations include the following considerations:

- **Format**—Is the website user friendly, aesthetically appealing, and appropriate for the target audience, not heavily graphic or time-consuming to download?

- **Accessibility**—Does the site work with multiple browsers (i.e., Netscape, Explorer)? Does the site work with Text to Speech devices? Does it conform to accessibility standards such as Bobby?

- **Content and Accountability**—Is the purpose of the site instantly clear? Is the author/organization immediately recognizable and reliable? Is the content accurate, complete, up-to-date, and useful? Will the site be revisited?

- **Learning Process**—Does the information promote engagement of the learner, use of multiple intelligences or multiple talents, and higher-order thinking at different levels (think, reflect, discuss, hypothesize, compare, challenge, classify, etc.)?

Kathy Schrock's Guide for Educators includes sites to help teachers and parents evaluate websites (school.discovery.com/schrockguide/eval.html).

Software and webpage evaluation rubrics developed by Maury Greenberg, Director of Technology Resources for the Jewish Education Center of Cleveland, are reprinted in this volume with permission and can also be accessed online at the JECC website (www.jecc.org).

CASE STUDY: BJE/CHAI LIFELINE TELECOMMUNICATIONS NETWORK—CHAILINK/SCHOOLLINK

In the spring of 1996, the Board of Jewish Education of Greater New York, in cooperation with Chai Lifeline and supported by a grant from the Butler Family Foundation, created Chailink. Chailink is a distance learning program that connects hospitalized and youngsters who are at home with their schools via videophones. The goal of the program is to provide children academic and social links to their schools and friends while recuperating from serious illnesses. Through this mechanism children can maintain their academic levels without losing a year's schoolwork or have to repeat grades. Furthermore, maintaining an ongoing relationship with school and peers is often believed to aid in the recuperation process. The advantages of using videophones are their flexibility of use and their quality of communication. Because these phones work on regular telephone lines, no additional equipment or hookups are necessary, and one can connect the child to virtually any location with great ease. The child can hear and view all classroom activities and be heard and seen by teachers and students alike—true virtual classroom participation. Since its inception, scores of children have been linked through the BJE/Chai Lifeline program.

This case study concerns the use of Chailink for Arele. Arele was a middle school student in a Chassidishe yeshiva in Monsey, New York. Arele was diagnosed with leukemia at the beginning of the 1997–98 school year and received treatment at Hackensack University Medical Center in New Jersey. The home and school were desperate to keep his mind active and knowledge current, and all agreed that the Chailink project was a viable solution. Rabbi Martin Schloss and Sara Seligson of the BJE of Greater New York set up the videophones at both the school and the hospital. Shortly thereafter, Arele was learning along with his classmates. Rabbi Farber, the principal of the yeshiva, sent Rabbi Schloss a letter describing the experience. He wrote:

> All his classmates and many other schoolmates would each pass by the telephone every day to wish Arele a *refuah sh'leimah* [speedy recovery] and talk…with him. The *melamed* [teacher] himself felt as if he were teaching Arele alone, since the telephone faced him constantly. Also Arele felt that his rabbi was teaching him privately.
>
> It was astonishing to see how Arele in his painful situation sat glued to the telephone for hours listening to his rebbe's *shiur* [lecture]. The nurses and doctors were all bewildered.…
>
> Arele himself once commented to Rab [Rabbi] (his guardian), while listening on the telephone to his rabbi, that if the nurse will come to him, he should inform her that he is not available. He is in _heder_ [school] now.

Among the many experiences Arele encountered during his stay at Hackensack University Medical Center, two stand out in particular. The first is a somewhat humorous situation. It seems that one of the students was throwing paper at another student during class. The rabbi was quick to put an end to the classroom disturbance and called the perpetrator to task for his classroom behavior. At the end of the session Arele asked to speak to the rabbi privately. "Off the air," so to speak, he informed the rabbi that he had seen the disturbance take place, and in fact, it wasn't the boy who was punished that had committed the act, but the rather the one sitting next to him who was actually the guilty party. The rabbi thanked Arele and righted the wrong.

The second experience occurred as Arele's class celebrated the conclusion of a Talmudic tractate. Such a celebration is called a *siyum*. During the *siyum* each student dressed up in his "Shabbos best" and recited a particular selection of the Talmud. Arele dressed accordingly and recited his prepared Talmudic selection. He also joined them virtually for the meal. Arele had special food brought to the hospital so that he could truly participate in all facets of the event. At the conclusion of the celebration, Arele's classmates recited *Tehillim* [Psalms] on his behalf in the hope of a speedy recovery. Arele asked if he could be visually present as the *Tehillim* were being recited. In describing this event, Rabbi Farber writes:

> Since the boys saw him while reciting the *Tehillim*, they all said it with extreme enthusiasm and feeling. When they finished everyone passed by the telephone to wish him a quick recovery. We watched Arele then wipe away the tears from his eyes. Rabbi (his guardian) was present with Arele at that time. He related that the nurse (not Jewish) who was present at that time watched the whole scene and commented that it was worth for her to be born just to see all this.

A few days later, on the day before Purim, Arele died.

This experience teaches that although the length of one's days is in the hands of God, technology allows us to enhance the quality of those days.

CONCLUSION

Assistive and educational technologies are most successful when they help students become effective, active, and creative learners. Technology is not an end in itself, but rather an educational tool, and perhaps more than that. When it is used by educators to integrate different learning modalities and to create inclusive and enriched learning environments that correlate to school goals for Jewish living, technology not only enhances the learning experience, it transforms it.

REFERENCES

Barrett, Helen. *Electronic Portfolios = Multimedia Development + Portfolio Development: The Electronic Portfolio Development Process.* Available from http://electronicportfolios.com.

Harris, Judi. *Design Tools for the Internet-Supported Classroom.* Alexandria, VA: Association for Supervision and Curriculum Development, 1998.

Harris, Judi. *Virtual Architecture Designing and Directing Curriculum-Based Telecollaboration.* Eugene, OR: International Society for Technology in Education, 1998. Supporting materials are available online at http://virtual-architecture.wm.edu.

Hasselbring, Ted S., and Candyce H. Williams Glaser. "Use of Computer Technology to Help Students with Special Needs." *The Future of Children: Children and Computer Technology*. Volume 10, Number 2. The David and Lucile Packard Foundation. Fall/Winter 2000. Available from www.futureofchildren.org.

Pugach, Marleen, and Cynthia Warger. "How Does Technology Support a Special Education Agenda?" In *Technology, Curriculum and Professional Development: Adapting Schools to Meet the Needs of Students with Disabilities*. Woodward and Cuban, eds. Thousand Oaks, CA: Corwin Press, 2001, pp. 226–239.

Reed, Penny R. *Resource Guide for Teachers and Administrators about Assistive Technology*. Available from www.wati.org.

Rose, David, and Anne Meyer. *The Future Is in the Margins: The Role of Technology and Disability in Educational Reform*. Available from www.cast.org.

Woodward, John, Deborah Gallagher, and Herbert Rieth. "No Easy Answer: The Instructional Effectiveness of Technology for Students with Disabilities." In *Technology, Curriculum and Professional Development: Adapting Schools to Meet the Needs of Students with Disabilities*. Woodward and Cuban, eds. Thousand Oaks, CA: Corwin Press, 2001, pp. 3–26.

SUGGESTIONS FOR FURTHER LEARNING

In addition to the books and websites listed below, be sure to check resources and recommendations available from local central agencies for Jewish education and other educational organizations.

Please note that websites and web addresses are subject to change.

Barrett, Helen. *Electronic Portfolios = Multimedia Development + Portfolio Development: The Electronic Portfolio Development Process*. Available from http://electronicportfolios.com.
Resources for using technology for assessment, with a focus on developing electronic portfolios.

Brunner, Cornelia, and William Tally. *The New Media Literacy Handbook: An Educator's Guide to Bringing New Media into the Classroom*. New York: Anchor Books, 1999.
An introduction to media literacy and curricular integration with a focus on history and social studies, arts education, language arts, and science.

Curtis, Michael, Bard Williams, Cathleen Norris, David O'Leary, and Elliot Soloway. *Palm Handheld Computers—A Complete Resource for Classroom Teachers*. Eugene, OR: ISTE, 2003.
Rationale, sample lessons, templates, and tips for using handheld computers in the classroom, including a companion CD-ROM with Palm OS freeware programs.

Dockterman, David A. *Great Teaching in the One Computer Classroom*. Watertown, MA: Tom Snyder Productions, 1998.
Provides a rationale and suggestions for using computers in the classroom, with an emphasis on successful ways of incorporating even one computer into the setting.

Dodge, Bernie. "FOCUS: Five Rules for Writing a Great WebQuest." *Leading and Learning with Technology*, 28:8 (May 2001). Available from www.iste.org.
Recommendations for creating educationally productive and challenging WebQuests.

DO-IT *Working Together* publications (www.washington.edu/doit).
A series of downloadable publications and online videos to promote assistive technologies, including *Working Together: People with Disabilities and Computer Technology* (an overview of adaptive technology); *Working Together: Computers and People with Learning Disabilities* (an overview of computer-based tools for people with learning disabilities); *Working Together: Computers and People With Mobility Impairments* (an overview of computer-based accommodations for people with mobility impairments); *Working Together: Computers and People with Sensory Impairments* (an overview of accommodations for people with sensory impairments); and, *Adaptive Technology Used by DO-IT Scholars* (technology used by participants and students with disabilities). DO-IT also publishes information about accessibility standards for website and software design.

The Future of Children 10:2, Fall/Winter, 2000. "Children and Computer Technology." The David and Lucille Packard Foundation. Available from www.futureofchildren.org.
Publication devoted to issues related to technology and its impact on children.

Kimball, Walter H., Libby G. Cohen, Deb Dimmick, and Rick Mills. "No Special Equipment Required." *Learning and Leading with Technology* (31), 4, 2003, pp. 12–15.
Discussion of accessibility features found in Windows and Macintosh computer systems and their application for learners with special needs.

Harris, Judi. *Design Tools for the Internet-Supported Classroom*. Alexandria, VA: ASCD, 1998.
Resources for designing inquiry-based educational activities and projects using the Internet.

Gordon, David T., ed. *The Digital Classroom: How Technology Is Changing the Way We Teach and Learn*. Cambridge, MA: Harvard University Letter, 2000.
A compilation of articles and essays addressing the challenges of educational technology for the classroom.

Isaacs, Leora, and Caren Levine. *Technology Planning 101*. New York: JESNA, Jewish Education Service of North America, 1999 (available from www.jesna.org).
A planning guide for integrating technology into educational settings.

Isaacs, Leora; Caren Levine, and Rebecca Goldwater. *Preliminary Survey of Distance Learning in Jewish Education*. New York: Jewish Education Service of North America, 2002. Available from www.jesna.org.
A study of different models of e-learning for Jewish education, with an emphasis on programs for the professional development of Jewish educators.

ISTE, International Society for Technology in Education (www.iste.org).
ISTE is the leading organization for educational technology professionals. The organization also works to develop national educational technology standards for students, teachers, and administrators.

ISTE/SETSIG (www.iste.org)
ISTE's special interest group to advance knowledge concerning specialized technology products and effective practices for enhancing opportunities for children, youth, and adults with disabilities and for students who are gifted.

The Jossey-Bass Reader on Technology and Learning. San Francisco, CA: Jossey-Bass, 2000.
A collection of articles, reports, and essays by leading experts on educational technology and its impact on learning.

Jewish Educational Leadership, 1 (1), Spring 2003, 23-28. Available from www.lookstein.org.
Issue devoted to the use of technology in Jewish schools, including theory, practice, and learnings from secular education that can be applied to Jewish educational settings.

Jewish Education News 23:2, Summer 2002. "Technology and Jewish Education."
This issue of JEN includes articles on integrating technology, teacher training and professional development, the school setting, and special projects in Jewish education.

Levine, Caren. "Jewish Learning in the Digital World." In *The Ultimate Jewish Teachers Handbook*, edited by Nechama Skolnik Moskowitz. Denver, CO: A.R.E. Publishing, Inc., 2003.

AN OVERVIEW OF HOW THE INTERNET AND SOFTWARE CAN BE INTEGRATED INTO JEWISH LEARNING SETTINGS WITH AN EMPHASIS ON RESOURCES FOR JEWISH EDUCATION AND DEVELOPING TECHNOLOGY-ENHANCED MATERIALS.

Mandel, Scott. *Wired into Teaching Jewish Holidays*. Denver, CO: A.R.E. Publishing, Inc., 2003.
——*Wired into Teaching Jewish Virtues: An Internet Companion*. Denver, CO: A.R.E. Publishing, Inc., 2002.
——*Wired into Teaching Torah: An Internet Companion*. Denver, CO: A.R.E. Publishing, Inc., 2001.

——*Wired into Judaism: The Internet and Jewish Education*. Denver, CO: A.R.E. Publishing, Inc., 2000
A series of books designed for teachers without Internet access at school, but who are online at home. Step-by-step methodology helps Internet novices as well as those with experience.

March, Tom. *Working the Web for Education: Theory and Practice on Integrating the Web for Learning*. Available from www.web-and-flow.com/help/formats.asp.
An article on different formats for online curricular design.

Matanky, Leonard A. "What We Know About...Computers in Jewish Education." In *What We Know About Jewish Education: A Handbook of Today's Research for Tomorrow's Jewish Education*, edited by Stuart L. Kelman. Los Angeles, CA: Torah Aura Productions, 1992.
An overview of Jewish education and educational technology, research, and implications for Jewish settings.

Mulligan, Sarah A. "Assistive Technology: Supporting the Participation of Children with Disabilities." *Beyond the Journal: Young Children on the Web*. Journal of the National Association for the Education of Young Children (NAEYC). Available online from www.journal.naeyc.org/btj/200311/assistivetechnology.pdf.

Introductory article describing assistive technology for early childhood classrooms.

Romm, Diane. *The Jewish Guide to the Internet* (3rd edition). Northvale, NJ: Jason Aronson, 2003.

A guide to the Jewish Internet, including resources for Jewish education.

Schneider, Roxanne. "Homework Helpers to the Rescue." *Technology and Learning*, October 2001 (Available from www.techlearning.com).

OVERVIEW OF DIFFERENT MODELS OF HOMEWORK HELPERS.

Tomlinson, Carol Ann. "Mapping a Route Toward Differentiated Instruction." *Educational Leadership*, 57:1 (September 1999). Available from www.ascd.org.

INTRODUCTION TO DIFFERENTIATED INSTRUCTION BASED ON CASE STUDIES OF TWO TYPES OF CLASSROOMS.

Woodward, John, and Larry Cuban, eds. *Technology, Curriculum and Professional Development: Adapting Schools to Meet the Needs of Students with Disabilities*. Thousand Oaks, CA: Corwin Press, 2001.

TAM Monograph Series: "Helping Practitioners Use Assistive Technology" (www.tamcec.org).

TAM is the technology and media division of the Council for Exceptional Children. Print publications include *A School Administrator's Desktop Guide to Assistive Technology*, *Technology and Media for Accessing the Curriculum—Instructional Supports for Students with Disabilities*, and *Considering the Need for Assistive Technology within the Individual Education Program*. TAM also publishes *Technology in Action*, available online.

JUDAIC SOFTWARE PUBLISHERS

Below is a partial listing of publishers of Jewish software.

Davka (www.davka.com)

Dor L'Dor (www.dorldor.com)

JeMM Productions (http://ejemm.com)

MATACH: Centre for Educational Technology, Israel (www.cet.ac.il)

T.E.S.—Torah Educational Software (www.jewishsoftware.com)

SPECIAL NEEDS SOFTWARE PUBLISHERS

Below is a partial listing of publishers of assistive technologies and software for learners with special needs.

Ablenet (www.ablenetinc.com)

Attainment Company (www.AttainmentCompany.com)

Crick Software (www.software.com)

Don Johnston (www.donjohnston.com)

Intellitools (www.intellitools.com)

Kurzweil Educational Systems (www.kurzweiledu.com)

Laureate Learning Systems (www.LaureateLearning.com)

WYNN Freedom Scientific (www.FreedomScientific.com)

Please note that there are many other websites and software/hardware publishers and distributors. Those listed are intended to make readers aware of available resources and do not necessarily reflect endorsements of these products.

CHAPTER 25

THE LEARNING CENTER MODEL

Ann Litwack

WHAT IS A LEARNING CENTER?

A learning center is an area that is set up in a classroom and focuses on a specific topic or subject. The materials at a center offer different learning modalities and are displayed in such a way that the students can explore them independently.

For example, a *V'ahavta* learning center might include the following:

- an audiotape of the prayer for students so students can listen
- worksheets to reinforce important roots and vocabulary words found in the prayer
- games to provide students with practice in reading the prayer and translating key words and phrases
- a writing or art project connected to the meaning of the prayer

Centers should provide opportunities for students to work individually as well as collaboratively with other children.

The goal of learning centers is for the students to be actively involved in learning, making choices in a variety of ways, and exploring topics through different modes of learning. The learning center approach to teaching enables students to construct their own understanding of the materials, providing them with a strong foundation on which to build as they increase their Hebrew and Judaic knowledge.

The terms "learning center" and "learning station" are often used interchangeably but are actually different approaches. A "station" contains one specific activity, and generally there are three or four of them so that students can rotate through them. As with learning centers, stations provide opportunities for students to be actively involved in learning and can be set up to include different learning modes. For example, a set of stations for Shabbat might include making *hallah* (tactile), listening to the Friday night blessings (oral), and creating a Shabbat *brakhot* book (visual). The main difference between these two approaches is that learning centers are set up over a long period of time—weeks or months—while stations can change daily. Many of the Shabbat learning center ideas that will be shared in this chapter can be done as individual projects at stations. Both approaches enable students to work in small groups and get more individualized attention from the teacher and peers.

HOW ARE LEARNING CENTERS HELPFUL FOR STUDENTS WITH SPECIAL NEEDS AND DIFFERENT LEARNING STYLES?

Learning centers offer many benefits for students with special needs and their diverse learning styles. Children work independently at centers, allowing the teacher more time to interact with individual students. Centers give teachers the opportunity to meet the needs of individual children through the varied activities offered and the small group size. Since students keep a daily learning log and the teacher has the flexibility to meet with them on a regular basis, the teacher can easily identify the students who need extra help and provide them with the guidance they require.

Students with special needs often have one strong learning mode, while the other modes may be less developed. Learning centers can provide many different learning opportunities, giving students the chance to choose activities at each center that work best for them. In this way, all students are provided with equal opportunity to master the material being taught. Centers help to build self-esteem as students experience success and also help to alleviate behavior problems as the students are actively involved in learning and are allowed to make choices. While whole-class instruction can be successful for a small group of students, learning centers offer exploration, discovery, practice and application of skills, problem solving, and mastery of skills for all children.

HOW DO I SET UP LEARNING CENTERS IN MY CLASSROOM?

A learning center environment looks quite different from a traditional classroom. First divide the room into four or five separate areas. Each center should include a table and some type of small bookshelf or storage bins to make materials easily accessible to the students. Shelves or drawers on wheels allow for easy setup and rearrangement of centers. It is important for each center to have its own space. Dividers or moving bulletin boards are helpful in separating centers. To keep track of students' progress, it is a good idea to have a folder for each child. A good method is to have a storage file crate and file folders of a different color for each class. This allows for easy access for the students and the teachers. At the end of each class session the students can put their work-in-progress in their folders so they can easily find it the next day.

Each center should be clearly labeled. You might want to give each center a Hebrew name; it is a great way for students to begin to recognize important Hebrew words. With young children who are not yet reading, use pictures of Jewish objects or Hebrew letters to identify the centers. Below the title of each center it is important to have clear directions for the students to follow. Directions for young children can be created with pictures, each depicting the different activities they can choose. In addition to the general directions for the center, each individual activity or game should have instructions. Clear labels and directions are the key to successful independent work.

THE TEACHER'S ROLE

The teacher's role in a learning center environment is quite different from that in a traditional classroom, but equally important.

1. The teacher must introduce each new set of learning centers, explaining the materials, location, and name of each center. When using centers for the first time it is important to clearly state and enforce rules:

- maximum number of students at any one center at a time
- respect for the materials at the center
- expectations for cleanup

   During the first couple of weeks the rules should be reviewed regularly, and individual students should be reminded as needed.

2. Each student receives a Student Learning Center Sheet. This sheet contains a list of the centers and the activities available at each one. The students check off each activity as they complete it. The last item on each center sheet is a meeting of the student and teacher. The teacher will look at the work that was completed at the center and, if necessary, ask questions or give the child a check sheet to see if the material at the center has been mastered. If the teacher determines that a child still has work to complete at the center or needs more practice to master a skill, specific activities are then marked on the Student Learning Center Sheet. The student returns to the center and completes the activities.

3. When not meeting with a student, the teacher can float around the room and make sure the students are on task. The teacher is available to answer any questions students may have.

THE STUDENT'S ROLE

It is a privilege for students to be able to work independently and with their peers. Before students can participate at the learning centers, special rules must be established. Consequences need to be set up for students who abuse materials and/or "goof off". The students need to be clearly told that they are responsible for their learning. One way to hold students accountable for their learning is have them fill out a learning log at the end of each day (see _____). Each student enters the date, the center at which he or she worked, what was accomplished, and what the plan is for the next day. Younger students can have learning logs with pictures of the different activities at each center and can circle what they completed on that day and what they plan to do during the next class session. The students' job is to use the Learning Center Sheet to guide them through the centers and to independently complete the activities that will best help them master the material. Before going on to a new center each student must have a conference with the teacher and share the work he/she did at the center. At any time a student can decide whether he or she needs help and can choose to meet with a teacher.

EVALUATION

Evaluating each student's progress may prove to be easier in a learning center classroom. Since children work independently at centers, it frees the teacher to interact with and monitor students on a regular basis. There is more time for the teacher to confer with each student and to keep anecdotal records.

It is important that a regular evaluation procedure be established. When a student completes the activities at a center, an evaluation conference can be set up with the teacher. At this time the student can share his or her accomplishments and discuss any concerns. The conference time is spent in dialogue, which allows both the teacher and the child to ask and respond to questions and concerns. The teacher might also ask the student to demonstrate his or her newly acquired skills or knowledge. This can be done through questions asked by the teacher or by having students complete a test that covers the concepts and skills learned at the center. The teacher should create a specific block of time when s/he can be available for conferences and establish a procedure for students to sign up for a meeting. One good method is to have the students write their names on the chalkboard when they are ready to meet. The teacher can call the child over at the appropriate time. This allows the students to continue to work while waiting for their conference. Students should know in advance what materials they are responsible for bringing to the conference. The teacher might create a conference preparation checklist that could be kept in each student's folder for future reference.

The daily learning log, mentioned above, is another important evaluation tool. These logs should be checked regularly by the teacher and be evaluated for patterns that might show where a child is having difficulty. For example, if a child records doing the same thing over several days and does not appear to be making progress, the teacher should have a conference with the child and help to find a successful way for the student to complete the necessary work at the center. The most important aspect of the evaluation conference is that leadership and responsibility should be shared by the student and the teacher.

FINAL NOTE

Learning centers can be a challenging and exciting experience for both students and teachers. Here are some responses to centers by students: "Wow, has it really been two hours? I can't believe it has been that long." "I remember sitting at my desk last year, and the time went so slowly." Learning centers can provide an opportunity for exploration, discovery, problem solving, and mastery for both the teacher and the students.

SHABBAT LEARNING CENTERS (K–3rd grade)

INTRODUCTION

This cluster of Shabbat centers was created to provide students with the opportunity to explore the Kabbalat Shabbat rituals, learn the blessings, and create special Shabbat objects. An important additional component of this unit is to have a parent education session. Parents have the opportunity to learn about the Shabbat rituals and how to bring them into their homes in a meaningful way. This can be done through a family Shabbat program in which the parents are invited to come to class with their children and learn about Shabbat together. Having parents involved makes the learning centers more meaningful as the students connect what they are learning with their own personal Shabbat experiences.

PREPARATION

There are four kindergarten–third grade Shabbat learning centers:

- The Shabbat Table
- Creation
- Shabbat In A Box
- Shabbat Games

The room is divided into five areas. The four main areas contains the following:

- table
- four to six chairs (depending on the number of students in the class)
- materials
- drawers or shelves for the materials to be stored in
- sign containing the name of the center
- instruction sheet for the center and for individual activities

The fifth and smallest area of the room is for evaluation meetings and is set up with a small table and a couple of chairs. A learning center sheet is created that contains the name of each center and the activities that are available there. These are the basic preparations for all the centers. The specific materials and individualized setup for each center is listed below.

1. THE SHABBAT TABLE CENTER

This center includes five different activities:

1. Setting the Shabbat table
2. Learning Friday night *brakhot*,
3. Using the Shabbat *brakhot* book,
4. Creating a Shabbat placemat
5. Celebrating Shabbat at home

At this center it is helpful to have several small tables, each set up for one of the activities, or a box/drawer for each activity that contains all the necessary materials for completing the project.

1. SETTING THE SHABBAT TABLE

Materials needed:

1 small table

1 tablecloth
1 hallah cover
1 kidush cup
1 set Shabbat candleholders and candles
1 hallah (*hallot* made from baked play dough or plastic hallah will work best)
4 kippot
Various ritual object used for other Jewish holidays, such as a menorah, seder plate, and shofar
Pictures of Shabbat objects and rituals
Index cards

Goal: The goal of this activity is for the students to become familiar with the ritual objects and foods used for Kabbalat Shabbat and with their names.

Setup: A small table is set up with ah tablecloth on it and chairs around it. A shelf or drawer nearby contains a hallah cover, hallah, kiddush cup, set of Shabbat candle holders, candles, kippot, and various other ritual objects such as a menorah, seder plate, and matzah cover. Index cards are created containing the Hebrew word for each Shabbat item with a picture of it. Pictures of Kabbalat Shabbat objects and rituals are put up on the walls or bulletin boards at the Shabbat Table center. Having a tape recorder and a tape of the blessing for children to listen to is a great addition to this activity.

Activity: The object ofthis activity is for the students to select the correct items for setting the Shabbat table, to learn the Hebrew names of Shabbat objects, and be introduced to the Kabbalat Shabbat blessings. The students begin by setting the Shabbat table with the correct ritual objects. Once the table has been set, the students will take the index cards with the name of each Shabbat object in Hebrew and a picture of the object and match them with the Shabbat icons on the table. This provides even the youngest students the opportunity to begin to recognize Hebrew Shabbat words. Children can check themseles and see if they have put the right object on the table. After setting the table the children practice the rituals of lighting the candles, saying Kiddush over the wine, and *ha-Motzi* over the hallah. It is beneficial to have a teacher or aide available to talk with the students while they are setting the table. He/she can ask the students about what objects they are putting on the table and why they chose them. The teacher can also introduce the students to the Hebrew names for the objects through dialogue with the children. For example, if a child says that he is putting the bread on the table, the teacher can respond by saying, "Yes, you ar putting the hallah on the table." The teacher can then ask the student again what he has put on the table, give the child an opportunity to use the new Hebrew word that he has learned. In this way the teacher validates the student's response and introduces him to the Hebrew word "*hallah*". With older students you might want to focus on recognizing and reading the Hebrew Shabbat words associated with each of the objects and/or reading the blessings. The teacher can also help the students to practice the blessings over the candles, wine, and hallah.

Evaluation: To evaluate a student's understanding of the Shabbat ritual objects, their uses, and Hebrew names, you might have the child draw a picture of a table with all the objects needed to welcome Shabbat on Friday night. Talk to the child about the drawing when it is completed. Ask the name of each of the objects drawn and what is the function of each. This will enable you to see if the student is familiar with the Hebrew name of each object and its use. Older students can be asked to label their objects in Hebrew or to read and match the Hebrew Shabbat names with pictures of the objects.

Conclusion: When a child has completed the activity, he/she should put all of the objects away carefully so that they are ready for the next person. Some children may want to do this activity more than once, especially the younger ones. The more the students practice, the more comfortable they will be with the Shabbat words and rituals.

2. FRIDAY NIGHT *BRAKHOT*

Materials needed:

    2 tape recorders

    Earphones

    Tape with the blessings for Shabbat candles, wine, and hallah.

    Blank tapes

    2 sets of blessings cards (each card should contain one of the blessings in Hebrew with an English translation and a picture of what it is for)

Goal: The goal of this center is for the students to learn the blessings that are said over the Shabbat candles, the wine, and the hallah and to create a tape of themselves singing the blessings that they can take home and use to teach the blessings to their families.

Setup: Set up the tape recorder with the Shabbat blessing tape and earphones at a table, along with two sets of blessing cards. Encourage older students to use the blessing cards to follow along with the tape. For younger students you can create a special tape with turn-the-page signals and the blessings in a booklet format. This way they can connect the blessings with the objects. The second tape recorder can be set up at the other end of the table. Once a student feels he/she knows the blessings, he/she can record him/herself singing them.

Activity: A student begins this center by putting on the earphones and listening to the blessings over the candles, wine, and hallah. Students are encouraged to listen to the blessings several times. When a child feels he knows the blessings well, he/she can move to the other tape recorder and make his/her own blessing tape.

Evaluation: To evaluate what the student has learned from this activity, the teacher listens with the student to the recording he/she made to check for accuracy or has the child sing the blessings to her. In addition, the student could match the blessings to pictures of what is being blessed.

3. SHABBAT *BRAKHOT* BOOK

Materials needed:

    Construction paper

    Marking pens

    Old magazines

    Scissors

    Glue sticks

    Copies of the blessings (one for each child)

Goal: The goal of this center is for each child to create a Shabbat *brakhot* book to use at home. For this book to be useful for the whole family, it should contain each blessing in Hebrew, transliteration, and English. Remember, some family members may not know Hebrew and will be left out if there is no transliteration available.

Setup: The materials listed above, along with an instruction sheet, should be set up at the table or put together on a shelf or in a drawer that is easily accessible.

Activity: The students create a special page for each Shabbat blessing. They either cut out or write the blessing in Hebrew, transliteration, and English. The children then decorate their blessing pages with corresponding pictures. After completing a page for each blessing the students create a cover. This is a good opportunity to teach or review the Hebrew word Shabbat, guiding the students to write it in Hebrew on the cover of their books. They can decorate their covers with symbols of Shabbat.

Evaluation: To evaluate a student's understanding of the *brakhot* book, look through the book with the student and have each student read and explain the blessings.

4. SHABBAT PLACEMATS

  Materials needed:
  - Construction paper
  - Sequins
  - Glitter
  - Marking pens
  - Contact paper
  - Scissors

Goal: The aim of this activity is for the students to review the Shabbat symbols they know while creating a special placemat to use at home for Shabbat.

Setup: The supplies listed above are placed together. The contact paper should be precut to fit over the construction paper. For really young students it may be helpful to precut some Shabbat symbols out of construction paper, such as a ḥallah, ḥallah cover, Torah, candlesticks, and kiddush cup. Older children can include Hebrew Shabbat words with their Hebrew names or the Friday night blessings on their placemats.

Activity: A student creates a Shabbat placemat by taking a piece of construction paper and arranging Shabbat symbols, Shabbat words, sequins, glitter, and Shabbat pictures they have made. It is helpful to have an aide or teacher available to help students put the contact paper over their designs to seal them onto the construction paper. There are many variations that can be done with this project depending on the age of the children. Placemats can be created to show how Shabbat is celebrated in each child's home, in another country, or illustrating a new Shabbat tradition they would like to begin.

Evaluation: To evaluate what a child has learned, have a conversation with the teacher about what he/she has created. Through this dialogue you will be able to get a sense of the child's understanding of Shabbat and the rituals connected to it.

5. CLASS BOOK: SHABBAT AT YOUR HOUSE

  Materials needed:
  Tag board paper
  Marking pens
  Pencils

Goal: The goal of this project is for students to gain knowledge about different Shabbat traditions and to create a personal connection to Shabbat by writing and drawing about how they celebrate it in their homes.

Setup: The materials listed above are placed where the children can easily access them. For younger students who do not have the writing skills, it may be helpful to have a teacher or aide available to take dictation.

Activity: Each child takes a piece of tag board paper and draws and/or writes about how his or her family celebrates Shabbat at home. Students who do not have the writing skills can dictate their stories to the teacher. An interesting addition to this assignment might be having students bring pictures of their families celebrating Shabbat together to add to their pages. All of the pages will be put together to make a class book. One book can be made, allowing the children to take turns bringing it home to share with their families. The book can also be copied so that each child can have a copy to take home and keep.

Evaluation: To evaluate the child's understanding of this project, have him/her share the page that he/she created. Ask him/her questions about the family traditions that he/she has written about and illustrated.

THE CREATION CENTER

This center contains three different activities:

1. The Story of Creation
2. Make a creation book
3. Play the "Creation" game

Each of these activities is designed to enhance the students' understanding of the story of Creation and its connection to Shabbat.

1. The Story of Creation: This activity enables the children to become familiar with the story of Creation by reading, looking at illustrations, and listening to different versions. Having several different picture books of the story available allows students to compare and contrast how the story was interpreted by different authors and artists. For children who are not yet reading, provide a tape of the story with turn-the-page signals .

2. Make a Creation Book: The students create their own Creation book. For each day of Creation they make a separate page on which they will illustrate what was created on that day and write the day of the week on it. Older students can write the days of the week in Hebrew. For the seventh day the students write Shabbat in Hebrew and illustrate how they think God rested on that day. Once they have created all of the pages for their book they are ready to create a cover. Younger students might title the book "In the Beginning" or *Bereshit*, while older ones write *Bereshit* in Hebrew as their title. The students can practice reading their books to each other and can take them home to share with their families.

3. Play the "Creation" Game: This game is played like "Old Maid". The deck contains four sets of cards depicting the six days of Creation and one "Shabbat card". The children collect pairs of the different days of Creation by picking cards from their teammates' hands. If they get a pair, they put it down in front of them. The person who is left with the "Shabbat" card is the winner. For older students, the Hebrew names for each day of Creation can be added to the cards. When a child gets a pair, he/she says the Hebrew name before putting it down.

SHABBAT IN A BOX CENTER

This center contains three different activities:

1. Shabbat Feely Box
2. Create Your Own Shabbat Objects
3. Make a Shabbat Box

These activities enable the students to explore the Shabbat ritual objects through touch.

1. Shabbat Feely Box: To create a Shabbat feely box for the students, take a large box and cut a hole in the lid or on the side of the box so that children can put their hands inside and feel objects without seeing them. Inside the box put a candle, candlestick, hallah cover, hallah, and Kiddush cup. The students take turns putting their hands in and feeling the different Shabbat objects, guessing what they are. For older students, have cards containing the Hebrew word for each object that the students match with the object after pulling it out of the feely box.

2. Create Your Own Shabbat Objects: The students will be able to create their own hallah cover, Kiddush cup, and candle holders. A variety of different materials can be used to create these ritual objects. See Appendix for books containing Shabbat craft ideas.

3. Create a Special Shabbat Box: Ask each student to bring a shoebox from home. The students can use fabric, sequins, glitter, and fancy papers to create a Shabbat box in which to keep all of their Shabbat ritual objects. On the top of the box they can write the word "Shabbat" in Hebrew. After rotating through all the Shabbat centers they can take this box home. It should contain candle holders, Kiddush cup, hallah cover, recipe for hallah, Shabbat placemat, and the Shabbat tape and book created by the students. An interesting addition to this activity can be to have the students take a picture of their families using the items in the Shabbat box on a Friday night and write about their experience of celebrating Shabbat using their new ritual objects.

SHABBAT GAMES CENTER

This center contains four different activities:

1. "Set the Shabbat Table" game
2. Shabbat sequence cards
3. Shabbat Charades
4. Make your own Shabbat Memory game

These activities enable the students to review and practice the Shabbat rituals, Shabbat objects and their Hebrew names, and the order of the Kabbalat Shabbat table service.

1. "Set The Shabbat Table" Game: This game is played much like "Go Fish". Each student has a rectangular or square piece of felt that represents the Shabbat table. The object of the game is to get all of the Shabbat objects and people on your Shabbat table, making pairs of Shabbat objects with the Hebrew letter with which they begin. The deck of cards contains four sets of *yeled, yaldah, ima, abba, dag, narot, yayin,* and hallah cards. It also contains enough *yud, alef, dalet, nun,* and hallah cards to match with each of the Shabbat object cards that begin with that letter. There are two special cards in the deck: (1) Clear the Shabbat table—if this card is picked, all items on the player's Shabbat table must be returned to the Shabbat bag. (2) Pick any item for your Shabbat table—this card enables the student to choose any item he/she needs from the Shabbat bag. The Shabbat bag contains pictures (four of each one) of: *ima, abba, yeled, yaldah, dag, narot, yayin,* and *hallah* with Velcro on the back so that they can attach to the felt tables. Each student is given a felt table and is dealt four cards. The players check to see if they have any pairs (picture and Hebrew letter with which it begins). If they do, they put the pairs down, and for each pair they have, they take the item from the Shabbat bag. For example, if a child had an *alef* and an *abba* card, he/she takes an *abba* picture card from the Shabbat bag. The players take turns asking for picture or letter cards to make pairs. If the person they ask does not have the needed card, he/she says "Shabbat Shalom," and the player picks a card from the pile. Play then goes to the next person. If a child gets a pair, he/she puts it down and chooses that item from the Shabbat bag. The first player to get all the Shabbat people and items at his/her table and to make pairs with all his/her cards is the winner.

2. Shabbat Sequence Cards: Each of these cards contains a picture of a different part of the Kabbalat Shabbat table service: (1) setting the table, (2) lighting the candles, (3) saying Kiddush, (4) saying *Ha-Motzi* over the *hallah* and eating the Shabbat meal, and (5) singing *z'mirot* after dinner. The children try to put the cards in the correct order, checking themselves by looking on the back of each card and seeing if the numbers are in the correct order. To personalize this game, photos of the children doing the Shabbat rituals in the classroom can be used.

3. Shabbat Charades: Students take turns acting out different parts of the Shabbat service, having the others guess what they are doing. Older students, in addition to guessing the part of the service, guess what blessing is being said. Pictures of the Friday night table rituals can be put on different cards. These can be folded and put in a basket, having the children take turns picking a card and acting out what is on the card.

4. Make Your Own Shabbat Memory Game: The students create their own Shabbat Memory games using index cards and marking pens. Depending on the age of the children, they can make matching Shabbat object cards, Shabbat object and first letter of Hebrew word matching cards, or Shabbat object and Hebrew name matching cards. They can use the cards to play with their classmates and to take home to practice with their families.

SHABBAT LEARNING CENTERS—FOURTH–SIXTH GRADE LEVEL

A. FRIDAY NIGHT *BRAKHOT*

1. Listen and practice singing the Friday night blessings.
    a. Candles
    b. Full Kiddush
    c. *Ha-Motzi*
    d. *Birkat ha-Mazon*
2. Learn key vocabulary words, roots, and meanings of the blessings by completing worksheets from each of the *brakhot* folders.

B. FRIDAY NIGHT SYNAGOGUE SERVICE

1. Siddur Scavenger Hunt. Locate different prayers in the siddur and answer questions about them.

2. Prayer Boxes. Each prayer box contains objects and words that are clues to the meaning of each prayer. The object is to guess the name of the prayer represented by each box. The students can check their answers.

3. Create Your Own Prayerbook
   a. *Lekha Dodi*
   b. *Barkhu*
   c. *Shma/V'Ahavta*
   d. *Mi Khamokha*
   e. *Avot/V'Imahot*
   f. *Shalom Rav/Oseh Shalom*

4. Prayer Posters. Research one of the prayers and create a poster that includes the meaning of the prayer, the prayer in Hebrew with your own translation, and key words and roots from the prayer.

C. SHABBAT CUSTOMS

1. Research how Shabbat is celebrated in another country. Create a poster or diorama that shows the Shabbat traditions in the country researched.

2. Create interview questions to ask your parents and grandparents about how they celebrated Shabbat growing up and what they do today.

3. Write and illustrate a page for a class book about Shabbat traditions in your family. Include information you learned in the interview with your parents and grandparents.

4. Create a Shabbat tradition you would like to start with your family. Describe the tradition and why you chose it.

D. HAVDALAH

1. Create a Havdalah kit:
   a. Havdalah candle
   b. *Besamim* box
   c. Havdalah *brackot* book

2. Learn the Havdalah blessings
   a. Listen to the blessings on tape
   b. Practice reading and singing the brakhot

E. BONUS CENTER

1. Shabbat Newspaper—create a puzzle, game, or article based on what you have learned about Shabbat at the different centers.

2. Create a game, activity, or worksheet to add to one of the centers.

CHAPTER 26

INSTRUCTIONAL GAMES

Jennifer Malka Rudo

Instructional games provide a variety of services in the classroom. They can be used to review, re-teach, drill, and introduce material. What an instructional game provides is based on how the game is structured and where it is used in the lesson. Keep the following questions in mind when deciding if a game is the appropriate activity:

1. Do the students possess the social skills required to play the game?
2. Will the game provide a different way to teach the material so those students with different learning styles can benefit?

Instructional games provide numerous benefits through their ability to employ a variety of teaching styles so that students who are auditory, visual, and kinesthetic learners are able to access information easily. An issue a teacher may encounter when implementing games is the social aspect. Students need to have a clear understanding of what is considered acceptable behavior in the class. *Derekh Eretz*, translated as "way of the land" or "manners", can be a catch-phrase meaning how to act.

Prior to playing any game in the class it is wise to teach students appropriate social skills. It is important to make certain that the students feel good about their level of participation.

Classroom game rules should be set up by the students with the guidance of the teacher. The following is a sampling of rules.

- Each group is a team. Team members help other team members.
- Every team member must be consulted prior to asking the teacher for help.
- Knowledge, effort, and support are rewarded.
- It is equally important to teach students how to help one another.

How do I help my teammates?

1. Identify the problem. (Point to the letter, vowel, etc.)
2. Identify what is correct. (Point to the beginning, middle, end, letter, etc.)
3. Give clues.

Reading	Vocabulary
Similar-sounding letter or vowel	Roots
Write another word that is similar	Prefixes
Visual tricks	Suffixes
Vowel / Letter chart, etc.	Context, etc.

4. Give part of the answer—the very LAST step.

Instructional games are used for a variety of educational purposes. Two primary aims are skill reinforcement and enabling students to apply a previously taught skill to a new task. The purpose of the game should be to teach a skill, not the game. Therefore, when selecting a game, keep the following questions in mind:

1. Do the students possess the independent work skills required to play the game?
2. Do the students possess the social skills needed to work as a team?
3. Is there enough time for the activity? Will every child get an opportunity to engage in the activity?
4. Are the directions clearly stated and/or written?
5. Is there a plan to transition in and out of the game?

When introducing a new game, it is a good practice to teach it to the whole class. Everyone should play, including the teacher. The teacher's participation can be an excellent way to model the behavior and educational goals desired in the game. Students can be preoccupied with the accumulation of points. Therefore, depending on the class, it may be a good practice to set up a point system to be used for all games.

Below is a sample point system:

Complete the task independently: 2 points.
Complete the task with help: 1 point.
Person or team that assists: 1 point.

Participation, teamwork, and effort are rewarded. A point system that allows and gives credit to students who help each other fosters an environment based on community and learning. not winning.

Once the structure is in place, it is time to play. The initial work to ensure that games are used in a meaningful manner may seem overwhelming, but in the long term it is critical to student success. Give one of the following examples a try!

SELECTED INSTRUCTIONAL GAMES

Game/Brief Description	Rules	Learning Styles Utilized
Dot Game (Teams) Corrected answers are rewarded by connecting dots. Obj: Draw a shape	Draw 5 rows of 6 dots each on the board. Students need to complete a task (e.g., read a word). Students who complete the task correctly may draw a line connecting two dots. No diagonal lines. The person who draws the last line to make a box writes his team's name in the box. Points are awarded for the most boxes.	Visual, auditory
Baseball (2 teams) Allow students to choose the topic and difficulty level of question. Each corner of the room is a base.	Three corners in the room are bases. Home is your seat. Write the batting order on the board so you are not confused. Pick a topic for the game (e.g., reading or vocabulary). When a student goes to bat he chooses a single, double, or triple. There are no home runs. The difficulty of the question should increase with the number of bases. A correct answer allows the player to move around the bases. An incorrect answer is a strike. Three strikes for a team and everyone sits down. Alternate between the two teams for batting. One team should not wait until the other is out to bat.	Auditory and kinesthetic primarily

SELECTED INSTRUCTIONAL GAMES

Game/Brief Description	Rules	Learning Styles Utilized
Chalkboard Draw (2 teams) Teacher says a letter, and the first student to write it down and turn around gets the point.	Draw a line down the center of the board. Teams pick a letter for their team. Call up one person from each team to the appropriate side of the board. Dictate a letter and vowel (i.e., write one letter and vowel that makes the sound "Sa." The correct answer is either *Samekh* or *Sin* and any "ah" vowel) The first person to write the correct answer and turn around gets the point. If the student doesn't turn around, the assumption is that student is still thinking, and no points are awarded.	Auditory and kinesthetic
Stuffed Animal Toss Say a vocabulary word and get the meaning back.	Everyone stands in a circle. Toss the stuffed animal to a student. Say a word in Hebrew for him to translate. The student translates the word and tosses the animal back. One can play with outs or not. Student sits down if the answer is incorrect. The person left standing is the vocabulary master for the day.	Auditory and kinesthetic
Stuffed Animal Hot Potato Pass the animal until someone says stop. Teacher reads word; if student is correct, then he says "stop" next.	Sit in a circle on the floor. Select a page for reading. The teacher is in charge first. The teacher passes the animal around the circle. Students' eyes are closed. When the teacher says stop, the person holding the animal must read from the page. If he reads correctly, the student is in charge; if not, the teacher remains in charge. The student closes his eyes and gets to say stop.	Kinesthetic
Hebrew Dice Game (multiple groups) Roll the die. Find all the words on a selected page that use the letter on the die. Take turns reading them.	Divide into several groups or partners. Select a Hebrew page to work with. Give each group a die with Hebrew letters. Each group rolls the die. Using the letter on the die, they must find all the words that begin with that letter (or you could do end with that letter). As a group they may decode the words. When they are ready they raise their hands to get teacher's attention. The group must read all the words they found. For each word read correctly, give 2 points. They then roll again. The winning group is the one who managed to read the most words in the time allotted for the game.	Kinesthetic, visual

SELECTED INSTRUCTIONAL GAMES

Game/Brief Description	Rules	Learning Styles Utilized
Dice Reading Game (multiple groups or partners) Roll the dice. Count that many words from the last word read and read it.	Divide into groups or partners. Select a reading page. Give each group regular dice. Each person gets an individual turn. Roll the dice. Start at the first word and count the number of words rolled. This is the word the person reads, or the teacher can have that person read the number of words rolled. If he reads correctly, it is worth 2 points. If he reads with help, it is worth 1 point. The next person rolls the dice. He starts counting where the last person stopped. He continues to the end of the page and then goes back up to the top. Points can be gotten individually in the group or by a team point count. The team point count fosters the feeling of community.	Primarily visual; kinesthetic
Flashcard Round Robin (teams or partners) Students show their card, allowing all to have an opportunity to try to read it correctly.	1. Divide the students into groups or partners. 2. Each student has 5 flashcards. 3. They take turns showing their cards to each other. 4. The cards are shown until all the cards are read. 5. Points are awarded for correct reading. 6. Points can be tracked as a team or individually.	Primarily visual Auditory
In-line Reading or Vocabulary (teams) Students stand in line and read as they come to the front.	Divide the students into two groups. Have the students stand in two lines in front of teacher. The teacher holds flashcards for the students to read or state the meaning. Show the card to one team and then the other until one team gets it correct. That team receives a point. As each student takes his turn he goes to the end of the line.	Visual, kinesthetic
Find That Word Student reads word on page. The first person who successfully finds the word gets to read the next word to be found.	Give the students a few minutes to study a page of text. Each student should pick out 3–4 words he likes. Select one person to start. This student will read the word selected. The first person to find it and raise his hand gets to read a word of his or her choosing. Keep finding words until the time has elapsed. This is a great sight-reading builder.	Visual
Flashcard Tic-Tac-Toe (teams) Earn a square by reading the word correctly. Earn a bonus point for stating the meaning of the word.	Create a Tic-Tac-Toe board on the blackboard. Instead of it being 3 x 3, make it 8 x 8. Place flashcards in each empty space on the board. Above the board place Hebrew letters or numbers. Divide the class into two teams. When it is a student's turn, he picks a flashcard using the coordinates provided (Column 2, Row Gimel, etc.) The student completes the task. Read; state the meaning, etc. Take the card off the board and mark it with the team's letter. When all the cards are gone, count up how many tic-tac-toes (3 in a row) each team has. That is the winner.	Visual

SELECTED INSTRUCTIONAL GAMES

Game/Brief Description	Rules	Learning Styles Utilized
Syllable Bingo (individual or teams) Students paste words under the column that corresponds to the number of syllables. When complete, play Bingo.	Give the students a sheet with words to cut up. The bingo sheet has columns labeled 1,2,3,4. The students glue the words in the columns that correspond to the number of syllables in the word. Each board should be different but should show evidence that the student can break down a difficult word. Play Bingo with the boards they created.	Kinesthetic, visual, auditory

Points to remember:

- Games should be first utilized in whole-class settings.
- Model and ask other students to model how to earn helping points in the game, if applicable.
- Keep rules and point structures consistent from game to game.
- Have fun!

CHAPTER 27

BUILDING BRIDGES THROUGH MUSIC AND MOVEMENT EXPERIENCES IN THE CLASSROOM

Ronna S. Kaplan

WHY MUSIC?

Music transcends cultural and language barriers. It is a universal language.

Premature infants in the neonatal intensive care unit (NICU) "calm to music stimuli."[1] A lullaby sung and recorded by a mother and played frequently for the infant in the NICU "becomes familiar and comforting, promotes bonding, and provides a familiar reference for the infant when the transition to the home environment is made."[2] Research has shown that the "portions of the brain that respond to music are the last to deteriorate in illnesses affecting the brain."[3] We can therefore come full circle in sharing music with people of all ages, from babies to *bubbies*. It is also interesting to note that "language/speech and language/music appear to follow similar developmental patterns and have been found to occupy adjacent areas of the brain."[4]

Music occurs naturally in our environment in many settings. It is a key component of daily and weekly Jewish worship as well as of all our holidays and life-cycle events. It links us with our families, friends, and fellow Jews all over the world and with past and future generations. We learn the music of our ancestors and pass it on, ever broadening the repertoire. We create rich memories of past important events and often experience strong emotional reactions to particular selections.

Not only do we Jews experience music in our liturgy, but we experience it in many other everyday events. There is music at sporting events, at concerts, to accompany other cultural events such as plays and ballets, in shopping malls, in elevators, and in doctors' offices. The actual practice of music therapy occurs in early intervention centers, preschools, schools, hospitals, hospice programs, community-based facilities, home-based programs, day care settings, group homes, residential treatment centers, nursing homes, prisons, and more.

Music is a socially appropriate activity and leisure skill. One can act as listener, player, singer, dancer, composer, or a combination thereof. Participation in movement and music experiences

---

[1] Collins, S. K. & K. Kuck. "Music Therapy in the Neonatal Intensive Care Unit." *Neonatal Network*, 1991, 9 (6), pp. 23—26.

[2] Standley, J. M. *Music Therapy with Premature Infants: Research and Developmental Interventions.* Silver Spring, Maryland: The American Music Therapy Association, 2003, p. 31

[3] Chavin, Melanie. *The Lost Chord: Reaching the Person with Dementia through the Power of Music.* Mt. Airy, Maryland: ElderSong Publications, Inc., 1991, p. 1.

[4] Michel, Donald & Janet Jones. *Music for Developing Speech and Language Skills in Children: A Guide for Parents and Therapists.* Denton, Texas: 1991, p. 7.

may provide a predictable time-oriented and reality-oriented structure while offering opportunities for participation at one's own level of functioning and ability. A child with a severe physical disability may simply activate a switch or augmentative communication device to make a sound on an instrument to play his part, while someone else may sing or play independently. These experiences may be adapted for group or individual involvement as well.

It should be noted that people with disabilities are not necessarily disabled in their musical skills. Not only may music and movement experiences "be opportunities for a child to 'shine,'" but also they may be used to reinforce nonmusical goals."[5] "Particularly for the child who excels in music these activities can be used to help overcome weaknesses or to reinforce what the student has already learned."[6]

Music stimulates more than one sense and involves the child at many levels. Music can be highly motivating but also may have a calming and relaxing effect. Music and movement experiences in the classroom can be designed to be success-oriented and to help children feel good about themselves. Music and movement experiences may encourage socialization, self-expression, communication, and motor development.

In general, both research and practice in music therapy have greatly influenced the use of music and movement experiences adapted to the needs of children with special needs in educational settings.

USES OF MUSIC AND MOVEMENT IN THE CLASSROOM

Music as a carrier of information: Song lyrics often carry information that gives directions, signals transitions, or teaches academic concepts/skills. The song "Put Your Finger in the Air" tells us where to put our finger in each verse. In teaching Hebrew vocabulary and body parts, lyrics could incorporate *rosh* for head, *regel* for foot, and so on. At the end of an activity or class the teacher can sing *"Shalom Haverim,"* at first to the entire group and then to each child, inserting his/her name instead of *"haverim"* to signal when it is time for each student to walk to the door.

Music as a reinforcer: Music listening, singing chosen songs, playing instruments, and/or moving and dancing serve to reinforce completion of less preferred tasks. Music as a reinforcer may be delivered either individually or in a group. Headphones are frequently used to individualize the experience. Hearing one's own music (sung or played) is often very reinforcing and motivating to the child. One example of this principle is to allow a student to complete musical lessons and play musical games on the computer following his Torah portion chanting practice.

Music as a background for learning: Listening to music is utilized in some classrooms or other environments to help filter out sounds that might otherwise be distracting. Background music can also be used to set a particular mood, either calming or stimulating. Music can easily be related to classroom themes such as holidays, seasons, or special topics being studied in the classroom.

Music as a physical structure for a learning activity: Certain music and movement experiences can be systematically designed to provide structured opportunities to practice a particular skill or to set the occasion for a behavior to occur. For example, the dance to

---

[5] *Music Therapy and the Young Child Fact Sheet.* Silver Spring, Maryland: American Music Therapy Association, 1999.
[6] Davis, Ronna. "Living with Learning Disabilities: How Music Therapy Can Help Kids Cope." *Wellspring.* Sarasota, Florida: Ruggles Publishing Company, 1987, p. 27.

the song *"Akhshav"* could be introduced to give children a structured opportunity to cooperate and interact appropriately with a partner. Likewise, the dance *"Tcherkiziya"* with the following lyrics: "You don't do the hora/ You just take a step or two/ It's called the *Tcherkiziya*/ Here's all you gotta do/ La, la, la…" offers a chance for the children to be leaders and to follow the leader in the "La" section.

Music as a reflection of skills or processes to be learned: Finally, some musical tasks are similar to nonmusical tasks. For example, one could compare hitting a woodblock to hitting with a hammer. Using two hands to play an instrument is similar to other bilateral tasks. And reading a song sheet is another venue in which to practice the nonmusical skill of visually tracking from left to right and top to bottom.

SUCCESS STORIES

Children with varying disabilities and levels of functioning may be included and participate effectively in general music classes in Jewish day or supplementary schools. They may sing, play instruments, and move within their capabilities. Adaptations may be made for their success. Large-print song sheets for those with visual impairments or sitting next to a peer partner may help encourage appropriate interaction. Color coding may be utilized to signify the various Torah and Haftarah trope symbols. Backward chaining, where one teaches the last verse first and then adds each prior verse one by one to the entire portion, gradually increases the complexity and length of the task as well as the duration of participation, while helping the child feel secure and gain a sense of accomplishment.

Children with disabilities may participate successfully in the congregational junior choir. Even if a child with a learning disability cannot read the song sheets well, he/she may learn the music by rote. And of course, children with physical disabilities need to be given accessibility to the space where the performance will take place and a chair in which to sit, if necessary. Participating in the junior choir is another way in which the child may excel and feel more a part of the life of the synagogue and congregation.

Music in self-contained classes for children with special needs in engaging the more resistant students. For example, with older, high-functioning students, playing "Name That Prayer," a variation on "Name That Tune," encourages recognition, participation, reading, and singing Shabbat prayers necessary in preparation for their bar and bat mitzvah ceremonies.

Use of accompaniment instruments such as the QChord (an electronic instrument where one pushes chord buttons and strums)[7] is a way to engage a nonverbal student in musical experiences. It also provides variety for the verbal students, and can be used as a reinforcer.

Finally, teaching the entire class the sign language for the first line of the *Shema* was helpful in preparing a nonverbal student and typical students enjoy learning sign as well.

A few years ago I taught a class called *Kol Ivrit*, the premise of which was that Hebrew could be taught through music and voice, mostly by rote, as the two students were not yet successful English readers. In this class we frequently played the rhythm sticks or hand drums to echo lines of prayers. An "echo microphone" was passed from student to student to signal when it was each one's turn to sing or chant portions of *brakhot*. Movement activities such as passing a beanbag to another person while reciting one word of a prayer, or walking on one construction-paper footstep per word, maintained attention and provided repetition and review. Both boys' abilities to recite all or part of the Shabbat candle blessing, Kiddush, *Motzi*, Havdalah

---

[7]Suzuki Corporation, San Diego, California (www.suzukimusic.com).

blessings, *Shema, Barkhu, Mi Khamokha,* and *Oseh Shalom* increased from when the prayers were initially introduced to later in the year. It should be noted that two teenagers acted as "shadows" and role models for the students in this class.

The following are some tried and true suggested *general teaching strategies/techniques* for children who are "typically developing" or who have varying abilities/disabilities.

- **Modeling/imitation (motor/vocal/verbal):** Many songs and movement games have this built into them.

- **Hand-over-hand physical assistance** may be given if it is truly needed, and then the teacher or aide should try to fade out this extra help.

- **Rehearsal:** Practice is an important part of learning. Repetition strengthens association and improves memory. Music and movement activities can add variety to otherwise potentially boring drills.

- **Visual cues:** Pictures, symbols (including *Boardmaker* Picture Communication Symbols), and words, e.g., "stop" and "go" signs, are useful.

- **Holding objects near one's face** may help the adult gain a child's eye contact.

- **"Chunking":** This is a technique described to me by a speech therapist. She states that we learn phone numbers through "chunking." We do not memorize each isolated number. Rather, we piece together the first three numbers as a unit and then the second group of four numbers as a unit. Now, of course, we have to deal with area codes as well! Children might learn the sequence of the Hebrew alphabet in this manner, by singing Debbie Friedman's "Aleph Bet" song in its echoed sections.

- **Word recall-completion:** Start saying or chanting a line of a prayer and see if your students can fill in the blank when you stop.

- **Variation of pitch/volume:** Teachers can vary the volume of their voices to denote something important (loud voice), or they might change the pitch of their voices to signify size (little could be connected to a high voice and big to a low voice). This can be quite effective in storytelling. Movements could be made big, little, loudly, or softly as well to fit the occasion.

- **Preparing the child: Warnings** such as "Five minutes" or "Two minutes" may signal to a child that he needs to finish what he is doing in a given time frame, and then hopefully he will not be surprised or resistant when the activity draws to a close. **Schedules/agendas** are very functional for many students, either with actual objects, pictures, or words to denote the predictable order of events/tasks. **Participation in planning,** giving the student an opportunity to choose some of the activities or the order in which they occur, may help him/her feel more a part of the classroom routine.

- **Framing time into more concrete entities** is often done if traditional time concepts have not been mastered. One can announce that the child needs to read five more lines, sing one more verse, or complete one more page in his/her workbook. Numeric cues, such as holding up a certain number of fingers or displaying a numeral flash card, may be useful to concretely show how many turns remain.

- **Reciprocal reading and singing** (Quill, 1995), particularly with repetitive and/or rhyming patterns, enhance joint activity and two-way discourse.

- **Ignoring** is an important skill for any adult in the classroom. Choose wisely which behaviors you can safely ignore.

- **Approving incompatible responses:** If a student is singing, he is less likely to be talking out of turn. If his hands are clapping or playing an instrument, they are less likely to be touching someone else. Verbally praise appropriate participation. Teach your students skills to replace the inappropriate behaviors they display.

- **Differential reinforcement of others:** As a teacher you must be very observant of all the students in your class. Sometimes praising or rewarding those who are doing what is expected to be doing serves as an incentive and model for those who are off task or not actively engaged in learning.

- **Hesitation:** Be sure to allow ample time for a child to respond.

- **Pairing music with other cues** often strengthens the likelihood of the desired response's occurring.

- **Structure the music or movement (or other) experience to elicit specific responses.**

- **Peer tutoring:** Partners of varying abilities can teach or cue their peers.

- **Shadowing:** High school students may be assigned to work with individuals in the lower grades to help them participate successfully in inclusion classes.

- **"Social stories™"**, developed by Carol Gray (1993, 1994), are utilized to teach students social strategies and concepts. They help students identify behaviors expected in various social settings and may be presented to the individual through written or visual information or may be read aloud. They include "descriptive" sentences (who, what, where, why), "perspective" sentences (explaining reactions and feelings of others), "directive" sentences (individualized statements of desired responses), and "control" sentences ("I will...," "I can...," strategies for recalling information). **Musically adapted social stories** (Brownell, 2002), **social scripts and songs** (Dacus and Harmon, 2004), and **therapeutic prescriptive songs** (Pasiali, 2004) are musical variations on this theme.

- **Games** are excellent methods to practice skills and concepts. For example, "Simon Says" may be renamed *"Shimon Omeyr"* and offers a simple opportunity to follow movement directions with Hebrew vocabulary.

Listed below are extra tips to use when working with students with specific disabilities. Remember that many tips listed as related to one disability area may be used successfully and appropriately in other areas, depending on individual students' needs.

Extra tips when working with students with hearing impairments are summarized from resources written by Buechler (1982) and Gfeller (1990):

- Do not stand in front of a strong light, such as a window.

- Do not exaggerate your lip movement.

- Do not change topics abruptly; help the child make the transition, perhaps with a few key words on the blackboard.

- Have the child sit or stand close to you, if possible.

- Face the child when giving instructions and information.

- Speak slowly and clearly.

- Give instructions and engage in dialogue that is realistic. Be aware of the length and complexity of phrases and sentences, as well as tenses and vocabulary.

- Have one adult in charge in the room, so the student knows where to look.

- Real contact and experience with musical instruments will provide real memories (holding, watching, and/or feeling vibrations).
- Use musical instruments with large amounts of vibration and materials with varied textures. Some examples of instruments are bass bars (which look like individual xylophone bars), a woodblock, maracas, claves or rhythm sticks, the cabasa (a hand-held percussion instrument with strings of metal "beads" on it), autoharp, and guitar.

Paul (1982) and Graham (1975) provided these **extra tips when working with students with emotional disturbances or behavior disorders:**

- Be consistent.
- Use successive bringing into the group (Increase the length of time during which a child participates in the group).
- Encourage self-evaluations to help students realize their own behaviors and internalize their control over them.
- Use rapid pacing if necessary.
- Provide structure.
- Give directions clearly and concisely.
- Provide much positive reinforcement.
- Use movement activities frequently.
- Provide repetition, but intersperse new activities to maintain interest and motivation.

Extra tips when working with students with learning disabilities are condensed from Graham (1975) and Davis (1987):

- Give students specific items (instrument sounds, words, etc.) to listen for in songs or recordings to help focus their attention.
- Tell what is expected before an activity begins.
- Start with short experiences.
- Establish limitations/boundaries for movement.
- Add structure. For example, call students one by one to leave the room.
- Give extra cues as needed.
- Use charts to show progress. Secondary reinforcers such as checks, stickers, or privileges may work to motivate students.
- Reduce to a minimum the space where a child works.
- Additional marks on instruments—e.g., stickers—may be useful as targets to be hit.
- Be consistent in using the same attention-getting devices and cues as other teachers/professionals working with the child. Common cues include "Eyes up here" to receive eye contact, touching students, or asking them to repeat a direction back to the adult instead of asking, "Do you understand?"
- Be consistent in using the same discipline techniques and consequences for inappropriate behavior as others do, if possible.
- Individualize.

Extra tips in working with students with autism come from Grandin (1995), an adult with autism, Furman (2000), and Berger (2002).

- Many people with autism are visual thinkers. Teachers should demonstrate words like "up" or "down" to help children learn.
- Avoid long strings of verbal instructions. If the child can read, write the instructions down.
- Use a child's fixations, such as trains or maps, to motivate schoolwork.
- If the child has a difficult time with handwriting, let him/her type on the computer to reduce frustration and to help the child enjoy writing.
- Be sensitive to and provide for varied sensory motor needs of students, as students with special needs, particularly those with autism spectrum diagnoses or regulatory dysfunctions, may respond to, process, and interpret incoming sensory information in different ways than students who are "typically developing."
- Certain repetitive movements may be calming or organizing.
- Children with autism may need to be protected from sounds that hurt their ears. Adults in the classroom may put tape on school bells or slit tennis balls on the ends of chair legs to muffle these sounds.
- Some children with autism are bothered by visual distractions and fluorescent lights. Try to place the child's desk near the window, or avoid using fluorescent lights.
- Some children with autism who are very hyperactive and fidgety will often be calmer if they are given a padded weighted vest to wear for some periods during the school day. Pressure from the vest helps to calm the child's nervous system.
- Some children with autism sing better than they can speak. They may respond better if words and sentences are sung to them rather than spoken. Some children with extreme sound sensitivity will respond better if the teacher talks to them in a low whisper.
- Some children who are nonverbal cannot process visual and auditory input at the same time. They should not be asked to look and listen at the same time but instead should be given either a visual or an auditory task.
- For many older nonverbal children, touch is often their most reliable sense. Letters can be taught by letting them feel plastic letters. They can learn their daily schedule by feeling objects a few minutes before a scheduled activity—e.g., holding a spoon fifteen minutes before lunch.
- Expand/generalize your activities into social interactions and games.
- Be flexible yourself. Stick with your plan only when it is working.
- Watch for and reinforce the small changes, sounds, or movements your students make and then use this information to develop new activities they find reinforcing and fun.

Let's talk about **sound** for a moment. Music is "organized sound," but there are many other sounds in our environment.

Sounds that are rhythmic, soft, and constant may be calming. Sounds that have these qualities may help calm children who are loud and who become easily aroused by environmental sounds. Examples of this type of sound include the soft whir of a fan, the hum of a humidifier, or someone softly humming a song or whispering.

Sounds that are loud and variable, however, may be more alerting. Environmental sounds with these features may arouse children who are lethargic. Examples of this type of sound include loud voices, intercom announcements, rock music, vacuuming, school bells, alarms, and sirens.

Possible remedies for the problem of **hypersensitivity to sound**, when a child is easily distracted by and fears loud noises, include using soft talking to focus attention; playing soft music or setting a metronome to a slow rhythm to help calm the child; allowing him/her to wear ear protectors or headphones—unplugged—to buffer classroom noise; limiting or forewarning the child about intercom announcements, buzzers, and alarms; and vacuuming, playing music, or watching TV only when it is least distracting.

Suggested solutions to the problem of **hyposensitivity to sound**, where the child has difficulty processing sounds, include giving directions slowly, one at a time; using body gestures and tone of voice to help the child process what he/she hears; being sure the child is looking at you when you give directions; and reinforcing what the child hears by supplementing words with written lists.

GENERAL HINTS IN PROVIDING MUSIC AND MOVEMENT EXPERIENCES

- Start with short, repetitive songs with a limited range, including the "natural chant" (using the interval of the minor 3rd—"sol-mi"—when kids sing "na-na-na-na-nah"). Such songs are particularly good initially for lower-functioning students or for quick rapport building.
- *Niggunim* or songs without words are also helpful for quick, easy participation.
- Rounds and part-songs are nice for higher-functioning students or for intergenerational activities.
- Sing about what children are doing.
- Change words to familiar tunes.
- Use children's names frequently in songs.
- Use readily available materials—body percussion; items found at school, at home or outdoors; common objects.
- Think about how children can feel vibrations from speakers, instruments, etc.
- Find the optimum position for a child or for the instruments and equipment for talking, singing, moving, and/or playing.
- Expose children to a variety of musical styles and languages (English, Hebrew, Yiddish, Ladino).
- Provide some structure so that children know what to expect and can feel comfortable and secure.
- Remember that repetition is extremely important in learning new material and that it may add to enjoyment.
- Choose music that is age-appropriate, developmentally appropriate, and acceptable in the child's community.
- Give additional cues (visual, verbal, gestural, hand-over-hand) as needed to aid children in participation.
- Be a good role model yourself and participate in the activities.

Suggestions for Song-leading

- Know your song well. Do not rely on the printed music if you can help it.
- Make eye contact, even if intermittent, with the children.
- Move around within the group if necessary.

- Smile and nod encouragement.
- Give verbal cues before a line if necessary.
- Exaggerate words—enunciate.
- Sing in a comfortable range.
- Give clear signals for when to begin and when to end.

SUGGESTIONS FOR TEACHING NEW SONGS

- Try breaking the song into smaller parts.
- Teach the chorus first, and those who know verses already may help sing the verses.
- Leave words out at the end of a phrase for children to fill in the blanks.
- Echo words.
- Clap the rhythm of the lyrics.
- Use backward chaining (teach the last line first, then sing the last two lines, then last three lines, etc.). Keep building upon what was already learned.

EXAMPLES OF MUSIC AND MOVEMENT EXPERIENCES IN THE CLASSROOM

In addition to the many music and movement experiences already briefly described above, here are more creative ideas for you.

- **Orchestrate a Jewish folktale:** For example, with *It Could Always Be Worse* (Zemach, 1976), different instruments, short melodies, or sound effects could be created and assigned to children to correspond to the various characters—the man, rabbi, chickens, rooster, goose, goat, and cow. Children work together to create the whole story and learn to wait for their turns to play.

- **Combine music and movement:** The teacher distributes two of each Hebrew letter to students in the class, one letter per student. She instructs the students to walk to her drumbeat and keep walking until they find their partners with the like letter. If desired, the teacher may count how many beats it takes to find a match, and the children could try to beat their previous scores.

- **Songwriting.** *Filling in the blanks:* The song "To the Sukkah I Will Bring" (composer unknown) allows children an opportunity to say what items they would like to hang in a sukkah. Writing new personal or group verses to Cotler and Marx's "Thank You God" (1988) provides for individual creativity, self-expression, and expanding understanding of the concept of giving thanks.

Creating entire new verses: Here is an example written by a fourth grade religious school class about their favorite Jewish people, one of many original verses to "My Favorite Jewish Things," a take-off on "My Favorite Things" from *The Sound of Music*.

> Abraham, Isaac, Jacob, and Moses,
> Adam and Eve, Joseph, and us,
> Rabbis and cantors, Leah, Einstein,
> These Jewish people are really FINE!

Commercials: Choose a character—e.g., from the Purim story—and write a commercial (usually using the tune from a TV or radio commercial) about that person, embodying the character traits of that person.

- **Song choice cards:** Write song titles on index cards, and have children choose the next song for the class to sing. Choices could be related to the week's topic or an upcoming holiday. Children may also vote on what song to sing next.

- **Use recordings:** Play a recording of a Jewish song or prayer. Stop it in the middle and have the student say the word that comes next. If it is a large class, passing a ball or bean-bag around and having the person caught holding it when the music stops be the one to respond helps provide structure.

- **Play instrumental accompaniments:** Songs with repeated parts such as "Dundai" and "*Atzey Zeytim Omdim*" could be opportunities for children to have special privileges to play a repeated "ostinato" melodic accompaniment on bells (C-C-G-G-C-C for "*Atzey Zeytim Omdim*" or C-E flat-C-E flat for "Dundai, dundai") or a rhythmic accompaniment on tambourine.

- **Moving on a specific word:** In songs such as "<u>Hag</u> Purim" children can be instructed to stamp their feet or clap on the phrase "rash, rash, rash."

- **Action songs** such as "*David Melekh Yisrael*" or "My Hat It Has Three Corners" (*Lakova Sheli*) are fun experiences that provide some variety and allow children to move in a socially acceptable manner. Children may also take turns in leading the motions to these and other songs.

- **Israeli dancing:** There are many recordings of music for common Israeli dances. Weikert's series entitled *Rhythmically Moving* has several tracks with Israeli dance music. Use of these dances is particularly appropriate for *Yom Ha-Atzm'ut* or in relation to the study of Hebrew, Israel, or of wedding and b'nai mitzvah ceremonies/celebrations. Dance may also be used as a classroom management technique, to provide a break or a reinforcer.

- **Musical games:** Klepper (1986) suggested a game entitled "Sing Down," where teams list as many songs as they can that contain a specified word or pertain to a given theme in a specified time frame. Each team then sings a line from one of their songs, and that round of the game continues until all but one team runs out of songs or sings a song that another team has already sung.

- **Jewish music in the Learning Center:** Klepper (1986) also proposed a listening center in the classroom. Songs and stories related to classroom themes and topics are made available to the students. In addition, students may listen to and compare and contrast different versions of prayers or songs. Rossel (1987) also suggested having students listen to music of famous Jewish composers such as Bloch or Mahler or performers such as Yitzhak Perlman or Isaac Stern. The study of American Jewry might be enhanced by listening to music of American Jewish composers such as Irving Berlin or Leonard Bernstein. Likewise, the introduction of Yiddish folk music during a unit on Eastern European Jewry, becoming familiar with Ladino music when studying Sephardic Jews, or listening to a Yemenite seder when studying Oriental Jewry makes sense. Rossel further suggested that teachers make listening a bit more activity-centered by allowing students to draw or color or by asking them to write poetry or jot down random thoughts while the music plays.

- **Song parodies:** Jewish rock groups such as Schlock Rock have created humorous song parodies on many topics or pertaining to holidays or ceremonies that may become adjuncts to traditional teaching materials. One of my favorites is *"Under the Huppah"* to the tune of "Under the Boardwalk." Many other song parodies, such as "The Ballad of the Four Sons" to the tune of "Clementine," are readily available. Students, individually or in groups, may write new parodies as well on various topics.

- **Song lyric discussions:** Especially with older, higher-functioning students, this activity can lead to many insightful classroom dialogues about a variety of topics. "Tribute," by Safam (1991), is a particularly moving song written by the composer upon his father's death. Discussion of the lyrics might tie in nicely to lessons on Jewish rituals related to death and mourning.

CONCLUSION

A teacher need not be musically inclined to plan and lead music and movement activities. Creativity, patience, and persistence are valuable traits for those who wish to engage in this worthwhile endeavor. It is important to use music and movement in whatever way you feel is appropriate for your students. Not only may these experiences help them succeed in the classroom, but their lives may become enriched and their connections to their heritage may be strengthened through music and movement classroom experiences.

The inclusion of music and movement in the classroom builds many bridges—bridges between students, bridges between teacher and students, bridges between the music or dance and the students, bridges between text and students, bridges between generations, bridges between countries, and much, much more.

ADDITIONAL REFERENCES/RESOURCES

Berger, D. S. *Music Therapy, Sensory Integration and the Autistic Child.* Philadelphia: Jessica Kingsley Publishers, 2002.

The Best of Debbie Friedman. Cedarhurst, New York: Tara Publications, 1987.

Brownell, M. D. "Musically Adapted Social Stories to Modify Behaviors in Students with Autism: Four Case Studies." *Journal of Music Therapy, 34 (2),* 2002, pp. 117–144.

Buechler, J. *Music Therapy for Handicapped Children: Hearing Impaired.* Washington, D.C.: National Association for Music Therapy, Inc., 1982.

Craig Taubman Songbook. Los Angeles, California: Sweet Louise Productions, 1987.

Dacus, D. & C. Harmon. *Teaching Social Skills through Scripts and Songs: A Powerful Approach to Communication.* Grapevine, Texas: Prelude Music Therapy Products, 2004.

Doug Cotler Songbook. Woodland Hills, California: A-Major Studio, 1992.

Furman, A. "Come on Over and Sit Right Down…Group Music Therapy for Children along the Autism Spectrum." In *Proceedings of the Institute on Music Therapy with Young Children.* Silver Spring, Maryland: American Music Therapy Association, 2000.

Gfeller, K. "A Cognitive-Linguistic Approach to Language Development for the Preschool Child with Hearing Impairment: Implications for Music Therapy Practice." *Music Therapy Perspectives,* 1990, 8, 47–51.

Grandin, T. *Thinking in Pictures and Other Reports from My Life with Autism.* New York: Vintage, 1995.

Gray, C. *How to Write Social Stories.* Jenison, Michigan: Jenison Public Schools, 1993.

Gray, C. *The New Social Story Book.* Jenison, Michigan: Jenison Public Schools, 1994.

Hackett, P. *The Melody Book.* Englewood Cliffs, New Jersey: Prentice-Hall, Inc., 1983.

A Harvest of Jewish Song (T. Jochsberger and V. Pasternak, eds). Cedarhurst, New York: Tara Publications, 1980.

Hirschorn, L. *Gather Round*. Cedarhurst, New York: Tara Publications, 1989.

Klepper, J. "Chai on Music—18 New Ideas/Resources for Jewish Music Education." In *The Jewish Teachers Handbook, Volume I* (Audrey Friedman Marcus, ed.). Denver, Colorado: Alternatives in Religious Education, Inc., 1986.

Manginot: 201 Songs for Jewish Schools (S. Richards, Ed.). New York: Transcontinental Music Publications and New Jewish Music Press, 1992.

Mesirow, L. *A Ladino Songbook*. New York: Global Village Music, 1989 (recording).

Music for the Exceptional Child (R. Graham, ed.). Reston, Virginia: Music Educators' National Conference, 1975.

Nash, G. C., and J. Rapley. *Holidays and Special Days*. Los Angeles: Alfred Publishing Company, Inc., 1985.

Nelson, E. *The Great Rounds Songbook*. New York: Sterling Publishing Company, Inc., 1985.

The New Children's Songbook (V. Pasternak, ed.). Cedarhurst, New York: Tara Publications, 1981.

NFTY Chordster. New York: North American Federation of Temple Youth, 1981.

NFTY's Fifty Songbook (M. Arian et al, eds.). New York: Transcontinental Publishing Company, 1989.

Paul, D. W. *Music Therapy for Handicapped Children: Emotionally Disturbed*. Washington, D.C.: National Association for Music Therapy, Inc., 1982.

Pasiali, V. "The Use of Prescriptive Therapeutic Songs in a Home-based Environment to Promote Social Skills Acquisition by Children with Autism: Three Case Studies." *Music Therapy Perspectives*, 22 (1), 2004, pp. 11–20.

Quill, K. A. *Teaching Children with Autism: Strategies to Enhance Communication and Socialization*. New York: Delmar Publishers Inc., 1995.

Richard Wolfe's Legit Professional Fake Book. New York: The Big 3 Music Corporation.

Rossel, S. *Managing the Jewish Classroom: How to Transform Yourself into a Master Teacher*. Los Angeles: Torah Aura Productions, 1987.

Safam's Greatest Hits, Volume I. New Centre, Massachusetts, 1991 (recording).

Schlock Rock. *Purim Torah*. New Jersey, 1987 (recording).

Shaarei Shira: *Gates of Song* (C. Davidson, ed.) New York: Transcontinental Publications, 1987.

Therapy Skill Builders. The Psychological Corporation, 1995.

Weikert, P. *Rhythmically Moving*. Ypsilanti, Michigan: High/Scope Press (recordings).

Zemach, M. *It Could Always Be Worse*. New York: Scholastic Inc., 1976.

CHAPTER 28

THE MAGIC AND THE ART OF STORY: STORYTELLING AND CREATIVE DRAMATICS IN THE CLASSROOM

by Cherie Karo Schwartz

Stories are the mirror and the memory of our Jewish soul. They interweave five thousand years of our wishes and wisdom into a magical feast of history, ethics, customs, holidays, rituals, and world view. We, the tellers and listeners, as participants in the world of story, enter the enchantment of word weaving—and we listen and remember. Storytelling is the most ancient of our arts, and the most enduring. It is the perfect blend of all that we are as the Jewish people. We are more than "The People of the Book;" we are The People of the Never-ending Story.

Our Jewish tradition is filled with the power of story. There is a tale of the Rhizhiner Rebbe, a great Hassidic master. As a very old man he was presented with two books for which to write letters of recommendation: one a book of law and one a collection of stories. He knew he only had the strength to write one, and he chose the book of stories. Why? He explained that even God knows the power of story; the Torah begins with "In the beginning..." and proceeds through story after story before presenting the laws!

The Jewish world is blessed with story: tales of our Matriarchs and Patriarchs, Sages and Rebbes, heroes and common people from throughout time and place. Our history unfolds in holidays and life-cycle events. The dreidel helps tell the Hanukkah story; Elijah is invited to the *Brit Milah*; we act out the story of Esther on Purim. All of Passover is rich with symbol and story, from foods to rituals: symbolic foods on the seder plate, *Maggid* (telling the story), the Four Questions, opening the door for Elijah, and the story-song "<u>Had Gadya</u>" all help us to remember to "tell it to the children that we will remember." Judaism draws from the well-spring of story to help preserve and perpetuate our five thousand years of tradition. It is a lesson of lifetime learning.

As our sages knew, there is simply no better way to teach and to learn than through the use of story. Watch children's eyes as they enter the spell of a well-told story. Research tells us that participants in story actually enter a light trance state: endorphins released, synapses strengthened, and senses heightened. It has been proven that the teller and audience actually begin to breathe together, and their hearts beat together! What a deep connection is made, and what better connection could there possibly be for learning and retention to occur?

While the telling of a story is an essential teaching tool, stories are also read and experienced. Children grow from infancy through the use of story. They take the information they are experiencing in the world and "story" it from their earliest years. They move in improvisation, create songs and rhymes, "play house," and make up games to process the knowledge they receive from around them. Story helps them make sense of the world. They use all of their senses in their creations, and story helps to make order and sense of the knowledge they are gaining.

As children grow in experience and knowledge, the safety and fantasy of story still helps them to learn. By involving students of any age in the story world, they are gaining knowledge and are also integrating and synthesizing what they know into their lives.

These story techniques and skills are especially appropriate for working with diverse special audiences. Storytelling, stories, improvisation, and creative dramatics allow for a wide spectrum of learning and learners. Using many learning styles (oral, aural, kinesthetic) and senses (feeling, taste, touch, smell, sight), the world of story involves students in participatory, engaging, fun learning experiences.

Our Jewish sages and teachers knew how to use stories to impart important life lessons. Judaism is infused with story from infancy through adulthood, from holidays to life-cycle events. So how can modern teachers tap into this great reservoir of Jewish tales, allowing stories to gently and powerfully weave their magic to clarify and extend our Jewish knowledge and love for learning?

Here are some examples of how to "story" the classroom to maximize teaching and learning. Let imagination and heart combine with subject matter to help create a vibrant environment and develop a lifelong passion to learn.

STORYTELLING AND CREATIVE DRAMATICS ACTIVITIES AND IDEAS

WHAT KINDS OF STORIES TO TELL

There are as many Jewish stories as there are stars in the sky and blades of grass on earth! Find a story that makes a connection for you and by learning it, your listeners will love it, too. There are Jewish stories on every subject, and they can be used to more deeply and joyously teach any Jewish subject. Books like Ellen Frankel's *The Classic Tales* have several indexes, and stories are categorized by theme and type. You can tell stories for holidays, life-cycle events, Israel study, history, values, rituals, customs, and traditions. The uses of stories are endless.

BEFORE TELLING THE STORY—GETTING READY

STORY ENHANCERS

Before you even start to tell a story, you can help set the stage.

- Wear something (color, pattern, jewelry, pin, scarf, hat, etc.) that has a connection to the story.
- Establish ground rules for story time: stay together, listen, observe, be ready to participate, respond.
- Devise a way to get to the place of the story. Take an in-place hike, light a candle, recite a poem, take a magic carpet ride, close eyes and then open them to story, open eyes and heart.
- Use sensory input. Set the stage with the group with description of sounds, smells, colors, feel.

- Create a sound symphony. Let the group help build the sound of a place: animals, people, environment.
- Build object memory. At the beginning of the story, describe some objects in the story; at the end, see who remembers.
- Present new vocabulary at beginning of story (foreign words, foods, ideas, time, and place).
- Become a character in the story to help introduce it (news reporter, archeologist, friend, descendant).
- Use a prop. Bring in something to show or refer to, helping to attract and keep interest.

STORYTELLING FROM THE START

Here are some easy story starters to help students open up to creatively thinking of stories.

NAMES STORIES: Have the students find out about and share the stories of their names: first, last, Hebrew, their nicknames. Where do they come from? What do they mean? Were they named after someone in family or history or Torah?

FIVE-PART STORIES: These are stories that the students create from five disparate pieces of information. Ask the group to name a Jewish holiday, a place in the world, a Jewish object, an unusual color, and a Jewish food. Then have them, individually or in groups, combine these items into stories. You can use the story elements (beginning, middle, and end; plot, action, and characters) to add to the learning. They can tell their stories out loud or act them out for each other.

CREATE A CHARACTER FOR STORIES: Have the group suggest the name for a fictional character who will be with your class for the whole year. (Perhaps you can use some Yiddish words like *kugel*, *tsimmes*, or *gribbeneh*!) This is along the lines of K'Tonton, who was created by Sadie Rose Weilerstein with her religious school classes over fifty years ago. Decide on one or a couple of characters. Then for each holiday or life cycle event studied in class, have students help make up a story using the character. They will enjoy creating, and they will be reinforcing their knowledge of the subject. You can have students write out and illustrate the stories so that by the end of the year you will have a whole class book of stories!

READING STORIES ALOUD: Choose short, easy stories to start, and set up a specific time to read a whole story or a portion of the story. Use an enthusiastic, expressive voice, sound effects, and pauses for effect. Feel free to add explanatory historical or cultural comments as you read. Get the students involved with sound effects, answering questions, or guessing what will happen next. Read the story more than once to the class, and see how much they can remember and tell back. Have the students draw or move to the story. Let them try guessing the ending.

TAKING THE STORY OFF OF THE PAGE: It is an easy step to move from reading to telling a story, and the experience becomes much more immediate for the listeners. Try reading the story out loud to yourself three times, and then close the book and see if you can remember the story. You can! Go back and find the stick points, make an outline, put important points on a note card, or "web"[1] the story visually to help remember it. Use the magic of voice and movement to help carry the story as you tell it to the class. Catch their eyes and their spirit and feel the power of the told story. Then add to your repertoire, one story at a time.

TELLING THE TALES

TORAH TALES: Read a short version of a story in the Torah (favorites include Steven Rosman's *Sidra Stories* and Stan Beiner's *Sedra Scenes*) Then have students act out the story, retell it, do it as a consecutive narrative, become one of the characters, or answer questions as a character in the story.

Bibliodrama can be very effective for special audiences. With the whole group, ask them a question and let them respond as one of the characters in the story. Or with more advanced groups, set the scene by reading it from Torah, then let them interact with each other as characters in the scene, with the teacher as guide and director of the scene.

MAKING MODERN MIDRASHIC TALES: Read a good short version of a Torah text

to the students. Then read them a classic Midrash on the same story (favorites include Barbara Diamond Goldin's *A Child's Book of Midrash* and Peninnah Schram's *Ten Classic Jewish Children's Stories*). What is the same? What is different? Read them another Torah story. Then ask them what questions they have about things not really explained in the story. This will start them on the path to creating their own midrashic tales. They can create them as a whole class, in small groups, or in improvisation, or they can write them or draw them.

FOLKTALES: Depending on the reading and comprehension level of the students, either

read to them or have them read short versions of Jewish folktales (some favorite books include Simon Certner's *101 Jewish Stories* and Howard Schwartz and Barbara Rush's *The Diamond Tree* and *The Wonder Child*). Then they can try remembering the tales and retelling them, recreating them in their own words or acting them out.

LITERARY TALES: There are hundreds of wonderful children's books that can easily be

used for storytelling. Choose a favorite tale, simple for the time of year or occasion. Read it aloud three times. Ask the students questions about the characters and the situations. Then have them tell the story back to you. How much can they remember? You can create cards with short descriptions of the scenes and then have the students act out the play of the story. Make sure to acknowledge the author of each book.

ARTIFACTS HAVE STORIES TO TELL

RITUAL OBJECTS CAN TALK: Show the students a Jewish object and have them tell you what they might know about it. Then have it "introduce[1]" itself to them (you become the object and speak in first person). Let it tell about its use, when and how it came to be here, its memories of being used, and so on. After the teacher has demonstrated the activity, have each student choose one object to "become". You can use pictures of the objects or the objects themselves. Or you can have the students each come in with an object from home.

MORE STORY PROJECTS

FAMILY FOLKLORE: Students find a Jewish family story (foods, holidays, immigration) to tell the class.

INTERGENERATIONAL TELLING: Get parents, grandparents, or Senior Center residents to share stories with the class. The students and adults can tell each other stories of holidays, foods, school, and life-cycle events. Then they can tell the stories, write them down, or act them out.

STORYTELLING FESTIVAL: Have each student or pair of students learn a story and tell it to the class in a one-day festival. Invite other classes or parents as audience.

STORIES AND FAMILY TREASURES: Each student brings in (or obtains) a Jewish object, researches its story (or creates a plausible story about it), and then presents the story speaking as the object itself, as an archeologist in the future who found it, or as a descendant of the original owner.

STORIES AND FOODS: Each student (or small group) chooses a Jewish food from a country, researches it, prepares it, and tells a story about it and perhaps about a family who eats this certain food (time period, place in the world, holiday, or occasion). You can feast on foods and the stories!

EASY STORIES TO PLAY

Any story can easily be transformed into a play, allowing kinesthetic learners and all to be involved joyously in the story process. Here are some easy suggestions on the process.

- Choose a simple, short story to present.
- Read over the story three times, then have the class tell the story back in sequence.
- Make an outline using each element of the story as one scene (write on board or make copies).
- Decide on characters (everyone can have a part, or some may choose to participate).
- Take one scene at a time; teacher is director and guide and keeps the play moving.
- Practice three times.
- Create simple scenery on large white paper; add small costume and set pieces.
- Practice again. Teacher can provide cues and dialogue narration and keep the action moving.
- Present the masterpiece of theater, with or without an audience!

READERS' THEATRE AND CHORAL READING

For students who have more difficulty with movement and/or learning lines and/or speaking individually, there are other forms of storytelling: readers' theatre and choral reading. Readers' theatre involves reading the lines of a play or story while seated and facing front. There is a narrator to keep the story moving. The reliance is on voice, pacing, and sound effects (some students can provide a whole chorus of sound effects to great advantage). Everyone can participate this way, with the more verbal taking the major parts.

Choral reading means that each part or section of a story, play, or poem is read by a group of people together. This way the volume is increased, students feel that they are really active participants, and everyone learns as they follow each other in their parts. Again, one group can create the sound effects for the story. Add repetitive lines (either a repeated theme or line or an echo) to a story to add texture. Start with an easy poem or very short story, make sure that each choral grouping has at least one strong reader, and then gradually increase the reading length and challenging vocabulary and concepts.

AND A LAST WORD...

Remember: There is a whole wide world of Jewish stories waiting to be told and retold. We as storytellers and teachers know the essential and vital role that stories have played in the development, nourishment, preservation, and continuation of the Jewish people. Five thousand years of stories open us to the heart of our people wherever and whenever we have lived. Revel in the riches of our heritage through story, and may the stories continue!

BIBLIOGRAPHY

Here is a list of books mentioned in this chapter, plus others that can be useful resources for storytelling and creative dramatic projects.

Beiner, Stan. *Sedra Scenes: Skits For Every Torah Portion*. Denver: Alternatives in Religious Education, Inc., 1982.

Certner, Simon. *101 Jewish Stories*. NY: Board of Jewish Education of Greater New York, 1987.

Frankel, Ellen. *The Classic Tales: 4000 Years of Jewish Lore*. Jason Aronson, Inc., 1989.

Gellman, Marc. *Does God Have a Big Toe? Stories About Stories in the Bible*. NY: HarperCollins Children's Book Group, 1993.

——*God's Mailbox*. NY: HarperCollins Children's Book Group, 1995.

Goldin, Barbara Diamond. *A Child's Book of Midrash*. NJ: Jason Aronson, Inc., 1990.

Jaffe, Nina, and Steve Zeitlin. *While Standing On One Foot: Puzzle Stories and Wisdom Tales From the Jewish Tradition*. NY: Henry Holt and Co., 1993.

Jaffe, Nina. *The Uninvited Guest and Other Jewish Holiday Tales*. NY: Scholastic Inc., 1993.

Noy, Dov. *Folktales of Israel*. Chicago: University of Chicago Press, 1968.

Rosman, Steven M. *Sidrah Stories: A Torah Companion*. NY: UAHC Press, 1989.

Rossel, Seymour. *Sefer Ha-aggadah: The Book of Legends for Young Readers* (Vols. 1, 2). NY: UAHC Press, 1997, 1998.

Rush, Barbara. *70 and 1 Tales for the Jewish Year*. NY: A.Z.Y.F., 1980.

Schram, Peninnah. *Ten Classic Jewish Children's Stories*. NY, Jerusalem: Pitspopany Press, 1998.

Schwartz, Cherie Karo. *My Lucky Dreidel: Hanukkah Stories, Songs, Poems, Crafts, Recipes, and Fun for Kids*. NY: Magnolia Editions, 1994.

——*The Kids' Catalog of Passover: A Worldwide Celebration*. Philadelphia: Jewish Publication Society, 2000.

Schwartz, Howard. *Next Year in Jerusalem: 3000 Years of Jewish Stories*. NY: Viking Penguin, 1998.

——*The Day the Rabbi Disappeared*. NY: Viking Penguin, 1999.

Schwartz, Howard, and Barbara Rush. *A Coat For the Moon and Other Jewish Tales*. PA: Jewish Publication Society, 1999.

——*The Diamond Tree: Jewish Tales From Around the World*. NY: HarperCollins Children's Book Group 1998.

——*The Wonder Child and Other Jewish Fairy Tales*. NY: HarperCollins Children's Book Group, 1996.

Stavish, Corinne. *Seeds from Our Past, Planting for Our Future: Jewish Stories and Folktales.* Washington, DC: B'nai B'rith Int. Commission on Jewish Education, 1997.

Weilerstein, Sadie Rose. *The Best Of K'tonton.* Philadelphia: The Jewish Publication Society, 1980.

PART 5:
CLASSROOM
AND MATERIAL
ACCOMMODATIONS

FOR ALL STUDENTS AND ESPECIALLY STUDENTS WHO MAY HAVE A VARIETY OF LEARNING DISABILITIES

1. Use the clearest copy of material to photocopy. Make sure the material is written clearly and simply and coded when necessary (e.g., write directions in italics or in a box, or underline).
2. Make sure the students are sitting close to the teacher, board, or work area in the least distractable place (i.e., away from movement, noise).
3. Write clearly in an uncluttered fashion on the board and on worksheets.
4. Use a card to block out material that is not being focused on at the moment.
5. Use visual clues when appropriate (e.g., highlighting to indicate where to begin working or reading).
6. Introduce copying activities at the students' desks, later moving on to copying from the board, allowing the students to sit near the material. Realize that some children will always have difficulty copying.
7. Allow students to use index cards to keep their place. Cut cards for appropriate usage (i.e., to block out a word, phrase, etc.).
8. Color code vowels, prefixes, and suffixes.
9. Keep oral directions short and simple. Have student repeat directions or paraphrase.
10. Speak slowly and clearly.
11. Use visual aids frequently.
12. Circulate around the room providing individual recognition of good work.
13. Be sure students' desks are cleared except for material being used for the lesson.
14. Modify workload (i.e., homework, classwork, minimal copying, and in some cases, writing activities).
15. Teach students to organize written material, distance between words, lines.
16. Give students material from a workbook one page at a time (i.e., tear out sheets).
17. Consistently place directions, schedules, and homework assignments in the same location on the board or chart.
18. Establish a procedure for changing activities.
19. Establish daily routines.
20. Set up a reward system.
21. Allow extra time to finish assignments.
22. Review frequently.
23. Use different color coverings for books.
24. Teach students to self-correct materials.

25. Encourage oral as well as written presentations.
26. Allow time for students to ask and answer questions.
27. Structure tests or review quizzes for success (i.e., review material, discuss test format, read test with students, write test clearly).

Source: S. Fagen, "Promoting Successful Mainstreaming." Montgomery County, Maryland Public Schools, 1984. Excerpt from *The Resource Program Guide for a Congregational School* by Phyllis S. Greene and Sara Rubinow Simon, 1992.

CLASSROOM MODIFICATIONS

AUDITORY PROCESSING PROBLEMS	VISUAL PROCESSING PROBLEMS	EXPRESSIVE LANGUAGE PROBLEMS
1. Preferential seating 2. Short oral directions 3. Oral with written directions 4. Student repeats directions 5. Alert to directions 6. Talk slower 7. Vary voice tone and pitch 8. Quiet work area 9. Key points on board 10. Notes written out 11. Explanation with visuals 12. Classroom charts 13. Manipulations 14. Wait time	1. Preferential seating 2. Clear writing (board and dittos) 3. Verbal with written directions 4. Visual focusing cues 5. Oral directions 6. Tape recorded material 7. Color coding 8. Summarize questions 9. Wider spacing on worksheets	1. Mnemonic devices—hints 2. Every student response card 3. Wait time 4. Notes, visuals with oral 5. Silent reading vs. oral reading 6. Drawings, diagrams with verbal response
VISUAL MOTOR PROBLEMS	ORGANIZATIONAL PROBLEMS PROBLEMS	
1. Matching and multiple choice activities 2. Grade content only 3. Oral quizzes, tests 4. Specially lined papers 5. Paper placement 6. Reduced writing requirements 7. Allow more time 8. Check with a model	1. Daily routine 2. Factual/abstract 3. Clear, concise directions 4. Notebook dividers 5. Review & summarize 6. Samples of finished product 7. Block and/or folded worksheets 8. Enumerate steps for specific assignments 9. Uncluttered worksheets 10. Clues—page number where answer is found 11. Focusing techniques	(Summary of Classroom accomodations from S. Fagen's *Promoting Successful Mainstreaming*)

CHAPTER 29

SUGGESTED CLASSROOM ACCOMMODATIONS FOR STUDENTS WITH ATTENTION DEFICIT DISORDER

Gary Smith, Marilyn Eyler Conaway, and Carolyn Croft Lodwig

WHEN YOU SEE THIS BEHAVIOR	TRY THIS ACCOMMODATION
1. Difficulty following a plan (has high aspirations, but lacks follow-through); sets out to "get straight A's, ends up with the F's; sets unrealistic goals.	• Use a questioning strategy with the student; ask, What do you **need** to be able to do this? Keep asking that question until the student has reached a obtainable goal. • Assist student in setting long-range goals; break the goal into realistic parts. • Have student set clear timelines for what he needs to do to accomplish each step or part and monitor student's progress frequently.
2. Difficulty sequencing and completing steps to accomplish specific tasks (e.g. writing a book report, term paper, organized paragraphs, division problem, etc.).	• Break up task into workable and obtainable steps. • Provide examples and specific steps to accomplish task.
3. Shifting from one uncompleted activity to another without closure.	• Define the requirements of a completed activity (e.g. your math is finished when all six problems are corrected; do not begin on the next task until it is finished.
4. Difficulty following through on instructions from others.	• Gain student's attention before giving directions. Use alerting cues. Accompany oral directions with written directions. • Give one direction at a time. Quietly repeat directions to the student after they have been given to the rest of the class. Check for understanding having the student repeat directions. • Place general methods of operation and expectations on charts displayed around the room and/or on shelves to be included in the student's notebook.

WHEN YOU SEE THIS BEHAVIOR	TRY THIS ACCOMMODATION
5. Difficulty prioritizing from most to least important.	• Prioritize assignments and activities. • Provide a model to help students. Post the model and refer too often.
6. Difficulty sustaining effort and accuracy over time.	• Reduce assignment length and strive for quality (rather than quantity). • Increase the frequency of positive reinforcements (catch the student doing it right and let him know it).
7. Difficulty completing assignments.	• List and/or post (and say) all steps necessary to complete each assignment. • Reduce the assignment into manageable sections with specific dates. • Make frequent checks for work/assignment completion. • Arrange for the student to have a "study buddy" with phone number in each subject area.
8. Difficulty with any task that requires memory.	• Make frequent checks for work/assignment completion. • Arrange for the student to have a "study buddy" with phone number in each subject area
9. Difficulty with test taking.	• Allow extra time for testing; teach test-taking skills and strategies; and allow students to be tested orally. • Use clear, readable and uncluttered test forms. Use a test format that the student is most comfortable with. Allow ample space for student response. Consider having lined answer spaces for essay or short answer tests.
10. Confusion from non-verbal cues (misreads body languague, etc.)	• Directly teach (tell the student) what non-verbal cues mean. Model and have student practice reading cuse in a safe setting.
11. Confusion from written material (difficulty finding main idea from a paragraph, attributes greater importance to minor details.)	• Provide student with copy of reading material with main ideas underlined or highlighted. • Provide an outline of important points from reading materials. • Teach outlining, main-idea/details concepts. • Provide tape of text/chapter.
12. Confusion from spoken material, lectures and A.V. material (difficulty finding main idea from presentation, attributes greater important to minor details).	• Provide student with a copy of presentation notes. • Allow peers to share carbon-copy notes from persentaiton (have student compare own notes with copy of peer's notes). • Provide framed outlines of presentations (introducing vusual and auditory cues to important information. • Encourage use of tape recorder. • Teach and emphasize key words (the following..., the most important point...etc.).

WHEN YOU SEE THIS BEHAVIOR	TRY THIS ACCOMMODATION
13. Difficulty sustaining attention to tasks or other activities (easily distracted by extraneous stimuli).	• Reward attention. Break up activities into small units. Reward for timely accomplishments. • Use physical proximity and touch. Use earphones and/or study carrels, quiet place, or preferential seating.
14. Frequent messiness or sloppiness.	• Teach organizational skills. Be sure student has daily, weekly and/or monthly assignment sheets; list of materials needed daily; and consistent format for papers. Have a consistent way for students to turn in and receive back papers; reduce distractions. • Give reward points for notebook checks and proper paper format. • Provide clear copies of worksheets and handout and consisten format for worksheets. Establish a daily routine, provide models for what you want the student to do. • Arrange for a peer who will help him with organization. • Assist student to keep materials in specific place (e.g. pencils and pens in pouch). • Be willing to repeat expectations.
15. Poor handwriting (often mixing cursive with manuscript and capitals with lower-case letters).	• Allow for a scribe and grade for content, not handwriting. Allow use of a computer or typewriter. • Consider alternative methods for student response (e.g. tape recorder, oral reports, etc.). • Don't penalize student for mixing cursive and manuscript (accept any method of production).
16. Difficulty with fluency in handwriting, e.g. good letter/word production but very slow and laborious.	• Allow for shorter assignments (quality vs. quantity). • All alternative method of production (computer, scribe, oral presentation, etc.).
17. Poorly developed study skills.	• Teach study skills specific to the subject area—organization (e.g. assignment calendar), textbook reading, notetaking (finding main idea/detail, mapping, outlinining, skimming, summarizing).
18. Poor self-monitoring (careless errors in spelling, arithmetic, reading)	• Teach specific methods of self-monitoring (e.g. stop-look-listen). • Have student proof-read finished work when it is done.
19. Low fluency or production of written material (takes hours on a 10-minute assignment).	• Allow for alternative. completing assignments (oral presentations, taped report, visual presentation, graphs, maps, pictures, etc. with reduced writing requirements). • Allow for alternative methods of writing (e.g. a typewriter, computer, cursive or printing, or a scribe).

WHEN YOU SEE THIS BEHAVIOR	TRY THIS ACCOMMODATION
20. Apparent inattention (underactive, daydreaming, not there).	• Get student's attention before giving directions (tell student how to pay attention (look at me while I talk, watch my eyels while I speak). Ask student to repeat directions. • Attempt to activiely involve student in less (e.g. cooperative learning).
21. Difficulty participating in class without being interruptive; difficulty working quietly.	• Seat student in close proximity to the teacher. • Reward appropriate behavior (catch student "being good"). • Use study carrel if appropriate.
22. Inappropriate seeking of attention (clowns around, exhibits loud excessive or exaggerated movement as attention-seeking behavior, interrupts, butts into other children's activities, needles others).	• Show student (model) how to gain other's attention appropriately. • Catch the student when appropriate and reinforce.
23. Frequent excessive talking.	• Teach student hand signals and use to tell student when and where not to talk. • Make sure student is called when it is appropriate and reinforce listening.
24. Difficulty making transitions (from activity to activity or class to class); takes an excessive amount of time to "find pencil", gives up, refuses to leave previous task' appears agitated during change.	• Program student for transitions. Give advance warning of when a transition is going to take place (now we are completing the worksheet, next we will...) and the expectation for the transition (and you will need...). • Specifically say and display lists of materials needed until a routine is possible. List steps necessary to complete each assignment. • Have specific locations for all materials (pencil pouches, tabs in notebooks, etc.). • Arrange for an organized helper (peer).
25. Difficulty remaining seated or in a particular position when required to.	• Give student frequent opportunities to get up and move around. Allow space for movement.
26. Frequent fidgeting with hands, feet or objects; squirming in seat.	• Directly teach (tell the student) what non-verbal cues mean. Model and have student practice reading cues in a safe setting.
27. Inappropriate responses in class often blurted out; answers given to questions before they have been completed.	• Seat student in close proximity to teacher so that visual and physical monitoring of student behavior can be done by the teacher. • State behavior that you do want (tell the student how you expect him to behave).

WHEN YOU SEE THIS BEHAVIOR	TRY THIS ACCOMMODATION
28. Agitation under pressure and completion (athletic or academic).	• Stress effort and enjoyment for self, rather than competition with others. • Minimize timed activities; structure class for team effort and cooperation.
29. Inappropriate behaviors in a team or large group sport or athletic activity (difficulty waiting turn in games or group situations).	• Give the student a responsible job (e.g. team captain, care and distribution of the balls, score keeping, etc); consider leadership role.. • Have student in close proximity to teacher.
30. Frequent involvement in physically dangerous activities without considering possible consequences.	• Anticipate dangerous situations and plan for in advance. • Stress Stop-Look-Listen. • Pair with responsible peer (rotate responsible students so that they don't wear out).
31. Poor adult interactions, defies authority, sucks up, hangs on.	• Provide positive attention. • Talk with student individually about the inappropriate behavior (what you are doing is....A better way of getting what you need or want is....).
32. Frequent self putdowns, poor personal care and posture, negative comments about self and others, low self esteem.	• Structure for success. • Train student for self-monitoring, reinforce improvements, teach self-questioning strategies (What am I doing? How is that going to affect others?). • Allow opportunities for the student to show his strengths.. • Give positive recognition.
33. Difficulty using unstructured time—recess, hallways, lunchroom, locker room, library, assembly..	• Provide student with a definite purpose during unstructured activities (The purpose of going to the library is to check out.... The purpose of ...is....). • Encourage group games and participation (organized school clubs and activities).
34. Losing things necessary for tasks or activities at school or at home (e.g. pencils, books, assignments before, during and after completion of a given task).	• Help students organize. Frequently monitor notebook dividers, pencil pouch, locker, book bag, desks. A place for everything and everything in its place. • Provide positive reinforcement for good organization. Provide student with a list of need materiasl and their locations.
35. Poor use of time (sitting, staring into space, doodling, not working on task at hand.	• Teach reminder cues (a gentle touch on the shoulder, hand signals, etc.). • Tell the student your expectation of what paying attention looks like (You look like you are paying attention when...).. • Give the student a time limit for a small unit of work with positive reinforcement for accurate completion.

Remember: Any of these accommodations are part of an on-going process. Students with Attention Deficit Disorder need frequent and continued re-teaching and review of expected behaviors and learning strategies.

This chart *Suggested Classroom Accommodations for Students with Attention Deficit Disorder*, 1991, was developed by a team, including Gary Smith (Special Education Teacher Consultant for the Anchorage School District), Marilyn Conaway (Principal, Anchorage School District), and Carolyn Croft Lodwig (retired teacher and parent of an A.D.D. student).

CHAPTER 30

CLASSROOM MODIFICATIONS

Anita Naftaly

THE NEED FOR MODIFICATIONS

As adults, we all use tools to aid our daily lives. Some of us need glasses for reading, calculators to help balance our checkbooks, and planners to keep our schedules organized. If we commit to a healthier lifestyle, we may turn to our treadmills, calorie counters, and personal trainers. We utilize all of these modifications to help us achieve our goals.

Within each classroom there are children who likewise may need modifications to achieve their academic goals. They may be children who have learning difficulties or other special needs with their own various challenges. Some of them may need the assistance of tape recorders to help them remember or an FM unit to sharpen their auditory processing. Others may need a bookmark to keep their place while reading or a highlighter pen to distinguish parts of similar-looking letters. By providing adaptations for struggling students, we can help them learn more effectively. We can also help decrease their feelings of frustration, failure, and low self-esteem while increasing their independence and, inevitably, their self-image.

Effective teaching strategies tell us that one size does not fit all—not all children learn in the same way. As Richard D. Lavoie, M.A., M.Ed., nationally-known expert on learning disabilities, often reminds us, "Fair doesn't mean that every child gets the same treatment, but that every child gets what he needs." We need to create an equal-opportunity setting in our classroom. Modifications are the vehicles to meet those needs and enable a child to function comfortably and successfully within a classroom.

WHO NEEDS OUR HELP?

Many children attending a supplemental religious school are receiving support in their secular school settings. It is quite helpful when the religious school teacher is aware of the identified learning difficulties and the modifications that have worked effectively with a student. This confidential information may have been provided by the parent via a registration form/questionnaire or conversations with the school director and/or religious school special education consultant. In some instances the Jewish education central agency special education consultant can provide consultation and recommendations for a specific child. With parental permission the consultant or special education professional may be able to contact the secular school special education teacher to find out which classroom modifications have been successful. These modifications can then be adapted to the subject matter in a religious school setting. A meeting can be convened using a team consisting of the classroom teacher, parents, school director, and special educator to share information regarding the child's strengths and interests, types of assistance the child might need, present levels of functioning, and the parent's specific goals and expectations for their child.

Some children may not be formally identified as having learning or behavioral difficulties, yet their performance is a concern to us. Our role as religious school teachers is not to diagnose or label behaviors, but rather to make appropriate modifications that will enable the child to receive a positive Jewish education. We can achieve that through a keen awareness and sensitivity as we observe our students. There are three simple questions that we can ask ourselves:

- What are the behaviors we see?
- When and where do they occur?
- What can we do to modify them?

WHAT ARE THE BEHAVIORS?

Let us look closely at a child and observe *consistent* patterns of behavior. Students may display some behaviors that can signify a red flag or trigger to act upon. These may include academic and/or behavioral issues. For instance

- What subject area is causing difficulty?
- Is Hebrew reading a "problem"?
- Is the child struggling when writing Hebrew?
- Are Judaic studies such as Bible, history, or the holiday cycle areas of weakness?
- Are key concepts not understood?

Some of the typical behaviors displayed in a religious school setting may include:

- The child who confuses Hebrew letters that look similar, e.g., the *resh* and a *daled,* or a *nun* and a *gimel*
- The child who cannot identify the consonant or vowel sounds
- The child who confuses the right-to-left orientation of Hebrew (i.e., writing from the left side of the *maḥberet* or reversing the actual letter)
- The child who does not remember the cursive form for the printed letter (i.e., he can read the word *melekh* in the *Siddur* but can't reproduce it in cursive [script] form)
- The child who is unable to copy items from the blackboard correctly so that he never completes the entire list of vocabulary words
- The child who always asks you to repeat directions or is unable to pay attention
- The child who has difficulty remembering familiar blessings in correct sequence—such as the *Hamotzi* or *Kiddush*
- The child who is disorganized and/or forgets to bring books or supplies to school

WHEN AND WHERE DO THEY OCCUR?

Some thoughts to consider: Do I observe these things primarily when the child is in my classroom? Where is the child seated—close to classmates, close to the windows or doorways? Do these behaviors occur in the sanctuary during services? Do these behaviors consistently occur during special sessions like music or in the media center? Is the child having difficulty during whole-class activity or during independent work? Do the behavioral concerns occur during transition times or when the child first arrives at school or near the end of the school day? Do these behaviors occur with a change of routine? Do they occur during a structured or non-structured activity?

WHAT CAN I DO TO MODIFY THEM?

When some of these behaviors are consistently observed, it is our cue to acquire a "modification mindset" and begin to ask ourselves what simple modifications or adjustments we can make that might enable this child to learn more effectively.

- Can I implement them in a reasonable amount of time with a reasonable amount of effort?
- How can I make these modifications fit into my existing class structure and expectations?
- Can I choose appropriate modifications that don't stigmatize the student but can make an immense difference in a child's religious school experience?

Let's explore the various types of modifications. Close observation is the key to effectively evaluating the situation, making modifications, and adjusting them accordingly while teaching. There is no magic formula or recipe that we can use. Just a willingness to try and try again. Be creative in your thinking! It is worth the effort to help a child be more successful and achieve a positive and appropriate Jewish educational experience.

OUR CHOICES

There are general areas of modifications to consider. Modifications can be grouped into categories. These options can be used as a springboard for ideas and help us focus on specific variables of change. The following chart contains the general types of modifications followed by specific explanations and samples.

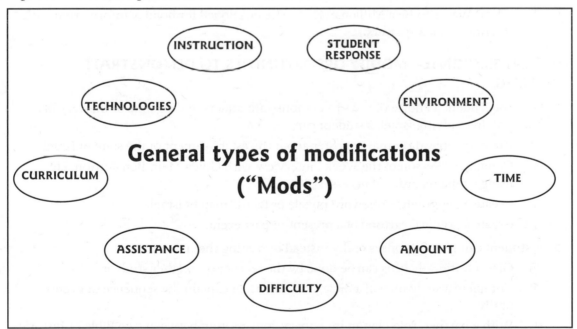

Our main charge is to prioritize the behavior—decide on the general area that needs adjusting—choose a modification that is appropriate—try it—evaluate its effectiveness!

In our next section we will explore examples of how this can be accomplished.

INSTRUCTION—MODIFY THE DELIVERY OF INSTRUCTION

1. Get the student's attention and prompt him before giving directions. Examples:
   A. Establish a secret code word with a student and say it aloud, or use a secret tap, or snap your fingers to help him focus.
   B. Say to the whole class, "Eyes (*aynayim*) towards me."
   C. Say to the whole class, "If you can hear me, clap once (class claps)…If you can hear me, clap twice."

2. Use multi-sensory modalities including the visual (sight), auditory (sound), tactile (touch), and kinesthetic (movement) senses. Examples:
   A. Use three-dimensional Hebrew letters with glitter glue or puff paint so a student can see and touch the distinct characteristics of the letter.
   B. Use a sand tray or desktop to trace the Hebrew letters while saying the letter sounds.
   C. Sing a vowel rap song with accompanying hand signals, such as (fist to stomach) ‎ו‎ ‎וּ‎ (oo oo) "I caught the flu." Then (punch fist in the air) ‎..‎ ‎..‎ (ay ay) "Have a nice day"

3. Limit "lecture-type" presentations to five-minute chunks of time.

4. Use games to engage active learning and to reinforce material. Examples:
   A. "Jeopardy" can be adapted for Bible facts.
   B. "Concentration" game can be used to match ritual objects such as Torah scroll, *mezuzah*.
   C. "Fish" game can be played to match words such as *mitzvah* and *tzedakah*.
   D. "Who Wants to Be a Millionaire?" can be developed for holiday information with multiple-choice answers.

STUDENT RESPONSE—MODIFY OPPORTUNITIES TO DEMONSTRATE LEARNING

1. Give the student a choice of ways to demonstrate understanding and/or mastery of material. In studying Israel, a student can
   A. Create poetry, diorama, or poster about the establishment of the state of Israel.
   B. Conduct a "Person of the Week" interview with Golda Meir, Ben Gurion, etc., using a tape recorder, if necessary.
   C. Create a geography crossword puzzle or tactile map of Israel.
   D. Create a political cartoon of a present or past event.

2. A student can give responses orally instead of writing them down.
   A. Give a test orally (this can be done by the teacher or another student).
   B. Complete a story-map of a Bible story and then explain the sequence of events orally.
   C. With a partner, role-play an imaginary conversation between two Bible or historic figures.
   D. Use Bibliodrama to actively involve the student.

E. Reenact Bible events such as various dream scenes.

ENVIRONMENT—MODIFY THE SETTING FOR THE STUDENT

1. Place desks in "pods" or small groupings of four chairs in a semicircle.
2. Distance students from distractions. Examples:
   A. Place a bookcase or room divider strategically.
   B. Place student desks away from windows, noisy heating vents, and doorways.
3. Provide study carrels or private work areas when concentration is necessary.
4. Establish a standing workstation or "office" for freedom of movement.

   Example: A countertop or freestanding bookcase can be used at the rear of the room a student can stand and complete work.

TIME—MODIFY THE TIME TO COMPLETE A TASK OR A TEST

1. Use a calendar timeline for a project.
2. Provide additional breaks after student completes "chunks" of a task.
3. Break tests down into ten-minute periods.
4. Provide increased time for work completion in class or at home.
5. Give time cues to aid time management. Provide prompts:
   A. Say "There are two minutes left before we begin our writing."
   B. Say "There are two minutes left before we finish."
6. Prioritize steps of an assignment and provide checklists.

   Example: Number 1-2-3 with check-off for each part completed

AMOUNT—MODIFY THE NUMBER OF ITEMS THE STUDENT IS EXPECTED TO LEARN.

1. Reduce amount of work/length of tests.
   A. Use ample space between items.
   B. Reduce the number of choices in a multiple-choice question.
   C. Provide a word bank for choice selection.
2. Assign only the even- or odd-numbered questions on a page.
3. Only grade what the student has completed.
4. Expose only one section of a worksheet at a time.

DIFFICULTY—MODIFY THE SKILL LEVEL FOR THE STUDENT.

1. Provide a study guide of key concepts.
2. Rewrite text passages at a lower readability level.
3. Provide multi-level questions in a game or project.

   Questions may range from facts and knowledge to application and finally analytical questions.

4. Pre-teach or have a student preview the material.

5. Select different vocabulary words to learn based on ability level.

ASSISTANCE—MODIFY THE SUPPORT GIVEN TO THE STUDENT.

1. Pair students with peer buddies or partners for work assignments.

2. Arrange for a teen assistant or *madrikh* to assist a particular student or act as a class aide to avoid singling out a student.

   Example: The *madrikh* can write teacher presentation notes on the chalkboard.

3. Utilize cooperative learning groups.

   Example: One student can be the reader, another student the scribe, etc.

4. Provide outline or key facts of lesson presentation for the student to follow.

CURRICULUM—MODIFY WHAT IS BEING TAUGHT.

1. Provide simplified goals and objectives.

2. Provide alternative text or worksheets at a lower readability level.

3. Use films and tapes to enhance a textbook lesson. Examples:
   A. Use the movie *Exodus* to discuss the settling of Israel.
   B. Use the movie *The Ten Commandments* to portray Biblical events.
   C. Use a *tefillin* video demonstrating the procedure of fulfilling this mitzvah.

MATERIALS—MODIFY MATERIALS USED BY THE STUDENT.

1. Use large-print textbooks. Examples:
   A. A *Siddur* or *Haggadah* that has larger print can help a student see the distinctive characteristics of the Hebrew letters more easily.
   B. Create a student study guide for Judaic content areas.
   C. Add pictures and symbols to text.

2. Provide individual desk charts for reference.

   Example: An *Alef Bet* chart with print and corresponding script letters can make it easier for a student to remember.

3. Use color-coding, highlighting, underlining. Examples:
   A. Color-coding the Hebrew vowels can help a student remember them.
   B. Highlight the unique characteristics of a letter, such as the "dent" in the letter *daled;* or on worksheets or flash cards, highlight (red) a vocabulary word and highlight (blue) the definition.
   C. Circle the key words in the written directions such as "Match" or "Compare".

4. Use individual dry-erase boards instead of paper and pencil.

5. Use hands-on manipulatives.

   Example: Bingo chips and tongue depressors can be used to represent vowel sounds.

6. Use visual aids such as a web to chart prior knowledge and organize ideas.

Example: Make a web and put the main topic or character in the center with traits and descriptions stemming from the center.

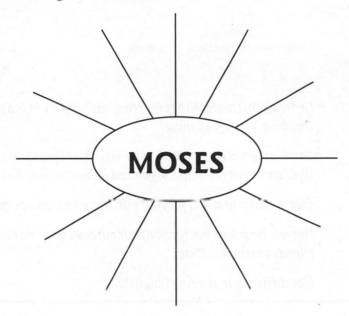

7. Shorten, alter, or eliminate some homework assignments.

8. Provide uncluttered worksheets and reduce the amount on a page.

TECHNOLOGIES—MODIFY THE EQUIPMENT USED BY THE STUDENT.

1. Use taped materials for reinforcement. Example: Prayers (*tefillot*) or Torah service can be taped; holiday songs such as the Four Questions can be taped with pauses for student responses.

2. Use computer software games for reinforcement.

3. Use a computer for a student to research a topic.

4. Use assistive equipment. Examples:
   A. Laptop computer
   B. Voice recognition computer program for children who are nonverbal
   C. Computer wand that scans and reads words aloud

PLAN OF ACTION

In the previous sections we have shown the necessary steps to take when considering academic or behavioral adjustments for individual students. We begin by gathering information to learn as much as possible about the student, observing and analyzing the behaviors of concern, and selecting the appropriate modifications. Our final step is to evaluate modification effectiveness after implementation. In this section we will give examples of how to implement modifications.

STUDENT PROFILE

Information provided by parents

Student:	Brian
Grade:	4
Religious School: General Classroom	Congregational school, 2x a week
Secular School:	*General classroom with resource room support in language arts (reading, writing, spelling)*
Strengths:	*Good imagination, curious, creative, attention span strong if Brian likes an activity. Brian is organized in his thinking but not on paper.*
Interests:	*Enjoys music and art, playing with Nintendo, computer Wizards game*
Goals:	*Hebrew language instruction, bar mitzvah and "doesn't have a lot of friends in temple school."*
Weaknesses:	*Has difficulty in reading (English).*

Information provided by student

Likes to play Nintendo, Play Station. Favorite game is Wizards (computer).

I'm good at drawing. I play soccer.

Invention: computers to communicate with aliens on different planets

Collects Crazy Bones

Observable behaviors of concern: Brian has difficulty in reading Hebrew words. He often mistakes the similar-looking letters and seems unfamiliar with the final letters. He sometimes has trouble distinguishing left and right orientation of letters. He has trouble following oral and written directions. He doesn't get started on his work right away and procrastinates about doing the work, rarely finishing it, resulting in incomplete work.

Concerns about how to evaluate his learning? Does he comprehend the material and just not demonstrate it in this way? He appears to be distractible, opening and shutting the book, restarting and throwing away paper, sharpening his pencil, leafing through his desk, shuffling papers, etc. He loses his place when called upon to read a sentence or stumbles over his reading of prayers and seems embarrassed about his mistakes.

When and where do they occur? They are seen during religious school when the student is in Judaic studies, which include reading and answering questions independently. They also are observed midweek, during the reading of the Hebrew prayers. Most of the time he has difficulty with paper/pencil tasks such as worksheets or working in the Hebrew *mahberet*.

Strengths observed: Brian participates when we are discussing things such as current events as a whole class. He is quite creative with his art projects. He assists in the synagogue youth choir. He participated in a lower grade on a school project recently and was recently very helpful with the younger children.

NEXT STEP

After gathering and analyzing the above data, the classroom teacher discusses it with the religious school special education consultant. A decision is made regarding possible modifications that might enhance Brian's performance in the classroom. Several adaptations are noted, keeping in mind that they should be simple and easily implemented and within the limited timeframe of the supplemental school program. For modification planning forms, see Appendix F.

MODEL REFERRAL PROCEDURE

TEACHER IDENTIFICATION
• General Classroom Teacher Completes Referral Forms

PARENT IDENTIFICATION
• Writes/Phones Contacts School Registration Form

SCHOOL DIRECTOR
• Reviews Forms
• Contacts Parents (phone approval or consent form)

RESOURCE TEACHER/SPECIAL EDUCATOR/ LEARNING SPECIALIST
• Informally Evaluates Student
• Formulates Individualized Education Plan
• Confers with School Director, Parents, Classroom Teacher
• Provides Consultative Services to Parents and Teachers
• Makes Academic/Behavioral Recommendations to Teachers
• Provides Direct Instruction
• Writes Progress Reports

Opening the Doors: Special Education Partnership Program, Agency for Jewish Education, Southfield, Michigan

Date_____		**MODIFICATION PLANNING FORM**	
Student *Brian*	**Age** *10*	**Phone** _____	**School** _____
Teacher(s) *Mrs. Cohen*		**Class** _____	**Grade** *4*

Brief description of concern: *Difficulty in reading English. Weak in completing independent written work, avoiding and showing frustration. Difficulty in ascertaining level of comprehension.*

Judaic Studies / Hebrew Lesson and/or Activity	*Modification Selections*
Bible Story: *Joseph and His Brothers*	**Instruction:** *Present movie of story to whole class followed by discussion so that Brian doesn't struggle with the reading and he can learn through different modality.* **Student Response:** *He can illustrate the story through sequence of drawings (comic strip), then explain it orally to the class. (This is also a way we can see if he is comprehending). He can work with buddy and have buddy do written part of story to go along with the pictures.* **Environment** _____ _____ **Time** _____ _____ **Amount:** *Reduce paper/pencil worksheets by half. Do a portion of the story at a time.* **Difficulty**_____ _____ **Assistance:** *He can do comprehension questions/worksheets paired with a classmate who can record his answers as Brian dictates them or he can try a small group.* **Curriculum:** *Study guide—highlight key concepts. Give alternatives: choice of art project or own creative project.* **Materials:** *Copy graphic story map and have him complete it, adding setting, characters, theme, etc. Drawing or brief answers accepted.* **Technologies:** *Have Brian research on the computer the various interpretations of Joseph's dreams.*

Form Completed By ☐ Classroom Teacher ☐ Special Educator
Form provided by Federation's Alliance For Jewish Education, Opening the Doors Partnership Program

MODIFICATION PLANNING FORM

Date_____			
Student *Brian*	**Age** *10*	**Phone** _____	**School** _____
Teacher(s) *Mrs. Cohen*		**Class** _____	**Grade** *4*

Brief description of concern: *Reading Fluency and accuracy.*

Judaic Studies / Hebrew Lesson and/or Activity	*Modification Selections*
Hebrew Prayer: *Ashrei*	**Instruction**: *Use flashcards of high-frequency sight words found in the Siddur in "Fish" game format. Play "Bingo" with Siddur phrases. Put specific prayer on tape (by song) and choral-sing short "chunks" at a time.*
	Student Response: *Tape record "echoing"—he is to repeat 1-2 lines of singing prayer.*
	Environment _____
	Time: *Give additional time for mastery.*
	Amount: *Decrease to half page of worksheet. He should be graded on progress and effort.*
	Difficulty _____
	Assistance: *Classmate buddy can play games to reinforce word recognition. Have him use a bookmark as a line marker to follow text. Highlight key direction words on worksheet and have him repeat directions in own words before beginning. Show/model the task for him at his work space.*
	Curriculum _____
	Materials: *Enlarge whole prayer. Cut into sentence strips and highlight specific difficult letters. Use green dots and arrows to show directions. Leave large spaces between each word. Use "foldable" letter for final letter form and desk chart.*
	Technologies: *Ashrei may be located on Hebrew computer software.*

Form Completed By ☐ Classroom Teacher ☐ Special Educator

Form provided by Federation's Alliance For Jewish Education, Opening the Doors Partnership Program

FINAL STEP

After the modifications are implemented, the special education teacher and the classroom teacher reconvene to evaluate the effectiveness of the modifications and make further recommendations as necessary. (See sample evaluation forms below)

Date_____ **Teacher Evaluation Modifications Implemented**

Student *Brian*　　　　**Age** *10*　　**Phone** _____　　**School** _____

Teacher(s) *Mrs. Cohen*　　　　**Class** _____　　**Grade** *4*

☒ **Judaic Studies Activity:** *Joseph and His Brothers*

☐ **Hebrew Lesson:**

What worked? *Brian liked the movie—it kept his attention. He had a lot of comments and questions during class discussion. He drew a detailed illustration of the story as other students wrote brief text in a small group. He seemed to really excel and got positive feedback from peers about his ability to draw well (his strength). He did a fantastic "web."*

What did not work? *Brian worked on the web but did not do the corresponding question-and-answer sheets required. The format of the study guide and worksheet has to be redesigned—still too hard for him to read. (Maybe a tape or a buddy would be more effective). We should try multiple choice, matching, or true and false.*

Form Completed By　　☐ Classroom Teacher　　☐ Special Educator
Form provided by Federation's Alliance For Jewish Education, Opening the Doors Partnership Program

---

Date_____ **Teacher Evaluation Modifications Implemented**

Student *Brian*　　　　**Age** *10*　　**Phone** _____　　**School** _____

Teacher(s) *Mrs. Cohen*　　　　**Class** _____　　**Grade** *4*

☐ **Judaic Studies Activity:**

☒ **Hebrew Lesson:**

What worked? Brian showed improvement with Siddur word recognition after repeated practice playing Fish & Bingo games. Enlarging the words seemed to help him see letter difference. Calling on Brian (with previously reviewed words) had a positive effect—he seemed to want to study more in order to get positive peer feedback. Tape of prayers seemed to improve his pronunciation of words and chunking phrases.

What did not work? Hebrew computer software wasn't effective because Hebrew font was different than what's used in class. (Reminder: Ask school computer consultant if other software is available with traditional font.) He preferred playing games with peer buddy as opposed to studying independently. (We need to achieve a balance.)

Form Completed By　　☐ Classroom Teacher　　☐ Special Educator
Form provided by Federation's Alliance For Jewish Education, Opening the Doors Partnership Program

---

CONCLUDING REMARKS

Our overall goal as Jewish educators is to enable our students to receive a quality and appropriate Jewish education. We need to invest our time and commitment so that we can truly make a difference in a child's life. In this chapter we have demonstrated the necessity of being flexible and creative when assisting our students and assuring them a successful and rewarding educational experience with their peers. By implementing modifications we can meet our students' challenges by creating a positive learning environment for them. In addition, we can decrease their common feelings of frustration, failure, and low self-esteem. We have included ways to help a student by implementing adaptations in order to foster success and impact a child's life and view of him/herself as a Jew. There is no one magic answer! Just be willing to try and try again. Be creative in your thinking. The rewards are great for you and your students.

REFERENCES

Janney, Rachel Ph.D., and Martha E. Snell, Ph.D. *Modifying Schoolwork*. Paul H. Brookes Publishing Co., 2000.

Javorsky, James, M.Ed. *Alphabet Soup*. Minerva Press, Inc., 1993.

IDENTIFYING SPECIAL NEEDS AND ACCOMMODATING THEM IN THE CLASSROOM

Identifying Special Needs	Accommodations
Visual Perception Problems	
• Frequently loses place when reading or copying • Has trouble discriminating similar shapes, letters, words • Does not enjoy pictures, slides or books • Shows signs of eye strain, e.g., squinting, blinking • Has trouble following written directions from board or printed page • Works slowly on printed assignment or tests • Displays poor sight vocabulary • May use fingers to keep place while reading • Skips words or reverses words when reading aloud • Cannot visualize things in mind • Demonstrates erratic spelling or incorrect letter sequences • Does not notice details on pictures, maps, photographs • Confused by worksheets containing a great deal of visual stimuli • Has difficulty remembering what is seen • May whisper to self while working with visual material	• Preferential Seating • Clear writing (board and dittos) • Verbal with written directions • Visual focusing cues • Oral directions • Tape-recorded material • Color coding • Summarize questions • Wider spacing on worksheets • Buddy reader/peer reading aloud • Highlighted text • Use of index cards • Comprehension discussions • Reading/discussion groups
Auditory Perception Problems	
• Has trouble distinguishing fine differences between sounds and words, e.g., d-t, pin-pen • Loses interest or concentration during lectures • Has difficulty following a series of oral directions • Cannot accurately record notes from oral presentations • Displays poor receptive vocabulary • Repeats what is told before acting or responding • Often repeats the same question • Asks questions about oral directions and facts previously given • May watch the speaker's face intently or lean forward toward the speaker • Does not enjoy listening to records or rhythmic activities • Becomes irritated by extraneous noise • Has difficulty learning and applying phonic rules • May have difficulty remembering what is heard	• Preferential seating • Short oral directions • Oral with written directions • Student repeats directions • Alert to directions • Talk slowly • Vary voice tone and pitch • Quiet work area • Key points on board • Notes written out • Explanation with visuals • Classroom charts • Manipulations • Wait time

Identifying Special Needs	Accommodations
Fine Motor Problems	
• Displays poor handwriting, including difficulty forming letters and numbers • Has difficulty in activities requiring cutting or pasting • Finds it hard to trace or color within the given borders • Has trouble with speed and neatness in taking notes • Shows fatigue and restlessness during writing or drawing tasks • Handwritten work often appears sloppy and disorganized • Has difficulty manipulating or using small objects and tools, e.g., nuts and bolts, screwdrivers, puzzle pieces • Usually works slowly in completing written work • Has trouble making straight lines to connect points, match answers, or label maps • Is clumsy with tasks requiring sorting, cutting, etc. • Displays poor copying skills	• Model good handwriting • Adjust expectations • Paper placement • Teach erasing • Few copying activities • Appropriate writing materials • Reduce writing requirement • Student types • Write every other line • Tracing • Large motor activities
Organizational Problems	
• Demonstrates poor organization of work on paper • Frequently misplaces books, pencils, homework, etc. • Becomes disoriented during confusing situations such as fire drills, assemblies • Is easily distracted by extraneous stimuli and is often off task • Has difficulty getting started on assigned activities • Has difficulty distinguishing main ideas from details • Has trouble developing an outline • Has trouble making choices and identifying priorities • Loses track of time, tends to get disoriented when moving from place to place • Always seems to be doing things at the last minute • Has a messy desk, locker, or notebook • Frequently forgets assignments, directions, schedules • Has difficulty adjusting to changes in routine	• Daily routine • Clear, concise directions • Notebook dividers • Review & summarize • Sample of finished product • Block and/or folded worksheets • Enumerate steps for specific assignments • Uncluttered worksheets • Clues—page number where answer is found • Focusing techniques • Work area clear • Workbook pages one at a time

Identifying Special Needs	Accommodations
Written/Motor Expression Problems	
<ul><li>Has difficulty writing answers on paper, but may be able to give correct answers orally</li><li>Written vocabulary is much weaker than spoken vocabulary</li><li>Handwritten work may appear sloppy and disorganized</li><li>Has difficulty shading in answers on score sheets</li><li>Written ideas and concepts are usually stronger than writing mechanics, e.g., spelling, syntax, vocabulary level</li><li>Has trouble writing a sentence with a complete thought</li><li>Demonstrates poor spelling skills</li><li>Tests better on objective tests than on tests that require writing, e.g., essays, definitions</li><li>Frequently does not complete written assignments</li></ul>	<ul><li>Allow more time</li><li>Use short answers</li><li>Stress accuracy</li><li>Class time to work</li><li>Use pictures with written product</li><li>Proofreading checklist</li><li>Oral reports</li><li>Reduce writing requirements</li><li>Modify original tasks</li><li>Tape answers</li><li>Distraction-free work area</li></ul>
Verbal Expression Problems	
<ul><li>Does not enjoy discussions, oral presentations, or reading aloud</li><li>Has difficulty explaining self clearly and coherently</li><li>Displays poor speech, e.g., articulation, fluency, expressiveness</li><li>Is unable to vocalize thought rapidly</li><li>Uses slang or colloquial terms instead of more precise words</li><li>Spoken vocabulary is much weaker than written vocabulary</li><li>Is reluctant to volunteer ideas or respond verbally to questions</li><li>Remarks, when made, are often irrelevant, confusing, or inaccurate</li><li>Appears to be uncomfortable speaking in a group</li><li>Has difficulty recalling a word he/she wants to use</li><li>Uses grammatically incorrect sentences</li></ul>	<ul><li>Extra time to answer</li><li>Hint</li><li>Notes with oral report</li><li>Visual with oral report</li><li>Read silently/orally</li><li>Time limit on oral reports</li><li>Specific questions</li><li>Small group discussion</li><li>Written instead of verbal</li><li>Projects</li><li>Tape their oral reports</li></ul>

PART 6: BEHAVIOR

V'KHOL BANAYIKH—JEWISH EDUCATION FOR ALL

CHAPTER 31

BEHAVIOR—WHAT IS THE STUDENT TRYING TO TELL US?

Miriam Gluck

INTRODUCTION

Can information on behavior address diverse ages and settings? Are the issues the same for children and teens, from early childhood to post-confirmation, whether in a day school, supplementary school, or camp setting? The answer is yes. The underlying needs that drive behavior are similar across all ages.

The need for food is an active need from the moment of birth. The need for holding and attachment may be less apparent, but if unmet, it can lead to distortion in behavior. The need for social contact is a need that begins at birth and grows stronger as the individual grows. In fact, an infant deprived of social contact will not thrive and may even die. An adult deprived of social contact is likely to become depressed, but probably not die. The same needs that motivate the behavior in a child also motivate behaviors in an adult. However, the adult may try to meet those needs by different and, one hopes, more mature behaviors.

Behaviors may look different at different ages and stages, but the causes remain the same. To better understand the reasons for a particular behavior, the adult should look at the child with this question in mind: "If I were his age, what might cause me to behave in this way?"

All behavior is purposeful; individuals try to communicate through actions. Often the individual himself is unaware of the purpose behind a particular behavior. This is why it is usually useless to ask a child, "Why did you do that?" One's actions can be due to various reasons—for instance, a physiological reason that regulates sensory input to keep from becoming overloaded. Or it may be a matter of feeling driven to ward off an unpleasant thought. The difficulty arises when the person's efforts to meet his or her needs come into conflict with others' needs and goals.

This is often the issue in a school setting. Regardless of concerns that may be affecting individual class members, the teacher has overall goals for the class that need to be accomplished. Students are not usually able to leave class to resolve whatever might be upsetting them. Though the teacher may not like the observed behavior nor agree with the purpose of the behavior, a child's behavior is not for the teacher's benefit, but to achieve relief for the child. If the teacher can understand what it is the child is trying to accomplish through this behavior, then neither student nor teacher has to adopt an adversarial position. Thus it becomes much easier to deal with the unacceptable behavior.

CAUSES OF DISRUPTIVE BEHAVIOR

If teachers want to understand and help their students, it is important to begin from the correct premise. If a teacher thinks a student is misbehaving "on purpose" to make the teacher's life miserable, then it will be extremely difficult for change to occur, and both the student and the teacher will most likely have a long, miserable year. On the other hand, if the teacher is sensitive to issues that may be affecting a child and is able to tune into what motivates the child to do what he or she does, disruptive behaviors are more likely to decrease. Nonetheless, disruptive behaviors take many forms and present for many reasons.

A. ENVIRONMENTAL

All people react to their environment. Industries have been built around the use of color and placement of environmental props to create the appropriate atmosphere. Imagine yourself walking into a classroom that is neat and clean and has interesting items displayed on the walls. There are inviting things to do on the table or the board. The teacher greets you with a big "Hello!" Now walk into the following room. There is clutter everywhere, the tables or desks are not clean, the walls have had the same material on them for months, and there are only a few activities available for the student. In fact, it looks as if the teacher is not ready. How would you feel in each environment? It is critical to establish an environment that provides appropriate activities and learning opportunities for all students.

Students learn best in a calm, organized, predictable environment. They need to know what comes next. Anxiety can be exacerbated when a student does not to know the class schedule and the expectations for the class. Few individuals can be productive in an anxious state. Students may go to great lengths to reduce anxiety, which often means acting out in some way.

Many children have difficulty paying attention when there is too much visual or auditory stimulation. For some it is distracting; for others it is actually painful. Class size and seating arrangement can also be a factor in behavior. Each person has a personal space or boundary that should be honored.

B. FAMILY ISSUES

The Jewish community is no longer immune to the plagues of the rest of society. Divorce, alcoholism, drugs, abuse of spouses and children, illness, death, job loss, and poverty affect Jewish families. People cannot function at an optimal level if they are preoccupied with any of the above issues. It is possible for a student who seems disinterested in class to be concerned with personal problems. These distractions can impact students, making it very difficult for a child to concentrate.

Teachers take for granted that when the children arrive at school they have had breakfast and there will be a well-balanced meal available for lunch. Unfortunately, this is no longer a valid assumption for some of our children. A child who comes to school hungry or worried about the contents of lunch will not be able to function well and may not be able to, or may be too ashamed to, verbalize what is wrong. The teacher will only see a child unable to concentrate on the school activity.

Teachers must be aware that simchas also interfere with the performance of a student. The excitement of an impending wedding, bar mitzvah or brit milah ceremony can impact a child's ability to concentrate in class. Preparations, out-of-town family members, additional activities, late bedtimes, and little time for homework, to name a few problems, can have an adverse affect on a student's performance. With today's families so scattered, it is important for children to have a sense of rootedness in the extended family and family celebrations. The memories a child carries with him of grandparents, aunts, uncles, and cousins are more beneficial than the schoolwork required for that week. We as teachers must keep things in proper perspective for our students.

C. PHYSICAL/BIOLOGICAL

A child is not just a cognitive, emotional being. He is also governed by his biology and his physical being. A part of a child's biology is his sensory system. This includes the auditory, visual, and tactile systems and the sense of smell and taste. Each person has what is called the "threshold", the point at which input from a particular system begins to register. Most individuals have the ability to regulate the amount of information that comes into a particular system at any time. Some people, however, lack the ability to discriminate what is important. How does this knowledge assist us when working with students of various ages and in different types of settings? As teachers we need to be most aware of the auditory, visual, and tactile systems, as it is these modalities that have the most impact on learning.

- **Auditory:** A child can have a low threshold for sound. This means that certain prolonged sounds, such as an air-conditioner or a fan, can be extremely disturbing. Also, some children are overwhelmed or frightened by loud sounds; it is too much for the auditory system to handle. There are some children with the opposite problem. They have a very high threshold for auditory stimulation, and if the sounds are too low or too similar, they will not register.

- **Visual:** The same problem can occur with the visual system. The child may be overwhelmed by too many things on the walls, board, or even on paper, especially if the material is not presented in an organized fashion. They easily become overstimulated by too much input. Paper-and-pencil tasks can cause similar problems.

- **Tactile:** The tactile system is involved with the sense of and reaction to touch. Most people can tolerate being touched even when they don't particularly want it. There are people, especially some children, who for purely sensory reasons cannot tolerate a slight or unexpected touch. The child that flinches when touched, strikes out when bumped into, or refuses to put on a particularly stiff jacket because he only wants to wear soft clothing may fall into this category. Any of these sensory issues can explain why a particular child has difficulty paying attention to a lesson.

Another biological component in all people is their level of reactivity. Reactivity refers to the manner in which individuals react to incoming stimuli and how they regulate their physical state of being. It is best to think of reactivity on a continuum, with hyporeactivity and hyperractivity at each end. The middle sixty percent is considered within the normal range. These people usually react appropriately to stimuli, while those at either end have difficulty reacting appropriately.

- **Hyporeactivity:** Individuals who fall on the low end of the continuum often have difficulty reacting to normal levels of stimulation and appear disinterested, lethargic, or sleepy. They move slowly and are generally last to finish their work. The problem lies in the level of stimulation. For these students the stimulation must be animated and of interest and volume, otherwise they won't respond. This is called hyporeactivity. Often a child with hyporeativity will try to arouse himself by becoming over-reactive or appearing to be hyperactive.

- **Hyperreactivity:** At the other end of the continuum is the child who is hyperreactive. Hyperreactivity refers to one's difficulty regulating the amount of sensory input to his or her system. Because of this deficit he becomes easily overstimulated.

While these may be biological reasons for a child's behaviors, other issues might cause a similar effect. A child who is hungry will have difficulty concentrating. For older children, particularly girls, dieting can interfere with learning. Powers of concentration will decline. Children who are sleep-deprived will not be able to pay attention; they will marshal all their energy just to stay awake. Since adolescents seldom get the proper amount of sleep, concentration problems can surface. Add to that the fact that Hebrew school and confirmation class often meet in the late afternoon, when the body's natural rhythms dip. Students will have difficulty giving their full attention to learning. Other problems that can interfere with learning may include ear infections and fluid in the ears. In summary, any physical illness or pain can potentially alter the child's ability to function in the class. If a child suddenly displays unusual behavior, it is always best to investigate and rule out any physical cause before looking for other reasons.

D. GOODNESS OF FIT

Children and adolescents are put into a particular school and class for a variety of reasons, not all of which take a student's needs into account. All people have different learning styles. Some can sit for long periods. Some cannot. Some are quiet, and some speak up. There is no one right way. But an active, inquisitive child who has difficulty with prolonged periods of uninterrupted quiet work is going to experience stress if placed in a setting that does not make allowances for his or her needs. It is important that educators not only listen to the parent's needs for the child, but also to the child's needs as expressed in words and actions. There is no guarantee that the match between student and environment will be a good fit. When problems arise, parents and educators should determine the best fit.

E. ATTENTION SEEKING

Developing children need attention. All living things need light from the sun to grow, including humans. From birth on, a child turns to his "sun," the parent. When this "sun" is not there, the child may wither and fail to thrive. A child who does not get attention from his primary care givers has a very difficult time developing fully. Unconsciously the child will seek attention, because the alternative is so unacceptable. If a child is unable to elicit a response from the parent for positive behavior, because the parent is either disinterested or too busy, then the child has no recourse but to use negative or disruptive behavior to say "Look at me! Here I am."

How does this need impact the teacher and classroom? If a child has learned that the only way to be noticed at home is to act out through challenging behaviors, he most likely will not change because he is now in a classroom. Similarly, if the class is very large or the teacher is not particularly fond of a child and pays him little attention, the child may feel that there is no place in the "sun" for him. If his "good" behavior and quality of work is not getting acknowledged, he may turn to disruptive behavior. He then gets acknowledged while being reprimanded. The adage "A negative response is better than no response" is still very accurate.

There is another type of attention-seeking child. That is the one that always receives a lot of attention and has never been told "Not now" or "Later". This child expects that the world is just waiting to do whatever he or she wants and needs. Unfortunately, the child should not be blamed in most cases, as it is the parent who never allowed the child to experience the reality of the larger environment. This type of attention seeking is no easier for the teacher who tries to show the child that there are other people with wants and needs in the world.

HOW TO ASSESS STUDENTS' BEHAVIOR

Good observation over a period of time is one of the best ways to assess behavior. To observe a challenging behavior out of its context misses seventy-five percent of the behavior. It is only when the particular piece of behavior can be put into the larger picture that it begins to make sense. The teacher then may determine what must be done in this particular situation and what to do to prevent it from recurring. The following is an orderly way of thinking about an incident.

There are five simple but very necessary steps to instruct the teacher as to what to do.

A. DESCRIBE WHAT HAPPENS JUST BEFORE DISRUPTIVE BEHAVIOR.

What happened in the classroom before this incident happened?

Was it noisy? Confusing? Unstructured? Transition time?

Many children can have difficulty maintaining themselves in these situations.

What about the other children?

Are they subtly "nudging" the child, either physically or verbally?

Is this child excluded from the community of children?

Does the child lack the necessary social skills to become part of a group in an appropriate way?

B. DESCRIBE THE BEHAVIOR.

It is wonderful when the teacher has witnessed the episode firsthand. More than likely, the teacher will not have seen it and must rely on reports of others. This in itself can be problematic. Each will have a different perspective.

This means that the teacher cannot come to an immediate conclusion about what really happened and who is responsible. The teacher must be a seeker of facts. When a child feels threatened it becomes very difficult for him to give an even-handed report. The normal inclination is to protect oneself, which, of course, biases the report. Therefore, the goal is for the teacher to gather as much information as possible to reconstruct the event. The consequences decided upon should be consistent with the inappropriate behavior. If the teacher is not certain about what really occurred, it is best to acknowledge this and then discuss the problem in a general way, either in a small group situation or using the whole class to make it a learning experience for everyone.

There is also the matter of primary and secondary responsibility. If David hit Sara, David did something wrong and is primarily responsible. However if, prior to David's striking out at Sara, Sara said or did something to provoke David, Sara is secondarily responsible. This does not excuse David's behavior or its consequences. But it is very important for David, Sara, and the rest of the class that Sara's provocation be addressed. David needs to know that he is not "being picked on," Sara needs to learn that her provocative behavior will not be tolerated, and the class needs to see that the teacher deals fairly with all the children in the class.

C. DESCRIBE THE BEHAVIOR FOLLOWING THE INCIDENT.

How does everyone react?
Are the child's classmates amused? Disturbed? Jealous?
Does an adult come right over and give attention to the child?

A teacher must be aware of very subtle reinforcements a child receives. A smile from one friend may be enough for a child to justify the teacher's displeasure. Is class activity interrupted as a result of the behavior? To extinguish a disruptive behavior, positive feedback, to the extent possible, must be eliminated.

D. STUDENT GAINS FROM THE BEHAVIOR.

Actions do not occur in a vacuum. Even if it is not obvious at first, the student perceives a benefit from his behavior that helps meet his needs. It is rare that a person puts himself at risk for punitive action unless the need is very great. One of the primary motivators is the attention that is generated by the negative behavior. The need may be for attention from the adult. One way to say "look at me" is to do something that will draw the teacher's attention. The price of the punishment is secondary to the need to be acknowledged. The need for peer recognition becomes greater as peers become an increasingly important factor in the young person's world. For some students, recognition by one's peers overrides the inner voice of the parent's rules and values. Some students find it exceedingly difficult to be "one of the group," and they feel slightly out of step. They don't get the rhythm of social interaction and rarely feel that they fit in easily. These students will often adopt negative means to attract and keep the attention of their peers. In an effort to show off, they typically act out, take unnecessary chances, become disrespectful, or are verbally abusive. They often adopt the "I don't care" stance to cover the underlying feelings of being outside.

Disruptive behavior is often employed to keep secret the student's limited understanding of the material. Often these young people are the "class clowns". This can be a diversionary tactic used to divert attention away from the underlying problem. What looks like a disruptive behavior may really be a child with a learning disability or someone that is struggling academically.

APPROPRIATE WAYS TO REACT TO BEHAVIOR

There are basically two different ways to react to a situation: the knee-jerk reaction and a planned response. The knee-jerk reaction is often the typical reaction to misbehavior from a child, especially when the adult has a full classroom. However, it really is not the most effective way of reacting.

When a person reacts immediately, without thinking, the disciplinary action taken may not be the most appropriate and effective. It probably has not been well thought out, and more harm than good can result. If a teacher does not feel calm enough, it is perfectly permissible to share this with the student. The teacher should feel free to tell the child that she will look at the situation and assess the steps to be taken. It helps the child understand the magnitude of the event and can be beneficial at the same time.

A second and much more effective way to react is to take a deep breath, stop the behavior, make sure everyone is safe, and evaluate. The teacher should evaluate the following:

A. What is taking place?
B. Why is it happening?
C. What is the student telling me?

D. What can I do to alleviate the cause?

E. What can I do to assist the student in coping?

SETTING APPROPRIATE EXPECTATIONS FOR EACH SCHOOL SETTING

A. ISSUES FOR SUPPLEMENTARY/CONGREGATIONAL SCHOOLS

Teachers in congregational school programs confront unique educational issues. Religious/ Hebrew schools are supplementary in nature, creating an added burden to the teacher. The teacher must recognize this hurdle and seek ways to overcome it.

Children need a mixture of quiet and active activities. The combination is necessary to regulate their sensory systems. Without this they are likely to become hyporeactive (lethargic) or hyperreactive (ADHD-like). Unfortunately, most schools expect children to sit still for long periods of time little time given for physical activity. This can result in ineffective learning opportunities. The Hebrew teacher must take this into account when planning. It may not be productive to begin with a serious lesson. Many of the children are not able to "learn" again. The first portion of the class needs to be devoted to stimulating activities, both physically and verbally. Some time devoted to physical activity can be very beneficial. When a person exercises, there is increased blood flow to the brain. This increased blood flow brings increased oxygen and chemical activity to the centers of the brain. The brain wakes up and is ready to begin to take in information.

Every teacher is aware that students spend the last half hour of the school day watching the clock, counting the minutes until they are out of there. If children were polled as to what they want to do when school is out, going to another school would probably not rank very high. This is the challenge facing every teacher of Hebrew school. It is not productive to blame the children or adolescents. It's not a question of how they feel about their Judaism. It is just reality. The most productive way to deal with it is to acknowledge it, not take it personally, and devise creative ways to enliven the classroom. If a teacher does not, the children will devise their own ways to make the time pass as painlessly as possible, and their means and goals often work against the teacher and class.

B. ISSUES FOR DAY SCHOOLS

Administrators and teachers should consider themselves blessed. The expectations the day school puts on a child and the fact that most children rise to the occasion, are amazing. The student copes with eight to ten subjects with minimal time for large-muscle activity, little time for play, at least two languages to read and speak, and several hours of homework! This is what the day school asks of the child. Many schools are teaching two complete curriculums each day and expect the child to be able to operate in two languages. And to make matters more difficult, they need two alphabets and use one language that goes from left to right and one that goes from right to left! The quantity of material that could be taught is enormous. Often what doesn't get taught in school is given for homework. However, to ask a child to sit for hours at home after sitting for hours in school is a call for trouble. Again, most children can cope, but at the expense of a piece of their childhood. But twenty-five percent are at risk for difficulty. The pressure is too much. And the child will manifest symptoms of one kind or another, from acting out in class to headaches or stomachaches.

C. ISSUES FOR PRESCHOOLS

Often the expectations for children are not developmentally appropriate. School boards (usually composed of lay members), administrators, and parents each have a set of expectations in regard to what a child should accomplish in the preschool. Society often places unrealistic goals upon the school and the child. In past years children were expected to come to first grade ready for academic learning. Today children are expected to come to first grade already knowing a large part of the curriculum that used to belong in first grade. This increases the pressure upon both the teacher and the child. Fortunately, most children can cope with the program; but for about twenty-five percent of children the demands are too great. The child is well within normal limits of development, but because of external or internal factors is progressing at slower pace.

The danger is that this child will come to be regarded as having a "problem". Often he or she will begin to act out due to frustration and lack of positive support, or we will have planted the seeds of failure: "Everyone else can do it but me." Parents and teachers will also view this child as different or difficult or not as bright when all he or she needs is time.

As educators it is our job to protect these children by maintaining realistic expectations for them and not be caught up in the concept that the earlier the child learns the academics, the better. A teacher must provide a safe, nurturing, stimulating, and challenging environment. Then all the children will learn as much as they are able. Behavior may be saying "I'm not ready for all of this. Did you forget that at my age I learn best through play?"

In summary, there can be a number of reasons for challenging behaviors that can occur in the classroom. It is important that the teacher look carefully for clues to the cause of the disruptive behavior. Strategies should be identified and implemented to eliminate the behavior. Consistency in the enforcement of the strategies is important for a change in behavior. Lastly, one must remember the student is not a bad person; it is the actions the student is displaying that may be inappropriate.

BIBLIOGRAPHY

Greenspan, Stanley I., M.D. *The Challenging Child.* Reading, MA: Addison-Wesley, 1995.

Kranowitz, Carol Stock, M.A. *The Out-of-Sync Child.* New York: Parigee, 1998.

Pipher, Mary, Ph.D. *Reviving Ophelia.* New York: Ballantine Books, 1994.

CHAPTER 32

BEHAVIOR MANAGEMENT CONCEPTS AND TECHNIQUES

Sara Portman Milner

Behavior management involves a variety of techniques designed to reduce or eliminate unacceptable behavior and to increase socially acceptable behavior. *Not all techniques are appropriate for all situations or for all students.*

SETTING LIMITS

WHY IS IT IMPORTANT?

- Children need to be clear as to what is expected of them. (They love to <u>test</u> the limits!)
- Children need consistency. They become confused when adults are inconsistent in their responses.
- Consistency provides children with a feeling of security and safety. (Flexibility is crucial, but this is most applicable after relationships have been established and the children are comfortable with the rules set.)
- Children will learn values, sharing, and fairness with staff as role models.
- Firm and clear limits decrease manipulation by both individuals and the group. Once a decision is made for a child or the group, stick with it. There will be plenty of time for flexibility later. (Kids have a tendency to take advantage if staff is indecisive.)
- Children learn appropriate behavior and alternative ways of expressing feelings, allowing for emotional growth in a positive manner (e.g., talk about being angry instead of hitting.).
- Allowing children to respond to the limits placed will provide the teacher with the opportunity to notice children with specific problems.

HOW DOES ONE SET LIMITS?

- The teacher should use a *level* tone of voice when asking a child to cease a certain behavior. The request should be firm but fair. Compassion should be used. If the teacher starts raising his or her voice or argues with the student, s/he may be experiencing one of several things:

- Power struggle: a fight for control through arguing or shouting. Sometimes giving up control will result in gaining it.
- The pressure of a personal issue. Teachers need to be aware of their own moods and feelings.
- Inexperience: The teacher should instruct the child or group a few times. If the instructions become repetitive or one is losing control, try a new tactic.

If there is repeated difficulty with one particular child, speak with him/her separately from the group. There are several reasons for doing this:

- Attention by being reprimanded in front of the group may be what the child wants (negative attention).
- Some children may genuinely be having difficulties controlling themselves. They may become embarrassed at being reprimanded in front of the group.
- The child may be troubled and in need of talking. This may be the only way the child can get staff's attention and help.

POINTS TO CONSIDER

- A teacher should treat each child with respect and show him or her that she cares about his or her feelings.
- Decisions and limits must be followed through. Children know when teachers are floundering, and they love taking advantage. However, there is nothing wrong with the teacher telling children that he or she will think about it. That in itself is a decision.
- Limits should be set in a positive manner. Other children will observe the positive attention the teacher has given and will try to receive it without having to misbehave.
- Nonverbal communication can be used. Sometimes a raised eyebrow, sideward glance, or finger on lips is all that is needed.
- Honesty is the best policy. If the teacher becomes increasingly frustrated or angry, telling the child will help.

Try to avoid:

- Being punitive
- Showing favoritism
- Being judgmental
- Threatening, especially when no follow-through is planned

POSITIVE REINFORCEMENT

Positive reinforcement is the **first and most important** technique. It should be used often, but at appropriate times. The reinforcement should be specific to a child's behavior.

Example: *Thank you for cleaning up after yourself without my having to remind you. That shows me you are responsible.*

Appropriate behavior is maintained when a child is told that what he is doing is what is expected.

It is important to reinforce the child when h/she is trying to change a negative behavior. In changing a negative behavior, it is important to let the child know what is acceptable through reinforcement, not just identifying what is unacceptable. Every unacceptable behavior has an acceptable alternative that should be encouraged and nurtured through positive reinforcement.

Examples: *If a child frequently hits, the child should be lavishly reinforced for interacting with peers in appropriate ways.*

If a child whines, the child should be praised for speaking appropriately.

If a child tends to disrupt a group activity, the child should be told how well he/she is participating.

REDIRECTION

Redirection can be a very useful technique. Instead of acknowledging the unacceptable behavior, redirect the child with a substitute behavior. The child's attention has been redirected, and no incident has occurred.

Redirection can be used with most unacceptable behaviors as long as they are not dangerous to others. Make a point to reinforce the acceptable behavior.

Example: *Student shares information about another child's behavior with the teacher. The teacher redirects by having the student focus on his own behavior.*

PREVENTIVE CUEING

Preventive cueing is a technique for stopping disruptive behavior before it begins and for avoiding confrontation or embarrassment of the student in front of peers. The teacher arranges privately with the student a predetermined hand signal or work signal to cue the student to calm down, pay attention, stop talking out, etc. These are all quiet reminders.

Examples: *The teacher can tap own chin a few times to indicate to the student it is time to focus on the task.*

The "two thumbs up" sign can be used by the teacher to indicate that the student can get up and move around the room or outside area.

A hand sign can be established with the student to indicate it's time to be quiet.

PROXIMITY CONTROL

Circulate around the room during an activity. A hand on the shoulder or a direct look with a quiet reminder is effective when trying to get a student back on task.

Seat students who have difficulty paying attention or completing a project next to a staff person or a well-focused student. Avoid seating them along the periphery or next to doors, windows, or other distractions.

MODELING

Modeling is a positive and effective way to increase appropriate behavior by giving teacher's attention to students who are "modeling" the behavior an activity requires. By giving this attention the teacher can see other students adopting the model behavior in order to receive positive attention. This can be accomplished by either:

    A. modeling the specific actions of an individual

      B.   modeling an appropriate group

Example: *"David has his book open, so he may take his turn first."*

IGNORING

Ignoring can be a very effective technique, but one that can be difficult to use. When a child repeatedly does something irritating for the teacher's attention or the attention of the group or something that is disruptive to the group, ignoring can be a good technique to use.

IMPORTANT: *Do not ignore when a student is trying to hurt him/herself or, someone else or is destroying property.*

Ignoring is especially effective if the child is seeking the teacher's attention before the misbehavior. The child who checks to see who is watching before engaging in the misbehavior is overtly seeking attention. Pay no attention to the child's unacceptable behavior. Any kind of attention, including redirection or stares from others, can be rewarding to the child. Ignoring will often cause the behavior to stop. The unacceptable behavior may increase slightly before it decreases or stops. When a child gets no attention for negative behaviors and plenty of attention for appropriate behaviors, his/her behavior will begin to improve. It is also useful to positively reinforce the other children in the group for displaying appropriate behaviors.

PERSONAL CONNECTION AND DISCUSSION

Discussion works well with students who understand that what they are doing is unacceptable. Students may not feel good about their behavior. If the student wants to change the behavior, the teacher should discuss the behavior and ways to change with the child. It is important to find a private place for the discussion.

The teacher should take the student aside to discuss the behavior. Talk calmly and concisely and discuss the facts. Warnings and consequences of breaking the rules should be shared. The following techniques can be used when talking with students:

- Passive listening—hear the student out without interrupting.

- Acknowledge responses—give verbal and/or nonverbal feedback that the student has been heard.

- Active listening—respond; request more information, saying, "Tell me more," "Keep going," or "I'd like to hear more."

- When asking questions, it should be done like one who is recording information rather than a like police officer challenging the student.

- The teacher should give direct verbal praise, such as "This is good," "This helps me understand what you are thinking/feeling," "This is important," "I am glad you can tell me," "I am glad you are saying this out loud instead of keeping it to yourself."

- It is best for the teacher to sit with the student when engaging in a discussion.

- The teacher should state understanding of the student's message by saying, "So you're saying/feeling...," "You're angry because...," or "Is this what you're saying?" When the conversation is complete the teacher should summarize with the student all that was gathered from the discussion.

BEHAVIOR ACTION PLAN

Date:_____

Student's Name: _____

Define the behavior. _____

_____

How often does it occur?_____

How long does it occur?_____

Who is involved? _____

Where does it occur? _____

When does it occur? _____

- Discuss with the parents both your perspective and their perspective regarding this behavior. _____

_____

- List others who can provide information.

Name   Information

_____   _____

- Cite two or three reasons why this particular behavior needs to be decreased. _____

_____

_____

- Note what happens just BEFORE the target behavior occurs. (Consider time of day, number of students involved, what the students were doing, and what you were doing.)

_____

_____

- Note what happens just AFTER the target behavior occurs. (Consider how the other students respond to the child's behavior, how you respond, and the child's reaction to these responses.) _____

_____

_____

- Try to identify at least three possible reasons for the behavior. _____

_____

_____

- List strategies tried. _____

_____

continued on page 320

- List strategies to use. Describe the plan. _____
  _____
  _____
  _____

- Who is going to implement the plan? List the names below. _____
  _____
  _____
  _____

- After you have had some time to actually implement the plan, evaluate the impact on you, the student, other children, family, and other staff members. _____
  _____
  _____
  _____

- Does your assessment require changes? Gather all involved to explore modifications. _____
  _____
  _____
  _____

Adapted from "Child Care Plus Twelve Step Action Plan"

TEACHER SELF-ASSESSMENT: Points to Ponder

TO BUILD A SOLID FOUNDATION FOR LEARNING	always	never
I encourage the student's positive behaviors throughout the day.		
I recognize the student for positive contributions.		
I use encouragement to give students information about their behavior.		

TO STRUCTURE THE LEARNING ENVIRONMENT FOR SUCCESS	always	never
I encourage behaviors that are most acceptable.		
I rearrange the classroom so the student's behavior changes.		
I change the schedule so the student's behavior changes.		
I provide enough interesting and challenging materials for the student.		
I organize the classroom so that the student finds it intriguing.		
I give the student plenty of time to complete assignment/activity.		
I allow the student to decide when to be finished with an activity.		
I provide for student choice throughout the day.		
I provide easy transitions from one activity to the next.		
I ensure productive alternatives during wait time.		
I eliminate wait time to change the student's behavior.		

TO HELP STUDENTS LEARN ACCEPTABLE BEHAVIOR	always	never
The rules/guidelines for behavior are easy to understand.		
The rules and guidelines are reasonable for the student.		
I am able to ignore some behaviors.		
I teach natural consequences for this behavior to help the student learn.		
I provide a variety of activities that are satisfying for the student.		

TO RESOLVE PROBLEMS WHEN THEY OCCUR	always	never
I teach this student problem-solving skills.		
I check to see that the student understands the impact this behavior has on other children.		
I help the student get back on track when he/she disrupts a group activity.		
I stop the behavior immediately if it poses imminent danger.		

CODE OF CONDUCT

Ohr Kodesh, Chevy Chase, MD

SCHOOL ATMOSPHERE—*SH'LOM BAYIT*

Hillel and Shammai received from them. Hillel said: Be of the disciples of Aaron, one that loves peace, that loves humanity and brings them near to Torah (Avot 12).

At _____ we see the classroom as a place to build community. We need to respect one another, and this premise leads to certain behaviors on everyone's part. The strategies and philosophy we use promote and create *sh'lom bayit*, a harmonious school atmosphere. Our students will learn Jewish sources and Jewish life skills that will help them to develop "menschlikite" behavior. Judaism is a lifestyle; the more we live it, the more it becomes our lifestyle.

THEREFORE, OUR HOPE IS THAT OUR STUDENTS WILL:

1. Feel good about themselves as Jewish individuals.

2. Feel that Judaism is to be their way of life.

3. Not only learn the prescribed subjects, but truly understand and relate these teachings to their everyday lives.

4. Be able to question that which puzzles and concerns them in an open atmosphere.

WE RECOGNIZE THAT:

1. Each child is unique, and our aim is to help him/her grow.

2. We must strive to provide an atmosphere in which our children will attain success, confidence, security, love, and recognition of classmates and teachers.

3. In order to achieve these goals, we will place children where this can best be accomplished.

WE ARE ASSURED THAT WE CAN BEST SUCCEED WHEN:

1. Parents help their children understand the importance of their commitment to a Jewish education.

2. Parents are involved in their children's education and take an active interest in the questions, ideas, and communications they bring home from religious school.

3. Parents make every effort to keep the lines of communication open with the teachers and administration of our religious school.

APPROPRIATE BEHAVIOR—*DEREKH ERETZ*

STUDENTS WILL:

- Use acceptable language.
- Respect personal and school property both inside and outside of the building.
- Attend all classes.
- Dress appropriately.
- Arrive at school on time.
- Treat all people with respect.
- Be prepared for class and have appropriate materials.
- Respect the right of all to learn and express opinions.
- Keep the classroom clean and neat.
- Walk quietly in hallways and classrooms.

STUDENTS WILL NOT:

- Threaten and/or physically attack or verbally abuse anyone.
- Vandalize, damage, or otherwise abuse school or synagogue property.
- Smoke or bring alcohol, drugs, fireworks, or other hazardous objects to school.
- Bring anything that can bother other people, is a safety hazard, or disrupts learning or studying.
- Leave classroom or school grounds without permission.

CAUSE FOR IMMEDIATE SUSPENSION:

- Vandalism to school or synagogue property. The parents will be financially responsible.
- Possession and/or use of drugs, alcohol, or weapons.
- Physical attack.

The president of the congregation/school will be notified in writing immediately upon suspension of any child. The family has the right to appear and defend the actions before the Education Committee (convening a special meeting, if necessary) and the right to appeal any committee decision to the Executive Committee of the Board of Directors.

SCHOOL PROCEDURES

Rules are designed to create a safe, orderly school and learning environment for all involved. In addition, they protect and foster respect for the synagogue, school, and private property.

The synagogue has made school-wide rules that will benefit the total student population, parents, teachers, and administrators. These rules will be enforced by the staff and administration with the full support of the board. Teachers may make rules appropriate to their particular classrooms.

If a student is not adhering to the school discipline policy or classroom rules, thus interfering with the right of other students to learn, or is not participating in classroom activities, the following procedures will be observed:

1. Every effort will be made by the faculty and administration to involve the student in the resolution of the problem.

2. If the teacher is unable to resolve the problem with the child, the teacher will inform the Education Director and contact the parent by phone to discuss the behavior and agree to action(s) to correct the situation.

3. If the behavior persists, the teacher will refer the problem to the Education Director, and the parents will be required to attend a conference involving the child.

The maintenance of discipline in the school is essential to an effective learning climate and is the responsibility of students, parents, teachers, and administrators. Student conduct that for any reason materially disrupts class or involves substantial disorder or involves the rights of others will not be tolerated.

Parents wishing to discuss a school concern should observe the following procedure:

a. Contact the teacher to discuss the matter.

b. If the concern is not satisfactorily resolved, contact the Education Director.

c. If the concern is still not satisfactorily addressed, contact the chairperson of the Education Committee, who will bring the matter to the committee for resolution.

We consider the resolution of problems a priority and will make every effort to address all issues in a timely and fair manner.

BEHAVIORAL INTERVENTION PLAN

The Ariella Joy Frankel Keshet Day School Program

Keshet High School and Transition Program

In the event of an emergency involving a student's aggressive behavior, the following steps should be taken:

FIRST The student shall be protected from hurting himself/herself and others. An immediate assessment must be done by those staff present and/or those staff that can be quickly summoned to determine whether:

1. The student shall be removed from the current setting and taken to a safe place

OR

2. The student shall remain in the current setting and his or her classmates taken to a safe place.

3. A staff member shall remain with the student at all times.

SECOND Any staff member who has been trained in crisis prevention may apply a physical restraint to the student if so indicated to protect the student from hurting himself/herself or others, if other means to subdue the student have not been successful.

THIRD A member of the school's administrative team and school social worker shall be notified immediately and will intervene as necessary.

FOURTH If necessary, parents shall be called and will be told to pick up their child.

FIFTH The appropriate team, consisting of the Director, the site supervisor, social worker, teacher, and other staff deemed necessary, along with the parents and private physicians and therapists, will convene to develop

PART 7:
HEBREW LANGUAGE INSTRUCTION

PART 7:
HEBREW LANGUAGE
INSTRUCTION

CHAPTER 33

NATURAL HEBREW: A COMMON-SENSE FRAMEWORK FOR TEACHING HEBREW READING

Sharon S. Schanzer

INTRODUCTION

According to Hayim Nachman Bialik, poet laureate of Israel, "The key to Jewish education is the Hebrew language." And in the words of Dr. William Chomsky, a twentieth-century pioneer in the field of Jewish education, "Hebrew is the nerve center which unites and integrates the Jewish people in land and space. It serves as an intellectual and emotional bond among all Jews throughout all generations and throughout the lands of dispersion." Due to the continuity of Hebrew over the centuries, the twenty-first-century Jew who speaks, reads, or writes Hebrew evokes the voices of the past.

The material in this chapter is based on the premise that Hebrew is necessary for the continuity of the Jewish people. It presents methods for teaching Hebrew to the "typical" child as well as accommodations helpful for children with special needs. Specific suggestions for students with special needs are highlighted in shaded boxes throughout.

In general, the "special needs" herein refer to learning disabilities. A learning disability is a handicapping condition in which the individual has average or above average intelligence but is delayed in academic achievement. Learning disabilities refer to a group of disorders that interfere with the ability to listen, think, speak, read, write, or do mathematical calculations. These disorders are presumed to be due to central nervous system dysfunction and are not the result of sensory impairment, mental retardation, serious emotional disturbance, cultural difference, or inappropriate instruction. Learning disabilities can interfere with the acquisition of Hebrew as a second language. Specific perceptual problems (such as fine-motor, visual-motor, auditory perception, and visual perception) will be defined in other sections.

The three major sections are:

1. General methods for teaching the Hebrew language

2. Assessment of skills

3. Teaching Hebrew text

The suggestions for methodology are based on good teaching practices and are examples rather than an exhaustive list of techniques. This material is intended for teachers and directors of Jewish schools.

GENERAL METHODS FOR TEACHING THE HEBREW LANGUAGE
LISTENING

One's first language usually develops in the following order: listening, speaking, reading, and writing. The child generally speaks thousands of words before ever learning anything about the relationship between the spoken words and the graphic symbols required for reading. In teaching second languages, many schools immerse students in spoken language before exposing them to the written word. The underlying premise is to use the natural progression and order of language acquisition. Giving children the opportunity to hear a language lays the groundwork for speaking, reading, and writing later on (see Figure 1).

Since most children who are four years old already speak thousands of words in their first language, this would appear to be a good time to introduce a second language orally. Moreover, children at this age are generally not self-conscious about speaking or imitating a language. Thus preschool is a good setting in which to introduce the Hebrew language. For those youngsters who did not attend a Jewish preschool, it would still be advisable to emphasize listening to the spoken language in the *mekhinah* and *aleph* grades. *Mekhinah* refers to first to second grade in secular school. *Aleph* corresponds to third grade in secular school, and *bet* to fourth.

Specific methods of teaching children to listen to Hebrew are listed below.

1. Teach Hebrew songs, blessings, and prayers. This provides a basis for learning the phonemes (sounds) of a second language. Teaching Hebrew through music also provides emotional links to the language. Hebrew music can continue to be part of the school curriculum throughout the grades.

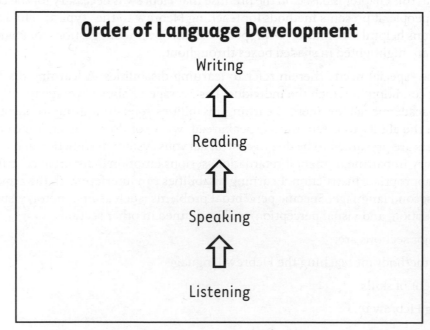

Order of Language Development

Writing

⇧

Reading

⇧

Speaking

⇧

Listening

Figure 1.

2. Expose the child as much as possible to listening and following directions in Hebrew. This should continue throughout the grades. Examples of easy directions that can be used are:

a. Open the book!　　　　　　　פְּתַח (פִּתְחִי) אֶת הַסֵּפֶר!

b. Take the pencil!　　　　　　קַח (קְחִי) אֶת הָעִפָּרוֹן!

c. Please close the door.　　　בְּבַקָשָׁה, לִסְגֹּר אֶת הַדֶּלֶת

d. Listen to the directions!　　שִׁמְעוּ לְהוֹדָעוֹת!

Examples of questions that can be used in the classroom include:

a. How are you?　　　　　　　מַה שְׁלוֹמְךָ? מַה שְׁלוֹמֵךְ?

b. What's the weather today?　מַה מֶזֶג הָאַוִיר הַיּוֹם?

c. Where are you going?　　　　לְאָן אַתָּה הוֹלֵךְ? לְאָן אַתְּ הוֹלֶכֶת?

In developing the listening skills of children with special needs, the following accommodations may be helpful:

1. Use simpler, shorter prayers, songs, and directions.

2. Slow down the pace of instructions.

3. Increase the amount of reinforcement and repetition.

4. Immediately translate directions.

5. Use a visual cue (e.g., picture) for the spoken word.

6. Make tapes of the prayers, songs, vocabulary, and directions for children.

7. Have children sing along with the tape at home and at school.

SPEAKING

Children should be encouraged to speak Hebrew after listening skills in Hebrew have begun. The teacher should encourage older children to understand that Hebrew is a spoken language and that it is the basis for future reading and writing. Specific methods for helping typical children learn to speak Hebrew as their second language are listed below.

1. Model (say aloud) Hebrew sentences for the child to repeat.

2. Translate new phrases or sentences. The translation can later be phased out.

3. Use some routine questions and answers every day. These include:

How are you?　　　　　　　מַה שְׁלוֹמְךָ? מַה שְׁלוֹמֵךְ?

What day is today?　　　　　אֵיזֶה יוֹם הַיּוֹם?

What month is it?　　　　　　בְּאֵיזֶה חֹדֶשׁ אֲנַחְנוּ?

What's the weather today?　מַה מֶזֶג הָאַוִיר הַיּוֹם?

4. Have children act out a play or a television or radio show. Audiotapes or videotapes can be made of the shows. Examples of radio shows include interviews about where a person lives or goes to school; a television show might include a scene from a holiday dinner or holiday celebration.

5. Build a bank of key words and phrases that can be reinforced during each lesson. These should be put on flashcards. Teach the words and phrases thematically. For example, children can be taught the names of fruits, holiday words, family members, or words relating to Shabbat.

6. Show children videotapes of conversations and real-life situations such as *Rehov Sumsum* ("Sesame Street").

7. Set up a play store in the room and have children practice phrases that begin with אֲנִי רוֹצֶה (רוֹצָה) לִקְנוֹת _____ ("I want to buy").

8. Teach as many Hebrew songs as possible. These can be standard songs or those created by teacher and children.

9. For older children, use verbal games such as "I'm going on a trip and taking a "_____." Children will have to use a Hebrew word.

10. Use CD-ROMs that provide opportunities to listen to and speak easy Hebrew. Examples include: *Triple Play Plus Hebrew* (available through the Davka Corporation), *Hebrew World: A Multimedia Course for the Family* (Davka), and *Rosetta Stone—Language* (available from Fairfield Language Technologies, Harrisonburg, VA).

Throughout the day teachers should use Hebrew words and expressions and encourage children to use them as well. Resources for Hebrew words and expressions that are useful appear in the bibliography and include the following:

1. *Eileh HaDevarim,* published by Auerbach CAJE, Melrose Park, PA, 2001, is designed to teach Jewish literacy and includes vocabulary related to holidays, daily practices, and life-cycle events.

2. *How to Teach Hebrew in the Elementary Grades* by William Chomsky, Ph.D., New York, NY, The United Synagogue Commission on Jewish Education, 1946.

3. *Mabey Hakitah—A Curriculum of Classroom Hebrew Expressions* by Debby Leibenstein, Brooklyn, New York, Torah Umesorah Publications, 1993.

4. *A Practical Guide for Teaching Hebrew, Volumes I and II* by Rebecca Kohn Mosenkis, New York, NY, Board of Jewish Education of Greater New York, 1965. These books include word lists and stories in simple Hebrew.

5. *Sefer T'munot* by Zehavah Blackman, student workbook, and teacher's guide translated and edited by Nancy M. Messinger, Auerbach CAJE, Melrose Park, PA, 1999, helps children listen to and speak short Hebrew sentences. Students "read pictures" in Hebrew and play games with the learned vocabulary.

In teaching children with special needs how to speak Hebrew, the following accommodations may be helpful:

1. When modeling Hebrew words or phrases, translate them immediately and repeat/ reinforce them more frequently.

2. Slow down the pace of teaching.

3. Put phrases and their translations on tape for children to use at home.

4. Use shorter sentences (two or three words long).

5. Limit the number of new vocabulary words introduced. One or two words may be appropriate for some children.

6. Teach Hebrew through songs—both standard and teacher-created.

7. Use picture cues for children who benefit from using a visual stimulus combined with the auditory stimulus.

READING

Reading is the process of getting information from the printed word. It is basically comprised of both word recognition and comprehension. Word recognition can be further divided into three parts: sight or whole words (words that children recognize immediately without phonetic decoding), phonetic decoding (understanding the sound symbol relationships of letters), and word recognition in context (understanding words in sentences). Comprehension can be subdivided into understanding areas such as main ideas, factual information, inferential material, vocabulary, and contextual clues (see Figure 2).

If we assume that children have been exposed to listening to Hebrew and have had opportunities to speak Hebrew (as described in the two previous sections), then children have heard the phonemes (speech sounds) over a period of years. A major problem in many religious schools occurs when children are taught to read before they have had adequate exposure to listening to and speaking Hebrew. Basically, it is jumping into the third step of language development without the building blocks. This can lead to feelings of frustration and lack of accomplishment on the part of children and their parents.

According to Dina Maiben, a contemporary Jewish educator, there is considerable evidence to indicate that learning some language can actually enhance a learner's decoding skills. She recommends that children be introduced to a limited amount of "authentic Hebrew vocabulary" or "key words" that can include general vocabulary of Jewish life, such as holiday terms, greetings, and ritual items.

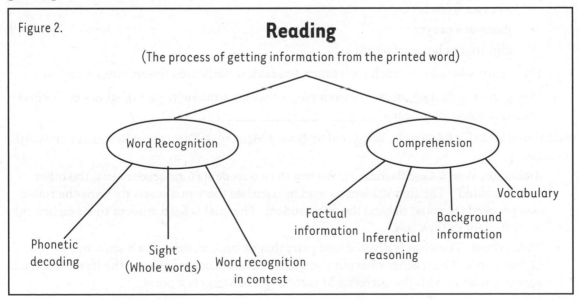

Figure 2.

Reading

(The process of getting information from the printed word)

Word Recognition

- Phonetic decoding
- Sight (Whole words)
- Word recognition in contest

Comprehension

- Factual information
- Inferential reasoning
- Background information
- Vocabulary

In reality, there are many children who enter *kitah aleph* without the preparation in listening to and speaking Hebrew. The *aleph* teacher can use the first few months to develop their listening and speaking skills before beginning to teach Hebrew reading.

Again, if educators follow the progression of language development, the first step in reading would be to expose children to sight words (or whole words). Children learning to read in their native language generally learn to recognize words on signs and in other places in their environment before they learn formal phonics. Thus it would be appropriate to teach children in religious school as many sight words as possible throughout the grades.

Teaching sight words (whole words) has two purposes. First, since sight words are words for which children know the translation or meaning, they learn meaningful words. Second, since some phonetic elements can be inferred from sight words, the more sight words a child has mastered, the easier it will be to learn formal, explicit phonics later on.

Flashcards and labels of objects in the room can be reviewed a few minutes a day throughout the years of religious school. Over the six or seven years of school children can accumulate hundreds or even thousands of sight words that they can recognize automatically.

Teachers should use professionally labeled flashcards or create their own by using stencils or peel-and-press letters. It is important to be consistent and careful in making the letters. Specific suggestions for teaching sight words include:

1. Have a print-rich environment. Immerse children in Hebrew print. Label items all around the room and use the words whenever possible.

2. Put common phrases and directions on flashcards and review them daily—e.g., weather terms, months, holidays, family members, directions ("open your book").

3. Put Hebrew songs on charts. Have children read them after they have learned the song. Emphasize songs that repeat words, e.g., דָּוִד מֶלֶךְ יִשְׂרָאֵל and סֹב, סֹב, סֹב סְבִבוֹן.

4. Have students keep word banks in shoeboxes. These words can include functional words אֲנִי צָרִיךְ (צְרִיכָה).
   * phrases from texts
   * parts of a prayer
   * children's choice of words

5. Have pairs of students teach each other and review flashcards ten minutes a day.

6. Play games with flashcards. For example, see which student or pair of students can find the sight word that means "_____."

Additional ideas for flashcards, suggested by Nancy Messinger, Director of Resources at ACAJE, include:

* *Around the World*: One flashcard is flashed to two students (one student sits, the other stands behind). The first student to read or translate the word correctly wins the round and proceeds to stand behind the next student. The goal is for a student to stand behind each student in the class.

* *Match Game*: The class is divided into pairs that sit back to back. Each student has a pack of flashcards. The teacher calls out the question, and students choose the flashcard. Each pair of students with the correct and matching answer gets a point.

- *Reading Bee* (play is similar to a spelling bee): The class is divided into two teams and lines up along the sides of the classroom. A card is flashed to one team, and the person at the head of the line reads it. If correct, he or she remains in the game and goes to the end of the line. If incorrect, he or she returns to his or her seat. The student who remains in the game the longest is the winner.
- *Blackboard Words*: Flashcards are used instead of writing on the board. This saves time, and the words are legible and quickly changed. Attach the words using masking tape, poster board thumbtacks on a bulletin board, or paper clips on poster board.
- *Concentration* (for the whole class or a small group): The class is divided into two teams. Twenty flashcards (two each of ten different words) are randomly placed in a twenty-pocket board or on the floor. Students (in turn) choose a card, read it aloud, and try to locate its match. The team with the most matches at the end wins.
- *Team Bingo*: The class is divided into two teams. Each player on the team has ten flashcards in front of him or her. As the teacher reads the word from the master list (of fifty words) the child with the word hands the word in. When all of a student's words are called, that student stands. When all the players on a team are standing, the team wins.
- *Flashcard Card Games* (for small groups): With several sets of four cards each–e.g., four picture cards, four flashcards of the same word, four words that are on one theme—play games like "Go Fish" or "Old Maid."

Flashcards can also be made from the list of words in *Eileh HaDevarim* (see above speaking section on teaching Hebrew).

In an ideal setting, children would hear and begin to speak Hebrew in preschool. An emphasis on listening to and speaking Hebrew would continue through *mechinah*. Sometime around the age of eight years, corresponding to *kitah aleph* in many religious schools, children would begin to learn explicit phonics. An advantage to waiting until this age is that most children will have mastered much of the phonics of their native language before beginning a completely different alphabet and sound-symbol system. Another advantage of waiting until a child is close to eight before teaching a new graphic system is that most children will have had a chance to master Hebrew reading readiness skills. Some of these skills include:

- auditory discrimination (the ability to hear small differences between sounds)
- visual discrimination (the ability to detect small visual differences between letters)
- laterality (the ability to know the difference between left and right on one's own body)
- directionality (the ability to know the difference between left and right on paper, in books, and in the world in general)

WHEN TO TEACH HEBREW

Shlomo Haramati, a leader in Israel in teaching the Hebrew language to immigrants, has devoted a chapter in his book on teaching methods to the teaching of reading to American youngsters. Haramati (1972) states that there are two essential factors that affect the decoding process: the characteristics of the language to be learned and the age of the students. Haramati states that six-year-olds aren't ready for systematic phonetic instruction in a second language from a psychophysiological point of view. On the other hand, he agrees with the notion that children who are eight or nine have the psychophysiological ability and have already learned to read in their mother language; they have mastered the symbolic essence of an alphabet.

HOW TO TEACH PHONICS

Over the decades the pendulum has swung many times regarding the best methods to use to teach reading to children. On one end of the continuum is the emphasis on teaching phonemes before whole words and sentences. This method, referred to as explicit phonics, involves teaching the sound-symbol (phoneme/grapheme) relationship of every letter. On the other end of the continuum is the "whole language" method of teaching reading. In this method, implicit phonics instruction is used. This involves teaching phonics inferentially through reading literature. The "whole language approach" dominated reading instruction in elementary schools in the United States for most of the 80's and 90's, but there has been a notable swing back to explicit, systematic, and sequential teaching of phonemes.

Many religious school teachers, as well as the parents of children in the schools, complain about the number of children who are ready to become bar or bat mitzvah who still cannot read Hebrew fluently. One wonders why this occurs so frequently. The answer is multifaceted.

In May 1997 the Orton Dyslexia Society published a position paper entitled *Informed Instruction for Reading Success: Foundations for Teacher Preparation.* The paper was written for all reading teachers, not just those who teach children with reading disabilities. The authors emphasize that research and teaching practice show that children profit from instruction in reading that is explicit, systematic, and sequential, and that effective instruction requires multiple opportunities to practice reading, spelling, and writing. Children first must be taught sensitivity to the individual sounds in words. Next they should learn to link the speech sounds (phonemes) with their corresponding letter patterns (both graphemes and spelling patterns). However, the authors warn that the frequent practice of teaching "a minimum amount of decoding in first and second grade and then discontinuing any focus on the structure of words leaves too many children without sufficient guidance."

Of course, the above discussion of teaching methods is based on the concept of teaching reading in one's first language. The question at hand is how this applies to teaching Hebrew reading to children whose first language is English.

In looking at how to help youngsters learn to decode Hebrew well, we can apply some of the principles detailed by the Orton Dyslexia Society. There are two key elements that appear to be relevant:

- Phonics needs to be taught explicitly and systematically. Children must be taught the sound-symbol relationship of every consonant and vowel in a systematic, logical sequence.

- There must be multiple opportunities to reinforce reading skills after *kitah aleph* and *bet*. This means that children must continue to receive practice and guidance throughout the grades to assure fluency in decoding.

These additional specific guidelines are suggested for teaching Hebrew decoding:

- Teach for mastery (100 % accuracy) for every letter and vowel. If children recognize the letter or vowel 75% or 80% of the time, they have not reached mastery level.

- Since the visual discrimination of letters is often confusing, emphasize the minute discriminations and go from simple to more complex. From the point of view of visual perception, easy features are standard vertical (|) and standard horizontal (-), while more difficult features include dots and the diagonal (/). Examples of easy letters include (1%).

- When teaching pairs of letters, first teach those that are not easily confused with one another, such as " and %, rather than highly confusable pairs, such as 9 and

- The most confusing pairs of Hebrew letters, those that have many overlapping features, are listed in Figure 3.

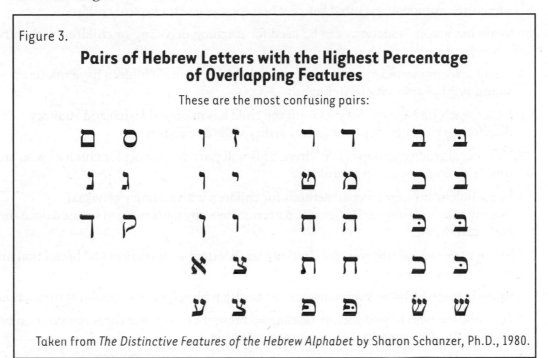

Figure 3.

Pairs of Hebrew Letters with the Highest Percentage of Overlapping Features

These are the most confusing pairs:

Taken from *The Distinctive Features of the Hebrew Alphabet* by Sharon Schanzer, Ph.D., 1980.

The importance of teaching phonics systematically, along with multiple opportunities for reinforcement, cannot be overemphasized. The goal is to have students who are able to read any new Hebrew word that they encounter. Ultimately students would be able to read various Hebrew texts and not just the siddur. Although the emphasis on learning Hebrew phonics should be stressed in the early grades of religious school, *phonics must be reviewed frequently in every grade through bar/bat mitzvah.* Since many texts for teaching Hebrew are geared for younger children, there will need to be additional texts written to help teachers reinforce decoding skills for older students. Presentations should be varied to avoid boredom and frustration.

Among the many difficulties encountered in Hebrew decoding is the understanding of how to pronounce the vowel *sheva* (שְׁוָא). The correct pronunciation of the *sheva na* (נָע שְׁוָא) and *sheva nah* (שְׁוָא נָח) is a key element in Hebrew syllabication and Hebrew reading fluency. It is important for teachers to emphasize the difference between the two sounds.

Specific methods for teaching Hebrew decoding are listed below.

- Use overlays on the overhead projector to provide reinforcement activities.
- Create games and other materials to reinforce Hebrew. A good example of a decoding game format is a "spin and say."
- A good source of phonics games for beginning students is *Fun with Phonics* prepared by Rita Silverman and edited by Sarah M. Siegman.
- Model fluent reading for the class.

- Use choral reading with the children so that the entire class has an opportunity to read aloud in unison.
- Reinforce phonics (once the letters and vowels have been taught) with CD-ROMs such as *Learning to Read Hebrew* (Davka Corporation).
- Use the accommodations listed below when appropriate for typical children.

The following accommodations can be used for teaching decoding to children with varying special needs:

1. Delay teaching sound-symbol associations in Hebrew until children have mastered sound-symbol associations in English.

2. Delay teaching Hebrew phonics until the child has mastered visual and auditory discrimination, laterality, and directionality skills (see above).

3. Use choral reading groups of children. This will provide support for children who are unable or do not want to read aloud.

4. Use whole-word (sight word) methods for children with auditory or visual discrimination problems. Linguistic patterns (rhyming patterns) can be used once the child can rhyme.

5. Teach easier visual features first. Initially teach letters with vertical and horizontal lines rather than diagonals.

6. Initially teach Hebrew letters that are dissimilar with respect to visual discrimination.

7. For children who have difficulty reading Hebrew, make tapes of the *Aleph-Bet*, numbers, months, etc. Use songs to help with memorization.

8. Have children read words/stories into a tape recorder and play back the tape so children can hear their voices.

9. Use flashcards that have Hebrew letters made of sandpaper or other tactile materials such as buttons, and have children trace the letters.

10. Have children use their fingers to draw Hebrew letters on one another's backs and then try to guess the letters.

11. Use large foam letters that children can trace.

12. Teach the root of the word, if the root is consistent, so that children learn visual patterns.

13. Use reading texts that have the following characteristics:
    no clutter
    good spacing between words
    simple font
    large print
    pictures kept to a minimum and used for context clues

A good source of games for teaching Hebrew reading to children with special needs is *The Resource Program Guide for a Congregational School* by Phyllis S. Greene and Sara Rubinow Simon.

WRITING

In order to learn handwriting skills, children should have acquired several readiness skills. First they must have the fine-motor skills to hold the pencil properly. Most youngsters are able to do this by age six. Second, they need to have adequate visual-motor-integration skills. This refers to the ability to copy from a book or a chalkboard and write on paper. Third, children should have adequate visual discrimination to distinguish the small differences among vowels and consonants. Fourth, they should have mastered laterality and directionality. These latter three skills are generally in place by the time a child is seven or eight years old. The following are specific methods for teaching Hebrew handwriting to typical children:

- Begin by teaching manuscript letters until reading is fluent so that the child only has to learn one new alphabet. Block print reinforces the letter shapes that students are reading.
- Teach the easiest vowels first. This means that the *patah* and *kamatz* should be taught before the vowels with dots.
- Teach the easiest consonants first. The easiest ones have vertical and horizontal lines.
- Do not teach confusing letters together (see Figure 3).

Specific suggestions for teaching writing to children who have difficulty with handwriting include:

1. Have children practice writing letters in sand.
2. Have children practice tracing stencils of letters.
3. Have children trace dotted lines. Gradually reduce dots as handwriting becomes more proficient.
4. Have children use wide pencils and rubber pencil grips, which may help them hold the pencil more firmly.
5. Use extra wide "primer paper."

GRAMMAR

Hebrew is a logical language, much of which is based on three-letter root words. As soon as children have mastered Hebrew decoding they can be taught that certain combinations of letters are related to root words (e.g., אמר). Highlighting the root letters of sight words will help the child read for meaning and expand sight word recognition. Teaching key prefixes and suffixes will also enhance meaning. For example, without teaching formal grammar, a child can be taught that the word "וְאָמַרְתָּ" has three parts: a root word, a prefix, and a suffix. Young children can be exposed to informal grammar in this manner.

Specific methods of teaching root words appear below.

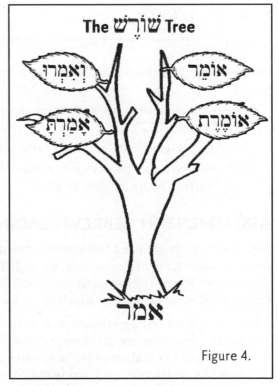

Figure 4.

341

1. Make different *shoresh* (root) trees. Write the *shoresh* at the bottom of a tree trunk. Add a leaf to the tree with each new word containing the *shoresh* "אמר."

2. Use root words in which all three letters remain constant.

3. Write words on the chalkboard or on flashcards in color. All three-letter root words should be in one color, all prefixes in a different color, and all suffixes in another.

4. Play Scrabble and use words with prefixes and suffixes.

5. Make flashcards with different forms of the *shoresh*. The *shoresh* should always be in the same color.

6. When children are ready to learn formal grammar—tenses, singular and plural—use boxes as grammar cues for students to write the *shoresh* letters. See Figure 5 for an example of creating the cues.

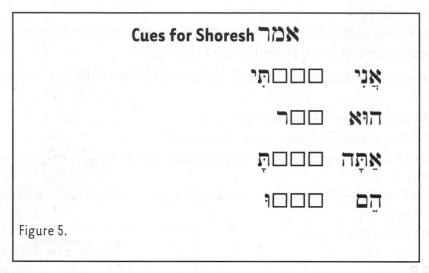

Figure 5.

For teaching grammar to children with special needs, the following techniques are suggested:

- Use the *shoresh* tree, but with fewer *shorashim*. The most common ones can be used, such as (אָמַר and שָׁמַר).

- Keep formal grammar in the *kal* conjugation, the most simple of Hebrew's conjugations.

- Use repetitive oral practices. For example, go around the room and have each child say, "My house is white (or blue or black)."

ASSESSMENT IN HEBREW READING

Assessment tools are used to measure students' skill levels in various areas of reading. Unless one uses some form of assessment, it is difficult to know what students have learned and what they need to learn. Testing instruments can be standardized, informal, or criterion-referenced. Each school must determine which of the following tests are appropriate for its students.

1. Standardized testing is based on norms to which a child's scores are compared. There are norms that compare children of different ages or grades. Often there are hundreds or thousands of children in the normative sample, which includes children from cities and suburbs, from different parts of the country, and from different socio-economic groups.

The *California Achievement Tests* is an example of a standardized group test, and *Woodcock Reading Mastery Test* is an example of a standardized individual reading test.

2. Informal testing is not based on norms. Informal diagnostic testing in reading measures a student's level of achievement as well as strengths and weaknesses in the areas of word recognition and comprehension. The diagnostic information can be used to understand what students have learned and what they need to learn in specific skill areas.

3. Criterion-referenced testing also is not based on formal norms. It refers to testing in which scores are compared to a set performance standard. An example of a set performance standard is "Can say all letters of the Hebrew alphabet in order."

One of the goals of assessment in Hebrew reading is to learn how much the student or class has mastered. Another goal is to find out the strengths and weaknesses of the individual students in order to find out what needs to be retaught or taught next.

The Hebrew tests listed below are samples of informal diagnostic reading tests.

1. The *Diagnostic Hebrew Reading Test* (Behrman House, Inc., 1982) has 75 questions and evaluates the ability to identify letters and vowels, recognize their sounds, distinguish letters that look alike, and read the letters when they are combined into words. There are forms to show areas of difficulty for the entire class and for individuals. The test takes 45 to 50 minutes to administer.

2. The *Hebrew Decoding Inventory* (Sharon Schanzer Ph.D., Auerbach CAJE, 1999) assesses pure Hebrew decoding skills by using nonsense words. It tests the ability to read all Hebrew consonants and vowels in isolation and in one- and two-syllable words. It can be used at the end of *kitah aleph* to measure progress or at the beginning of *bet* and *gimel* to diagnose what to teach. It provides both class and individual analyses of what has or has not been mastered. It takes 15 minutes per student to administer.

3. The *Koallen Diagnostic Criterion-Referenced Tests of Primary Hebrew Reading* (distributed by The Learning Plant, 1981) is designed for use in the "individualization of reading instruction for students who have completed at least one year of formal Hebrew reading instruction." The 20 sub-tests can be administered to groups or to individuals. The following skills are evaluated: directionality (knowing left and right), auditory discrimination (the ability to perceive similarities and differences among sounds), visual discrimination (the ability to perceive similarities and differences among graphic symbols), and sound to symbol/symbol to sound relationships. The test requires two hours to administer.

4. The *Kriyah Scan for Hebrew Reading Skills* (Rabbi Aharon Hersh Fried Ph.D., Torah Umesorah, 1999) allows a teacher to identify a child's specific areas of reading strengths and needs. The reading SCAN is designed to assess the attainments in Hebrew reading of children who have completed a program of reading instruction in a Hebrew day school. The SCAN measures standard basic words with vowels, standard sight words without vowels, fluency in reading paragraphs, and children's ability to read script and Rashi orthographies. This test requires approximately 15 to 30 minutes per student to administer.

5. *A Diagnostic Hebrew Reading Test for the Second Grade of the Hebrew School* (Council on Jewish Education, Pittsburgh, PA, 1960) is designed to aid in the diagnosis of an individual's reading difficulties. It consists of 45 isolated words taken from the prayer curriculum and ten phrases of 38 words taken from the same prayer curriculum. The

words and phrases in the test include all consonants, vowels, and phonic combinations. The test is given orally and requires five minutes per student to administer.

It is difficult to imagine teaching reading without using an assessment tool. The importance of pinpointing individual needs is at the core of good teaching. In addition, testing can be a time saver in the long run. By knowing what each individual student needs as well as what the class as a whole needs, the teacher does not have to reteach every consonant and vowel at the beginning of each year. That time can be used for reinforcement and/or teaching Hebrew texts.

TEACHING HEBREW TEXTS

The ultimate goal of reading is to get meaning from the printed word. Before moving into reading text, children need to develop and master decoding skills. Development of sight words should also be part of a firm foundation. An understanding of grammar (prefixes, suffixes, and root words) will enhance fluency and meaning. The greater the mastery of phonics, sight words, and grammar, the more fluency the reader brings to the text. This fluency allows the reader to concentrate on reading for meaning.

Hebrew text should not be used to teach and/or reinforce basic decoding skills. Teachers should use other methods (such as flashcards and games) for this purpose. If the Hebrew text is used to teach phonics, it takes away from the meaning of the text. In addition, if children start reading text before they have mastered decoding skills, they may form negative feelings towards the text, be it *siddur* or *humash* or general Hebrew readers.

TEACHING *SIDDUR*

Many children come to the reading of *siddur* with portions memorized. Rote memorization is an excellent way to begin to learn prayer. However, memorized material may not correspond to accurate decoding. One is reminded of the child who was surprised when he finally decoded the Pledge of Allegiance. For years, he had been saying "...and to the Republican Richard Sands."

Before students actually begin to read the prayers from the *siddur*, they should have mastered Hebrew decoding through games, flashcards, and decoding books. The *siddur* should NOT be used as a means to teach decoding.

Listed below are some specific methods to help children prepare for reading the *siddur*.

- Teach children as many *siddur* sight words as early as possible. Teachers can make their own flashcards. See figure 6, which shows a list of 34 frequently used sight words from the *siddur*. The original author/publisher of this list is unknown.
- Have students practice decoding individual words and phrases using the overhead projector. An excellent kit for learning several specific prayers through overlays on the overhead projector is Dr. Nathaniel Entin's *Prayer Overlays*, published by the Learning Plant. The goal of the program is to have students become fluent in reading several prayers such as the *Kiddush* and the *Aleinu*. The overlays contain *siddur* words divided first into syllables and then into meaningful phrases. The entire prayer is eventually put together.

An excellent variation of teaching prayer through phrasing is found in *Bo Kra*, also written by Nathaniel A. Entin and published by United Synagogue of Conservative Judaism.

According to Dr. Entin, "Good phrasing is the secret to good reading. Pronouncing the words correctly is very important, but that is just the first step to mastery. The meaning of a sentence is carried by the phrasing, that is, knowing when to pause and when to 'run on'."

Accommodations for children who are not able to read *siddur* follow.

- Teach prayers through songs and memorization. While this method may appear to contradict what was recommended above, it is appropriate for children who are non-readers.
- Make tapes for children to use at home and at school.

TEACHING *ḤUMASH*

Once children are decoding fluently, have a fund of sight words, and have some knowledge of *shorashim*, they are ready to begin *ḥumash*.

Below are some methods to introduce children to *ḥumash*.

- Introduce key Hebrew words and phrases through games and flashcards before children begin to read the text.

Teach through the *parashah* (the weekly Torah portion). Take the storyline and choose certain *p'sukim* (passages). Make an abridged version of the story.

- Use the *shoresh* tree for all root words.
- Continue to reinforce basic grammatical structures of prefixes, suffixes, and singular and plural forms.
- Use comprehension questions that include the main idea, facts (e.g., "Who said…?" "Who did…?"), inferential thinking, and background information.

Specific accommodations for teaching *chumash* to children with special needs include:

- Use more English in teaching the *parashah*. Teach the most commonly used Hebrew words, such as names (מֹשֶׁה and אַבְרָהָם) and concepts (צֶדֶק and אַהֲבָה).
- Have children present plays of the *parashah*.
- Have children make dioramas based on the storyline.
- Use puppets to say the dialogue of the *parashah*.
- Record one or two *p'sukim* on a tape so that the children can listen to and practice the words at home.
- Ask the comprehension questions and develop vocabulary in both Hebrew and English.
- Explain the meanings of biblical translations such as "Be fruitful and multiply" in both Hebrew and English.
- Use a linear *ḥumash* in which each *pasuk* is written phrase by phrase and translated phrase by phrase. The Metzudah Company has such a text.

TEACHING HEBREW READING FOR PLEASURE

After children have an initial mastery of phonics, they can begin to learn through reading stories. The sight words they have mastered can be the basis for reading for pleasure. Specific suggestions for teaching reading for fun appear below.

- Use short books (20–30 pages) in which the vocabulary is controlled. The *Sifriyah Oneg* series is fun to read. It includes such books as *El Hayeladim B'Tayman* and *Chanah Senesh* by Aharon Meged and *B'reḥovot New York* by Meir Michaeli (see bibliography).
- Use easy Hebrew newspapers such as *Lamatkhil* (Israeli newspaper), *Lamishpaḥa* and *Sulam Ya'akov* (both from Histadruth Ivrith of America, New York).

- Teachers can write stories and plays in which the students are the characters. Real-life situations can be used. Students can read their parts.

In teaching reading for fun to children with special needs, the teacher can use the following suggested activities:

- Create a newspaper with the vocabulary that the students know. It can be just headlines.
- Create stories and plays that have the vocabulary that the students know.
- Try to create high-interest, easy-readability materials whenever possible.
- Have children be Hebrew pen-pals with each other, using reinforced Hebrew words in English sentences.

CONCLUSION

Hebrew is the thread that has bound Judaism over the centuries. It permeates prayer, Bible, holidays, literature, and the essence of modern Israel. This connection with the language of the Jewish people is important and necessary for Jewish continuity. All Jewish children, regardless of ability, can achieve some degree of Hebrew learning. Teachers must be willing to make accommodations for students with special needs so that they can feel this connection with the Hebrew language. These accommodations may include going at a slower pace, covering less material, and increasing opportunities for reinforcement.

On a practical level, there may be some teachers and principals who are wondering how to incorporate this framework of reading into their schools. It *is* possible to integrate the framework and specific suggestions on a gradual basis. It is imperative, however, that teachers who teach reading have an understanding of the theory of teaching language as it relates to Hebrew.

Some of the basic suggestions for teaching typical children, as well as those with special needs, include:

- Have students listen and speak some Hebrew before learning to decode. (This means that there must be teachers on staff who are competent Hebrew speakers.) Teachers should be encouraged to expand their Hebrew skills through in-service learning, *ulpanim*, and study in Israel.
- Use lots of games to reinforce decoding skills.
- Reinforce decoding every day.
- Teach for mastery (100%).
- Reinforce decoding every year through bar/bat mitzvah.
- Do not use the *siddur* or *humash* to teach decoding.
- Teach simple letters first (with vertical and horizontal lines).
- Initially, teach pairs of letters that are dissimilar.
- Model correct reading for children.
- Use choral reading.

BIBLIOGRAPHY

Auerbach Central Agency for Jewish Education, compilers. *Eileh HaDevarim: These Are the Words—A Vocabulary for Jewish Living.* Melrose Park, PA: The Auerbach Central Agency for Jewish Education, 2001.

Blackman, Zehava. *Sefer T'munot: Learning Hebrew through Pictures*. Melrose Park, PA: Auerbach Central Agency for Jewish Education, 1999. Student Workbook and Teacher's Guide edited and translated by Nancy M. Messinger.

Castberg, C., & Lillian W. Adler. *Diagnostic Hebrew Reading Test*. West Orange, NJ: Behrman House, 1982.

Chomsky, William. *How to Teach Hebrew in the Elementary Grades*. New York, NY: The United Synagogue Commission on Jewish Education, 1946.

Entin, Nathaniel. *Bo Kra*. New York, NY: United Synagogue of America, 1991.

——*Prayer Overlays*. West Palm Beach, FL: The Learning Plant, 1967.

Fried, Aharon Hersh. *The Kriyah Scan*. Monsey, NY: Torah Umesorah, 2000.

Greene, Phyllis S., & Sara R. Simon. *The Resource Program Guide for a Congregational School*. Rockville, MD: The Board of Jewish Education of Greater Washington, 1990.

Haramati, Shlomo. *Sugueot B'hanhalat Halshon H'ivrit*. Tel Aviv, Israel: Amichai Limited, 1972.

Informed Instruction for Reading Success: Foundations for Teacher Preparation. Baltimore, MD: The Orton Dyslexia Society, 1997.

Kessler, Aharon. *A Diagnostic Hebrew Reading Test for the Second Grade of the Hebrew School*. Pittsburgh, PA: Council on Jewish Education, 1960.

Leibenstein, Debby. *Mabey Hakitah: A Curriculum of Classroom Hebrew Expressions*. Brooklyn, NY: Torah Umesorah Publications, 1993.

Lenchner, Orna. *Z'man Likro, Books I and II*. Denver, CO: A.R.E. Publishing Inc., 1989.

Lowy, Martin, et al. *Koallen Diagnostic Criterion-Referenced Test of Primary Hebrew Reading*. West Palm Beach, FL: The Learning Plant, 1991.

Maiben, Dina. "After the Primer: Where Do We Go from Here?" *Jewish Education News*, Fall 1997.

——"Issues in Hebrew Reading Instruction" in *The New Jewish Teacher Handbook,* Audrey Friedman Marcus and Raymond A. Zwerin, editors. Denver, CO: A.R.E. Publishing Inc., 1994.

Megged, Aharon. *El Hayeladim B'tciman*. New York, NY: United Synagogue Commission on Jewish Education, 1948.

——*Chanah Senesh*. New York, NY: Jewish Education Committee Press, n.d.

Michaeli, Meir. *B'rehovot New York*. New York, NY: Jewish Education Committee Press, n.d.

Mosenkis, Rebecca Kohn. *A Practical Guide for Teaching Hebrew, Volumes I and II*. New York, NY: Board of Jewish Education of Greater New York, 1965.

Schanzer, Sharon S. *Distinctive Features of the Hebrew Alphabet*. Bryn Mawr, PA: Bryn Mawr College, 1980.

——*Hebrew Decoding Inventory*. Melrose Park, PA: Auerbach Central Agency for Jewish Education, 1999.

Silverman, Rita. *Fun with Phonics*. Baltimore, MD: Baltimore Board of Jewish Education, 1983.

Zana, Hillary, with Orna Lenchner. *Z'man Likro Teacher's Guide*. Denver, CO: A.R.E. Publishing, Inc., 1990.

For more information, contact ACAJE, 215-635-8940, www.acaje.org.

READING PROBLEMS IN HEBREW

PRE-TEST

READING DIFFICULTIES IN HEBREW

VISUAL PROCESSING DIFFICULTY

THINGS TO LOOK FOR
- Constantly uses a finger or a pointer
- Confuses letter shapes
- Skips a line in reading
- May not be looking at the page but recites from memory
- Writing and copying are poor (poor letter formation and/or spacing of letters)

TECHNIQUES TO AID PROBLEM
- Have the student use a paper or cardboard place marker, blocking out other printed material
- Print vowels in a different color than consonants
- Work carefully on visual discrimination of lookalike letters; use color coding and/or tracing to emphasize distinctions
- Use "see and say" method
- Use cassette tapes and shadow reading
- Encourage memorization of sight words

AUDITORY PROCESSING DIFFICULTIES

THINGS TO LOOK FOR
- Difficulty learning to pronounce polysyllabic words
- Very easily distracted and has a short attention span
- Super-sensitive to noise
- Difficulty learning phonetics
- Difficulty blending sounds in word attack process

TECHNIQUES TO AID PROBLEM
- Seat student where she/he can see teacher's lips
- Teacher reads a new word or phrase first so that student knows how it should sound; be sure not to let the student struggle and mispronounce a word or phrase continuously
- Work carefully on sound blending, starting with simple consonant–vowel combinations in familiar words
- Provide sufficient examples of monitored repetition

- Provide opportunities for choral recitation, cassette tapes with earphones, and shadow reading

Be aware of the **reading instructional material** you use.

Do the materials emphasize a phonetic approach and therefore make heavy auditory demands on students?

Do the materials emphasize a sight vocabulary and therefore make heavy visual demands on students?

Adapted from R. Malter

DIAGNOSTIC READING TEST SCORE SHEET

SARAH SIEGMAN, BJE BALTIMORE

Name _____   Class _____

School _____   Teacher _____

Score Sheet

1	2	3	4	5	6	7	8	9	10	11	12	13	14	15	16	17	18	19	20	21
פָּ פַּ	פֶּ פֵּ	דְ	גָ אָ	חַ הַ	בְּ	אַ ﭏ	הֵ בֵ	הֵ תֵ	וֹ וֹ	סֻ	כְ	וֵ	וָ וֻ	ו with vowel	final letters	silent י	◼	ִ	vowel followed ו	vowels

5	5			13	9		5	5		10	10		16	7
מְכַלְכֵּל			פּוֹתֵחַ			כַּלְכֵּל			בֵּרְכֵנוּ			מִצְוָה	

13 18   17 19 10 9   19   11 11 19   18 1 4 1

מְשִׁיחַ   וּבְלֶכְתְּךָ   תִּשְׁמְעוּ   בְּחַסְדְּךָ   טַעֲמֶיהָ

9 2   16 1   17 6 6   1 1 7   4 4

שְׂרָפִים   נִצְטַוּוּ   הָרַחֲמִים   אֲרוֹמִמְךָ   עַצְמוֹתַי

16 16   13 8 2   6 6   6 6 6   4

וְהִתְחַוִּיתֶם   לְשַׁבֵּחַ   תְּחִלָּה   לְהַחֲיוֹת   צוּרִי

17   10/5 10   2 2   19   14 14

וְזוֹקֵף   בָּרְכִי   שִׁשִּׁים   מֶמְשַׁלְתְּךָ   וָעֹז

5 5   13 9   5 5   10 10   16 7

דּוֹרוֹתֵינוּ   נוֹגַעַת   יָדוֹן   מְפַרְנֵס   גָּלוּי

3   12 12   17   12 12   11 11 11

גִּנָּה   סְלָעִים   וּבָאָרֶץ   הַסְכִים   הִדְרִיךְ

20   8 8   15 15   15 15   7 7

תִּקְוֹת   בִּלְבַב   וַיַּעַן   וִילוֹן   אֶמְצַע

20   17   14   8 8   20

מִצְוֹת   אֲרוֹמִמְךָ   מָזוֹן   מְבַלְבְּלִים   עֲוֹנוֹת

NOTES

1. The test page contains rows of Hebrew words that gradually decrease in size from top to bottom.
2. The examiner records errors on the scoring sheet by circling the syllables misread by the student on the examiner's master copy of the test page, which includes the numbers above the letters.
3. The errors are then tallied.
4. There are twenty-one groupings that correspond to these numbers.

This test pinpoints elements that require re-teaching or drilling to achieve decoding accuracy and mastery.

THE HEBREW ALPHABET IN SIGN

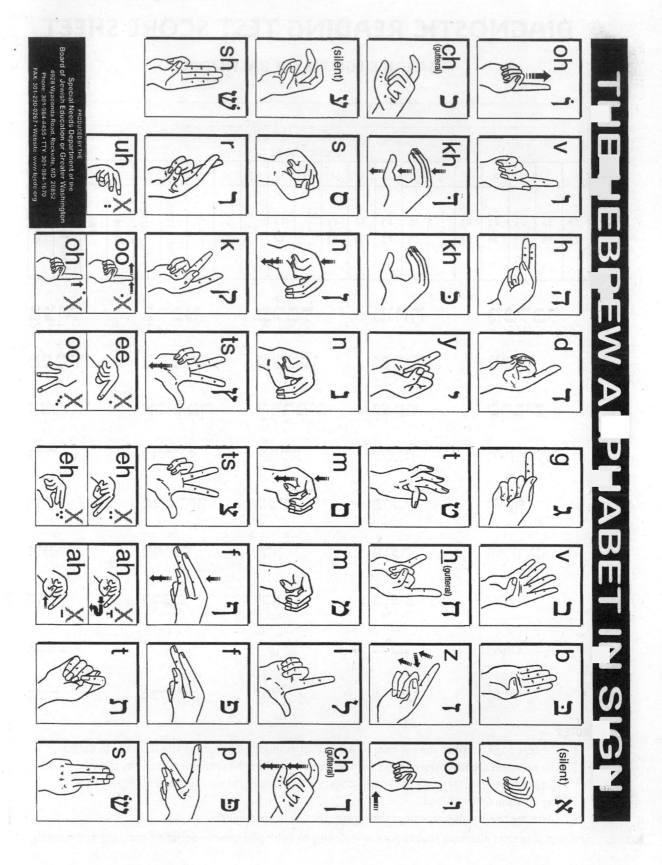

PRODUCED BY THE
Special Needs Department of the
Board of Jewish Education of Greater Washington
4928 Wyaconda Road, Rockville, MD 20852
Phone: 301-984-4455 · TTY: 301-984-1670
FAX: 301-230-0267 · Website: www.bjegdc.org

PART 8: CURRICULAR EXCERPTS

CHAPTER 34

SH'MA V'EZER PROGRAM
BJE of Greater Washington

A SUMMARY OF CURRICULAR EMPHASIS

Sh'ma V'Ezer's goal is to develop pride in and a sense of kinship with the Jewish people as well as an understanding of the relevance of the Jewish way of life to the students.

The curriculum is intended to flow on a continuum that is regulated by the students' capabilities. The levels are therefore only approximate.

LEVEL I: Introduction to the elementary stages of the Jewish cultural heritage

- Holidays and customs
- Bible heroes
- Simple prayers and blessings
- Functional Hebrew vocabulary related to holidays and Jewish symbols
- I am a Jew: symbols of the Jewish home and the synagogue
- Israel as the Jewish homeland and our link to it
- Opportunities for pleasurable experiences in Jewish living

LEVEL II: Continuation of Level I to broaden and deepen Jewish understandings

- Systematic study of Jewish tradition and practices involving intelligent use of the Jewish calendar and a knowledge of the origin, meaning, and observance of Shabbat and holidays
- Introduction to the arrangement of the *siddur* and general sequence of prayers
- *Tefilah* as individual and group worship
- Stories of selected Jewish personalities through the ages, stressing identification with their social and ethical qualities as related to the students' lives as American Jews
- Study of Israel as the land of the Bible
- I am a Jew: Mitzvot such as *tzedakah, kashrut, gemilut hasadim*
- Where appropriate, a multi-sensory approach to reading Hebrew

LEVEL III: Reflecting the special needs and interests of students in pre-adolescent and adolescent age ranges

- Jewish life cycle
- Implications of becoming a bar/bat mitzvah
- Jewish concerns in today's world *(Klal Yisrael)*
- Further development of synagogue skills

- Investigation of *tefilah* as communication
- Study of Zionist history and our link with it
- Where appropriate, development of accuracy and fluency in Hebrew phonetic reading skills
- Continuation of study of selected Jewish personalities

Holiday Curriculum (Shabbat)

SHABBAT WEB

CONCEPTS/THEMES

Queen/Bride	Rest	Joy
Peace	Holiness	Worship
Creation	Connection with God	Home/Synagogue
Weekly		

CUSTOMS/OBSERVANCES/RITUALS

Preparing for Shabbat	Family/friends	Singing
shopping	cooking	cleaning
Rest	tzedakah	Meals
Shabbat dinner	Kiddush lunch	*Melave Malkah*
Seudah Shlisheet		

PRAYERS/BLESSINGS

Kabbalat Shabbat	Kiddush	Candles
Motzi	*Birkat ha-Mazon*	Order of the service
Havdalah		

SYMBOLS

2 candles/candlesticks	braided hallah	hallah cover
twisted Havdalah candle	spice box	Kiddush cup/wine

VOCABULARY

Shabbat	*Malave Malka*	Ha-Motzi
Zmirot	*B'samim*	*Neirot*
Se'udah Shleesheet	*Oneg Shabbat*	Kiddush
Havdalah		

CHAPTER 35

ETGAR HOLIDAY CURRICULUM
Jewish Education Center of Cleveland

SHABBAT

CYCLE A: RITUALS AND SYMBOLS

OBJECTIVES

Students will be able to:

1. Identify symbols and describe their significance to the beginning of Shabbat
   - Candles
   - *Hallot*
   - Wine

2. Distinguish what makes a Shabbat meal different from others
   Blessings/songs
   Ritual objects
   Nicely set table
   Timing of the meal (i.e., sundown)
   Special meal/food

3. Identify & use Hebrew words that constitute basic functional vocabulary for Shabbat

4. Sequence the day's cycle
   Showering & dressing for Shabbat dinner   *Shaharit* (morning) services
   Setting table & cooking for dinner   Kiddush after morning services
   Kabbalat Shabbat   Meal
   Shabbat dinner   Afternoon rest
   Friday night services   *Se'udah Shlisheet*
   Oneg Shabbat   *Malave Malka*
   Havdalah

5. Sing Shabbat prayers and songs

6. Distinguish Shabbat from the rest of the week

7. Explain that Havdalah ends Shabbat, begins a new week and separates it from Shabbat

8. Identify symbols of Havdalah and demonstrate their use
   B'samim (spice box)   Braided candle   Wine

9. Recognize blessings for Havdalah

10. Sing the prayers associated with Havdalah

TACTILE	
1	• Make *hallah*. • Collect 3–7 pairs of Shabbat candlesticks. Mix up the sets, then have the students work to re-sort them into matching pairs. Provide candles for students to put into completed sets. • Place a *hallah* inside a large feely bag (perhaps a pillowcase). Ask students to feel inside and identify it (this activity may be done with a variety of ritual objects). • Make a *hallah* cover. • Create a *tzedakah* box. • Create Shabbat symbols out of clay or other material. • With assistance, set the Shabbat table. • Put the spices in the spice box for Havdalah. • Smell the Havdalah spices. • Participate in a Shabbat dinner. • Make a Shabbat tablecloth using handprints dipped in fabric paint. • Hold the objects used for a Havdalah ceremony. • Solve easy Shabbat puzzles in the classroom.
2	• Sort pictures indicating what we do on Shabbat and what we do during the regular week. • Create a mobile with three stars signifying the end of Shabbat. • Before class, cut out pictures of things we do on Shabbat and those we do during the regular week. Mount on construction paper. Students identify the behaviors as Shabbat or regular-week activities using stickers or stamps. • Using beeswax, create a Shabbat *or* Havdalah candle. For the latter, discuss the reason for the braided candle. • Offer a feely bag of Shabbat ritual objects. Have students reach inside and identify them by touch.
3	• Create a picture/collage that describes all of the aspects of Shabbat. • With supervision, follow the steps of a recipe to make *hallah*. • With supervision, prepare a Shabbat dinner. • Create the symbols that are necessary for the game "What Do We Like About Shabbat". • Make ritual objects for the Shabbat table using more "sophisticated" materials than clay. • Offer a feely bag of several items, some for Shabbat and some not. Have students feel for a Shabbat object, identify it, and show it to the class.
MOVEMENT	
1	• With assistance, set the Shabbat table. • Try on clothing related to the holiday and take pictures. • Wash hands (*n'tilat yadayim*) before Shabbat dinner. • Clean for Shabbat. • Prepare centerpiece for the Shabbat table and practice presenting flowers to the host family. • Give students a variety of rhythm instruments. Sing or play a variety of songs, some for Shabbat and some not. Have students play the instruments when the song is for Shabbat, but not play for a secular song.

2	• With assistance, practice lighting the Shabbat candles. • Welcome a Shabbat guest in and invite him/her to come sit at a set Shabbat table. • Attend a Shabbat dinner. • Dance to Shabbat music. • Play musical chairs while the teacher sings a Shabbat song. When the teacher switches to a non-Shabbat song, sit in the chairs. • Do a "Shabbat dance," acting out the various things our bodies do for Shabbat—light candles with our hands, eat _hallah_ with our mouths, walk to set the table, etc. • Walk through the week—students take a step on each day, Sunday through Friday, then stop (rest) on Shabbat.
3	• Go on a field trip to purchase flowers, candles, wine (grape juice), ingredients for _hallah_. • Attend Shabbat services. • Attend a Shabbat dinner. • Prepare a Shabbat dinner. • Participate in a pantomime play going through the sequence of a Shabbat day.

AUDITORY

1	• Listen to chanting of the blessing over the Shabbat candles, _Kiddush_ & _motzi_ • Practice chanting blessings. • Listen to appropriate holiday greetings. (e.g., _Shabbat Shalom_) • Listen to Shabbat songs. • Practice singing Shabbat songs. • Listen to Shabbat stories. • Play "What Do We like About Shabbat".
2	• Listen to and repeat the first verse of _Kiddush_. • Chant the remainder of _Kiddush_ with assistance. • Chant _Hamotzi_ with cues. • Sing Shabbat songs in choral form. • Listen to a Shabbat blessing and match it to the appropriate ritual object. (_Hamotzi_ to _hallah_) • Listen to and identify Havdalah blessings. • Listen to a variety of songs and identify those that are for Shabbat.
3	• Chant _Kiddush_. • Chant _Hamotzi_. • Chant blessing over the candles. • Sing Shabbat songs. • Play Shabbat "Jeopardy". -Chant Havdalah blessings and associated songs. • Students read Shabbat stories to others.

	VISUAL
1	• Place variety of loaves of bread, including a *hallah*, on the table. Ask students to locate the *hallah*. • Using pre-cut pictures of the symbols, paste and create a picture. • Watch someone light the Shabbat candles. • Identify pictures of people nicely dressed for synagogue. • Take pictures of students as they make *hallah* (see tactile level 1). Use the pictures to remind students of the order of the process. • Using pictures, identify parts of the cycle of Shabbat. • When presented with the symbols, point to each.
2	• Place on the table various symbols of the holidays. Give a description of one object's significance and have students pick out that object. • List activities that are appropriate for Shabbat and have students explain them. • Sort clothing worn to synagogue (bring in actual clothing). • Using pictures, sequence the cycle of Shabbat events. These pictures may be taken during other learning activities—e.g., while *hallah* is baking, while candles are lit or the table set, or doing the table blessings. • Using pictures, sequence the order of the blessings. • Make a Shabbat book about the cycle of the day, including Havdalah. • Present students with symbols. With assistance, have students identify the Hebrew names for each. • With assistance, have students discriminate objects for Shabbat and the regular week. • Have students close their eyes. Place on a table set for Shabbat several non-holiday items (e.g., a comic book, a video game). Ask students to identify what does not belong. • Place on the table a variety of ritual objects that match as pairs: 2 candlesticks, a *hallah* and cover, a *Kiddush* cup and small bottle of grape juice, etc. Mix up the items and have students match the pairs.
3	• Discuss the significance of the symbols. • Show a Jewish calendar. Identify Shabbat as occurring each week. • Create a poster "What do we like about Shabbat?" Have students play. • Present students with symbols. Have them identify the Hebrew name for each. • From a variety of symbols and ritual objects, students choose those that are related to Shabbat. • Be outside at the end of Shabbat, locate 3 stars, then do Havdalah. • Hide various ritual objects around the classroom. Students "spy" out the Shabbat items.

For more information, contact www.jecc.org.

CHAPTER 36

MY BOOK OF JEWISH HOLIDAYS
BJE of Greater Washington

Marlene N. Marcus and Mary F. Meyerson

These pages are from an experimental edition, utilizing adaptations of Mayer-Johnson Board-maker picture communication symbols.

For more information go to www. PJLL.org.

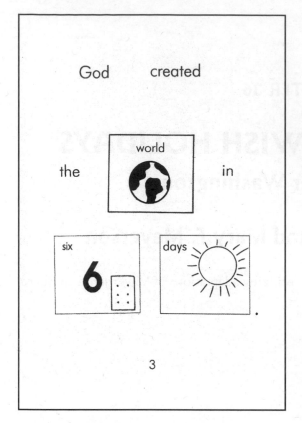

7

8

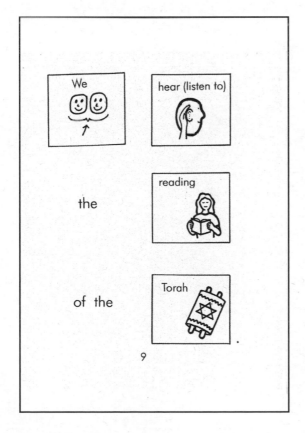

9

10

CHAPTER 37

A TIME TO REJOICE
Bureau of Jewish Education of Los Angeles

Miriam Wolf, Marlynn Dorff, Kenneth Schaefler

INTRODUCTION

"A Time To Rejoice" holiday series was developed to try to meet the differing learning needs of Jewish children in various educational settings. The curriculum is suitable for students who may have a variety of learning disabilities or mild developmental delays. If teachers choose activities that emphasize different strengths and skills, all children should be able to participate actively and enthusiastically. Finally, this material is a resource for any teacher who is sensitive to the individual needs of children and who is looking for alternative strategies to teach the Jewish holidays.

The curriculum is set up using a multi-sensory approach to teaching Judaic ideas and values. The material is presented using many modalities: visual, auditory, and tactile. A child who has a visual perception problem is given a model he/she can touch rather than a picture. A child with language problems is given the choice of writing, acting, or drawing to convey comprehension of a concept, rather than an oral response. To reinforce the concepts and skills presented, the learning center model is incorporated into the curriculum.

The following unit focuses on giving children tools to celebrate Shabbat in their homes with their families. The unit is structured around the creation of the ritual objects necessary for Friday night home ceremonies, making a booklet that explains the rituals and includes the *brakhot*, and it culminates in the children creating a taped oral guide to facilitate these observances. Because this is a lengthy unit, Lessons 1-6 are provided to give the reader a complementary format to teach Shabbat. The complete holiday series curriculum manual can be purchased from Bureau of Jewish Education, Los Angeles.

LESSON 1
OBJECTIVES

- Students will distinguish between the concepts of "special" and "ordinary."
- Students will identify the symbols that help the Jewish people create a special day called Shabbat (Kiddush cup, Shabbat candles, ḥallah).

MATERIALS NEEDED

- Copies of the story "The Shabbat Snowstorm" (Melton Curriculum Level Aleph, Shabbat Unit)
- Tablecloth
- Candlesticks
- Kiddush cup
- Wine or grape juice
- Hallah
- Hallah cover
- Pitcher of water

These items should be set up on a table before the students arrive.

Activity 1: Opening Discussion (approximately 5 minutes): As students arrive in class, listen to comments about the Shabbat items set out on the table. Once students are seated, reiterate some of the comments you overheard and state that today you will be beginning to study the very special Jewish holiday of Shabbat. First you will read a story about how two children celebrated Shabbat.

Activity 2: Story, "The Shabbat Snowstorm" (approximately 15 minutes): The teacher should present the story "The Shabbat Snowstorm" using the set Shabbat table for visual cues and as a way to introduce Shabbat rituals. For example, in the story Sarah lights the Shabbat candles. Here the teacher should circle the candles three times with his/her hands, cover his/her eyes, and say the blessing.

Activity 3: Review the Story (approximately 10 minutes): You can review the story verbally or by acting out students' favorite parts of the story. Students can describe in pantomime, using the objects, those parts of the Friday night home ceremony that they do in their homes or have seen in someone else's home.

Activity 4: Concluding Activity (approximately 10–15 minutes): Choose one or more of the following activities to conclude the lesson.

a. The children can draw a picture of the Shabbat table that can be hung up in the classroom. You could play a Shabbat record while the children are drawing.

b. Make a "sense box" into which the children have to reach, feel the objects, and try to identify them and their function by the way they feel.

c. Have a "fishing" activity where the children "fish" with a pole and string behind a curtain and "catch" one of the objects, which they either write about or draw on a section of a class mural that can be hung up in the classroom

d. Find and circle "hidden" Shabbat symbols on a teacher-made worksheet.

e. Make a class collage by cutting out pictures from magazines that depict "special" or "ordinary" activities.

LESSON II

OBJECTIVES

- To help students learn the order and significance of the Friday night home ceremony.
- To make candlesticks for inclusion in a "Shabbat Box."

MATERIALS

- 3 large poster boards, one with a large picture of candlesticks, one with a large picture of a Kiddush cup, one with a large picture of ḥallah (a fourth with *kos n'tilat yadaim* cup for washing is optional)
- String
- Clay
- Pencils
- Old newspapers
- Candlesticks
- Candles
- Matches
- Kiddush cup
- 2 ḥallot

Activity I: Scavenger Hunt (approximately 20–25 minutes): This activity can be presented in a number of ways, depending on space and number of adults available.

Option I (if more than one adult is available): The children begin in the classroom with the teacher and assistant. The teacher explains that they will be embarking on a scavenger hunt for Shabbat symbols within a defined area. They will go in a group with the assistant and search for the same symbols they learned about in the previous lesson. (Review the items briefly, orally.) At this point, the *teacher* goes out and first hides the candlesticks, candles and matches. The assistant (or other participating adult) brings the group to the area to be searched. When the object is found, the teacher, wearing the candlesticks posterboard around his/her neck, explains the significance and use of the item in *first* person.

A sample presentation follows.

"Hi! You found me! Since you found me first, then you must know that I am the first symbol to be used on Friday night.

"By lighting me, you welcome in the Shabbat. Usually I am placed somewhere special in the house where everyone can see me. People know that Shabbat has started because they see me glowing brightly. I get lit in a special way, too. The person who lights me circles his/her hands three times around me (demonstrate) and then covers his/her eyes (demonstrate). I used to think that was silly—I mean, I'm so beautiful, why wouldn't they want to look at me? But then I learned the reason. See, they need to say a *brakhah* (a blessing) over me.

"Now usually, when you say a *brakhah,* you say it first and then do something afterwards. But I get lit *before* the *brakhah* is said. I know it's kind of funny, but that's the way it's done. I know that's kind of confusing, so let's practice how to do it."

Practice lighting, circling three times, opening eyes. Let students know that there's a *brakhah* for the candles, but they'll be learning it another day. You can also let the children know that the candles have a Hebrew name and have them practice saying it, e.g.:

"By the way, in Hebrew I'm called נֵרוֹת *neirot* Shabbat. Who thinks they can call me by my Hebrew name, instead of just calling me 'candles'?"

The *neirot* can ask if there are any questions and can retreive information verbally by asking "How many times do you circle me?" etc.

When most of the class seems to grasp the main ideas, the teacher hides the Kiddush cup and again hides. When found by the class, the teacher should appear, wearing the Kiddush cup posterboard, and present information about the Kiddush cup in a manner similar to that above. The information that should be conveyed is:

- Kiddush is the *second* ritual performed.
- Kiddush is said to make the Shabbat meal special and different from ordinary meals during the rest of the week.
- The Kiddush cup is held up during the blessing for all to see.
- Its Hebrew name is כּוֹס יַיִן *kos yayin*.
- The teacher performs the Kiddush while everyone drinks or sips from the *kos yayin* (or you can pour the grape juice into small cups for everyone to sip).

When the students have had a short question-and-answer period with the *kos yayin,* the teacher should hide the ḥallah and cover. Imparting of information should take the same format, covering the following material.

- The ḥallah is the *third* ritual (unless you have chosen to also present the כּוֹס נְטִילַת יָדַיִם *kos n'tilat yadaim,* in which case it would be the fourth).
- It's covered, so as not to be jealous of the wine, with the ḥallah "saying" that it got so jealous that it now gets covered up so it can't see or hear the wine being blessed.
- The ḥallah is braided. Can the children think of reasons that the ḥallah is twisted up?
- There is a blessing over the ḥallah that the children will be learning.
- The ḥallah has a delicious smell when it is baking, which reminds us that Shabbat is coming.
- Uncovering ḥallah is like opening a present. Each week there is an element of surprise and anticipation as we uncover the ḥallah and taste it. Ask the children how it is possible to still be surprised when we know what is under the cover.

Again, have a short question-and-answer period with the students.

Option 2 (if only one adult is available or space is limited): Before children arrive in class, set up four stations in your classroom—an introductory one and one for each of the symbols. Have the children rotate from station to station. The teacher still speaks for the symbol and wears the poster board as in Option 1.

Option 3: Hide the objects within your room. The child who finds an object can assist the teacher in the presentation. The teacher still speaks for the symbols and wears the poster board as in Option 1.

(Options 2 and 3 will probably take less time than Option 1.)

Activity 2: Making Candlesticks (approximately 20 minutes): Introduce the children to the idea of a "Shabbat Box" (a box with all the necessary materials to make Shabbat in their homes). Ask them to guess which objects they will be making during the next few lessons to be included in the box.

Begin making candlesticks, or follow an idea of your own. You will probably only have time to roll, shape, and design the candlesticks during this lesson, so the candlesticks should be stored in a safe place to dry and will be painted during the next lesson.

Directions for Making Candlesticks

MATERIALS NEEDED
- Clay (air-hardening)
- Pencils and other textured items to decorate clay
- Optional: paint and paintbrushes

DIRECTIONS
1. Give each student two lumps of clay (approximate size: medium apple).
2. Roll and shape clay into a ball.
3. Flatten the bottom so it stands securely.
4. Insert a Shabbat candle about halfway down into the clay to make a hole. Wiggle the candle slightly to enlarge the hole. Remove the candle.
5. Decorate the candlesticks using pencil points and other textured objects.
6. Let candlesticks dry.
7. Optional: paint.

Activity 3: Concluding Activity: If you have some extra time, use one of the review options from the concluding activity choices in Lesson 1, Activity 4.

LESSON III

OBJECTIVES
- The students will review the steps of the candle lighting ceremony.
- The students will be able to recite the *brakhah* over the candles.
- The students will paint their candlesticks.

MATERIALS NEEDED
- Old newspapers (for desks)
- Clay candlesticks from previous lesson
- Paint
- Paintbrushes
- Items for learning center activities (see below)

Activity 1: Brief Review of Last Lesson and Teaching of Candlelighting Brakhah (approximately 10–15 minutes):

Briefly review orally what was covered in the previous lesson. Then teach the blessing. (Some children may know the blessing, in which case the lesson will be more of a review, and you can move on to the learning centers.) If the blessing is new for a majority of the children, teach the blessing in the following manner:

- Have words written on the board or on a large poster in Hebrew or in transliteration. (Some students might also benefit from individual copies.)

- Practice the words לְהַדְלִיק נֵר שֶׁל שַׁבָּת *l'hadlik ner shel Shabbat* first. (Ask if any of the words–e.g., *"ner Shabbat*—sound familiar.)

- Practice first in a group and then ask individuals (everybody in a red shirt, everybody in jeans, etc.) to say the words.

- Then practice אֲשֶׁר קִדְּשָׁנוּ בְּמִצְוֹתָיו וְצִוָּנוּ *asher kidshanu b'mitzvotav v'tzivanu* one or two words at a time.

- Then practice from the beginning. This part will probably be familiar to a majority of students.

Then practice entire *brakhah* with circling motion and eyes closed.

Note to teacher: By the end of the unit, the children should be able to recite all the *brachot* for candles, wine, and ḥallah (and washing hands, if you are including that). In each of the subsequent lessons review and practice time should be allotted both as a group and with individual children. Many of the subsequent lessons have quiet work or learning centers as culminating activities. While children are working independently, the teacher or assistant should pull individual children to practice the *brakhot*.

Activity 2: Page for Booklet (approximately 5–10 minutes):

As children finish their painting they should complete a sheet on *neirot Shabbat* that will be included in a Shabbat Box booklet. Some students will be able independently to write three or four sentences describing the candle lighting ceremony. Others should be encouraged to use a fill-in form such as the example below. Nonreaders can go over this sheet with a partner or the assistant.

Example: Lighting candles is the ___(first)___ thing we do to welcome ___(Shabbat)___. We circle our hands ___(3)___ times, cover our ___(eyes),___ and say the blessing:

בָּרוּךְ אַתָּה יי אֱלֹהֵינוּ מֶלֶךְ הָעוֹלָם אֲשֶׁר קִדְּשָׁנוּ בְּמִצְוֹתָיו וְצִוָּנוּ
לְהַדְלִיק נֵר שֶׁל שַׁבָּת

(Teacher can write the blessing or have a separate sheet for inclusion in the booklet.)

LEARNING CENTERS

If students finish painting early, they should be encouraged to use a learning center that the teacher can set up before class. Students can be assigned by the teacher or can choose which center they want to use. There should be activities that emphasize varying modalities—something for every child.

Here are some examples.

a. A listening center with a tape recorder and earphones to practice the *brakhah* and corresponding movements.

b. A self-checking puzzle game with the Hebrew names of Shabbat objects and pictures of the objects.

c. Creative writing/drawing/drama center. Children can write about the *neirot* in first person, or there can be some kind of related theme such as "In some homes, an extra set of Shabbat candles is left unlit to remind us that some Jews are still not free to practice Judaism." Ask children to write/draw/act out what it would be like not to be able to celebrate Shabbat.

d. Puppet corner where kids can practice the *brakhot* using puppets.

e. Stained-glass picture of candles as described on previous page.

LESSON IV
OBJECTIVES
- Students will learn the *brakhah* over the wine and Shabbat Kiddush.
- Students will make Kiddush cups for the Shabbat box.

MATERIALS NEEDED
- *Kiddush* cup
- Plastic or glass wine glasses for each child (available at any five and dime store)
- "Liquid embroidery" pens (available at any crafts store)
- Paper
- Pencils
- Sheets with the *brakhah* over the wine and the Shabbat *Kiddush*

Activity I: Teach *Brakhah* over Wine (approximately 10 minutes): Remind children of the part in the story "The Shabbat Snowstorm" when they make a blessing over the wine. (You can reread that part if necessary.) Ask if anyone remembers *why* we drink wine. If not, remind the children that we drink wine at many Jewish celebrations to make them special and as a sign of joy.

Teach the *brakhah* over the wine in the same manner in which you taught the candle blessing in small chunks, beginning with (Hebrew) *borei pri ha-gaffen.* Children will probably notice that the beginning parts are the same. (You will be doing a mini-lesson on *brakhot* during Lesson VI, but for now you might want to introduce *very* briefly the notion that there are a lot of *brakhot* that begin with those words, because we stop to thank God before we do things.)

Activity 2: Introduce Shabbat Kiddush (approximately 10 minutes): Tell the children: Whenever we drink wine we say the *brakhah* we just learned. It is called the Kiddush. On Shabbat we add some words when we say the *brakhah*. This is called the "Shabbat Kiddush." These words thank God for giving the Jewish people the special gift of Shabbat. This is how it goes (the teacher should sing):

בָּרוּךְ אַתָּה יי אֱלֹהֵינוּ מֶלֶךְ הָעוֹלָם בּוֹרֵא פְּרִי הַגָּפֶן.

בָּרוּךְ אַתָּה יי אֱלֹהֵינוּ מֶלֶךְ הָעוֹלָם אֲשֶׁר קִדְּשָׁנוּ בְּמִצְוֹתָיו

וְרָצָה בָנוּ וְשַׁבַּת קָדְשׁוֹ בְּאַהֲבָה וּבְרָצוֹן הִנְחִילָנוּ

זִכָּרוֹן לְמַעֲשֵׂה בְרֵאשִׁית.

כִּי הוּא יוֹם תְּחִלָּה לְמִקְרָאֵי־קֹדֶשׁ זֵכֶר לִיצִיאַת מִצְרָיִם.

כִּי בָנוּ בָחַרְתָּ וְאוֹתָנוּ קִדַּשְׁתָּ מִכָּל הָעַמִּים

וְשַׁבַּת קָדְשְׁךָ בְּאַהֲבָה וּבְרָצוֹן הִנְחַלְתָּנוּ.

בָּרוּךְ אַתָּה יי מְקַדֵּשׁ הַשַּׁבָּת.

Barukh Atah Adonai Eloheinu Melekh ha-Olam Borei Pri ha-Gafen.

Barukh Atah Adonai Eloheinu Melekh ha-Olam Asher Kidshanu b'Mitzvotav v'Ratzah Vanu

v'Shabbat Kodsho b'Ahavah u'Vratzon Hinhilanu,

Zikaron l'Ma'asay V'reishit.

Ki Hu Yom T'hilah l'Mikra-ei Kodesh, Zeikher l'Tzi'at Mitra'im.

Ki Vanu Vaharta, v'Otanu Kidashta, mi-Kol ha-Amim,

V'Shabbat Kodsh'kha b'Ahavah u'v'Ratzon Hinhaltanu.

Barukh Atah Adonai m'Kadesh ha-Shabbat.

The teacher should decide if he/she wants to devote time during this lesson to begin teaching this now, or whether introduction of the concept is enough. Regardless of when it is taught, it should be done in small chunks and reinforced in a learning center in subsequent lessons.

Activity 3: Make Kiddush Cups (approximately 20–25 minutes)

MATERIALS NEEDED

- Wine cups
- Liquid embroidery pens

DIRECTIONS

1. Buy stemmed wine glasses.
2. Cover ½" of the upper rim of each glass with scotch or masking tape so that you will not decorate the area your lips will touch.
3. Using liquid embroidery pens (available at any crafts store), draw designs on the glass. (Designs can be at students' discretion: squiggly lines, dots, flowers, or Shabbat symbols, or teacher can assist student in writing "Shabbat" [Hebrew]).
4. Let paint dry.
5. Wash by hand in warm water, no soap.

Activity 4: Concluding Activity (approximately 5–10 minutes): As you did

with the candles, summarize the wine ceremony in writing—either creative writing or a fill-in exercise such as:

(Wine) is used in many Jewish celebrations to make them special and to show that we are happy. The blessing we say is called the (Kiddush) . On Shabbat we say a special prayer over the wine call the (Shabbat Kiddush) .

If you have lag time at the end of this lesson, or if a group of children have finished their wine cups and sheet quickly, a fun way to review and evaluate is a beanbag game in which the teacher starts off the *brakhah* and throws the beanbag to a child who must supply the next word.

LESSON V

OBJECTIVES

- Students will use the sense of taste to explore the idea of the "specialness" of Shabbat.
- Students will make <u>h</u>allah covers.

MATERIALS NEEDED

- Materials for <u>h</u>allah covers
- Grape juice or Concord grape wine
- Paper cups
- Dry white wine
- <u>H</u>allah
- Regular white or wheat bread
  - Story "The Sabbath Taste" by Sadie Rose Weilerstein, Melton Holiday Curriculum, Level Aleph, Shabbat Unit.

Activity 1: "Science" Experiment (approximately 15–20 minutes): Tell the students that today we will be trying an experiment to see if Shabbat foods taste more special than foods during the rest of the week. Tell the children:

"Usually scientists make predictions—guesses—about the way their experiment will turn out. Let's try to guess the result of our experiment. Raise your hand if you think Shabbat foods will taste better than ordinary foods. Raise your hand if you think Shabbat foods will taste the same as ordinary foods." Chart the results on the board.

"Scientists also try to guess *why* experiments come out in certain ways. Why did you vote the way you did?

"Now we are going to run the experiment."

Have the children taste white grape juice and purple grape juice.

"Who likes the white grape juice better?

"Who likes the purple grape juice better?"

Chart the results.

Have children taste a piece of <u>h</u>allah and a piece of regular white bread.

"Who likes the <u>h</u>allah better?

"Who likes the white bread better?"

Chart the results.

Make observations about predictions and outcomes.

Discussion: "What is different or special about the wine and <u>h</u>allah?"

Discussion: "Would the wine and <u>h</u>allah be so special if we had them every day?"

Give time for opinions. Teacher should sum up the discussion by saying that we will be hearing a story that helps to explain why Shabbat foods taste special.

Activity 2: Read the Story "The Sabbath Taste" (approximately 10–15 minutes): Read the story. Discuss with the children the following questions:

1. Have you ever tasted the Shabbat spice? When?

2. What is the special message of this story? (The *effort* that goes into celebrating Shabbat is what makes it special.)

3. What about the story reminds you of our experiment?

Activity 3: Making <u>H</u>allah Covers (approximate time: remainder of lesson): Ask students to recall (from Lesson II) why we need <u>h</u>allah covers. Summarize.

Make the covers. (You will not have time to finish them in this lesson; time is allotted in Lesson VI.)

MATERIALS NEEDED

- Pieces of cloth (white or beige) approximately 11" x 16"
- Black indelible ink marking pens
- Rit dye in two colors
- Rubber bands
- Four buckets or pails
- Water
- Clothesline or rope
- Aprons (or have children wear old clothes)

DIRECTIONS—FIRST LESSON

1. Before children arrive, prepare Rit dye according to directions on package.

2. Hand out cloths, one to a child.

3. Help children write Shabbat (Hebrew) or make other relevant drawing on their cloth.

4. Gather cloth in rubber bands at various points. (This will make designs when cloth is dyed.)

5. Dye cloth using ONE color on various poionts. (Do not dye entire cloth, as you will need to let it dry before adding second color.)

6. Rinse and dry according to directions on package. (Remove rubber bands.)

7. Hang on line to dry (preferably outside).

DIRECTIONS—SECOND LESSON

Repeat steps 4–7, dyeing remainder of cloth in second color.

NOTE: You can simplify this project by using one color dye only.

Following this lesson or Lesson VI, you can include an optional project of a *hallah* board easily made by sanding and varnishing a piece of wood.

LESSON VI

OBJECTIVES

- Students will demonstrate understanding of the meaning of *brakhot* by acting out scenes thanking God for different foods.
- Students will learn *ha-Motzi*.

MATERIALS NEEDED

- Story "The Sabbath Taste," Melton Holiday Curriculum, Level Aleph, Shabbat Unit
- Props for the story (apron, grocer's apron, bowl, wooden spoon, straw hat, overalls, loaf of bread and, if possible, a stalk of wheat)
- Cards with the following captions and corresponding pictures: BREAD, MOTHER, GROCER, BAKER, MILLER, FARMER
- Card with no picture: God

Activity 1: Active Storytelling (approximate 10–15 minutes): Tell the story using the above props to make the characters and process concrete. For example, when the grocer is speaking, put on the grocer's apron and speak his part in first person. The children will enjoy seeing you alternate characters and will be able to attend to the sequence of the story.

After reading the story, place caption cards with pictures of the baker, the miller, etc. (see attached illustrations) on the floor or board where they are visible to the students. Mix the cards up so that they are *not* in the order presented in the story. Have the kids recall the story by sequencing the cards.

Activity 2: Drama (approximately 20 minutes): Split the class into two groups—one with the teacher, one with the assistant. Assign each group a food such as pizza or ice cream. Have the group brainstorm steps for thanking God for that food (limit it to four or five steps). For example, for ICE CREAM: store clerk—factory worker—milker—cow—God. (This activity will necessitate giving children information such as that ice cream is made from milk.) In each case, the steps should culminate in thanking God.

Each group should develop a *short* skit with their food and perform it for the other group. Ask the children, after the performances, what the three skits (yours on bread included) have in common. (We thank God for them all.)

Activity 3: Return to Ha-Motzi (approximately 10–15 minutes): Teacher should say, "Eating is something we do every day. We could easily forget how wonderful it is that we have food. We could take food for granted. Rabbis long ago decided that there had to be a way to help us remember not to take food for granted. They decided that whenever a Jew eats a meal, he/she should say a special phrase to remind him/her of how lucky we are to have food. We thank God with *ha-Motzi*. Today we're going to learn this *brakhah*."

Teach this *brakhah* using the same method as in previous lessons. (Chances are that most of the children will be familiar with it, so it will not require much practice.) Ask if anyone hears any familiar words and point out *lekhem* (bread) and *aretz* (earth).

Activity 4: Continue Work on Hallah Covers:

Work on hallah covers. (If some children have already finished their hallah covers, they can participate in any learning center-type activity in the unit.)

For more information, contact www.bjela.org.

PART 9:
PROFESSIONAL
DEVELOPMENT/
STAFF TRAINING

CHAPTER 38

SH'LOM KITAH: A MODEL TO TRAIN CONGREGATIONAL SCHOOL LEARNING SPECIALISTS

Partnership for Jewish Life and Learning (Washington, D.C.)

Lenore Layman

RATIONALE

Sh'lom Kitah (Peace in the Classroom), a mentoring program for congregational school teachers, was developed to provide training for teachers to learn the techniques necessary to successfully integrate students with learning differences into their classrooms. Approximately 10–20 percent of students enrolled in congregational schools have learning difficulties of varying degrees of severity. These are primarily students in regular classes that require teachers with appropriate training and specialized resources to help them learn to the best of their abilities. Lack of training and knowledge about materials on the part of the teachers can lead to frustration for both students and teachers as well as to behavior management problems.

PROGRAM DESCRIPTION

The *Sh'lom Kitah* program matches selected teachers at area synagogues with mentors who have degrees in special education or a related field, as well as experience in the field of Jewish education. The mentors observe the teachers in their classroom approximately eight times during the course of the year and provide guidance, support, and feedback to them so that the teachers can work more successfully with diverse types of learners in their classroom. In addition to the on-site observations, the mentors and teachers come together four to five times during the course of the year for Sunday afternoon seminars on a variety of topics. At these seminars the mentors make presentations on subjects such as individual learning styles, goal setting in the classroom, behavior management, remedial Hebrew, curriculum modification, and multisensory teaching and activities.

Information describing the program is sent out to education directors at area congregational schools. Education directors are asked to select specific teachers who might be willing to make the commitment and have the interest to participate in such a training program. Applications are filled out by educational directors and teachers, résumés are reviewed, and appropriate teachers are selected to participate in the program. The Mashkon Initiative provides a financial stipend to the mentors, teachers, and synagogues that participate in the program. Upon completion of the program synagogues receive an allocation to use in purchasing resource materials for their school. Teachers receive a stipend, and mentors are paid for their commitment of time to this training program.

Upon completion of the year-long *Sh'lom Kitah* program teachers are given the opportunity to continue refining their skills in working with students who have special learning needs. Funding exists to underwrite a series of professional seminars on a variety of topics in the field of special education. The seminars are held on Sunday afternoons and are open to teachers in both congregational and day schools in addition to teachers who have participated in the *Sh'lom Kitah* program. Seminars are generally held four times during the course of the year and are two to three hours in length. Teachers who have completed the mentoring program are encouraged to attend by being offered an additional financial stipend for attending the seminar series.

CONCLUSION

In conclusion, the *Sh'lom Kitah* mentoring program is an exciting model that can be replicated in other communities to train committed congregational school teachers to work with students with multiple learning needs within regular classrooms, self-contained special needs classes, and resource room programs. This type of mentoring program plays an important role in providing teachers with techniques to successfully integrate students with special learning needs into congregational schools.

SH'LOM KITAH FACT SHEET FOR TEACHERS

WHAT IS *SH'LOM KITAH*? *Sh'lom Kitah* is a mentoring program for congregational school teachers. The goal of the program is to provide training for strong, committed congregational school teachers to become learning specialists, resource room teachers, or special education consultants within their congregational school.

WHAT IS INVOLVED IN BEING PART OF THIS PROGRAM? Teachers who are selected to participate will be matched with a mentor (a special education professional). This mentor will observe you in your classroom eight times during the course of the academic year. Your mentor will provide feedback after each observation either in person or over the phone. Your mentor will provide ongoing support and guidance to you throughout the school year. In addition, you will be required to attend four to five *Sh'lom Kitah* seminars sponsored by the BJE along with the other teachers and mentors in the program. Seminars will be on a variety of topics related to special education. Tentative dates and times of the seminars can be found below.

FINANCIAL INCENTIVE You will receive a stipend of $_upon completion of the program. In addition, your synagogue will receive a stipend of $_that can be used to purchase materials for students with special learning needs.

DATES OF THE PROGRAM The program will begin on September and end on June .

Tentative dates and seminar topics are as follows:

If you are interested in applying for this exciting training program, please ask your educational director for an application and send it along with a résumé by
to:

SH'LOM KITAH GUIDELINES FOR PRINCIPALS

WHAT CAN *SH'LOM KITAH* OFFER YOUR SCHOOL?

Sh'lom Kitah provides a special education professional who will observe a teacher in your school eight times during the academic year and provide ongoing feedback, support, and guidance. Additionally, the mentor will be available to work with you for ten additional hours during the course of the year. In the role of professional consultant the mentor will be available to observe in other classrooms, meet with other teachers, present at faculty meetings, and offer professional guidance to you.

WHAT IS THE ROLE OF THE *SH'LOM KITAH* MENTOR?

The *Sh'lom Kitah* mentor will observe the *Sh'lom Kitah* teacher eight times during the course of the year and provide feedback about each observation either in person or by phone. In addition, the mentor will be available to provide ongoing support and feedback to this teacher as needed during the course of the year.

The mentor will be available ten additional hours during the year for professional consultation (as specified above). Each principal and mentor will collaborate to determine the ways the school can best utilize this consultation time.

The mentor will also attend three of the teacher seminars.

WHAT IS THE OBLIGATION OF THE PRINCIPAL?

The principal is required to set up an initial meeting in September with the mentor to discuss the role of the mentor in the school. During the course of the year the principal is required to identify areas of need in terms of special education and to utilize the mentor's expertise in this area in ways best suited to his/her school. The principal is required to fill out four mentor logs during the course of the year, detailing the work that the mentor has done in the school. In addition, the principal is required to fill out an end-of-year evaluation.

For more information, contact www.pjll.org.

TO PREPARE FOR INITIAL MEETING WITH MENTOR

Teacher_____

Synagogue _____

Date_____

What are the challenges in your class this year? _____

_____

_____

_____

How would you like to see things change?_____

_____

_____

_____

List several goals you would like to accomplish in your classroom over the next year through participation in the mentoring program. _____

_____

_____

_____

_____

_____

_____

_____

MENTOR OBSERVATION LOG

Mentor: _____

Teacher: _____

Date of Observation _____

School: _____ Grade: _____

Components of lesson: (e.g., Hebrew reading, prayer, Bible, Israel, etc.) _____

_____

_____

_____

Strengths of the lesson: _____

_____

_____

_____

Recommendations/goals for teacher: _____

_____

_____

_____

Date of post-observation: _____

_____

_____

_____

Outcome of post-observation meeting: _____

_____

MENTOR EVALUATION FORM

Name:_____

Teacher's Name _____

Synagogue school where teacher taught: _____

Were you able to observe and/or meet with your teacher eight times during the course of the program? _____

If not, please describe the reasons why. _____

Do you feel that the teacher benefited from these observations/meetings? Please describe how. _____

What changes did you observe in the teacher's classroom (e.g., physical setup, organization, types of lessons, behavior management, etc.)? _____

How did you communicate your observations to the teacher? Did you meet in person or talk on the phone? Was the teacher receptive to your comments? _____

In your opinion, after this program would the teacher be comfortable and/or does the teacher have the skills to work with students with special learning needs in a resource room, self-contained class, or inclusionary setting within a supplementary school?_____

Did you feel that the seminars were helpful in providing useful information to the teachers? Why or why not? Please comment on the specific seminar topics.

  Behavior and Classroom Management_____

  Curriculum Modifications _____

  Multisensory Teaching_____

  Hebrew Reading _____

  Hebrew Games _____

Did you think that the seminar topics were on target in terms of the teacher's needs? Why or why not?_____

Did you enjoy presenting information at the seminars? Did you feel that you were given enough advance notice to prepare? _____

What other topics do you think would be useful to include in a series of seminars for the mentoring program?_____

Do you have any suggestions about changing the structure of the mentoring program? _____

Any additional comments or suggestions would be welcomed and helpful in planning for the future. _____

TEACHER EVALUATION FORM

Name:_____

Synagogue School: _____

Mentor: _____

Did your mentor observe you and/or meet with you eight times during the course of the program? _

If your mentor came less frequently, please describe reasons why. _____

Do you feel you benefited from these observations? Please specify. _____

In what ways, if any, do you think your teaching techniques and/or class management techniques have changed? Please specify. _____

How did your mentor communicate observations to you? Did you meet in person or talk on the phone? Did you feel that your relationship with your mentor was a comfortable one? _____
_____

Did you feel that the seminars were helpful in providing useful information to you? Why or why not?

Which topics were the most useful to you as a teacher (Behavior and Classroom Management, Multisensory Teaching, Curriculum Modifications, Hebrew Reading, Hebrew Games, Humash Strategies, Sensory Integration Techniques, Talking Tips)?_____
_____

What other topics do you think would be useful to include in a series of seminars? _____
_____

Did you use your mentoring handbook during the course of the year? If yes, in what way? If no, why not? _____

Did you ever share any information or techniques that you learned in the mentoring program with other teachers or the principal in your school? If yes, please specify._____

Would you feel comfortable informally sharing information and suggestions that you received with other teachers in your school in the future? Would you feel comfortable if your principal publicized to other teachers that they could come to you as a resource if they were struggling with a particular student or classroom situation?_____

Would you feel comfortable working with students with special learning needs in a resource room program, self-contained classroom, or inclusionary classroom? If you are already working in this capacity, do you think your teaching skills have improved? Please specify. _____

Do you have any suggestions about changing the structure of the mentoring program? _____

Any additional comments or suggestions would be welcomed and helpful in planning for the future.
_____

PRINCIPAL EVALUATION FORM

Name:_____

Supplementary School:_____

Teacher's Name: _____

Did the mentor come out to observe your teacher on a regular basis? _____

If the mentor came less frequently, please describe the reasons for this. _____

Do you feel that your teacher benefited from these observations? Please specify. _____
_____

What changes, if any, have you observed in your teacher's classroom (e.g., teaching techniques, classroom management, behavioral strategies, physical setup of room, accommodations for specific students, etc.)?_____
_____

Has the teacher given you any feedback about whether the seminars were useful? If yes, please specify. _____

Do you know if the teacher shared any information or techniques learned in the mentoring program with other teachers in your school? If yes, please specify. _____
_____

Would you feel comfortable calling upon this teacher in the future as a resource to assist other teachers who were experiencing frustration in their classroom with a particular student or classroom situation? Why or why not? _____
_____

Do you feel that your teacher has gained the expertise to begin to work with students with special learning needs in your school or will be able to work more effectively with these students in the future?_____
_____

Do you have any suggestions about changing the structure of the mentoring program for the future?_____
_____

Any additional comments or suggestions would be welcomed and helpful in planning for the future. _____

CHAPTER 39

THE ROLE OF INSTRUCTIONAL AIDES IN A DAY SCHOOL SETTING

Ellen Fishman

Instructional aides are critical personnel who help bridge the differences between children with special needs and their typical peers to achieve successful inclusion. These individuals are also responsible for direct instruction to their assigned students. While there is no argument about the credentials they should possess, the reality is that most come to our schools with little or no training and experience. Still we should strive to hold them to certain standards and be prepared to provide professional development opportunities for them and the teachers with whom they work.

The responsibilities that an instructional aide assumes are comprehensive in nature, as the work impacts every aspect of the life of the classroom. Instructional aides should have the educational background and experience to perform their role. They must understand the special needs of the child they will be assisting. The instructional aide is responsible for facilitating the student's direct participation with other students and adults, providing individual support to the student as necessary, and incorporating goals in activities and interactions as directed.

RESPONSIBILITIES INCLUDE BUT ARE NOT LIMITED TO:

- Greeting the student upon arrival at the school and being prepared to begin the school day in a timely manner.
- Modifying curriculum and incorporating goals in concert with educational coordinator and other appropriate personnel in the school, such as the classroom teacher and/or school administrator.
- Assisting student by implementing methodologies and utilizing materials designed to meet the student's individual needs as suggested by the educational coordinator.
- Adapting written assignments and assessments in all academic areas as needed.
- Facilitating daily interaction with the student's peers.
- Assisting in making transitions, especially during periods of unexpected classroom activity or changes in routine.
- Monitoring playground, lunch, and classroom social situations to promote socially appropriate behavior.
- Assisting student's participation in daily school activities.

- Reinforcing positive behavior.
- Completing the substitute folder and bringing completed folder to the school office.
- Assisting in monitoring behavior.
- Encouraging participation in class discussion.
- Assisting during large-group time, independent seatwork, and other areas as needed.
- Assisting with fine motor activities, use of the computer, or other adaptations as necessary.
- Keeping a communication booklet that documents work that has been completed, homework for the day, etc., and sharing this information with the student's parents on a daily basis.
- Working cooperatively with the classroom teacher.
- Participating in meetings with classroom teacher and educational coordinator.
- Attending all professional development sessions.
- Working cooperatively as a member of the education team.
- Informing designated personnel of absences with as much advance notice as possible.
- Abiding by all rules and regulations of the assigned school.
- Reporting to work on days that particular student is absent.
- Performing additional tasks as requested.

Adapted from Keshet, Chicago

CHAPTER 40

TEENADE: JEWISH CONTINUITY THROUGH SPECIAL EDUCATION

Bureau of Jewish Education of Greater Boston

Sandy Miller-Jacobs

OVERVIEW

"I felt better connected because I was able to teach Hebrew and meet other Jewish teens." TeenAder

The Bureau of Jewish Education of Greater Boston (BJE) created an outreach program for Jewishly under-engaged teens in September 2002. TeenAde targets teens interested in community service and prepares them to work as aides for children with special needs in congregational schools, offering them another way to remain connected to the Jewish community. The program consists of a series of seminars in which teens learn about disability awareness, Jewish views on disabilities, and teaching strategies. Simultaneously, the teens work in our Jewish supplemental schools as *madrikhim*, offering additional support for children with special learning needs. Teens might work with children individually, in small groups, or in inclusive classrooms. All the teens receive indirect and/or direct supervision.

Over the past four years this highly successful program prepared thirty-five teens, known as TeenAders, who worked in seventeen synagogues. Many of the teens have returned for a second year, and some have even returned for a third year! The teens are a mixed group socioeconomically as well as religiously. Since the teens are under-engaged, most are not involved in youth groups, few attend Jewish camps, and only a few have been to Israel. We have included some students who attend a Jewish day school (Orthodox and pluralistic), enabling a more diverse group of teens who learn much from one another.

"It gave me a stronger connection to other Jewish teens with different backgrounds."

TeenAder

TeenAde provides a new way for our teens to identify with the Jewish community, engage in Jewish community service, develop professional skills, and appreciate the importance of an inclusive Jewish community. This program has been well received by the teens, education directors, teachers, and especially by the teens' parents.

PROGRAM GOALS

There are five major goals for the TeenAde program:

1. Expand inclusion possibilities for children in congregational/community schools.

2. Reach out to unaffiliated teens.

3. Increase sensitivity to and skills in teaching children with special needs.

4. Create a *hevrah* for teens.

5. Foster careers in Jewish special education.

EXPAND INCLUSION POSSIBILITIES

Over the past ten years, meeting the needs of individuals with disabilities has become a high priority for the Jewish community. In the Boston area our federation, Combined Jewish Philanthropies (CJP), established a Committee on Services for People with Disabilities that raised awareness about the importance of the Jewish community's being more inclusive and accessible to individuals with special needs. In August 2001 the first full-time special educator position was funded by CJP and hired by the BJE, with a directive to create new programs for children with special needs, to support existing educating programs for children with disabilities, and to offer professional development for teachers.

One of the difficulties our educational programs encounter is locating adequately prepared Jewish special educators. By providing a skilled group of teens who can do this, TeenAde enables school programs to expand their services to students with special needs. The teens serve as tutors and classroom assistants, working individually, in small groups, and in self-contained and inclusive classrooms. TeenAde tells our schools that we expect children with special needs to receive a Jewish education and that we will help these children succeed.

OUTREACH TO UNAFFILIATED TEENS

Many of our teens seem to drop out of the Jewish community after becoming bar/bat mitzvah. According to the BJE's Research Report 11, "Reach and Retention: Challenges from the 2001–02 Jewish School Census in Greater Boston" (A. Koren, 2003), attrition of teens in Jewish education is a significant problem. Enrollment during the teen years (post b'nai mitzvah years) is 32% of enrollment in grades 3–7. Based on the 1995 population survey (S. Israel, 1997), we are reaching only 18% of teens in grades 8–12.

"One of the surest ways to engage Jewish teens is through social action projects" (S. Schwartz). Rabbi Schwartz, president of The Washington Institute for Jewish Leadership and Values, states that there are five ideas central to engaging teens in *tikkun olam*:

- Inform: Teens should interact with knowledgeable people.

- Empower: Teens should be given the message that they can make a difference in society. Community service is one avenue by which teens can engage with the world around them.

- Inspire: Teens respond best to passionate role models.

- Motivate: Teens must know they are needed.

- Contextualize: All of these principles must show a connection to Judaism. Without being placed in a Jewish context, doing good deeds can become its own religion.

TeenAde employs each of Schwartz' principles in its structure. In the seminars our teens learn from knowledgeable people and begin to develop their own knowledge base for work with children with special learning needs. Working in congregational schools with students with special needs is an empowering experience. These teens understand that their work provides them with the opportunity to give back to their community. The seminars are given by qualified BJE staff and guest speakers who are passionate about the importance of Jewish special education. In their roles as aides in classrooms it is obvious to the teens that they are needed by the school in order to successfully include students with special needs. In addition, their relationships with these students are a powerful testament to the impact they can have on another person. The seminars incorporate Jewish texts and Jewish views on disabilities. As they work in congregational schools they are learning and working with students directly in a Jewish setting.

INCREASE SENSITIVITY AND DEVELOP TEACHING SKILLS

TeenAde provides our teens with an opportunity to develop sensitivity and appreciation for children with special needs while simultaneously developing skills necessary to teach them in Jewish schools. Through the seminars and their work in classrooms teens become aware of social and academic issues facing children with special learning needs, and they develop the skills to help them learn.

TeenAde staff place the teens in congregational schools and give them stipends for attending the seminars. Teens are interested in earning money. Having their own money makes them less dependent on their parents and provides them with added independence as they budget for their expenses.

TeenAde gives them skills needed to obtain jobs in Jewish educational institutions throughout their high school, college, and young adult years. Depending on the synagogue and the wishes of the teens, they can volunteer or receive payment from the school. However, all the teens say it is not money that motivates them to participate in TeenAde.

CREATE A _HEVRAH_ FOR TEENS

While teens have many opportunities to become involved in Jewish activities through youth groups, Israel programs, and Hebrew high schools, there are relatively few community service opportunities for them within the Jewish community. High school students become involved with organizations such as Habitat for Humanity (constructing homes) and Los Amigos (building latrines in South America). TeenAde provides another way for teens to serve their own community through teaching children with special needs.

> In a White House conference on teaching, Mrs. Bush noted "the intangible rewards of making a difference in children's lives."

> "Wherever I go," she said, "people tell me they are reassessing their lives. They are considering public service because they want to make a difference in their communities. Teaching is the greatest community service of all." (_Washington Post_, March 6, 2002)

As the teens join together for the seminars they become a cohesive group despite their diversity, instant messaging each other, inviting others to school performances, and sharing information about events that might be of interest. TeenAde enables them to meet other teens interested in education and disabilities in a Jewish context. Their different backgrounds, socioeconomically and religiously, enable them to learn about different Jewish practices, and they connect as fellow Jews—*K'lal Yisrael*.

> "I have become close friends with the other aides. We are all like family. I would have never had the chance to meet all these amazing people had I not become a TeenAder." *Participant*

FOSTER CAREERS IN JEWISH SPECIAL EDUCATION

> "Being an aide has helped me realize my love for teaching, and maybe I'll take it up as a career when I get older." *TeenAder*

After high school graduation TeenAders are able to get private tutoring positions as teachers or teacher aides in schools near their colleges, thereby increasing the number of teachers who are prepared to work with children with special needs in congregational schools. Our ultimate goal is that some teens will see the field of Jewish special education as a possible career path.

RECRUITMENT

A unique feature of TeenAde is the focus on under-engaged teens resulting from funding by CJP's *No'ar* Committee, whose mission is outreach to teens. We defined "under-engaged" as little to no involvement with youth movements, limited Jewish camp experience as teens, and lack of participation in teen trips to Israel. This program recruits teens who are rarely seen around their synagogues and brings them back through their work in the school. One recruitment strategy is through discussions with the youth educators of synagogues, whom we ask to locate those teens who are on their list but who do not come to events. We also ask education directors to tap those teens who are interested in being *madrikhim*. Some of our schools employ these teens in 8th and 9th grades, but not throughout high school. Over time we have found our TeenAders recruit their younger friends and siblings. We have even had parents who know about the program ask us to call their teen children.

PROGRAM CONTENT

The Sunday seminars are devoted to teaching the teens about disabilities, the Jewish perspective on disabilities, and special education teaching strategies. At the first seminar each TeenAder receives a binder with his or her name on it containing a variety of readings that relate to the seminar topics. The seminars are planned to engage the teens; they are highly interactive, using case studies and simulations. Many of the seminars are designed for the teens to learn about themselves as well as about those with disabilities. For example, as the teens learn about multiple intelligences they have many "aha" moments about who they are as learners. TeenAders make materials such as folder games and felt boards that they can use in their schools. Videos spark discussions and highlight issues faced by people with disabilities. Guest speakers, including those with disabilities and their families and other professionals who work in special education, are invited to talk with the teens about their work and their lives.

> "I was amazed that you had them for so many hours…and you kept them interested. He came home so excited by what he had learned." *Parent of a TeenAder*

Although the teens attend approximately thirty hours of seminars, completed end-of-year evaluation forms always include requests for more seminars. The seminars are divided into two parts. The initial twenty hours of seminars are preparatory, giving them the important skills they need to work with their children. The final ten hours provide an opportunity to learn additional content that supports their work and offers the teens the opportunity to reflect on their work. These seminars are spread over the rest of the year and are only two hours in length.

The seminars present information on the following topics:

- Disability Awareness—What are the different types of disabilities, and what are their implications for behavior and learning? How does it feel to be different? How do you feel around people who are disabled? What are the differences between visible and invisible disabilities?

- Jewish Views on Disabilities—What do the Jewish sources say about our treatment of people with special needs? How has the Boston Jewish community responded to people with special needs? How does our community effort compare to other community's programming?

- Special Education—What is the field of special education? What is "special" about special education? What do commonly used special education terms and diagnoses mean (e.g., inclusion, mainstreaming, learning disabilities, AD/HD, PDD, Autism Spectrum Disorders)? What laws (e.g., IDEA, ADA) protect people with disabilities? What are the models of service delivery?

- Being a Professional Aide—What makes you a teacher and not just a "buddy?" How do you write a lesson plan? How do you interact with the other aides and teachers? How do you find time to talk with the teacher so you can plan? What are the expectations for your job? How do you ask questions so that you get answers? What are the protocols for getting things done at your school? (Whom do you ask for what? What do you have to do for yourself?) What are the "nitty gritty" things that you have to learn? (Where's the snack food? How do you run the photocopy machine?)

- Teaching Strategies—What are multiple intelligences and learning styles? How do you match teaching to children's learning styles? How do you set expectations for children's learning? How do you teach Hebrew reading using multi-sensory techniques? How do you break tasks down for children with special needs? What instructional materials (e.g., manipulatives, charts, cards) can you use for children with different special needs? How can games help reinforce learning? How can you incorporate music and art to help children learn?

- Handling Behaviors—How do you set and enforce limits? What purpose do children's behaviors serve? How do you give positive reinforcement for children's behavior (academic and social)? How do you keep children on task? How can you help children get organized for learning? What is conflict resolution, and how does it work?

- The Boston Jewish Community Response—What programs are available for individuals with special needs in the Boston community? What are the opportunities for education, synagogue life, social, work, and residential facilities for Jewish children and adults with special needs?

Seminars also allow for reflective discussions on these topics:

- Case studies—Who are the children you work with? What kinds of problems do they have? What are their strengths? What are their areas of weakness? What challenges do they present to you?

- Behavior Management—What strategies are working? What problems are you experiencing? Does positive reinforcement work?
- Teaching Strategies—What materials have you created? What instructional strategies work well? What strategies didn't work?
- Professional Relationships—How do you work with the teaching staff? What kinds of questions get the best responses? What do you do when you are frustrated with the children or your teacher?

"Ever since participating in the TeenAde program, I've thought more about the tutoring and aiding that I do. I realize that what I do actually affects people's lives, and I like to see the positive effects I produce because of my knowledge, which comes from the program."
TeenAder

PROGRAM RESULTS

"I am not the only one out there with issues. Other people face greater things than me." *TeenAder*

The teens talk about how much *TeenAde* has affected their lives, from feeling more connected to their Judaism to learning about the different movements within Judaism. In the end-of-year evaluation questionnaire, 100% say they would recommend the program to their peers. While some indicate the best part of the program is the actual teaching, others find the seminars to be the high point of the program. Many indicate they learn from the seminars, and many say they learn from their children. All the teens feel they have learned about themselves through this program.

The education directors find the extra hands in the classrooms working directly with children to be helpful. They are thrilled that these teens know about special needs and have learned new ways to reach the children with learning problems. The children indicate they are better able to read and enjoy working with their TeenAder. The variety of approaches makes learning more interesting for them. Our schools that use younger teens as *madrikhim* ask us to provide workshops of a less intensive nature for these teens as well.

Many of the teens found the program opens new doors. They integrate their experiences into their lives in a variety of ways.

- They apply their learning to their own lives. As they tackle school assignments they break tasks into manageable pieces; they create multi-sensory ways to learn. One teen began to explain math to himself by visualizing graphs and using his fingers to trace patterns.
- Many write about their experiences in TeenAde in their college application essays.
- Several take summer jobs working with children with special needs.
- Several use their TeenAde experience as the basis of their high school senior projects:
  - Two teens worked weekly in a residential school for children with autism.
  - One teen collaborated with the education director of his synagogue school to create a summer "Pizza and Practice" program where children could come once a week to practice Hebrew. Several teens volunteered to staff this program and thought the children learned and enjoyed the experience. The following September the teachers saw a real difference in the reading skills of the children who participated. This synagogue has continued to implement the program even after the TeenAder who helped create this program graduated.

- Three teens developed a video documenting the program. They took a video of teens working with children and interviewed the children, the TeenAders, the education directors, and the TeenAde staff. This CD is used in recruiting efforts.

Parents of the teens have unexpectedly endorsed this program. They comment on how their teens have talked with them about what they learned and how much the teens got from this experience. The parents appreciate the thoughtfulness with which the program and the teaching materials have been organized. They are pleased that the Jewish community has given their teens this opportunity to give back to the community and to develop a new group of Jewish friends. Several have commented that perhaps their teens have found an area of expertise that will serve them throughout their lives.

The teens have been overwhelmingly enthusiastic about the program. After the first year, *all* the teens who were not graduating returned for a second year. Those who entered the program in their sophomore year have asked to return for a third year. To accommodate this unanticipated demand we created new topics to present in the seminars and are slowly instituting a mentoring and leadership program for the second- and third-year TeenAders.

Another unexpected result has been the enthusiasm with which the program has been received by other professionals. A presentation about TeenAde to the Consortium of Jewish Special Educators in Central Agencies received enthusiastic support. With information from the presentation, this program was successfully replicated in Philadelphia and is currently in the planning stages in Washington, DC, New Jersey, and Cincinnati.

As one teen said, "I had fun and learned *a lot*; where can you go wrong?" Another teen reported, "It was the best experience of my life." It is not our obligation to complete the task, just to take the first step. TeenAde may be one successful step toward fostering Jewish continuity through special education.

BIBLIOGRAPHY

Israel, S. *Comprehensive Report on the 1995 CJP Demographic Study.* Boston: Combined Jewish Philanthropics, 1997.

Koren, A. Research Report 11: *Reach and Retention: Challenges from the 2001–02 Jewish School Census in Greater Boston.* Newton, MA: Bureau of Jewish Education of Greater Boston, 2003.

Schwartz, S. *Educators and Teachers: Teens and* Tikkun Olam, www.socialaction.com/eduteach.html

For more information, contact www.bje.org.

PART 10:
BAR/BAT MITZVAH
PREPARATION

CHAPTER 41

BAR/BAT MITZVAH PREPARATION FOR CHILDREN WITH SPECIAL LEARNING NEEDS: AN OVERVIEW

Sara Rubinow Simon

Significant changes have taken place in communities across North America in recent years. It is no longer unacceptable to be "different." In fact, it is common for people to strive to be unique and innovative. In the religious world also there are new opportunities to be creative and distinctive during the worship service. With this greater latitude comes the chance for different modes and levels of involvement requiring varying skill levels so that individuals who may have been excluded in the past are able to take part in religious services in many different ways.

Driven by federal legislation in the past thirty years mandating equal access and an appropriate education for all, awareness of individual differences and also of the existence of people with previously untapped ability has been heightened. The ensuing emphasis on the field of special education has intensified the challenge to find the methodology and the setting that will enable each person to achieve his or her full potential.

The impact of special education has also been felt within the Jewish community. With this new perspective it becomes incumbent upon the Jewish community to ensure that every Jew be given the opportunity to receive an appropriate Jewish education, including a chance to celebrate the bar/bat mitzvah milestone. Congregations have increasingly become more flexible regarding what they consider appropriate public affirmation of the attainment of adult status. There are now few instances in which synagogues refuse to allow a person with special needs to participate (to the best of his or her ability) in congregational programs and services. Modern rabbinic responsa are reinterpreting traditional practices in light of new information regarding the ability of people with special needs to function effectively in society. Technological and attitudinal advances have helped sensitize us to our responsibility to view each person as a unique individual.

In the past, parents of children with special needs, frustrated by the absence of a suitable synagogue school situation, either hired a private tutor or gave up hope that their children would be able to receive a religious education. Occasionally, a small class would meet for a short time and then disband through lack of support and direction.

As the stigma of having special needs disappears, synagogue religious schools are finding it increasingly easy to obtain data from parents that help them to identify and accommodate students who have a broader range of learning styles and special learning needs. Teachers are acquiring the requisite skills to individualize instructional strategies and materials. They are able to adapt teaching methodology and materials to dovetail with strategies utilized in the students' secular schools.

It is strongly recommended that youngsters with special learning needs becomes part of an ongoing religious education program for as many years as the regular program lasts, albeit with appropriate modifications in curriculum and behavioral objectives. Within this framework the bar/bat mitzvah ceremony is then only one facet of preparing to lead a rich Jewish life rather than the single focus. Goals are geared to a suitable cognitive level, guided by a Jewish literacy checklist so that there will be familiarity with the elements of the Jewish home, Shabbat, the Jewish holiday and life cycles, basic prayers and blessings in Hebrew and/or English, the synagogue, the Jewish community, Bible heroes, *mitzvot* and Jewish values, Israel, etc. It is possible to adapt the curriculum to fit the special learning profile so that maximum mastery can be achieved in each area. In this way, the youngster will have a chance to acquire the tools necessary to function competently in the Jewish mainstream.

When approaching bar/bat mitzvah preparation, it is important to consider the youngster's wishes and expectations as well as the family's so that there can be cooperative planning and support. It is critical that the synagogue clergy and educational staff be involved well in advance of the proposed date to begin the collaborative planning process.

- Can the family feel comfortable with the outcome should there be unplanned glitches?
- Does the family regularly attend services so that the youngster feels at home in the synagogue and has absorbed parts of the service by osmosis or by living through siblings becoming b'nai mitzvah?
- Can he/she stand up in front of a large number of people, particularly strangers?
- Will he/she have the chance to use the skills acquired again in the future?
- Selection of the date and time of the bar/bat mitzvah service must take into account the youngster's ability to sit through a longer or shorter service in the main sanctuary or chapel.
- Would a Rosh Hodesh or a Monday or Thursday morning service be more suitable than Shabbat?
- Can he/she participate alone, or is it preferable to have somebody by the child's side to prompt or accompany him/her?
- Can he/she learn a *Haftarah*? A Torah portion? Chant or read either? Deliver a speech or message? Lead an English prayer? Lead a Hebrew prayer? Read or recite by rote? Perform nonverbal roles such as opening or closing the ark? Wrapping the Torah? Holding the Kiddush cup? Saying "Amen"? There are merely some examples of options and there are others to consider.

It is all too common to assume that children with special learning needs cannot master the Hebrew portion of the service, yet there is no necessary correlation between Hebrew and English reading ability. If a youngster can read English, there is a good chance that he or she can also learn to read Hebrew on some level, although it may be time- and labor-intensive. Even if only minimal decoding ability is achieved, there is a great delight in being able to identify letters or words in any *siddur* or Hebrew book. By learning the geography or layout of the page, the familiar elements can be located. There are lists of high-frequency words similar to the Dolch lists used in English reading that can be used for whole-word recognition. It is possible for someone who has been labeled dyslexic to learn to read Hebrew fluently and accurately. It is therefore important to make a serious attempt at helping the student learn to read utilizing a variety of approaches and materials and providing adequate drill time. Transliteration, rather than being a help, is limited to a single selection and cannot be transferred. If transliteration must be used, it is advisable to dictate the Hebrew passage and have the youngster write it down in English characters the way he/she hears and processes it so that the child can read it back according to his/her notation system. Chanting also helps to bind the Hebrew into a structure that can be retained more easily.

Frequently Used Sight Words from the Siddur

The following list of 34 words includes one-third of the word to be found in the Siddur. If the class can read these words, it is well on the way to reading the siddur.

לִפְנֵי	הִיא	אָב
מֶלֶךְ	חַיִּים [חַיֵּי]	אֲדוֹנִי [ה]
מָלַךְ	חֶסֶד	אֵל
נָתַן	טוֹב [טוֹבָה]	אֱלֹהִים
עוֹלָם	יוֹם	אָמַר
עַל	יִשְׂרָאֵל	אֶרֶץ
עִם	כִּי	אֵת
עָשָׂה	כֹּל [כָּל]	אַתָּה
קֹדֶשׁ	לֹא	בַּיִת
רַחֲמִים	לִי [לְךָ]	בָּרוּךְ
שֵׁם	לְעוֹלָם וָעֶד	בֵּרַךְ
		הוּא

Unfortunately, children with special needs can still be "handicapped" by the attitudes of others. The others are, in some cases, their own parents. Even parents who have come to terms with their child's limitations in the secular world may have a particularly hard time as the bar/bat mitzvah period approaches. Some parents, as well as psychologists and Jewish educators, think that they are being kind to these young people by not "burdening" them with all the extra lessons, expectations, and tensions involved in bar/bat mitzvah preparation. But it is not a burden! The bar/bat mitzvah ceremony and celebration can be the most normalizing and memorable milestone these youngsters have. In the same way, the joy of adults with special needs who become bar/bat mitzvah at a later age attests to the tremendous power of this event. These adults never had the chance to celebrate becoming bar/bat mitzvah when they were teenagers because it was unacceptable that the process be made available to them at that time. It is hoped that there will be fewer such delays in future years because attitudes in the Jewish community have changed.

Approaching each bar/bat mitzvah student as a unique individual, whether or not special learning needs have been identified, greatly increases the chances of success and achievement. Educators must be aware of different teaching and learning styles. They must be eclectic and pragmatic, flexible, make educated guesses, and be ready to try many different methodologies to find what works for each child. Success is a magical motivator. The potential exists. This is the message of special education!

CHAPTER 44

BAR MITZVAH STORIES

Rabbi Daniel T. Grossman

The most common doorway to Jewish education for a special needs person is life cycle. It usually happens when parents walk through the door and ask, "Can we somehow have a bar or bat mitzvah ceremony for my child?" This is a reasonable question. It reflects several different needs: The need to link this child to the Jewish people. The need to share a "normal" life-cycle event with the extended family, especially grandparents. The bar or bat mitzvah ceremony provides for the possibility of a shared family success. Over the last twenty years I have learned what I can and cannot do in the area of bar and bat mitzvah. I have learned what becomes a meaningful effort and what is seen only as a show event. Let me share a sampling of bar and bat mitzvah stories with you.

A LESSON TO BE LEARNED

When I left NTID (National Technical Institute for the Deaf) I worked as a congregational educator and then as a pulpit rabbi. About a year into my first pulpit, a family came to me from the community. They walked into my office, Mom, Dad, and a young boy with severe retardation. "Can our son become a bar mitzvah?"

I focused on this challenge and began a plan of action. I met with his special needs teachers to find out how best to reach out to him. I spent hours at play just to build a bond between us. I established a regular time to meet and study and prepare for him to become a bar mitzvah. The lessons took place twice a week, each for about twenty minutes. That was the realistic limit of his attention span. He loved to play with a large green plastic box tape recorder. I used that tape recorder frequently, and he enjoyed memorizing short phrases in Hebrew. He kept up this system for about a year and a half. Eventually the evening of his bar mitzvah ceremony was upon us. I had wanted the event to take place on Shabbat morning, as other b'nai mitzvot services had taken place in the congregation. The parents had wanted a Saturday evening service where only their friends and family would be present. Saturday evening came, and we began the Havdalah bar mitzvah service. The Torah is read Saturday evening before sundown with three short *aliyot*, Torah honors. He had memorized the Torah blessings and two sentences of Torah text. The minimum is three sentences. I would complete the third sentence of the section he had learned.

What followed that evening were a series of shocking and awkward events that changed the way I would teach special needs bar or bat mitzvah students in the future. We were about to begin the service, but our bar mitzvah boy was not in the room. I asked his mother why the delay, and she informed me that he would be kept in another room till the last possible moment so as not to disturb their guests. I began to protest that he absolutely had to be present, and not just for his *aliyah*. The mother began to cry, the grandfather began to yell at me, and the father just ran from his wife to his father-in-law trying to calm them both. I caved in.

I allowed the mother to keep him in the classroom down the hall until his *aliyah*. He appeared, chanted his few lines like a trained parrot, and disappeared.

Later I was informed that because loud noises and sound disturbed him, he was being sent home with a babysitter while his family celebrated his becoming bar mitzvah at a catering hall without him. That was the last time I ever saw him or his family despite numerous phone calls.

Hopefully we learn from our mistakes. Certainly I tried to find some lessons from this experience, which had a very hopeful beginning and a less-than-satisfying ending for me. These are the insights that grew from this bar mitzvah.

I never again prepared anyone for bar or bat mitzvah without insisting that the family join the synagogue and become part of the community. A life-cycle experience done outside the context of community sends a very different message to the participants. It implies that such an event takes place isolated in time, without any context. Joining the synagogue means more than membership. Affiliation means attending synagogue and family education events and an active integration of the entire family into synagogue life. Because many families in this circumstance are reticent to join groups because of their special needs, the synagogue must also make active efforts to include all the family members in synagogue life.

The focus of the bar or bat mitzvah ceremony must be Jewish education. The parameters of the education need to be determined by the students' abilities and the reality of the situation. It is not appropriate for the student or the rabbi to participate in a "show event."

The entire service, whether on Friday night, Saturday morning, or Saturday night, must be integrated to involve the student on several levels. While it is appropriate to adjust certain factors in this service, it is not appropriate to have the student's contribution exist as if it were outside the service.

I would make these particular principles clear to the parents before we began our studies together. I would insist on the above principles and reinforce them as often as necessary. Without these guidelines, I would not allow this life-cycle event to take place under my guidance. I would encourage the family to find other means to satisfy their needs.

Over the years I have kept to these principles, and the impact has been significant. I would like to share an example of positive bar/bat mitzvah training and worship, giving you some sense of the possibilities.

THE PICTURE ON MY WALL

On my office wall there are diplomas, awards, paintings, and a photograph of a bar mitzvah ceremony. This is the photograph of the first sign-language bar mitzvah service I ever participated in. This family was unique within the deaf world. Mom, Dad, and both of their sons are deaf. It is very rare for all the members of a family to be deaf. The boys had very positive self-images. Everyone signed and also spoke orally with confidence. During the learning process the entire family came to every lesson.

Together they learned history, life cycle, holidays, and the Hebrew language. The bar mitzvah candidate made it very clear that he wanted to read and chant the Hebrew as well as signing the text of the Torah and Haftarah. I can recall many wonderful moments of our lessons together.

Once, after five or six weeks of Hebrew lessons beginning with *shin*, (sh), *lamed*, (la), and *mem* (mi), letters that were easier to sound out because of the vibrations associated with them, we then focused on *aleph* and *ayin*. When studying Hebrew with deaf students we focus on parallel English sounds: l, m, sh, etc.

Having isolated the particular sounds one by one, I asked the parents and their children to touch my face as I sounded out the letters with various vowel combinations. There is a point where the jawbone forms a right angle up to the ear. This particular spot is the most sensitive to vibration on the entire body. Touching my cheek and jaw at this point as I spoke added sound and vibration to letter association. We did this day by day as we learned each letter.

That day I said, "We will learn *aleph* and *ayin*, the silent letters." No sooner had I spoken these words than the younger brother, about six years old, fell on the floor convulsed in laughter. Looking up from the floor with a big grin, he signed, "Don't you get it, Rabbi? They are *all* silent letters!" There ended the lesson. For the next half hour we howled over dozens of jokes about sounds and strange words in English and Hebrew.

On the morning of the bar mitzvah ceremony I had arranged for Carol Chopinsky, of blessed memory, to sign the service with me. Carol was one of the best interpreters in the country and a very close friend. Usually I did my own signing, but on this occasion, needing to be focused on several different responsibilities at once, I knew that I would need an interpreter to help things move smoothly. This time Mom, Dad, the bar mitzvah boy and his little brother all took part in the service. Whenever he chanted in Hebrew, he would sign in English. At the same time Carol would speak the English words so that deaf guests who were speech readers could read both the sign and the speech. Later in the morning, when our bar mitzvah gave his original speech, he focused on the liberating joy of fully participating in Jewish life. He spoke about the fact that while neither of his parents had had a Jewish education or become bar or bat mitzvah, their learning together as a family and their taking *aliyot* that morning meant that this was really his parents' bar and bat mitzvah service as well as his own.

His picture, in the homemade frame he made for me, remains on my wall to remind me of how wonderful it can be when all of the parts of the puzzle fit together properly. As a postscript, through a variety of contacts I can tell you that the bar mitzvah boy, now almost thirty years old, teaches for a school for the deaf and remains active in the deaf Jewish world.

CHAPTER 43

MICHAEL'S PERFECT BAR MITZVAH

Beverly Weaver

When he was two years old he spoke in complete sentences, but his behavior was so impulsive that the china closet had to be bolted to the wall to prevent him from pulling it over!

When he was five years old he could whistle Beethoven concerti, but when asked "What's one plus one?" he replied, "Give me a hint!"

When he entered fifth grade he still did not know multiplication tables, but he could (and did) cook an entire Thanksgiving dinner—making everything from scratch, including stuffing, cranberry sauce, and several varieties of pies!

When he was thirteen years old, he became a bar mitzvah—a perfect bar mitzvah.

BACKGROUND

Our son Michael is learning disabled and has been identified as such since he was four years old. When he was in the fifth grade school was a daily struggle, coping with homework was worse, and coping with Hebrew school beyond worse. Yet in spite of it all he was a neat, funny kid with all kinds of special talents and abilities. When we got a letter from our synagogue inviting us to a parent meeting to assign bar/bat mitzvah dates for our son's Hebrew school class it dawned on us that this neat kid was going to face the pressures of bar mitzvah before we knew it, and we needed to plan for it. I don't mean that we started to call caterers and listen to bands, but that we made a conscious decision that we wanted our son's bar mitzvah memories to be pleasant; and we felt that under the circumstances, that would not happen unless we planned for it.

At our synagogue the philosophy of the rabbi and the director of religious education is that bar/bat mitzvah preparation is a learning experience designed to lead teenagers into observant adulthood. Consequently students learn, among other things, to chant Friday night services, Saturday morning *Shaharit*, Torah and *Musaf* services, the trope for Haftarah and Torah portions; and then they study English translations of their Haftarah and Torah portions in order to be able to prepare discussions.

On the other hand, both the rabbi and the director of religious education make it well known that *halakhah* states that a boy is bar mitzvah when he turns thirteen and is automatically obligated to the *mitzvot* whether or not he has a bar mitzvah ceremony; that bar mitzvah is not a contest; and that if pre-bar mitzvah study is non-negotiable, at least some aspects of the bar mitzvah ceremony are.

The first decision we made was that Michael deserved to choose the bar mitzvah option comfortable for him—even if his choice was no bar mitzvah ceremony.

I recalled an incident that occurred several years before, when I was a Sisterhood catering vice-president. In that position I helped parents plan the *kiddushim* for children's *simhot*. I got a call one day from the mother of a boy in the current bar/bat mitzvah class. She called to tell me that her son's ceremony had been rescheduled for the next year because he had learning disabilities and simply could not be prepared in time. The family moved shortly after their son's bar mitzvah ceremony, and I never learned how the bar mitzvah boy felt about celebrating his special day one year later than planned, with another bar/bat mitzvah class. But I did know that my own son was sensitive to the difference his learning problems presented and (rightly or wrongly) would be embarrassed by such a time change for his celebration.

The next decision we made was that if he had a bar mitzvah ceremony at *shul,* our son's ceremony would take place as scheduled—with his bar/bat mitzvah class.

I also recalled something my son had said to me one day: "I'm so tired of being different. Just once I wish I could be like everyone else."

Another decision we made was that if our son's bar mitzvah ceremony was held in the synagogue, it would be like everyone else's. What he did from the *bimah* would not be noticeably different from what others do.

Our final resolution occurred as a result of contact with a long-lost cousin. In the course of relating family stories he shared a poignant story about his younger brother. It seems the brother had unidentified learning problems as a child that interfered with bar mitzvah training. Our cousin said that they still had a practice tape that had been made for the brother's bar mitzvah study—a tape that contained the *hazzan* screaming in the background. Even with all the practicing (and screaming), the bar mitzvah boy could not learn a Haftarah or the Saturday morning service, and he ended up doing only the *aliyah* blessings. To this day, he cringes at the memory of the whole experience.

The final decision we made was that our son's bar mitzvah experience would be something positive he could store in his heart and carry into his Jewish future.

OUR STORY

My husband and I took the issue to Michael. We thought it best to discuss the matter with him privately—no siblings allowed. So two years ahead of the bar mitzvah year the three of us went for a walk to discuss an event that didn't even have a date yet!

As we walked we made the case to Michael that the decision rested solely with him, and we would not be disappointed if he chose not to have a bar mitzvah ceremony at thirteen, or ever. If this was one thing too many for him to do, that was truly okay with us, and he was still a good Jew and a great son. This was not something he needed to do for us. However, if he chose to have a bar mitzvah ceremony, my husband and I already had a resolute position: Our son had to agree to work hard and to see it through; and tougher yet, no daily complaints about the workload. Those were tough conditions for a pre-teen boy to accept, and we knew it, but we would accept no less.

Not surprising to us, Michael quickly ruled out the no bar mitzvah ceremony options as well as becoming bar mitzvah in Israel (too different from all his friends). He worried over a bar mitzvah ceremony in the synagogue but again chose to do it for much the same reason—being different was not desirable at this stage in his life. Michael has always had a strong work ethic, and he readily agreed to try to learn as much of the bar mitzvah curriculum as possible.

Later that night, my husband and I discussed the situation and, for practical reasons, decided that I would essentially manage the bar mitzvah study plan. My livelihood is earned by tutoring students with learning disabilities. I already helped with our son's secular education, so it made sense to do the same for his bar mitzvah education. Michael always says that his LD problems are like speed bumps—they slow him down but don't stop him cold. My first job was to figure out how many of those speed bumps currently stood between him and a successful bar mitzvah ceremony.

The next day, I got to work. I had observed from attending synagogue services that although the bar/bat mitzvah curriculum was all-inclusive for study, there was variability in what each child actually did at his or her ceremony. I concluded that Michael could concentrate his efforts on the items everyone, or almost everyone, did and still have a bar mitzvah ceremony he would find acceptable.

I made a list of every selection in the Torah and *Musaf* services and had Michael try to chant each selection. Next to each I made a notation of whether or not he could reliably chant it. That list gave me a concrete understanding of how much had yet to be accomplished. After that I poured over the *Humash* and made a list of every Haftarah and how many sentences each contained. Then I highlighted those that had the fewest sentences.

Next, I made an appointment to meet privately with our rabbi and director of education. I explained everything to them, stressing that I was not looking for an easy way out for my son but rather for a viable path to a successful bar mitzvah ceremony for a kid with special needs. Together we chose a Haftarah of just thirteen sentences that also was an available Shabbat on the calendar. Speed bump number one was cleared.

Unfortunately, speed bump number two popped up fast and was more of a hurdle. Both services and the Haftarah were in Hebrew—common practice in a Conservative synagogue but still a formidable problem. Since Hebrew is written with consonants on top of vowels, it takes some visual integration to read even the simplest word. Michael could not integrate those visual images. The only way he could read Hebrew was to try to read the consonant to himself, remember it, read the vowel to himself, remember it, and then try to put it all together orally. It was a painfully slow and often inaccurate process. But I knew that time and knowledge were on my side. First, I knew I had a full two years for focused study, and second, I knew that Michael was a good auditory learner.

To successfully manage the time component I made what I call a "rigidly flexible" schedule. I roughly divided the months between the current date and the bar mitzvah date into thirds, with the last third slightly larger than the other two. The first time span would be devoted to the Torah service, the second would be devoted to *Musaf*, and the third would focus on the Haftarah, with one month set aside at the end for review and work on the speeches. If things went faster than planned, we could add the *Maftir* Torah portion. If things went slower than planned, the review month gave us time to regroup.

My son and I worked together five out of almost every seven days for all those months. That was the rigid part—making sure we kept to a schedule. The flexible part was that we varied the days and amount of time we spent each day according to my son's wishes and needs: his mood, his secular school workload, vacations (we *never* worked on vacations), etc. On the best days we worked as long as 30-45 minutes. On not-so-good days we literally worked 5–10 minutes. On days when Michael felt more relaxed we worked on something new. On less relaxed days we reviewed work already learned.

At first I set days and the time of day, making it convenient for me. But I found that my son was grumbling if he had to be interrupted at something else. So we compromised. As long as he chose five days out of every seven, he could select the day and time and even change it daily, just as long as he did not pick an entirely inappropriate time.

Making good use of my knowledge of learning strategies was tougher than scheduling. By definition, an auditory learner usually "gets" more information when it is explained orally than when it must be read from a written page. Knowing Michael was such an auditory learner, I initially assumed that he could learn everything by listening to a tape. But I quickly found that he needed more input than just his ears. The information was simply too unfamiliar to master with only one sense. So by trial and error we ended up doing the following: I listened to the tape and mastered each selection. Then I taught it to Michael—in very small doses—using a multi-sensory approach. That is, Michael listened to me sing (auditory input) while he looked at the written page (visual input) and followed along with his finger, touching each word (tactile input). He practiced new information daily for five minutes and integrated it into already learned information on a weekly basis.

For the most part, this plan worked because it set realistic goals and gave Michael a say in its operation. However, I won't lie and say it all went smoothly. One difficulty occurred each time we started something new. Michael would often be sulky and demanding (you're singing too fast, too slowly, too loudly; I'm tired, thirsty, bored, etc.) Once I recognized this pattern, I explained it to him, and he really did try not to let it happen. But I think he truly dreaded beginning each new selection.

Once, when tensions were heating up, I slammed the book shut and made Michael leave the house with me. I told him we were going for a walk to clear the air. We started out with me in the lead, furiously walking and pumping my arms as fast as I could. Michael was doing the same, but making sure not to give me the satisfaction of walking with me—he was about half a block behind. As I cooled down and slowed down he must have cooled down, too, because the next thing I knew he was walking with me. After a while we actually talked to each other, and by the time we got home we were both feeling okay. I never kept track of how many times we had to resort to walking, but I know I lost five pounds without dieting that summer!

When I mentioned to others what I was doing with my son, their common response was surprise that I would take on the responsibility of tutoring my own son for bar mitzvah. But I never saw myself as Michael's tutor. I was the bar mitzvah facilitator. My goal was not to bypass the religious school program but to prepare Michael well enough so that he could participate in that program. This method is called "pre-teaching." It involves giving a student with learning disabilities information at a slower speed and with a method more appropriate for him to learn, so that he becomes familiar enough with the information to get it when it is taught in class.

In Michael's case it worked like this. Instead of learning to first read and then chant each selection in bar/bat mitzvah class (the standard teaching method), he did the opposite. He auditorially learned to chant each selection at home until he was familiar enough with the Hebrew to recognize it and read it in class. Michael's classmates were unaware of his pre-teaching and his many hours of work at home. They only saw this kid who seemed to learn how to chant everything immediately. Michael loved feeling "smart" in Hebrew school for the first time and especially loved it when classmates asked him for help.

A month prior to his ceremony Michael had satisfactorily completed everything on our initial list. His teacher suggested that he add either the *Shaharit* service or Torah reading, but I resisted. Michael seemed comfortable and knowledgeable with what he had already learned. But I have seen kids with learning disabilities "lose" knowledge as unexpectedly and completely as a computer whose hard disk crashes, and I concentrated on repetition and relaxation during those last precious weeks.

And then it happened. Our son walked into the synagogue one Shabbat morning, a boy. Sometime about mid-morning he put on the tallit of a man and flawlessly led the congregation in prayer and study as though it were the easiest and most natural task in the world. And nothing will ever be quite the same again. That day really did mark the first step toward Michael's adult life and his independence from his dad and me. Michael had a bar mitzvah ceremony, a personally successful one—with good memories—in fact, a perfect bar mitzvah.

HELPFUL HINTS FOR PARENTS AND EDUCATORS

Empower every child. Bar/bat mitzvah is a major life-cycle event in the life of a child. Every child deserves a major say in how the bar/bat mitzvah goes but must also take the major responsibility for the success of the event.

Time can be one of your biggest allies. But keep in mind that there is a difference between planning and obsessing. Too much pressure for too long will do in any child—LD or not. Especially in the last week before the bar/bat mitzvah ceremony, it is important that the house be calm. Don't leave too many last-minute errands and jobs, and don't plan on *any* last minute learning. Repetition and relaxation are the keys.

Selectively share the situation. It is important that LD information is shared with the key players in each child's religious education, bar/bat mitzvah planning, and bar/bat mitzvah training. However, those pre-teen/teen years can be especially difficult for students who have learning disabilities because they desperately want to fit in. If a child doesn't want to share this information wholesale, respect that. When my son was writing his speech I encouraged him to talk about how difficult his bar mitzvah study was and how hard he had worked to achieve his goal. He adamantly refused. He wanted everyone to think he had breezed through!

Accommodations. There are as many ways to accommodate learning disabilities as there are disabilities. Accommodations must be matched to specific problems—they don't work if they are generalized. The key is to pinpoint the child's learning styles.

Enjoy! Too many times, everyone gets so involved with worry over the details of bar/bat mitzvah celebrations that they really don't enjoy them. That goes double when the child has a learning disability. Keep in mind that the congregation at a bat/bar mitzvah ceremony is the least critical audience in the world. They are already sure the child will be wonderful—and, somehow, he or she always is.

HELPFUL HINTS FOR STUDENTS

Believe in yourself. Your learning problems are the direct result of identified learning disabilities, not low intelligence. You can have the bar/bat mitzvah celebration you want if the correct educational approach is used. Also keep in mind that bar/bat mitzvah is not a contest. Measure success by the level of effort you expended and your commitment to Judaism.

Be your own advocate. No matter what you are studying, it can be taught in a manner appropriate for you to learn. Speak up—either to the teacher or to your parents—when something does not make sense. People do not look down on you for advocating for yourself—they respect you for it.

Enjoy! Becoming bar/bat mitzvah happens only one time in your whole life. It is natural to be nervous, but don't let worry get out of hand and take away from your celebration. Keep in mind that those in the congregation on the day of your bar/bat mitzvah ceremony already know you are wonderful!

This article originally appeared in the *United Synagogue Review*, Spring 1995.

BAR/BAT MITZVAH PREPARATION FOR CHILDREN WITH SPECIAL LEARNING NEEDS

BJE of Greater Washington, D.C.

POINTS FOR CONSIDERATION

PREPARATION

1. Is my child self-motivated?

2. Is s/he anxiously awaiting become a Bar/Bat Mitzvah or is s/he just anxious?

3. Does my child work well one-on-one?

4. Can my child read Hebrew or does s/he have the potential for learning to read Hebrew?

5. Does my child learn better auditorially or visually?

6. Would my child do better with frequent, short lessons or longer lessons once a week?

7. What are my child's expectations?

SELECTION OF TUTOR

1. Does this person understand my child's strengths and challenges?

2. Can the tutor be flexible in teaching methods?

3. Is the tutor familiar with the form of the service in my congregation?

SELECTION OF DATE AND TIME

1. Can my child sit through a service?

2. Is my child able to stand up in front of a large number of people, particularly strangers?

3. If my child is capable of learning a Haftarah, should I look for a week that has a shorter Haftarah selection?

4. Would my synagogue permit a Bar/Bat Mitzvah service at another time, e.g., *Havdalah*, *Rosh Hodesh*, Monday or Thursday morning, afternoon or evening service?

5. What other responsibilities can my child take in the service, e.g., *Shema, Ein Keloheinu*, readings in English, opening/closing of the Ark, dressing or carrying the Torah, etc.?

6. What other options does my congregation offer?

HOW ELSE CAN I HELP?

1. Take your child to synagogue at least once a month.

2. Give your child frequent opportunities to meet the rabbi, cantor, and congregants.

3. Encourage your child to recite *Kiddush* and *Ha-Motzi* for the family each Shabbat.

4. Emphasize the "Mitzvah" not the "Bar."

5. Involve your child in as much of the planning as possible.

6. Give your child new opportunities and responsibilities as an "adult" Jew.

7. Meet with all the synagogue people who have roles that day: rabbi, cantor, gabbai, executive director, etc..

8. Be sure the tutor, the rabbi, and the religious school (if your child is enrolled) are in touch with each other.

SIDDUR TEFILLAH
YEHOSHUA ḤAZAK

Siddur Tefillah Yehoshua Ḥazak was developed by the Masorti Movement's Bar/Bat Mitzvah Program for Children with Special Needs.

It utilizes Mayer-Johnson Boardmaker picture communication symbols along with the Hebrew prayer text and is adaptable for use in many settings.

סדר ההתעטפות בטלית ■

בָּרוּךְ אַתָּה יְהֹוָה אֱלֹהֵינוּ מֶלֶךְ הָעוֹלָם
אֲשֶׁר קִדְּשָׁנוּ בְּמִצְוֹתָיו וְצִוָּנוּ לְהִתְעַטֵּף בַּצִּיצִית.

סדר הנחת תפילין ■

בָּרוּךְ אַתָּה יְהֹוָה אֱלֹהֵינוּ מֶלֶךְ הָעוֹלָם
אֲשֶׁר קִדְּשָׁנוּ בְּמִצְוֹתָיו וְצִוָּנוּ לְהָנִיחַ תְּפִלִּין.

בָּרוּךְ אַתָּה יְהֹוָה אֱלֹהֵינוּ מֶלֶךְ הָעוֹלָם
אֲשֶׁר קִדְּשָׁנוּ בְּמִצְוֹתָיו וְצִוָּנוּ עַל מִצְוַת תְּפִלִּין.

בָּרוּךְ שֵׁם כְּבוֹד מַלְכוּתוֹ לְעוֹלָם וָעֶד.

וְאֵרַשְׂתִּיךְ לִי לְעוֹלָם

וְאֵרַשְׂתִּיךְ לִי בְּצֶדֶק וּבְמִשְׁפָּט וּבְחֶסֶד וּבְרַחֲמִים

וְאֵרַשְׂתִּיךְ לִי בֶּאֱמוּנָה, וְיָדַעַתְּ אֶת יְהֹוָה

5

For more information contact www.masorti.org.

PART 11: INFORMAL EDUCATION

CHAPTER 44

SOCIAL/RECREATIONAL ACTIVITIES FOR CHILDREN WITH DISABILITIES

Jewish Community Center of Greater Washington, D.C.

Sara Portman Milner

Children with disabilities benefit from informal education in ways that far outreach academic or cognitive gain. When a child with autism participates as a member of an audience at a puppet show that brings Israel to life, he/she not only is exposed to Israeli music, concepts, etc., but also practices staying in a seat, not making noises, and looking in the direction of the performers. The other members of the audience who are typical children serve as role models and help prompt the child to maintain appropriate behavior.

While many recreational activities in a Jewish setting can provide meaningful learning experiences, camp is probably the most effective. Camp offers a concentrated block of time of two, four, or even eight weeks, with whole days (and in the case of residential camps, nights) for experiencing the practice of Jewish values and rituals. Repeating Hebrew prayers, learning Jewish songs, doing Israeli dancing, observing Shabbat, making gifts for others, doing acts of loving kindness for those in need, learning from the implementation of a Jewish theme, and observing *kashrut* are just some of the many experiences a camp setting can offer a child with special needs. The naturalness of these experiences, without pressure to achieve certain milestones, is a major factor in the tremendous growth that can occur over a summer. When total inclusion is the modality for serving children in a camp setting, then the benefits increase multifold.

An important aspect of the inclusion experience is the education of the non-disabled peers. Children are able to get to KNOW a child, not just as "the boy who uses a wheelchair and speaks differently," but also as Adam, a kind, fun guy who is a major sports fan. They become sensitive and knowledgeable of not only the disabilities with which the campers appear at camp, but also the many *abilities* they demonstrate throughout the summer. The typical peers not only become comfortable with children with a wide range of differences, but they also become loyal advocates, continuing their advocacy not only during the summer months, but also throughout the year and from year to year.

Over the thirty summers that the Jewish Community Center of Greater Washington has provided an integrated summer camp program, there have been dramatic demonstrations of this. Children have grown up with peers with disabilities, experiencing one of their favorite times of the year together, creating shared Jewish memories. Typical children have grown up to be understanding, compassionate, and helpful toward others with disabilities. Counselors who had their first experience with a child with disabilities at camp have changed their majors and gone on to be speech and language pathologists, physical therapists, special education teachers, psychologists, and social workers. Even those who have pursued law have utilized their own experiences in their practice in order to make their practice more accessible, non-discriminatory, and just. Doctors who worked as counselors, swim instructors, etc. have a heightened awareness and greater level of comfort when treating patients with disabilities and working with their families.

Camp is a springboard to many other aspects of life in a typical Jewish community. The relationships formed in camp are probably the greatest guarantors of continued successful integration in the community. During the school year, children with a wide range of disabilities participate in all activities at the Jewish Community Center. In most cases children receive additional support from a designated staff person in order to participate in a Jewish holiday crafts workshop, for example. The extra staff person works alongside the child or children with special needs, repeating directions, giving physical assistance, implementing a behavior management program, encouraging, interpreting, and modeling how to be part of a larger group. Whether it is participating in the Pesah school-break program, the daily after-school program, or one of the story-hour activities at the annual Jewish Book Fair, with support, the children with disabilities not only participate and learn but are also welcomed by the former campers who have gotten to know them over the summers.

"Attitudinal accessibility" is a key component in the successful integration of children with disabilities. Any agency or organization involved in formal or informal Jewish education of such children must believe that the children have a right to be there, and indeed belong there. Then they must put their beliefs into practice, removing all barriers—physical, political, financial, and attitudinal. Only then will they be truly successful in teaching the true meaning of *hesed* and *gemilut hasadim*.

Some children may require a tremendous amount of structure, staff intervention, and small group size in order to be successful, even in an informal learning situation. At these times a self-contained option should be made available. Many children need such a setting in their earlier years but can gradually be included totally as they improve their abilities to maintain self-control and develop appropriate ways to relate to typical peers in a group situation. For some children this takes only days or weeks, for others it takes years to achieve, but there must be a starting point available.

Having a continuum of services available makes it possible to meet the varied needs of individuals. For example, a weekly activity group for children with disabilities can provide opportunities for structured practice of social skills while the children are engaged in a fun experience, such as preparing treats to eat in the Sukkah. When their family participates in a community or synagogue-sponsored Sukkah party, they are more prepared for what is appropriate in that integrated setting.

The Jewish community has a unique opportunity to enhance the quality of life for its children with disabilities. These children already know how different they are from other children. They need opportunities to learn how like other children they are. They are thrilled to learn that other children also light Shabbat candles, say the *motzi,* and attend their synagogue.

In order to make activities and programs available to all members of the community, parents are excellent consultants, as are adults with disabilities. When a community-wide event is planned, such as a *Yom Ha'Atzmaut* celebration, it would be critical to make sure that the location is physically accessible in every way, from parking to rest rooms to removable seats in an auditorium or sanctuary, for someone using a wheelchair. In fact, staff providing information regarding the event should either be skilled in communicating via the community's TTY-linked phone system, or the sponsoring organization should provide that person with a TTY in order to provide information to those people who may be deaf or hearing-impaired. Sign language interpretation not only should be available, but should be advertised along with the program. These kinds of accommodations encourage participation by people with disabilities. Aside from being the law, such accommodation is the right thing to do.

CHAPTER 45

RECRUITMENT AND TRAINING OF "NON-PROFESSIONAL" SUPPORT STAFF

Jewish Community Center of Greater Washington, D.C.

Sara Portman Milner

Professionals with experience, training, and highly developed skills are critical to the successful implementation of many programs. However, that alone does not guarantee success. In the experience of the Jewish Community Center of Greater Washington's Special Needs Programs, it has been found that the majority of informal educational programs rely heavily on a cadré of well-trained, involved volunteers or paid aides to provide the extra direct service needed in order for all participants to experience success. Whether in a self-contained social group or in a general camp group where children with disabilities are included, these non-professional support people are the key.

Recruitment and training of these people deserves serious time and attention. The benefits return many times over. The recruitment begins as soon as the need is identified. Adults, college students, and even high school students should not be overlooked for the contributions they can make. A critical screening factor is willingness to try. One might think that prior experience would be a major screening factor. While this is desirable, it may not be as important, because it could have been a very negative or inappropriate prior experience. There may be too much wrong to undo before getting the person oriented to where you are headed.

While people learn from reading and hearing, a visual exposure jump-starts the process. If there is a video of the specific program for which people are being recruited, that is optimal. Even if there is not a video of the specific program, a video of a similar program can help recruits see the nature of the population being served as well as the role of the aide, companion, helper, peer volunteer, facilitator, or whatever the title. A major benefit of sharing this visual presentation is that the mystery or unknown factor becomes minimized, as everyone involved has the same image in mind as they move forward.

Indeed, training starts with the interview. As information is shared, responses of the interviewees are weighed, and direction begins toward the most appropriate role for each interviewee. In the interview one can assess some comfort-level factors regarding both specific disabilities and age group. For recruits, the gender preference in terms of those with whom they would work is not as much a factor with younger children as it is with teens and adults. Many teens

423

are more comfortable working with people with disabilities of the same sex when they are closer to their age or older.

If possible, select more applicants than you currently think you need. In that way you not only have the opportunity to train your substitutes, but you retain a trained pool for the next program. Sometimes staff who are hired begin the process with good intentions but later find that the commitment is more than they expected, at which time you can immediately draw from your backup pool.

Training of non-professionals to work with children with disabilities in an informal educational or recreational setting is geared toward building confidence and competence. Therefore, it is important to continually assess the comfort level of the trainees. Teenagers who spend a majority of their waking lives in a formal learning mode may be more open to the experience than adults who have been out of the learning mode for a while. In either case, the continual monitoring of the comfort level will prove useful.

It is important to determine your philosophy or approach before you can teach it to anyone else. Spend some time developing what you want to be the guiding light in not only the training, but also the implementation of programs. For example, in the camp programs at the Jewish Community Center of Greater Washington a guiding principle is "We want everyone to have a positive experience in the least restrictive environment. Do not focus on why something won't work; focus on what has to be done to make it work." This reflects the *attitudinal accessibility* mentioned in the previous chapter. That principle then guides the training, giving a common direction in hope of reaching a common outcome.

Disability awareness training is a critical piece of training people to work with individuals with disabilities. To the greatest extent possible, experiential activities should be used. When a person experiences what it feels like to talk with an articulation problem or to do simple math problems and experience the frustration of a person with a severe learning disability or mental retardation, it is retained on not only an intellectual level, but also on a personal level. That seems to have a longer-lasting impact.

Each summer, staff is trained using activities found in Disability Awareness programs. Those experiences address mental retardation, articulation, motor dexterity, attention deficit disorder, and learning disabilities. In addition, an overview of learning disabilities should go into greater depth in explaining the five senses and how learning disabilities affect learning far beyond the classroom through all sensory avenues.

Because a typical person is not usually aware of the range and impact of learning disabilities, this can prove helpful on many levels. It causes the participants to think about how people are perceiving information, not just how information is presented. Thus, when a group of volunteers or trainees sees the jumbled, disorderly, intermittently reversed paragraph as perceived by a child with dyslexia or other visual, figure-ground, or spatial relationships problems, they recognize the need for ways of presenting information other than print. All five senses should be addressed, giving everyday examples of how learning is affected. For example, the need to physically model where to stand on a kickball field and to run alongside someone in the correct direction for first base may not have been considered before by someone who is volunteering in a camp group. The necessity to close doors and windows or to pull a child aside to a quieter area to further explain directions would be important for a child who is auditorially distractible. Practicing an Israeli dance movement, focusing on the appropriate amount of pressure to use when holding hands, would be important for children whose sense of touch is affected, so they won't squeeze their partners' hands too tightly or become tactilely defensive when it is time to touch another dancer. The concept of tactile defensiveness is not a generally known concept but would need extensive explanation to any assistants helping children in sports, dance, or other movement activities.

The people who are recruited to help need to learn some basic behavior management skills. A Behavior Management Concepts and Techniques guide provides a uniform approach to behavior that can be used in many different settings and programs. When combined with sample scenarios for each technique, it has proven to be highly effective. Also, the format is such that is provides a handy "cheat sheet" for future reference.

It is important to take a proactive stance. Think of all things that could go wrong, and allow the staff to develop a response to the situation at hand. Scenarios should be drawn from actual happenings within the program or activity. This will make it relevant for the aide and will trigger the memory when it arises in the actual situation.

Throughout the training the prospective volunteers and staff should be encouraged to ask questions. It is important to share that "There is no such thing as a stupid question. Probably someone sitting next to you wants to know the same thing and is hesitant to ask." This not only helps people feel less intimidated about asking, but also encourages people to ask, giving you the opportunity to see how information is being received. It allows you to emphasize those areas that are being received with greatest difficulty.

Throughout the training it is important to provide a lot of positive reinforcement, to model that concept of the behavior management plan. It is also important to acknowledge people's discomfort when they indicate it. Reassure them that it is all new, unknown, and scary at this time, but it will become second nature to them within weeks. Let them know that at the beginning they will be focusing on all the things that their person can't do, rather than what they can do. Yet that will change and they will quickly get to know the total person, not only his/her disabilities, but the many abilities, the feelings, and the uniqueness as a human being, more like others with various strengths and weaknesses.

JEWISH DAY AND RESIDENTIAL CAMP RESOURCES FOR CHILDREN AND TEENS WITH SPECIAL NEEDS

American Camp Association, (800) 428-2267, www.acacamps.org

Association of Jewish Sponsored Camps, (212) 751-0477

Foundation for Jewish Camp, (647) 278-4500, www.jewishcamps.org

JCC Association of North America, (212) 532-4949 www.jcca.org

Camp Ramah, (212) 678-8881, www.campramah.org

Jewish Education Service of North America (JESNA), 212) 529 -2000, www.jesna.org

Orthodox Union of America: National Jewish Council for the Disabled/Yachad/Our Way, (212) 563-4000, www.ou.org

United Synagogue of Conservative Judaism, (212) 533-7800, www.uscj.org

Union for Reform Judaism, (212) 650-4294, www.urj.org

CHAPTER 46

THE TIKVAH STORY

Howard Blas

(Presentation at the Ramah at 60 Conference, 2007)

The Camp Ramah Tikvah Programs are among the many fine day and overnight programs for young people with special needs offered in Jewish camps. These programs are sponsored by Jewish community agencies such as Jewish Community Centers, the denominational streams, and others.

For more information, contact Foundation for Jewish Camp (FJC) at www.jewishcamp.org.

STORY OF "MITCH"

Earlier this week I had reason to phone a couple in our New Haven community. Both are in their mid 60's or early 70's. They are empty nesters, in a sense, with grown children. "In a sense," I say, because their son, "Mitch", in his mid 40s, has special needs.

I have met Mitch on a few occasions, as he drops by on his bike to join his parents for Shabbat lunch at the home of friends in the community. What I did not know until this particular conversation—which was about the upcoming bat mitzvah of one of my children, is that Mitch had HIS bar mitzvah at Camp Ramah in New England. Mitch was a Tikvah camper in the early 70's. Mom replies, "A very nice man (that is Herb Greenberg, founder of Tikvah and director, with his wife, Barbara for 29 years) agreed to accept Mitch." "It wasn't the best fit for him. I think they were trying to decide the kinds of campers they were looking for, and I don't think anyone knew much about Asperger Syndrome back then—but it was a good experience for Mitch. And it was a perfect place for him to celebrate his bar mitzvah."

WHAT IF MITCH WAS AN APPLICANT IN 2007/2008

Tikvah New England in the early 70's may not have been right for Mitch. But surely, if Mitch was an applicant for Ramah Camps for Summer 2008, the Ramah movement could have offered Mitch several wonderful options.

Tikvah in Wisconsin *may* have been right for—as it is more geared for young adults with Asperger Syndrome. In fact, Mitch could have possibly grown to become part of the Vocational Program there, and maybe even attended the special Birthright Koach Israel trip for young adults with Aspergers.

If the family had been thinking about camp for a younger Mitch, ages 9-12, perhaps Breira (in the Berkshires) would have been a great choice. Or possibly, an even younger Mitch, ages five to eleven, may have been a good candidate for their program, offered in partnership with Keshet, a Chicago area inclusion program for Jewish children with a wide range of special needs. Our Inclusion Program at Camp Ramah of New England, now entering its 4th summer, may have also been an option.

And Ramah camps without formal special needs programs have been supporting campers without a "formal" label of Aspergers, language processing disorders, Attention Deficit Disorder, Obsessive Compulsive Disorder, social skills impairments, etc. They are showing up at all of our camps, and at camps everywhere, for that matter. We should have an entire conference on ways camps are, and should be, supporting ALL campers, regardless of strengths and weaknesses!

Thanks to the pioneering work of Ramah Darom, Mitch's family might have entered the "Ramah System" through Camp Yofi, the wonderful weeklong Family Camp at Ramah Darom in Georgia, for children with autism, their parents and siblings.

If Mitch presented with such developmental disabilities as mental retardation, or autism, or neurological impairments, or if he had cerebral palsy, he might have been a better fit for one of the Tikvah Programs at Ramah Camps in New England, Canada, or California, which have all evolved from the days when Herb and Barbara Greenberg kindly and lovingly accepted Mitch.

Look how far we've come! We in the Ramah movement are truly *halutzim*/pioneers, and we continue to be on cutting edge in offering Jewish camping for children, young adults and, in some camps, adults, with a wide range of special needs. California and Canada offers vocational education opportunities until age twenty four or twenty five, and New England will take appropriate candidates "forever" if hired to work as full staff. And we frequently receive praise and requests for consultations from other camps—from Orthodox camps, to Young Judea, to Jewish Community Center camps, seeking guidance on how they can incorporate some of our successes and experience in to their planning for campers with special needs.

PRE-HISTORY AND HISTORY OF TIKVAH:

The history of the Tikvah Program has appeared in articles in various journals and publications--mainly written by the Greenbergs.

"The concept of a camping program for Jewish adolescents with special needs was first proposed in the late 1960's. The Subcommittee on Special Education of the United Synagogue's Commission on Jewish Education requested that a Jewish summer camp incorporate a group of adolescents with developmental disabilities into its population."

Much like that famous *midrash* about the many nations of the world rejecting the "gift" of the Torah, various Jewish camps had already rejected this proposal. In early 1970, this proposal was presented to the National Ramah Commission. Ramah camps and directors expressed fears that the presence of a mentally and/or emotionally handicapped (sic) group in the camp community would disrupt the structure of the camp, and leaders of Ramah felt that a program that introduced children with disabilities into the camp would create anxiety, both among the other campers and among the staff. They also worried that some parents might be afraid to send *their* children to camp if THESE children were there…"

Donald Adelman, the Director of Camp Ramah in Glen Spey, New York, notes Greenberg, "was the lone dissenter, the only Ramah director who really wanted this program. He took an enormous risk, and he staked his whole career on it. He saw it as a moral responsibility toward those with special needs."

428

Herb Greenberg reports, "Years later, we learned that Don had stated that if there was no room at Ramah for Tikvah, then the whole point of the camp would be lost. This is what Ramah should be, and I insist on having it."

The original plan for the first Tikvah summer was for a group of adolescents with mental retardation. Things didn't quite work out as planned as recruitment was difficult. The initial group of eight campers in 1970 consisted of children classified by their respective school systems as "brain-injured," "learning disabled," and "emotionally disturbed." Perhaps Mitch was part of this original group of campers!

Other Ramah camps soon followed the lead of the pioneering Camp Ramah in New England Tikvah Program:

> In 1973, Camp Ramah in Conover, Wisconsin.
>
> In the early 1980's, Camp Ramah in Ojai, California
>
> In 1993, Camp Ramah in Canada

We now have Breira and Yofi as well as Keshet, as mentioned earlier.

CAMPERS

Tikvah campers, like all Ramah campers, have multiple opportunities to experience and master different things.

Over the years:

- Tikvah campers have learned how to say *hamotzi*, or *birkat hamazon*, or the Torah blessings—in many cases leading them, or even davening *kabbalat Shabbat* and *maariv* or *musaf* in front of the entire camp.
- Tikvah campers go on *"etgar,",* hiking, and canoeing, cooking on an open fire, and sleeping in tents which they built in teams.
- And Tikvah campers put on a play, mainly in Hebrew, for the entire camp—in some cases—in conjunction with another *edah* or division. And they proudly and confidently presented a song and dance in front of the entire camp at the *zimkudiyah,* the camp-wide song and dance festival. But these are obvious—so obvious that we often take them for granted.

Some Tikvah campers have acquired job skills at camp which have lead to amazing jobs both in camp and in their communities upon return from camp: from Aaron serving as a security guard at the Camp Ramah in New England guard house; to working for the U.S. Postal Service; to the team of Jason and Marie single-handed, with a little help from a few other Tikvah campers and a job coach, maintaining our prized six room New England guest house.

Ramah alumni of all ages surely recall one or more b'nai mitzvah they have experienced at a Ramah camp. Without a doubt, the bar/bat mitzvah experience has had a tremendous, life-long effect on camper, family and community.

Rabbi Michael Panitz, rabbi in Nortfolk, Virginia, former Camp Ramah in New England staff member, and father of a Tikvah alum, recently devoted his Rabbi's Column to thoughts on his daughter Emily's (Rivkah), thirteenth anniversary of her bat mitzvah, NOT because it took place at camp, but because, thirteen years later, she continues to read Torah, attend daily minyan and teach *alef-bet* in the Hebrew school.

I am pleased that Rivkah has a strong desire to give back. This is something she has learned at home and something we have tried to instill in our campers—from baking and selling *hallah* in camp to raise money for *tzedakah* (in memory of a camper who died several years ago); to pushing the stroller or wheelchair in camp of a campers who has some mobility issues; to doing *bikkur holim,* visiting the sick, *erev Shabbat* at a hospital in Jerusalem, giving out gifts to Israeli Jewish and Arab children on Hadassah's Pediatric unit. Two campers wanted so badly to give back they convinced the Israeli *nagar,* carpenter, a long-time friend of Tikvah, to help them design and build an *aron kodesh* for the Tikvah Program—and it is GORGEOUS! Our campers truly understand the concept of *mitzvot,* *hesed,* and *kol Yisrael areivim zeh b'zeh*, all Jews are responsible for each other. (During a recent Ramah Israel Trip, Rivkah gave her friends the opportunity to reciprocate by helping others. In the Old City of Jerusalem, we could not find an accessible path. They looked at us, said there was none, and then reached down and lifted Rikvah, in a wheelchair, up 10 steps!)

A FEW WORDS ABOUT PARENTS

Parents marvel that their children even have the OPPORTUNITY to participate in something as basic as Jewish camping, something they often enjoyed, and their more typically-developing children enjoyed—but which they doubted their children with special needs would EVER enjoy:

The mother of a Ramah New England camper with Down Syndrome who is hard of hearing and unable to speak a single word appreciates that **B** "has the same opportunity that other children have, to attend a summer camp." At camp, he learns how to live away from home, and interact with many different people—in a well-staffed, safe, Jewish environment. She appreciates the fact that B has opportunities to expand his social circle, and notes what we already know from our research that "other kids learn to be more accepting and tolerant. It opens their eyes to something they may otherwise never have been exposed to."

The **Y's** similarly worried they would never find a Jewish camp to offer Jacob the same experiences their other sons had. After eleven years as a camper and voc ed-er, the Y's report, "The best part of being able to have Jacob at overnight camp is that when things come up with my other boys and they talk about camp, Jacob can join into the conversation because he has had those same experiences. And he has learned to be independent of my husband and myself and knows that he can go places and survive nicely without us. If he were to tell you his favorite place in the world, it would be Camp Ramah!"

This sentiment is expressed by so many families, in ALL Ramah camps:

Another family,**The K's**, comment on what so many Tikvah families have experienced in the past—the lack of opportunities, in so many communities, for a proper Jewish education. "Lindsay has received a wonderful Jewish education. This is very important to us. Because of her disabilities, she has not been able to attend religious school and receive a Jewish education." The K's are also pleased that Lindsay has grown, matured, and become so independent, all in a happy friendly loving environment!"

The H Family is similarly pleased with the Jewish immersion environment Ramah and Tikvah offer. "The program has enhanced Jeremy's understanding and participation in Judaism. He now understands (although sometimes he doesn't want to admit it) the Shabbat Service, Shabbat Dinner, and Shabbat observances. The Tikvah Program has been a tremendous growth experience for Jeremy."

And **The S Family** is pleased with Marie's friends, both campers and staff, the skills she has learned, and the self-confidence she has developed, all in a safe, Jewish environment. "That gives my husband and me great peace of mind."

Other parents speak about more specific successes such as camp teaching campers to use a fork at the table, make their bed, and try new foods. I have received two emails in the past month and a half from a delighted mother of a new camper, a fifteen year old boy with Down Syndrome, who, prior to his Ramah days, was a "fussy eater":

"At dinner tonight, I sat and kvelled as my son at a salad of heirloom tomatoes, micro greens, beets and red onions, all covered in ketchup of course. Thank you for helping open him up to so many new pathways of life. My thanks and gratitude to all at the Tikvah Program." (I'm not sure we deserve all that credit. I know our new catering company was wonderful, but I don't even remember beets!)

And the follow up was actually from his teacher, telling the parents how much Matthew enjoyed the stir fry he made in class earlier this week. The teacher, remembering his resistance last year to new things, especially vegetables, was concerned about how much he would want to try the new vegetables. "First, Matthew set the table. Then, to my surprise, Matthew loved the stir fry. He ate the entire plate and then asked for more. He would have eaten thirds if we had more!"

OTHER CAMPERS, STAFF AND *SH'LIHIM*—A WORD ABOUT OUR RESEARCH

Clearly campers in other *edot* and staff members—from *edah* counselors, to *mumhim*, specialists, to *hevrei mishlahot*, Israeli staff members, have benefited and been transformed by the presence of Tikvah in camp.

I get calls each winter from campers and parents, usually of eleven or twelve year olds, asking how they might involve Tikvah as they prepare for bar and bat mitzvah: is there anything Tikvah needs (art supplies?), or is there something I can do over the summer? (one girl very successfully came alone, then with friends, to help with letter writing during the rest period, *sha'at menuhah*).

I patiently speak to each caller. For I **know** where good feelings about Tikvah and positive relationships with Tikvah campers, from a young age, can lead. It can lead to a lifetime and sensitivity and comfort around people with special needs.

Campers of all ages have opportunities to "experience Tikvah" at Ramah camps with Tikvah Programs—from a distance, and from up close—sometimes in the same day. Campers from many *edot* come, by bunk or *edah*, to experience the upbeat, musical, Tikvah *tefillot*; campers do *pe'ulot tzrif*, bunk activities, or *pe'ulot edah*, division activities, with Amitzim, the Tikvah kids; campers participate together in the *zimkudiyah,* the song/dance festival, plays, Friday night services, meals, etc. And campers from ages fourteen to sixteen may choose to participate in such long-standing programs as Bogrim Buddies, Machon Helpers and CITs. And the experience of working with Amitzim truly brings out the best in our teenagers.

Many former buddies, helpers and CITs are the ones who call me years later to be on staff (note: in 1984, almost all Tikvah campers came from outside of Ramah to gain experiences working with people with special needs; in the past few summers, 100% of Tikvah counselors have been "home grown talent.")

Counselors often come our way after years of observing Tikvah from a distance. Perhaps they worked in another *edah*, or *anaf*, branch, or even in the office, the *misrad* (two came this way and they were so transformed that both become professionals: one, a social worker, and I just wrote recommendations for the other, who was applying to graduate school in profound and severe disabilities).

Our vocational education advisors created a brilliant program a few years back called "Staff Buddies." After all, the peer group of workers is workers! Our advisors have matched each voc ed program participant in a one to one buddy relationship which meets over Shabbat and one weeknight for games, walks, schmoozing and hanging out. One particularly wonderful *shaliah*, was a *madrikh*, counselor, one summer, then was a *rosh edah*, division head, this past summer. He was the product of an Israeli *hesder yeshivah*. He took it one step further: he also volunteered to learn Torah, *parshat hashavua*, the weekly portion, each Shabbat afternoon with a Tikvah camper who did not wish to swim on Shabbat.

This Israeli is one of literally hundreds who have been touched by Tikvah. Suffice it to say that no fewer than ten *shelihim* met our recent Tikvah tour group at Ben Gurion airport, both at our 7 pm arrival and then saw us off at midnight! That says something!

In the summer of 2006, Ramah New England and Ramah California were lucky enough to be selected by researchers Michael Ben Avie and Jeffrey Kress of Yale and JTS respectively. They developed the Learning and Development at Camp Ramah Inventory to help Ramah establish a data-driven process of educational change. Within the survey was a 12-item scale on the impact of Tikvah on typical campers—at last, data on what we already know anecdotally!

Some very very **preliminary findings** from 64 Solelim, Shoafim and Magshimim Campers (ages eleven to thirteen) at Ramah New England:

- 79 percent strongly agreed or agreed that "The Ramah experience has helped me to feel more comfortable around people with special needs."
- 63 percent strongly agreed or agreed that "My experiences with campers from this camp's special needs program will carry over into other areas of my life."
- 58 percent strongly agreed or agreed that "My experiences with campers from this camp's special needs program has made me a better person (for example, more patient, more tolerant)."

We can't wait to expand this study!

WHAT ARE THE CHALLENGES AND OPPORTUNITIES AHEAD?

We have come a long way: Let's build on our strengths and keep going. Let's continue to reflect on our work, challenge our assumptions, innovate for today and for tomorrow. Let's challenge ourselves to meet the needs of those we don't yet meet.

I feel terrible when I need to turn away a camper—and I can't turn to a fellow director for help. This has happened in the case of two campers who were deaf, campers with multiple handicaps, and campers with serious psychiatric issues. We in New England have proudly begun to meet the needs of campers with mobility issue by paving of roads, building ramps, and renovating bunks to have fully accessible toilets and showers. But we also need accessible *hadrei okhel* or dining rooms, waterfronts, and buses for out of camp *tiyulim*, trips which are fully accessible. And we need more camps to strive for accessibility.

We need staff, families and donors in all of our camps to fully believe that we are all created *b'tzelem Elohim*, in God's image, and that each camper, regardless of need, deserves to be a Ramah camper. Let's work together towards this goal. We have a great product—one which transforms lives!

For more information, contact 212-678-8881, www.campramah.org/tikvah.

PART 12: TRANSITION TO ADULTHOOD

CHAPTER 47

TRANSITIONING FROM SCHOOL TO ADULTHOOD: A PARENT'S PERSPECTIVE

Becca Hornstein

Transitions are a universal experience. Transitions are times of elation and depression, of adventure and trepidation. We linger, not quite certain about letting go of what we know before we rush headlong to embrace the unknown. You've experienced this yourself, perhaps when you awaited the arrival of your first child.

I still remember the dreams I had about my baby's future. They extended beyond the horizon formed by my burgeoning belly. My husband and I talked constantly about the baby-to-come. My husband Barry wanted a complete basketball team, and he even had names selected. I dreamed about practical things, like would the baby look like his daddy or his mommy. A month before our first child was born I had a remarkable dream and clearly "saw" the delicate little blue-eyed, blonde-haired daughter I was carrying. Inspired by this nocturnal revelation, I awoke and quickly drew a portrait of my vision. Four weeks later I gave birth to our husky brown-eyed, black-haired son Joel.

Dreams are not reality. I learned that lesson quickly as Joel's disability, autism, surfaced at age twenty-one months. We went from doctor to doctor, therapist to therapist, and city to city looking for answers about Joel's condition. It took two years to get a diagnosis, and it was quickly followed by a devastating prognosis: This child will never be anything but profoundly mentally retarded, will never speak, will never acknowledge your existence, will never be toilet trained or feed or dress himself. This child will never be capable of giving or receiving love. If I had any dreams left before that prognosis, they were destroyed at that moment.

But it's not fair to take away parents' dreams! Dreams are what give us the motivation to make it through those scary, difficult transitions. At first Barry's and my dreams were born of desperation:

- Will this child ever be toilet trained??
- Will he ever sleep for more than two hours a night?

Some were practical—Please talk to us, Joel. Please look me directly in the eye and acknowledge that I exist in your world!

And some were silly:

- Oh, Joel, whatever will you do when you grow up?

- You have phenomenal math skills, Joel. Have you considered going into the stock market?
- You learned to play the piano in just two hours. Maybe we can find an autistic piano bar to hire you!

But when silliness subsided, we had to seriously consider how to prepare Joel for his transition into the adult world, and we couldn't wait to begin that process at age eighteen. The first steps toward planning the future for a child who has a disability should start very early. It necessitates taking a realistic look at that child and asking "What are his strengths and his weaknesses, his skills and his behavior?" We needed to honestly assess Joel and his finger-flipping, echolalia-spouting, highly vulnerable personality. Based on that assessment, we started to set goals for his future.

Because children with developmental disabilities need extra time to learn things, and because behaviors that become implanted are hard to extinguish and redirect, it's important to lay the foundation early for appropriate adult living skills. For example, Joel had household chores to teach him to respond to directions and also to learn about cause and effect. He had to empty the trash, set and clear the table, and make his bed. He learned that when he did those things, he received a reward! To make that reward meaningful, it had to be either something Joel wanted or, when Joel understood delayed gratification, a token that he knew would translate into something he wanted.

Joel loves a schedule, and we used one at home and one at school. Because Joel was fixated on numbers and letters, he learned the concept of time at a very early age. His teachers and I discovered that we could alleviate his anxiety about the uncertainty in his life by giving Joel a daily written schedule. It reassured him that there was a pattern to his daily routine, and children with autism are comforted by repetition in their lives.

Learning to follow a schedule from an early age established a pattern that Joel continues to use in his job today. His work assignments are in half-hour blocks and are posted on a daily worksheet for him to read. Using a schedule, though it may seem rigid and stultifying for some, provides the structure for adult responsibilities in the workplace as well as developing a social calendar for some people who have cognitive impairments.

Another essential early lesson was teaching Joel how and when to seek help. Many parents focus so completely on teaching their child who has a disability to be fully independent that they sometimes miss an important point. Those children may feel that they have failed or were defeated if they seek assistance, when it is actually more appropriate to request help sometimes. There are also times in the adult world when insisting "I can do it myself!" is counterproductive. Employers need to see the ability to work as a team in potential employees. As adults, in jobs or out in the community, they will need to learn how to evaluate situations and determine when asking for help is the most beneficial and expedient solution.

While there are many more ways to teach children how to prepare for the adult world of work and play, the most important lesson may be learning how to interact with those around you. More jobs are lost by people who are disabled because they act inappropriately in the lunchroom than for any other reason. Lou Brown at the University of Wisconsin shared a wonderful story:

A young man who had a severe cause of autism was placed at a work site. He did his job well but made his co-workers very uncomfortable at lunch and break time with his incessant rocking and chattering nonsense. When the young man moved on to another job they taught him to wear a pair of headphones attached to a tape player during his breaktime and lunch hour.

His co-workers saw him rocking and humming. One of the workers glanced at the young man and commented, "Hey, my kids do the same thing when they listen to that junk they call music. Leave him be." And no one was upset by his behavior after that!

How can the Jewish community provide support and assistance to the family of a child with disabilities as they move toward transition?

In our day schools and supplemental schools we can build a warm and accepting place for each and every child. Our schools become microcosms of society in general, training grounds in which to learn the skills described above. In an academic setting where ethical behavior, *gemilut hasidim* (deeds of loving kindness), and *tikkun olam* (healing the world) are part of the curriculum, teachers can guide all the students through such lessons as when to help someone and when to enable someone to help himself. Examples of challenging social situations can be constructed and appropriate behaviors modeled for group discussion. Students who have mental or physical impairments can learn to advocate for themselves in a safe environment. Their peers provide the best role models as well as influential counselors to impress upon them the importance of issues like shared responsibility, promptness, attention to detail, and setting and reaching goals. Teachers can learn how to include a system of tasks and rewards in a child's curriculum as well as providing opportunities for students with special needs to learn how to make wise choices, all of which will be used in adult life on a daily basis.

Our Jewish community centers, camps, youth groups, and social clubs provide an additional opportunity to prepare for life among the unimpaired. In all of these settings the essential ingredient is reality. Children and teens with disabilities need to learn how to manage in the fast-paced world of typical people, a world that won't always slow down to accommodate them. For example, Gary, who has Prader-Willi syndrome, a condition that involves obsessive eating, is given the opportunity to attend a day camp. The camp setting allows him, outside of home and school, to learn the consequences of grabbing other people's lunches or snacks and how to work on his own behavior in a different setting. For Sammy and Dina, both of whom are deaf, the camp counselors are instructed to "fade away" from being the children's interpreters as soon as possible. The camp becomes a training site for them to develop communication skills outside the protected, insular bubble of special schools. And for Leah, who has Down syndrome, and Ari, who has been blind since birth, participation in synagogue youth groups means learning to employ self-advocacy techniques on a frequent basis.

The Jewish social service agencies should offer workshops and support systems for families and teens-about-to-become-adults long before the safety-net of the public school years falls away. Those agencies should offer support groups for the individual who has a disability and for family members; mentoring programs for experienced parents to assist those who are just learning how the system works; social skills training for teens and adults with special needs; and informative workshops on issues that are relevant to those who are disabled. Every Jewish Family and Children's Service agency should have a social worker on staff who can help a family work their way through the multitude of issues facing them, such as applying for Social Security, filing for guardianship or durable medical power of attorney, and learning about other government programs.

Finally, congregations can assist families in the most important way. If a child with a disability becomes an active and frequent participant in Shabbat and holiday services, he will develop a sense of belonging that will carry through for the rest of his life. During the period of transition from school to adulthood, when all that is familiar and comforting is taken away from a young adult, being able to return to the security and regimen of weekly prayer and participation in synagogue activities will become the reassuring anchor. Attending services and being greeted by fellow congregants will remind this young adult that he is still respected and valued in his community.

We have been lucky. Joel made remarkable progress, and we were able to dream again as he made successful transitions from private school to public school, from elementary grades to high school, and now from childhood to adulthood. Joel works full-time at the county library, earning a paycheck and paying taxes like everyone else. He has the respect and affection of his co-workers at the library, and he is treated with dignity. Joel also lives in a Jewish group home that is fully supervised, and he proudly leads his housemates in chanting *Kiddush* every Shabbat. Joel has proven wrong those experts who predicted that he would be a person of very little capability. My husband and I continue to dream our dreams and help Joel become the very special young man that he is.

CHAPTER 48

JEWISH LIVING IN GROUP HOMES

Jewish Foundation for Group Homes, Washington, D.C.

Marcia Goldberg

As children age, so do their parents. The time comes when families are no longer able to care for, or wish to encourage the independence of, their members with special needs. The United Jewish Appeal Federation of Greater Washington (UJAF) provided the seed money that brought a new agency, the Jewish Foundation for Group Homes (JFGH), into being. The first group home opened in 1983. JFGH is now a major agency with national recognition. Nearly 2,000 people attend its annual gala in support of twenty group homes, twenty-five apartments, and several alternative living units—and the numbers are growing.

The group homes are designed for four to six residents. Some residences are coed. Depending upon the need in the group home, one to four staff people may be on duty, and staff may be awake through the night. Every resident must have a day program—a competitive paying job, a highly supervised position, a workshop, or volunteer work. They only remain in the home during the day when ill.

The apartment residents live in single apartments or with another resident in a two-bedroom apartment. These folks function much more independently but have a counselor who sees them at least once a week to help with things such as money management and social skills.

WHAT MAKES JFGH A JEWISH PROGRAM?

Each group home maintains a kosher kitchen with separate pots, pans, and dishes for meat and dairy. All foods brought into the home are kosher. Shabbat is observed every Friday evening with the lighting of candles and the blessings over grape juice and _hallah_. All the Jewish holidays are celebrated. The fall harvest festival of Sukkot is celebrated with a _sukkah_ in the yard of each home. Homes are thoroughly cleaned before Passover, and all items used the rest of the year are sealed away. Special pots, pans, and dishes are brought out for the eight days.

Because of the level of independence of the apartment residents, _kashrut_ is an option. But they celebrate Shabbat and holidays as a large group or in the company of a few friends.

The dedication of each group home is a wonderful community event with hundreds of people in attendance from Jewish communal leadership, elected officials, rabbis, families, neighbors, and, of course, the new residents. The benefactor's congregational rabbi officiates in the ceremony of affixing the mezuzah to the front door.

Many residents join their families for the high holidays and for Passover. Congregations donate tickets for Rosh Hashanah and Yom Kippur to the other residents. People within the community invite residents to join them for the Passover seder or come to a group home to lead the seder for the remaining residents of several group homes. Rabbis and other volunteers meet with the residents in advance of these holidays to discuss the rituals, to teach the songs, and to help them understand on their own level.

Each of the group homes has a special relationship with at least one congregation. That is the place of preference for High Holiday services and for Shabbat or holiday attendance. Residents go to the synagogue for Simhat Torah. They march around the sanctuary waving flags and singing with everyone else. And members who recognize them come over to say hello. They are also experienced *gragger* turners and enjoy listening to the Megillah.

Becoming Bar and Bat Mitzvah is an important rite of passage for Jewish youngsters at the age of twelve or thirteen. Some of the residents have been able to participate in this important ceremony when they lived with their families, but many have not. In addition, thirty or forty years ago it was rare for a woman to become Bat Mitzvah. In the larger Jewish community, men and women now study toward the goal of belated celebration of this milestone. JFGH does the same. To date there have been six adult B'nai Mitzvah classes. The residents study weekly for one year and participate in the service before family, friends, and leaders of the community.

Some congregations invite JFGH to take a major part in their regular Sabbath services—opening and closing the ark, reciting prayers, carrying the Torah scroll, being called up to the Torah, and basically handling all the honors. Services such as this are important so that congregants realize that the JFGH residents are able to participate and will therefore encourage them to do so on other occasions as well.

Residents participate in many Jewish communal events. On Super Sunday, residents help to make solicitation calls for UJAF and collect and sort pledge cards. Many congregations plan a mitzvah day when volunteers help to cook for the homeless, sort clothing donations for the needy, or prepare gift baskets for the needy. Our residents are not only on the receiving end—they help and give to others.

Jewish life is celebrated in the group homes, but illness and death are also noted in meaningful ways. Individuals who are seriously ill and their concerned housemates face illness in a Jewish context, with visits and appropriate prayers. Residents participate in funerals and interments of group home members, family, benefactors, and staff. Residents either sit *shiva* at the group home or at the home of relatives. Services are held in the group home for the week of *shiva* or at the end of the thirty-day mourning period, with residents standing to recite the memorial prayer—they are also family, the bereaved. Friends from the nearby synagogue come to comfort them. the Jewish Living Coordinator meets with residents to pray, sing, and, in general, help them to deal with the loss. Evening programs are held for apartment residents to help them handle the death of a friend in a Jewish way. There is a roster of rabbis willing to conduct funeral services for residents who no longer have a family connection in the area. Many residents have no living parent.

Staff members have also lost loved ones. In response to a stated need, the Jewish Living Coordinator conducts workshops for all staff on funeral and mourning practices in Judaism and other religions. *How to be a Perfect Stranger,* Volumes 1 and 2, published by Jewish Lights, is a valuable resource in this area.

The Jewish Living Coordinator works very closely with the volunteer Jewish Living Committee to create a Jewish ambience and foster Jewish identity, and with the Volunteer Coordinator to encourage volunteer and congregational involvement. In addition to presenting training workshops, they develop age-appropriate materials for different functioning levels.

CREATING A JEWISH IDENTITY IN GROUP HOMES WITH NON–JEWISH STAFF

The Jewish Living Coordinator and the Jewish Living Committee provide the bridge between the staff and the Jewish component of group home living with required training, ongoing support from volunteers, and integration into the community.

Many of our Jewish residents had some religious education and experiences in their early years, while the group home provides the Jewish atmosphere and involvement many residents did not have in the past. Whatever their background, they are now living within a Jewish environment in a kosher home.

In effect, the staff needs to be trained to act as teachers and facilitators, even though most of them come from other religions and cultures. Although eighty percent of the residents are Jewish, the majority of our direct care staff is not. Most staff members are not American–born, which presents an additional challenge. They have not come into contact with Jewish foods, expressions, or even a basic definition of what Judaism is. In addition to the support they may receive from other staff members from their homeland, they need training and reinforcement to enable them to understand this situation. They also need the involvement of volunteers and to experience integration of the residents into the larger Jewish community.

TRAINING

Training is a very important component of our program. Each staff member is required to attend training sessions in Judaism and in *kashrut*. Additional sessions are held on areas such as preparing for Passover, attending a synagogue service, and dealing with serious illness and death in Judaism. These trainings are a wonderful way in which to learn about other beliefs as people question and compare and build mutual respect.

"Basics of Judaism" touches on the Bible and commentaries, the Jewish calendar and holidays, the denominations within Judaism, and Jewish ritual objects. Among the goals are to show how Judaism differs from Christianity and Islam, and to present Judaism as a religion of ethics and values, with emphasis on the commandments serving as wisdom for us to live by rather than rigid rules. Ritual items are brought to the training session with demonstrations or photographs of how they are used. The Jewish Living Coordinator or a mentor also visits the group home when there is new senior staff to help them identify the Jewish ritual items there.

The *kashrut* (laws of keeping kosher) training addresses the origin of the laws for keeping kosher, the classification of foods, *kashrut* certification, planning menus, and revising recipes. Dishes, pots and pans, utensils, and silverware are color-coded. In this way, relief staff can readily identify meat and dairy in whatever home they are working in. The training includes looking at non-kosher recipes and seeing how to make them kosher as a way to encourage staff to make some of their own favorite foods.

Clearly, there is not sufficient time to cover all the questions that may arise. The trainer must have some understanding of other religions and cultures in order to present material in the best format. For example, staff from Muslim countries know they do not eat pork, but when they arrive in the United States they and other foreign born staff may not know the terms for pork products in the United States. Since some religions do not focus on individuals reading the Bible, they may not be familiar with the Bible stories that are known to many others.

In addition, special workshops are offered on holidays and on life-cycle events such as funerals and adult bar and bat mitzvah ceremonies, with reinforcement workshops provided as necessary. Workshops are led by the Jewish Living Coordinator or by local rabbis. Since new staff may be working in a home prior to *kashrut* training, they must view the "Kosher Kitchen" training video developed by JFGH as soon as they are hired. Each home also has a copy of the video for review as needed. This video is available for purchase by other agencies.

Each home has a basic Jewish library in response to staff who asked for texts to which they could refer. The books include *Gates of Prayer for Shabbat and Weekdays* (the Union of Reform Judaism prayerbook), *The Jewish Bible: Tanakh*, and *What is a Jew? A Guide to the Beliefs, Traditions and Practices of Judaism That Answers Questions for Both Jew and Non-Jew* by Rabbi Morris Kertzer, (Touchstone/Simon and Schuster).

VOLUNTEERS

Recognizing that staff cannot do it all, JFGH relies heavily on ongoing support from volunteers. Volunteers are members of local synagogues, youth groups, and social service organizations, or musicians, artists, or other individuals. A full-time volunteer coordinator on staff trains the volunteers and helps to schedule them for appropriate activities. In addition, members of the Jewish Living Committee serve as mentors to each home, providing an ongoing personal contact who can answer questions or step in to help plan a Jewish activity as needed.

Holidays are particularly busy times for the group homes. People come to the homes to help prepare special foods connected with the holiday, or the residents go to a synagogue to work with the members. A group of teens visit nearby homes for Shabbat and holidays.

Volunteers work on erecting the *sukkah*, others work directly with the residents in making decorations. Then everyone hangs the decorations and is invited to get together during Sukkot to eat in the *sukkah*. Families, friends, and benefactors are invited for holiday celebrations and Shabbat dinners on a regular basis.

Volunteers frequently join residents for singalongs. They help them make their own ritual objects in addition to the ones provided each group home at its dedication. Other groups have annual holiday parties at a synagogue with dancing or other entertainment.

JEWISH LIVING COMMITTEE MENTORS

The purpose of our mentor program is to develop an ongoing relationship between a committee member and residents and staff. The goal is to have someone the counselor can feel comfortable calling if there is a question about the observance of a holiday or *kashrut* or Passover. Sometimes this requires a visit; other times, a friendly phone call. The idea is to be regarded as a friend and supporter rather than a watchman.

Suggestions for establishing a relationship:

1. Arrange to meet the senior counselor to sit and talk about ways in which each of you believe you may be able to help.
2. Invite the residents and staff to meet you at your synagogue for the *Megillah* reading.
3. Offer to help the staff develop Passover menus.
4. Invite the home to your house for *Havdalah*, dessert, or some other activity.
5. Check in periodically to see how things are going.
6. Let the senior counselor know how to reach you and what are the best times.

RECOGNIZING DIVERSITY

Non–Jewish residents understand that they are living in a Jewish home, but we do not ignore their own religious and spiritual needs. We reach out to area churches to include our Christian residents in their holiday celebrations or provide volunteers. Residents are encouraged to attend the church of their choice and to celebrate their own holidays. Although the group home will not be decorated for Christmas, they are free to do what they want in their own rooms. They enjoy joining in with the others for Shabbat dinner and holiday celebrations. And memorial services are conducted in the group homes for their family members as well.

The task of recognizing staff diversity while creating a Jewish atmosphere in the home is an ongoing challenge. JFGH continues to update its training program and to seek volunteers and community involvement to ease the responsibilities placed on our staff. JFGH attempts to recognize cultural and religious diversity and differences in levels of observances while providing a home filled with Jewish tradition.

TRAINING MATERIALS—JUDAISM AND CHRISTIANITY

Concept	Christianity	Islam	Judaism
	Old Testament	Koran	Bible or Torah
	New Testament		within Judaism
God	God	God, Allah	God
Jesus	Son of God	A prophet	No special significance
Place of worship	Church	Mosque	Synagogue/Temple
Spiritual leaders	Minister, Priest	Imman, Alem, Malwes	Rabbi
Christmas, Easter	observed	not observed	not observed
Messiah	Jesus, awaiting second coming	no Messiah	Messiah has yet to come, speak more of a messianic era
Sabbath/ Shabbat	Sunday	Friday	Sundown Friday through Saturday evening

Holiday	Dates	Candles	Special Food	Jewish Stores	Work	Significance	Other
Rosh Ha-Shanah	Eve 9/29, 9/30-10/1	Yes 9/29& 9/30	Round *hallah*, apples, honey	Closed	No	Jewish New Year	Exchange New Year cards, ask forgiveness
Yom Kippur	Eve 10/8, 10/9	Yes• 10/8	No spicy food before fast	Closed	No	Day of Atonement	Holiest day of year•light candles AFTER dinner

Holiday	Dates	Candles	Special Food	Jewish Stores	Work	Significance	Other
Sukkot	Eve 10/13 10/14-21	Yes 10/13 & 10/14 & 10/20	Fall fruits and vegetables	Closed 10/14, 15 and 10/21	Observant Jews don't work 10/14 15, and 10/21	Fall harvest, thanksgiving	Custom: Build a *sukkah*, eat as many meals or snacks as possible in *sukkah*
Simhat Torah	Eve 10/21 10/22	Yes, 10/21	Apples	Closed	Observant Jews don't work	Celebrate cycle of reading the Torah	Special celebration in synagogue on the eve
Hanukkah	Eve 12/21 12/22-29	Yes,•• every night	Potato pancakes (latkes), jelly do-nuts	Open	Yes	First fight for religious freedom	Light special candlestick—menorah (see holiday binder for lighting details)
Tu B'Shevat	Eve 2/7 2/8	No	Dates, figs, raisins	Open	Yes	New Year for trees	Plant trees or other appropriate things
Purim	Eve 3/8 3/9	No	Hamantashen (3-cornered pastry)	Open	Yes	Jews in ancient Persia saved from wicked Haman	Special "noisy" celebration in synagogue on the eve, costumes, exchange gifts of food
Passover (Pesah)	Eve 4/7 4/8-15	Yes, 4/8,9,13,14	Matzah, special restrictions on processed foods	Closed 4/9,10, 14,15	Observant Jews don't work 4/9,10, 14/15	Festival of freedom from slavery in Egypt	Special meal (seder) first two nights (see holiday binder for food details)
Shavuot	Eve 5/27 5/28-29	Yes, 5/27,28	Blintzes, dairy foods	Closed	Observant Jews don't work 5/28,29	Celebrate the giving of the Law on Mt. Sinai	(see holiday binder)

WHAT MAKES MY HOME JEWISH

If a new friend walked into your apartment/home today, would he or she be able to see immediately that you are Jewish? Take a look around and check off the items on this list that you have.

☐ MEZUZAH on the door to the apartment

- ☐ SHABBAT CANDLESTICKS (for lighting candles on Shabbat and holidays)
- ☐ *KIDDUSH* CUP (for blessing wine or grape juice on Shabbat or holidays)
- ☐ *HALLAH* COVER (to cover the *hallah* on Shabbat and holidays while you are blessing the wine)
- ☐ HANUKKIAH—Hebrew word for Hanukkah menorah (for lighting the Hanukkah candles—should be electric rather than actual candles)
- ☐ *TZEDAKAH* BOX (to put money aside before Shabbat each Friday for charity)
- ☐ JEWISH ART (pictures of Israel, Jewish objects or other pictures, paintings on the walls or shelves)

If you are missing any of these items, here are some suggestions for how you can get them.

If someone asks you what you want for your birthday or Hanukkah, you can tell them what you need.

Call a family member, someone at a synagogue, Jewish Family Services, JCC, or Bureau of Jewish Education to help you buy what you need or make what you need.

For more information contact the Jewish Foundation for Group Homes at 301-984-3839 or www.jfgh.org.

CHAPTER 49

ADULT B'NAI MITZVAH

Jewish Foundation for Group Homes, Washington, D.C.

Marcia Goldberg

- Speeches no more than 1½ to 2 minutes each (this service took place on a Sunday during Hanukkah) and lasted about 45 minutes.
- A booklet was prepared with the prayers and readings, except for the following:
  1. *Amidah*, for which people were invited to use the weekday siddur .
  2. Torah reading, for which people will be invited to use the Humash at their seats.

Parts of service and page numbers announced by rabbi.

1. *Heveinu Shalom Aleikhem*—All
   Greetings from synagogue president
   Introduce members of the class—Marcia

2. Light the Hanukkiyah (no blessing)
   Sing "Hanukkah, O Hanukkah"—All

3. Placing of *tallitot*—Each student with family member or friend

4. *Birkat ha-Shahar*—President of JFGH

5. Rabbi Elazar said…
   Mitzvah project—Class representatives

6. *Barkhu*—Class and congregation preceded by reading "Prayer is praising God"—Class member

7. *Shma*—Class and congregation followed by reading on *V'ahavta*—Class member

8. *Amidah*—Congregation reads silently preceded by introduction—Class member reading based on *Al ha-Nisim*—Class member
   Oseh Shalom—Class and congregation

9. Torah Service
   Sing *Torah Tzivah Lanu Moshe* for processional—Class and congregation with Torah
   Torah reading—Class members
   Aliyot—Groups of class members
   All honors (ark, *hagba'ah*, *gelilah*, etc.)—Class members
   She'he'heyanu—Class and families

V'zot HaTorah—Congregation

Etz Hayyim Hi—Class and congregation

Reading preceding—Class member

10. *Eyn Keloheinu*—Class and congregation

11. Mourner's Kaddish—Congregation's rabbi

12. Class speech—Two class members

13. Greetings to class and presentation of certificates introduced by class member

President, Jewish Federation of Greater Washington

President, Board of Jewish Education of Greater Washington

JFGH Jewish Living Chair

14. *Alenu*—Rabbi

15. Closing songs—Class and congregation

S'vivon

Hinei Mah Tov

Shalom Haverim

The following is a sample letter inviting participants for the b'nai mitzvah program.

DATE

Dear (JFGH Family),

According to Jewish tradition, a boy or girl becomes bar or bat mitzvah at the age of thirteen. (Orthodox Jews give the age of twelve for bat mitzvah.) This is the age at which a Jew is considered to have reached the age of maturity to understand the *mitzvot* (commandments) given to us by God and can distinguish between right and wrong. The bar or bat mitzvah is usually celebrated during the course of a service as the culmination of a period of study.

What is accepted by most as a natural rite of passage has frequently been denied those with disabilities. JFGH, with the cooperation of the Board of Jewish Education of Greater Washington, plans to offer a study program concluding with a b'nai bitzvah (plural form of bar and bat mitzvah) service for our residents who did not have the opportunity to participate in one before. (In recent years as a part of the resurgence of interest in our Jewish heritage and Jewish learning, adults of all ages, particularly women who didn't have a bat mitzvah in their youth, are celebrating this rite.) Our goal is inclusion in the Jewish community as we demonstrate that our residents and the community can mutually benefit from one another.

Preparation for the b'nai mitzvah will include a course of study, a mitzvah project, and participation in a special service in one of the local synagogues. Classes will be held on a weekly basis at one of the group homes for approximately one year.

If your family member is interested in being considered for this special program, please complete the form below. I must know who is interested by_____. The fee of $_____ will cover the course of study and materials. Scholarship assistance may be considered if requested.

L'Shalom,

For more infirmation contact JFGH at 301-984-3839 or www.jfgh.org

CHAPTER 50

SHABBAT IN A BOX FOR JEWS
WITH SPECIAL NEEDS

Council for Jews With Special Needs, Phoenix

Becca Hornstein

Shabbat in a Box was developed to bring the practice of Shabbat rituals into the homes of teens and adults who have disabilities and have not been able to attend religious school, or who live in a Christian or secular "supervised residence." This program enables teens and adults who have not previously celebrated Shabbat to learn prayers, rituals, songs, stories, recipes, etc. to use in their own residences.

DESCRIPTION OF THE PROGRAM

Many older teens and adults who have developmental disabilities such as autism, Down Syndrome, mental retardation, and other cognitive/learning difficulties may not celebrate Shabbat or Jewish holidays because:

- they grew up at a time when a Jewish education was not available to them.
- their parents were too busy meeting the rigorous demands of raising a child with a disability to address Jewish issues.
- they presently live outside their parents' home in a supervised residence that is either Christian or secular.

While this population delights in monthly social programs sponsored by the Jewish community, they may not necessarily carry over the Jewish experience into their homes.

The idea of packaging Shabbat materials is not unusual in religious schools; however, it may not be considered for utilization with the special needs of a teen or adult who has a significant developmental or cognitive disability. Unable to learn in the "usual way," these individuals benefit from a multisensory, hands-on approach to learning.

To address this concern, the Shabbat in a Box project was created. This opportunity brings the beauty of Shabbat into their homes and has been welcomed and appreciated by all involved (parents, teens, adults, and staff).

A staff person visits each teen or adult in his/her residence on three Fridays. The staff person brings along a plastic box that contains the following:

- A book written at an appropriate reading level (sample included)
- A pair of candlesticks and candles

- A *kiddush* cup and a container of juice (wine is not provided, as many of these individuals take medication)
- A *tzedakah* box
- An audiotape of Shabbat prayers and songs
- A head covering for male or female
- A white dinner napkin and fabric paint to make a *hallah* cover (and two rolls)
- A stack of recipes for Shabbat meals

The staff member introduces each of the items with an explanation of how it is used in the celebration of Shabbat. A special Shabbat Book includes explanations of the rituals, objects, prayers, and other Jewish holidays. The blessings are presented in English, Hebrew, and transliteration. To involve the teen or adult in the learning process, the staff member assists him/her in decorating a *hallah* cover. Together they read the book, listen to the tape, and then practice the prayers.

The staff person makes three visits on consecutive Friday afternoons to reinforce the learning experience and encourage weekly use of the Shabbat in a Box materials.

RESULTS ACHIEVED

Parents of the teens and adults who may have stepped back from their Judaism during the stressful years of raising a child with a disability are now involving themselves in Shabbat celebrations. The teens and adults are actively participating in Jewish learning and practice in their homes. They eagerly display their new skills and knowledge to their families, housemates, and staff.

The teens and adults benefited in two ways:

- They have learned about their religion and the celebration of Shabbat in their homes
- They have begun to seek opportunities for more Jewish celebrations.

Truly, this project fulfills the mandate to "educate each child according to his ability," Proverbs 22:6.

The Shabbat in a Box project was a pilot project generously funded by a grant from the Jewish Community Foundation in 1997 and by additional funds donated by Dori and Cookie Shifris. Based on the enthusiasm and success with which the project has been greeted, we hope to put other Jewish holidays in a box and continue the learning process!

For more information, contact: Council for Jews with Special Needs, Inc., Phoenix, Arizona, (602) 277-4243, http://www.cjsn.org

CHAPTER 51

ADULT JEWISH EDUCATION: A MODEL FOR INDIVIDUALS WITH DEVELOPMENTAL DISABILITIES

Elliot Fix

As the adult population in our communities increases in numbers, the traditional youth-oriented focus of Jewish education needs to shift qualitatively to develop options for adults to become fulfilled in the mitzvah of study. As communities develop and implement these options, individuals with developmental disabilities must be included and offered both access and choice in regard to programs and services. In the parlance of diversity it is only recently that Jewish communities have begun to take seriously the rights of people with developmental disabilities to be included in educational programs that will satisfy their need to be cognitively challenged in their spiritual development.

The educational model presented consists of an ongoing course on Jewish Living that is part of a synagogue's adult educational program and the extended, inclusionary activities that enhance the skills and connections so vital to being an involved Jew. The program design was a response to a need to reach out to a growing population of Jewish adults who live in group homes, supervised apartments, or even on their own. Their connection to organized Jewish life ranged from no contact to some synagogue service attendance or participation in community center mass programming that included all levels of disabilities, both passive and interactive in format. Many of these individuals were the only Jewish person in their residence.

The cliché "You don't know what you don't know" applied to the need to create a meaningful adult educational program. Many of the professional and residential staff contacted to solicit Jewish individuals to participate knew little about Judaism and Jewish ethnicity. One woman regularly attended Sunday church services with the other residents; no other option was offered, even though a staff person accompanied her occasionally to Friday night services at a local synagogue. A man who recently lost his father was routinely taken to the cemetery every Saturday morning to visit his father's grave. While well meaning in intent, the religious inappropriateness of this act was difficult for the staff member to comprehend even with the alternative suggestion that this man attend services with a congregation to recite *Kaddish*. Some staff even viewed religious programming as secondary to meeting other scheduled activities such as bowling and movie night.

The themes of self-determination and person-centered planning should be considered when setting up a successful model for adult Jewish education for people with developmental disabilities. The individual is in the driver's seat, expressing his/her interests and preferences. A circle of natural supports is identified and involved in planning: family members, professional and residential staff, synagogue members, and religious leaders. These people are crucial to facilitate and encourage involvement in Jewish life, including adult education. To expect students to attend, a class schedule needs to be planned and set up with the individuals involved and their significant persons. Furthermore, if the goal of the educational enterprise is to develop skills, community connections, and participation, the course curriculum must extend beyond the classroom to support individual choice and partnerships that will enable inclusion in Jewish community life.

Residential staff and professionals are encouraged to receive in-service training on Judaism, its observances, and its practices to enable adequate Jewish life planning. Residents in group homes should be on mailing lists to receive synagogue bulletins and the local Jewish press. Jewish ritual objects, calendars, books, and music should become available as the concrete props to reinforce course content.

Given the groundwork that has been set up with the individual and his/her natural supports, the course itself becomes the focal point of the program from which inclusion and individual choice and observance can occur. A theory of learning laid out by Carl Rogers in his book *Freedom to Learn for the 80's* provides valuable characteristics for developing a dynamic curriculum that is student-centered:

- The affective and cognitive aspects of a person are involved in each learning event.
- A sense of discovery is cultivated.
- The learning "makes a difference" in the behavior and attitudes of the learner.
- The learner determines if the course experience is meeting his/her needs.
- The experiential learning is incorporated into one's total experience.

The Jewish Living course is the primary focus of the adult education program. Incorporating principles of active learning, the weekly schedule of ninety-minute sessions was designed for maximum participation and enjoyment. Potential participants were suggested by various Jewish agency personnel, case managers/service coordinators, and family members. The instructor spoke and met with the individual participants, staff, and families, insuring that regular attendance would be supported. A course fee was charged, but individuals could pay on a scale based on their financial ability.

Activities were developed that would appeal to all of the senses; hence music, food, props, role playing, crafts, special guest appearances, video, and slides were all utilized. The instructor needs to use expertise in applying the technology of teaching through well paced, organized lesson plans. However, it is the art of teaching expressed through an enthusiastic and energetic teaching style that creates the emotional bond between teacher and student. As students enter the room a song is heard from the CD player, creating the mood for the lesson, be it a Hasidic melody or a serious prayer. During one lesson students were given glow-in-the-dark sticks, similar to those at a rock concert, as songs were sung that had been learned. A folk story is acted out by the teacher to illustrate a lesson on *tzedakah* or Jewish continuity. An open discussion is conducted around the concept of preserving memory as a way of introducing the theme of the Passover holiday.

It is age-appropriate experiential learning that has been the most meaningful to the adult population. For example, a Purim lesson involved tasting several varieties of kosher grape juices. Each drink was followed by a cracker to cleanse one's palate. The students were then asked to judge which type they preferred. A professional circus clown also visited the class to explain and demonstrate the art of clowning, as along with a volunteer mitzvah clown from the community who frequently visits hospitals. For Shavuot, a florist assisted each class member in creating a floral centerpiece for the holiday table. A Rosh Hashanah lesson asked the students to judge various ethical scenarios as either "on target" or "missing the mark" behavior; one student, dressed in judicial robes, acted as a mediator. The theme of this lesson also focused on "How to be a Mensch." A Torah treasure hunt had clues hidden around the synagogue; each clue had a Torah fact written on it that also led to the next clue, until the final destination was reached at the Holy Ark/*Aron Kodesh*.

THE FOLLOWING COURSE OUTLINE ILLUSTRATES A SAMPLING OF AN INTRODUCTORY PROGRAM SCHEDULE,

- Overview of Jewish Living: Belief in Action
- Passing Down the Way of Life
- Review of Fall Holidays
- *T'fillah*/Prayers
- Celebrating Life Events: Special Ceremonies
- Birth and Naming
- Bar/Bat Mitzvah
- Jewish Marriage
- Death and Mourning
- Observing Shabbat/Going to Synagogue
- Friday Night Ritual
- Saturday Morning Service
- Saturday Night Havdalah
- Synagogue Geography
- People of the Synagogue: Rabbi, Cantor, Congregants
- Special Event: Shabbat Friday Night Dinner at a Special Location
- Falling in Love with Israel
- Special Friendship
- Getting to Know the Country
- Celebrating Hanukkah
- Getting Ready
- Customs
- Prayers and Songs
- Doing *Mitzvot*: Experimenting with Key Mitzvot
- Daily Life Practices
- Blessings/Prayers
- *Tzedakah*
- *G'milut Hasidim*: Being a Mensch
- Visiting the Sick
- Comforting the Mourners
- Hospitality

Application of the Jewish Living course content is realized through inclusionary activities organized and facilitated by the course instructor outside the classroom. While some agencies may advocate for volunteers to go inside group homes to conduct Jewish activity experiences, the intent of this model is to emphasize activities that would connect students to Jewish community life outside their community residence. These activities include a Shabbat dinner at a group home or with families, a Purim *Seudah* at a local synagogue, a community Hanukkah party, a Jewish music concert, and a community seder.

Too often, programs for people with disabilities are conducted as pre-holiday events. The main feature and goal here is to include the adults in Jewish experiences on the holiday itself. People with disabilities should be able to celebrate holidays and community events simultaneously with others.

A model of adult Jewish education that integrates course content and inclusionary events provides a stimulating and ego-boosting experience for the learner with special needs that has been traditionally neglected in formal Jewish education circles. These adults eagerly await the continuation of the program where they can gain new knowledge and skills and enjoy the beauty of their precious heritage.

PART 13:
DISABILITY AWARENESS/
SENSITIVITY

CHAPTER 52

LET MY HOUSE BE OPEN

United Synagogue of Conservative Judaism
Seaboard Region

Pearl Schainker

SUMMARY OF GOALS

Judaism teaches that we are all created in the image of God and should be treated with dignity and respect, that we are all responsible for each other, and that the community has an obligation to teach all our children as much as they can learn to make it possible for them to live fully as Jews.

We want our children to be aware of the differences among people and to be sensitive to special needs. We want them to ask questions so that they begin to understand disabilities that people have.

We hope to raise future generations that welcome all Jews into synagogues, Jewish schools, and Jewish organizations. In order to accomplish, this we have to eliminate physical barriers that stand in the way. We need access to all facilities by ramps, drinking fountains and bathrooms that can accommodate people in wheelchairs, cooperation between home and school in arranging for Braille Hebrew textbooks before the school year begins, tutoring for children with learning disabilities, interpreters to sign for Jews who are deaf, and so on.

However, what is even more challenging is eliminating the emotional and psychological barriers that exist. Only through understanding disabilities and truly integrating into one's actions the ideals that Judaism expresses about the intrinsic value of every single human being can the community honestly accept all Jews into their midst.

RELATED JEWISH CONCEPTS

We are all created in God's image, and so Judaism teaches us to treat every person with dignity and respect (Genesis 1:27).

God created differences as well as similarities among people. The blessing "Blessed are You, Lord our God, King of the Universe, who makes people different" can help us express fear and embarrassment when we see people who were born with visible differences and can help us deal with those feelings so that we treat all people as people and help make all Jews welcome in the Jewish community.

Jews are part of a community whose members assume responsibility for one another: "All Israel is responsible one for the other" (Shavuot 39a).

All Jews have something that they can contribute to the community and to the world, as expressed in *Pirke Avot* 4:3: "Do not despise any person and do not disparage any object. For there is no one who does not have his/her hour, and there is no object that does not have its place."

We need to provide opportunities for the realization of those contributions and not hinder them in any way. Moreover, it is our responsibility to do whatever is possible to remove or mitigate physical and/or attitudinal obstacles, as we can learn from "Do not curse a person who is deaf and do not put a stumbling block in front of a person who is blind" (Leviticus 19:14).

SIH̱AH I: EXPERIENCING DISABILITIES
GOALS
To increase awareness about people with various disabilities

To experience adapting to several disabilities

To increase sensitivity to the challenges encountered by those with disabilities

PROCEDURE
Participants are divided into pairs. Each pair will have five minutes at each task. At each task the pair should take turns. One member of the pair is disabled; the other is not. Then they switch.

The group leaders circulate around the room raising general questions. For example, what conditions might cause a person to experience the kinds of difficulties you had with a particular activity?

After all participants have completed the tasks, the group comes together for a debriefing and summary.

- How did you feel when you were trying to accomplish one of the tasks?
- If you experienced frustration, do you think people with a particular disability feel similarly or differently?
- You experienced each frustration for only a few minutes. How do you think someone feels who experiences such frustration repeatedly every single day?
- How did the non-disabled partner feel? Did you want to offer help? Did you feel uncomfortable about how to offer help?
- Why should we as Jews be concerned about people with disabilities?

DISABILITY STATIONS: MATERIALS AND DIRECTIONS

Fine Motor Impairment: Loss of sense of touch due to aging or stroke, stiffness in joints due to arthritis, loss of use of one hand due to injury or stroke, fine motor impairment due to birth trauma such as cerebral palsy.

Station A: Table is set up with one pair of heavy socks and straws. Task is to make a Jewish star with straws with hand inside sock. Try it with your left hand if you're right-handed and your right hand if you're left-handed.

Station B: Table is set up with one pair of heavy socks, index cards, and a book. Task is to count index cards and find a particular page in the book.

VISUAL IMPAIRMENT

Station A: Table with one pair of sunglasses smeared with Vaseline, book, and playing cards. Task is to read paragraph in book and identify playing card to sighted partner.

Station B: Table with blindfold. Task is for sighted guide to lead blindfolded partner on a "trust walk." To insure safety, they can move around the room, go out the door, and return. NO STAIRS. The sighted partner should introduce the "blind" partner to another person. Blindfolded partner takes the arm of guide at the elbow. Guide thus walks slightly ahead. Guide should explain where they are heading and identify obstacles.

Questions to ponder: What if you could not see the sunset? The faces of people you love? The glow of Shabbat and Hanukkah candles?

HEARING IMPAIRMENT

Station A: Table with bag of cotton balls and earmuffs. Index cards with a series of directions: Directions state: Please take off your shoes and sit on the floor.

Go to the door. Open it. Go out and return, closing the door behind you.

Please sit in a chair and place your right hand on your left shoulder.

Please stand on your left foot only and raise your right hand.

Task   One partner puts cotton balls in external ear canal and then puts on earmuffs. The other partner reads two of the directions to the hearing-impaired partner. The partners switch roles and read the other two sets of directions until the tasks are completed. The non-disabled partner may raise his or her voice and/or act out the directions.

Station B: Table with a set of directions and finger spelling charts. Task is to communicate with partner without writing or speaking.

Tell your friend to say *Kiddush*

Tell your friend that you like potato latkes.

Ask your friend if his/her sister is getting married.

Tell your friend the name of your favorite movie star.

Questions to ponder: What if you couldn't hear the latest song?

Hear the voices of your friend? Or the shofar?

What could you do?

SIHAH II: PROMOTING DISABILITY AWARENESS—JEWISH COMPONENT

ACTIVITY #1: COOPERATIVE LEARNING ACTIVITY—JIGSAW

Participants will discuss issues that children and teens with various disabilities are likely to face when beginning their Jewish school and/or participation in youth activities and will suggest ways to help in this process.

Divide the participants into groups of four. Groups can sit around a table or push their chairs into a circle. These are the JIGSAW groups.

Within each group each of the four participants is given a letter: A, B, C, D. These letters correspond to the biographies of children with disabilities. The A participant in each JIGSAW group will receive the A biography, and so on. The A participant will read the same bio as the A participant in all the other groups.

Give the participants the bios to read. Since the JIGSAW group has ABCD participants, each group will have four different bios being read by the four different participants in that group. Each participant will read his/her particular bio and then share in one or two sentences what the bio says.

All the As will then come sit together, and so on, when the signal is given. The participants are now in their EXPERT groups.

The EXPERT groups will read their bios together and discuss them. When they go back to their original JIGSAW groups they will report on their bio and answer the question: What problems could this child encounter and how can the situation be made easier for him or her?

At the signal, participants go back to their original JIGSAW groups.

Each participant will share in more detail what was discussed in each EXPERT group.

If time is available, the reporter from each A, B, C, and D EXPERT group summarizes what was discussed in that group.

CLOSING

How we can make our synagogue a place where everyone is welcome? Are these examples only for people with disabilities?

Biographies for Jigsaw Activity

A. DAVID used to drive his teachers crazy. He was constantly talking in class and never wanting to work on his assignments. Finally it was discovered he had dyslexia. He doesn't see the letters and numbers the same way other people do, making it hard for him to learn to read. Now, with special tutoring, his reading and writing skills have improved greatly, and he is performing better in school.

David used to go to Hebrew school, but because he had so many problems there his parents let him quit. Last year he joined a Little League baseball team, and he spends a lot of time practicing. He plays first base but really would like to try pitching. His parents have now enrolled him once again in religious school and have promised the principal that a special tutor will work with David and his teacher to help him with Hebrew.

This will mean that David will sometimes miss his Sunday ballgames when they are scheduled before Hebrew school ends at noon. His tutor has recommended that he also get involved with a youth group so he will have a better opportunity to meet more Jewish kids his age.

What do you think religious school and youth group will be like for David? What can his Hebrew school teacher, youth group advisor, and fellow students do to make it easier and more comfortable for him?

B. ALIZA was in a car accident a few months ago. Her legs were injured, and she will be using a wheelchair for a while. She will need a few operations, and with physical therapy the doctors are optimistic she will be able to walk again.

Aliza is twelve years old and very shy. She is a good student, but she doesn't like to raise her hand in class much. She is more relaxed and comfortable with her friends, but they usually do more talking than she does. She and her friends like to dance and were supposed to perform in the school show on Purim; unfortunately, Aliza won't be able to participate. This is a real disappointment for her, although she is glad to be out of the hospital and back to school, even if it is in a wheelchair.

What problems can Aliza face coming back to school using a wheelchair? What other problems should be considered? What can the teacher, students, and fellow youth groupers do to make it easier for her?

C. When she was a baby SARAH'S parents noticed that she smiled at toys and people when she saw them but didn't react to music, voices, or loud noises (fire engine sirens, loud thunder, etc.). She wasn't able to hear when people were talking and only knew that music was playing because of the vibrations she felt.

Sarah attended a special school where she learned to read lips, sign, and talk, although her speech was not always clear. People would have to ask her nicely to repeat something. Her family is religious, and her parents wanted very much for her to learn about being Jewish. She has had a private Hebrew tutor who taught her at home, so she knows how to read and write and even speak a little Hebrew. She doesn't like working with the tutor and would really prefer being in a class with other students her age.

The principal at the day school thinks that with a little extra help Sarah will be able to attend their school in September when she starts seventh grade.

What do you think the day school will be like for her? What can the teacher and students do to make it easier for her?

The students will be leading a Kabbalat Shabbat service. Do you think Sarah can participate? If so, how can she partake in the service?

D. JOSH is twelve years old. Ever since he was very little his parents and the doctors knew there was something wrong with his eyes. He has had some operations to make sure his eyes don't get any worse. He can see light and dark and some shapes, but if he isn't careful, he could walk into something that isn't in its right place. He can only read printed words if they are very big, and he has a special machine that looks like a little TV that magnifies the letters.

Josh attends a public school where they taught him to read Braille as well as printed letters. He loves school and is an outstanding student. He also loves all kinds of sports. He particularly likes to play baseball with a beeper ball.

Josh and his family very much want him to become bar mitzvah when he is thirteen. They have decided that it is time for him to start Hebrew school, and they will get him special help if he needs it.

What do you think Hebrew school and youth group will be like for Josh? What should the teachers, students, and fellow youth groupers do to make him feel comfortable?

This program was used for a Kadimah Kallah through the Youth Activities Department. For more information, contact www. uscj.org.

CHAPTER 53

JUSTICE, JUSTICE FOR ALL

Bureau of Jewish Education of Los Angeles

Marlynn Dorff, et al.

TEXT: EXODUS 4:10-17

OBJECTIVE

Students will be able to explain that Moshe was a different person because he had a speech impediment, but he was special because he led our people to freedom.

This is the story of the burning bush. God wants Moshe to speak to Pharoah and to the people and then lead them out of Egypt.

Teach this chapter the way you always do, but look for opportunities to bring in ideas that the children have learned from the puppet show and follow-up activities.

SUGGESTIONS

1. One of Moshe's concerns is that he is *Kvad Peh*—i.e., he has difficulty with his speech. (You may want to teach the class the midrash about the choice between the golden crow and hot coals.) People we know who do not speak clearly do so for a whole variety of possible reasons: physical structure of mouth, tongue, etc.; were in an accident; get very nervous; try to talk too fast; have hearing impairment; etc.

    This can be related to the blessing *Meshaneh ha-Briot*, who creates people differently. Moshe was different in the way he spoke, but he was special in many ways.

    It does not really matter how a person came to be the way she/he is; the important question is What do we do now? If a person cannot see well or has a hearing or speech impairment, how is that person going to live his/her life, and how is the rest of the world going to make that person's life easier or more difficult?

2. Why does God get angry at Moshe in verse 14? Does Moshe see his speech problem as a bigger obstacle than God does? What can we learn from this? (Example: Sometimes we make our own obstacles; sometimes we have to try to do something that we are not sure we can do; etc.)

    Have you ever had to speak in front of the class, the school, or another group of people? If so, how did you feel? If you were nervous, what could have made the experience easier for you? (Example: Practicing a lot and being sure of what you have to do; having others help you by being proactive and being supportive; people smiling at you from the audience; etc.)

What kinds of things might have made public speaking or just everyday conversation harder for some people? (lisp, stutter, foreign accent, speak too fast/slow…)

What can we do if someone with a lisp, accent, etc., is talking with us? (Example: pay close attention, not laugh.)

3. [If the children have studied this chapter in the past and you want to have this discussion now, you can ask the children how they feel about speaking in front of a group. Then ask them if they can think of a person in the book of Exodus who was asked to speak in front of others and found this very hard to do.]

Attending a Bar Mitzvah Ceremony

OBJECTIVE: Students will list on chart difficulties that people with various disabilities may encounter in attending a bar mitzvah ceremony and will suggest ways to help.

MATERIALS: copies of chart, pens/pencils

1. Have the class divided into small groups, two or three children working together.

2. Avi is very excited about becoming bar mitzvah and has invited all his family and his best friends to attend. Some of the guests have special needs.

   Tell the students to look at the list of guests, try to think of what their special needs might be in the activity the teacher assigned to you, and list them on the chart.

3. Assign each group of two to three students one activity—e.g., having an *aliyah*—and ask them to fill in that section of the chart for each of the guests.

4. Give the students fifteen or twenty minutes to do this. Bring the class back together and have the children briefly share their conclusions.

Guest	Difficulty	How we can help
1. Getting to the Synagogue		
Shoshana has a visual impairment		
Jon has hearing impairment		
Ben has a development disability		
Aliza has a learning diability		
Grandpa uses a walker		
Sam has CP and uses a wheelchair		
2. Getting Inside		
Shoshana has a visual impairment		
Jon has hearing impairment		
Ben has a development disability		
Aliza has a learning diability		
Grandpa uses a walker		
Sam has CP and uses a wheelchair		
3. Using Siddur or <u>H</u>umash		
Shoshana has a visual impairment		
Jon has hearing impairment		
Ben has a development disability		
Aliza has a learning diability		
Grandpa uses a walker		
Sam has CP and uses a wheelchair		
4. Rabbi and Avi Speak		
Shoshana has a visual impairment		
Jon has hearing impairment		
Ben has a development disability		
Aliza has a learning diability		
Grandpa uses a walker		
Sam has CP and uses a wheelchair		
5. Using the Bathroom		
Shoshana has a visual impairment		

Guest	Difficulty	How we can help
Jon has hearing impairment		
Ben has a development disability		
Aliza has a learning diability		
Grandpa uses a walker		
Sam has CP and uses a wheelchair		

6. Having an Aliyah

Shoshana has a visual impairment		
Jon has hearing impairment		
Ben has a development disability		
Aliza has a learning diability		
Grandpa uses a walker		
Sam has CP and uses a wheelchair		

7. Eat and Socialize at Kiddush

Shoshana has a visual impairment		
Jon has hearing impairment		
Ben has a development disability		
Aliza has a learning diability		
Grandpa uses a walker		
Sam has CP and uses a wheelchair		

4. Rabbi and Avi Speak

Shoshana has a visual impairment		
Jon has hearing impairment		
Ben has a development disability		
Aliza has a learning diability		
Grandpa uses a walker		
Sam has CP and uses a wheelchair		

For more information, contact www.bjela.org.

APPENDICES

APPENDIX A: DISABILITY/ ACCESSIBILITY STATEMENTS

JEWISH RECONSTRUCTIONIST FEDERATION

RECONSTRUCTIONIST VALUES SUPPORTING INCLUSION OF PEOPLE WITH DISABILITIES

- **HUMAN DIGNITY AND INTEGRITY.** Jewish tradition sees human beings as having been created in the "image of God" and, therefore, that each person is to be treated with dignity and respect. In the words of Rabbi Mordecai Kaplan, "All human beings are entitled to experience the dignity of selfhood or personality, the moral character of society and the reality of God."

- **HOLINESS.** The Jewish people have been commanded to "be holy, as God is holy"; to make holiness manifest throughout the world. We understand holiness as that which gives life moral and spiritual significance. One aspect of holiness consists of acts of caring about the people of the world. When we care about those with disabilities, recognizing their abilities and the holiness in them, it enhances the holiness in us.

- **EQUALITY.** The Torah teaches that the entire human race descended from a single person. We understand this to refer to the equality of all people and respect for human differences. Rabbi Kaplan said that "Every individual must be able to feel that the society in which he lives… recognizes him as an end in himself…" He also insisted that people can be said to have equal rights only when these include the right to worship in their community. "By discouraging any honest effort of men to commune with God…we deny them equality of spiritual status." Equality implies not only equal participation, but equal opportunity for leadership of the community.

- **INCLUSIVE COMMUNITY.** One of the basic tenets of Reconstructionism is the importance of community. It is through life in the community that people find support, protection, and companionship. We strive to make our congregations/*havurot* into "caring communities" and to include all who wish to participate in them. We believe in reaching out to those who have been, or have felt, excluded from the community. Caring communities show regard for the concerns of the individual, and individuals should also show regard for the concerns of their community.

- **JEWISH CONTINUITY.** The future growth and enrichment of Jewish life are goals of Reconstructionism. Our approach to Judaism teaches that for Judaism to remain authentic and compelling, it must adapt to the world without abdicating its fundamental values and teaching. We believe that the community's continued health and vitality can only be strengthened by being open to Jews with disabilities, even when that necessitates accommodation to new technology and/or new ideas. This creates possibilities where none previously existed.

- **DEMOCRACY.** The idea that every person should have a voice and a vote on matters affecting his/her life is a fundamental principle of Reconstructionism. Thus, lay members of congregations/*havurot*—including those with disabilities—must have a voice in deciding key issues facing the community—including how to make that community accessible to all who wish to participate in it.

- **PURSUIT OF JUSTICE.** Reconstructionism affirms that the improvement of conditions under which humans live is a central concern. Justice for vulnerable members of a society is a test of that society's values. We, as a people, have been vulnerable many times in our history. Thus, the Jewish people have a special concern for the just and fair treatment of all people.

JEWISH RECONSTRUCTIONIST FEDERATION GOALS OF THE TASK FORCE FOR INCLUSION OF PEOPLE WITH DISABILTIES

The overall goal of the Task Force is to encourage Reconstructionist communities, at the national, regional, and local levels, to be accessible to Jews with physical, sensory, intellectual, and emotional disabilities, their families and life partners, for religious services, social and educational programming, and all aspects of synagogue/*havurah* life.

In order to do this, the specific goals of the Task Force are to create awareness of and educate and sensitize members of the community to:

- The physical or architectural barriers which make it difficult or impossible for people with disabilities to enter or use the facilities with comfort and dignity.
- The barriers to receiving and participating in communication.
- The attitudinal barriers which make people with disabilities feel unwelcome.
- To work with the Reconstructionist community to overcome, as much as possible, physical and communication barriers.
- To create an atmosphere in the Reconstructionist community in which attitudinal barriers no longer exist.

In order to carry out these goals, the Task Force will urge the national Board of Directors of JRF (Jewish Reconstructionist Federation), regional councils, and all JRF affiliated congregations/*havurot* to adopt the following statement of principles:

- In keeping with the principles of Torah and in light of our understanding of Reconstructionist values, we will make every reasonable effort to welcome and actively include people with disabilities in all aspects of our Reconstructionist communities.
- Urge congregations/*havurot* to establish a committee or task force on inclusion which will evaluate the community's needs and the services it is providing.
- Serve as a resource and consultative service for JRF, congregations/*havurot*, the RRC and the RRA as they work toward inclusion.
- Work with the Education Commission on materials, programs, etc. which will enable our schools to better include children with disabilities.
- Work on a movement-wide level to create an atmosphere that is sensitive to and supportive of inclusion of people with disabilities.

ORTHODOX UNION

NATIONAL JEWISH COUNCIL FOR THE DISABLED MISSION STATEMENT

The National Jewish Council for the Disabled (NJCD) is dedicated to addressing the needs of all individuals with disabilities within the Jewish community. NJCD strives to enhance the life opportunities of people with special needs and to insure their participation in the full spectrum of Jewish life.

These goals are addressed through the following activities and services:

- Disseminating knowledge and information
- Advocacy on behalf of those with special needs
- Family counseling
- Sibling support groups
- Family retreats, conferences and workshops
- Conferences and workshops for professionals working with challenged individuals
- Respite care
- Promoting *inclusive* education and activities
- Sensitivity training for youth and adults through schools and synagogues
- Consultation to schools and synagogues on implementation of *Inclusion*

Inclusive social/recreational activities for the developmentally disabled and hearing impaired in chapters through the United States and Canada

Good Sports athletic training and sports activities

Jewish heritage classes providing Jewish education for developmentally disabled and learning disabled youth and young adults

Mainstreamed summer camping and touring experience for the developmentally disabled and hearing impaired

Vocational Resources and Job Placement

The National Jewish Council For the Disabled (NJCD) is composed of four major divisions which include:

Yachad for the developmentally disabled that provides unique social, educational and recreational "mainstreamed" programs for the developmentally disabled.

Our Way that provides both mainstreamed and self-contained educational and recreational activities for the hearing-impaired and deaf.

National Resource Center. A premier clearing-house which provides resource information, referral services, consultation, and direct services to individuals, families, and agencies regarding all kinds of disabilities.

National Inclusion Center. The National Inclusion Center promotes, facilitates, and provides for the inclusion of all children and adults throughout its departments of school and educational services, vocational resources and job placement, and clinical services.

These services which began with the Yachad program in 1983 have transformed the lives of thousands of challenged individuals and their families and has made dramatic changes within the Jewish community of which they are a part.

NATIONAL ORGANIZATION ON DISABILITY, RELIGION AND DISABILITY DIVISION

The National Organization on Disability (N.O.D.) promotes the acceptance and full participation in all aspects of life of American's forty-nine million men, women, and children with physical, sensory, or mental disabilities. Founded in 1982, N.O.D. is the only national disability organization concerned with all disabilities, all age groups, and all disability issues.

The N.O.D. Religion and Disability Program is an interfaith effort urging local congregations, national denominational groups, and seminaries to remove the obstacles to worship that alienate people with disabilities.

"THAT ALL MAY WORSHIP" CONFERENCES

The Religion and Disability Program conducts "That All May Worship" conferences throughout the U.S. These conferences bring together people with disabilities and religious leadership to plan improved access—both physical and spiritual—in houses of worship in their community. There have been over 100 conferences held to date.

2,000 IN THE YEAR 2000—ACCESSIBLE CONGREGATIONS CAMPAIGN

The Accessible Congregations Campaign sought to gain the commitment of 2,000 congregations by December 31, 2000 to include people with all types of disabilities as full and active participants. An Accessible Congregation acknowledges that it has barriers and makes the commitment to removing them and to welcoming people with disabilities into a full life of faith. The theme of the campaign is Access: It Begins in the Heart.

The following materials are available through the program to help religious communities identify and remove architectural, communications, and attitudinal barriers:

That All May Worship assists congregations, denominational groups, and seminaries in welcoming people with disabilities. This handbook is interfaith and concerns people with all types of disabilities. It is filled with common sense advice.

Loving Justice clarifies the relationship between the Americans with Disabilities Act (ADA), other relevant disability laws, and the religious community. It describes both legal and moral mandates.

From Barriers to Bridges fosters dialogue between people with disabilities, their family members, religious leaders, and the greater community. It provides guidance needed to hold a "That All May Worship" Conference and to promote other community-building activities.

For further information:
National Organization on Disability
910 16th Street, NW, Washington, DC 20006
  Phone: (202) 293-5960
     Fax: (202) 203-7999
   TDD: (202) 293-5968
   Web: www.nod.org

UNION FOR REFORM JUDAISM

Department of Lifelong Jewish Learning

PHILOSOPHY AND GOALS FOR SPECIAL NEEDS JEWISH EDUCATION

Our goal is to transform Reform synagogues and their related institutions into environments in which all Jews can experience Judaism. It is a founding belief of *Liheyot* that access reaches far beyond accommodation. We aim to create opportunities, to reach out and embrace those in our community with disabilities.

It is our duty to give every Jewish child a Jewish education.

It is difficult to imagine a Jewish community that does not uphold and even exceed the public laws that entitle a child to an appropriate and financially supported education. We are a community that bases its values and its understanding of God on a sacred text—the Torah. Our people's great prophet and teacher Moses, who led us to freedom in the Promised Land, had a speech impediment.

EVERY CHILD IS AN INDIVIDUAL.

As every child is unique, so is every child with special needs unique. The most beneficial learning will take place when the student's individual needs are the focus of the method of teaching.

THE REFORM COMMUNITY MUST ACCEPT ALL INDIVIDUALS AS EQUALS.

The way the community views a special needs education program is critical to its success. Acceptability is just as crucial as accessibility.

OUR SPECIFIC GOALS:

- To help Jews with special needs realize spiritual fulfillment.
- To make Judaism and Jewish education accessible to all Jews.
- To stimulate and inspire individuals with disabilities to develop their identities as enlightened, involved, and committed Jews.
- To establish a supportive environment in our synagogues that enables a person with special needs to take increased responsibility for his/her participation in synagogue life.
- To establish a national network that focuses on an agenda for individuals with disabilities and their families that deals with issues of Jewish identity, promoting feelings of self-esteem and inclusion.
- To broaden the experience and sensitivity of all our children.

HOW CONGREGATIONS CAN MEET THEIR GOALS

Open the doors to your religious schools and adult education programs, making adaptations and accommodations as needed.

Assess existing programs and evaluate accessibility.

Survey your physical surroundings and evaluate accessibility for people who are mobility disabled, visually or hearing impaired, or developmentally disabled.

Evaluate your policy of inclusion for all Jews, reviewing the attitudes conveyed by your written policies and your unwritten codes of conduct toward individuals who look or act differently from others.

Include people with special needs and parents of children with special needs in the development of new policies and programs that include all Jews.

Al Pi Darco,
According to Their Ways: A Special Needs Educational
Resource Manual.
URJ, 2000

www.urj.org

UNITED SYNAGOGUE OF CONSERVATIVE JUDAISM

Special Education Committee of the Commission on Jewish Education

MISSION STATEMENT

The mission of the Special Education Committee of the United Synagogue of Conservative Judaism is to encourage our affiliates to welcome and provide for the access and inclusion of all special populations within our Conservative synagogues, day schools, and synagogue schools. The committee is to be proactive in creating an awareness within the Conservative Jewish community of the availability of resources and programs.

TO WELCOME AND INCLUDE PEOPLE WITH SPECIAL NEEDS INTO OUR CONSERVATIVE INSTITUTIONS: A CAMPAIGN STRATEGY

The following guidelines have been compiled to assist congregations to welcome and include people with special needs.

IN OUR SCHOOLS

Our Congregation recognizes that every Jewish child is entitled to an appropriate Jewish education. To meet this goal, our school is committed to working with any family with a child requiring a specialized Jewish educational program.

Those families requesting a specialized program will meet with the Special Education Committee, which is comprised of the Rabbi, Educational Director, and Educational Vice-President, along with a Special Education consultant from our community, such as the Bureau of Jewish Education or Jewish Family Service. After careful evaluation (including observation, informal review of the student, input from parents, review of the public school I.E.P., if one exists) the committee will determine an appropriate individualized program of instruction for such a student.

Program modifications will be made on a case-by-case basis because learning needs may vary for each student in this category. Special provisions for these students may include, but are not limited to, remedial Hebrew/Judaic assistance, partial mainstreaming in a regular class, private tutoring, referral to another community-based special education program, or other appropriate measures determined by the committee.

The student's progress will be carefully reviewed and monitored by the Educational Director/Consultant and parent at least three times a year. Any adjustments will be made to the prescribed program as necessary.

The confidentiality of such students and their families will be protected at all times.

Special financial arrangements will be determined on a case-by-case basis to meet the individual student's religious school educational goals.

IN OUR CONGREGATIONS

For congregational advocacy and endeavor:

Establish a synagogue committee on accessibility (or special needs) to be made up of
> One-third "consumers" or family members
> One-third professionals in related fields
> One-third synagogue leadership with no "vested interest."

Prepare and disseminate mailings to membership

- Information
- Requests for input
- Revise membership application form to include questions on special needs
- Highlight accommodations already available
- Conduct individual outreach to known members with special needs
- Endow and name a special needs fund (perhaps considering a separate fund for the religious school)
- Arrange for speakers and handout materials for rabbinic groups, United Synagogue of Conservative Judaism regions, Women's League, youth directors, educators, synagogue administrators, Men's Clubs, and Sisterhoods

> United Synagogue of Conservative Judaism
> Committee on Accessibility
> 1991
> www.uscj.org

MEASURES FOR PERSONS WITH DISABILITIES

WHEREAS, by reason of the fact that a significant segment of the North American Jewish populace are persons with disabilities who have special needs regarding the ability to worship and participate in synagogue life which must be met by both public and private sectors; and

WHEREAS, many of the constituent congregations of the UNITED SYNAGOGUE OF CONSERVATIVE JUDAISM have not yet made adequate provisions for satisfying the needs of persons with disabilities; and

WHEREAS, the UNITED SYNAGOGUE OF CONSERVATIVE JUDAISM clearly has a moral, ethical, and practical obligation to encourage and support greater participation by persons with disabilities in the religious life of the community;

NOW, THEREFORE, BE IT RESOLVED that the UNITED SYNAGOGUE OF CONSERVATIVE JUDAISM provide guidance to its constituent congregations for the implementation of measures to make synagogues accessible to persons with disabilities; and

BE IT FURTHER RESOLVED that all member congregations of the UNITED SYNAGOGUE OF CONSERVATIVE JUDAISM are urged to take immediate steps to make all synagogues physically and programmatically more open and accessible to persons with disabilities, said steps including, but not limited to, the purchase of large-print prayerbooks for the sight impaired, infrared sound systems for the hearing impaired, and ramps for entry to the premises and to the bimah for those in wheelchairs; and

BE IT FURTHER RESOLVED that all segments of the congregations on the adult and youth levels become involved in the process of welcoming persons with disabilities into our synagogue; and

BE IT FURTHER RESOLVED that from this date forward all future conventions and public programs of the UNITED SYNAGOGUE OF CONSERVATIVE JUDAISM to be held within facilities that provide adequate accessibility to persons with disabilities.

APPENDIX B:
GLOSSARY OF SPECIAL NEEDS TERMINOLOGY

GLOSSARY OF SPECIAL NEEDS TERMINOLOGY

Ability grouping—The grouping of students based on their achievement in an area of study.

Accessible—Easy to approach, enter, operate, participate in, and/or use safely and with dignity by a person with a disability (i.e., site, facility, work environment, service or program).

Accommodations—Techniques and materials that allow individuals with disabilities to complete school or work tasks with greater ease and effectiveness. Examples include spellcheckers, tape recorders, and expanded time for completing assignments.

Adaptations—Special techniques or equipment that enable an individual with special needs to participate in an activity.

Adaptive behavior—An individual's social competence and ability to cope with the demands of the environment.

Adaptive equipment—Physical devices designed or modified to support the independence and participation of a person with special needs (communication board, computer, wheelchair).

Adaptive physical education—A specially designed program of developmental activities, games, sports, and rhythms suited to the interests, capacities, and limitations of pupils with disabling conditions who may not be able to safely or successfully engage in unrestricted activities of the regular physical education program.

Advocacy—A general term describing an individual, group, or agency working to bring to public attention their views/proposals in order to effect positive change.

Advocate—An individual, either parent or professional, who represents or speaks on behalf of another person's interests (i.e., establishing or improving services for exceptional children).

American with Disabilities Act (ADA) (Public Law 101-336)—A law that took effect in 1992 that defines "disability" as a substantially limiting physical or mental impairment that affects basic life activities such as hearing, seeing, speaking, walking, caring for oneself, learning, or working. The law prohibits discrimination by employers, by "public accommodations" (any facility open to the general public), and by state and local public agencies that provide such services as transportation.

American Sign Language (ASL)—A method of communication using hand signs. Each hand sign represents a word or concept that is expressed with several spoken words. For words that do not have a "sign," fingerspelling is used.

Animal aides—The use of animals who have been taught to help individuals with disabilities increase their mobility and independence and/or maximize their ability to communicate effectively.

Annual goals—Yearly activities or achievements to be completed or attained by the student with disabilities as documented on the Individualized Education Plan.

Annual review—An annual report/meeting to assess status of a person at risk or who has disabilities. The review will update the person's health status, needs, eligibility for services, current functioning level, family involvement, rights/legal status, involvement with service providers, assessment of progress toward meeting a goal, and discussion of any new implementation.

Aphasia—The impaired ability to express oneself and/or to understand spoken or written language, usually caused by damage to brain cells rather than a deficit in speech or hearing organs.

Apnea—A pause in breathing that lasts twenty seconds or longer.

Apraxia—A loss of the ability to perform voluntary, purposeful movements due to damage to the brain (although there is no actual paralysis). The brain is unable to make the transfer between the idea of movement and an actual physical response. (Examples: inability to perform movement of a command, repeat words correctly, or demonstrate understanding of the use of an object.)

Aquatic therapy—Rehabilitation done in a heated pool of water by a licensed physical therapist, physical therapy assistant, and athletic trainers trained in this procedure. This therapy can increase circulation, strength and endurance, range of motion, balance and coordination, and muscle tone. It can also protect joints during exercise, reduce stress, and decrease swelling.

Architectural barriers—Building design that limits usage by persons who are mobility impaired.

Articulation disorder—A speech disorder in which speech sounds are omitted or produced incorrectly. This disorder may be caused by a structural defect such as cleft lip or cleft palate, hearing loss, weakness or lack of coordination of the oral musculature, or language delay.

Assistive listening devices—Devices other than hearing aids, such as telephone amplifiers, voice amplifiers, personal FM systems, inductive loop systems, or infrared theater or television headsets, which enable people who have hearing impairments to make use of their residual hearing.

Assistive technology—Any item, piece of equipment, or product system either acquired off the shelf, modified, or customized that is used to increase, maintain, or improve functional capabilities of individuals with disabilities at home, work, and school. Examples include communication devices, computer adaptations, and tape recorders.

Asthma—A chronic respiratory disorder characterized by coughing, wheezing, and difficult breathing due to bronchospasm (abnormal contraction of the bronchi resulting in temporarily narrowed airways.) Asthmatic attacks may be caused by infection, inhaling allergens or irritating airborne substances, or exercise.

Ataxia—Difficulty with coordinating muscles in voluntary movement that may be caused by damage to the brain or spinal cord.

At risk—Usually refers to infants or children with a high potential for experiencing future medical or learning difficulties.

Atrophy—Wasting away or decrease in size of a cell, tissue, organ, or part of the body caused by lack of nourishment, inactivity, or loss of nerve supply.

Attention/concentration—The ability to focus on a given task or set of stimuli for an appropriate period of time.

Attention Deficit Disorder (ADD)—A group of symptoms believed to be caused by slight abnormalities in the brain. These symptoms include a developmentally inappropriate lack of ability to attend (i.e., difficulty in listening to and following directions) and possible impulsivity, distractibility, and clumsiness. Hyperactivity is not a feature.

Attention Deficit Hyperactivity Disorder (ADHD)—A group of symptoms believed to be caused by slight abnormalities in the brain. These symptoms include a developmentally inappropriate lack of ability to attend (i.e., difficulty in listening to and following directions), impulsivity, distractibility, clumsiness, and hyperactivity.

Audiogram—Graphic representation of an individual's hearing thresholds plotted by pitch (frequency) and loudness (intensity).

Auditory impairment—Hearing loss resulting from problems in any part of the ear or of the hearing center of the brain. Refers to a decrease in the range of perception of loudness and/or pitch.

Auditory training—Teaching individuals with hearing impairments to encourage full use of their residual hearing in order to facilitate development of receptive and expressive language skills with a focus on appropriate inflection patterns, rhythm, and rate of speech. The emphasis on this approach is on hearing speech rather than speech reading.

Augmentative or alternative communication—Use of various forms of communication other than speaking such as sign language, "yes, no" signals, gestures, picture board, and computerized speech systems to compensate (either temporarily or permanently) for expressive communication disorders.

Autism—A pervasive developmental disorder associated with social-communication problems that usually emerges before a child is three.

Auxiliary aids/services—Devices and services that accommodate a functional limitation of a person with a communication disability. This term includes qualified interpreters and communication devices for persons who are deaf or hard of hearing; qualified readers, taped texts, Braille or other devices for persons with visual impairments; adaptive equipment for persons with other communication disabilities.

Behavior assessment—Gathering (through direct observation and by teacher report) and analyzing information about a person's behaviors. The information can then be used to plan strategies to help change unwanted behaviors.

Behavior modification—Technique used to change behavior by applying principles of reinforcement learning.

Behavior specialist—Professional who assists teachers and parents in understanding effective techniques of behavior management.

Bilateral hearing impairment—Hearing impairment in both ears.

Blindness—A lack or loss of vision due to damage to the organs of vision or to the vision centers of the brain. A person is considered legally blind if he or she has corrected visual acuity of 20/200 (can best see at 20 feet what ordinarily be seen at 200 feet) or less in the better eye, or a visual field of no more than 20 degrees in the better eye.

Braille—A system that uses raised dots to represent numerals and letters of the alphabet that can be identified by the fingers.

Brain imaging techniques—Recently developed noninvasive procedures that study the activity of the living brain. This includes computerized axial tomography (CAT) and magnetic resonance imaging (MRI).

Brain injury—The physical damage to brain tissue or structure that occurs before, during, or after birth. When caused by an accident, the damage may be call traumatic brain injury (TBI).

Centers for Independent Living—Programs that offer a wide variety of independent living services for individuals with disabilities with the objective of helping them to function more independently in family and community settings and to secure and maintain appropriate employment.

Cerebral palsy—a functional disorder caused by damage to the brain during pregnancy or delivery or shortly after birth. The causes can include illness during pregnancy, premature delivery, or lack of oxygen supply to the baby. It is characterized by an inability to fully control motor function. Depending on which part of the brain has been damaged and the degree of involvement of the central nervous system, one or more of the following may occur: spasms, tonal problems, involuntary movement, disturbance in gait and mobility, seizures, abnormal sensation and perception, impairment of sight, hearing, or speech, and mental retardation.

Child Find—Program mandated by federal law to identify children birth through age twenty-one for developmental disabilities/delays.

Chronic illness—Illness of long duration or frequent recurrence (asthma, muscular dystropy, multiple sclerosis).

Cleft lip—A birth defect that occurs when the upper lip doesn't fuse together, leaving one or more vertical openings that may extend up to the nose. Cleft lips may be caused by genetic or environmental factors.

Cleft palate—A birth defect characterized by a split or opening in the roof of the mouth resulting from failure of the parts of the roof of the mouth to join together during pregnancy. Cleft palates may be caused by genetic or environmental factors.

Closed captioning—Allows individuals who are deaf or have limited hearing to view television and understand what is being said. The words spoken on the television are written across the bottom of the screen so the person can follow the dialogue and action of the program.

Cochlear implants—A device to treat severe sensorineural hearing impairment in which one or more electrodes are surgically implanted in the inner ear to electronically stimulate any undamaged inner ear nerves.

Collaboration—A program model in which the special education teacher demonstrates for or team-teaches with the general classroom teacher to help a student with disabilities be successful in a regular classroom.

College Board testing for learning-disabled students—Students who are learning disabled can arrange in advance to take College Board admission tests under special conditions such as extended time, separate test rooms, a reader, or a person to whom answers may be dictated and recorded.

Communication aid—Nonverbal form of communication such as gesture, sign language, communication boards, and electronic devices (e.g., computers and voice synthesizers).

Communication board/book—A board or book with pictures that a person with a disability can point to for communicating his/her needs.

Communication disorder—A disorder in one or more of the processes of speech, hearing, or language that interferes with the ability to speak, understand, or use language.

Communication notebook—Notebook sent to and from school between parent and student (typically a student with special needs or a young child) in order to maintain continuous communication on student's daily class activities and progress.

Companion animals—Animals who have been taught to provide personal assistance, companionship, and/or physical protection for people who have limited mobility.

Comprehension—Understanding of spoken, written, or gestural communication.

Conduct disorder—A disorder of childhood and adolescence that is characterized by a repetitive and persistent pattern of conduct in which either the basic rights of others or major age-appropriate societal norms or rules are violated.

Conductive hearing loss—Hearing loss caused by obstruction in the transmission of sound to the cochlea due to obstruction in the ear canal or the middle ear, which may result from otitis media or perforated eardrum.

Congenital—Referring to a condition present a birth that may be hereditary (a genetic disorder), may be the result of a problem during pregnancy (such as a maternal infection), or may occur due to injury to the fetus prior to or at the time of birth.

Consultant teacher—A supportive service for students with disabilities in which the services are provided by a specialist in the classroom.

Cystic fibrosis—An inherited disease that affects the pancreas, respiratory system, and sweat glands, which usually begins in infancy and is characterized by chronic respiratory infection, pancreatic insufficiency, and heat intolerance. There is no cure at this time, but antibiotics have prolonged the life of many individuals.

Deaf-blindness—A dual sensory impairment that is a combination of both visual and hearing impairments. An individual with deaf-blindness can experience severe communication, educational, and other developmental problems.

Deafness—A total or partial inability to hear.

Decibel—Unit used to measure the intensity or loudness of sound.

Discrete trial—a behavior teaching strategy, most often used with children with autism, characterized by direct, one-to-one instruction of specific behaviors such as saying a certain word or making eye contact. Training consists of intense repeated practice of specific, discrete trials consisting of a stimulus (e.g., "What is this?" and presentation of an object), a response (e.g., the child says "ball"), and a consequence (reinforcer, or if the response is incorrect, a negative consequence).

Depression—A biologically based psychological disorder marked by sadness, inactivity, difficulty with thinking and concentration, significant increase or decrease in appetite and sleep, feelings of dejection and hopelessness, and sometimes suicidal thoughts or actions.

Developmental age—Age at which a person is functioning (demonstrating specific abilities) based on assessment of the person's skills and comparison of those skills to the age at which they are considered typical.

Developmental assessment—A screening and diagnostic tool that measures cognitive/intellectual functioning, language and communication skills, independent living abilities, social and emotional development, and perceptual/motor functioning in order to identify people who show developmental delays, determine the nature and extent of the problem, and recommend a course of action.

Developmental delay—Refers to a child who is assessed to be delayed by 25% of his/her chronological age in one or more developmental areas: cognitive, physical, speech/language, social/emotional, and self-help. The term is commonly used in preschool and early intervention services and programs.

Developmental disability (DD)—Long-lasting disability that is the result of a mental and/or physical impairment, occurring before age twenty-two and likely to continue indefinitely. A person will have limitations in three or more areas: self-care, self-direction, economic self-sufficiency, independent living, learning, receptive and expressive language, and mobility, resulting in the need for specialized services.

Diabetes—A condition in which the pancreas produces insufficient or no insulin, a hormone that controls sugar levels in the blood. Without insulin the blood cannot absorb sugar into cells for energy and into liver and fat cells for storage. Principal symptoms are elevated blood sugar, sugar in the urine, excessive urine production, and increased food intake.

Direct instruction—An instructional approach that emphasizes the use of carefully sequenced steps that include demonstration, modeling, guided practice, and independent application.

Disability—A substantially limiting physical or metal impairment that affects basic life activities such as hearing, seeing, speaking, walking, caring for oneself, learning, or working.

Distractibility—Difficulty in maintaining attention.

Down syndrome—A condition caused by a chromosomal abnormality (trisomy 21) resulting in 47 instead of the usual 46 chromosomes. Characteristics may include poor muscle tone, slanting eyes, hyperflexibility, short, broad hands with a single crease across the palm, and broad feet with short toes. There is a wide variation in mental abilities, behavior, and developmental progress in individuals with Down syndrome.

Due process—The legal steps and processes outlined in the Individuals with Disabilities Education Act that protect the rights of students with disabilities.

Dwarfism—The condition of being abnormally small in stature, which may be hereditary or a result of endocrine dysfunction, deficiency diseases, renal insufficiency, or diseases of the skeleton.

Dysautonomia—A rare hereditary disease involving the autonomic nervous system that is characterized by mental retardation, lack of motor coordination, vomiting, frequent infections, and convulsions. It is seen almost exclusively in people of the Jewish faith.

Dyscalculia—Difficulty in understanding and using symbols or functions needed for success in mathematics.

Dysfluency—Hesitations, repetitions, omissions, or extra sounds in speech patterns.

Dysgraphia—Difficulty in producing handwriting that is legible and written at an age-appropriate speed.

Dyslexia—Difficulty in understanding or using one or more areas of language, including listening, speaking, reading, writing, and spelling.

Dysnomia—Difficulty in remembering names or recalling words needed for oral or written language.

Dyspraxia—Difficulty in performing drawing, writing, buttoning, and other tasks requiring fine motor skill, or in sequencing the necessary movements.

Early intervention—Recognition, diagnosis, and treatment of developmental delay or potential delay in children from birth to five years of age. Based on the theory that the younger the child, and the less well established the delay, the greater the likelihood that the delay can be minimized or eliminated. Interventions may include infant stimulation, therapy (i.e., occupational, physical, speech, etc.), family support and education, specialized health services, and coordination of services.

Echolalia—The constant repeating or parroting of words or phrases that have been said by others, often using the same intonation. It is normal for young children to echo another's speech to develop their own speech and language skills.

Education for All Handicapped Children Act (Public Law 94-142)—A law enacted by the 94th Congress in 1975 assuring that all children ages five to twenty-one with disabling conditions have available to them a free appropriate public education (FAPE) with special education and related services to meet their individual needs.

Education of the Handicapped Amendments of 1986 (Public Law 99-457)—A federal law passed in 1986 that amends and becomes part of Public Law 94-142 mandating that states provide preschool education for children with special needs beginning at age three. Part C of the law focuses on the identification and services to at-risk and developmentally delayed infants and toddlers.

Electronic communication aids—Computers, voice synthesizers, printers, and other electrical devices that enable an individual with speech difficulties to communicate.

Encopresis—Chronic soiling problem.

Enuresis—Chronic wetting problem.

Epilepsy—Condition characterized by recurrent seizures caused by abnormal electrical activity in the brain. Seizures can occur due to damage to the brain by infection, injury, birth trauma, tumor, stroke, drug intoxication, or chemical imbalance. Epilepsy is usually treated with antipileptic drugs to control seizures.

Exceptional children—Term coined at the 1930 White House Conference on Handicapped Individuals to refer to all children who are different from typically developing children.

Expressive language—Ability to communicate thoughts and feelings by gesture, sign language, verbalization, or written word.

Eye–hand coordination—Ability to use visual input to assist in manipulation of an object with the hands. Example: seeing a desired object and successfully reaching toward and grasping it.

Failure to thrive—Condition of undersized infants whose bodies do not receive or cannot utilize the nurturance necessary for proper growth and development.

Fetal Alcohol Syndrome—Group of symptoms exhibited by a child resulting from the mother's consumption of alcohol during pregnancy. Symptoms may include differing levels of mental retardation, low birth weight, small size, and underdevelopment of the upper lip.

Fine motor—Developmental area involving skills that require coordination of the small muscles of the body, including the hands and face. Examples: tracking an object with the eyes, smiling, stringing beads, grasping small items, holding a pencil, etc.

Fingerspelling—A form of sign language in which the fingers are used to represent letters of the alphabet. The letters (signs) are strung together to spell words.

Fluency disorder—Speech disorder such as stuttering that affects the rate and rhythm of speech production; characterized by frequent repetitions, prolongations, and blocking of speech sounds.

Fragile X Syndrome—A chromosonal abnormality associated with mental retardation. Individuals with this disorder often have distinctive physical features such as a long face and large, prominent ears. Along with having some degree of mental retardation, people with Fragile X Syndrome may also experience speech and language delays and exhibit behaviors associated with autism.

Free Appropriate Public Education (FAPE)—According to the Individuals with Disabilities Education Act (IDEA), FAPE is defined as special education and related services that 1) are provided at public school expense, under public supervision and direction, and without charge to the family; 2) meet the standards of the state educational agency; 3) include preschool, elementary, and secondary public school education in the state involved; and 4) are provided in conformity with the child's individualized education plan (IEP).

Full inclusion—Including children, teens, and adults with disabilities with their typically developing peers.

Functional—Having the ability to carry out a purposeful activity.

Functional behavior assessment—Evaluating the degree to which individuals' behaviors "work" to get them what they want and need.

Functional skills—Description of skills that are useful in everyday living.

Gait—the manner or style of walking or running.

Gastrostomy tube (G-tube)—Feeding tube inserted directly into the stomach through a surgically created opening in the abdominal wall. Used when individual is unable to receive adequate nutrition orally or if the esophagus is blocked; may be temporary or permanent.

Genetic disorder—Illness or condition that is inherited or caused by defective genetic material. A genetic evaluation can be done to determine the presence of a genetic disorder. Evaluation may include family health history (covering several generations), family's racial and ethnic background, parents' ages, mother's health during pregnancy, labor and delivery, and baby's health as a newborn.

Giftedness—Evidence of superior or unusual ability in areas such as intellect, creativity, artistic talent, physical agility, or leadership.

Glaucoma—Condition in which abnormally high pressure of the fluid in the eye causes damage.

Goals—General statements in a student's individualized educational plan (IEP) that state the desired outcomes for the student with special needs.

Gross motor—Developmental area that involves skills that require the coordination of large muscle groups in the arms, legs, and trunk. Examples: walking, jumping, throwing a ball, etc.

Group home—A housing option for individuals with developmental disabilities that allows them to live in residences within the community in a family-type setting supervised by live-in professional(s) and/or volunteer staff.

Handicapped parking—Access to designated parking spaces based on the use of registration plates for persons who are disabled.

Hand over hand—Physically guiding a person through the movement involved in a fine-motor task.

Head banging—A form of self-stimulation in which a person repetitively bangs his head on the floor or another surface.

Health impairment—Any type of chronic illness that affects how a person lives his or her life.

Hearing aid—Device for amplifying sound only; does not make the sound clearer. For a person to benefit from hearing aids, he must have some degree of hearing.

Hearing impairment—Any level of hearing loss, such as being hard of hearing or deaf.

Heart defect—Any structural abnormality of the heart that obstructs or creates abnormal blood flow through the heart.

Hemophilia—Hereditary blood disease that is characterized by greatly prolonged coagulation time. The blood fails to clot, and abnormal bleeding occurs.

Hepatitis—Inflammation of the liver of viral or toxic origin that usually is manifest by jaundice and, in some instances, liver enlargement. Fever and other systemic disorders are usually present.

Hepatitis B—Viral infection that attacks and causes inflammation of the liver. Can be transmitted either sexually or by exchange of blood.

High risk infants/children—Infants and children who are at risk for developmental delays or other problems because of congenital abnormalities; perinatal medical complications including anoxia, low birth weight, prematurity, respiratory distress syndrome, or metabolic or central nervous system disorders; medical problems that have their onset following birth; or environmental factors.

Human Immunodeficiency Virus (HIV)—The virus that causes AIDS, which damages the immune system and attacks the brain, increasing susceptibility to infection. HIV is transmitted when the virus enters the bloodstream. A person may carry the virus for several years before any symptoms of AIDS become apparent.

Hydrocephalus—A birth defect, sometimes referred to as "water on the brain," that can develop before birth in association with an infection, at the time of birth as a result of a brain hemorrhage caused by birth trauma, or later in childhood as a complication of meningitis. Hydrocephalus can be treated by the surgical insertion of a shunt (tube from the brain to another part of the body) that permits the fluid to be drained to a location where it can be absorbed into the bloodstream. Unless relieved quickly, brain damage may result and mental retardation, blindness, seizures, and motor impairment may occur.

Hyperactivity—A group of behavioral characteristics such as aggressiveness, constant activity, impulsiveness, and distractibility. Actual behaviors displayed may include fidgeting, inability to remain seated or still, excessive talking, and difficulty with playing/working quietly.

Hypertonic—Description of increased tone (stiffness) in the muscles.

Hypotonic—Description of decreased tone (floppiness) in the muscles characterized by excessive range of motion of the joints and little muscle resistance when parts of the body are being moved.

Impulsivity—Behavior characterized by acting on impulse or without thought or conscious judgment.

Inclusion—Education of students with disabilities in their neighborhood school, involving them in as many classes and extracurricular activities as possible, with special services and support provided.

Independent living—The belief that individuals with disabilities have the same rights as others in society; thus, services provided to the public should be accessible to persons with disabilities, and systems of support should be made available to help them lead more independent lives within their community.

Individualized Education Plan (IEP)—Mandated by Public Law 94-142, all students with a disability, ages three to twenty-one, classified for special education are required to have an IEP. The IEP is agreed upon by school staff, parents, and other relevant professionals and outlines type of program, related services (speech, physical therapy, etc.), and educational goals for the student. The IEP is reviewed on an annual basis or upon parental request.

Individualized Family Service Plan (IFSP)—Similar to an IEP, the IFSP describes services and support for children who are at risk or have developmental disabilities, birth to age three, and their families. It is developed and implemented by the child's parents and a multidisciplinary early intervention team overseen by a service coordinator.

Individualized Transition Plan (ITP)—Part of the Individualized Education Plan that identifies goals and activities to help a student with disabilities transition from the school environment to adult life.

Individuals with Disabilities Education Act (IDEA) (PL 101-476)—Federal law passed in 1991 that reauthorizes and amends the Education for All Handicapped Children Act (PL 94-142), ensuring that all children with disabilities, ages three to twenty-one, have available to them a free appropriate public education including an individually designed program (IEP). Part C of the law focuses on services to infants and toddlers who are at risk or have developmental disabilities.

Integration—Including individuals with disabilities in classes and activities with "typical" peers.

Intelligence—The ability to understand and apply knowledge.

Interdisciplinary approach—A method of evaluation and individual program planning in which two or more specialists (educator, psychologist, social worker, speech therapist, etc.) participate as a team in identifying the needs of the individual with a disability and developing a plan to meet the identified needs.

Intervention—Preventive, remedial, compensatory, or survival services provided to an individual with a disability.

Itinerant—Professional who provides specialized services in a variety of settings, traveling from site to site, frequently using a consultation model of service delivery.

Kinesthetic learner—A person who learns through movement and touch.

Language delay/disorder—An inability or difficulty with expressing, understanding, or processing language (oral or written information).

Learned helplessness—A tendency to be a passive learner who depends on others for decisions and guidance.

Learning disability—A significant discrepancy between ability and achievement in students with average or above average potential intelligence. This disorder occurs in one or more of the basic psychological processes involved in understanding or using spoken or written language. The disorder may manifest itself in an impaired ability to listen, think, talk, read, write, spell, or perform mathematical calculations. It includes perceptual disabilities, brain injury, minimal brain dysfunction, attention deficit disorders, dyslexia, developmental aphasia, etc. It does not include learning problems due primarily to visual, hearing, or motor disabilities, emotional disturbance, or environmental disadvantage.

Learning modalities—Approaches to assessment and instruction stressing the auditory, visual, or tactile avenues for learning that are dependent upon the individual.

Learning style—The way in which a person best acquires knowledge or processes information, emphasizing variations in temperament, attitude, and preferred manner of tackling a task.

Least restrictive environment (LRE)—The educational setting that permits a child with disabilities to derive the most educational benefit by participating in a regular classroom environment to the maximum extent appropriate.

Long-term memory—The ability to remember information from a while back (e.g., facts learned last month).

Mainstreaming—Integration of students with disabilities into settings available to children without disabilities for academic and/or social reasons. Supplemental resource services may be needed and provided.

Manual alphabet—An alphabet of hand signs that are used to spell out words. Each letter of the alphabet has its own sign. See **Fingerspelling**.

Manual communication—Use of manual signs as opposed to speech production (oral communication); a commonly preferred manual sign system is ASL, American Sign Language.

Medicaid—Jointly funded federal-state health insurance program for low income, elderly, and disabled individuals. Each state establishes its own eligibility standards; determines the type, amount, duration, and scope of services; sets the rate of payment for services; and administers its own program.

Medicare—United States' largest health insurance program, which provides insurance to people who are sixty-five years of age or older, individuals with disabilities, and people with permanent kidney failure. Two parts of Medicare: Hospital Insurance (Part A), covering inpatient hospital services, skilled nursing facilities, home health services, and hospice care; and Medical Insurance (Part B), which helps to pay for the cost of physicians, outpatient hospital services, medical equipment, and other health services and supplies.

Meningitis—An inflammation of the membranes of the spinal cord or brain that is usually caused by either a viral or a bacterial infection.

Mental illness—Any illness or disorder that has significant psychological or behavioral manifestations, is associated with painful or distressing symptoms, and impairs an individual's level of functioning in certain areas of life. Therapy and medication are the most common forms of treatment.

Mental retardation—A mental disability that limits the intellectual capacity of an individual. A person is considered to have mental retardation if he or she has an IQ below 70, the condition is present before age eighteen, and limitations exist in two or more adaptive skill areas (communication, self-care, home living, social skills, leisure, health and safety, self-direction, functional academics, and employment).

Mobility—The ability to move about in one's environment.

Mobility aid—Adaptive equipment that offers support, makes movement easier, or provides balance and stability. Examples: scooter, wheelchairs, and walkers.

Mobility specialist—Individual trained to teach children and adults with developmental disabilities or visual impairments how to move about independently.

Model—To provide an example for imitation, such as pronouncing a word to be repeated.

Motor control—The ability to voluntarily engage muscles in purposeful movements.

Motor planning—The ability to organize sensory information in order to plan and carry out the sequence of movements required to complete a task (example: climbing stairs).

Multidisciplinary team—Professionals who each represent areas of expertise useful in planning and implementing the educational, therapeutic, and/or medical treatment program of the person with special needs. Team members may include physician, psychologist, physical and/or occupational therapist, speech pathologist, social worker, educator, and family members.

Multiple disabilities—A combination of two or more disabilities that produce significant learning, motor, developmental, and/or behavioral problems.

Multiple sclerosis (MS)—A chronic, slowly progressive disease of the central nervous system in which the myelin sheath that covers the nerves hardens, resulting in difficulties with muscle control, involuntary movements of the eyeballs, speech problems, and tremors.

Muscle tone—A muscle's level of tension and resistance while at rest; abnormal muscle tone may be either hypertonic or hypotonic.

Muscular dystrophy (MD)—A group of inherited, degenerative muscle disorders characterized by progressive weakness. There are several forms, each of which varies in age of onset, pattern of inheritance, speed of disease progression, and level of resulting disability.

Music therapy—Programs that use music and music-related activities to help individuals who have mental, social, or emotional problems maintain/develop mental functioning, to facilitate social and emotional growth, to promote communication, to develop constructive use of leisure time, and to improve/maintain motor and perceptual skills.

Nonverbal communication—Information expressed through gestures, facial expressions, and sign language. The spoken word is not used.

Objectives—Behaviors and skills the student will learn en route to the achievement of long-term goals. Objectives are specific and measurable.

Obsessive-compulsive disorder (OCD)—A condition marked by persistent and recurring thoughts (obsessions) reflecting exaggerated anxiety or fears that have no basis in reality. Sufferers feel compelled to perform a ritual or routine to help relieve anxiety caused by their obsessions, realizing the ritual or compulsion makes no sense, yet they feel powerless to stop.

Occupational therapy—Therapeutic treatment aimed at helping individuals who are injured, ill, or disabled develop and improve self-help skills and adaptive behavior. The focus is on fine-motor skills, including coordinating the small muscles of the hands, developing eye-hand coordination, and working on sensory integration skills (tolerating touch, sounds, movement, and sights).

One-to-one aide—Adult assigned to shadow a specific student and provide specific kinds of support, such as physical support and mobility assistance, behavioral management, or medical assistance when needed.

Oppositional Defiant Disorder (ODD)—A pattern of negative, hostile, and defiant behavior up to, but not including, violating the basic rights of others (conduct disorder). Features of ODD include the following: persistent argumentative behavior with authority, frequent loss of temper, frequent use of obscene language, anger, resentment, and irritability. The person can exhibit "normal" behavior during an examination, often misleading the unsuspecting professional, and sees nothing wrong with his/her behavior, justifying it as retaliation to self-perceived or real injustices.

Oral communication—Approach preferred by some individuals with hearing impairments that focuses on auditory training and learning to understand and produce speech.

Oral speech aids—Devices such as amplifiers, clarifiers, and atificial larynges that make an individual's speech more intelligible.

Orthotic—A custom-made orthopedic appliance (such as a brace, splint, or cast) used to promote proper body alignment, to stabilize joints, or to passively stretch muscle or other soft tissue.

Otitis media—Chronic ear infection affecting hearing.

Parallel play—Play in which a child plays beside other children, rather than actually interacting with them, typical of the 18–24-month-old.

Paraplegia—Paralysis of the legs and lower part of the body involving loss of sensation and movement, caused by injury or disease in the low spinal cord or brain disorder.

Paraprofessional—Term used to describe a trained aide/assistant who assists a professional person (e.g., teacher aide).

Parent-professional partnership—The teaming of parents and professionals (teachers, therapists, physicians, etc.) to work together to facilitate the development of individuals with special needs.

Parkinson's Disease—A chronic nervous disease that is characterized by a fine, slowly spreading tumor, muscular weakness and rigidity, and a peculiar gait.

Part B of IDEA—Addresses special education services, ages three through twenty-one.

Part C of IDEA—Addresses early intervention services, ages birth to three (formerly Part H).

Pediatric AIDS—Disease of infants/children contracted from the mother during pregnancy. Afflicted children's immune systems are impaired, leaving them vulnerable to illnesses that would not otherwise occur.

People First Language (PFL)—Use of language in referring to people with disabilities that speaks of the person first and then the disability. Example: "a child with autism" rather than "an autistic child." This language emphasizes abilities rather than limitations.

Perception—Ability to process information that comes through the senses.

Perseveration—Continuous repetition of a behavior or response after it is no longer appropriate.

Physical therapy/therapist (PT)—A professional trained to help an individual strengthen, improve, or develop their gross motor skills. This includes coordinating the large muscles of the body for sitting, walking, crawling, etc. in order to move as independently as possible. A key function of a physical therapist is to recommend adaptive equipment (braces, walkers, wheelchairs) and help an individual with physical challenges learn to use it.

Play therapy—A diagnosis and treatment method used in child psychotherapy to help children resolve emotional or psychological conflicts. The therapist observes the child playing with a selected group of toys.

Portfolio—Carefully selected collection of a child's work that is used to document growth and development.

Positive behavior support—Behavioral technique that focuses on prevention of challenging behaviors and providing support for more positive behavior. The function of the challenging behavior is identified, and a replacement behavior is taught that is more acceptable. Antecedents of problem behaviors as clues to the possible "triggers" or causes of the behavior are identified, and attempts are made to modify and eliminate them.

Positive reinforcement—A stimulus or event, occurring after a behavior has been exhibited, that increases the possibility of repetition of that behavior in the future.

Prader-Willi Syndrome—A rare, incurable, and sometimes fatal disease that is characterized by short stature; lack of muscle tone, size and strength; underdeveloped or small genitals; an insatiable appetite that can lead to obesity if untreated; and mental retardation in most individuals.

Problem-solving—Ability to consider probable factors that can influence the outcome of each of the various solutions to a problem and to be able to select the most advantageous solution. Individuals with deficits in this skill may become "immobilized" when faced with a problem. Unable to think of possible solutions, they may respond by doing nothing.

Proprioception—Body's awareness of its position in space.

Pull-out services—A model of delivering specialized support services such as physical or speech therapy in which the student is removed from the classroom and taken to a resource room.

Psychologist—A professional specializing in counseling and/or testing to identify personality and cognitive functioning. The psychologist may provide individual or group psychotherapy for cognitive retraining, management of behavior, and development of coping skills by the client and members of the family.

Quadriplegia—A condition due to an illness or an injury to the spinal cord, generally at the level of the fifth or sixth vertebra, that is characterized by paralysis in all four extremities and, usually, the trunk. Can also affect the head and face.

Range of motion—The normal extent of movement of any body joint.

Receptive language—Ability to understand what is being expressed, including verbal and nonverbal communication (e.g., sign language).

Recreation therapist—Individual responsible for developing a program to assist persons with disabilities to plan and manage leisure activities, schedule specific activities, and coordinate the program with existing community resources.

Rehabilitation Act of 1973—Empowers individuals with disabilities to maximize employment, economic self-sufficiency, independence, and inclusion and integration into society through comprehensive and coordinated programs of vocational rehabilitation; independent living centers and services; research; training; demonstration projects; and the guarantee of equal opportunity.

Reinforcement—Behavior modification technique used to increase the likelihood of a desired response or behavior. Positive reinforcement is accomplished by immediately rewarding a desirable behavior. Negative reinforcement is ignoring the behavior.

Related services—Services provided to students with disabilities to assist in their ability to learn and function in the least restrictive environment. Such services may include in-school counseling, speech and language services, and math remediation.

Remediation—An educational program designed to teach students to overcome a deficit or disability through education and training.

Respite—Skilled caregiving service provided for the parent, caregiver, or guardian of a disabled or seriously ill person, allowing time away from home for several hours or overnight to rest or attend to other needs.

Response to Intervention (RTI)—Multi-tiered approach to early identification ad support of students with learning and behavioral needs. Struggling learners are provided with interventions at increasing levels of intensity (closely-monitored).

Rigidity—Extremely high muscle tone in any position, combined with very limited movement.

Savant—An individual who is unusually knowledgeable about one particular subject but is lacking in other areas of cognitive skill.

Seizure—Involuntary movement or changes in consciousness or behavior brought on by abnormal burst of electrical activity in the brain.

Self-contained class/program—A special classroom/program for students with disabilities.

Self-help—Skills that enable a person to care for his own needs (e.g., feeding, bathing, and dressing him or herself).

Self-stimulation—Abnormal behaviors, (e.g., head banging, watching fingers wiggle, rocking side to side) that interfere with the person's ability to "sit still," pay attention, or participate in a meaningful activity. Self-stimulatory behavior (aka "stimming") may occur if a person cannot readily participate with people and objects in his or her environment.

Sensory impairment—Problem with receiving information through one or more of the senses (hearing, vision, touch, etc.)

Sensory integration (SI)—The ability of the central nervous system to receive, process, and learn from sensations (such as touch, movement, sight, sound, smell, and the pull of gravity) to develop skills.

Sensory Integrative Disorder (SID)—Difficulty receiving and processing perceptions (tactile, proprioceptive, and vestibular) that are needed to orient and use the body in space. Problems may occur with tactile sensitivity, coordination of body movements, adaptation to the position of the body in space, and/or difficulty in muscle planning.

Sensory overload—Condition that occurs when one or more of the senses is overstimulated beyond the tolerance level, resulting in the individual becoming overactive, unable to attend to a task, or withdrawing. This may occur as a result of too much noise, light, or movement.

Sensorineural hearing loss—Hearing loss resulting from damage to the cochlea in the inner ear or to the auditory nerve, which interferes with the transmission of neural impulses to the brain.

Service coordinator—An interdisciplinary team member responsible for integrating services and keeping the family informed and involved.

Shaken Baby Syndrome—A group of symptoms that, occurring together, characterizes injury sustained by the infant who has been shaken (not necessarily with much force). The infant will have bleeding in the brain and in the retinas of the eyes, likely resulting in both mental and motor damage and often death.

Shunting—Process for implanting a tube (shunt) into the brain to allow proper circulation and drainage of fluids within the skull.

Short-term memory—Ability to remember something from one minute to the next (e.g., directions the teacher just presented).

Sign language—One method for communicating in which hand signs are used to express thoughts and feelings. American Sign Language (ASL) and Signed English are examples of forms of sign language.

Simian crease—A single transverse crease in the palm of one or both hands (instead of the typical two creases on the palm).

Spasticity—An involuntary increase in muscle tone (tension) that occurs following injury to the brain or spinal cord, causing the muscles to resist being moved.

Spatial orientation—Knowledge of where one is in relationship to his or her surroundings.

Special needs—The needs of a person who requires special services to assist with the acquisition of skills in one or more developmental areas: cognition, communication (language), gross and fine motor, social, and self-help (adaptive).

Speech impairments—Disorders that impair an individual's ability to verbally communicate. This could include the following: inability to speak, inability to maintain a flow or rhythm of speech (e.g., dysfluency or stuttering), or the inability to pronounce certain sounds. These impairments can be caused by hearing loss, neurological disorders, mental retardation, or physical impairments such as cleft palate.

Spina bifida—A birth defect in which part of the spinal column (one or more vertaebrae) fails to close completely, exposing the meninges (membranes covering the spinal cord) or the meninges and the spinal cord. The severity of damage depends on the degree and placement of the exposure and can range from no apparent damage to paralysis below the level of the protrusion and severe brain damage.

Strabismus—Eye muscle imbalance problems correctable with eyeglasses.

Stuttering—Speech disorder in which there is a repeated hesitation and delay in uttering words or in which sounds are unusually prolonged.

Sudden Infant Death Syndrome (SIDS)—The unexpected and sudden death of an infant who had appeared to be healthy. Also known as crib death, SIDS occurs during sleep and is the most common cause of death in children between one month and one year of age. Peak incidence occurs between two and four months. The cause of SIDS is still unknown.

Syndrome—A grouping of related physical characteristics.

Tactile defensiveness—Being overly sensitive to touch, evidenced by withdrawing, screaming, or striking when touched.

Task analysis—Breaking a task into a sequence of steps to determine which components of a task the student can already perform and which need to be trained. A task analysis suggests the order in which steps should be taught.

Tay-Sachs—An inherited disorder caused by the absence of a vital enzyme called hexosaminidase (hex-A), which results in the destruction of the nervous system. An infant with Tay-Sachs develops normally for the first few months, then deterioration causing mental and physical disabilities begins.

Teachable moments—Points in time, perhaps associated with critical periods, when a child is highly motivated and better able to acquire a particular skill.

Telecommunications Devices for the Deaf (TDD)—Technological devices that enable persons with hearing and/or speech impairments to communicate over standard telephone lines. To operate successfully, both the transmitting and receiving parties must have compatible TDDs in which the users type messages by phone instead of voicing them. Messages are received on a display screen at the receiving end and/or by a printer that records the conversation on paper.

Temperament—The individual's psychological makeup or personality traits.

Tongue thrust—Strong involuntary (reflexive) protrusion of the tongue. Tongue thrust can interfere with eating and create dental problems.

Total communication—A method of communication using a combination of the following: facial expression, gesture, sign language, fingerspelling, lip reading, speech, writing, and augmentative communication devices.

Tourettes Syndrome—A genetic, neurological disorder characterized by repetitious, involuntary body movements and uncontrollable vocal sounds. Usually detected before age eighteen, it most commonly affects males.

Traumatic brain injury (TBI)—Damage to living brain tissue caused by an external, mechanical force usually characterized by a period of altered consciousness (amnesia or coma) that can be very brief (minutes) or last for months/indefinitely. The specific disabling condition(s) may be orthopedic, visual, aural, neurologic, perceptive/cognitive, or mental/emotional in nature.

Unilateral hearing impairment—Hearing impairment in only one ear.

Ventilator—A mechanical device used to provide assisted breathing for a person who cannot breathe on his own. The ventilator pumps humidified air (with a measured amount of oxygen) into the lungs via an endotracheal tube or tracheostomy tube. The elasticity of the lungs allows the air to be expelled.

Visual impairments—Impairments of sight that cannot be corrected by glasses or contact lenses. This includes individuals with low vision as well as people who are legally blind.

Visual learner—Person who learns by what he or she sees, as compared to what he or she hears. Example: watching a demonstration of a task rather than listening to an explanation of how it is done.

Vocational rehabilitation—Programs designed to assist individuals with disabilities to enter or reenter gainful employment.

Voice synthesizer—Computer that can produce spoken words; type of assistive technology often used by individuals with significant communication disabilities.

APPENDIX C: OVERVIEW OF EXCEPTIONALITIES

LEARNING DISABILITIES

(National Dissemination Center for Children with Disabilities)

WHAT IS A LEARNING DISABILITY?

A learning disability is a neurologically based disorder that can interfere with a person's ability to store, process, or produce information. According to the Individuals with Disabilities Act, these individuals are of at least average intelligence (many are far above average), and their academic problems are not caused by an emotional disturbance, by social or cultural conditions, or by a primary visual, hearing, or motor disability. Instead, the reason for their learning problems seems to be that their brains are "wired" in a way slightly different from the average person's. About 20 percent of children with learning disabilities also may have attention deficit disorder (ADD) or attention deficit hyperactivity disorder (ADHD).

INCIDENCE

Many different estimates of the number of individuals with learning disabilities have appeared in the literature ranging from 1% to 30% of the general population. The U.S. Department of Education (1999) reported that slightly less than 5% of all school-aged children received special education services for learning disabilities. Differences in estimates perhaps reflect variations in the definition.

CHARACTERISTICS

Learning disabilities are characterized by a significant difference in the individual's achievement in some areas, as compared to his or her overall intelligence.

LEARNING DISABILITIES MAY OCCUR IN THE FOLLOWING ACADEMIC AREAS:

Spoken language: delays, disorders, or discrepancies in listening and speaking

Written language: difficulties with reading, writing, and spelling

Arithmetic: difficulty in performing arithmetic functions or in comprehending basic concepts

Reasoning: difficulty in organizing and integrating thoughts

Organization skills: difficulty in organizing all facets of learning

TYPES OF LEARNING DISABILITIES

Four stages of information processing used in learning:

Input—process of recording in the brain information that comes from the senses.

Integration—process of interpreting this information.

Memory—storage for later retrieval.

Output of information through language or motor (muscular) activity.

Learning disabilities can be classified by their effects at one or more of these stages. Each student has individual strengths and weaknesses at each stage.

INPUT

The first major type of problem at the input stage is a **visual perception disability**.

Some students have difficulty in recognizing the position and shape of what they see. Letters may be reversed or rotated; for example, the letters d, b, p, q, and g might be confused.

The child might also have difficulty distinguishing a significant form from its background. People with this disability often have reading problems. They may jump over words, read the same line twice, or skip lines.

Other students have poor depth perception or poor distance judgement. They might bump into things, fall over chairs, or knock over drinks.

The other major input disability is in **auditory perception**.

Students may have difficulty understanding because they do not distinguish subtle differences in sounds. They confuse words and phrases that sound alike—for example, "blue" with "blow" or "ball" with "bell."

Some children find it hard to pick out an auditory figure from its background; they may not respond to the sound of a parent's or teacher's voice, and it may seem that they are not listening or paying attention.

Others process sound slowly and therefore cannot keep up with the flow of conversation inside or outside the classroom. Suppose a parent says, "It's getting late. Go upstairs, wash your face, and get into your pajamas. Then come back down for a snack." A child with this disability might hear only the first part and stay upstairs.

INTEGRATION

Integration disabilities take several forms, corresponding to the three stages of sequencing, abstraction, and organization.

A student with a **sequencing** disability might recount a story by starting in the middle, going to the beginning, and then proceeding to the end. The child might also reverse the order of letters in words, seeing "dog" and reading "god." Such children are often unable to use single units of a memorized sequence correctly. If asked what comes after Wednesday, they have to start counting from Sunday to get the answer. In using a dictionary they must start with "A" each time.

The second type of integration disability involves **abstraction**. Students with this problem have difficulty in inferring meaning. They may read a story but not be able to generalize from it. They may confuse different meanings of the same word used in different ways. They find it difficult to understand jokes, puns, or idioms.

Once recorded, sequenced, and understood, information must be organized—integrated into a constant flow and related to what has previously been learned. Students with an **organization** disability find it difficult to make bits of information cohere into concepts. They may learn a series of facts without being able to answer general questions that require the use of these facts. Their lives in and outside of the classroom reflect this disorganization.

MEMORY

Disabilities also develop at the third stage of information processing, memory. **Short-term memory** retains information briefly while we attend to it or concentrate upon it. For example, most of us can retain the ten digits of a long-distance telephone number long enough to dial, but we forget it if we are interrupted. When information is repeated often enough, it enters **long-term memory**, where it is stored and can be retrieved later. Most memory disabilities affect short-term memory only; students with these disabilities need many more repetitions than usual to retain information.

OUTPUT

At the fourth stage, output, there are both language and motor disabilities. Language disabilities almost always involve what is called "demand language" rather than spontaneous language. Spontaneous language occurs when we initiate speaking—select the subject, organize our thoughts, and find the correct words before opening our mouths. Demand language occurs when someone else creates the circumstances in which communication is required. A question is asked, and we must simultaneously organize our thoughts, find the right words, and answer. A child with a language disability may speak normally when initiating conversation but respond hesitantly in demand situations—pause, ask for the question to be repeated, give a confused answer, or fail to find the right words.

Motor disabilities are of two types: poor coordination of large muscle groups, which is called **gross motor** disability, and poor coordination of small muscle groups, which is called **fine motor** disability. Gross motor disabilities make children clumsy. They stumble, fall, and bump into things; they may have difficulty in running, climbing, riding a bicycle, buttoning shirts, or tying shoelaces. The most common type of fine motor disability is difficulty in coordinating the muscles needed for writing. Children with this problem write slowly, and their handwriting is often unreadable. They may also make spelling, grammar, and punctuation errors.

EDUCATIONAL IMPLICATIONS

Because learning disabilities can be manifested in a variety of behavior patterns, a team approach is important for educating a student with a learning disability.

The following are general strategies that have been effective with some students who have learning disabilities:

Capitalize on the student's strengths.

Provide high structure and clear expectations.

Use short sentences and a simple vocabulary.

Provide opportunities for success in a supportive atmosphere to help build self-esteem.

Allow flexibility in classroom procedures (e.g., allowing the use of tape recorders for note-taking and test-taking when students have trouble with written language).

Make use of self-correcting materials, which provide immediate feedback without embarrassment.

Use computers for drill and practice and teaching word processing.

Provide positive reinforcement of appropriate social skills at school and home.

Recognize that students with learning disabilities can greatly benefit from the gift of time to grow and mature.

ORGANIZATIONS

Council for Learning Disabilities (CLD)
P.O. Box 40303, Overland Park, Kansas 66204
(913) 492-8755

Division for Learning Disabilities Council for Exceptional Children
1110 North Glebe Road, Suite 300, Arlington, VA 22201- 5704
(703) 620-3660

International Dyslexia Association (formerly the Orton Dyslexia Society)
Chester Building, Suite 382, 8600 LaSalle Road, Baltimore, Maryland 21286-2044
(800) 222-3123 (toll free)

Learning Disabilities Association of America (LDA)
4156 Library Road, Pittsburgh, PA 15234
(412) 341-1515

National Center for Learning Disabilities (NCLD)
381 Park Avenue South, Suite 1401, New York, NY 10016
(888) 575-7373

ATTENTION DEFICIT HYPERACTIVITY DISORDER

Shana R. Erenberg

"If she would just pay attention, she would do so much better." "He can't sit still for a minute!" How many times have you, as a teacher, uttered these words? Most teachers have experienced students who have difficulty focusing and maintaining attention in class. While the causes of inattentiveness and restlessness can be multifaceted, it is important to understand and recognize the symptoms of Attention Deficit Hyperactivity Disorder (ADHD).

DEFINITION

Attention Deficit Hyperactivity Disorder is a neurobiological condition that affects 3–5% of school-age children. ADHD affects both males and females; however, boys tend to be diagnosed with the disorder more readily than girls. ADHD is characterized by difficulties with focusing and sustaining attention, impulsivity, and in some cases, hyperactivity. Until recently it was thought that children with ADHD outgrew the condition as they became teenagers, as the symptoms of hyperactivity tended to decrease with age. Current research, however, indicates that ADHD is a lifelong condition with implications for adults with regard to employment, life skills, and social interactions. Proper identification and early intervention are crucial to avoid the serious consequences of ADHD, which include academic failure, and anxiety, social problems, conduct disorder, substance abuse, and job failure.

The DSM IV identifies three subtypes of Attention Deficit Hyperactivity Disorder: attention deficit that is predominantly inattentive, with minimal or no signs of hyperactivity; attention deficit that is predominantly hyperactive and impulsive; and ADHD combined type, in which individuals manifest symptoms of inattentiveness, hyperactivity, and impulsivity. Diagnostic criteria indicate that symptoms of ADHD arise by age seven unless associated with some type of brain injury later in life. The presence of symptoms for six months or more and the exclusion of other causes of inattentiveness, such as mood disorders, cognitive impairment, or pervasive developmental delay, are included in the diagnostic profile. While differential diagnosis is indicated in determining the presence of ADHD, it is important to note that the disorder can co-occur with other disabilities such as depression, anxiety, behavior and conduct disorders, tics or Tourette's syndrome, or learning disabilities. National Institutes of Mental Health research indicates that two thirds of all children with ADHD have a least one other coexisting condition. The presence of another condition increases the complexity of associated academic and behavioral problems.

CHARACTERISTICS

What do children (and adults) with ADHD look like in the classroom and at home? Students with Attention Deficit Disorder without hyperactivity have difficulty arousing, focusing, sustaining, and shifting attention. They often fail to pay close attention to details and tend to make careless mistakes in their work. These students may frequently appear to be daydreaming and do not seem to be listening in class. They tend to avoid tasks that require sustained mental effort, even when the task is well within their ability level. Individuals with ADHD often have difficulty with organization and tend to lose materials and assignments. They are forgetful, easily distracted, and may struggle to follow through on instructions. They need frequent repetition of directions, hands-on examples, and visual cues and reminders. Individuals with ADHD tend to do better with one-on-one intervention. Paradoxically, individuals with ADHD may have periods of long attention spans, particularly for stimulating activities such as video games.

Individuals with an Attention Deficit Disorder that is predominantly hyperactive and impulsive are always on the go. They have a high energy level and difficulty remaining seated. These students may be bouncy and tend to fidget with hands or feet or squirm in their chair. They may be constantly touching things, seemingly unaware of appropriate boundaries or restrictions regarding others' property. Individuals with this type of ADHD may run about or climb excessively. Symptoms of impulsivity include a low tolerance for frustration and a tendency to give up easily. Impulsive individuals manifest a high level of risk-taking behaviors and thus may be more accident-prone. These students do not seem to understand the consequences of their actions or cause-and-effect relationships. They may talk excessively, interrupt others, and blurt out answers (often inaccurate) before questions have been completed. These individuals may have difficulty waiting or taking turns and can be excitable or explosive. These behaviors often impact social relationships, making it difficult for children with ADHD to make and maintain meaningful friendships. Individuals with the combined ADHD subtype meet both sets of inattention and hyperactive/impulsive criteria.

Children with ADHD often display developmental and emotional delays that make them appear less mature and responsible than their peers. In addition, those with ADHD present a complex challenge due to the increased academic and social demands they face. Teens with ADHD may be more susceptible to peer pressure, particularly if they are impulsive and have difficulty understanding consequences. They may be more inclined to self-medicate, using drugs or alcohol. ADHD complicates the issues adolescents typically encounter, including identity and independence, sexuality and social concerns, self-esteem and self-confidence, and learning to make appropriate choices.

DIAGNOSIS

Diagnosing ADHD is a multifaceted and multidisciplinary process. Differential diagnosis based on DSM-IV criteria is crucial, as there are many conditions that produce similar symptomology. There is no single test to diagnose ADHD; thus a comprehensive evaluation is necessary to establish a diagnosis. The evaluation should include a physical exam; rating scale assessments of attention and behavior completed by parents and teachers; an analysis of the learning environment; an assessment of cognitive and academic skills, social and emotional functioning, and developmental levels; as well as hearing and vision exams. A careful history should be taken from the parents, teachers, and, when appropriate, the child.

Individuals must meet six of nine diagnostic criteria as indicated in the DSM-IV. Symptoms must be more frequent or severe than in other children the same age and must be present in two or more settings, such as home, school, work, or social settings. In adults the symptoms must affect the ability to function in daily life and persist from childhood. Symptoms must be present for at least six months.

The causes of ADHD are not well understood. Research indicates that the disorder is neuro-biological in nature and not the result of "poor parenting". Inheritance may play a factor in the disorder. Current studies are investigating neurochemical relationships and imbalances, neuro-structural anomalies, and genetic roots of ADHD.

TREATMENT

It is important to correctly identify and treat ADHD as early as possible to minimize the impact of the disorder on academic achievement, self-esteem, behavioral repercussions, and social interactions. Treatment plans for ADHD must be multifaceted and may include a combination of medical, educational, behavioral, and psychological interventions. Research has shown that a combination of approaches in a treatment plan is more effective than a given single intervention. Education and counseling for parents and family members of individuals with ADHD is also beneficial. ADHD is a disorder that affects the child in all situations, not just school. Therefore, it is important for parents to learn strategies that will provide consistency and structure for the child with ADHD.

Psychostimulant medications are most frequently used to treat the symptoms of ADHD. Seventy to eighty percent of individuals with ADHD respond favorably to the medications, with increased attention and concentration as well as decreased activity levels and impulsivity. The use of medication requires a period of adjustment with regard to dosage and frequency. Medications such as Ritalin are effective immediately, with a reduction in symptoms noted thirty minutes after a dose is taken. Other medications such as Adderall or Concerta require an additional time for the full effect to be achieved. Strattera, a relatively new, non-stimulant medication, also requires additional time to be fully effective. Parents may find that there is a period of experimentation before the proper medication and dose are determined. For some children medication will not be effective and may exacerbate symptoms. In these instances it is important to re-examine the diagnosis of ADHD and determine if other conditions are causing the inattentiveness, distractibility, hyperactivity, and/or impulsivity. Other conditions that mimic ADHD include sensory integration deficits, ocular motor problems, anxiety, depression, and learning disabilities.

While psychostimulant medications work effectively in the majority of cases, they do have potentially harmful side effects. Insomnia and loss of appetite are the most frequently reported side effects. Individuals may also experience nausea, headaches, and dry mouth. Children who take Ritalin or other short-acting forms of medications may experience peaks and valleys in their attentiveness and behavior. A particular problem may arise for children on medication who attend after-school programs. The effects of the medication may have worn off by that time, and the parents may be reluctant to give a dose later in the day due to subsequent problems with sleeplessness. In these instances children may do better with a time-released version of the medication.

Many parents, teachers, and physicians are concerned about the over-prescribing of Ritalin and other ADHD medications. The following statistics illustrate the basis for such apprehension:

- About six million children, roughly one in eight children, take Ritalin, Adderall, Concerta, or other ADHD medications.

- Since 1991 prescriptions for ADHD medications have increased fivefold.

- In that same time period Ritalin use for the symptoms of ADHD increased 700 percent.

- ADHD medications prescriptions for children ages 2 to 4 increased almost 300% between 1991 and 1995.

Effective treatment plans must include an appropriate behavior management component and classroom accommodations. Consistency, structure, and predictable routines are fundamental aspects of any plan. Individuals with ADHD need a proactive rather than punitive approach to dealing with learning and behavior, as well as positive reinforcement. They need to learn effective problem-solving, communication, and self-advocacy skills. Children, especially teenagers, should be actively involved as respected members of the school planning and treatment teams. Classroom accommodations may include minimizing distractions in the classroom, preferential seating, visual schedules, assistance with organization and planning, goal setting, and breaking long-term tasks into manageable segments. Students with ADHD need to develop a repertoire of study skill and time management strategies.

SUGGESTIONS FOR THE SUPPLEMENTARY SCHOOL SETTING

Students with ADHD face unique challenges in the supplementary school setting. First, if the student is taking medication, it may not be as effective in the late afternoon when he or she is in class. Some parents do not give their child medication on weekends, making it difficult for the student to focus and concentrate in a religious school setting. In either case it is important to communicate with parents regarding the behavioral symptoms noted in class and the implications of those behaviors for the child's ability to learn in that setting. Perhaps modifications to the medication schedule can be made. Be as specific as possible in this communication, detailing the behaviors observed but remaining positive about the child. Clearly convey to the parents that you are on the same side. Understand that parents of children with ADHD (as well as parents of children with any special needs) want an environment where their child can be "just a regular kid". For many, the religious school is the setting where normalcy is desired most. Brainstorm with the parents to develop strategies that will help the child perform well in class and verbally reaffirm your commitment to the child's success. Keep the lines of communication with parents open; a team approach to dealing with ADHD will be most effective.

Another challenge to teachers in supplementary schools is the length of time the children are in class and the frequency of those classes. Individuals with ADHD need structure, consistency, and predictable routines that may be difficult to implement in classes that meet for two hours once or twice each week. Nevertheless, it is crucial for the success of the child with ADHD that these sessions are as familiar and routine as possible. Advance notice should be given to the child (and the parents) if there are going to be changes in the schedule. Work with the student to develop a plan for dealing with unexpected changes or activities.

The following tips are effective for children with ADHD but will also work for the majority of students in your class. Remember: Best practices in special education are, in actuality, just best practices to insure the success of all learners.

TIPS FOR THE TEACHER

- Learn about ADHD. The greater your understanding of the disorder, the more effective your interventions will be.
- Maintain regular communication with parents.
- Consult with other professionals in your school, or with the individuals who work with the child in his or her regular school placement.
- Protect the child's self-esteem. In doing so, you also protect his Jewish self-esteem.
- Have clear and consistent rules and expectations. Teach the rules as routines in the class.
- Repeat directions and check for understanding. Use visual cues and schedules.
- Make adaptations in assignments and give extended time when needed.
- Use cooperative learning groups that allow each child to demonstrate his/her multiple intelligences.

DIFFERENTIATED INSTRUCTION

- Understand that one size does not fit all.
- Develop an understanding of learning styles and special needs.
- Conduct a task analysis. Identify the skills necessary for successful completion of the task.
- Incorporate metacognitive strategies into instruction. Teach *how* to approach the task as well as the content.
- Address executive functioning skills—organization, planning, time and assignment management

MODIFY THE PRESENTATION OF MATERIAL

- Break assignments into shorter segments.
- Use concrete materials to introduce abstract concepts
- Relate information to student's experiences.
- Reduce the number of concepts covered at one time.
- Provide an overview of the lesson "why and what" before beginning.
- Monitor the level of language used to communicate concepts.
- Monitor the rate at which the information is presented.
- Schedule short, frequent conferences to check for comprehension.
- Provide consistent review of lessons before introducing new information.

MODIFY THE ENVIRONMENT

- Consider students' needs and strengths in relation to the classroom environment.
- Use proximity seating.
- Use study carrels.
- Reduce distractions.
- Provide organizational support or books and materials.
- Use checklists and visual schedules.
- Reduce clutter.

MODIFY TIME DEMANDS

- Increase the amount of time given to complete assignments and tests.
- Use contracts.
- Reduce the amount of work or length of tests.
- Teach time management skills.
- Space work periods with breaks based on student's needs.
- Alternate demanding tasks with simpler activities.
- Alternate quiet and active times.
- Give a specific task to perform within a specified time.

LINKS

Attention Deficit Disorder Help Center
ADD Resources
CHADD: Children and Adults with Attention Deficit Hyperactivity Disorder
National Institutes of Mental Health

AUTISM SPECTRUM DISORDER/ PERVASIVE DEVELOPMENTAL DISORDER

National Dissemination Center for Children with Disabilities

INTRODUCTION

The term Pervasive Developmental Disorders (PDD) was first used in the 1980s to describe a class of disorders that has the following characteristics in common: impairments in social interaction, imaginative activity, verbal and nonverbal communication skills, and a limited number of interests and activities that tend to be repetitive.

In the latest revision (1994) of *Diagnostic and Statistical Manual of Mental Disorders* (DSM-IV), the manual used by physicians and mental health professionals as a guide to diagnosing disorders, five disorders are identified under the category of Pervasive Developmental Disorders:

(1) Autistic Disorder

   (2) Rett's Disorder

   (3) Childhood Disintegrative Disorder

   (4) Asperger's Disorder

   (5) Pervasive Developmental Disorder Not Otherwise Specified, or PDDNOS

All of the disorders that fall under the category of PDD share, to some extent, similar characteristics. To understand how the disorders differ and how they are alike, it's useful to look first at the definition of the general category of PDD and its specific disorders.

DEFINITION OF THE PERVASIVE DEVELOPMENTAL DISORDER (PDD) AND ITS FIVE SPECIFIC DISORDERS

All types of PDD are neurological disorders that are usually evident by age three. In general, children who have a type of PDD have difficulty in talking, playing with other children, and relating to others, including their family.

According to the definition set forth in the DSM-IV (American Psychiatric Association, 1994), Pervasive Developmental Disorders are characterized by severe and pervasive impairment in several areas of development:

- social interaction skills,
- communication skills
- the presence of stereotyped behavior, interests, and activities

THE FIVE TYPES OF PDD

(1) AUTISTIC DISORDER

Autistic Disorder, sometimes referred to as *early infantile autism* or *childhood autism*, is four times more common in boys than in girls. Children with Autistic Disorder have a moderate to severe range of communication, socialization, and behavior problems. Many children with autism also have mental retardation.

(2) RETT'S DISORDER

Rett's Disorder, also known as Rett Syndrome, is diagnosed primarily in females. In children with Rett's Disorder, development proceeds in an apparently normal fashion over the first six to eighteen months, at which point parents notice a change in their child's behavior and some regression or loss of abilities, especially in gross motor skills such as walking and moving. This is followed by an obvious loss in abilities such as speech, reasoning, and hand use. The repetition of certain meaningless gestures or movements is an important clue to diagnosing Rett's Disorder; these gestures typically consist of constant hand-wringing or hand-washing (Moeschler, Gibbs, & Graham 1990).

(3) CHILDHOOD DISINTEGRATIVE DISORDER

Childhood Disintegrative Disorder, an extremely rare disorder, is a regression in multiple areas of functioning (such as the ability to move, bladder and bowel control, and social and language skills) following a period of at least two years of apparently normal development. By definition, Childhood Disintegrative Disorder can *only* be diagnosed if the symptoms are preceded by *at least* two years of normal development and the onset of decline is prior to age ten (American Psychiatric Association, 1994).

(4) ASPERGER'S DISORDER

Asperger's Disorder, also referred to as Asperger's or Asperger's Syndrome, is a developmental disorder characterized by a lack of social skills; difficulty with social relationships; poor coordination and poor concentration; and a restricted range of interests, but normal intelligence and adequate language skills in the areas of vocabulary and grammar. Asperger's Disorder appears to have a somewhat later onset than Autistic Disorder, or at least is recognized later. An individual with Asperger's Disorder does not possess a significant delay in language development; however, he or she may have difficulty understanding the subtleties used in conversation, such as irony and humor. Also, while many individuals with autism have mental retardation, a person with Asperger's possesses an average to above average intelligence (Autism Society of America, 1995). Asperger's is sometimes incorrectly referred to as "high-functioning autism."

(5) PERVASIVE DEVELOPMENTAL DISORDER NOT OTHERWISE SPECIFIED

Children with PDDNOS either (a) do not fully meet the criteria of symptoms clinicians use to diagnose any of the four specific types of PDD above, and/or (b) do not have the *degree* of impairment described in any of the above four PDD specific types.

THE CONFUSION OF DIAGNOSTIC LABELS

Doctors are divided on the use of the term PDD. Some doctors are hesitant to diagnose very young children with a specific type of PDD, such as Autistic Disorder, and therefore only use the general category label of PDD. However, amidst all the confusion, it is important to remember that regardless of what the label is within the PDD category, the treatment is similar.

Note that the term PDD will be used throughout this paper in reference to all categories in the spectrum, including autism and Asperger's Disorder.

THE CAUSE OF PDD

The cause is unknown at this time. Currently researchers are investigating areas such as neurological damage and biochemical imbalance in the brain. These disorders are not caused by psychological factors.

THE SYMPTOMS AND SIGNS OF PDD

Generally, children are three to four years old before they exhibit enough symptoms for parents to seek a diagnosis. There is no set pattern of symptoms and signs in children with PDD. It is important to realize that a very wide range of diversity is seen in children with PDD.

DEFICITS IN SOCIAL BEHAVIOR

In early childhood children with PDD may show a lack of eye contact, but they may enjoy a tickle or may passively accept physical contact. They do not develop typical attachment behavior, and there may seem to be a failure to bond. Many such children show a lack of interest in being with or playing with other children. They may even actively avoid other children. In middle childhood such children may develop a greater awareness of or attachment to parents and other familiar adults. However, social difficulties continue. They still have problems with group games and forming peer relationships. Some children with less severe symptoms may become involved in other children's games.

As these children grow older they may become affectionate and friendly with their parents and siblings. However, they still have difficulty understanding the complexity of social relationships. Some individuals with less severe impairments may have a desire for friendships. But a lack of response to other people's interests and emotions, as well as a lack of understanding of humor, often results in these youngsters saying or doing things that can slow the development of friendships.

IMPAIRMENT IN NONVERBAL COMMUNICATION

In early childhood, children with PDD may develop the concrete gesture of pulling adults by the hand to the object that is wanted. They often do this without the typical accompanying facial expression. They seldom nod or shake their heads to substitute for or to accompany speech. Children with PDD generally do not participate in games that involve imitation.

In middle and late childhood such children may not frequently use gestures, even when they understand other people's gestures fairly well. Some children do develop imitative play, but this tends to be repetitive.

Generally children with PDD are able to show joy, fear, or anger, but they may only show the extreme of emotions. They often do not use facial expressions that ordinarily show subtle emotion.

IMPAIRMENT IN UNDERSTANDING SPEECH

Comprehension of speech in children is impaired to varying degrees, depending on where the child is within the wide spectrum of PDD. Individuals with PDD who also have mental retardation may never develop more than a limited understanding of speech. Children who have less severe impairments may follow simple instructions if given in an immediate context or with the aid of gestures (e.g., telling the child to "put your glass on the counter" while pointing to the counter). When impairment is mild, only the comprehension of subtle or abstract meanings may be affected. Humor, sarcasm, and common sayings (e.g., "it's raining cats and dogs") can be confusing for individuals with the mildest PDD.

IMPAIRMENT IN SPEECH DEVELOPMENT

Many infants with PDD do not babble or may begin to babble in their first year but then stop. When the child develops speech he or she often exhibits abnormalities. Echolalia (seemingly meaningless repetition of words or phrases) may be the only kind of speech some children acquire. Though echolalic speech might be produced quite accurately, the child may have limited comprehension of the meaning. Recent studies have found that echolalia can serve several functions, such as self-stimulation (when a child says words or phrases repeatedly without a communicative purpose just because it feels good); as a step between a child being nonverbal and verbal; or as a way to communicate (Prizant & Rydell, 1993). Other children develop the appropriate use of phrases copied from others. This is often accompanied by pronoun reversal in the early stages of language development. For instance, when the child is asked "How are you?" he or she may answer "You are fine."

The actual production of speech may be impaired. The child's speech may be like that of a robot, characterized by a monotonous, flat delivery with little change in pitch, change of emphasis, or emotional expression.

Problems of pronunciation are common in young children with PDD, but these often diminish as the child gets older. Some children have a chanting or singsong speech, with odd prolongation of sounds, syllables, and words. A question-like intonation may be used for statements. Odd breathing rhythms may produce staccato speech in some children.

Abnormal grammar is frequently present in the spontaneous speech of verbal children with PDD. As a result:

phrases may be telegraphic (brief and monotone) and distorted;

words of similar sound or related meaning may be muddled;

some objects may be labeled by their use;

new words may be coined; and

prepositions, conjunctions, and pronouns may be dropped from phrases or used incorrectly.

When children with PDD do develop functional speech, they may not use it in ordinary ways. Such children tend to rely on repetitive phrases. Their speech does not usually convey imagination, abstraction, or subtle emotion. They generally have difficulty talking about anything outside of the immediate context. They may talk excessively about their special interests, and they may talk about the same pieces of information whenever the same subject is raised. Ordinary to-and-fro conversational chatter is lacking. Thus they give the impression of talking "at" someone rather than "with" someone.

UNUSUAL PATTERNS OF BEHAVIOR

The unusual responses of children with PDD to the environment take several forms.

1. RESISTANCE TO CHANGE

Many children are upset by changes in the familiar environment. Even a minor change of everyday routine may lead to tantrums. Some children line up toys or objects and become very distressed if these are disturbed. Efforts to teach new activities may be resisted.

2. RITUALISTIC OR COMPULSIVE BEHAVIORS

Ritualistic or compulsive behaviors usually involve rigid routines (e.g., insistence on eating particular foods) or repetitive acts, such as hand flapping or finger mannerisms (e.g., twisting, flicking movements of hands and fingers carried out near the face). Some children develop preoccupations; they may spend a great deal of time memorizing weather information, state capitals, or birth dates of family members.

3. ABNORMAL ATTACHMENTS AND BEHAVIORS

Some children develop intense attachments to odd objects, such as pipe cleaners, batteries, or film canisters. Some children may have a preoccupation with certain features of favored objects, such as their texture, taste, smell, or shape.

UNUSUAL RESPONSES TO SENSORY EXPERIENCES

Many children may seem underresponsive or overresponsive to sensory stimuli. Thus they may be suspected of being deaf or visually impaired. Some children avoid gentle physical contact, yet react with pleasure to rough-and-tumble games. Some children carry food preferences to extremes, with favored foods eaten to excess. Some children limit their diet to a small selection, while others are hearty eaters who do not seem to know when they are full.

DISTURBANCE OF MOVEMENT

The typical motor milestones (e.g., throwing, catching, kicking) may be delayed but are often within the normal range. Young children with PDD usually have difficulty with imitation skills, such as clapping hands. Many such children are very overactive, yet tend to become less overactive in adolescence. Children with PDD may exhibit characteristics such as grimacing, hand flapping or twisting, toe walking, lunging, jumping, darting or pacing, body rocking and swaying, or head rolling or banging. In some cases the behaviors appear only from time to time; in other cases they are present continuously.

INTELLIGENCE AND COGNITIVE DEFICITS

Generally, children with PDD do very well on tests requiring manipulative or visual skills or immediate memory, while they do poorly on tasks demanding symbolic or abstract thought and sequential logic. The process of learning and thinking in these children is impaired, most particularly in the capacity for imitation, comprehension of spoken words and gestures, flexibility, inventiveness, learning and applying rules, and using acquired information. Yet a small number of children with PDD show excellent rote memories and special skills in music, mechanics, mathematics, and reading.

ASSOCIATED FEATURES

The emotional expression of some children with PDD may be flattened, excessive, or inappropriate to the situation. For no obvious reason they may scream or sob inconsolably one time, yet giggle and laugh hysterically another time. Real dangers, such as moving vehicles or heights, may be ignored, yet the same child might seem frightened of a harmless object, such as a particular stuffed animal.

DIAGNOSING PDD—NO SPECIFIC TEST AVAILABLE

Currently, no objective biological test, such as a blood test or an X-ray examination, can confirm a child's PDD diagnosis. Diagnosing PDD is complicated and much like putting together a jigsaw puzzle that does not have a clear border and picture. Therefore, it is reasonable to say that when a PDD diagnosis is made, it reflects the clinician's best guess. Assessment and evaluation can be done through the child's local public school or a private practitioner who specializes in developmental disorders (i.e., child psychiatrist, developmental pediatrician, pediatric neurologist, developmental pediatrician, child psychologist, developmental psychologist, or neuropsychologist).

The assessment should include the following:

1) Medical assessment

2) Interviews with parents, child, and child's teacher

3) Behavior rating scales

4) Direct behavioral observations

5) Psychological assessment

6) Educational assessment

7) Communication assessment

8) Occupational assessment

EDUCATION AND PDD

If the child is attending a school program, teachers need to be told of the symptoms of PDD and how those symptoms may affect the child's ability to function at home, in the neighborhood, in school, and in social situations.

ADDRESSING BEHAVIOR ISSUES

As children with PDD struggle to make sense of the many things that are confusing to them, they do best in an organized environment where rules and expectations are clear and consistent. The child's environment needs to be very structured and predictable.

Many times a behavior problem indicates that the child is trying to communicate something—confusion, frustration, or fear. Think of the child's behavior problem as a message to be decoded. Try to determine the possible cause of the behavior.

Has the child's routine or schedule changed recently?

Has something new been introduced that may be distressing or confusing the child?

When a child's communication skills improve, behavior problems often diminish; the child now has a means of expressing what is bothering him or her without resorting to negative behavior.

The use of positive behavioral support strategies for these children has proved effective. It is important to remember that:

1. Programs should be designed on an individual basis, because children vary greatly in their disabilities and abilities. Treatment approaches that work in certain cases may not work in others.

2. Children with PDD have difficulty generalizing from one situation to another. The skills they have learned in school tend not to be transferred to the home or other settings. It is very important to be consistent across all areas of the child's life—school, community, and home. This encourages generalization of behavior changes.

APPROPRIATE EDUCATIONAL PROGRAM

Many children with PDD experience the greatest difficulty in school, where demands for attention and impulse control are virtual requirements for success. Behavioral difficulties can prevent some children from adapting to the classroom. However, with appropriate educational help, a child with PDD can succeed in school.

The most essential ingredient of a quality educational program is a knowledgeable teacher. Other elements of a quality educational program include:

- structured, consistent, predictable classes with schedules and assignments posted and clearly explained;
- information presented visually as well as verbally;
- opportunities to interact with nondisabled peers who model appropriate language, social, and behavioral skills;
- a focus on improving a child's communications skills using tools such as communication devices;
- reduced class size and an appropriate seating arrangement to help the child with PDDNOS avoid distraction;
- modified curriculum based on the particular child's strengths and weaknesses;
- using a combination of positive behavioral supports and other educational interventions; and
- frequent and adequate communication among teachers, parents, and the primary care clinician.

MEDICATION

There is no one specific medication that helps all children with PDD. Some medications have been found to be helpful, but for many children with autism or PDD, medication levels need to be experimented with until the optimal combination and dosage are found.

OTHER THERAPIES AND TREATMENTS

FACILITATED COMMUNICATION

This is a method of encouraging people with communication impairments to express themselves. By providing physical assistance, a person called a facilitator helps the individual to spell words using the keyboard of a typewriter or computer or other letter display. Facilitation may involve hand-over-hand support or a simple touch on the shoulder. The individual with the impairment initiates the movement while the facilitator offers physical support.

AUDITORY INTEGRATION THERAPY (AIT)

AIT uses a device that randomly selects low and high frequencies from a music source (a cassette or CD player) and then sends these sounds through headphones to the child.

SENSORY INTEGRATION THERAPY

Sensory integration is the nervous system's process of organizing sensory information for functional use. It refers to a normally occurring process in the brain that allows people to put sights, sounds, touch, taste, smells, and movements together to understand and interact with the world around them (Mailloux & Lacroix, 1992).

On the basis of assessment results, an occupational therapist who has been trained in sensory integration therapy guides an individual through activities that challenge his or her ability to respond appropriately to sensory stimulation. This type of therapy is directed toward improving how an individual's senses process stimulation and work together to respond appropriately.

THE LOVAAS METHOD

This method (which is a type of Applied Behavior Analysis [ABA]), developed by psychologist Ivar Lovaas at UCLA, is an intensive intervention program originally designed for preschool-aged children with autism. It uses behavioral techniques—molding and rewarding desired behavior and ignoring or discouraging undesirable actions—to achieve its goals. Generally, this method consists of 30 to 40 hours a week of basic language skills, behavior, and academic training. Therapy usually consists of 4 to 6 hours per day of one-on-one training, 5 to 7 days a week.

CONCLUSION

Children with PDD happen to have a unique disorder that will make certain parts of life more challenging. Learning and understanding their special needs can be of enormous emotional and practical help to those who are involved with and who care about these special individuals.

Organizations

Autism Hotline, Autism Services Center
P.O. Box 507, Huntington, WV 25710-0507
(304) 525-8014
www.autismserviccenter.org

Autism National Committee
635 Ardmore Avenue, Ardmore, PA 19003-1831
www.autcom.org.

Autism Society of America
7910 Woodmont Avenue, Suite 300, Bethesda, MD 20814
1-800-328-8476 (Toll-free)
www.autism-society.com

FEAT (Families for Early Autism Treatment)
P.O. Box 255722, Sacramento, CA 95865-5722
www.feat.org

Indiana Resource Center for Autism
2853 East 10th Street, Indiana University, Bloomington, IN 47408-2601
(812) 855-6508 (V/TTY).
www.iidc.indiana.edu\irca

New Jersey Center for Outreach and Services for the Autism Community (COSAC)
1450 Parkside Ave., Suite 22 , Ewing, NJ 08638
(609) 883-8100
www.cosac.org

Division TEACCH
310 Medical School Wing E, 222H, University of North Carolina
Chapel Hill, NC 27514
www.unc.edu/depts/teacch

Other helpful websites:

Autism: Family Village:

Autism-PDD Resources Network:

Autism Research Institute:

Autism Resources:

Center for the Study of Autism:

SENSORY INTEGRATION DISORDER

Mimi Goss

INTRODUCTION

Sensory integration is the central nervous system's organization of sensory input for use. It involves how the brain integrates or processes sensations in order to enhance appropriate motoric and emotional responses. Sensory integration gives us the ability to take in, sort out, and connect sensory information from the world around us. This provides us with information about our body and its interaction with the environment.

Think of the senses: sight, hearing, touch, smell, and taste. There are many other sensations, all of which are significant for survival. These sensory systems include:

Vestibular System (movement and gravity). This system, with its receptors located in the inner ear, gives us information about our body in relation to gravity and movement. The vestibular system contributes to the development of our equilibrium reactions, muscle tone, motor coordination, oculomotor responses, and ability to learn.

Proprioceptive System (muscle and joint information). This system provides awareness of sensation in the muscles and joints. This sensory system is important for developing a sense of our body's position in space as well as developing motor planning skills, good balance, and coordination. It is the proprioceptive system that gives us the ability to walk up uneven stairs.

Tactile System (touch). This system gives us information related to touch. This sensory system gives us information about our bodies to help develop motor planning skills and gross and fine motor coordination. This system helps us discriminate "touch" information. Light touch such as tickling tends to be aversive and alerting. Heavy touch such as a bear hug tends to be inhibitory and calming.

Our brains must interpret and organize information from all of these systems so that we may function in everyday situations. The central nervous system is constantly focusing, screening, sorting, and responding to sensory information. This information comes both from the external environment and from internal receptors. It is the brain's interpretation of these stimuli that provides the information that allows the body to perform purposeful activities. Imagine the amount of sensory integration needed to sit in a chair, pay attention in an active classroom, copy an assignment, or read a book.

DYSFUNCTION OF SENSORY INTEGRATION

Dysfunction of Sensory Integration (DSI) occurs when the brain is not processing or organizing the flow of sensory impulses and therefore lacks good, precise information about our body and the world around us. Children with these difficulties interpret this information as a distorted image. Because they don't know what to compare it to, they feel the information is

527

accurate and reliable. In reality, the information that they are receiving is unreliable, inconsistent, or threatening.

SIGNS OF SENSORY INTEGRATION DISORDER

There are many signs or behaviors displayed by a child who has a sensory integration disorder. It is possible for a child to display a few or many of these characteristics at one time:

- Oversensitivity to touch, movement, sights, or sounds.
- Behavior issues may include distractibility, withdrawal when touched, or reacting in an explosive manner when touched.
- A child may display a fearful reaction to ordinary movement activities.
- Underreactivity to sensory stimulation.
- The child may sit on the sidelines and have a difficult time jumping in and getting involved with activities.
- The child may actively seek out increased exploration of movement, such as spinning, or may enjoy crashing into objects in order to achieve an alert state.
- Unusually high/low activity levels.
- Constant movement.

Slowness at getting started and quickness at reaching fatigue.

- Coordination problems.
- Balance issues.
- Clumsiness or awkwardness.
- Difficulties learning a new task that requires motor planning.
- Difficulties with learning.
- Problems with academic areas even if a child has average or above average intelligence.
- Difficulties coping with ordinary demands and stresses.
- Difficulty with activities of daily living.
- Difficulty dressing (tying shoes, buttoning and zipping clothes).
- Difficulty sequencing tasks.
- Uncomfortable about body.
- Appears lazy, bored or unmotivated.
- Avoids tasks and appears stubborn.
- Lacks impulse control.
- May be reactive.
- Doesn't anticipate the results of an action or exhibit poor safety awareness.

HOW COMMON IS DYSFUNCTION OF SENSORY INTEGRATION (DSI)?

The Sensory Integration Dysfunction Treatment and Research Center at Children's Hospital in Denver, Colorado, estimates that 10% of all children ten years of age or younger have DSI.

HOW CAN YOU TELL IF A CHILD HAS A SENSORY INTEGRATION DISORDER?

If a child is displaying any of the above characteristics, it is important that a trained professional evaluate the child. If the child is age appropriate (4 years to 8.11 years), a Sensory Integrative and Praxis Test (SIPT) is strongly recommended. This is a standardized tool used to obtain a diagnostic understanding of irregularities in learning and behavior. This evaluation should be administered by an occupational therapist who is certified in this area.

WHAT ABOUT THE TREATMENT?

An occupational therapist with training in sensory integration provides therapeutic activities to facilitate child-directed treatment sessions. Treatment is based on improving processing within the central nervous system. Building a neurological foundation helps the brain understand and process incoming sensory stimulation. An older child learns how to facilitate certain messages and inhibit others. An older child can also interpret all of the incoming messages, allowing age-appropriate perceptions and behaviors. A therapist can provide sensory stimulation in an organizing manner to help the brain organize and process information optimally and respond appropriately.

SENSORY INTEGRATION IN THE SCHOOLS

Children with DSI are unable to recognize their distorted interpretation of stimuli. They do not realize that they may interpret stimuli differently than their peers. With intervention, children should be able to cognitively identify what is bothering them so that they are able to self-regulate.

One of the biggest issues common in school-age children who have DSI is poor self-esteem. Their poor sensory processing can leave them confused, resulting in poor behavior and academic issues.

The teacher needs to have a basic understanding of what type of stimuli will increase a child's attention and focus. Each child with DSI may require different input to achieve this goal. With consultation from the child's therapist, the teacher can access the type of input a child may need to help with organization. For the child who requires a lot of movement, an example may be to allow the student to be the messenger for the classroom. This would provide him or her with the opportunity to walk down to the office often, allowing him or her to obtain the movement and receive proprioceptive input. This organizing opportunity may cause the child to be more attentive to other classroom activities.

It is important to look at the classroom and understand how the environment and/or tasks can be adapted (e.g., alter how assignments are given and/or length of assignments). It is also important to look at the classroom and control the distractions. Each child needs to be viewed on an individual basis, although often the entire class can benefit from the increased organizational stimuli that help one child succeed at a task.

RESOURCES

Kranowitz, Carol Stock. *The Out-of-Sync Child: Recongizing and Coping with Sensory Integration Dysfunction.* New York: Skylight Press, 1998.

Koomar, Jane, M.S. Szklut, and Sharon Cermak. *Making Sense of Sensory Integration*. Belle Curve Records, Inc., 1998. (1-888-357-5867)

Szlut, Stacey, and Carol Stock Kranowitz,. *Teachers Ask About Sensory Integration*. Belle Curve Records, Inc., 1999. (1-888-357-5867)

Watson, Linda, Elizabeth Crais, and Thomas L. Layton. *Handbook of Early Language Impairment in Children: Assessment and Treatment*. Delmar Thomson Learning, 2000.

ORGANIZATIONS

The American Occupational Therapy Association, Inc. (AOTA)
4720 Montgomery Lane, Bethesda, MD20824-1220
 (301) 652-AOTA or 1-800-668-8255, FAX: (301) 652-7711
www.aota.org

Sensory Integration International (SII)
1602 Cabrillo Ave, Torrance, CA 90501
(310) 320-9986, FAX: (310) 320-9934
www.sensoryint.com

Zero to Three / National Center for Clinical Infant Programs
734 15th Street, NW, Suite 1000, Washington, DC 20005-1013
(202) 638-1144 or 1-800-899-4301, FAX: (202) 638-0851
www.zerotothree.org

Henry OT Services
P.O. Box 145, Youngtown, AZ 85363
1-888-371-1204
www.henryot.com

TEACHING THE "TWICE EXCEPTIONAL" STUDENT: GIFTED AND LEARNING DISABLED

Limor Dankner

Incorporated into the scope of special education, or education of exceptional children, is the area of individuals who are gifted and talented. In recent years education of the gifted has become a focus of attention beyond theoretical research. Today programs for the exceptionally able child are numerous. An infrastructure exists in this country, as well as in many others around the globe, to address and support the needs of the gifted and talented members of our society. This infrastructure, comprised of numerous organizations on the national, state, and local levels, attempts to disseminate information and deliver programs that address the needs of this very complex segment of the population.

The attempt to understand and cultivate "giftedness" has also given rise to a great deal of controversy and question.

How should we address the needs of the gifted?

Are we being elitist when labeling giftedness?

Is it ethical to fund enrichment programs when our population of individuals with debilitating special needs is constantly on the rise?

We now know that gifted children are, in fact, children with special needs facing many challenging issues. Those who demand "equal opportunity" and "equality in education" fail to take into account a very important variable—that of potential. If we alter the principle of equality in education to include this variable, we would say "equal opportunity according to individual potential." Furthermore, some suggest that differentiated educational programs for students who are gifted grant them some form of undue privilege. In fact, gifted children are underprivileged when they are not provided with the opportunity to realize their full potential. Distinct and qualitatively different programs for them should be considered a right rather than seen as "elitist." Another ethical dilemma centers on the time, energy, and resources allocated to gifted students who are perceived as being "well equipped". Being gifted does not imply that one is over-bestowed, so there is no need for intervention and guidance. Differentiated quality education is as much a right of the gifted child as it is the right of any other child, including the child with learning disabilities. If deprived of this opportunity, gifted children are at significant risk of developing aggressive behavior, delinquency, social isolation, poor self-image, and underachievement.

WHAT IS GIFTEDNESS, AND HOW IS IT IDENTIFIED?

For many years educators and researchers have grappled with this question in their attempt to establish universal criteria by which to define this term. In schools, the concept of "giftedness" was defined as "above average" ability. Students who were labeled "gifted" were those individuals who were able to excel in their academic pursuits. This definition excluded those individuals whose talents and gifts were not readily identifiable through conventional academic achievement. Another criterion by which giftedness was measured involved the scoring of Intelligence Quotient tests. It was, and still is, believed that a high I.Q. score (usually over 130) was indicative of superior intellectual ability and, therefore, giftedness. I.Q. tests can be very useful instruments; however, caution must be used when these tests are the only diagnostic tool. Intelligence Quotient scores do not measure the entire scope of intellect, particularly the creative abilities; they are culturally and regionally biased; they are language based; and they fail to take into account affective factors such as inadequate motivation. When used as a *part* of an evaluation of an individual, I.Q. scores can be extremely informative and useful. While we can often rely on a significantly above-average I.Q. score to indicate giftedness, we must be cautious to not exclude individuals whose scores are not consistent with giftedness. Today we recognize giftedness as multifaceted and multidimensional. Similarly, we acknowledge the need to utilize various tools in identifying giftedness. These include intelligence tests, creativity measures such as the Torrance or Yamamoto tests, teacher and parent referrals, school records, and the child's input. This "individual portfolio" approach enables us to better understand the whole person and any gifts or talents that may be present.

CHARACTERISTICS OF THE GIFTED INDIVIDUAL

When considering the multifaceted nature of giftedness, we acknowledge gifted children as those whose skills are distinctly above average in *one or more* areas. These children usually exhibit exceptional performance in a given field of activity. Children capable of high performance include those with demonstrated achievement and/or potential ability in any of the following areas, singly or in combination:

- Creative or productive thinking
- Interpersonal and leadership ability
- Specific talent in visual and performing arts
- Specific academic aptitude
- General intellectual superiority
- Superior psychomotor ability

Regardless of the gift and/or talent, highly able children are characterized by common behaviors. Most are able to utilize their creativity to form abstract concepts and largely remote elements into new, valuable, and meaningful combinations. These children are highly curious, creative, self-motivated, and independent.

EDUCATIONAL PROGRAMS

Highly able students require differentiated educational programs and/or services beyond those usually provided by a regular school program. Comprehensive programs for gifted learners include four components:

- Differentiated educational curriculum
- Specialized teacher training

- Support and guidance to parents
- Counseling for the children

The curriculum should reflect differentiated content, instruction, and end product consistent with the gifted learner's needs for greater complexity and depth of study, novelty and interest-based learning experiences, and flexible pacing in both teaching and learning. Teachers require adequate training so that they are able to recognize not only the "typical" gifted student, but more importantly the "atypical" gifted individual with other learning issues. They must have access to resources and be provided guidance in differentiating the curriculum and instruction for their gifted students. Parents need to be educated about the unique gifts and issues of their children and be assisted in creating a home environment that is both nurturing and challenging. In addition, parents of gifted children often benefit from a support group, not only to alleviate stress and worry, but to serve as a resource to parents on the availability of services and programs for gifted children in the community. Finally, counseling is a key component of any program for the gifted. Many highly able children lack appropriate social skills and present social/emotional issues. Counseling is a very effective method of intervention, particularly in cases of aggressive behaviors, perfectionism, low self-esteem, inability to understand social cues, and stress.

THE DEVELOPMENT OF THE GIFTED CHILD—A BRIEF SKETCH

INFANCY

- Will have difficulty in establishing sleeping patterns. S/he may require very little sleep.
- Will quickly develop in one or more areas, both motor and intellectual skills. May skip a developmental stage (e.g., crawling).
- Will develop verbal skills at a young age. At times, will withhold verbal communication until ready for phrases and sentences.
- Alert, inquisitive, constantly manipulating objects in the environment.
- Will often reject close physical contact. Not as likely to need constant holding and cuddling.

THE PRESCHOOL YEARS

- Continues to be extremely inquisitive. Constantly manipulates the environment.
- Is very independent.
- Has a long attention span.
- Has a high level of verbal ability and language development.
- Is able to think at advanced levels of complexity.

ELEMENTARY SCHOOL YEARS

- Is curious, and the desire to learn is most evident.
- Is resistant to routine and drill.
- Wants to question, express an idea, and receive a reaction.
- Shows an interest in exploring topics beyond chronological age and maturity level.
- Has the ability to process ideas very rapidly, almost without being aware of the steps involved.

THE TEEN YEARS

- Continues resistance to routine and drill.
- Possesses an intense sensitivity to fair play, honor, and truth.
- Possesses an advanced sense of humor.
- Has the need to interact with mental peers.
- Has the need to concentrate on areas of great ability and to master many skills.
- Often disregards the need for social activities and physical development or exercise in favor of intellectual pursuits.

CHALLENGING THE HIGHLY ABLE STUDENT

- Create a safe space where students are encouraged to explore and feel successful.
- Let the student take the lead—show, guide, direct.
- Encourage use of sensory perception.
- Avoid workbooks that "teach" rote-level academic tasks.
- Encourage higher level thinking skills: "What do you think just happened?" "Would you do it in the same way?" "What do you think would make it more successful next time?"
- Ask "Why?" Help him/her understand relationships and make connections.
- Put aside set agendas.
- Point out sequences, patterns, and cause-and-effect relationships in day-to-day life.
- Encourage play. Rule-governed games are necessary and important, but should not substitute for exploration.
- Ask questions rather than explaining what is "correct." Ask open-ended questions ("What if… ?").
- Establish firm limits and predictable routines. Structure clear and consistent guidelines.
- Challenge facts. Engage children in the discussion of moral dilemmas.
- Encourage articulation of feelings.
- Play games of strategy such as chess and Battleships.
- Allow him/her to make choices and live with the consequences.

SUPPORTING THE HIGHLY ABLE STUDENT

- Support the student who has strengths and gifts in only one or two areas.
- Support the evenly developed perfectionist. His/her vision of what is possible clashes with time and energy constraints, leading to dissatisfaction and often frustration. Solution: time, patience, and modeling of the behavioral process that exhibits compromise and reasonableness.
- Help the student clarify self-expectations. Give constructive criticism.
- Allow the student to make mistakes without experiencing the stress of being judged or judging himself/herself to be a failure. Compliment the process. He/she needs to feel empowered to deal with his/her environment and supported when he/she falls and skins emotional, social and intellectual knees.
- Help the student evaluate the worst-case scenario for a failure—e.g., average grades. Practice active listening. Paraphrase back what he/she said and validate his/her feelings.

- Identify the problem and establish strategies for rectifying similar situations in the future. "How will you do this differently next time?"
- Encourage noncompetitive activities such as hobbies, research, family field trips. Avoid intense pressure!
- Assist the student (and parents) in making choices from among the many activities and options in and outside of the school, so that s/he is not over-scheduled.
- Assist with time management and organizational skills, but do not give the impression that success is not possible without your involvement.
- Help locate or obtain the resources and materials that help accomplish many of the ideas his/her mind can envision.
- Teach tolerance and respect of others with certain personality types or limitations. Encourage rather than pressure so that the channels of communication can remain open between you and the student.

CHARACTERISTICS OF THE GIFTED STUDENT

COGNITIVE

- Advanced vocabulary for age
- Possesses large storehouse of information
- Quick mastery and recall of information
- Has rapid insight into cause-effect relationships
- Asks provocative questions
- Wants to know how and why of things, unusually curious
- Has sophisticated and/or unusual sense of humor
- Can quickly make valid generalizations about events, people, or things; abstract thinking ability
- Has high level of visual and spatial ability
- Is a keen and alert observer
- Reads a great deal on his/her own
- Reasons things out for himself/herself
- Has ability to generate original ideas
- Is a metacognitive learner
- Is creative and task-committed

AFFECTIVE

- Is persistent, absorbed in certain topics
- Is easily bored by routine tasks
- Needs little motivation to follow work that is exciting to him/her
- Strives for perfection and is self-critical; heightened self-awareness accompanied by feelings of being "different"
- Prefers to work independently
- Is interested in adult problems
- Is assertive and stubborn in beliefs

- Likes to organize and bring structure to things, people, and situations and at times can seem "bossy"
- Is concerned with right and wrong; evaluates and passes judgment
- Is unusually sensitive to expectations of others
- Has unusual emotional depth and intensity
- Is highly active; may need less sleep

BRIGHT CHILD	GIFTED LEARNER
Knows the answers	Asks the questions
Is interested	Is highly curious
Is attentive	Is mentally and physically involved
Has good ideas	Has wild, silly ideas
Works hard	Plays around, yet tests well
Answers the questions	Discusses in detail, elaborates
Is in the top group	Is beyond the group
Listens with interest	Shows strong feelings, opinions
Learns with ease	Already knows
6–8 repetitions for mastery	1–2 repetitions for mastery
Understands ideas	Constructs abstractions
Enjoys peers	Prefers adults
Grasps the meaning	Draws inferences
Completes assignments	Initiates projects
Is receptive	Is intense
Copies accurately	Creates a new design
Enjoys school	Enjoys learning
Absorbs information	Manipulates information
Is a technician	Is an inventor
Is a good memorizer	Is a good guesser
Enjoys the straightforward	Thrives on complexity
Uses sequential presentation	Is a spatial thinker
Is alert	Is keenly observant
Is pleased with own learning	Is highly self-critical

By: Janice Szabos (*Challenge*, copyright 1989, Issue 34)

THE "TWICE EXCEPTIONAL" INDIVIDUAL

Included in the population of the gifted are the gifted/learning disabled, also known as the "twice exceptional" student. In recent years, improved identification of this group has enabled educators to better understand their unique behaviors and needs. However, identification of gifted/LD remains extremely problematic. Standardized tests and checklists are often inadequate, as significant discrepancies exist between verbal/oral and written expression. Giftedness is often masked by the disability, while disabilities are sometimes masked by the gift, making accurate diagnosis extremely difficult. High ability combined with learning disabilities may lead to frustration, boredom, aggression, underachievement, discouragement, or disruptive behaviors. Whereas the highly able student with mild learning disabilities can learn to compensate early in life so that both exceptionalities appear less extreme, the gifted child with significant learning disabilities appears to be unable to cope and achieve. This behavior often encourages educators to remediate deficits while overlooking gifts and talents. Consequently, the student perceives that something is wrong and must be "fixed," resulting in lowered self-esteem and a sense of inadequacy. Underachievement can be one of the most reliable indicators of gifted/LD, although it may also account for social and emotional issues, perfectionism, cultural and socioeconomic considerations, and level of interest. Nevertheless, when gifted children present themselves as underachievers, learning disabilities must be considered as a possible explanation. Subtle learning disabilities seldom impact intelligence quotient scores, though over time the gap widens between expected and actual performance. For this reason, we must consider nonconventional indicators of intellectual talent. Keeping in mind that scores will be depressed due to the disability, we must adjust cutoffs appropriately and allow children to participate in educational programs for students who are gifted on a trial basis. Subtest scores must not be aggregated into a composite score, but rather weight must be given to those characteristics that will allow the child to effectively compensate for the disability. When in doubt, it is recommended to include gifted/LD children in programs for the gifted, since addressing the gift supersedes the need for remediation.

CHARACTERISTICS OF THE TWICE EXCEPTIONAL STUDENT

- Is usually an underachiever
- Shows a vast gap in quality between oral and written work
- Is a test phobic and therefore usually has poor results
- Does not consistently finish schoolwork
- Has difficulty with memorization, computation, phonics, and/or spelling—weak decoding skills
- Has difficulty organizing work belongings and self
- Has difficulties with sequential tasks, following directions; easily disoriented
- Is often immature in all areas
- Is not school oriented and therefore is not motivated by usual devices such as teacher enthusiasm, praise, group interest, etc.
- Derives no apparent satisfaction from successful demonstration of acquired skill
- Is a very autonomous spirit, quite focused on self and resistant to external influences
- Is unable to function constructively in a group of any size
- Is rigid in his/her interests and may have a profound interest in an area in which he/she is an "expert"
- Has tendency to set goals and standards too high
- Has very low self-esteem, lacks self-confidence, and may sincerely believe to be unliked
- Is frequently absent from school with real or imagined illness
- Has intense feelings that may lead to power struggles with authority
- Tends to withdraw or be aggressive
- Has poor social awareness; unable to figure out what other people expect

- Displays attention deficit behaviors, including poor attention and daydreaming (will begin a project but will see very few to completion); impulsivity; high level of activity; restless; often talks excessively; often interrupts or intrudes on others, etc.
- Displays hyperactive behavior; is frequently inattentive; is easily distracted (DSM-IV-R Diagnostic criteria for Attention-Deficit Hyperactivity Disorder)
- Is talented in certain areas, yet "autistic-like"—preoccupied, intensely focused, "wandering mind," discourteous, argumentative, stubborn, uncooperative, egocentric, indifferent to conventions of socialization and dress, resistant to teacher domination, compulsive, preoccupied with words, ideas, numbers, and foods, perfectionistic. Has a rigid fascination with an interest, a need for precision, lack of social skills, the need to monopolize conversations and situations, intense need for stimulation, a tendency toward introversion.

QUESTIONS TO ASK IN DIFFERENTIATING BETWEEN GIFTED AND TWICE EXCEPTIONAL

- Are the behaviors manifested in all settings?
- Are the behaviors more problematic in certain settings?
- Could the child be bored in the non-challenging, slow-moving classroom? Have any curricular changes been made?
- Are behaviors responses to inappropriate placement, lack of intellectual peers?
- Is the hyperactive-like behavior focused and directed?
- Has the child been asked what his/her feelings are about the behavior?
- When engaged, is the child able to maintain attention?
- Does the confrontational, non-conformist behavior stem from intellectual judgment calls?
- Do the adults in the child's life perceive the child as "out of control"?

REMEDIATION AND INTERVENTION
FOCUS ON THE DEVELOPMENT OF THE GIFT

- Provide access to challenging material at an advanced level and intellectual peers with whom to interact.
- Emphasize high-level abstract thinking and problem solving (higher end of Bloom's Taxonomy).
- Consider Howard Gardner's theory of multiple intelligences and provide activities appropriate for areas of strength.
- Provide opportunities for self-directed learning, independent projects with structure, creative self-expression, and interest-based exploration.
- Promote active inquiry, experimentation, and self-direction.
- Provide exposure to a wide variety of subjects.
- Provide opportunities for intellectual debates and discussions.
- Expect participation in all classroom activities.
- Create opportunities for success.

School programs must provide remediation in conjunction with an academic challenge so that high potential may be developed!

ENCOURAGE COMPENSATION STRATEGIES

- Organize information at different levels of difficulty.
- Provide outlines, study guides, pretests and post-tests, visual structures, etc.
- Teach brainstorming and webbing strategies ("inspirations").
- Allow the child to tape-record lessons.
- Allow the child to use computer (in-class laptop), especially in the case of labored writing.
- Teach short-term memory strategies such as mnemonics and visualization.
- Provide for a variety of modes of communication—encourage use of technology, fine arts, dramatics.
- Provide alternate reading materials.
- Stress kinesthetic learning—simulations.
- Integrate the disciplines as much as possible to provide for creative self-expression.
- Provide instruction in test taking, study, time management, organization, self-monitoring, and learning skills.
- Modify the evaluation methods—oral spelling tests, recorded book reports, visual representations, etc.
- Use criterion-referenced testing to identify areas of mastery and deficiency.

PROVIDE A NURTURING AND SAFE ENVIRONMENT

- Be respectful of individual differences; allow children to feel valued, needed, and welcomed.
- Enable children to work in cooperative groups to achieve goals.
- Acknowledge multiple intelligences.
- Provide for group self-esteem activities to improve self-concept.
- Provide for group process skills to improve peer relationships.
- Provide for leadership training groups.
- Facilitate interactions with peers; simulations help with social problems.
- Offer a counseling program to students and parents.
- Encourage awareness of individual strengths and weaknesses so that children can make intelligent choices about their future.

The key in supporting students who are twice exceptional lies in the differentiation of instruction. It is important that the strategies for differentiation be in alignment with student needs:

- Acceleration and pacing
- Depth of subject
- Complexity of subject
- Novelty

When differentiating, keep in mind the following:

- Content
- Process
- Product

Possibilities for differentiation of instruction include:

- Problem solving

- Individual research
- Independent projects
- Learning centers
- Role-playing and dramatics
- Integration of disciplines
- Group work
- Process-oriented activities
- Question-based learning
- Open-ended approach to learning
- Student-selected activities
- Self-directed learning
- "Real" product, "live" audience
- Student contracts

"Gifted behavior…is not confined to a select few. It is defined as behavior that shows a creative, productive commitment to accomplish a particular task. Gifted behavior is displayed when a child uses intelligence or ability in a creative way and follows through to the completion of a task" (Eby, *Gifted Behavior: A Non-elitist Approach* from Educational Leadership, May, 1983, page 35).

In conclusion, many valuable and stimulating opportunities can be provided effectively and efficiently in a regular classroom for students with above-average ability, creativity, and task commitment. Consider the following suggestions:

- Use pre-tests and mastery tests to enable students to "test out" so that student are not required to spend unproductive time on skills and materials that they have already mastered.
- Use programmed instructional materials, learning packets, modules, and mini-courses to "compact" the role, pace, and content of instruction in selected areas.
- In each unit, include optimal learning activities that involve more advanced content and independent projects requiring originality and unique products.
- Provide time for students to engage in concentrated, uninterrupted work in individual or small-group investigations.
- Offer a choice of projects and assignments involving varying degrees of student planning.
- Develop a classroom library dealing with topics beyond the usual curriculum areas.
- Utilize bulletin boards and displays to heighten awareness and curiosity.
- Include at least one challenging question each week that is open-ended and that could lead to methodological discussions as well as independent study.
- Incorporate idea-generating techniques such as brainstorming, attribute listings, or forced relationships.
- Develop a unit with multiple starting points and multiple activities so that students may start and continue their work at different levels according to their ability, experience, prior learning, and interests.
- Work with other teachers to plan for cross-age and peer-tutoring opportunities.

- Develop record-keeping sheets so students can handle routine drill and practice tasks by themselves.

- Provide some "Do Not Disturb" signs for students to use when they are doing concentrated work.

- Encourage students to establish specific personal goals and objectives for school time and follow-up at home.

For more information, check "The Identification and Nurturing of 'Twice Exceptional' Students in Jewish Educational Settings: An In-Service Professional Development WebQuest" by Blanche E. Sosland, Ph.D. www.jesna.org.

THE NON-ELITIST GIFTED STUDENT

> "Gifted Behavior....is not confined to a select few. It is defines as behavior that shows a creative, productive commitment to accomplish a particular task. Gifted behavior is displayed when a child uses intelligence or ability in a creative way and follows through to the completion of a task."

(Eby, "Gifted Behavior: A Non-elitist Approach", Educational Leadership, May 1983, p. 35)

Suggestions for meeting the special learning needs of students with above-average ability, creativity, and task commitment in the regular classroom:

Many valuable and stimulating opportunities can be provided effectively and efficiently in a regular classroom for these students.

Consider these suggestions that provide:

Individualized instruction

Appropriate enrichment

Independence and self-direction

Personal and social growth

- Use pre-tests or mastery tests to enable students to "test out" so that they are not required to spend unproductive time on skills and materials they have already mastered.
- Use programmed instructional materials, learning packets, modules and mini-courses to "compact" the role, pace, and content of instruction in selected areas.
- In each unit, include optimal learning activities that involve more advanced content and independent projects requiring originality and unique products.
- Provide time for students to engage in concentrated, uninterrupted work in individual or small group investigations.
- Offer a choice of projects and assignments involving varying degrees of student planning.
- Develop a classroom library dealing with topics beyond the usual curriculum areas.
- Utilize bulletin boards and displays to heighten awareness and curiosity.
- Include at least one challenging question each week that is open-ended and that could lead to methodological discussions as well as independent study.
- Incorporate "idea-generating" techniques such as brainstorming, attribute listings, or forced relationships.
- Develop a unit with multiple starting points and multiple activities so that students may start and continue their work at different levels according to their ability, experience, prior learning, and interests.
- Work with other teachers to plan for cross-age and peer-tutoring opportunities.
- Develop record-keeping sheets so students can handle routine drill and practice tasks by themselves.

- Provide "Do Not Disturb" signs for students to use when they are doing concentrated work.
- Encourage students to establish specific personal goals and objectives for school time and follow-up at home.

THE CHILD WITH A HEARING IMPAIRMENT IN THE JEWISH CLASSROOM

"Our Way"
Orthodox Union

Batya Jacob

MODES OF COMMUNICATION

There are many different ways that the deaf and hearing-impaired communicate. You may find that students will primarily use of menthod but will sometimes mix other modes of communication.

- **Oral Communication**. The goal is to utilize amplification, lip-reading skills, and speech to communicate. The student will be able to use his/her voice to speak to the teachers and classmates. S/he will understand spoken language by using residual hearing, lip-reading skills, and facial expressions.

- **Manual Communication**. Use of American Sign Language and fingerspelling as the primary mode of communication. The student will use a hand sign to represent words and concepts. S/he may use a handshape to represent individual letters and fingerspell the word if the sign is not known. A sign language interpreter may be present in the classroom if the student uses this form of communication. Manual communication is also called American Sign Language (ASL) or Signed English. ASL utilizes a different grammatical structure than spoken English. Not every spoken word is represented by a sign. In Signed English, the signer conveys the message in English word order. The signs, grammar, and syntax vary in different languages and countries. Israeli Sign Language is not the same as American Sign Language.

- **Cued Speech**. An easy-to-learn visual system based on phonemics in spoken language. There are eight handshapes that represent consonant sounds and four body locations that represent vowel sounds. Cued Speech is not a language and can be used to convey any spoken language, including its syntax, pronunciation, and structure. Cued speech is used to allow the child with a hearing impairment to see the sounds, through vision alone, of English, Hebrew, or any other language.

- **Total Communication**. Use of any combination of the above methods of communication by the student. Students will use sign language, cued speech, speechreading, oral language, and amplification to communicate. This method is the most prevalent method presently used by the deaf and hearing impaired.

DO:

- Use as many visual aids as possible.
- Seat the student in the front of the classroom.
- Ask the student is s/he is getting the information.
- Encourage the student to ask the teacher to repeat what s/he had not gotten.
- Encourage the student to ask questions and raise his/her hand.
- Use attention-getting signals set up with the student's involvement. Hand signals or flashing classroom lights are effective.
- Seat the student in front of the auditorium and use an interpreter, transliterator, or auditory trainer for all assemblies as well as field trips.
- Send home a written schedule of assignments and tests.
- Send a copy of new vocabulary words and new topics of instruction to the student's supplemental teachers and to the student's parents at the beginning of each week.
- Allow the student with a hearing impairment to use a tape recorder to tape classes. Parents can then help transcribe classroom instruction and discussions to fill in gaps.
- Set up a buddy system to help ensure that the student takes accurate notes and gets assignments. Classmates can take turns doing this <u>h</u>esed (good deed.)
- Communicate daily with the student's parents through a written journal.

Excerpted from *The Hearing-Impaired Child in the Jewish Classroom*. For more information, contact www.ou.org.

APPENDIX D: SYNAGOGUE ACCESSIBILITY SURVEY

SYNAGOGUE ACCESSIBILITY SURVEY

An accessible congregation is one that explores barriers to the full participation of people with disabilities and makes a commitment to begin removing them. The congregation has committed to these principles:

In our congregation, people with disabilities are valued as individuals, having been created in the image of God.

Our congregation is endeavoring to remove barriers of architecture, communications, and attitudes that exclude people with disabilities from full and active participation.

People, with and without disabilities, are encouraged in our congregation to practice their faith and use their gifts in worship, service, study, and leadership.

Note: A person with a disability is anyone who requires assistance in order to participate in any synagogue service, program, or activity.

SYNAGOGUE ACCESSIBILITY QUESTIONNAIRE

Place a check mark next to each item that pertains to your synagogue. Even if you only check one item on the survey, your synagogue is on the way to becoming fully accessible.

Our congregation has the following accessible features for people with disabilities:

PARKING AND PATHS

YES   NO   Clearly marked accessible parking spaces on a stable surface are provided close to accessible entrances for lift-equipped vans and cars with handicapped parking stickers.

YES   NO   A clearly marked level "path of travel" exists from the accessible spaces in the parking lot to the synagogue's entrance.

YES   NO   Pathways are at least 48 inches wide with a slope of no more than 5 percent.

YES   NO   Curb cuts are provided from the parking lot to sidewalks and entrances.

YES   NO   At least one building entrance is wheelchair accessible.

DOORS AND DOORWAYS

YES   NO   Door openings are at least 32 inches wide.

YES   NO   Doors can be opened by exerting no more than 5 pounds of pressure.

YES   NO   Automatic doors are installed at one or more entrances.

WORSHIP SPACE

YES   NO   The sanctuary is wheelchair accessible.

YES NO The chapel is wheelchair accessible (entrance door is at least 32" wide)

YES NO The bimah is accessible by ramp or wheelchair lift.

YES NO Seating spaces are provided with extra leg room for people using crutches, walkers, braces, or casts.

YES NO Scattered spaces or "pew cuts" are provided for the users of wheelchairs who prefer to be seated in the main body of the congregation, not in the front or back of the sanctuary and not in the aisles.

YES NO Bookstands or lapboards are available for those unable to hold prayer books.

YES NO Choir area is accessible, allowing wheelchair users to participate.

YES NO A railing is installed next to any steps leading to the bimah.

YES NO An adapted lectern is provided for Torah readings from a wheelchair.

YES NO The social hall(s) is wheelchair accessible.

YES NO At least one classroom is wheelchair accessible.

RESTROOM AND WATER FOUNTAIN ACCESS

YES NO Lever-type faucet controls and hardware on doors are provided.

YES NO One or more restrooms are wheelchair accessible (including grab bars, widened stalls, lowered sinks, levered controls on faucets, etc.)

YES NO Towel dispensers are no higher than 40 inches from the floor.

YES NO Water fountains, if provided, are, mounted with basin no more than 36 inches from the floor and are easily operated from wheelchairs.

YES NO Water fountains are *not* located in alcoves.

YES NO Public telephones are lowered for wheelchair access and provide a volume control.

COMMUNICATION/PROGRAM ACCESS

YES NO Large-print prayerbooks are provided for people with visual impairments.

YES NO Assistive Listening Devices are provided for people with hearing impairments.

YES NO Sign language interpreters are available upon request for people who are deaf.

YES NO Specialized programming and/or tutoring is available for people of all ages and disabilities for life-cycle events (e.g., bar/bat mitzvah, Torah study, etc.). If **YES**, describe: _____

_____

YES NO Services and messages are presented verbally and visually.

YES NO Sermons or entire services are available on tape.

YES NO Lighting is adequate.

YES   NO   A TDD (text telephone for the deaf and speech-impaired) is available in the office or religious leader's study.

ATTITUDINAL BARRIERS

YES   NO   Persons with disabilities are welcome to worship with your congregation.

YES   NO   Persons with disabilities are given opportunities to serve others within the congregation and in the outreach programs.

YES   NO   Positions of leadership are offered to qualified individuals who happen to have a disability.

YES   NO   Efforts are made to respond to religious or lay leaders and congregants who acquire a disability.

YES   NO   Outreach efforts include people with disabilities.

YES   NO   A comfortable way is provided for people with disabilities within the congregation to offer suggestions for reducing barriers.

YES   NO   Educational resources about disability are in the library.

YES   NO   A religious education is provided that intentionally plans experiences for children, young adults, and older adults with disabilities to increase awareness about disability.

YES   NO   Provisions are made in your religious education program for all people, including children and adults with disabilities.

OTHER ACCESS FEATURES

YES   NO   Our congregation has an Inclusion of People with Disabilities Committee to address access issues. The chairperson is:

Name: _____

Address: _____

Telephone: (_____)_____

E-Mail: _____

YES   NO   Information about accessibility is included in our synagogue bulletin.

Adapted from United Synagogue of Conservative Judaism, **Accessible Congregation Campaign Survey**

WELCOMING A PERSON INTO OUR HOUSE OF WORSHIP: THAT ALL MAY WORSHIP

National Organization on Disability

WELCOMING A PERSON WITH A MOBILITY IMPAIRMENT

Mobility impairments are the most visible of all disabilities. Of the 43 million Americans estimated to have disabilities, 1.4 million use wheelchairs. There are also millions of others who use walkers, canes, braces, and crutches. Causes of physical disability range from accidents to genetic conditions or diseases. Aging increases the chance of broken bones and deteriorating strength.

Most congregations think about ramps, curb cuts, and designated parking arrangements. These adaptations are also useful to movers of heavy equipment, shoppers with bundles, and pushers of baby strollers.

Attitudes can keep people out as easily as architectural barriers. Surprisingly, there are people who think someone in a wheelchair cannot hear or that someone with cerebral palsy is not intelligent because speech is slow and labored. Often, when people who use wheelchairs participate in classes and social settings, they find that people talk over their heads or behind their backs. One explanation, not an excuse, for this rudeness is that people may feel somewhat guilty that they are able to get around easily when the other person can't.

IMPROVING PERSONAL INTERACTIONS

- Sit in order to be at eye level when talking with a person using a wheelchair.
- Do not move a wheelchair, crutches, or walker out of reach. Ask if assistance is needed.
- Do not lean on the wheelchair or otherwise "invade" the person's space.
- When buffet or cafeteria lines cause inconveniences, get suggestions and offer to carry the person's plate or tray.

WIDENING CONGREGATIONAL HOSPITALITY

- Provide outside barrier-free access including curb cuts, street-level or ramped entrances, and 32" doorways with adequate and level of entry space.
- Designate 12' 6"-wide parking spaces near the accessible entrances.
- Lower elevator control panels.

- Provide an accessible source of water. If a drinking fountain or cooler cannot be lowered, provide a cup dispenser beside it.
- Adapt a bathroom (which may be unisex) and install grab bars, raised toilet seats, sinks at appropriate levels, lever-type faucets, towel dispensers, and appropriately positioned mirrors.
- Extend hand rails beyond the top or bottom step, a feature helpful to those with braces, crutches, canes, and walkers.
- Install firm carpeting and reduce floor slickness.
- Shorten several pews so one or more wheelchairs can fit into the main body of the congregation and not be placed awkwardly in aisles. Scatter these pew cuts throughout a sanctuary to allow a choice of seating near companions.
- Build a ramp to the altar or bimah and to all raised portions of the sanctuary.
- Move the location of any classroom that is inaccessible.
- Contact the national denominational headquarters to see if there is a low-interest loan fund to assist local congregations in remodeling buildings for accessibility.
- Think about room arrangements for all meetings, coffee hour gatherings, or receptions. Is there clearance in halls? Is the meeting or eating table a convenient height? Are there loose or curling rugs that will impede travel? Are there enough chairs for people who tire easily?
- Set microphones at the appropriate height and location to be easily accessible.
- Have someone available to open heavy doors.
- Offer a note taker if manual dexterity is impaired.
- Have a supply of straws available for those who have difficulty holding a cup, glass, or can.

Note: The metal stall dividers in most bathrooms represent a major barrier for people in wheelchairs. If it is not possible to remodel immediately to include an accessible stall, remove the metal walls entirely and surround the toilet area with a hospital curtain. This temporary measure allows privacy and is easily accomplished.

WECLOMING A PERSON WHO IS BLIND OR HAS A VISUAL IMPAIRMENT

All congregations include people with varying amounts of vision. Fortunately, there are ways that a person with low vision or no vision can be active in the worship, education, and social life of the congregation.

IMPROVING PERSONAL INTERACTIONS

- To get a person's attention before speaking, speak the person's name. In a conversation group, identify people by name as each is speaking.
- Do not pat a guide dog in harness. It is not a pet when on the job.
- Feel free to use words such as "see" and "look."
- When guiding, give verbal clues to what is ahead, such as steps, curbs, escalators, or doors.
- Inform the person when you are leaving.

WIDENING CONGREGATIONAL HOSPITALITY

- Describe materials being distributed to a group that includes a blind person. Summarize information displayed on a screen.
- Accept a guide dog in the sanctuary as you would any guide.
- Produce bulletins and the words to hymns, litanies, and prayers in large print by using copy machine enlargers. Provide brailled versions if requested.
- Have available large-print Bibles and prayerbooks.
- Make audio tapes of entire services, sermons, speeches, or seasonal spiritual study guides.
- Offer a volunteer reader service.
- Improve sanctuary and hallway lighting, especially around staircases and other areas of potential difficulty for people with low vision.
- Place brailled information plaques on elevator panels.

WELCOMING A PERSON WHO IS DEAF OR HARD OF HEARING

Each congregation includes people, young and old, who are hard of hearing or deaf. They may read lips so well that they appear less deaf than they truly are. Indeed, they may understand only 80% of what is spoken, chanted, or sung but may be reluctant to complain. Knowing this, a congregation will want to replace poorly functioning sound systems and consider additional measures.

People who are **hard of hearing** communicate through enhanced sound and lip reading. Sound systems that serve everyone are important additions to the sanctuary and meeting rooms. But in order to be fully involved in worship and study, a person with partial hearing may benefit from assistive listening devices (ALDs) such as a hearing aid, an audio loop worn around the neck, and a small microphone worn on the speaker's lapel.

People who are **deaf** prefer interpreted conversation using American Sign Language (ASL), signed English, or Cued Speech. Since ASL is a language with its own syntax allowing for the exchange of ideas on many levels, it forms the basis for what is known as the Deaf Culture.

Signing is a beautiful art form. It will greatly enrich the worship experience for all once the congregation becomes accustomed to it. For many people who are deaf, however, it is more than an art form. It is the primary way to understand the full content of worship.

Many deaf people prefer to worship in a deaf congregation. Others seek a mainstream religious community that is able to arrange for sign language or oral interpretation of worship services and activities. This is particularly important for deaf parents who have hearing children and wish to worship as a family.

IMPROVING PERSONAL INTERACTIONS

- To get a person's attention before speaking, tap on elbow and speak face to face.
- Look at and speak to the person rather than the interpreter. The interpreter may be greeted privately, but when the interpreter is working, he or she is a transmitter for the person who is deaf, not a participant.
- Speak at a moderate pace, clearly but without exaggeration.
- Avoid covering the mouth while speaking. Beards and moustaches also make it harder to lip read.

- Do not stand in front of a window or bright light, since it puts the face in shadow and makes lip reading more difficult.
- Do not pretend to understand if the speech of a person is unclear. Request that the person rephrase until the point is clear.
- Communicate by telephone with deaf members at home by using relay services, available in most states. Consult the telephone book for the local number.

WIDENING CONGREGATIONAL HOSPITALITY

- Provide seating near speakers and interpreter. Usher the person to an appropriate seat.
- On important holy days, provide an interpreter and reserved seating in the main sanctuary. If there is televised broadcasting of the service to overflow crowds, provide an interpreter in that room as well.
- Be sure that important announcements are also provided in print form. Remember to inform someone bringing an interpreter of cancellations or any change of time or place.
- Use pencil and paper to communicate when necessary.
- Reduce background noise from radios, television sets, and loud fans.
- Purchase assistive listening devices (ALDs) for large assembly areas and small meeting areas.
- ALDs are systems that combine with a person's hearing aid to augment and clarify sound in a group setting. Examples are personal and group FM systems (using radio waves), loop systems (using magnetic waves), infrared systems (using light waves), and hardwire systems (directly connecting the speaker and listener). The key to the success of ALDs is in the speaker's use of a lapel microphone, which reduces background noise as it transmits the voice to the person wearing the hearing aid.
- Do a weekly check of batteries in listening devices.
- Encourage those who use equipment to inform someone if ALDs are not working properly.
- Purchase a telecommunications device (TDD) for the synagogue office so that a deaf or hard-of-hearing person can call the staff and religious leaders. Advertise the availability of the TDD.
- TDDs allow deaf people and non-deaf people to talk to one another over telephone lines using a small terminal with a screen and an abbreviated keyboard, something like a typewriter. A TDD may be purchased for under $300.
- Encourage some members of the congregation and staff to learn American Sign Language, Signed English, and/or finger spelling as a way to increase degree to which the deaf person feels at home within the congregation.

WELCOMING A PERSON WITH A MENTAL ILLNESS

A person with a mental illness has a biological dysfunction in his or her brain that may cause serious disturbances in the way the person thinks, feels, and relates to other people. Because of the disorder the person may find it difficult to cope with the ordinary demands of daily life. Such disorders affect individuals of all ages, and they occur in families across all boundaries of income, education, race, and ethnicity.

People with mental illnesses agree that the hardest part of living with their situation is the stigma and lack of understanding they encounter from others. Since their disabilities are not physically visible, it is hard for others to adjust to unexpected and different behaviors. Sadly, most people have limited knowledge about mental illness and may believe some of the myths about it. Because of this, they may not know what to do or say, and they turn away in their uncertainty.

There are also persons in all congregations who do not have a major mental illness but suffer from episodes of poor mental health. Their poor mental health is often due to environmental stresses and traumatic life experiences. Professional counseling and a caring congregation will help these people to experience a better quality of life.

In welcoming a person with a mental illness:

- Try to remain noncritical when encountering unusual behavior, giving responses that are supportive of the person
- Cultivate the ability to listen.
- Ask the person how the congregation might be supportive.
- Offer either community or private intercessory prayer.
- Make referrals to professionals when appropriate.
- Do not deny that the person has serious difficulties that may continue a long time.
- Offer choices of opportunities and tasks appropriate to the person's ability.
- Be sensitive to the fact that physical touch, such as a friendly pat, a hug, or a squeeze of the hand, affects people differently. Some appreciate the caring, but others find touch threatening.

WELCOMING A PERSON WITH DEVELOPMENTAL DISABILITIES

People with developmental disabilities have lifelong disabling conditions that occurred at or before birth, in childhood, or before the age of twenty-two. The conditions include mental retardation, spinal cord injury, epilepsy, sensory impairment, cerebral palsy, autism, and traumatic brain injury as well as other conditions resulting in limitations. This legal definition of developmental disability dictates who may or may not be served by certain government programs.

The term "developmental disability" is complicated by the fact that some people with cerebral palsy, autism, or traumatic brain injury may have advanced intellectual skills but limited speech or physical function, while people with mental retardation have slower rates of learning and limited capacity for abstract thinking.

Today religious and lay leaders are beginning to understand that those with developmental disabilities who have been lovingly included in family and community are able to have a meaningful relationship with God and have much to offer any congregation.

It is not wise to assume that a person will "get nothing" from attending services. Faith is not measured by how fast it develops, nor are we fully aware of the depth and breadth of what any one of us grains from worship. When we restrain someone with developmental disability from participating, we may be more worried about our own potential embarrassment than concerned about his or her religious experience.

IMPROVING PERSONAL INTERACTIONS

Treat adults with developmental disabilities as adults, not as children.

Talk to the person directly, not through a companion or family member.

Be patient. Give instructions slowly, in short sentences, one step at a time.

Allow the person to try tasks on his or her own, to make mistakes, to take a longer time, and to persevere. Do not impatiently take over dong things for the person that she or he can do alone.

WIDENING CONGREGATIONAL HOSPITALITY

Provide opportunities for participation in all congregational activities.

Find concrete ways for the child or adult with retardation to assist before, during, and after the worship service. Some possibilities include:

- Passing out programs and bulletins
- Filling the water glass for the religious leader
- Collecting materials left in pews after services

Find appropriate ways to increase knowledge and understanding among the members of the congregation, especially among peer groups of children.

Offer an older child with developmental disability the opportunity to help the teacher of younger children with cutting, pasting, reading, and straightening the classroom.

Assist persons with developmental disability to participate in denominational activities such as retreats, camping programs, conferences, and assemblies.

Sponsor a self-advocacy program such as "People First" or "Speaking for Ourselves".

Integrate students with developmental disabilities into regular classes whenever possible.

Form a relationship with a group home in the neighborhood. Activities can take place in the congregation's building or out in the community. Possibilities include everything from worship to hockey games! Don't overlook home improvement projects at the group home, such as painting a room, weeding the garden, or sewing new curtains.

WELCOMING A PERSON WITH LEARNING DISABILITIES

A person who has one or more learning disabilities has constant interruption in the basic brain-centered processes that affect listening, thinking, speaking, reading, writing, spelling, and sometimes calculating. The person has average to above-average intelligence, although learning is slower or different in the affected areas. The frustrations experienced usually result in low self-esteem and uneven performance, and frequently in behavioral difficulties. The person with a learning disability does not have developmental disability, mental illness, or a communicable disease.

Some symptoms of learning disability include:

- Short attention span
- Poor memory
- Difficulty following directions
- Inability to discriminate between and among numbers, letters, and sounds

- Poor reading ability
- Problems with eye–hand coordination

Some people with these learning differences miss social cues, do not learn easily from experience, and are physically and socially immature. In addition, there may be an uneven ability to retain information, resulting in failure in school and in the workplace.

Feeling impatient and somewhat inadequate themselves, teachers, supervisors, peers, parents, and siblings may have difficulty understanding why "he/she won't try harder". It is not hard to see that the accumulated frustrations experienced by someone with a learning disability may lead to emotional problems.

The religious congregation can be a welcoming haven of acceptance and affirmation for children and adults with learning disabilities, free from the rejection and extreme stress they experience in most other places.

IMPROVING PERSONAL INTERACTIONS

- Build confidence and skill by helping to develop interests and the opportunity to share them.
- Be direct and specific in conversation and in teaching. Give instructions simply.
- Use teaching techniques appealing to different senses.
- Be patient and flexible.
- Have realistic expectations.
- Help the person understand how the disability is connected to social interaction with peers, families, teachers, and employers.

WIDENING CONGREGATIONAL HOSPITALITY

- Help teachers and parents to examine expectations within the faith tradition that relate to educational achievement.
- Provide a personal teacher and advocate for the child or young teenager who is being baptized or confirmed or is joining the church or synagogue.
- Find creative ways to adapt the teaching of Hebrew, Latin, Greek, or other languages important to religious expression. This is, of course, essential in preparing a young boy to become a bar mitzvah or a girl preparing to become a bat mitzvah.
- Adapt seminary curricula for those with learning disabilities studying to be priests, rabbis, or ministers.

WELCOMING A PERSON WITH A CHRONIC ILLNESS

Every congregation has members who have one of the many chronic illnesses that persist for months or years and generally interfere with an individual's everyday ability to function. The effects of the particular illness may be invisible or can be camouflaged until the most acute stages begin. Thus, few people in the congregation may know that the person is ill. For others, periodic flareups may require hospitalization and result in some of the disabling conditions described elsewhere in this handbook.

Among the many types of chronic disabilities are psychiatric disorders, AIDS/HIV, seizure disorders, respiratory conditions, diabetes and other metabolic disturbances, head trauma, sickle-cell anemia, cardiac conditions, multiple sclerosis, muscular dystrophy and other neuro-muscular degenerative diseases, gastrointestinal disorders, allergies, the many forms of cancer, arthritis, chronic back pain, lupus, osteoporosis, glaucoma, retinitis, cataracts, and numerous other visual impairments.

Question: Why would someone hide the fact of such an illness from members of the synagogue? Is it fear of rejection? The dread of pity?

Answer: Yes. Previous negative experiences, even subtle or inadvertent thoughtlessness, result in fear of further rejection.

From the point of view of the congregation, if people do not really know how a disease is spread, they may think they can "catch" mental illness or AIDS or epilepsy in casual social situations. Feeling apprehensive and not understanding the illness, they may avoid those whose behavior or appearance makes them uncomfortable.

As lay and religious leaders learn about conditions that are present within the congregation they can provide a loving example of how to offer spiritual, physical, and moral support.

IMPROVING PERSONAL INTERACTIONS

Be sensitive to the possibility of hidden chronic illness if a person repeatedly declines to participate in activities.

Persist in efforts to find suitable avenues of involvement.

Accept their fears about the future. Sometimes apprehension about increasing dependency affects motivation and willingness to join activities in the present.

Invite the person to be part of the Task Force on Disability Issues. Planning for others with disabilities may provide an atmosphere where self-acceptance grows.

WIDENING CONGREGATIONAL HOSPITALITY

Include in congregational prayer and private intercessory prayer "those with chronic illnesses." In other words, offer an atmosphere of support.

Make the congregation aware, clearly but tactfully, that some people with allergies or other respiratory conditions are very sensitive to strong perfume and smoke. Sever respiratory distress can be triggered if the air is not clear.

Provide opportunities to learn about the two types of chronic illness that are most feared: AIDS and psychiatric disorders. As members of the congregation study these illnesses, ways to offer compassionate hospitality will be discovered and put into practice.

For more information, contact www.nod.org.

BY USING WORDS WITH DIGNITY, WE ENCOURAGE EQUALITY FOR EVERYONE

WORDS WITH DIGNITY	AVOID THESE WORDS
person with a disability	cripple/handicapped/handicap/invalid (Literally, invalid means "not valid." Don't use it.)
person who has/person who has experienced/person with (e.g., person who has cerebral palsy)	victim/afflicted by/afflicted with (e.g., victim of cerebral palsy)
uses a wheelchair	restricted, confined to a wheelchair/wheelchair bound (The chair enables mobility. Without the chair, the person is confined to bed.)
non-disabled	normal (Referring to non-disabled persons as "normal" insinuates that people with disabilities are abnormal.)
deaf/without speech/nonverbal	deaf mute/deaf and dumb
disabled since birth/born with a disability	birth defect
person with mental illness	crazy/insane
seizures	fits
developmental disability	slow

OTHER TERMS THAT SHOULD BE AVOIDED BECAUSE THEY HAVE NEGATIVE CONNOTATIONS AND TEND TO EVOKE PITY INCLUDE:

abnormal	disfigured	palsied	special	spastic
burden	incapacitated	pathetic	stricken with	suffer
condition	imbecile	unfortunate	retard/retarded	moron
deformed	maimed	pitiful	tragedy	invalid
poor	unfortunate	physically challenged	differently abled	

PREFERRED TERMINOLOGY

person who is blind (no visual capability)	person with hemiplegia
person with a visual impairment	person who has quadriplegia
person who is deaf or hard of hearing	person with paraplegia
person who uses a wheelchair	person with an intellectual impairment

APPENDIX E: RESOURCES FOR JEWISH EDUCATORS

SPECIAL NEEDS RELATED RESOURCES

JEWISH RESOURCES

Abrams, Judith Z. *Judaism and Disability: Portrayals in Ancient Texts from the Tanach through the Bavli*. Washington, D.C.: Gallaudet University Press, 1998.

Astor, Carl. *Who Makes People Different: The Jewish Perspective on the Disabled*. New York: United Synagogue of Conservative Judaism Department of Youth Activities, 1985, revised 2005. www.uscj.org

Christensen, Shelly. *Jewish Community Guide to Inclusion of People with Disabilities*. Minneapolis: Jewish Family Services of Minneapolis. 20007. www.jfcsmpls.org.

Consortium of Special Educators in Central Agencies for Jewish Education Newsletter. New York: Jewish Educational Service of North America (published annually) www.jesna.org

Council for Jews with Special Needs, Inc. *North American Disability Resource Directory of Jewish Agencies, Schools, Camps,Support Groups, Residential and Vocational Programs*. Phoenix. (480) 629-5343. www.cjsn.org

Curtis, Sandra. *Gabriel's Ark: An Instant Lesson*. Los Angeles, CA: Torah Aura Productions, 1996. A loving family helps a fearful boy with special needs through a wonderful Bar Mitzvah experience.

Dorff, Marlynn, et al. *Justice, Justice for All: Promoting Disability Awareness in the Jewish Community*. Los Angeles: Bureau of Jewish Education of Greater Los Angeles, Inc., 1991. www.bjela.org.

Elkins, Reuven. *Unconventional Wisdom: Torah Perspectives on the Child who Has Difficulty Learning*. Southfield, MI: Targum Press, 1997

Feldman, Jennifer. *The Four Questions From the Passover Haggadah*. Rockville, MD: The Partnership for Jewish Life and Learning (formerly the Board of Jewish Education of Gr. Washington) www. pjll.org.

From Barriers to Bridges: A Community Action Guide for Congregations and People With Disabilities.

Washington, D.C.: National Organization on Disability, 1996. www.nod.org.

Fulda, Yehoshua. *The Dikduk Difference: A Beginning Workbook*. New York: Ptach, 1986. www.ptach.org.

Goldman, Paula. *Teaching Hebrew Reading to Students with Learning Disabilities*. Rockville, MD: Partnership for Jewish Life and Learning (formerly The Board of Jewish Education of Greater Washington), 1995. www.pjll.org.

Greene, Phyllis S. and Simon, Sara R. *The Resource Program Guide for a Congregational School*. Rockville, MD: Partnership for Jewish Life and Learnng (formerly the Board of Jewish Education of Greater Washington), 1990. www.pjll.org.

Greene, Roberta and Heavenrich, Elaine A. *A Question in Search of an Answer: Understanding Learning Disability in Jewish Education*. New York: Union for Reform Judaism, 1981. www.urj.org

Grossman, Dan. *Bible Play: An Instant Lesson.* Los Angeles: Torah Aura Productions, 1987. (Grades 6–Adult)

A midrashic play which explores varying reactions to people with physical challenges.

Hammer, Reuven. *The Other Child in Jewish Education: A Handbook on Learning Disabilities*. New York: United Synagogue of Conservative Judaism Commission on Jewish Education, 1979. www.uscj.org.

Isaacs, Leora W. *So That All May Study Torah: Communal Provision of Jewish Education for Students with Special Needs*. New York: Jewish Educational Service of North America (JESNA), 1995. www.jesna.org.

Jacob, Batya. *The Hearing-Impaired Child in the Jewish Classroom*. New York: Orthodox Union, 1999. www,ou.org.

Kupferman, Flora. *Handbook for Special Education Programs in the Synagogue Schools*. San Francisco: Bureau of Jewish Education of San Francisco, 1996. www.bjesf.org.

Loving Justice: The ADA and the Religious Community. Washington D.C.: National Organization on Disability, 1994. www.nod.org.

North American Disability Resource Directory of Jewish Agencies, Schools, Camps, Support Groups, Residential and Vocational Programs. Phoenix: Council for Jews with Special Needs, Inc. www.cjsn.org

Schein, Jerome D. Ed., *The Deaf Jew in the Modern World.* New York: Ktav, 1986.

Schwartz, Elliot S. *Organizing Classes for Jewish Special Children.* Providence: Board of Jewish Education of Rhode Island and United Synagogue Commission on Jewish Education, 1979.

Schwartz, Rabbi Joel. *Special Child ~Special Parent: The Special Child in Jewish Sources.* New York: Feldheim Publishers, 1998.

That All May Worship: An Interfaith Welcome to People with Disabilities. Washington, DC: National Organization on Disability, 1992. www.nod.org.

Union for Reform Judaism Department of Jewish Family Concerns. *AIDS in the Jewish Community, A Synagogue Response.* New York: 2000. (study guide to the UAHC video) www.urj.org

Union for Reform Judaism Department of Jewish Family Concerns. *Al Pi Darco, According to Their Ways: A Special Needs Educational Resource Manual.* New York: UAHC, 2000. www.urj.org.

United Synagogue of Conservative Judaism Commission on Jewish Education *Parent Education for Parents of Jewish Special Children.* Teacher's manual. www.uscj.org.

Wolf, Miriam et al. *A Time To Rejoice: The Harold and Libby Ziff Jewish Special Education Holiday Curriculum.* Los Angeles: Bureau of Jewish Education, 1995.www.bjela.org.

SIGN LANGUAGE

Biatch, Rabbi Miriam. *Celebrating Judaism in the Home: A Manual for Deaf Jewish Families.* Arleta, California: Temple Beth Solomon of the Deaf, 1996.

Costello, Elaine. *Religious Signing: New Comprehensive Guide for All Faiths.* Toronto, New York: Bantam Books, 1986.

NCSY Signs of Shabbos. New York: Orthodox Union Our Way, 1992.

Stuart, Adele Kronick. *Signs in Judaism: A Resource Book for the Jewish Deaf Community.* New York: Published for the National Congress of Jewish Deaf by Bloch Publishing Co., 1986.

CHILDREN'S BOOKS

11th Commandment: Wisdom From Our Children. Jewish Lights Publishing, 1996. Admonitions from children such as "do not be mean or stare at people with disabilities" will help everyone get along. Presented in five sections: living with other people, with the earth, with family, with ourselves, and with God. Name, age, and religious affiliation of the child is noted with each maxim.

Cohen, Floreva G. *My Special Friend.* New York: Board of Jewish Education of Greater New York, 1986. Doron introduces us to his special friend Jonathan at synagogue and at his Bar Mitzvah.

Gartenberg, Zachary M. *Mori's Story: A Book about a Boy with Autism.* Minneapolis: Lerner Publications, 1998. A boy discusses his autistic brother, including his home life, foster home, schooling and how the disease affects the whole family.

Gellman, Ellie. *Jeremy's Dreidel.* Rockville, MD: Kar-Ben Copies, 1992. Jeremy signs up for a Hanukkah workshop to make unusual dreidels and creates a clay dreidel with braille dots for his dad, who is blind.

Goldin, Barbara Diamond. *Cakes and Miracles: a Purim Tale.* New York: Puffin Books, 1991. Young Hershel who is blind finds that he has special gifts he can use to help his mother during the holiday of Purim.

Millman, Isaac. *Moses Goes to a Concert.* Farrar, Straus and Giroux, 1998. Moses, who is deaf, joins his deaf classmates as they visit an orchestra concert. They meet the percussionist, who is also deaf and feels the vibrations of the music through her stockinged feet.

Peterseil, Tehila. *The Safe Place.* New York: Pitspopany Press, 1996. The story of a child with special learning problems and how the school special education teacher gave her the confidence and strategies to succeed in learning.

Peterseil, Tehila. *Unjust Cause.* New York: Pitspopany Press, 1997. Davey is struggling to please a demanding father and teachers who don't understand him. The author delves deeply into the thoughts and motivations of the father and gives readers information and insight about children with dysgraphia.

Rosenfeld, Dina. *Yossi & Label on the Ball*. Brooklyn, NY: Hachai Publishing, 1998. When Avi, a new boy moved in next door to the two brothers, it does not look like he will be a good ball player, but Yossi and Label soon learn that it is not appearances that count but what's inside.

Ruthen, Gerald C. *Daniel and the Silver Flute: An Old Hassidic Tale*. New York: United Synagogue of Conservative Judaism Commission on Jewish Education, 1986. Old Hassidic tale that deals with a High Holy Day theme stressing the acceptability of all tefillah (prayer) by God. Especially meaningful when working with disabled individuals and sensitizing all to special needs.

Sabin, Ellen. *The Autism Acceptance Book: Being a Friend to Someone With Autism*. New York: Watering Can Press. 2006. This book offers educational information, conversation-starters, and engaging exercises. The Covenant Foundation commissioned companion guides for educators in Jewish settings. Lessons wrtiten by Rebecca E. Starr. Free downloads (pdf).

Sabin, Ellen, *The Special Needs Acceptance Book: Being a Friend to Someone with Special Needs*. New York: Watering Can Press. 2007). This book offers educational information, conversation-starters, and engaging exercises. The book covers a range of disabilities including autism, Down syndrome, cerebral palsy, cystic fibrosis, learning disabilities like dyslexia, ADHD, blindness and deafness. The Covenant Foundation commissioned companion guides for educators in Jewish settings. Lessons wrtiten by Rebecca E. Starr. Free downloads (pdf).

Sanford, Doris. *David Has AIDS*. Portland, OR: Multnomah, 1989. A little boy with AIDS turns to God to help him cope with the pain, fear, and loneliness that surround him.

Sose, Bonnie. *Designed By God, so I Must Be Special*. Winter Park, FL: Character Builders for Kids, 1988. A book filled with warmth and love describing what God gives us that makes us unique and special.

Topek, Susan Remick. *A Turn for Noah*. Rockville, MD: Kar-Ben Copies, Inc. 1992. Noah has trouble learning to spin the dreidel as his preschool class celebrates Hanukkah.

Weinberg, Yona. *The Diamond Bird*. Brooklyn, NY: Mesorah Publications, 1991. Twin boys, Shaya and Shua, meet Yossi, their "special"

cousin. Yossi has Down Syndrome and the twins include him in their many adventures.

Webb-Mitchell, Brett. *God Plays Piano, Too: The Spiritual Lives of Disabled Children*. New York: Crossroad Publishing Co., 1993.

VIDEOS/DVD'S

AIDS IN THE JEWISH COMMUNITY: A SYNAGOGUE RESPONSE—Union for Reform Judaism Department of Family Concerns www.urj.org

BAR MITZVAH OF JOSHUA KARP—Union for Reform Judaism Department of Family Concerns. Bar Mitzvah ceremony of a boy with autism. www.urj.org

BAR MITZVAH OF MATTHEW CASO—Union for Reform Judaism Department of Family Concerns. Bar Mitzvah ceremony of a boy with significant cerebral palsy. www.urj.org

EUGENE—The Jewish Theological Seminary of America, 1995. The story of Eugene Chernyakhovsky, a boy with cerebral palsy who overcomes many challenges as he prepares for his Bar Mitzvah. Assisted by a team of experts and volunteers from his Philadelphia community, Eugene transfers his entire Torah portion to a computer that serves as his voice using only one foot. Eugene's journey is culminated in the Bar Mitzvah service and celebration at which he addresses the congregation in both English and Russian. www.jtsa.edu

PRAYING WITH LIOR—This popular documentary film shows Lior, who has Down Syndrome, as he passes through his Bar Mitzvah to manhood. Some people believe that he is a spiritual genius. www.prayingwithlior.com

SOMEONE IS LISTENING—United Synagogue of Conservative Judaism Commission on Jewish Education. www.uscj.org. The first 28 minutes relate the story of a deaf teenager who meets a rabbi, communicates with him in sign language and with the rabbi's guidance, becomes a Bar Mitzvah. The additional 10 minutes is a sign teaching segment.

SPECIAL CHILDREN—SPECIAL NEEDS—Jewish Education Center of Cleveland (formerly Bureau of Jewish Education), 1989. Presents Isador Reisman of the Cleveland BJE demonstreating his pioneering techniques and methods for teaching children with special needs. www.jecc.org.

TIKVAH... MEANS HOPE—The video describes the Tikvah program, a summer camp program for Jewish children with special needs at Camp Ramah in Ojai, California. www.campra-mah.org

TRIUMPH: THE STORY OF THE JEWISH BRAILLE INSTITUTE—JBI International (formerly The Jewish Braille Institute of America). Four families show how the Jewish Braille Institute helped them feel connected to Judaism. How to donate and volunteer is also included in the video. www.jbinternational.org.

DISABILITY-RELATED ORGANIZATIONS

SECULAR CLEARINGHOUSES

Clearinghouse on Disability Information
Office of Special Education and Rehabilitative Services (OSERS)
Room 3132, Switzer Building
330 C Street S.W.
Washington, DC 20202-2524
(202) 205-8241 (Voice/TTY)
www/ed/gov/about/offices/list/osers/codi.html

Council for Exceptional Children (CEC)
1920 Association Drive
Reston, VA 20191-1589
(800) 328-0272 (Voice/TTY)
www.sped.org

ERIC (Education Resources Information Center)
www.eric.ed.gov

National Health Information Center
P.O. Box 1133
Washington, DC 20013-1133
(800) 336-4797
www.nhic-nt.health.org

National Organization for Rare Disorders (NORD)
P.O. Box 8923
New Fairfield, CT 06812-8923
(800) 999-6673
(203) 746-6927 (TTY)
www.rarediseases.org

NICHCY
National Dissemination Center for Children with Disabilities
P.O. Box 1492
Washington, DC 20013
1-800-695-0285 (Voice/TTY)

(202) 884-8200 (Voice/TTY)
www.nichcy.org

ORGANIZATIONS

American Association of People with Disabilities (AAPD) Interfaith Initiative
Ginny Thornburgh, Director
1629 K Street NW, Suite 503
Washington, DC 20006
(202) 457-0046
(800) 840-8844 (TTY/V)
www.aapd.com

Association of Jewish Family and Children's Agencies
557 Cranbury Road, Suite 2
East Brunswick, NJ 08816-5419
1-800-634-7346
www.ajfca.org

CAJE (Coalition for the Advancement of Jewish Education)
261 West 35th Street, Floor 12A
New York, NY 10001
(212) 268-4210
www.caje.org

Consortium of Special Educators in Central Agencies for Jewish Education
Jewish Education Service of North America (JESNA)
111 8th Avenue
New York, NY 10011
(212) 284-6998
www.jesna.org

JBI International (formerly Jewish Braille Institute)
110 East 30th Street
New York, NY 10016
(212) 889-2525
www.jbiinternational.org

JCC Association of North America
15 East 26th Street, 10th Floor
New York NY 10010-1579
(212) 532-4949
www.jcca.org

Jewish Children's Adoption Network
P.O. Box 147016
Denver, CO 80214
(303) 573-8113
Contact: Steve and Vicki Krausz
http://jcan.qwestoffice.net

Jewish Reconstructionist Federation
1299 Church Road

Wyncote, PA 19046
(215) 782-8500
www.jrf.org

National Organization on Disability Religion and Disability Program
910 16th Street NW, Suite 600
Washington, DC 20006
(202) 293-5960
(202) 293-5968 TDD
www.nod.org

PTACH (Parents for Torah for All Children)
4612 13th Avenue
Brooklyn, NY 11219
(718) 854-8600
www.ptach.org

Orthodox Union
National Jewish Council for the Disabled/ Yachad Program/Our Way
333 Seventh Avenue
New York, NY 10001
(212) 563-4000
(212) 564-9058 (fax)
www.ou.org

Union for Reform Judaism
Department of Family Concerns
633 Third Ave
New York, NY 10017
(212) 650-4294
(212) 650-4119 (fax)
www.urj.org

United Jewish Communities
111 8th Avenue
New York, NY 10003
(212) 686-8670
www.ujc.org

United Synagogue of Conservative Judaism
Commission on Inclusion of People with Disabilities
155 Fifth Avenue
New York, New York 10010-6802
(212) 533-7800
www.uscj.org

ISRAEL

ALYN Pediatric Hospital and Rehabilitation Center for Physically Handicapped Children
Shmariyahu Levin Street,
Kiryat Hayovel
Jerusalem 91090, Israel (972) 2 649 4222
www.alyn.org

Beit Issie Shapiro
Raanana, ISRAEL
200 West 57th Street, Suite 609
New York, NY 10019
(212) 586-2464
www.beitissie.org.il

Gan Harmony
POB 37011
Jerusalem 91370, Israel
(972) 2- 651-9929
www.ganharmony.org

Bar/Bat Mitzvah Program for Children with Special Needs
Masorti Movement in Israel
www.masorti.org

Rosh Pina Mainstreaming Network
Chana Zweiter
9 Press Street
Jerusalem 94705, Israel,
(972) 2-500-2120
rpmn@netvision.net.il

ONLINE RESOURCES FOR JEWISH SPECIAL NEEDS

These sites were selected because they provide a sampling of resources that can be found online; it is not intended to be a comprehensive list, and the authors are not responsible for, nor do they necessarily endorse, their content. Be sure to check resources available from local central agencies for Jewish education. Please also note that websites and web addresses change over the course of time.

Board of Jewish Education of Greater New York Special Education Center
www.bjeny.org
Information about the BJE's Special Education Center and its programs including its Resource Listing of Congregational Jewish School Programs for Children with Special Needs, Parent Education program, and, Volunteers in Education program.

Coalition for the Advancement of Jewish Education (CAJE)
www.caje.org
CyberCAJE offers information about the organization, the annual conference, articles from Jewish Education News, and access to CyberCAJE's curriculum bank for CAJE members, including

a network for learning differences and resources for special needs and early childhood education. Also see the CAJE Network on Diverse Learners.

e-Chinuch.org: Pinchas Hochberger Creative Learning Pavilion
www.chinuch.org
Online resource center based on Torah Umesorah's Creative Learning Pavilion. The site houses and collects down loadable teacher-made materials and curricular resources for Judaic studies teachers and administrators, including, but not limited to early childhood education, special needs, classroom and school management, weekly "parsha pages" and a "Bais Midrash" of resources for Jewish text study, teaching tips, lesson plans, worksheets, crafts, digital slideshows and multimedia, clip art, program banks, moderated message boards, and more.

Etta Israel Center
www.etta.org
Website of the Etta Israel Center, developed in part through a grant from the Covenant Foundation; includes information about programs and services that help Jewish children, young adults, and families achieve inclusion and integration in the community and works to raise community awareness and sensitivity toward people with special needs.

Jewish Deaf Resource Center (JDRC)
www.jdrc.org
The Jewish Deaf Resource Center (JDRC) is a bi-cultural, bi-lingual organization facilitating equal participation and decision making in Jewish life for Deaf and Hearing Jews. The JDRC was created to take on the challenges of assuring that Deaf and hearing participate equally in the Jewish community. Among other services, the JDRC offers Jewish home schooling opportunities using videophones.

Jewish Education Service of North America (JESNA)
www.jesna.org
JESNA's goal is to make engaging, inspiring, high quality Jewish education available to every Jew in North America. Online resources include annotated listings of general and Judaic websites and other resources for special needs education, as well as publications related to the field and information about the Consortium of Special Needs Educators in Central Agencies for Jewish Education and its Newsletter.

Lookstein Center
www.lookstein.org
The Lookstein Center was established to promote the advancement of Jewish education in the Diaspora. Resources include access to lesson plans, classroom activities, opportunities for distance learning, and publications such as *Jewish Educational Leadership*, a professional journal for Jewish educators.

MATAN
www.matankids.org
MATAN is a multi-disciplinary team of Jewish educators, special educators, and mental health professionals committed to designing and implementing modifications that enable Jewish day schools and supplemental schools to serve all children regardless of ability. The website also includes links to its newsletter.

National Jewish Council for the Disabled
www.ou.org/ncsy/njcd
The National Jewish Council for the Disabled is dedicated to enhancing the life opportunities of people with special needs, insuring their participation in the full spectrum of Jewish life. The website includes links to programs and resources affiliated with Yachad, National Resource Center; National Center for Inclusion; Yachad; Social Skills Training; School Programs; birthright Israel; Summer Programs; Vocational Programs; Our Way for the deaf and hard of hearing; and, The National Association of Day Schools for Exceptional Children for yeshivot and day schools across the United States and Canada providing programs for students with varying special needs.

PTACH
www.ptach.org
Advocacy organization to encourage and assist every yeshiva and day school meet the needs of its students; focuses on teacher training, parent outreach, early identification and screening, and more. The website includes links to professional development services and curricular publications.

Pirchei Shoshanim: Special Education Resources
www.pirchei.co.il

The site includes resources for Jewish special education.

Union for Reform Judaism
Department of Lifelong Jewish Learning
http://urj.org
Resources for special needs education, including programs, curricular material, links to other sites, and "Dear Shana: Frequently Asked Questions on Special Needs."

United Synagogue of Conservative Judaism
www.uscj.org
USCJ's Department of Education includes a section for Jewish special education resources, materials, and organizations. The USCJ web site also hosts the Accessibility Web Site Commission on Inclusion of People with Disabilities which includes resources for making participation in Jewish life more inclusive.

GENERAL RESOURCES

AbilityHub
www.abilityhub.com
Resource for locating information on adaptive equipment and alternative methods available for accessing computers.

ABLEDATA
www.abledata.com
ABLEDATA provides objective information on assistive technology and rehabilitation equipment available from domestic and international sources to consumers, organizations, professionals, and caregivers within the United States. It serves the nation's disability, rehabilitation, and senior communities. ABLEDATA is sponsored by the National Institute on Disability and Rehabilitation Research (NIDRR), part of the Office of Special Education and Rehabilitative Services (OSERS) of the U.S. Department of Education. The site includes an online library with references to a wide variety of books, articles, papers and other paper and electronic publications that deal with topics relating to assistive technology such as reviews of products; research to develop products and improve existing ones; guidance for selecting assistive products or finding information about funding; or general information on a class of products.

ADA Technical Assistance Program
www.dbtac.vcu.edu

A comprehensive Resource for Information on the Americans with Disabilities Act, Accessible Information Technology, and more. The National Institute on Disability and Rehabilitation Research (NIDRR) has established ten regional centers to provide information, training, and technical assistance to employers, people with disabilities, and other entities with responsibilities under the ADA. The centers act as a "one-stop" central, comprehensive resource on ADA issues in employment, public services, public accommodations, and communications.

Adaptive Technology Resource Centre
http://atrc.utoronto.ca
The Centre advances information technology that is accessible to all through research, development, education, proactive design consultation and direct service. Resources include a technical glossary, online resources for adaptive technology, and research and development.

ADD: National Attention Deficit Disorder Association
www.add.org
Attention Deficit Disorder Association, ADDA, provides information, resources and networking opportunities to help adults with Attention Deficit/Hyperactivity Disorder (AD/HD) lead better lives. Resources include research, treatment information, books, family issues, legal issues, school and career support, and areas for kids and teens.

All Kinds of Minds
www.allkindsofminds.org
Co-founded by Dr. Mel, Levine, All Kinds of Minds is a non-profit Institute that helps students who struggle with learning measurably improve their success in school and life by providing programs that integrate educational, scientific, and clinical expertise.

ARC's Disability-Related Web Sites
www.thearc.org
The Arc of the United States works to include all children and adults with cognitive, intellectual, and developmental disabilities in every community.

Assistive Technology Industry Association
www.atia.org
ATIA serves as the collective voice of the Assistive Technology industry.

Assistive Technology Training Online Project (ATTO)
www.atto.buffalo.edu
The Assistive Technology Training Online Project (ATTO) provides information on AT applications that help students with disabilities learn in elementary classrooms, including resources for decision making, options for assistive technology, resources for adapting curricula, and online tutorials for professional development.

ATSTAR, Assistive Technology Strategies, Tools, Accommodations, and Resources
http://aimstar.knowability.org
Collaborative effort to build technology-enhanced learning environments and to increase assistive technology expertise among educational professionals, parents, and consumers. The site includes information and resource about assistive technologies and their uses.

Center for Applied Special Technology (CAST)
www.cast.org
CAST is a nonprofit organization that works to expand learning opportunities for all individuals, especially those with disabilities, through the research and development of innovative, technology-based educational resources and strategies. CAST promotes Universal Design for Learning and the National Instructional Materials Accessibility Standard (NIMAS) to guide the production and electronic distribution of curricular materials in accessible, student-ready versions, including Braille and Digital Talking Books. CAST also developed Bobby, a tool for Web page authors to help them identify changes to their pages so users with disabilities can more easily access them.

Council for Exceptional Children (CEC)
www.cec.sped.org
The Council for Exceptional Children (CEC) is the largest international professional organization dedicated to improving educational outcomes for individuals with exceptionalities, students with disabilities, and/or the gifted. CEC advocates for appropriate governmental policies, sets professional standards, provides continual professional development, advocates for newly and historically underserved individuals with exceptionalities, and helps professionals obtain conditions and resources necessary for effective professional practice. Their Technology and Media division is found at www.tamcec.org.

CHADD, Children and Adults with Attention-Deficit / Hyperactivity Disorder
www.chadd.org
CHADD serves individuals with Attention Deficit / Hyperactivity Disorder. Through collaborative leadership, advocacy, research, education and support, CHADD provides science-based, evidence-based information about AD/HD to parents, educators, professionals, the media and the general public.

Child Development Institute
www.childdevelopmentinfo.com
Site for information on child development, psychology, parenting, learning, health and safety as well as childhood disorders such as attention deficit disorder, dyslexia and autism.

Closing the Gap
www.closingthegap.com
The organization focuses on computer technology for people with special needs through its bi-monthly newspaper, annual international conference and extensive web site.

disAbility Resources on the Internet
www.makoa.org
Listings of resources, organizations, accessibility sites, and more.

DO-IT, Disabilities, Opportunities, Internetworking, and Technology
www.washington.edu/doit
The Center promotes the use of accessible information technology and universal design. The site includes resources for K-12 educators, students with disabilities, librarians, employers, and parents and mentors.

EduHound: Everything for Education K-12
www.eduhound.com
Online educational directory of resources for educators and parents compiled by T.H.E. Journal according to subject area, including links to teacher resources, worksheets, software demos, home schooling resources, special education, early childhood education, and more.

ERIC Clearinghouse on Disabilities and Gifted Education
www.eric.ed.gov

Database of resources for exceptional children archived from the ERIC Clearinghouse system.

Get Ready To Read!

www.getreadytoread.org

Get Ready to Read! (GRTR!) is a national program to build the early literacy skills of pre-school children. GRTR! brings research-based strategies to parents, early education professionals, and child care providers to help prepare children to learn to read and write. Our goal is to ensure that all children have opportunities to become successful readers. Get Ready to Read! is an initiative of the National Center for Learning Disabilities. The site includes resources and interactive games and activities for reading readiness.

Hoagies' Gifted Education Page

www.hoagiesgifted.org

Resources and links related to gifted education for parents, for educators, counselors, administrators and other professionals, and for kids and teens. Resources include information on identifying gifted children, learning styles and socio-emotional issues, a glossary of gifted education, materials about testing and measurement, support systems and conferences, publications, research.

The Inclusion Network

www.inclusion.org

The Inclusion Network is a non-profit organization whose staff and volunteers partner to promote inclusion of people with disabilities in the Greater Cincinnati community. Resources include information about inclusion, and an organization self-study on inclusion.

Internet Resources for Special Children

www.irsc.org

Online directory of resources including websites and online communities dedicated to children with disabilities and other health related disorders worldwide.

KidTools Support System

www.kidtools.missouri.edu

The KidTools Support System (KTSS) is a federally-funded project to provide performance support software for children, ages 7-13, who have learning disabilities and/or emotional and behavioral problems. The KTSS software includes a library of tools provided as easy-to-use templates for children to personalize and use independently in school and home settings. The KidTools program includes template tools to assist children in self-management, problem solving, and making plans and contracts.

LD Online

www.ldonline.org

LD OnLine is a national educational service of public television station WETA in Washington, D.C. It offers online services and produces video programs dedicated to improving the lives of children and adults with learning disabilities and ADHD. Resources include guides to learning disabilities for parents, teachers, and children, learning strategies, information on adaptive technologies, and an area for children to share and learn.

LD PrideNet

www.ldpride.net

Includes explanations of learning styles and multiple intelligences as well as self-tests, articles on LD and ADD, and other resources.

National Association of Private Special Education Centers (NAPSEC)

www.napsec.org

NAPSEC is a non-profit association mission is to represent private special education centers and their leaders to promote high quality programs for individuals with disabilities and their families and to advocate for access to the continuum of alternative placements and services.

National Center for Learning Disabilities

www.ncld.org

NCLD provides essential information to parents, professionals and individuals with learning disabilities, promotes research and programs to foster effective learning, and advocates for policies to protect and strengthen educational rights and opportunities.

National Clearinghouse for Professions in Special Education (NCPSE)

www.special-ed-careers.org

NCPSE is committed to enhancing the nation's capacity to recruit, prepare, and retain well qualified diverse educators and related service personnel for children with disabilities.

National Cristina Foundation

www.cristina.org

National Cristina Foundation (NCF) provides

computer technology and solutions to give people with disabilities, students at risk and economically disadvantaged persons the opportunity, through training, to lead more independent and productive lives.

National Dissemination Center for Children and Youth with Disabilities

www.nichcy.org

NICHCY is the national information and referral center that provides information on disabilities and disability-related issues for families, educators, and other professionals; special focus on children and youth (birth to age 22); includes listings of national resources and camp directories. NICHCY also hosts Zigawhat, a website for learning, connecting, growing, coping, and fun for young people with disabilities and their peers.

National Organization on Disability (NOD)

www.nod.org

The National Organization on Disability promotes the full and equal participation of America's 54 million men, women and children with disabilities in all aspects of life. Their Religion and Disability program encourages congregations and seminaries of all faiths to become more accessible and welcoming to people with disabilities.

Office of Special Education and Rehabilitative Services, U.S. Department of Education (OSERS)

www.ed.gov/about/offices/list/osers/index.html

The Office of Special Education and Rehabilitative Services (OSERS) is committed to working with internal and external partners in ensuring that every individual with a disability maximizes their potential to participate in school, work, and community life. OSERS provides a wide array of supports to parents and individuals, school districts and states in three main areas: special education, vocational rehabilitation and research.

PACER Center: Parent Advocacy Coalition for Educational Rights

www.pacer.org

PACER Center's mission is to expand opportunities and enhance the quality of life of children and young adults with disabilities and their families, based on the concept of parents helping parents. Resources include the Simon Technology Center, (used/assistive technology; software lending library, etc). parent advocacy, early childhood, employment strategies, emotional behavioral disorders, legislation, and more.

Rehabilitation Engineering and Assistive Technology Society of North America (RESNA)

www.resna.org

RESNA's mission is to improve the potential of people with disabilities to achieve their goals through the use of technology by promoting research, development, education, advocacy and provision of technology; and by supporting the people engaged in these activities.

RTI (Response to Intervention) Action Network

www.rtinetwork.org

Contains glossary, descriptions of RTI multi-tier models of school supports that use research-based academic and/or behavioral interventions, links and related readings

SchwabLearning.org

www.schwablearning.org

SchwabLearning.org is a "parent's guide to helping kids with learning difficulties be successful in school and life" and provides useful information and practical strategies for parents of children in kindergarten through high school. SchwabLearning.org offers parents what they need to understand the concepts and consequences of learning and attention problems for themselves, their children, and their families.

SERI: Special Education Resources on the Internet

seriweb.com

Special Education Resources on the Internet (SERI) is a collection of Internet accessible information resources of interest to those involved in the fields related to special education; includes information on specific disabilities and support organizations as well as resources on gifted and talented and for parents and educators.

Starlight*Starbright Foundation

www.starlight.org

The STARBRIGHT Foundation is dedicated to the development of projects that empower seriously ill children to combat the medical and emotional challenges they face on a daily basis.

STARBRIGHT projects do more than educate or entertain: they address the core issues that accompany illness—the pain, fear, loneliness, and depression that can be as damaging as the sickness itself.

Web-Based Tutor Training (WBTT)
www.nwrel.org/learns/web-based/index.php
The site was designed to make it easier to provide training to tutors in reading programs and meet CNCS guidelines. It includes resources and ideas for working with tutors, reading comprehension, and more.

Wisconsin Assistive Technology Initiative (WATI)
www.wati.org
A clearinghouse of resources to ensure that every child in Wisconsin who needs assistive technology (AT) will have equal and timely access to an appropriate evaluation and the provision and implementation of any needed AT devices and services. A primary goal is to improve the outcomes and results for children and youth with disabilities through the use of assistive technology to access school programs and curriculum. The project is designed to increase the capacity of school districts to provide assistive technology services by making training and technical assistance available to teachers, therapists, administrators and parents throughout Wisconsin. Resources are also useful for other states and includes best practices, assessment forms, online guides, etc.